Strategic Management
in Developing Countries

Strategic Management
IN
Developing Countries

Case Studies

James E. Austin
Harvard Business School

WITH

Tomás O. Kohn
Boston University

THE FREE PRESS
A Division of Macmillan, Inc.
NEW YORK

Collier Macmillan Canada
TORONTO

Maxwell Macmillan International
NEW YORK   OXFORD   SINGAPORE   SYDNEY

The Free Press
A Division of Macmillan, Inc.
866 Third Avenue, New York, N.Y. 10022

Collier Macmillan Canada, Inc.
1200 Eglinton Avenue East
Suite 200
Don Mills, Ontario M3C 3N1

Printed in the United States of America

printing number
1   2   3   4   5   6   7   8   9   10

Library of Congress Cataloging-in-Publication Data

Austin, James E.
    Strategic management in developing countries : case studies /
James E. Austin with Tomás O. Kohn.
        p.   cm.
    Includes bibliographical references.
    ISBN 0-02-901105-1
    1. Industrial management—Developing countries—Case studies.
2. Strategic planning—Developing countries—Case studies.
I. Kohn, Tomás O.   II. Title.
HD70.D44A97   1990
338.7′4′091724—dc20

                                                90-37736
                                                CIP

To Our Students

For Whom We Work
and
From Whom We Learn

Contents

Acknowledgments   *xi*

1. Overview   *1*

     Objectives of the Book   *2*
     Importance of LDCs   *2*
     LDC Diversity   *4*
     An Approach to Management in Developing Countries   *8*
     Organization of the Cases   *15*

2. Investing in Developing Countries   *23*

     Key Issues   *23*
     Case Study Questions   *26*
     Nike in China   *29*
     Hitchiner Manufacturing Company, Inc.   *59*
     Enterprise Development Inc.   *83*
     Industrias del Maiz S.A.   *107*

3. Managing the Business-Government Nexus   *129*

     Key Issues   *129*
     Case Study Questions   *132*
     John Deere, S.A. (Mexico)   *135*
     Background Note on Mexico   *151*
     Mexico and the Microcomputers   *159*
     Dow Indonesia   *171*
     State Timber Corporation of Sri Lanka   *185*
     Bribery and Extortion in International Business   *203*

Standard Fruit Company in Nicaragua   *205*
Pandol Brothers, Inc. and Nicaragua   *231*

4. Production   *245*

Key Issues   *245*
Case Study Questions   *247*
Leather Industry in India   *249*
Packages Limited   *269*
Thai Polyester Fiber (B)   *293*
Evans Food Corporation   *303*
Rio Bravo Electricos, General Motors Corporation   *321*

5. Marketing   *333*

Key Issues   *333*
Case Study Questions   *335*
Sabritas   *337*
Milkpak   *359*
Nestlé Alimentana S.A.—Infant Formula   *377*
Population Services International   *399*

6. Finance   *417*

Key Issues   *417*
Case Study Questions   *419*
Electrohogar, S.A.   *421*
Compañía Telefónica Mexicana S.A. (CTM)   *427*
Colgate-Palmolive in Mexico   *453*
Citibank in Zaïre   *471*
International Pharmaceuticals Incorporated   *497*
Thai Farmers Bank   *515*

7. Organization   *537*

Key Issues   *537*
Case Study Questions   *538*
Selecting a New Manager at Milkpak   *541*
Turrialba Mining Company   *549*
The Case of the Untouchable Water-Carrier   *563*
Thai Polyester Fiber (C)   *571*
Ashamu Holdings Limited: Let the Goat Eat Salt   *577*

8. **Exporting from the Developing Countries**   *595*

Key Issues   *595*
Case Study Questions   *597*
Empresa Brasileira de Aeronáutica S.A.   *599*
The Cut Flower Industry in Columbia   *625*
Daidong Mould & Injection Co.   *649*
Countertrade and the Merban Corporation   *667*

Acknowledgments

This casebook is the collective result of many persons' efforts over several years. Most of the cases in this book emerged from the development of the Harvard Business School course Management in Developing Countries, originally created in 1978 and taught by me, and subsequently refined, extended, and taught by my colleague, Professor Lou Wells. The course development was made possible through the financial and administrative support of the School's Division of Research. This lengthy journey to publication was facilitated by the continual encouragement of HBS Dean John McArthur and Professor Tom McCraw, Head of the School's Business, Government, and Competition Area. The President and Fellows of Harvard College, the copyright holder of most of the cases in this book, generously gave permission for their publication here.

These case studies required extraordinary field research efforts by many case writers who adeptly captured the complex realities of business situations in developing nations around the world. The case writers and supervising faculty skillfully crafted that field data into exceptionally rich and effective teaching cases. For those cases in which I was involved in the preparation, I again express to these colleagues my appreciation for their work and for the opportunity of collaborating with them. I am especially grateful to those colleagues at Harvard Business School, Instituto Panamericano de Alta Dirección de Empresa, International Management Development Institute, Euro-Asia Centre-INSEAD, Lahore University of Management Sciences who kindly allowed us to abridge and include their cases in this book. The collaborative spirit of these individuals and institutions was an important source of encouragement. The inclusion of these cases has significantly enhanced the educational value of the book. The names of these creative and skillful academics who were involved in the case preparation are noted on the title page of their respective cases.

The case studies would not have been possible without the generous cooperation of the companies and institutions about which the cases were written. I thank them for sharing their experiences and contributing to the management education of thousands of students. It is a tribute to their good citizenship.

I am also grateful to the multitude of students who have discussed these cases in the classroom. Their analyses and insights have consistently revealed ways in which the cases or teaching plans could be refined. The book is better because of them.

The preparation of the manuscript benefited from the exceptional word-processing and organizational skills of my assistants, Nancy Hayes and Leslie Cadwell, and the efficient assistance of the HBS Word Processing and Case Services staff.

Bob Wallace, Vice President and Senior Editor of The Free Press, and his staff provided outstanding support in ensuring a high-quality publication.

Finally, my deep thanks go to my collaborator, Dr. Tomás Kohn, whose intellect, pedagogical perceptiveness, business experience, and warmth were invaluable in creating this book. He enhanced not only the quality of the final work but also the pleasure of producing it. It has been a treasured dividend.

JAMES E. AUSTIN
Boston, Massachusetts

1

Overview

$\mathbf{A}$s the economy floundered during Mexico's 1982 crisis, Dietrich Hermann, CTM's controller, scrambled to hedge the company's $20 million-denominated debt. The cost of hedging seemed unreasonably high, yet the risk of not doing so seemed even greater. Decisions had to be made on the spot, yet standard operating procedures for such transactions called for multiple-level approvals. The race was on! Could the company approve the financial operation before it was too late? Would the banks sign the needed documents in time? With the firm's survival in his hands, yet seemingly out of his control, Hermann suddenly understood why, when he accepted the controllership of Compañía Telefónica Mexicana, he was told that it would be the challenge of his life. On the other side of the globe, in India, Sundara Raman couldn't sleep. That morning he had hired a new water carrier to serve the employees in the branch of the state-owned bank he managed. All of a sudden work at the bank seemed to come to an abrupt halt. The word had spread that the new water carrier was an "untouchable." The next day Raman would have to find a solution to the problem, but which?

Raman's and Hermann's problems are just two of many the reader will wrestle with while analyzing the cases we present in this book. The problems are challenging, and the less-developed country (LDC) environments managers must face are complex and diverse. To master the art and science of managing in developing country environments is a demanding task, given their distinctive features. The government seems to be everywhere, controlling prices and foreign exchange, restraining raw material imports, providing credit, buying finished products, regulating expansion, entry, and exit. Conventional strategic planning tools seem inadequate, as demand gyrates, inflation soars, exchange rates tumble, costs change by leaps and bounds, and competitors come and go when borders are opened and closed to international competition.

1

OBJECTIVES OF THE BOOK

Maybe the picture painted just now is somewhat extreme; not all of those changes take place in every developing country, and in those where they do, not necessarily all come at the same time. Yet the picture is revealing. Managing in LDCs is different and requires new analytical tools and a heightened awareness to cope with the ever changing environment. This book will provide the reader with an opportunity to wrestle, through a series of real-life cases, with the distinctive problems and special opportunities that managers working in, or dealing with, LDCs are likely to encounter. By analyzing the cases students will get their feet wet before having to dive head first into the turbulent yet invigorating waters of LDC management. The hope is also that for managers in developed countries the book will provide vivid illustrations of the issues with which their colleagues in LDCs must deal, thereby improving the understanding of each other's problems and the ability to interact.

Through the analysis of the cases, we hope readers will (1) deepen their understanding of the managerial realities of developing countries' environments, their commonalities and their diversity, and (2) increase their ability to deal systematically with the strategic and operating issues, problems, and opportunities facing them. As will become apparent, the problems are tough but manageable, and the opportunities are exciting and abundant.

IMPORTANCE OF LDCs

If indeed the difficulties of LDC management are great, one might ask, Why bother? The answer is simple: Developing countries are much too important in economic and human terms to be ignored. Given the interdependence of today's global economy, the incentives to learn how to handle the problems are significant. Firms that master the intricacies of operating in LDCs can achieve competitive advantage, while contributing to economic development in the Third World.

Over two-thirds of the world's surface area belongs to developing countries, and so most of the world's supplies of certain minerals and agricultural products come from those countries. LDCs are, and can be expected to remain, key suppliers of many vital commodities.

Some three-quarters of our planet's 5 billion people live in developing countries. Since LDC workers receive low wages relative to their DC counterparts, developing countries have an enormous pool of low-cost labor that gives them a potential comparative advantage in labor-intensive products. The global sourcing strategies of many DC-multinationals, along with the increased emphasis on export-led development strategies

of many LDCs, make it realistic to expect that these countries will continue to play an increasingly vital role as exporters of manufactured
goods and of services to DCs. Developed country imports of manufactured goods from low- and middle-income countries increased forty-five-
fold, from $4 billion to $180 billion, in the twenty years between 1967 and
1987.[1] (Imports from other developed countries increased only fourteen
times during the same period.) In general, while total exports by DCs grew
at an average rate of 3.3% between 1980 and 1987, LDC exports grew at
5.0%—a reversal of the relative growth rates of DC and LDC exports
during the 1965–80 period.[2]

The demand for goods by the developing countries' 4 billion inhabitants is enormous. LDCs' population is expected to grow during the next
decade at an average annual rate of 1.9%, more than twice the DCs' rate
of growth. By the year 2000, in the developing countries there will be 5
billion potential customers, 1 billion more than today! Even with relatively low levels of per capita GNP, 5 billion people represent monumen-
tal markets. The demand, moreover, is not only for consumer goods.
LDCs are continually increasing their manufacturing capacity, creating
what appears to be an insatiable demand for producer and capital goods.
This demand is heightened by the large infrastructure development
needs of such countries: additional transportation, education, and health
care facilities; expanded energy generation and distribution systems; and
effective telecommunications networks, to name some. In short, LDCs'
demand for goods translates into opportunities for exports from DCs and
for productive investments in LDCs by multinational corporations and
local investors alike.

Developing countries need capital to develop. LDCs have imported
capital from private lenders, investors, and governments. The total
amounts of capital transferred and its sources have fluctuated widely.
Capital flows to LDCs more than doubled between 1970 and 1981, reaching U.S. $135.7 billion, and then were halved in the next five years.

While government lending, in the form of development assistance and
as nonconcessional flows, has traditionally represented the bulk of capital
transferred to LDCs, private flows became increasingly important in the
late 1970s and early 1980s, reflecting the recycling of petrodollars by the
international banks. Capital flows to LDCs peaked in 1981; that year
private lenders provided over half of all transfers. By 1986, not only had
the total amount transferred shrunk, but the private portion of those
transfers fell to less than one-third of the total as the international banks
cut their lending in the face of the LDC debt crisis.

The large indebtedness accumulated during the 1970s and early 1980s
has created a critical situation for most developing countries. Real interest rates soared while commodity prices and LDC-exports plummeted, as
recession in the industrial countries sharply reduced their demand for
imports. The result was an ever growing debt that could not be serviced

adequately. In the ten years between 1979 and 1989, debt for all LDCs climbed from approximately one-quarter to one-half of GNP. The result is that today approximately one out of every four dollars of LDC exports must be devoted to debt service payments, hobbling these countries' development efforts.

As LDCs struggled to service their debt, as developed countries curtailed the flow of new funds, and as eroding confidence gave rise to massive capital flight from LDCs, the net flow of funds reversed itself. Since 1984 the developing countries became net suppliers of capital to the industrial nations. With ever increasing need for new funds, ongoing debt servicing repayments, and the imperative of alleviating the human suffering pervasive in so many LDCs, these countries need a new reversal in the flow of funds. With declining private bank lending, the importance of attracting new foreign direct investment and official assistance has become paramount in most LDC governments' financing agendas. LDCs will continue as important actors in the international financial markets.

LDC DIVERSITY

Developing countries stand out by their differences as much as by their similarities, and providing a broad picture, as we have done above, risks creating an impression of homogeneity. LDCs, of course, differ in many ways, including geography, culture, surface area, population, resource endowments, economic growth patterns, industrial structure, political stability, economic stability, and health status. One of our objectives in choosing the cases in this book has been to provide the reader with a broad picture that highlights this diversity. While we cannot be comprehensive in this endeavor, the reader will find in the next few paragraphs that the cases chosen capture considerable diversity.

Geography and Culture

We include cases that take place in Latin America (Brazil, Colombia, Ecuador, Mexico, Nicaragua, Peru, and Puerto Rico), in Africa (Nigeria, Zaïre, and Zambia), and in diverse regions of Asia (Bangladesh, China, India, Indonesia, Korea, Pakistan, Sri Lanka, and Thailand). Geographic diversity also gives our sample cultural variety.

Economic Growth and Level of Economic Development

In the "Citibank in Zaïre" case we find a major international bank struggling to put together a syndicated loan for Zaïre, a country that in the

1965–87 period had a negative (—2.4%) average growth in GNP per capita. Zaïre's per capita GNP was a scant U.S. $150 in 1987. This contrasts sharply with "Daidong Mould and Injection Co.'s" home country, Korea, where per capita GNP grew during the same twenty-two-year period by an impressive average annual rate of 6.2%, reaching U.S. $2,690 by 1987.[3]

The relatively high per capita GNP places Korea among the so-called newly industrialized countries (NICs). Brazil and Mexico (1987 GNP per capita of U.S. $2,020 and $1,830, respectively) are other NICs included in our sample.

Size and Population

"Nike in China" exposes the reader to the largest developing country. China's enormous land mass—more than 9,500 square kilometers (sq. km.)—harbors the greatest population in the world—more than a billion. India, another mega-population country with some 800 million inhabitants, is where "The Untouchable Water Carrier" case is set.

In sharp contrast with vast India and China stands tiny Nicaragua. This country, where the "Standard Fruit Co." and "Pandol Brothers, Inc." cases take place, has barely 3.5 million inhabitants and occupies 130,000 sq. km. It would require some two hundred ninety Nicaraguas to make one country with China's population! When we look at "Industrias del Maiz," we find ourselves in Ecuador, another small country, with under 10 million inhabitants and 284,000 sq. km. Yet not all small countries are small along both dimensions, population and geography. The site of "Population Services International's" (PSI) social marketing program for birth control contraceptives is Bangladesh, the world's most densely populated country with more than 110 million inhabitants crowded into less than 160,000 sq. km. Bangladesh's 685 inhabitants per sq. km. contrast sharply with Zaïre's 14.

Industrial Structure and Resource Endowment

Our sample countries include diverse industrial structures. We find "EMBRAER" exporting aircraft from Brazil, where agriculture represents only 11% of the GDP, while PSI works in Bangladesh, where almost half of the country's gross domestic product comes from agriculture.

When agriculture represents a small percentage of a country's GDP, one might assume that the country is fairly industrialized, but such a conclusion can be erroneous. For example, in Peru, home of "Industrias del Maiz's" parent, agriculture represents only 11% of GDP, the same as in Brazil. That results not from a comparable level of industrial development in Peru but from the large role played by mining in that country's economy. Our sample includes a sprinkling of countries that are natural-resource–rich—Peru, Indonesia, Nigeria, and Zaïre—and countries that are natural-resource–poor, such as Korea and Sri Lanka.

Political Stability and Economic Systems

We include several cases that take place in Mexico. That country's political stability, with more than sixty-five years of uninterrupted peaceful presidential transitions, contrasts sharply with the turbulent revolutionary changes taking place while "Pandol Brothers, Inc." develops an export market for Nicaraguan bananas.

Not only do we include countries with different rates of political change, our sample includes also countries with vastly different economic systems. "The Leather Industry in India" case reflects India's rather centralized economic system; and "Nike" must operate in China's highly controlled economy. The "Thai Polyester Fiber" company, by contrast, operates in Thailand's free-market economy, and "The Cut Flower Industry in Colombia" case is an example of private sector cooperation, rather than central government control.

Economic Stability

One of the great challenges often facing LDC managers is coping with economically unstable high-inflation environments, so we include cases in Brazil, Nicaragua, and Mexico, all with 1980–87 average inflation rates of over 50%. But not all LDCs suffer from high inflation, as is seen in the cases in Thailand, China, India, Zaïre, and Korea, countries with rates well below 10%.

Physical Quality of Life Indicators

Our sample of countries includes variety along other dimensions. In Sri Lanka, China, and Korea, life expectancy at birth hovers around seventy years, while in Zaïre, Nigeria, and Bangladesh, a newborn is hardly expected to live past the age of fifty. Infant mortality rates are around 100 per thousand live births in Zaïre and Nigeria and about 30 in China and Sri Lanka. Behind such statistics lie differences in, among other factors, health care services. The population per physician in our sample of countries ranges from lows of around 1,000 in China, Korea, Ecuador, Colombia, and Brazil, to highs exceeding 6,000 in Zaïre, Bangladesh, Nigeria, and Thailand.

To summarize, we provide in Table 1.1 some statistics for our sample of countries.[4] In general, the diversity of countries in our sample reflects the

Table 1.1

Characteristics of the Sample of Countries

Country	GNP per Capita Dollars (1987)	GNP per Capita Ave. Annual Growth Rate (%, 1965-87)	Population (millions) (mid-1987)	Area (sq. km.) (000)	Ave. Annual Infl. Rate (%, 1980-87)	Life Expectancy (years, 1987)	Agriculture as % of GOP (1987)	Average Pop. Growth (%, 1980-87)
Africa								
Zaïre	150	−2.4	32.6	2,345	5.3	46	32	3.1
Zambia	250	−2.1	7.2	753	28.7	53	12	3.6
Nigeria	379	1.1	106.6	924	10.1	51	30	3.4
Asia								
Bangladesh	160	0.3	106.1	144	11.1	51	47	2.8
China	290	5.2	1,068.5	9,561	4.2	69	31	1.2
India	300	1.8	797.5	3,288	7.7	58	30	2.1
Pakistan	350	2.5	102.5	796	7.3	55	23	3.1
Sri Lanka	400	3.0	16.4	66	11.8	70	27	1.5
Indonesia	450	4.5	171.4	1,905	8.5	60	26	2.1
Thailand	850	3.9	53.6	514	2.8	64	16	2.0
Korea, Rep.	2,690	6.4	42.1	98	5.0	69	11	1.4
Latin America								
Nicaragua	830	−2.5	3.5	130	86.6	63	21	3.4
Ecuador	1,040	3.2	9.9	284	29.5	65	16	2.9
Colombia	1,240	2.7	29.5	1,139	23.7	66	19	1.9
Peru	1,470	0.2	20.2	1,285	101.5	61	11	2.3
Mexico	1,830	2.5	81.9	1,937	68.9	69	9	2.2
Brazil	2,020	4.1	141.4	8,512	166.3	65	11	2.2

diversity in LDC environments. However, one must not lose sight of the many shared characteristics that distinguish developing countries' business environments and that enable one to use a common analytical framework to tackle LDC-management issues.

AN APPROACH TO MANAGEMENT
IN DEVELOPING COUNTRIES

Given the diversity among developing countries, it is necessary to search for systematic ways of analyzing and understanding the LDC environment and the variables that create that diversity. We contribute to the search by presenting the core elements of an analytical framework, designed to help the manager examine the LDC business environment and understand the links that join it to the firm. This framework, presented in detail in Austin's *Managing in Developing Countries*,[5] is called the Environmental Analysis Framework (EAF). It is our conviction that adequate analysis of the business environment and clear understanding of the environment's influence on operations of the firm are keys to successful management in LDCs.

As we summarize the EAF in the following pages, we use examples from this book's cases to highlight the conceptual framework's relevancy to the managerial settings and problems the reader will analyze in subsequent chapters.

The EAF starts by categorizing the factors that shape a firm's environment into four groupings: economic, political, cultural, and demographic. These factors influence each level of a firm's environment, starting from the most distant, international level and progressing to the national, the industry, and finally the company level, as illustrated in Figure 1.1.

Environmental Factors

The usefulness of the EAF lies in its ability to focus the manager's analysis systematically on the multiple variables that impinge on a business. For example, isolating demographic, economic, political, and cultural factors is vital to understanding the issues "Population Services International (PSI)" must resolve to achieve its ambitious goals in Bangladesh. Similarly, the business problems faced by "Standard Fruit Company in Nicaragua" cannot be understood without delving into the political, economic, and social factors shaping revolutionary Nicaragua in the early 1980s.

However, focusing on broad variables, as described above, is only an organizational starting point. The EAF probes these broad categories

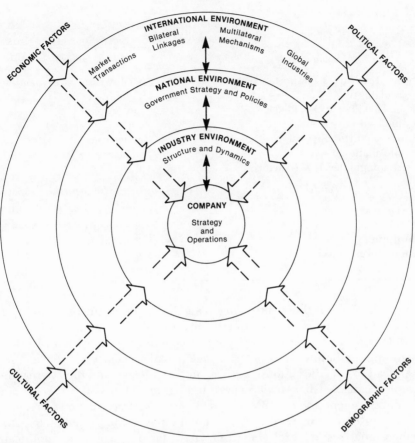

Figure 1.1. Environmental Analysis Framework

through their more specific components. For example, the EAF subdivides the economic factors into the three classical divisions of natural resources (land), labor, and capital, and adds two categories that are of particular relevance to developing countries: infrastructure and technology. Colombia's cut flower operations had to overcome transportation difficulties, and Milkpak's new venture in Pakistan faced problems of inadequate refrigerated storage facilities in the distribution channels. EMBRAER's efforts to enter the aircraft industry required overcoming technological barriers. Table 1.2[6] summarizes the EAF's environmental categories' subcomponents. Although identified separately for analysis, the interrelationships among these components also need to be examined.

A detailed evaluation of any of the environmental factors will point to the typical differences between developing and developed countries. An

Table 1.2
Environmental Factors

Economic	Cultural
Natural resources—importance and availability	Social structure & dynamics
Labor—skilled & unskilled	Human nature
Capital—domestic & foreign	Time & space
Infrastructure—physical & informational	Religion
Technology—levels & structure	Gender roles
	Language

Political	Demographic
Instability	Population growth
Ideology	Age structure
Institutions	Urbanization
International links	Migration
	Health status

understanding of those differences can clarify the distinctive nature of LDC business environments, and the direction of change can be surmised as LDCs move forward on the path of economic development. Under-standing the implications of a shortage of skilled laborers, for example, can lead to specific actions as we see in the "Mexico and the Microcomputers" case: Sensing Mexico's need to upgrade labor skills to accelerate its development process, IBM included in its investment proposal a scholarship program for training Mexican nationals in the United States. Detailed analyses of each environmental factor—economic, political, demographic, and cultural—will help LDC managers develop viable policies and implement sound strategies for their firms.[7]

Environmental Levels

1. The International Level

Environmental levels, like factors, need to be refined further to be analytically useful. At the international level it is appropriate to identify the cross-border flows that link countries together. One can classify four types of flows.

First, normal market transactions—as LDCs act as buyers, suppliers, competitors, and users of capital—link LDCs to each other and the DCs. Zaïre is linked with the United States and other DCs when Citibank puts together a sydicated loan in the "Citibank in Zaïre" case; and when American teenagers wear sneakers made by "Nike in China," flows of international trade strengthen the supply links between the United States and China. Second, special bilateral linkages join many countries into particular "partnerships." The special trading arrangements that exist between the United States and Mexico form the foundation on which the businesses discussed in "Compañia Telefónica Mexicana" and in "Rio Bravo Electricos, General Motors Corporation," are based. Third, multilateral mechanisms such as the Multi-Fiber Agreement (MFA), General Agreement on Tariffs and Trade (GATT), and the International Monetary Fund (IMF) ease the functioning of the international system. In the "Citibank in Zaïre" case, for example, one sees how the IMF's actions are central to continuance of private bank financing of Zaïre's development. And fourth, global industries and corporations link together LDCs and other countries as they all form part of globally distributed research, production, and distribution systems. The role of Mexico as a production site for General Motors' global sourcing strategies forms part of the analysis of the "Rio Bravo Electricos" case. On a smaller scale, we also find "Hitchiner Manufacturing Company, Inc.," exploring its first venture into "global" sourcing by considering a Mexican production site. Nike's incorporation of China into its international supply network is another example of links through a global industry.

2. *The National Level*

Within the EAF the focus is on the business environment of developing countries. Therefore, the stress is on the influence of international-level links on the national level of the firm's environment. Given the central role of governments in shaping the business environment, the focus at this level is on the strategies of governments.

Governments can be viewed as organizations striving to achieve national goals, which are shaped by economic, political, cultural, and demographic factors. To achieve their goals, governments devise development strategies, expressed in terms of national policies. These in turn are implemented through policy instruments and institutions, which affect industries and firms. Yet goals are not always explicitly stated, and the manager's first task is to understand what policy the government is following and why. From that understanding comes an assessment of possible future policy changes, as shifts in the factors that shape government strategy are foreseen. Finally, the manager's role is to assess the impact that policy changes—and their implementation via policy instruments and institutions—will have on the industry and the company. The resulting chain of events can be illustrated, as in Figure 1.2, using what Austin terms the "Public-Policy Impact Chain."[8] Figure 1.2 also illustrates the iterative nature of the process. Firms and industries, by their actions, can influence policy-makers and alter national strategies, policies, and implementation mechanisms.

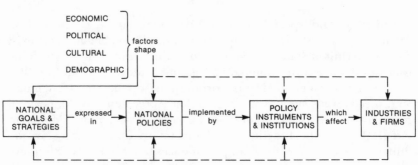

Figure 1.2 Public Policy Impact Chain

National Strategies. To achieve their goals, countries adopt development strategies, which can be classified in terms of their orientation or their main focus. Two strategies that stand out are the so-called import substitution industrialization (ISI) and export promotion industrialization (EPI) strategies. An ISI strategy is inward-oriented and focuses on serving the domestic market, protecting so-called infant industries from international competition. Managers like Reinaldo Richardson of "John Deere, S.A. (Mexico)" face specific challenges when operating in ISI environments. John Deere had to invest in Mexico or be shut out of the Mexican market. The decision that had to be made was far from routine: The investment required was substantial, yet project profitability depended on uncertain government policies.

An EPI strategy, on the other hand, focuses on serving international markets and gives incentives that foster international competitiveness. Korea's "Daidong Mould & Injection Co." and the exporters in "The Cut Flower Industry in Colombia" compete for exports in the international marketplace, and their success, while dependent on the favorable export-promoting policies of their home countries, rests primarily on their international competitiveness. Daidong's Mr. Jung-Myun Kang's outward vigilance contrasts with the inward preoccupations of John Deere's Mr. Richardson.

As one observes, each development strategy has rather specific effects on the business environment and on individual firms. The LDC manager, therefore, needs to understand the country's development strategy and the factors leading to its choice. The manager also needs to understand the dynamics involved, since countries sometimes change the strategies they follow. The EPI-based economic success of the "four dragons" (Korea, Taiwan, Hong Kong, and Singapore) has attracted attention of many observers. Several Latin American countries, traditionally devoted to ISI strategies, are shifting to EPI strategies. Chile, Brazil, and Mexico stand out as examples of countries that are doing so with rather positive results. "Empresa Brasileira de Aeronautica S.A." (EMBRAER) shifted from supplying a closed domestic small aircraft market to knocking on the doors of the U.S. market, which paralleled Brazil's development strategies. EMBRAER's U.S. competitor, Cessna Aircraft Company, needs to understand the forces behind these competitive moves to devise appropriate strategic responses.

Sometimes export promotion strategies are centered on exports of natural resources rather than manufactures, as was the case in copper-rich Zaïre and petroleum-rich Indonesia. In the "Citibank in Zaïre" case, one observes how lending policies depend on the prospects of the international copper market, while in the "Dow Indonesia" case Dow's executives must manage the tension between export promoting and import substituting policies of the government.

National Policies and Policy Instruments

The managerial implications of development strategies also depend on the policies and policy instruments used to implement them. As is done in other parts of the EAF framework, a breakdown into categories helps the manager understand the policies' potential impact. Policies can be grouped into six categories. The first five—monetary, fiscal, incomes, trade, and foreign investment—affect the overall economy. The sixth category, sectoral policies, deal with specific sectors, such as industry, agriculture, education, or defense.

The three broad categories of policy instruments discussed in the EAF also have distinct managerial implications. Legal mechanisms, such as tax laws, tend to be sticky and hard to change, while administrative mechanisms, such as domestic content requirements or industrial capacity licenses, are sometimes more flexible. The other broad government policy instrument, direct market operations, tends to have wide-ranging and hard-to-predict outcomes, as governments, frequently through state-owned enterprises (SOEs), participate as buyers, sellers, or creditors in the economy. Different instruments may impose quite different constraints and opportunities on affected firms. For example, getting an unfavorable law changed might be much more difficult for a company than negotiating a modification in an administrative procedure or regulation.

Just as policies and policy instruments have varying effects on the business environment, they also tend to affect different aspects of the firm's operations. Being aware of points at which policies impact firms, what Austin calls the policy impact points, will help managers establish the appropriate locus of the firm through which to monitor and react to shifts in policies and policy instruments.[9]

3. The Industry Level

Having understood the national level of the firm's environment, the manager must also analyze the industry level. Here the structure of the industry and the competitive dynamics among its players are the key elements. Since we are presenting the EAF as a tool of particular interest to managers in developing countries, we highlight the modifications that are needed to adapt Michael Porter's widely used "five forces" frame-work, to the LDC environment.[10] To the five competitive forces described by Porter: intensity of rivalry (between actual competitors), barriers to entry (against potential competitors), substitution pressures (from poten-tial substitutes), supplier bargaining power (as suppliers vie to benefit from selling to industry firms), and buyer bargaining power (from customers exerting their influence), we add the "mega-force" of govern-ment actions. Thus in our cases it is not surprising that "Pandol Brothers' " Jack Pandol is developing a partnership with the Nicaraguan government and "Dow Indonesia's" Colin Goodchild's project depends on the approval of Indonesian government officials. In order to do busi-ness, they all have to deal with the "mega-force." INDEMSA's effort to penetrate Ecuador's starch market requires dealing with the carton factories' larger buyer bargaining power derived from the government's import policies.

Bargaining with government is central to the business–government relationship. The "Mexico and the Microcomputers" case illustrates the dynamic interaction between governments and firms. Although its posi-tion departed from prevailing norms for foreign investments in Mexico, IBM insisted on a wholly owned subsidiary. A "policy tug-of-war" resulted between the foreign investor and the government. On a similar vein, Dow Chemical found itself proposing "creative" structures for its project in Indonesia to accommodate that country's interest in operating through a "contract of work" rather than through a Dow investment in a joint venture.

In addition to adding a sixth forth, the EAF modifies Porter's frame-work by explicitly exploring the role of the four environmental factors. Analyzing how economic, political, cultural, and demographic factors affect each of the competitive forces enables managers to undertake meaningful competitive analyses in vastly different environments. Only by incorporating political forces into the analysis, for example, can one understand the issues Citibank must resolve in Zaïre and the multiple constituencies tugging at Sri Lanka's "State Timber Corporation."

The EAF also places an institutional perspective on competitive analy-sis by highlighting the distinctive characteristics of five competitor cate-gories, starting with state-owned enterprises. In addition to shaping the competitive environment through its regulatory powers, LDC governments exert their influence through state-owned enterprises. Suddenly, the government is not only a shaper but a player within the industry, acting as buyer, supplier, competitor, or potential entrant. Brazil, for example, became a serious competitor in the aircraft industry through the actions of its state-owned enterprise "EMBRAER." The presence of state-owned enterprises in LDC industries highlights the need to take a closer look at the remaining distinctive actors that tend to be present in developing-country industrial environments. Private sector firms can be grouped into four broad competitor categories: (1) business groups like the Nigerian Ashamu Group described in "Ashamu Holdings Limited," the Pakistani Ali Group of the "Packages" and "Milkpak" cases, the Yipsoon Group involved in setting up the "Thai Polyester Fiber's" polymerization and filature factory, or the Peruvian-based von Rheineck Group that started "Industrias del Maiz S.A." in Ecuador; (2) local nonbusiness-group firms and cooperatives, such as "Daidong Mould & Injection Co." and the firms that make up the "Cut Flower Industry in Colombia"; (3) informal sector producers, such as the small-scale artisans in the "Leather Industry in India"; and (4) multinational corporations such as IBM, John Deere, General Motors, and Dow Chemical in the United States, and France's Chimie du Sud.

4. The Company Level

The EAF helps managers identify and understand the implications of the environmental factors for strategic decisions and operating actions at the firm level. In the chapters that follow we describe the key operating issues faced by LDC managers and give the readers an opportunity to apply the EAF to help resolve the problems presented in each chapter's cases.

ORGANIZATION OF THE CASES

We have organized the cases to focus on key issues of management in developing countries. Chapter 2 starts the case series by exploring issues surrounding the strategic decision to enter a developing country through direct investment. The issues we present in Chapter 2, "Investing in Developing Countries," are who invests in LDCs, why they invest, where do they invest, how do they invest, and what startup problems they must handle. Chapter 3, "Managing the Business-Government Nexus,"[11] is dedicated to issues surrounding the management of business–government relations. In LDCs, as has been pointed out in our brief discussion of the EAF, manging the "mega-force" of government intervention is of primary importance. Because of its overbearing significance, this aspect of LDC management precedes the chapters dealing with issues in the "traditional" functional areas of management. The key issues we highlight in this chapter deal with understanding the managerial significance of government policies and actions, negotiating with governments, and handling the uncertainties and demands that a powerful and changing "mega-force" imposes on firms.

In the four functional-area chapters, we stress once again key issues that are particularly relevant to operating in LDC environments. This is not to say that in those environments all the issues with which managers must deal normally are not present; they indeed are, and we assume that our readers are familiar with them. We emphasize, in these four chapters, the additional considerations that are eminently pertinent to developing-country environments.

In Chapter 4, "Production,"[12] we point to the key issues of choosing appropriate technology, transferring it from home-country to host-country, and operating it in the new environment. In Chapter 5, "Marketing,"[13] we once again highlight government intervention, bring out the influence of infrastructural and organizational problems in distribution channels, point to important factors affecting advertising and promotional techniques, and illustrate an effort in "social marketing." In Chapter 6, "Finance,"[14] we focus on the managerial problems caused by high inflation and currency devaluation, together with issues arising from LDCs' capital scarcity and the resulting debt crisis. In Chapter 7, "Organization,"[15] we concentrate on two sets of issues: relationships with employees and relationships with partners.

We close the book with Chapter 8, "Exporting from Developing Countries." In order to export successfully the LDC-company manager has to master the problems presented in the preceding chapters. Exporting, additionally, gives rise to specific operating issues that we address, including what are the barriers that exporters must overcome, how can governments affect export operations, and what should be the strategic focus of exporting firms? Table 1.3 at the end of this chapter gives an overview of the book's organization.

Even though cases appear in specific chapters, they embody broader issues and lend themselves to other avenues of inquiry: All the cases in Chapter 8 deal with export marketing, a topic that complements the domestic marketing issues addressed in Chapter 5's cases; Chapter 6's "Citibank in Zaïre," Chapter 3's "Standard Fruit in Nicaragua," and Chapter 2's "Industrias del Maiz, S.A.," all raise issues of managing in politically unstable environments; Chapter 6's "Colgate-Palmolive" and Chapter 5's "Sabritas" deal also with the business–government relations that are the subject of Chapter 3; Chapter 2's "Hitchiner Manufacturing" and Chapter 7's "Ashamu Holdings" bring out issues that must be considered in the choice between wholly owned and jointly owned ventures, and the concomitant problems of joint-venture-partner selection; and Chapter 4's "The Leather Industry in India" and Chapter 8's "EMBRAER" highlight the role of governments in promoting the growth of specific industries.

Another avenue of inquiry is provided by our inclusion in various chapters of several cases from the same country, Mexico. They enable analyses scrutinizing the evolution of a business environment over time and from multiple company perspectives, providing insights into the dynamic aspects of LDC environments and into the diversity of problems and opportunities managers face. The Mexico series starts in the oil-boom years of 1979, 1980, and 1981 ("John Deere," Chapter 3, "Sabritas," Chapter 5, and "Rio Bravo Electricos," Chapter 4), proceeds to deal with the 1982–83 economic crisis ("Hitchiner," Chapter 2, "Electrohogar," Chapter 6, and "Compañía Telefónica Mexicana," Chapter 6), and concludes with the hyperinflation and adjustment processes that followed the crisis (1984: "Mexico and the Microcomputers," Chapter 3; 1986: "International Pharmaceuticals," Chapter 6; and 1987: "Colgate-Palmolive," Chapter 6).

Other case series allow different perspectives: the Nicaragua series reveals changes in a single political environment and industry (bananas), from its prerevolutionary period in the late 1970s, through the 1979 revolution ("Standard Fruit"), to its postrevolutionary adjustment period ("Pandol Brothers"); and the Pakistan series follows the activities of a single company over time in different businesses and countries as "Packages Limited," founded in 1956, sets up a plant in Zambia in 1974, proceeds with a diversification program in Pakistan in 1979 ("Milkpak"), and deals with the resulting staffing problems in 1986 ("Selecting a New Manager at Milkpak").

Chapters 2 through 8, in addition to including the cases indicated in Table 1.3, contain introductory sections where we highlight the chapter's key issues and provide, as a starting point for analysis, study questions that may be considered for each case, as the reader embarks on the journey of exploring the challenge of strategic management in developing countries.

Table 1.3
Map of Cases and Issues

CHAPTER 2.	*Case*	NIKE IN CHINA	HITCHINER MANUFACTURING
	Countries	U.S. to China	U.S. to Mexico
	Industry	Shoe manufacture	Metal castings
INVESTING IN DEVELOPING COUNTRIES	*Issues*	• Startup problems • Global sourcing • Co-production agreements	• Foreign investment decision • Where to invest • Offshore sourcing • Global competition • Joint venture
CHAPTER 3.	*Case*	JOHN DEERE (MEXICO)	MEXICO AND THE MICRO-COMPUTERS
	Countries	U.S. to Mexico	U.S. to Mexico
	Industry	Farm equipment mfg.	Computer manufacture
MANAGING THE BUSINESS–GOVERNMENT NEXUS	*Issues*	• Dealing with government influence • Capacity expansion	• Negotiating with governments • Investing decision as bargaining tool • Global strategies • Role of MNCs
CHAPTER 4.	*Case*	LEATHER INDUSTRY IN INDIA	PACKAGES LIMITED
	Countries	Internal: India	Pakistan to Zambia
PRODUCTION	*Industry*	Leather manufacture	Paper products mfg.
	Issues	• Technology choice • Export	• Technology transfer • Third-World multinational

Table 1.3
Map of Cases and Issues (*Continued*)

ENTERPRISE DEVELOPMENT	INDUSTRIAS del MAIZ, S.A.		
U.S. to Sri Lanka	Peru to Ecuador		
Charcoal	Agroindustry		
• Foreign investment decision • Partner choice • Development vs. profit • Entrepreneurship	• Market entry • Transferability of strategy • Third-World multinational • Country choice		

DOW INDONESIA	STATE TIMBER CORPORATION	STANDARD FRUIT in NICARAGUA	PANDOL BROS. and NICARAGUA
U.S. to Indonesia	Sri Lanka	U.S. to Nicaragua	U.S. to Nicaragua
Petrochemicals	Wood Extraction	Bananas	Bananas
• Searching for firm–government goal congruency (ECBA) • Negotiating with governments	• SOE– government relations • SOE management • Pressures for SOE privatization	• Dealing with revolutionary change • Political analysis	• Dealing with revolutionary governments • Trading opportunities and problems

THAI POLYESTER FIBER (B)	EVANS FOOD CORPORATION	RIO BRAVO ELECTRICOS GENERAL MOTORS	
France to Thailand	U.S. to Puerto Rico	U.S. to Mexico	
Chemicals	Food packaging	Electrical equipment	
• Startup problems • Technology transfer when there are joint-venture partners	• Achieving operations management goals. • Cross-cultural management	• Organization of production with local workforce	

(Continued on next page)

Table 1.3
Map of Cases and Issues (*Continued*)

CHAPTER 5.	*Case*	SABRITAS	MILKPAK
MARKETING	*Countries*	U.S. to Mexico	Pakistan
	Industry	Snack foods	Food packaging
	Issues	• Dealing with price and advertising message controls • Implementing marketing strategy	• Altering traditional distribution systems • Lack of refrigeration in distrib.
CHAPTER 6.	*Case*	ELECTROHOGAR	COMPAÑIA TELE-FÓNICA MEXICANA
FINANCE	*Countries*	Mexico	U.S. to Mexico
	Industry	Appliance distrib.	Electronics mfg.
	Issues	• Adjusting operations to a high inflation environment	• Dealing with currency devaluation
CHAPTER 7.	*Case*	SELECTING a NEW MANAGER at MILKPAK	TURRIALBA MINING COMPANY
ORGANIZATION	*Countries*	Pakistan	U.S. to Latin Amer.
	Industry	Milk containers	Mining
	Issues	• Selecting managers in a family-owned business	• Managing union relations
CHAPTER 8.	*Case*	EMPRESA BRASI-LEIRA de AERO-NAUTICA, S.A.	THE CUT FLOWER INDUSTRY IN COLOMBIA
EXPORTING FROM DEVELOPING COUNTRIES	*Countries*	Brazil to U.S.	Colombia to U.S.
	Industry	Aircraft	Flowers
	Issues	• State-owned enterprises as exporters	• Export promotion by governments and industry assoc.

Table 1.3
Map of Cases and Issues (*Continued*)

INFANT FORMULA CONTROVERSY	POPULATION SERVICES INTERNATIONAL		
Switzerland to LDCs	Bangladesh		
Food; milk	Contraceptives		
• Dealing with consequences of mktg. practices • Government influence on marketing	• Modern promotion techniques for "social marketing" • Distribution channel problems		
COLGATE-PALMOLIVE IN MEXICO	CITIBANK IN ZAÏRE	INTERNATIONAL PHARMA-CEUTICALS	THAI FARMERS BANK
U.S. to Mexico	U.S. to Zaïre	U.S. to Mexico	Thailand
Soaps, detergents	Banking	Pharmaceuticals	Banking
• Dealing with hyperinflation and currency devaluation	• Debt financing • Country risk analysis	• Use of swap mechanisms to finance expansion	• Modern systems as competitive banking tools in LDCs
UNTOUCHABLE WATER-CARRIER	THAI POLYESTER (C)	ASHAMU HOLDINGS	
India	France to Thailand	Nigeria	
Banking	Chemicals	Diversified	
• Dealing with employees given cultural and regional differences	• Dealing with partners	• Dealing with partners • Business groups	
DAIDONG MOULD and INJECTION	COUNTERTRADE and MERBAN CORPORATION		
Korea to Japan	Indonesia		
Plastics	Trading		
• Technology and marketing required for exports	• Countertrade as an export tool		

NOTES

1. *World Development Report 1989* (New York: Oxford University Press, 1989), pp. 196–97.
2. *Ibid.,* p. 191.
3. Unless otherwise noted, statistics in this section come from, or have been calculated based on, *ibid.,* "World Development Indicators," pp. 157–232.
4. It is important to note that the statistics in Table 1.1 are all for the late 1980s. As such, they give a picture of the current differences between the LDCs discussed in this book's cases. The statistics, however, do not necessarily apply to the cases, because they take place during different time periods.
5. James E. Austin, *Managing in Developing Countries: Strategic Analysis and Operating Techniques* (New York: Free Press, 1990).
6. See *ibid.,* Chapter 3, Table 3.1.
7. See *ibid.,* Chapter 3, for a detailed description of environmental factor analyses and their implications for managerial action.
8. See *ibid.,* Chapter 4, Figure 4.1.
9. See Austin's *ibid.,* Chapter 4, Table 4.3, for a summary of policy impact points.
10. Michael E. Porter, *Competitive Strategy: Techniques for Analyzing Industries and Competitors* (New York: Free Press, 1980).
11. See Austin, *Managing,* Chapter 6, for more detail.
12. See *ibid.,* Chapter 8, for more detail.
13. See *ibid.,* Chapter 9, for detail.
14. See *ibid.,* Chapter 7, for more detail.
15. See *ibid.,* Chapter 10, for more detail.

2

Investing in Developing Countries

Developing countries have increasingly attracted foreign direct investment (FDI). In 1986 FDI flows amounted to $9.7 billion (in constant 1983
prices and exchange rates), more than double commercial bank lending,
which had declined dramatically because of the international debt crisis.
With bank loans drying up as a source of new capital, developing country
governments have aggressively sought FDI, not only for the capital but
also for the technology, management expertise, and export market access
that foreign companies often provide.

KEY ISSUES

The four cases in this chapter address five key dimensions of FDI: who
invests in developing countries, why they invest, where they invest, how
they organize, and what startup problems they have to deal with.

Who Invests?

There is great diversity in the companies investing in the Third World.
The main investors are the large multinational corporations (MNCs) from
a wide range of industries. In 1985, 55% of the 500 largest U.S. companies
reported having assets in developing countries.[1] The giant Japanese trading companies have about 80% of their foreign manufacturing investments in developing countries.[2] The first case in this chapter deals with a
multinational, Nike, and its strategic decision to set up operations in the
People's Republic of China.

Smaller companies also invest in LDCs. U.S. firms with fewer than 500
employees set up 17% of their overseas operations in developing coun-

23

tries.[3] Two of the cases in this chapter are about smaller companies considering investments in developing countries. Hitchiner Manufacturing Company is a medium-size firm in the castings industry looking at an investment opportunity in Mexico. Enterprise Development, Inc. (EDI) is a new entrepreneurial venture established to create companies in the Third World, with its first investment targeted to Sri Lanka.

Foreign investments in LDCs also come from companies in other developing countries, often nearby. These Third World multinationals had set up by 1980 more than 1,000 subsidiaries and had invested between $5 billion and $10 billion in other LDCs.[4] In some countries and industries these investments have become dominant; for example, Hong Kong's FDI in Taiwan accounted for over half of all foreign investment in the leather, pulp and paper, construction, and transportation industries.[5] The final case in the chapter, Industrias del Maiz S.A. (IDEMSA), is about a successful Peruvian company's becoming increasingly multinational by adding to its existing international investments by setting up operations in neighboring Ecuador.

Why Invest?

The motivations for FDI can vary considerably among companies. One theory holds that foreign investment follows an evolutionary pattern related to a product's life cycle.[6] The product is developed, produced, and marketed initially in a developed country, with exports being added subsequently to add volume and achieve economies of scale. As the product matures, the company sets up production operations in developed and developing countries to serve those markets previously handled with exports. Sometimes this FDI is prompted by tariff barriers raised by local governments to stimulate national production in protected markets. Those foreign production operations initially serve the local market but then may add exports, even back to the company's original home market. Meanwhile the company has been developing new products, for which the cycle begins again. To some extent such motivations prompted Hitchiner management's attraction to Mexico and IDEMSA's investment in Ecuador.

Although the product life cycle model provided a reasonable explanation for much of the FDI in the past, the growing globalization of industries and increasing interdependence of developed and developing economies have created new pressures and motivations for FDI. Setting up production operations in LDCs has been used as a defensive and an offensive competitive strategy. On the defensive side, many firms found their developed-country production operations progressively less able to compete against lower-cost and increasingly skilled producers in developing countries. Third World manufactured exports to the United States grew fivefold during 1978–87, accounting for almost 30% of U.S. manufactured imports.[7] The production of television sets in the United States, for example, was rendered economically unsustainable in the face of exports by LDCs, so all the U.S. producers moved their production offshore. Korea and Taiwan became the world's largest producers of televisions. Defending against lower-cost imports from Taiwan was one of the motivations propelling Hitchiner to consider investing in Mexico. Many firms have established LDC operations as part of a global production system aimed at creating competitive advantage. Most of the semiconductor companies, for example, carry out the lower-skilled, labor-intensive assembly activities in developing countries while retaining the more technologically demanding production steps in the developed countries. IBM sources most of the components for its personal computers from Asian production sites. The major auto companies are increasingly mounting global sourcing networks. In this chapter the Nike case study provides an opportunity to explore such a global production and sourcing strategy.

Where to Invest?

Between 1970 and 1983 Latin America and the Caribbean took 50% of the FDI going to LDCs, Africa's share of annual FDI flows fell from 23% to 11%, and Asia and the Middle East increased their share from 27% to 39%.[8] Although foreign investments are made throughout the Third World, more than half the FDI during 1973–84 went to five countries: Brazil, Mexico, Indonesia, Malaysia, and Singapore.[9]

Deciding which country to invest in involves assessing the fit between company needs and country characteristics. Each company's situation will be distinct in terms of its strategy, resources, other international operations, and competitive conditions. Those require a standard business policy and competitive strategy analysis. For the country analysis, the manager can apply the Environmental Analysis Framework delineated in the previous chapter and in Austin's *Managing in Developing Countries*. Failure to understand the country environment thoroughly can lead to unforeseen operating problems, noncorrectable incompatibilities, and even economic collapse. Each of the cases in this chapter provides an opportunity to assess the country variables in the context of the investing companies' situations. That assessment is central to the analysis of their strategic issues. The chapter's four cases, taken as a whole, will allow the reader to compare and contrast the distinct country environments in order to identify the implications of key country differences for FDI strategies.

How to Organize?

One of the key strategic entry issues for investing companies is whether to go it alone or to form a joint venture. As of 1985 about 38% of U.S. manufacturing subsidiaries in developing countries were joint ventures.[10] The desirability of a joint venture depends on the extent to which the needs and resources of the potential partners are complementary and their operating philosophies and styles compatible.[11] The managements of Hitchiner and the Mexican Lanzagorta group faced this difficult task of assessing the desirability of joining forces. Some companies, such as IBM, have a strong policy against joint ventures. In contrast, the business philosophy presented in this chapter's case on EDI considered joint ventures to be essential. Collaborative arrangements can take many different forms. Nike's co-production venture in China allows us to explore one such organizational permutation.

What Startup Problems?

Mounting new operations in a foreign country is a very demanding task. The challenge and the difficulty lie in understanding and adjusting to the new environment. Businesses approach new contexts armed with their operating experiences in other countries. At issue is the extent to which strategies and operating techniques successful in one business environment will be effective in a new one. Managerial focus must be on transferability and adaptability. Assessing what aspects can be transferred and what needs to be adapted requires a systematic approach to analyzing the new business environment. The EAF provides guidance in this task.

Two of the cases in this chapter reveal difficulties experienced in starting up operations. After successfully negotiating permission to operate in China, Nike finds itself confronted with a series of production and organizational problems quite different from those encountered in its other Asian operations. IDEMSA's effort to transfer its successful Peruvian strategy to its new operations in Ecuador encountered a series of problems rooted in differences in industry structure and political context.

CASE STUDY QUESTIONS

In studying the cases in this chapter, the reader might find the following questions to be useful starting points for analysis. They are not meant to be an exhaustive listing, but rather serve as doors opening into broader areas of analysis.

Nike in China

1. What were the strategic considerations and competitive forces that led Nike to invest in China?
2. How was it able to initiate its operations so quickly?
3. Why did it encounter the various startup problems?
4. What would you recommend that Phil Knight do about those problems and about Nike's China strategy?

Hitchiner Manufacturing Company, Inc.

1. What factors led Hitchiner to consider investing in Mexico?
2. Should Hitchiner make the investment?
3. Should Hitchiner and Lanzagorta form a joint venture?
4. What should the joint venture's strategy be?

Enterprise Development Inc. (EDI)

1. What is your evaluation of EDI's investment and operating philosophy?
2. What is your evaluation of the Sri Lankan charcoal project?
3. Would you invest in this new venture?

Industrias del Maiz S.A. (IDEMSA)

1. Why was IDEMSA successful in Peru?
2. Why did it invest in Ecuador?
3. Why did it encounter problems?
4. What should management do about those problems?

NOTES

1. Calculated from Compustat Business Segment Database using data through 1986.
2. Kiyoshi Kojima and Terutomo Ozawa, *Japan's General Trading Companies: Merchants of Economic Development* (Paris: OECD, 1984), p. 43.
3. Tomás Otto Kohn, "International Entrepreneurship: Foreign Direct Investment by Small U.S.-Based Manufacturing Firms," doctoral dissertation, Harvard University Graduate School of Business Administration, 1988, p. 10.

28 Investing in Developing Countries

28 Investing in Developing Countries

4. Louis T. Wells, Jr., *Third World Multinationals: The Rise of Foreign Investment from Developing Countries* (Cambridge: MIT Press, 1983), pp. 2, 10.

5. Edward K. Y. Chen, "Hong Kong," *World Development,* 12, no. 5/6 (1984): 482–83.

6. Louis T. Wells, Jr., ed., *The Product Life Cycle and International Trade* (Boston: Harvard Business School, 1972).

7. *Foreign Trade Highlights* (Washington, D.C.: U.S. Department of Commerce, Office of Trade and Investment Analysis, 1987), p. A-19.

8. *World Development Report 1985* (Washington, D.C.: Oxford University Press for The World Bank, 1985), p. 126.

9. David J. Goldsbrough, "Investment Trends and Prospects: The Link with Bank Lending," in Theodore H. Moran, ed., *Investing in Development: New Roles for Private Capital* (New Brunswick, N.J.: TransAction Books, 1986).

10. Stephen J. Kobrin, "Trends in Ownership of U.S. Manufacturing Subsidiaries in Developing Countries: An Interindustry Analysis," in Farok J. Contractor and Peter Lorange, eds., *Cooperative Strategies in International Business* (Lexington, Mass.: Lexington Books, 1988), pp. 129–42.

11. James E. Austin, *Managing in Developing Countries* (New York: Free Press, 1990), Chapter 10.

Nike in China

In April 1980 Nike, the leading U.S. sports footwear company, submitted a business proposal to the People's Republic of China (PRC). In a letter of transmittal, Nike's founder and president, Phil Knight, laid out the project's objectives and rationale:

> Primary among our objectives is to establish the means by which we would buy a finished shoe product from the People's Republic of China. We presently target a goal of 100,000 pair per month in the first phase, with growth to 1,000,000 pair per month, or US$30 million per year by the mid-1980s.
>
> We feel that the People's Republic of China, with its long tradition of excellence in this field of manufacture, would be an ideal additional source for our product. We see immediate benefits to be derived by each party in this business relationship, with even more important long-term benefits in the future.

Five months later the first production supply contract was signed; by October 1981 shoe production had begun. The rapidity with which Nike had maneuvered through the Chinese bureaucracy was hailed in the business press as "dazzling."

But by late 1984 production had reached only 150,000 pair per month. Many unforeseen problems led Knight to comment, "China has got to be about the toughest place to do business." In addition, the rapid growth of the sports shoe market was declining, and competition was increasing; this caused a drop in volume and major cutbacks in Nike's orders from its suppliers in South Korea and Taiwan (which provided 86% of its shoes).

David Chang, a Nike vice president and key player in the China project from its beginning, commented, "Unfortunately, China has not come on-stream as we expected. Although there have recently been encouraging changes in the government's policies, with our earnings going down there is pressure to get out of China." Given the importance of Nike's global sourcing strategy to its past and future success, Chang felt it was time to review the China experience and make recommendations on future actions.

This case was prepared by Professor James Austin, Professor Francis Aguilar, and Research Assistant Jian-sheng Jin as the basis for classroom discussion rather than to illustrate either effective or ineffective handling of an administrative situation. Abridged with permission.

Copyright © 1990 by the President and Fellows of Harvard College. Harvard Business School case #390-092.

COMPANY BACKGROUND

From a $1,000 investment and a small importing business in 1964, Nike had grown by 1984 into America's leading sports shoe company with sales approaching $1 billion. Return on equity averaged 46% over the 1978–82 period. During those years the business went public, but Knight remained the major stockholder and chief executive officer.[1]

Nike's product line proliferated as the fitness boom created new market opportunities. From high-performance racing shoes, Nike expanded into other sports (soccer, football, basketball, tennis), other user segments (joggers, nonathletes, children), and other product lines (leisure shoes, apparel). The number of basic footwear models increased from 63 in 1978 to 185 in 1983. Including model variations, the number of products totaled 340. Footwear accounted for almost 90% of Nike's 1982 revenues, with running shoes 34%, court shoes 30%, children's shoes 15%, cleated shoes 2%, and leisure shoes 2%; exports added 6%. Apparel sales were 10% of total revenue.

From its inception, Nike had sourced almost all its shoes from offshore producers. The original Japanese suppliers were replaced by South Korean contract factories, which provided 70% of Nike's needs. Other important suppliers were Taiwan (16%), Thailand, and Hong Kong. The remaining 7% were produced in Nike's own U.S. production and research facilities. China was the most recent supplier. (The Philippines had been phased out due to its political uncertainties. Brazil was no longer considered cost-competitive. Nike owned a factory in Ireland that supplied the European Common Market with 15,000 pairs of shoes per month in 1984—half its earlier peak. Nike had also built a rubber factory in Malaysia, which in 1984 had significant excess capacity.)

Nike held a commanding lead in the U.S. athletic footwear market, with a 30% share. Its strong R&D capacity, high quality, economical offshore sourcing, dependable delivery, and outstanding brand image lay behind its success. Its major competitor, West Germany's Adidas, had a 19% share in the United States and led in the world with $2 billion in sales, of which 40% was in apparel. While Nike's emphasis was on importing and marketing, Adidas developed as a manufacturer. It had its own and contract plants throughout the world, including the Soviet Union. Converse held the next-largest share with 9%; it manufactured 70% of its shoes in the United States and sourced the rest from the Far East. Puma (a spinoff from Adidas) and Keds (a leader in children's sneakers) accounted for 7%

---

[1]Data based primarily on the Nike (A)–(E) case series, Harvard Business School, 1984, prepared by Senior Research Associate David C. Rikert and Professor C. Roland Christensen.

each. Several other smaller companies specialized in certain categories; New Balance, for example, had 15% of the running shoe submarket. (*Exhibit 1* shows breakdown of competitor shares and market segment information.)

The 1970s' rapid market growth began to taper off in the 1980s. Some felt that a shift from a seller's to a buyer's market was in process, and that pricing would become more aggressive. The proliferation of shoe models accelerated. Nike's basic models were expected to rise from 196 in 1984 to 430 by 1986. Seasonality of sales emerged: About 65% of company sales were in the spring and during the August–September back-to-school period. (In the past, Nike had maintained level production year-round.)

As demand faltered, Nike cut back its orders significantly (by one-third from Korean factories) and closed a U.S. factory. It posted a $2.2 million net loss for the second fiscal quarter ending November 30, 1984. Industry observers projected a 6%–8% growth rate for the rest of the 1980s.

Nike shifted its attention to apparel. The Nike name and swoosh logo were believed to be transferable, but apparel, a very different business from footwear, was presenting new problems. Knight commented:

> Adidas sells $700 million in apparel. We should get a portion of this, but with U.S. customs quotas, sourcing is a tough business. The quota on shoes is not so hard on us because we can get it better than our competitors due to our bargaining power with foreign suppliers. This is not true for clothes. Factories prefer to sell ski apparel rather than running warmups in their quota because of the higher value. In footwear we source 90% from abroad, but in apparel only 50%. Our apparel sales are growing; in 1984 they grew from $110 million to $180 million, but profit margins are lower this year. We would like to source apparel from China, but their quota is used up through 1987.

CHINA

Before its open-door policy in 1978, the Chinese government had relied on a "lean to one side" (toward the USSR) policy. Mao's Cultural Revolution had stressed self-sufficiency, isolationism, and anti-intellectualism. After Mao's death in 1976 and the Gang of Four's imprisonment, the government under Deng Xiaoping concluded that to modernize, China needed to tap Western technology, management, and capital. In 1979 Foreign Trade Minister Li Qiang described the break with old policy:

> We have made great changes in our trade practices and adopted various flexible policies. Not long ago we still had two important "forbidden zones" in our dealings with other countries: One, we

would not accept government-to-government loans; we would accept only commercial loans between banks. Two, we would not consider foreign investments. Recently we have decided to break down these "forbidden zones." By and large we now accept all the common practices known to world trade.

In 1981 Premier Zhao Ziyang described the rationale for the new strategy:

> By linking our country with the world market, expanding foreign trade, importing advanced technology, utilizing foreign capital and entering into different forms of international economic and technological cooperation, we can use our strong points to make up for our weak points through international exchange on the basis of equality and mutual benefit. Far from impairing our capacity for self-reliant action, this will only serve to enhance it. In economic work, we must abandon once and for all the ideal of self-sufficiency, which is a characteristic of the natural economy. All ideas and actions based on keeping our door closed to the outside world and sticking to conventions are wrong. . . . Ours is a sovereign socialist state. In accordance with the principle of equality and mutual benefit, foreigners are welcome to invest in China and launch joint ventures in opening up mines and running factories or other undertakings, but they must respect China's sovereignty and abide by her laws, policies, and decrees.[2]

Foreign investment flow into China in 1981 rose to an estimated $1.2 billion.

Also in Nike's favor was China's shift in emphasis from heavy to light industry, hoping to meet consumer demands and raise the standard of living closer to that of its neighbors. By exporting consumer goods, China would also earn foreign currency needed to achieve its goals of modernization before 2000.

China's Economic System

China's centrally planned economy did not rely on market mechanisms as the major tool for resource allocation. Rather, development priorities were set through decision-making at the highest levels of party and government, which then instructed the State Planning Commission to implement these policies through a series of economic plans. These plans were first defined as national programs to meet long-range objectives; later

[2]David G. Brown, "Sino-Foreign Joint Ventures: Contemporary Developments and Historical Perspective," *Journal of Northeast Asian Studies* 1, no. 4 (1982): 27.

they were specified in short-run, local directives and development targets, based on the various economic units' capacities. The commission allocated resources to ministries and provinces according to these plans. Ministries, organized by economic sector, controlled all important national economic units. Provinces, based on geographic divisions, ran their own economic activities like small nations. The commission had centralized control over the ministries; decentralized power was granted at the provincial level.

The bureaucracy tended to be vertical. But ministries were connected only horizontally by the State Planning Commission. As a result, production sometimes was disconnected, uncoordinated, and difficult to control. Prices were not based on market needs and demands; instead they were arbitrarily set by the commission to realize national goals. For example, food prices were kept low to meet consumption needs, and luxury items were priced high. Because output was geared to annual targets regardless of market demand, many goods became scarce and others were in oversupply.

Before the 1978 reforms, the Chinese "iron rice bowl" system guaranteed everyone a job and equal pay, regardless of performance. Promotions were based mostly on seniority or politics. With no tools to measure performance, workers had few incentives to produce more. The 1978 reforms provided bonuses to workers based on their performance, but these were still limited. Factory cadres able to institute rewards for their workers had little motivation to do so because they had few incentives for their own performance.

The Chinese Footwear Industry

In the past, most shoes produced in China had been manually made. Although the Chinese experience included the autoclave production technique for manufacturing canvas and rubber court shoes, the process for making more expensive jogging shoes was almost unknown to them. The government had previously neglected the footwear industry.

Workers in Chinese shoe factories generally had only an elementary school education. Also, Chinese factory managers lacked managerial training. Most had begun as workers 20 years earlier and advanced to managerial levels only because of seniority or politics.

Infrastructure

China's transportation and communication infrastructure was quite outmoded. The government had only just begun to rebuild port facilities to handle larger ships, and many new roads were under construction. Only the Beijing–Tianjin highway was close to U.S. standards. There was no direct-dialing telephone system between major cities; capacity within the cities was severely strained.

Cultural Environment

Trust and reliability were especially important components of business relationships in China, since China's formal legal system had yet to be completely institutionalized and channels for the free flow of information were often obstructed. Past experience with untrustworthy foreigners had made the Chinese reluctant to do business with strangers. "Friend of China" had a special meaning implying trust, patience, and understanding. The Chinese insisted that foreigners doing business with them treat them as equals and with respect.

NIKE'S ENTRY STRATEGY AND NEGOTIATIONS

Nike saw sourcing from China as a logical next stage in its global production strategy. It had shifted to South Korea and Taiwan from Japan when rising wages and the value of the yen pushed costs up. As costs in South Korea and Taiwan rose, Nike signed small production contracts in 1980 and 1981 with suppliers in the Philippines (250,000 pair), Thailand (250,000), Malaysia (75,000), and Hong Kong (50,000). A company study on future sourcing indicated India and China as the long-term, lowest-cost suppliers; China won out. (*Appendix A* provides a brief chronological summary of Nike's involvement in China during 1980–83.)

The company's director of Far East operations, Neal Laurinson, was the first Nike official to visit China; he went to the Canton Trade Fair in October 1979. Knight, deeply interested in Asia and China, waited in Hong Kong two weeks for a visa that never came. Like many other companies, Nike at first found the Chinese bureaucracy impenetrable. To gain access, management hired David Ping-Ching Chang as a consultant.

A Princeton-educated architect, Chang was born in China but left in 1941 at age ten. He was still a favored guest of the PRC and held a rare multiple-entry visa. His father had been China's ambassador to Czechoslovakia, Portugal, and Poland in the 1930s. The Chinese communists held ancestry in high regard; they also saw political value in dealing with their former class enemies. Before he joined Nike, Chang had helped arrange a deal between a Chinese factory and a U.S. auto parts company. His experience, contacts, language ability (he spoke Chinese but did not read or write it), and personality facilitated Nike's entry. Chang described the entry period:

One of the keys to Nike's success so far has been determining ongoing economic sources of supply. The president of the company had determined that China was the last major untapped source for a relatively labor-intensive product. We had to go. It was not a market; it was a production source. But we couldn't help but notice the two billion feet.

Success in China depends on common sense. The first thing we did was write a proposal to the Chinese, outlining the long-term nature of our commitment, the scope that would indicate to them that we were not just coming in to buy 100,000 pair of rack shoes and then heading over the hill. And we had the common sense to have the proposal translated into Chinese. This probably got our document to the top of the bureaucrats' stack. We wrote the proposal in April 1980 and got an invitation in July to come and hold a seminar. We were directed to the Ministry of Light Industry, which supervises the footwear industry. Our group of six visited 20 to 30 factories in Tianjin and Shanghai.

Negotiations continued in September and November 1980. The Nike team (Chang, the corporate counsel, and production and finance people) met daily with their Chinese counterparts, who numbered 20 to 30, de-pending on the issues discussed. Supply contracts were signed with two factories each in Tianjin, Guangzhou (formerly Canton), and Fujian prov-ince, and one in Shanghai. Ten trips over twelve months were required to complete negotiations involving provincial and municipal officials where the factories were located and the ministries of Light Industry, Chemistry (which controlled the rubber supply), and Foreign Trade.

Christopher Walsh (Nike's first resident managing director in China), who had worked two years in South Korea and three in Taiwan, stated:

The negotiations were some of the most strenuous I have ever participated in. The major issues we faced were issues we did not expect to arise. The Chinese were not familiar with the standard exclusivity clauses within our contracts. We wanted exclusive rights to these particular factories. We do not have difficulties enforcing these clauses in our other Asian countries and so tried to institute them in China.

The second issue was B-grade production. The Chinese will package almost 100% of what they make. There are certain standards that have to be adhered to which they were not familiar with, so that was a stumbling block for us.

The third issue was defective returns. A great deal of Nike's success today comes from standing behind its product. The Chinese could not accept that particular concept. They felt that once a shoe had been put in the container and was on its way to the United States, that was the end of the production agreement. In Taiwan or Korea that particular clause is long-standing and not questioned whatsoever. What we were able to procure from the Chinese was that they will guarantee the shoes for only 9 months after they depart China. This virtually eliminates that clause, for 9 to 12 months will have passed by the time the shoes reach the consumer.

Pricing was another key issue in the negotiations. Chang described Nike's approach:

One of the first things we told the Chinese was that their prices had to be more competitive with our other Far East sources because the cost of doing business in China was so enormous. We opened our books to them and showed what we were paying our other suppliers.

Walsh commented on the results of the price negotiations:

I think a lot of American corporations are misled in that you go to China expecting to pay much lower prices because people are earning $40 per month. However, the foreign trade corporations are of the opinion that since the standards are the same for them as for Nike in Korea or Taiwan, they deserve equal prices. We gave the Chinese a break on the first pricing round to get started, but we have to be more adamant in the future. The hope is for a 20% price advantage over Korea.

All contract agreements were negotiated with the ministries' staffs and the factory managers, and were based on specific shoe models' price, volume, delivery, and specifications. Because the factories had no foreign currency to purchase equipment, Nike entered into compensation trade arrangements whereby equipment was paid for in shoes. Nike would purchase B-grade shoes at a 20% discount during the first two years, then at a 40% discount. The agreements stipulated that factories could not sign contracts with Nike's competitors; they also granted Nike trademark protection.

Nike agreed to pay for purchases directly to the Ministry of Foreign Trade or its local offices. The factories would then receive Chinese currency at exchange rates higher than the fixed rate—as subsidies from the foreign trade unit (the only organization in China authorized to pay higher exchange rates). In Guangzhou the contracts were signed through the municipal government; new contracts were to be negotiated directly with the factory managers.

Operating Experiences

Walsh recounted the original production plans:

> In July 1981 we established forecasts for 10,000 pair per month in the
> initial 12-month period, with the gradual increase over 15 months to
> 100,000 pair. In retrospect those expectations were far too high. In
> the first 9 months we were able to export a total of only 35,000 pair.
> Not until 1984 did we reach 100,000 pair per month. We originally
> thought we would be producing a million pair a month by now.

The annual production figures were 140,000 pair in 1982, 263,000 in 1983
(9 models), and about 700,000 in 1984 (12 models).

Nike had to deal with a multitude of problems in technology transfer,
materials, quality control, inventory control, production flexibility,
worker and manager motivation, transportation, pricing, plant location,
expatriate staffing, and government relations.

Technology Transfer. Walsh described the transfer process:

> During the startup period, we had to arrange for technology transfer.
> The Chinese are looking for something in return. In the footwear
> industry the machinery was very antiquated; they expected us not
> only to import machines but to provide them with technical designs
> to help them get away from the cottage industry that had existed in
> China. Normally they would sit in small rooms and do most of the
> work by hand. A South Korean factory that makes 100,000 pair a day
> has good systems, so we brought those to China.
>
> We ran into difficulties, however. We did not really recognize what
> lay ahead for us. Lots of things evolve in these relationships with the
> Chinese that simply cannot be foreseen from overseas. It takes an
> onsite presence to get a feeling for the situation. As a result, six
> individuals and I located in Shanghai. We visited the factories daily.
> We attempted to institute inventory and transportation strategies. We
> assessed what these people could actually accomplish relative to our
> expectations.
>
> Communication is one of the chief liabilities in entering the
> Chinese market, and we went to great lengths to develop a
> communications system that would enable us to identify onsite
> problems and provide solutions to problems that arose in those
> factories. Only two Nike residents spoke Chinese, and no one at the
> factory spoke English, so we had to use interpreters.

Managers from the Fuzhou factory visited Nike headquarters in Beaverton, Oregon, in May 1981 and the Hong Kong factory in July 1983;
managers from the Tianjin #2 factory visited Nike's Thailand producer in
December 1982; and those from the Guangzhou and Quanzhou (Fujian)

factories traveled to the facilities in the Philippines and Thailand in November 1983.

Nike considered bringing native managers from South Korea and Taiwan to teach the Chinese the advanced technology. But the Taiwan factories were much smaller than those in China and the managers were unwilling or unable for diplomatic and political reasons to go to China. South Korean factories, on the other hand, were similar in size to those in China, and their managers were willing to cooperate.

Chang approached the Chinese about bringing South Korean managers to China to help in training. The Chinese leaders agreed, but only if the South Koreans obtained U.S. passports. The Chinese remained obstinate on this issue because of its political sensitivity. Unable to arrange entry for the South Koreans, Nike finally resorted to using videotapes of how the South Koreans operated different equipment. Walsh concluded:

> The biggest problem is that we are the buyers and they have to do it our way. It is difficult to convince them to use our processes and not theirs. For example, the factories need conveyor systems that are not now there. Our shoes, although simple, require a lot of preplanning and coordination on procurement. But their systems can't be changed overnight. There was give-and-take on processing methods. You have to be flexible.

Materials. The factories continually lacked local materials. Nylon, canvas, rubber, and chemical compounds were essential components in shoe production. Only about one-third of Nike's needs were available locally, and even these were sometimes difficult to obtain. When Nike offered foreign currency for domestically produced supplies, the Chinese were still not forthcoming because of bureaucratic obstacles. For example, although Shanghai had sufficient canvas for all Nike factories, to ship it to Tianjin required prior approval of at least six ministries. Nike found it easier to import canvas from Taiwanese and South Korean shoe exporters. Nylon also had to be imported. But suppliers were ambivalent about providing their competitor with materials: shipments often arrived deliberately damaged. This created strain between Nike and its South Korean and Taiwanese suppliers.

Walsh reflected on this aspect of the materials sourcing problem:

> The Taiwan issue went back and forth. Some months Beijing would turn its back on the issue, and some months they would lobby heavily to increase the trade via indirect avenues such as Hong Kong, Tokyo, or wherever, which increased our transport costs. South Korea was another issue. We did not really recognize the posture the Chinese had on South Korea. The Chinese knew very clearly that South Korea was our base for expansion and R&D in the Far East and that we had

to use these sources. But when we brought in material and machinery
marked properly with "Republic of South Korea" on the outside, it
just incurred a lot of wrath from customs officials, and fines were
assessed. But the major difficulties were the resultant delays. These
were 60 to 90 days, depending on the moods of the customs people.

Quality Control. Nike had a worldwide policy that its B-grade shoes
could not constitute more than 5% of a supplier's total production during
the first year, or 3% thereafter. B-grade shoes had cosmetic defects but
were structurally sound. Nike sold them as promotional items or in discount stores at a 40% discount. But because of quality-control difficulties
in China, Nike offered a 20% discount on all its PRC shoes for the first
two years and initially lowered its quality specs. After four years, still only
80% of the Chinese shoes were A-grade. Nike and the Chinese argued
constantly about the proper discount for B-grade shoes and the standard
measurements for A-grade. Nike felt that Chinese managers used more
energy arguing than improving production quality. Walsh commented on
the quality problem:

> The Chinese don't understand the brand concept. They couldn't
> grasp why C-grade shoes had to be destroyed and not sold locally or in
> another country. In fact, one batch of these was shipped to Australia
> without our knowledge.
>   We are educating factory managers that Korean, Taiwanese, and
> Chinese shoes are sold as equals and must, therefore, meet
> international standards. We are also getting the China Trading
> Company to understand the Nike production and marketing concept.
> The trading company staff and factory managers don't communicate
> enough with each other. Nike's people are physically in each of the
> factories almost daily. Our role is quality control, but we're looked on
> as educators. We prepared lots of manuals to define our methods.

Nike hired one Chinese inspector for each factory through the Foreign
Services Company, to which it paid $300 a month per inspector. The
inspectors received $60 monthly from the services company. They moni-
tored quality, production volume, new model development, and shipping
documentation.

One cause of the quality problem was the high level of dust in the cities
and factories, which impeded the gluing of insoles to soles. All the Tianjin
factory windows had to be shut to keep dust out. But this made the work
area too hot. Since air conditioning was too expensive, the factory had to
stop production during the summer. The cleaning procedure was to blow
dust off the soles with a squeeze bulb, but the workers tended not to do
this. Nike took factory managers to the Thailand plants, where they saw

the conditions and results of a less dusty environment and process. Dust-control procedures improved significantly after the visit.

Nike's national accounts, such as J. C. Penney, had been reluctant to take PRC shoes because of their presumed inferior quality. These buyers had at first been similarly reluctant when Taiwan began producing for Nike.

Inventory Control. Some shoe materials, unavailable locally, had to be imported. Ordering took six weeks. To guarantee normal production schedules, Nike had to know in advance what needed to be imported and when. But Chinese managers were unable to relay this information because they did not keep adequate inventory records. Planners did not recognize the importance of the time factor. In the Long March Factory in Guangzhou, the large storage room was on the top floor of the production building. A woman at the door checking materials in and out functioned more as a doorkeeper than a recordkeeper; she did not know what materials were needed for next month's production schedule and did not regularly coordinate her records with the planners. The planning staff responsible for ordering materials from Nike kept their own records based on a guess method of expected usage; very rarely did they check what materials actually remained in storage.

To remedy this, the Nike staff tried to keep track of materials needed for forthcoming contracts and to coordinate these needs with the supply room records to ensure that supplies were available. They also began teaching Chinese workers how to store the materials correctly to prevent damage.

Production Flexibility. Flexibility—a primary characteristic of South Korea and Taiwan—allowed Nike to expand production quickly. These factories were able to develop shoe models quickly from written specifications. Chang remarked on the contrasting situation in China: "Decisions in China are cast in concrete. You can't tell them, 'Stop making that shoe next month and start making this one.' Forget it! It's another round of meetings."

To increase flexibility, Nike hoped the Chinese would

- Build sample rooms enabling them to produce new models from patterns and specifications. This would require some new advanced equipment, about 19 more people, and an investment equal to about 2% of sales. The Chinese were unwilling to make such an investment.
- Produce, rather than import, lasts, molds, dies, and small tools necessary for the construction of each model. The initial investment could cost over $10 million, but individual factories had the authority to invest only $100,000. The Chinese were thus unwilling to accept small orders for different styles requiring different equipment. It was safer and easier for Chinese managers to import materials than to try

to develop or purchase local materials. Local suppliers tended to charge high prices because they did not want to incur losses; under the government's new policies, factories incurring losses risked being closed.

- Become more cooperative. But Chinese factory managers felt that as yet there was not real commitment from Nike. Furthermore, Nike's efforts to negotiate further price and quantity reductions had antagonized the managers.

Worker and Manager Motivation. Walsh described the basic, unexpected motivational problems encountered:

We set out more or less to emulate the South Korean and Taiwanese factories. We wanted to get Chinese factories up to where they could compete in development, pricing, and quality. We didn't realize the problems we would run into from the system. It's a planned economy: There are quotas in all sorts of different areas; pricing stipulations are established in Beijing. But most of all, there's the "iron rice bowl" concept that has long been a thorn in the side of the economy. It is hard to break. The factories are often poorly run because there is just no background in managing factory facilities.

By dangling big numbers we thought it would entice these people. It did not. We'd approach factories in midday and our production would be at a standstill, and they still had quotas to reach for that particular month. There was no motivation or incentive to increase the production.

A big problem is adhering to schedules. We've brought in graphics outlining schedules, and they don't grasp this. The problem is partly related to the lack of incentives. There is no difference in pay if they produce more shoes sooner. There is also a lack of talent on production scheduling. The talented business people are in the trading companies.

What we did was to institute our own incentive program. We lined up criteria based on productivity, quality, and delivery. We virtually put money on the table. If they would satisfy our demands, we would reward them with cash bonuses given to the factories. This concept was presented to Vice Premier Huan Lee in November 1981, and he was receptive to the idea. We instituted it in our first year there with mixed results. We saw a great leap forward for about 60 days. After that it was back to the same lack of motivation.

Transportation. In South Korea, where Nike had dockside factories, the products could be loaded directly into containers and shipped to world markets. In contrast, the PRC shoes had to be transported to the nearest harbor and shipped to Kobe, Japan, where they were transferred into container vessels. A Japanese trading company, Nissho-Iwai (Nike's primary supplier of working capital), handled all the company's exporting logistics from the Far East.

In Guangzhou, the two factories were close to each other and to the port. They had enough space for containerized trucks to drive in and out. But in Fuzhou the factory was on the main street; containerized trucks could not approach the entrance. The factory in Fujian, halfway between Fuzhou and Xiamen on a well-maintained road, also had no access for container vehicles. The dock was outmoded and could not be used on rainy days, causing many loading delays.

Pricing. Tensions in the initial pricing negotiations continued. The Chinese partners were used to the stable prices of a central planning system. Because of unexpectedly high overhead, the initial price had to be reduced by 25% after two years. Although Nike had to pay extra dollars because of inefficiencies and scarcities in the Chinese system, the Chinese felt that the costs for foreign firms to do business in China were still lower than in South Korea or Taiwan because of lower food and transportation costs. They also disagreed about which side should benefit from the dollar's relative strength. The Chinese felt Nike should first reduce its own costs before asking them to lower theirs. For example, they felt Nike could reduce costs if Nike employees were to live and eat right at the factories. Managers of one factory were dissatisfied because a price agreement reached with Nike's Shanghai representatives was later rescinded by Nike headquarters.

None of the Chinese participants in price negotiations—staff from the foreign trade bureau, factory directors, and local production bureau leaders—had authority to make price decisions. Everything had to be relayed to authorities in Beijing. Thus, compared with Korea or Taiwan, negotiations were slow. The lack of a cost accounting system and of market prices also made estimating actual costs very difficult. The amount of the government subsidy became a key factor in the costing.

Knight commented on the pricing process: "China has such a cumbersome bureaucracy. In our price negotiations, four ministries were involved. Three said yes, but the fourth wouldn't. Therefore, the agreement was delayed 90 days. In a market that's changing, you can't do this." A further complication in Nike's eyes was that the Chinese did not consider variations in the exchange rate in the price negotiations.

Plant Location. By 1983 Nike concluded that its original locations were not optimal. Remarked Walsh: "We were more or less forced to go to Tianjin and Shanghai. We were new to China and did not know which areas would give us the best opportunity and the greatest degree of cooperation. We followed the government's recommendations."

In Shanghai and Tianjin, a major problem was the length of negotiation periods. In Shanghai there was little support from the municipal authorities, who were more interested in larger industrial projects. In Tianjin there was support from the mayor, but product quality was low.

Nike terminated its supply arrangement in 1983 with the Shanghai factory and was attempting the same for Tianjin. In Shanghai, Nike had to make a small compensation payment to close. In Tianjin, officials were quite disgruntled about the original five-year agreement's early termination and, in May 1984, sent a strong letter of protest to Nike. In it they questioned Nike's sincerity and commitment to China in a slowing world market, charging that Nike had made many unreasonable requests (such as expecting the Chinese to import materials that were unavailable locally, or to develop several new shoe models too quickly). The letter also accused Nike of reneging on its own agreements (such as wanting sudden reductions on "fixed" prices, or reducing orders because of high inventory). The letter concluded that Nike would be responsible for losses incurred if production terminated, and to please reconsider its unfair "way of business" (see *Appendix B*). Nike risked not being able to recover all its equipment investment.

In the same period, Nike opened two new factories in the south. The Guangzhou and Fujian factories were located in Special Economic Zones, where there was less red tape and more decentralized authority for decision-making.

Expatriate Staffing. In September 1981 Nike opened its residential headquarters in Shanghai with a staff of six, all in their twenties and thirties, and all with previous experience in Nike's other Asian operations. The Beijing office was closed in December 1983 because it was deemed no longer necessary and because housing was scarce. Walsh commented on the expatriates:

> It's always been Nike's production philosophy to assign expatriates to foreign communities for control purposes. I think that has a great deal to do with out success in the Far East. The expatriate community for Nike in Asia is 80–90 people. In Shanghai we represent 20% of the American community. Most are from the State Department, but two other U.S. joint ventures are there. The Americans are a very small but close-knit community.

Shanghai was considered the best place in China for foreigners to live. It was China's commercial center; transportation and communications facilities were relatively more advanced than elsewhere in China. But there were few Western movies; TV consisted almost entirely of programs in Chinese and operated only from 5 P.M. to 10 P.M. It was rumored that the Shanghai city government wanted Nike to remove its office from the city because it had closed the factory. Meanwhile, the Guangzhou and Fuzhou city governments were trying to persuade Nike to move their offices south, but Nike employees resisted because of inferior living conditions and weather.

The Nike staff flew to the factories in the south and stayed for three or four days before returning. More than half the staff brought their families to China. They lived in Western-style apartments built in the 1940s. Nike paid their living expenses and a 30% salary supplement for working abroad. The staff also received a week's vacation every two months, when they could go anywhere with their families—fully paid by Nike. The staff usually rotated every two years.

Government Relations. From the beginning, Nike tried to establish a positive relationship with the Chinese government through contributions to the country's sports activities (e.g., holding sports clinics and equipping the national 1984 Olympic team). Nike also hosted various Chinese officials visiting the United States.

China received Nike with great hospitality. During banquets, the Nike staff met many high-level Chinese leaders, who listened carefully to its problems. But this interchange resolved nothing. The Chinese leaders seemed more intent on persuading Nike to sign joint-venture agreements.

Nike often did not know with whom it should talk to solve its problems. The combination of decision-makers for different problems was always changing, and it was not always apparent who was in charge of what. Sometimes officials failed to show up for appointments. The local Nike staff often felt it necessary for high-level managers from Nike headquarters to come to China to get the attention of and gain access to China's higher-level officials. At a banquet given by a city mayor for the Nike staff, one factory manager remarked that he was very happy to see so many leaders for the first time.

Nike sent a report to First Vice Premier Wan Li, reviewing the company's progress and problems in the 1980–83 period. An excerpt from Knight's letter of transmittal indicates Nike's approach to dealing with the government:

> In my country there is an old belief that in order for any relationship to grow and develop there must be a mutually candid and beneficial relationship. In our co-equal partnership effort in China, I feel I should, representing Nike, mention in candor some of the problems we must face and resolve together if our long-term goals are to be met.

The problems, according to Knight, were:

1. Nonavailability of local materials (a detriment to both Nike's and China's economic goals)
2. Inadequate shipping and transportation provisions (causing Nike's inability to meet delivery dates)

3. Inconsistent high quality in China's manufactured goods
4. Nonmotivation and noncommitment of Chinese workers (Nike's incentive programs had brought mixed results.)

Many factory managers had negative feelings about the $7 million Nike contributed to support the Chinese national sports teams. They felt that such extravagant PR expenses did not solve Nike's production problems and only increased Nike's overhead, and that the PR program attracted the attention of only the national leaders, thus fostering good relationships only at the top rather than at the local level. They felt a Nike joint-venture agreement would be stronger evidence of Nike's commitment to China's modernization program—and at a fraction of the cost. They also noted that the Chinese Olympic team was criticized in the Hong Kong media for wearing Nike apparel rather than Chinese-made clothing.

Chang reflected on Nike's approach to relations with China:

China historically has been exploited for so long by the West. As a Chinese, I am perhaps more aware of the sensitivity of the Chinese to past exploitation. So I want to do everything we can to come across, for lack of a better term, as good guys. We don't want to be the rapers and plunderers of colonial days, because the Chinese are very, very sensitive to any possible re-emergence of that kind of attitude.[3]

On the political dimension he added:

You talk about international diplomacy. We are really doing something with the Chinese, not just talking about it. We're pressing the flesh; we're down in the trenches. We're doing every bit as much as the politicians.[4]

FUTURE STRATEGIC CONSIDERATIONS

As Chang deliberated on possible recommendations for Nike's future course of action regarding China, he focused on six areas: (1) the situations of Nike's other suppliers, (2) recent changes in the business environment in China, (3) joint ventures, (4) new factory locations in China, (5) the domestic China market, and (6) Nike's competitors.

[3]"Nike Builds Firm Foothold in China," *Los Angeles Times,* February 16, 1982.
[4]Charles Humble, "China Connection," *Oregon Journal,* December 23, 1981.

Other Suppliers

Chang compared Chinese factories with Nike's primary supplier, using several criteria:

1. *Development and production startup time.* The time from when the factory received the shoe model's technical package to the point of shoe production was four months in South Korea and eight months in China (see *Exhibit 2* for timelines).

2. *Quality.* The A-grade to B-grade ratio was 99:1 in South Korea, 98:2 in Taiwan, and 80:20 in China.

3. *Quantity.* Taiwan produced 1 million pairs a month, South Korea 2.25 million (with installed capacity sufficient to double output), and China 100,000 (with current capacity for 180,000).

4. *Raw materials sourcing.* The Taiwanese and South Koreans sourced 100% of their raw materials domestically; the Chinese imported 70%.

5. *Financing.* South Korea and Taiwan provided their own financing and had a straight trading arrangement with Nike; China required compensation trade.

6. *Transportation.* Shipping time from Taiwan and South Korea was 20–25 days; from Shanghai it was 35–40 days.

7. *Labor costs.* For the factories, labor costs as a percentage of total costs were about 30% in Korea, 20% in Taiwan, and 10% in China.

8. *Landed costs.* The landed costs for a pair of shoes from South Korea were $7.86; from the PRC they were $9.87 (see Table A). Nike estimated it was losing $1.00 on each pair of Chinese-made shoes.

South Korean shoe manufacturers had been encountering rising labor costs. Between 1972 and 1979 the unit labor cost rose by more than 300% (see *Exhibit 3*) and was still rising in late 1984. In addition, the South Korean government in 1981 discontinued all its support, mostly financial, for the shoe industry. One Korean government official said, "We believe our shoe industry is now fully developed to compete internationally. Our limited resources for support should be directed to higher-growth-potential industries such as heavy, chemical, and high-tech industries."[5]

An executive from one of Korea's largest shoe-exporting firms (and a Nike supplier) had this to say about his country's rising labor costs:

In the athletic shoe industry, labor cost must not exceed 24% of total cost to maintain international competitiveness. As of 1984, our proportion of labor costs is between 22% and 24%. This is about 30%

[5]Direct interview by Research Assistant Seok Ki Kim in 1984.

Table A
Landed Cost Comparison

	Korea	PRC
Price paid at factory	$6.36	$6.36
Interest	.37	.47
Freight	.23	.45
Duty	.54	.79[a]
Commission	.25	.25
Nike local office overhead	.11	1.55
Total	$7.86	$9.87
Retail price needed to maintain equal margins	$18.75	$23.50

[a]Higher duty due to importation of rubber products.

higher than in Taiwan. To cope with this problem, we recently modified our production facilities; we reduced the capacity for cheap products [canvas and vinyl shoes] by 25%, and we increased capacity for more expensive products [nylon and leather shoes]. In simple and cheap products, we cannot compete with Taiwan and other countries with cheaper labor such as China, Sri Lanka, Thailand, and the Philippines. Moreover, in response to recent decreases in orders for canvas shoes, we are concentrating in high-end products such as aerobic shoes. But whatever market segments we may concentrate on, I do not think our international competitiveness with large-scale production can last more than five to ten years from now. We have to get out of this sunset industry successfully and as soon as possible.[6]

In 1983 Korea exported $928 million worth of footwear; in 1984, $1 billion worth. Taiwan exported about 50% more than Korea. About 70% of both countries' footwear exports went to the United States. As of late 1984, most Taiwanese footwear products cost $3 to $4; the Korean products cost $4 to $5.

Most Korean footwear firms were large, employing up to 17,000 people. This size gave advantages in dealing with large foreign buyers, rather than affording technical economies of scale. Almost all companies exported their footwear under foreign brand names.[7]

Chang remembered that "when we first went to China, Korea and Taiwan saw their meal leaving the table." He wondered now if it should be brought back, and if other newer suppliers should be expanded. The two

[6]*Ibid.*

[7]Yung Whee Rhee, Bruce Ross-Larson, and Garry Pursell, *Korea's Competitive Edge: Managing the Entry into World Markets* (Baltimore: Johns Hopkins University Press, 1984).

Thai factories' combined output was up to 260,000 pair a month, with a capacity for 400,000. The A:B-grade ratio was 97:3. Delivery time from Bangkok was 30 days. Price negotiations took two weeks. Thailand had been able to reduce its raw material imports to 40% for canvas and nylon shoes, but it would not be able to supply locally significant quantities of leather if these shoe types were to be manufactured there. Knight looked at Thailand positively but wondered if "it might turn into West Vietnam," given the political dynamics in Southeast Asia. India and Sri Lanka could also be reconsidered for future sourcing.

China's Changing Business Environment

Deng Xiaoping, China's eighty-year-old leader, continued to accelerate China's opening to the West. In December 1984 he proclaimed that "China is a good place to invest. China keeps its commitments." He asserted that the PRC would remain open to foreign investors for at least the next seventy years. A proclamation on October 20, 1984, stated that "factory workers will enjoy free-enterprise incentives—including the freedom to change jobs—and a wage scale keyed to the real difficulties of their jobs."[8] The *People's Daily* in Beijing also published an editorial stating that the country could not rely on Marx's and Lenin's doctrines to solve all present problems. This ideological shift was favorable to private and foreign investors, but many traditionalists within the Communist Party were reportedly disturbed by it. In late 1983 they mobilized a campaign against "spiritual pollution" caused by the mounting Western presence.

Joint Ventures

The joint-venture form of foreign investment was increasingly favored by PRC authorities: About 20 involving $20 million had been mounted by 1981, and the number increased significantly by 1984. Under the 1979 law, a foreign investor's participation could not be less than 25%, technology contributed was to be "truly advanced and appropriate to China's needs," and exports were encouraged. But joint-venture companies were allowed to sell their products in China. State subsidies were available to joint ventures, and the foreign partner could screen workers and require new employees to pass skill examinations. Presumably workers could be fired for violating work rules. But some existing joint ventures had met difficulties in exercising these management prerogatives. Salaries were about 20% higher than in local factories.

[8]Hobart Rowen, "Deng's Private-Enterprise Initiative," *Washington Post,* December 16, 1984, p. L1.

Such joint ventures, if undertaken by Nike, were estimated to require an investment of $500,000 per factory, which could reduce Nike's flexibility in later shifting production sites if necessary.

New Factory Location

Shenzhen was the most advanced of the Special Economic Zones (SEZs). By October 1984 it had signed 3,316 agreements and contracts with overseas firms, involving a total investment of 6 billion yuan (US$1 = 2.8 yuan). The SEZs were intended to attract foreign investment, particularly in light manufacturing industries catering to export markets. The Chinese government provided special facilities (infrastructure and services) and preferential tax treatment. Because Shenzhen was administered directly by the provincial authorities, the bureaucracy was simplified, and foreign trade and investment were granted broad latitude to protect investors' legitimate rights and privileges. Other special privileges included favorable consideration in land rent, choice of land sites, corporate income tax of 15% (half the normal rate), and import duties waived on production inputs. There were also favorable personal income tax laws for foreigners working in the SEZs. About 85 of the nearly 100 joint ventures in Shenzhen made profits, with an average rate of 15%. Considerable construction was under way to remedy Shenzhen's remaining infrastructure inadequacies with telephones, power, water, housing, and hotels.

Domestic Market

Visions of 2 billion feet still floated in Chang's mind. The numbers held inevitable market magnetism, but he was not optimistic about selling Nike shoes locally. The product was made for an affluent consumer, and the Chinese were more interested in Nike's exporting than in selling locally. But still, 2 billion feet.

Competitors

Finally, Chang wondered about the possible reactions of Nike's competitors:

> Puma, New Balance, Adidas, and Bata have visited China; none is sourcing from there yet. Dunlop has been buying canvas court shoes from the PRC, but we don't consider them to be a significant competitor. We are the point man for the industry. They are observing closely our experience and moves.

WHAT RECOMMENDATIONS?

The China project had brought Chang into Nike, and he had made a heavy personal and professional investment in it. Now well established in the firm and in charge of the company's apparel division, he believed it was important to analyze the China situation objectively and make recommendations that would best further Nike's success. He remembered Knight's words: "Winning is ultimately defined by the scorecard—which is financial results, but in the long run. We've had success, but we have to keep looking forward."

APPENDIX A
CHRONOLOGICAL SUMMARY OF NIKE IN CHINA, 1980–83

April 1980	Nike submits "A Business Proposal Between BRS, Inc., and the People's Republic of China," which outlines Nike's plans to trade with China.
July 1980	A Nike delegation including President Philip H. Knight visits the PRC for the first time for the purpose of entering into a long-term trade agreement with China.
September 1980	Second Nike delegation, headed by Vice President Robert J. Strasser, negotiates and signs the first supply agreements between Nike and the factories in Tianjin, Beijing, and Shanghai.
November 1980	Nike delegations return for further discussions with Sports Shoe Factory #2 in Tianjin. Agreements call for a total of about 1.5 million pair of shoes in the first year of production. Nike also signs an agreement with China Sports Service to equip Chinese national men's and women's basketball teams with shoes and apparel. Plans are begun for registering offices in Beijing, Tianjin, and Shanghai, and for establishing long-term residence for Nike's quality control managers in China.
March 1981	Nike's vice president, David Chang, hosts Luo Xin, first secretary of the Chinese embassy in Washington, D.C., at Nike's research and development facilities in Exeter, New Hampshire, and Saco, Maine. Nike signs basketball contract with China Sports Service at head office of Nike in Beaverton, Oregon.
May 1981	Fuzhou factory delegation visits Nike's operations in Beaverton, Oregon.

July 1981	Nike signs supply agreement with Shanghai #4 factory to begin production.
August 1981	Nike's resident teams selected for China under direction of Christopher Walsh, managing director, China operations. Nike sends three U.S. basketball coaches to Shanghai to conduct a clinic and assist in training Chinese athletes. China sends representatives of China National Light Industrial Products Import and Export Corporation to U.S. and to visit Nike.
September 1981	Nike sends three U.S. marathoners to participate in First International Beijing Marathon (placed 7th, 16th, and 25th in a field of 75). Nike's China office established at 65 Yanan West Road, Shanghai. Nike signs supply agreement with Shanghai #5 Rubber Shoe Factory.
October 1981	Nike's One-Line (nylon running shoes) production begins.
November 1981	Nike's president, Philip Knight, heads delegation, including David Chang, vice president, and Richard Holbrooke, former U.S. assistant secretary of state and Nike special counsel, to Beijing and Shanghai to hold high-level discussions concerning Nike's long-term plans for China, and to commemorate first "Made in China" shoes. Delegation received by Vice Premier Wan Li at Great Hall of the People in Beijing. Nike signs agreement with Quanzhou Rubber Shoe Factory to begin manufacturing canvas court (tennis) shoes for export. Ribbon-cutting ceremony held in Tianjin by Knight for first production of Nike One-Line shoes.
January 1982	Production schedules mutually agreed upon, calling for over 3 million pairs of athletic shoes to be produced in China by end of 1983.
February 1982	First workers' cash incentive plan begun in Tianjin. Other similar workers' programs are planned.
May 1982	Nike signs supply agreement with Long March Rubber Shoe (Guangzhou) and Fuzhou #1 Shoe Factories.
June 1982	Nike signs track and field agreement with China Sports Service, wherein Nike agrees to endorse, equip, and help train Chinese national men's and women's track and field teams.
July 1982	Nike hosts delegation of 10 Chinese coaches to attend clinics held at Washington State University.

August 1982   Nike's coaches conduct a 10-day clinic in Qunming.

September 1982   Nike sends 3 U.S. marathoners to participate in the 2d International Beijing Marathon (placed 6th, 10th, and 15th). Three U.S. coaches sponsored by Nike conduct track and field clinics in Nanjing, Shanghai, and Beijing.

November 1982   China's national track and field and basketball teams participate in Asian Games in New Delhi and capture overall title in Nike apparel and shoes. Nike hosts special trip for Shanghai #4 factory personnel to inspect Nike's production facilities in the Philippines.

December 1982   Nike hosts special trip for Tianjin #2 factory personnel to inspect Nike sources in Thailand.

January 1983   First shoes manufactured in PRC arrive in U.S. from Quanzhou factory; second shipment also arrives in U.S. from Tianjin factory.

March 1983   Nike signs supply agreement with Nan Fang factory in Guangzhou.

June 1983   Vice President David Chang meets Zhang Wen Jin, Chinese ambassador to the U.S., at the Tenth Anniversary Banquet of the National Council for U.S.–China Trade. Former President Nixon is keynote speaker. Zhu Jian Hua, in Nike shoes, breaks the world high-jump record of 2.37 meters at China's fifth National Games at Beijing Workers' Stadium.

July 1983   Delegation from Fuzhou factory inspects Nike operations in Hong Kong. Ron Nelson, vice president-production for Nike, visits factory sources in China with senior executives in charge of all shoe production scheduling and sales forecasting.

August 1983   Nike sponsors Nike China Summit for Foreign Trade Corporation meeting in Shanghai to discuss common problems and seek solutions. Meeting encompasses 24 individuals selected from Nike's source cities of Beijing, Tianjin, Fuzhou, Quanzhou, and Shanghai. High-jumper Zhu Jian Hua captures bronze medal in International Beijing Marathon, meets with board of directors of National Council for U.S./China Trade in Beijing.

November 1983   Guangzhou and Quanzhou factory personnel visit Nike's operations in Thailand and the Philippines.

APPENDIX B
CHINA NATIONAL LIGHT INDUSTRIAL PRODUCTS IMP.
& EXP. CORP. TIANJIN STATIONERY & SPORTING
GOODS BRANCH

TIANJIN

May 10, 1984

Scott Thomas
Managing Director,
NIKE, INC.
Shanghai International Club,
65 Yaman West Road, RM. 304 SHANGHAI
PEOPLE'S REPUBLIC OF CHINA

Dear Mr. Scott Thomas:

We have read your letter of May 2, 1984 and wish to reply as below:

Tianjin and Nike have been cooperating for shoe production for three years. Although we are still behind our designated goal, we have been making progress all the time both in quality and quantity of the products. Now, let us take the last 90 days evaluation period—Jan. 1 to March 31, 1984—as a case in point. The goal was 1,200 pairs of shoes per day for quantity and over 90% of A-grade shoes for quality while the daily output of TJ2 was over 1,000 pairs of A-grade shoes was around 90% by the end of March 1984. This means we have created the conditions for further cooperation.

On April 11, 1984 in Tianjin, you talked about the market changes and raised the subjects of price, new models, etc. We clearly expressed our willingness to consider your requests, meaning the prices would be lower and adoption faster for future new models. Our relative department already said we would set up specialized factories to make moulds and materials for large-scale production and quick adoption of new and varied models of NIKE shoes.

However, we must not be divorced from the present reality while considering things in future. In your letter, you definitely asked us to reduce the prices of the present models by 26% and specified the prices of different sizes of all the three models. You asked TJ2 to develop eight new models in September 1984, one new model per month from September to February and two per month after February 1985. Finally, you said that price and adoption of new models were the two prerequisites of our cooperation. If we accept them, our cooperation will continue. Otherwise, you will come to talk with us to cancel the supply agreement. May we ask, even if we accept your requirements on these two points, would you raise further points or put forward higher criteria two months later? We therefore cannot but feel doubtful about your sincerity in the cooperation.

We signed the five-year supply agreement in September 1980. In the spirit of that agreement, we signed the first sales contract for about 80,000 pairs of

ONE-LINE shoes for which you supplied some of the necessary materials unavailable locally in China. Later on, you said you would not supply the materials and asked us to do the import. That was a great change. But in consideration of our long-term business, we agreed to do so and imported part of the materials enough for the production of 300,000 pairs of shoes. After two years of cooperation, the factory is actually producing only two models—OCEANIA and OLLIE OCEANIA. Production for the third model—DYNO is not started yet. Now you ask the factory to develop eight new models in about four or five months (from May to September). Is this a realistic attitude toward continued cooperation with Tianjin? On more than one occasion, your people said: NIKE is recession proof (not affected by recession) and that your business is expanding very fast while many others in this line collapse because of market changes. With this in mind, we were all very surprised when you said that your inventory of shoes was very high and that you had more shoes than you could sell at the recent FU ZHOU Conference held in March this year. During our talk in Tianjin on April 11, you again said the prices must be reduced since the market was not good. We said we were ready to cooperate relating to the prices of future new models and even to a certain extent for those of the present three models for which prices have been fixed. You should not refuse to let us have orders for the models already in production such as OCEANIA and OLLIE OCEANIA and DYNO of which prices were just confirmed in February. You must be responsible for the losses arising from the suspension of production. So far we have not received any fresh orders from you after P.O. #84-3-5-TJ while in your letter you asked to reduce all the prices for OCEANIA, OLLIE OCEANIA, and even DYNO. For more than one reason, TJ2 has suffered heavy losses owing to the long suspension and abnormal situation of production. For NIKE production, TJ2 has set up new buildings and purchased special equipments and are heavily in debts now. How can a sudden reduction of prices by 26% be possible? Do you really think this is a reasonable request? The prices of DYNO were just confirmed in Feb. 1984 by your Shanghai Liaison Office, but you also asked to reduce them two months later on April 11. We expressed on the spot it was not a right way of business while you said it was the decision or instruction of your American Head Office. If your Shanghai Office did not represent your head office and prices confirmed or decisions made by your Shanghai Office could be negated by your American Head Office, it would be very difficult for us to accomplish things.

In your letter of May 2, 1984, you put forward two prerequisites for continued cooperation with Tianjin, i.e., reduce FOB prices by 26% and develop eight new models in September 1984. If we are not able to accept them, you will come to talk with us to cancel the supply agreement. Does it mean that you are ready to stop NIKE-TIANJIN cooperation?

Finally, we wish to advise that we should cherish our mutual relations already established and abide by the signed agreement. We should have further negotiations on prices, new models, etc. on the principles of mutual understanding and accommodations and in consideration of the market changes and actual situation of the factory so as to reach an agreement on main issues to let our cooperation continue. Cancellation of the supply agreement will be good to neither party, especially to NIKE's reputation. If you intend to terminate the agreement unilaterally by not giving fresh order to the factory while TJ2 has made preparations for the production, you will be held responsible for any loss of the factory arising from the suspension of production, etc.

It is hoped that you will carefully consider the above frank opinions of the five points mentioned by Mr. Li Guang Zeng of Tianjin Second Light Industry Bureau at our last meeting. Please come to Tianjin soon so that we may talk further in detail.

L. Yanji
General Manager

cc: Philip H. Knight of NIKE Beaverton head office, U.S.A.
David Chang Ping Chong of NIKE Beaverton head office, U.S.A.

Exhibit 1

Branded Athletic Footware Submarkets, 1982 Market Shares (%)

Submarket	Racquet	Running	Basketball	Field	Other
% of total market	*35%*	*30%*	*15%*	*15%*	*5%*
Leading competitors (% market share)	Nike 40% Adidas 20 Tretorn 6	Nike 50% New Balance 15 Adidas 10	Converse 36% Puma 30 Nike 20	Puma 30% Adidas 20 Hyde 10	Hiking and walking: Small but growing as older people discover walking.
Comments	Common for street use; tennis has not been growing but may in coming years.	Growth of 6% to 8% expected, depending on how long people continue to run and how many are diverted to home exercise.	Beginning to decline; fewer teens; Title IX[a] bulge over.	Team sports, so depend on increase in industrial leagues; soccer will grow but at expense of football.	Leisure: Moderate growth unless a model captures imagination of young people.

NOTE: Data based on sales in athletic specialty and sporing goods channels *only*.

[a]Title IX, a federal statute, required that educational institutions provide for women athletic programs and facilities similar to those provided for men.

SOURCE: "Nike (A)," HBS No. 9-385-025.

Exhibit 2 Current Models Development Timelines

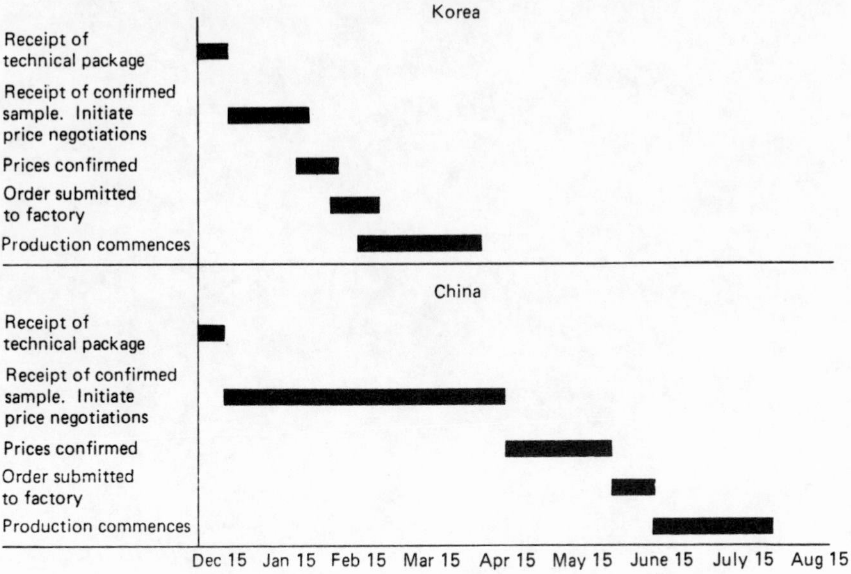

Exhibit 3
Comparative Changes in Unit Labor Cost

	1972	*1973*	*1974*	*1975*[a]	*1976*	*1977*	*1978*	*1979*
Korea	65.4	71.1	85.5	100.0	126.7	149.0	173.2	196.9
Taiwan	65.2	70.5	100.9	100.0	95.3	94.8	90.1	94.3
Singapore	—	71.4	90.7	100.0	99.7	120.4	—	—
USA	74.6	76.7	84.9	100.0	100.7	107.3	115.7	123.2
Japan	59.8	62.0	80.4	100.0	99.4	104.0	102.0	99.1

[a]1975 = 100 in national currency.

SOURCE: *Financial Times*

Hitchiner Manufacturing Company, Inc.

In April 1983 Nicholas Babich, president of Hitchiner Manufacturing Company, thought back to eight months earlier, when a feasibility study by a Harvard intern concluded that Hitchiner should expand its operations into Mexico via a joint venture with an influential private industrialist and entrepreneur. The arguments supporting an expansion into Mexico were simple then: The move would allow Hitchiner to enter an untapped foreign market and would establish a low-cost manufacturing base from which to import into an increasingly price-competitive U.S. market. Since then, however, Mexico had had a series of devaluations totaling 460% and was facing a liquidity crisis that was driving many companies bankrupt. Furthermore, questions still remained about Mexico's domestic market size and potential cost advantages of manufacturing there.

A letter from José "Pepe" Lanzagorta, a private investor in Mexico City, indicated that he was willing to negotiate with Hitchiner about an acceptable arrangement for proceeding with a joint venture. "Well," Babich thought, "one issue is clear; now we must decide whether and how to proceed with the Mexican project."

HITCHINER MANUFACTURING COMPANY

Hitchiner, founded in 1946, had become the world's largest diversified investment-casting company, with 1,000 employees and record net sales in 1981 of $54,600,000 (see *Exhibit 1*). Privately held and, according to its bankers, with the best balance sheet in the state, the company was headquartered in Milford, New Hampshire, and had three production facilities.

A plant in O'Fallon, Missouri, cast nonferrous metals; the Milford plant ferrous metals; while the Wallingford, Connecticut, plant served the local

This case was prepared by Javier Lanzagorta and Joseph Gonzalez-Rivas, MBAs '83, under the supervision of Professor James E. Austin, as the basis for class discussion rather than to illustrate either effective or ineffective handling of an administrative situation. Abridged with permission.

aerospace market. Each plant operated as a profit center. Sales were nationwide through a ten-person direct sales force and a network of 43 manufacturers' representatives. The manufacturers' reps were part of 13 separate rep organizations that carried Hitchiner investment castings and other industrial products. Commission was 5% of sales. (*Exhibit 2* shows Hitchiner's organization chart.) In a fragmented, price-competitive industry, Hitchiner was best known for quality and technological achievements. It held several patents and had experience in technology transfer due to two prior joint ventures in Brazil and Australia and numerous licensing arrangements in the United States and abroad. Its Milford plant was considered the industry's best for high-volume production, and it was the first investment-casting company to sell in large volume to the automotive industry.

Hitchiner's past growth had been strong and steady; sales records were set each year in 1976–81. Sales and earnings dropped in 1982 as a result of the recession and increased import competition. The company's long-term objectives were to continue to develop new metallurgical and ceramic processes for licensing, to remain privately held, and to grow through increased share of the commercial (nonaerospace) market.

INVESTMENT-CASTING PROCESS

In foundry terminology, casting is the production of parts by solidifying molten metal in a mold. Investment casting, named from the ceramic shell produced in the process and known as the investment, is the modern form of the "lost wax" method. Of the various casting processes, investment casting gives the best dimensional accuracy and finish.

In investment casting, one first constructs a very accurate wax, plastic, or frozen mercury model of the desired part. The model part(s) are then attached to a shaft or sprue of like material for handling during coating. In coating, the sprue is covered with a semifluid slurry that soon hardens much like concrete. Heat then melts the model, leaving a very accurate cavity on the hardened investment, which can stand temperatures up to 2,000°F. Metal poured into the investment produces a casting of excellent accuracy and very fine finish.

Capital equipment costs in investment casting are relatively low, from $0.20 per dollar of sale for a large, fairly automated facility like Milford to $0.31 per dollar of sale for a smaller plant like the proposed Mexican operation. Operating costs are fairly high, but the reduction in later machining permitted with investment castings makes its overall cost competitive with other manufacturing processes. (Hitchiner's operating costs are in *Exhibit 3*.) With mechanization the process is reasonably fast; skilled labor is unnecessary. In fact, only in the fabrication of the metal die from which the wax models are made is skilled labor required.

COMPETITIVE SITUATION IN THE U.S. MARKET

The noncaptive U.S. investment-casting market in 1981 was $828 million among 202 competitors. Only about half of these recorded 1981 sales over $1 million. Hitchiner was third, behind two large aerospace suppliers with sales between $64 million and $97 million. The commercial ferrous sector, Hitchiner's largest market, was estimated at around $430 million in 1981.

Overall, the commercial ferrous sector was a low-tech, low-capital investment industry. Competition in most product segments was in price; quality was secondary in all but a few. For instance, handguns and automotive precombustion chambers were very quality sensitive. Most companies focused on a few products. The many customers ranged from the very small to the largest, like General Motors. Average order size, even for a large firm like Hitchiner, was around $3,000. Because of either the industry's fragmentation or the many small customers, the market was somewhat divided geographically.

Commercially, Hitchiner was rather unusual. With production capacity to do about $90 million in sales, it had the largest, most modern facility in the commercial industry at Milford. It competed across 60 different products. (A breakdown of Hitchiner's competitive situation versus some competitors for 1980 and 1981 is in *Exhibit 4*.) By 1981 Hitchiner was concerned about its ability to compete in some products. For instance, price competition in valves (a large and growing market) would not support Hitchiner's high overhead, which included corporate staff and an R&D technical center.

Besides domestic pressures, investment-casting imports from Korea, Taiwan, and Japan began arriving in the United States in 1981. (*Exhibit 5* compares competitive bids that a U.S. valve producer received from Hitchiner and Hanton International of Taiwan.) Both Taiwan and Korea were focusing on the valve, golf, and other price-sensitive sectors, and Japan was going after higher-quality sectors. By April 1983 it was clear that Japan would be exporting automotive precombustion chambers in significant volume to U.S. car manufacturers. In fact, Hitachi Metals, which had investment-casting experience in Japan, made inroads into the U.S. precombustion chamber market as early as 1981. For 1982 Hitchiner's sales of precombustion chambers were $2.7 million, with around a 24% market share, a dramatic drop from 1981. The shift was due partly to a subcontract change in the parts, which caught Hitchiner unprepared, and partly to Hitachi's aggressive selling. Hitachi's and Hitchiner's precombustion chambers were of comparable quality, and Hitchiner's quoted price was slightly lower than Hitachi's for one of the two models supplied.

MEXICAN INVESTMENT-CASTING MARKET

As of August 1982, there were only two small investment-casting suppliers in Mexico, with a combined capacity between 100 and 250 tons per year. One of these suppliers, Eutectic Investment Casting, was located about an hour from Mexico City. Of Eutectic's 70 workers, about 45 were in production, and half of these were women. Eutectic estimated that it had produced over 400 different parts. Among its customers were two large valve manufacturers; it claimed to be producing transmission parts for General Motors, Renault, and Chrysler. Wax and shell materials (estimated at around 50% of all material costs) were imported from the United States. Although the parts' quality appeared lower than U.S. standards, two different customers indicated satisfaction with Eutectic. The other investment-casting supplier, smaller than Eutectic, was thought to have operating problems. The cost structure of neither company was known, but typical cost data for the Mexican casting industry were available (*Exhibit 6*).

The import market for investment castings in Mexico was not well quantified because most import parts were categorized by end use, not by manufactured process. Interviews with Singer, which controlled about 70% of the sewing machine market in Mexico, revealed that about 40 tons of investment castings were imported annually from Taiwan. Some sewing machine parts could be made only as investment castings. It was not known how many more investment-casting imports existed, but sources felt the amount was not large.

The estimated demand for investment castings in Mexico was based on the annual consumption and projected growth rates of relevant user segments in Mexico and on available demand figures for investment castings in Brazil (*Exhibit 7*). Brazil was used as a proxy for an industrially developing country (like Mexico) where an industry such as investment castings was thought to be in early stages of its life cycle.

IDENTIFYING A MEXICAN PARTNER

Hitchiner had participated in joint ventures in Australia and Brazil, but by 1982 only the Brazilian one, of which it owned 30%, was still ongoing.

Overall, Hitchiner felt joint ventures were not very satisfactory. Lessons learned from those past experiences perhaps led John Morrison, chairman of Hitchiner's board, to comment, "We've learned to be cautious. A key understanding of the partners is crucial to the outcome of any joint venture. We at Hitchiner work on a personal basis: If we like people, we will work with them." Others attributed the problems to Hitchiner's past role as mainly a financial partner. They felt Hitchiner had not been active in running the business and had not insisted adequately on management training for overseas partners.

In identifying Mexican candidates, Hitchiner focused on 30 firms selected from Dun & Bradstreet International as possible consumers and/or interested parties in investment castings. The firms' executives were interviewed to determine their interest in a joint venture and compatibility with Hitchiner. (The evaluation criteria are in *Exhibit 8*.) In September 1982 Hitchiner notified José "Pepe" Lanzagorta that it considered him the most suitable candidate with whom to establish an investment-casting operation in Mexico.

THE MEXICAN PARTNER

Lanzagorta's Background

Lanzagorta was president and CEO of Grupo Lanzagorta, a company that had sales close to $1 billion, employed 8,500 people, and had 28 Mexican and U.S. plants and subsidiaries. Headquartered in Mexico City, the Lanzagorta Group manufactured and sold a wide range of petroleum equipment—offshore platforms, drilling rigs, turbo compressors, etc. It also made industrial valves, pipe fittings, castings, forgings, and welding equipment and offered galvanizing services.

The oldest (at forty-eight) of four brothers, Lanzagorta was 25% owner of the privately held group and most responsible for its fast growth. A totally bilingual CPA, he began working in Lanzagorta at sixteen by selling over the counter when the group was a modest industrial supply business his father had founded in 1931. Lanzagorta described its long-term goals and strategy: "Growth with profitability, full reinvestment of profits, world penetration with international quality, vertical integration through incorporation of acquired technology and development of its own, and majority ownership and control of its subsidiaries."

Because of his long, successful business career in Mexico, Lanzagorta had extensive political and market contacts, which helped him solve many fiscal, legal, labor, political, and PR problems. With a long history of collaborating with U.S. companies (Atlantic Richfield, J. R. McDermott, and Dresser Industries, to name a few), he had ample experience in joint venture negotiations and a reputation for being able to make these ventures profitable in Mexico.

Finally, as a closely held and relatively unstructured company, the Lanzagorta Group was viewed in Mexico as an aggressive, flexible, and fast-growing company that provided a great opportunity for young executives to develop and grow. This *modus operandi* very much reflected Lanzagorta's entrepreneurial style and his way of expanding the group by creating and controlling companies. (Of the group's 28 plants and subsidiaries, 24 were started from scratch and 4 were acquisitions; 17 started as joint ventures.)

Lanzagorta's Interest in a Joint Venture

To preserve a healthy business, the four Lanzagorta brothers had agreed on a corporate policy of no nepotism that prohibited the owners' children to work for Lanzagorta. With this in mind, José "Pepe" Lanzagorta offered his only son, Javier (a recent MBA graduate), an opportunity to participate in the creation of a new business, work in it, and eventually buy out the company based on the business's earnings. They first had to find a small but highly promising business; the Hitchiner joint venture seemed to be the perfect choice. With an operation very similar to what Lanzagorta had in Mexico (i.e., manufacturing and selling metal castings for industry), Hitchiner was a relatively small and flexible company, and its products were in the growth stage in Mexico. It appeared to be a very good opportunity to develop the domestic market and penetrate the U.S. market through exports.

MEXICO'S ECONOMIC OUTLOOK

In December 1982, as de la Madrid became president, Mexico was undergoing a most traumatic period. A year earlier it had been riding high: its economy growing at 8% when other countries were in recession and the peso at 26.5 per US$1. But rapid inflation, excessive foreign borrowing, and softening oil prices led to devaluations totaling 460% and a meager 1% economic growth rate in 1982.

Since then, Mexico had turned to the IMF for a $4.65 billion loan and committed itself to decrease its deficit from 17% in 1982 to 8.5% in 1983. De la Madrid planned to do this by cutting public spending and raising taxes. But these measures were already causing social unrest. Unemployment was running high; wage increases were limited and could not keep up with inflation of about 100%. Price controls of many essentials were lifted, and subsidies for many products such as gasoline and tortillas were severely decreased, boosting prices to unprecedented levels.

Early in 1982, under the prior administration of president Lopez Portillo, the peso's overvaluation weakened exports and eroded confidence in its stability. Capital flight caused dollar scarcity, payment arrears, and loss of external credit. In August 1982 the government instituted exchange controls, nationalized the private banks, and limited the availability of dollars. (Nationalization did not significantly affect Lanzagorta's relations with its domestic creditors, but local credit became increasingly tight.) By April 1983, Mexico had to pay interest and principal of $14 billion on a total foreign debt of $80 billion. This represented 56% of its export revenue, estimated at $25 billion for 1983. Of the $11 billion left, Mexico had to pay for all imports of vital raw materials, already thought to be around $14 billion.

Priorities for foreign exchange use had to be set, so dollars at a subsidized rate were available only for certain imports.[1] Many imports were prohibited; others had to be paid with dollars bought at the "free" market rate of about 150 pesos to US$1. Because of the need to cut government spending and the belief that a weak peso made exports much cheaper, additional export incentives were not being granted.[2] Finally, dampening the economic outlook were high interest rates, an oil glut, and depressed prices that had greatly reduced the government's foreign exchange revenues. (For major economic indicators, see *Exhibit 9.*)

LANZAGORTA'S PERSPECTIVE ON THE JOINT VENTURE

Regarding the joint venture, Lanzagorta stated, "The main objective of the joint venture with Hitchiner would be to make a sound, growing profit. The key to achieving this is that the partners agree to commit themselves and view this company as their baby and be willing to sacrifice for it. They have to get along very well." He also commented on some of his past experiences with joint ventures:

In addition to compromising and making an effort, the partners have to realize that the only way of doing business in Mexico is having

---

[1] It was estimated that Hitchiner's raw materials could all be imported at a "preferential" rate of 110 pesos to US$1. This rate was slowly devaluating at a pace that would catch up with the market rate by year-end. It was also thought that importing the necessary machinery and equipment would not be a problem as long as they were not available locally.

[2] It was believed, though, that as the economy recovered and more funds were available to the government, traditional export incentives would return. These had been promotional, fiscal, and financial stimuli that could significantly enhance the attractiveness of an export business.

"Mexican know-how," i.e., knowing the right people, union leaders, politicians, lawyers, etc., and the way things are done in Mexico. I have seen many ventures fail because the U.S. company tried to apply the U.S. strategy without considering Mexican circumstances. Also, it is very important that both partners agree not to make a profit outside the regular operations of the company, that is, without trying to make money on the sale of old equipment, raw materials, technology, etc. This is essential for the survival of the business and should be specified from the very beginning. Written contracts are of little importance. If both partners are not morally committed to getting along with each other, the venture will not last long.

Regarding general guidelines to be followed to form the venture, Lanzagorta stated:

The technology has to be the same that Hitchiner is using in the U.S. Mexico needs new equipment, the same raw materials, and the very same process to be able to compete in quality. Also, the Mexican operation should be run as soon as possible by Mexicans. This maximizes the benefits of having a Mexican subsidiary as a supply source for the product in the U.S. market. About production and selling strategy, I think the Mexican operation should place quality and low cost before quantity. In the long run the Mexican operation should be an exporter, for the natural reason of market size. The margins in Mexico may be larger but not the volume. In the short run I can contemplate some 40% of domestic sales, but decreasing steadily to a minimum.

Concerning the compensation of partners, I think neither Hitchiner nor Lanzagorta could do it on their own. Therefore neither should pay any kind of royalties or fees to the other partner. Hitchiner would provide the technical know-how, the initial personnel training, and the U.S. market contacts, and I would provide Mexican know-how and experience, the contacts and relations, and whatever leverage as president of the Lanzagorta Group I may have.

(The Lanzagorta Group, for example, was already a large consumer of investment castings.)

Asked about the benefits and risks of entering a venture like this, Lanzagorta commented:

If we can take advantage of the Mexican economic depression and position ourselves in a good competitive base, we will be able to beat low-cost producers exporting to the U.S. like Taiwan and Korea and grow like mad. We will be creating employment in Mexico and bringing dollars to this country and can become leaders in the growing Mexican investment-casting industry. On the other hand, it is a big challenge to prosper in the depressed economy of Mexico and to compete in international markets with high-quality castings. Finally, I see a strong need to maintain a healthy relationship with our U.S. partner.

HITCHINER'S PERSPECTIVE ON THE JOINT VENTURE

On the joint venture's objectives, Babich replied:

The Mexican operation would be a clear opportunity for growth through presence in a new, industrially developing market. It would also provide us with a low labor and energy cost manufacturing base adjacent to the U.S. from which to penetrate the low-cost sectors of the investment-casting market. The company has been losing ground to small shops and imports from Taiwan and Korea. This new plant could really help us to fight back.

(*Exhibit 10* has direct cost comparisons between Mexico and Hitchiner U.S.) About overall guidelines for ventures, Babich commented:

We have to start small and build quality. Anything the Hitchiner name is associated with must be of the highest quality. Although this could be a problem at the beginning, we think that it is achievable. We would start with a few basic parts for which a Mexican market exists and within two years plan to sell in the U.S. through our own sales force. Such segments as textiles, valves, and automotive parts are important in the Mexican market. We could use the latest process and equipment in Mexico with no problem. Most of it we would manufacture ourselves. We could also use some good but idle equipment we have here in our plants.

About management and finances, he said:

I think 49% of the equity in Hitchiner's hands is O.K. as long as the growth objectives and management techniques to be used are agreed upon in advance. [Majority ownership by Mexicans was required by the government's foreign investment law.] We need a U.S. factory in Mexico, not a Mexican company with a U.S. flag. In Mexico we would have no control, but I think that José "Pepe" Lanzagorta has what is necessary to bring the business about. The way I see it, Hitchiner would contribute the technology, equipment, U.S. sales organization, and training for the people that are going to run the company. For this, some kind of fee would have to be negotiated and sent back to Hitchiner through sales commissions, transfer pricing, or other arrangement. At the same time José "Pepe" Lanzagorta could contribute the land, the building, and the Mexican know-how.

The joint venture would also require the government's approval. (See Appendix for criteria.)

Intending to start negotiations as soon as possible, Hitchiner had prepared sales, capital equipment, and personnel requirement estimates. These were then incorporated in a pro forma income statement and a cash flow analysis (*Exhibit 11*). An initial sales target of $5 million was to be achieved in the third year of operations with an estimated average sales price of $6 per pound and an export/domestic sales mix of 50/50. Requirements to start the operation included the training of Mexican operators and staff in U.S. facilities for a period of up to a year and the presence of U.S. technicians in the Mexican plant while the desired quality level was ensured. As Babich thought about the Mexican project, he wondered whether this venture would improve Hitchiner's competitive positions.

Exhibit 1
Hitchiner Manufacturing Co., Inc.
Statement of Income and Retained Earnings
Years ended December 31, 1982 and 1981

	1982	*%*	*1981*	*%*
Net sales	**$44,669,948**	**100.0**	$54,612,535	100.0
Operating costs and expenses:				
Cost of sales	**35,983,398**	**80.6**	41,877,290	76.7
Selling	**3,063,340**	**6.9**	2,962,141	5.4
General and administrative	**4,959,891**	**11.0**	6,266,239	11.5
	44,006,629	**98.5**	51,105,670	93.6
	663,319	**1.5**	3,506,865	6.4
Other income (expense):				
Interest expense	**(554,212)**	**(1.2)**	(1,258,498)	(2.3)
Interest income	**148,134**	**.3**	213,848	.4
License income	**437,694**	**1.0**	440,759	.8
Other	**42,474**	**.1**	71,008	.1
	74,090	**.2**	(532,883)	(1.0)
Income before income taxes	**737,409**	**1.7**	2,973,982	5.4
Provision for income taxes (Note 1):				
Federal	**68,500**	**.2**	725,885	1.3
State	**61,400**	**.1**	245,358	.4
	129,900	**.3**	971,243	1.7
Net income	**607,509**	**1.4**	2,002,739	3.7
Retained earnings at beginning of year	**17,813,346**		16,131,462	
Dividends on common stock ($25 per share)	**(310,930)**		(320,855)	
Retained earnings at end of year	**$18,109,925**		$17,813,346	
Earnings per share of common stock (Note 1)	**$48.28**		$160.05	

HITCHINER MANUFACTURING CO., INC.

Exhibit 2 *Organizational Chart* (effective January 15, 1983)

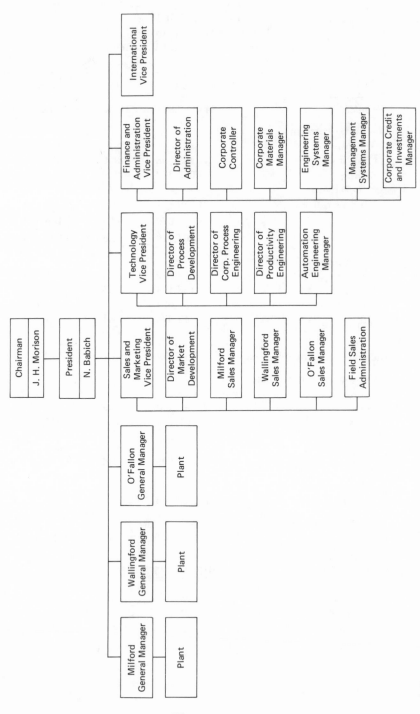

Exhibit 3
Investment-Casting Process Cost Breakdown (1981)

	% Sales	
Direct material	17.0	
Direct labor	15.0	
Direct overhead (including 4% energy)	18.0	
Total Direct Cost		50.0
Indirect material	5.0	
Indirect labor	10.5	
Indirect overhead (including 2.8% depr.)	11.2	
Total Indirect Cost		26.7
Total Cost of Sales		76.7

HITCHINER MANUFACTURING CO., INC.

Exhibit 4
Market Share (%) for 1980 and 1981

	Nonferrous		Auto Precombustion Chambers		Valves		Military Firearms		Hand- & Long Guns		Golf		Power Tools	
	'80	'81	'80	'81	'80	'81	'80	'81	'80	'81	'80	'81	'80	'81
PCC							32.6	33.0						
Arwood	14.2	11.9					16.3	17.0						
Hitchiner	7.6	6.9	67.2	85.0	13.0	6.8	14.1	12.5	10.0	8.2	14.5	13.2	40.0	31.0
Cercast	25.7	24.6												
Howmet														
Rex	4.0	3.8			3.4	2.8					14.5	NA		9.2
Hemet	12.5	10.0												
Golden State	5.3	NA					7.2	8.4						
Gray-Syracuse Casting									12.9	9.6				
Engineers					3.4	5.7			12.9	9.6			18.0	10.0
Southern Tool					18.3	14.8								
Post Precision					16.0	13.0								
Electroni-Cast									4.0	NA			18.0	NA
Other	30.7	42.8	32.8	15.0	45.9	56.9	29.8	29.1	60.2	72.6	71.0	86.8	24.0	49.8
Segment sales ($millions)	$113.0	$124.0	$6.5	$8.4	$43.8	$53.9	$9.2	$8.9	$31.4	$40.5	$11.0	$11.7	$2.5	$3.5
Hitchiner Sales	$ 8.6	$ 9.0	$4.4	$7.2	$ 5.7	$ 3.7	$1.3	$1.3	$ 3.1	$ 3.5	$ 1.6	$ 1.8	$1.0	$1.2

Exhibit 5
Hitchiner/H.I. Taiwan, Quote Comparison

			Hanton International		Hitchiner	
Valve Parts	Volume	Weight	Unit Price[a]	Tooling[b]	Unit Price	Tooling
1″ body	500	6.3 lb.	23.98	2,500	64.59	9,680
1″ bonnet	500	2.4 lb.	11.66	1,100	22.22	7,590
$1\frac{1}{2}$″ body	500	11.0 lb.	31.11	2,500	121.70	10,890
$1\frac{1}{2}$″ bonnet	500	4.3 lb.	15.55	1,300	33.20	8,030

[a]Unit price at Taipei, Taiwan. Transportation cost from Taiwan to Boston estimated at $.50/lb.

[b]Tooling represents the permanent metal die cost.

Exhibit 6
Mexico: Casting Industry Production
Cost Breakdown, 1975

Total	100%
Materials	
Raw materials	28
Direct materials	26
Indirect materials	3
Labor	
Direct	8
Indirect	4
SG&A	7
Maintenance	2
Energy	4
Depreciation	5
Scrap	13

HITCHNER MANUFACTURING CO., INC.

Exhibit 7

Mexico: Preliminary Market Growth Projections for Steel Castings
Without Including Potential Substitutions

Market Sector	1980 Consumption (metric tons)	1980–85 Projected Annual Growth Rate (%)	1985 Projected Consumption (metric tons)	
			Min.	Max.
Valves	22,000	13.7–24.7	41,800	66,300
Railroad equipment	17,200	6.3 (est. same as steel)	23,300	23,300
Mining equipment	17,200	6.8 (mining) 14.0 (petroleum)	23,900	33,100
Industrial equipment/tool	17,200	10.3–15.0	28,000	34,600
Construction equipment	8,770	11.1	14,800	14,800
Other (auto parts)	4,330	8.4–14.2	6,500	8,400
Total	86,700		138,300	180,500
Projected steel castings market growth rate			9.8% yr.	15.6% yr.

Source: SPP, NAFINSA, Mexico.

Exhibit 8
Candidate Evaluation Criteria

Criteria	Weight
Level of interest	1.0
Degree of financial and governmental clout	1.0
Joint-venture experience	0.8
Degree of management participation	0.8
Fit with corporate plans	0.7
Market contacts	0.7
Potential internal consumption	0.7
Foundry experience	0.6
Land/equipment availability	0.6

HITCHINER MANUFACTURING CO., INC.

Exhibit 9

Mexico Major Economic Indicators as of July 1, 1982

	'77	'78	'79	'80	'81	'82ᵉ	'83ᵉ	'84ᵉ	'85ᵉ	'86ᵉ
Billion Pesos										
Gross domestic product	657.7	712.0	777.2	841.9	910.3	898.8	870.5	901.3	947.4	1002.2
Output: agriculture	68.1	72.2	70.7	75.7	80.6	83.3	85.4	87.6	90.4	93.6
Output: industry	220.6	243.6	271.1	296.0	322.6	311.8	299.9	312.1	329.9	350.1
Output: Services	369.0	396.2	435.3	470.1	507.2	503.6	485.3	501.5	527.1	558.5
Private consumption	453.8	490.8	534.2	574.5	621.0	629.1	690.1	630.1	662.6	702.0
Government consumption	56.8	62.4	68.4	75.0	82.8	77.3	68.5	68.9	71.9	76.9
Gross fixed investment	124.0	142.8	171.7	197.4	227.1	190.5	167.1	170.4	179.8	191.1
Money supply	195.7	260.3	346.5	461.2	612.4	1018.1	1649.4	2372.1	3368.4	4715.7
Real per cap. disposable income (1970 Pesos)	9066.3	9446.7	10070.9	10670.6	11141.1	10725.2	10245.0	10116.9	10270.9	10467.3
Population (million)	61.4	63.4	65.4	67.6	69.4	71.2	73.0	74.9	76.8	78.7

Base Year: 1970 = 100

Wholesale price index	288.3	333.8	394.9	491.4	611.9	977.2	1912.6	2915.3	4247.3	5781.3
Consumer price index	263.3	309.3	365.6	461.9	591.2	937.1	1892.6	2988.9	4379.1	5973.0
Implicit GDP deflator	281.2	328.3	394.7	508.0	643.6	1021.8	2024.3	3155.6	4593.0	6262.3

Balance of Payments (Million US $)

Exports of goods	4649.8	6063.1	8817.7	15307.5	19379.0	18564.0	21116.3	26814.3	33139.3	40011.7
Imports of goods	5704.5	7917.5	11979.7	18486.2	23104.4	17841.9	15947.7	18955.4	23667.8	30339.3
Trade balance	−1054.7	−1854.4	−3162.0	−3178.7	−3725.4	722.1	5168.6	7858.9	9471.5	9672.4
Current account balance	−1596.4	−2693.0	−4875.8	−6760.8	−11704.1	−8695.8	−5030.8	−4114.2	−5065.3	−9236.2
Exchange rate, pesos/US$	22.6	22.8	22.8	23.0	24.5	53.5	112.7	168.8	229.4	286.9
Exchange rate, December avg.	22.7	22.7	22.8	23.2	26.0	80.3	137.6	191.7	260.6	325.9

Annual Percentage Changes

Gross domestic product	3.4	8.2	9.2	8.3	8.1	−1.3	−3.1	3.5	5.1	5.8
Output: agriculture	7.5	6.0	−2.1	7.1	6.4	3.5	2.5	2.6	3.2	3.5
Output: industry	2.6	10.4	11.3	9.2	9.0	−3.3	−3.8	4.1	5.7	6.1
Output: services	3.2	7.4	9.9	8.0	7.9	−0.7	−3.6	3.4	5.1	5.9
Private consumption	2.0	8.1	8.8	7.5	8.1	1.3	−3.2	3.4	5.2	6.0
Government consumption	−1.1	9.9	9.6	9.5	10.4	−6.6	−11.4	0.6	4.3	7.0
Gross investment	−6.7	15.2	20.2	14.9	15.1	−16.1	−12.1	1.9	5.6	6.3

(Continued on next page)

77

Exhibit 9

Mexico Major Economic Indicators as of July 1, 1982 *(Continued)*

	'77	'78	'79	'80	'81	'82ᵉ	'83ᵉ	'84ᵉ	'85ᵉ	'86ᵉ
Petroleum production, Tho, BPD	21.1	22.5	21.0	32.8	21.1	3.3	1.9	10.3	7.7	5.3
Money supply (million pesos)	26.4	33.0	33.1	33.1	32.8	66.3	62.0	43.8	42.0	40.0
Real per cap. disposable income	0.0	4.2	6.6	6.0	4.4	-3.7	-4.5	-1.2	1.5	1.9
Population (million)	3.3	3.3	3.3	3.3	2.7	2.6	2.6	2.6	2.5	2.5
Wholesale price index –End of year,	41.2	15.8	18.3	24.4	24.5	59.7	95.7	52.4	45.7	36.1
12-month rate	18.1	15.8	19.9	26.4	27.2	97.0	76.9	40.9	45.7	36.1
Consumer price index –End of year,	28.9	17.5	18.2	26.3	28.0	58.5	102.0	57.9	46.5	36.4
12-month rate	20.7	16.2	20.0	29.8	28.7	94.3	86.7	43.6	46.5	36.4
Implicit GDP deflator	30.4	16.8	20.2	28.7	26.7	58.8	98.1	55.9	45.5	36.3
Exports of goods	27.2	30.4	45.4	73.6	26.6	-4.2	13.7	27.0	23.6	20.7
Imports of goods	-9.5	38.8	51.3	54.3	25.0	-22.8	-10.6	18.9	24.9	28.2
Exchange rate	46.3	0.9	0.2	0.6	6.8	118.1	110.6	49.8	35.9	25.1
Exchange rate, December avg.	—	0.3	0.3	1.7	12.2	208.7	71.4	39.3	35.9	25.1

SOURCE: IMF, *International Financial Statistics.*   e: estimate.

Exhibit 10
U.S./Mexico Direct Cost Comparison[a] (dollars)

Part[b]	Weight (oz.)	U.S. Total Direct Cost (Milford)	Mexican Estimated Total Direct Cost[c]
1. Golf	9.7	2.63	1.26
2. Auto precombustion chamber	1.9	0.67	0.24
3. Auto precombustion chamber	2.4	1.35	0.93
4. Valve—1″ body	100.8	39.59	22.12
5. Valve—1″ bonnet	38.4	13.78	7.10
6. Valve—1$\frac{1}{2}$″ body	176.0	71.70	38.24
7. Valve—1$\frac{1}{2}$″ bonnet	68.8	20.70	11.45
8. Miscellaneous	23.8	3.97	2.61
9. Miscellaneous	376.0	105.14	40.30

[a]Total direct cost = direct materials + direct labor + variable overhead.

[b]Valve parts 4–7 are same as those quoted from Taiwan in Exhibit 9.

[c]Mexican direct labor cost including fringe = $0.81/hour (based on 150 pesos to $1). Electricity cost = $0.01/kwh. Import duties for raw materials = 25% of cost. Transportation cost Mexico to Laredo, Texas, estimated at $.07/lb., not included.

Exhibit 11

"Hitchmex": Pro Formas (constant 1982 dollars in hundreds)

	Income Statement				
	1985	*1986*	*1987*	*1988*	*1989*
Sales[a]	2000	4000	5000	5000	5000
Cost of goods sold[b]	850	1700	2125	2125	2125
Depreciation[c]	226	226	226	226	226
SG&A[d]	200	240	260	260	260
Interest expense[e]	125	125	125	125	125
Miscellaneous	50	50	50	50	50
Start-up costs[e]	500	—	—	—	—
Profit before taxes	49	1659	2214	2214	2214
Income tax @ 50%[f]	—	(440)	(1107)	(1107)	(1107)
Profit after taxes	49	1219	1107	1107	1107

[a]Estimated at an average $6/lb. and a 50/50 export/domestic sales mix.

[b]Estimated at an average $2.55/lb.

[c]Straight line with a life of 10 years on PP&E of $2.264 million.

[d]Estimated at $10,000/year average compensation per salaried employee.

[e]Estimated from experience on similar size plants.

[f]Includes tax-loss carryforward of $415 for year 1984 applied in 1985 and 1986.

	Cash Flow						
	1984	*1985*	*1986*	*1987*	*1988*	*1989*	*1990*
Profit after taxes	—	49	1219	1107	1107	1107	—
Interest expense	—	125	125	125	125	125	—
Depreciation	—	226	226	226	226	226	—
Changes in working capital[a]	—	(320)	(320)	(160)	—	—	—
Capital expenditures	(700)	(1564)	—	—	—	—	—
Startup costs	(130)	—	—	—	—	—	—
Residual value[b]	—	—	—	—	—	—	1934
Cash flow	(830)	(1484)	1250	1298	1458	1458	1934
IRR	45.62%						

[a]Estimated at 16% of sales from experience with similar size operations.

[b]Estimated as 5 years of undepreciated PP&E plus working capital in 1989.

APPENDIX I
MEXICAN GOVERNMENT'S FOREIGN INVESTMENT
REVIEW CRITERIA

To determine the covenience of authorizing a foreign investment and the percentages and conditions regulating it, the Foreign Investment Authority shall consider the following criteria and characteristics of the investment:

    I.   That said foreign investment be a complement to Mexican investment;

   II.   That it not displace Mexican corporations that are operating satisfactorily, and that it not be directed to fields adequately served by said Mexican corporations;

  III.   Its positive effects on the balance of payments and particularly on the increase in exports;

  IV.   Its effects on employments, considering the employment level created by it and the remuneration to labor;

   V.   Employment and training of technicians and administrative personnel of Mexican nationality;

  VI.   Incorporation of national materials and components in the manufacture of its products;

 VII.   Diversification of investment sources and the need to develop regional and subregional integration in Latin America;

VIII.   Its contribution to the development of the relatively lesser economic zones or regions;

  IX.   Not occupy monopolistic positions in the Mexican market;

   X.   Capital structure of the field of economic activity involved;

  XI.   Its technological contribution and its assistance to technological research and development in Mexico;

 XII.   Its effects on price levels and production quality;

XIII.   Conservation of the country's social and cultural values;

XIV.   Its importance within the Mexican economy;

 XV.   Identification of the foreign investor with Mexico's interest and its (his) relationship with foreign centers of economic decisions; and

XVI.   In general, the degree to which it helps achieve the objectives and complies with the policy of national development.

Enterprise Development Inc.

In September 1979 Thomas Barrett, a wealthy, socially concerned 1971 graduate of Harvard Business School, was presented with an investment proposal for a charcoal production venture in Sri Lanka to be undertaken jointly by Enterprise Development Inc. (EDI) and an indigenous firm (FINCO). The proposal came from an HBS classmate with the following note attached: "Tom, I thought you might be interested in this. It's one of the few opportunities I've seen where you can make money and also promote socioeconomic development. Steve Keiley, the president of EDI, is a good friend. If anybody can make this work, he can. But frankly, I don't know whether anybody can. If you're interested, let me know in a week or so."

CORPORATE PHILOSOPHY, OBJECTIVES, AND OPERATING PRINCIPLES

Barrett was struck by a brochure describing EDI's corporate philosophy:

> EDI believes the private enterprise system has a major role to play in the economic growth of developing countries. This role includes not only the provision of goods and services and local employment, but the building of indigenous capacity in developing countries to manage, own, and control the capital, technology, and other means of producing goods and services.
>
> The directors, officers, and investors in EDI seek to attain two coequal objectives through the activities of EDI. First, they will try to obtain a reasonable return on the investment made in the company by providing high-quality products and services that prove themselves in each relevant marketplace. Second, they will design EDI's activities to contribute significantly to the economic and social development of those most intimately involved with or affected by EDI operations in developing countries. EDI knows there will be constant tension between these two objectives, but it believes both are capable of

This case was prepared by Research Assistant John Ince, under the supervision of Professor James E. Austin, as the basis for class discussion rather than to illustrate either effective or ineffective handling of an administrative situation. Abridged with permission.

achievement and will consistently seek to realize both in all its operations.

A reasonable profit will be defined in advance for all EDI operations in light of the risks and uncertainties involved as well as the need for profit that may be necessary to contribute to the second objective. EDI pledges to be open about its return on investment.

EDI will define in advance of each new project, how and at what pace it will turn over its management control, technology, and ownership to host country nationals, and especially to those who work for EDI in the developing country. This transfer process will be designed to vest EDI's operations abroad in the hands of laborers, small businessmen, and others who would otherwise seldom have an opportunity to rise above their present economic status.

EDI will seek to be concerned about and involved with the interests of the entire community in which it operates in developing countries.

EDI operates on the following principles: (1) identification of development priorities in consultation with public and private officials; (2) determination of an approach sensitive and responsive to the country's needs and congruent with sound business practice; (3) utilization of a technology relevant and initially scaled for application by small business; (4) investment through a joint venture with a local company and an agreed formula for phasing out foreign investment when the operations are successful; (5) use of sound business practices to produce a top-quality product at a reasonable profit to investors; (6) selection of the most relevant technology and technical expertise without concern for national origin or political considerations; (7) promotion of international trade by linking suppliers in a developing country with prospective markets in the West; and (8) identification of value-added processes to enhance earnings from the export of natural products.

Barrett leaned back and smiled. He had never encountered an investment brochure like this before. He decided to give the investment a careful look.

THE CHARCOAL PROJECT

Country Background

The tropical island of Sri Lanka (formerly Ceylon) had 16.3 million acres and 14.5 million people. Politically stable, its government was democratically chosen in freely contested general elections. EDI viewed investment conditions in Sri Lanka as very favorable. The government was encouraging foreign investment. Allowed to float, the exchange rate was stable at 15.5 rupees to one U.S. dollar. (See *Exhibits 1 and 2* for government expenditures, balance of payments, and fiscal operations.) The World Bank and commercial banks were planning loans and credit arrangements to Sri Lanka of more than $450 million over 20 months to foster development. Sri Lanka's international credit rating was good. (See *Exhibit 3* for a description of important political and economic changes in Sri Lanka.)

The Sri Lankan Timber Industry

Sri Lankan forests covered about 3.3 million acres, or 22% of total surface area. In the late 1950s, forests covered as much as 45% of the area; the government was concerned about the recent rapid decline in forest area.

Broad forestry policies were framed by the Forest Department, part of the Ministry of Lands and Land Development. Most forests were controlled by the state; permission to clear an area had to be obtained from the Forest Department. The conservator of forests administered forest policies and implemented reforestation programs. The department was formerly also responsible for extracting timber from forests, but this activity (and necessary personnel) were transferred in 1968 to a newly created state-owned enterprise, the State Timber Corporation (STC). In 1981 STC enjoyed monopoly rights for timber extraction. It sold most of its extracted timber (80% logs and 20% sawn) through its own sales depots. STC had stepped up the volume of extracted timber considerably, from as little as 0.5 million cubic feet in 1968 to nearly 4 million cubic feet in 1977. Despite this, supply had always lagged demand. STC price increases had to be approved by the Prices Commission, under the Ministry of Finance; its prices were thus considerably below open market prices.

While timber extraction had grown rapidly, the rate of reforestation by the poorly funded Forest Department had been very slow, thereby gradually depleting the forests. The problem was exacerbated by illicit timber felling for what Sri Lankans called "chena cultivation" (clearing forest for firewood, then using the land for agriculture). It had been administratively and politically difficult to curb this practice by individual farmers.

The new government formed by the right-of-center United National Party (UNP) in 1977 was the first to take firm steps to arrest the alarming deforestation. In October 1977 it banned all tree felling in the wet zone (25% of the island's area) and permitted felling in only those forests of the dry zone (75% of the area) that would have to be cleared for developmental projects. Around the same time, the government also banned timber exports (including timber products such as charcoal) and liberalized timber imports so that any Sri Lankan could buy it abroad.

The government embarked on some major reforestation projects in addition to the Forest Department's program of reforesting 17,500 acres a year. Over five years they planned to reforest 15,000 denuded, degraded acres and to develop in 1980 a 25,000-acre plantation to supply firewood to settlers in the Mahaweli Development area. A plantation could be harvested in less than five years and would be productive for thirty years.

Charcoal Market

A large potential charcoal market existed in Sri Lanka. The demand could be about 160,000 tons a year with an approximate market value of Rs.192 million ($12.4 million). Commercial customers such as the tea industry represented half the market; urban households made up the rest. The potential export market was thought to be large, but figures had not been gathered. One international study reported that "wood fuels account for two-thirds of all energy other than human and animal energy used in Africa, for nearly one-third in Asia, for one-fifth in Latin America, and for 6% in the Near East. This compares with the one-third of 1% of total energy use which wood fuels account for in developed countries."[1] In developing countries, charcoal accounted for a minor but growing part of total wood fuel.

In Sri Lanka firewood was the main fuel source for both commercial and urban markets; about 60% of the country's total energy consumption was in the form of natural fiber. But firewood was becoming increasingly costly, for convenient supplies were limited and long-distance hauling was very expensive. Fuel oil was being substituted for firewood, but its price was also increasing rapidly. World prices had gone up 800% in six years but had moderated in Sri Lanka with heavy government subsidies that were now being removed. Recent removal of the government subsidy for kerosene had raised the retail price per gallon from Rs.1.10 to Rs.11.40, putting added pressure on fuel wood supplies. Because fuel oil was imported, it represented an outflow of scarce foreign exchange. Limited conversion to charcoal for commercial use could make possible net savings in foreign exchange of $10 million per year and modestly decrease dependence on foreign petroleum, the country's largest import.

EDI believed charcoal was competitive with wood because of low weight to heat energy output; it estimated that pound for pound charcoal produced at least five times as much heat value as wood. Thus, in Sri Lanka, where transport distance was a limiting factor for the economic use of firewood, charcoal was viewed as having a large potential market.

[1] J. E. M. Arnold and Jules Jongma, "Fuelwood and Charcoal in Developing Countries," 8th World Forestry Congress, September 1978, Djakarta.

Charcoal Production

There were three possible sources of wood for making charcoal. In 1980–85 about 24 million tons of fuel wood would come from the clear cutting of forest for the Mahaweli Development area. Less than a million tons would be needed for five years of charcoal production and could be in the form of slash or wastage from a timbering operation. The location posed prohibitive transport cost problems to move the wood as firewood. But it was economically feasible to transport charcoal the required distances, and charcoal did not have the storage problem of wood, which deteriorated rapidly in the climate.

Beginning in 1985 much charcoal could be produced from the surplus wood of fast-growing fuel wood plantations. Replenishment of these plantations and expanded acreage might provide a steady source of firewood for charcoal production and ancillary conversion technologies. Another source could be residue from a planned conversion of dry-zone forests to forest plantations and agricultural use. This was the subject of a World Bank Forestry Sector proposal that was favorably received by the Sri Lankan government in 1979.

Charcoal manufacture traditionally involved burning wood in pits or mounds where the air supply was restricted by covering burning wood with a layer of earth or metal cover. Control of carbonization was limited; yields were often low. This meant that often much wood was wasted. The charcoal produced was likely to vary in quality and to contain considerable amounts of earth and stones.

Portable metal kilns were ideal for charcoaling in developing countries with organized land clearance and reforestation programs. Owing to their size and cylindrical shape, they were easily rolled to new areas after forest clearance, thus minimizing the distance wood needed to be carried. The portable metal kiln developed and sold by Britain's Tropical Products Institute (TPI) was selected for charcoal manufacture in Sri Lanka. It was considered to be the best kiln available, but costly at $1,000 when compared to the $200–$300 cost of a traditional pit kiln. The TPI kiln was highly efficient, relatively pollution-free owing to its contained combustion, and simple to operate. Two men handling two kilns completed the charcoaling process in about two days.

TPI had agreed to provide in-country training and technical assistance for five years. Wood charcoaling expertise in Sri Lanka was scarce. The Sri Lankan partner had production and export market experience with activated charcoal using coconut shells. The STC had experimentally produced some charcoal in pit kilns to demonstrate local feasibility and to ascertain quality, but the pit kiln had proved unsatisfactory. The STC would experiment further with other production techniques and planned to test-market charcoal in the urban market.

Unit Cost and Profits

The costs of charcoal production were derived from STC and TPI data and an analysis by the Sri Lankan partner in the proposed joint venture with EDI. Cost figures were based on use of the TPI portable metal kiln with a production yield of 25%.

Wood for one ton of charcoal was estimated to cost Rs.300, based on the prevailing rate of Rs.75 a ton for wood cut and stacked. The cost was actually somewhat less: The wood could be obtained at little or no cost, for it was incidental to land-clearing operations.

Wages for firing, clearing, packing, loading, watering, etc. 1 ton of charcoal were estimated to be Rs.94, based on 1.5 men per kiln at a daily wage of Rs.25 with each kiln operating a seven-day week and producing 2.8 tons of charcoal per week. The packing cost was about Rs.115 per ton using coir net bags with polyethylene lining, costing an additional Rs.5 per bag.

Transport costs using a five-ton truck were estimated to be Rs.2.2 per ton per mile, including loading and unloading costs and allowance for recent cost increases for gasoline. Thus, transport costs for 100 miles would be Rs.220 per ton, adequate in most instances for a country the size of Sri Lanka. Administrative expenses and repairs were about Rs.68 per ton. Overhead was about Rs.303 per ton. A contingency allowance of Rs.100 per ton was included to cover unforeseen expenses.

A wood supply would be readily available. The charcoaling facilities would be situated close to the clear-cutting operations in the Mahaweli Development area; later charcoaling would be sited next to the fuel wood plantations. Unskilled labor would be readily available: The unemployment rate was high, especially in the rural sector.

In summary, the estimated cost of 1 ton of charcoal using the TPI portable metal kiln and including delivery of the charcoal to the industrial customer was Rs.1,200 per ton.

The market price of charcoal varied. The international market price was Rs.1,600 per ton FOB Colombo. STC was planning to introduce charcoal to the household market at Rs.2,000 per ton. The industrial market paid Rs.2,100 for the fuel-oil equivalent in BTUs for a ton of charcoal and had been notified of a 20–25% price increase in early 1980.

A preliminary price of Rs.1,750 per ton was for planning purposes. With charcoal costing Rs.1,200 per ton, a profit of Rs.550 per ton was projected, representing a 46% margin on cost or a 31% profit on the market price.

No allowance was made for taxes as a cost factor. It was assumed that a five-to-ten-year tax holiday could be negotiated with the government. Capital investment costs were modest next to other costs. A portable metal kiln costing $1,000 would produce about 100 tons of charcoal per year and would last five years or more. Thus, amortization of the kiln would be Rs.31 per ton if spread over five years.

Sales Projections

Discussions with the general manager of one prospective industrial customer (JEDB) indicated a sales potential of 30,000 tons of charcoal annually as a substitute for fuel oil and perhaps firewood. JEDB was willing to convert immediately to charcoal for tea-drying on two tea estates and to convert the rest contingent upon a five-year supply contract for charcoal. Several other large commercial customers represented a potential market for 60,000 more tons of charcoal per year. STC was strongly interested in the household charcoal market, which represented potential demand for another 70,000 tons. Thus, the potential Sri Lankan charcoal market could be as much as 160,000 tons per year valued at Rs.279 million with profits up to Rs.86 million or $5.5 million.

An export market for charcoal existed and could absorb excess charcoal production, but it seemed likely that the domestic market would initially purchase all the charcoal produced.

The intent of the proposed joint venture was to service a large, relatively secure industrial market. Long-term sales contracts with prospective customers were a realistic possibility. Total sales in the first five years were projected to be 200,000 tons over eight years, or $22.6 million. This was based on the production of 5,000 tons of charcoal in the first year, 15,000 tons in the second, and 30,000 tons per year thereafter.

The limiting factor was thought to be production capacity. Although the portable metal kilns were efficient, there was a point at which a profusion of small unit production kilns posed a technical and managerial problem. As experience was gained and a positive cash flow generated, it would perhaps be desirable to invest in relatively more capital-intensive methods of charcoal production to increase productivity and decrease unit costs with more efficient methods.

Investment by Enterprise Development Inc.

EDI was prepared to invest $165,000 in equity in the proposed venture: $60,000 cash and $105,000 in professional and technical services. A five-year $240,000 loan (repayable in annual installments) might be obtained in the second year from a U.S. lending institution. If certain conditions were met (mainly the equity participation of an investor satisfactory to the Overseas Private Investment Corporation [OPIC] and experienced in profitably owning and operating a business like the proposed project), OPIC would consider this debt financing. No assurances of this loan had yet been given in 1979. A commercial loan would carry a 20% interest rate.

Proposed Capital Structure

EDI would have a 49% equity position in the proposed joint venture; a local partner, FINCO, would hold 51%. (See *Exhibit 4* for a description of FINCO and *Exhibit 5* for the terms of agreement with FINCO.) Planned equity capital would be $227,000 ($122,000 in cash and $105,000 in professional services). Debt capital was planned to be $240,000. The anticipated combined equity and debt capital would amount to $467,000.

Complete ownership of the venture would eventually be turned over to Sri Lankan interests sometime between the fifth and tenth years of operations. EDI could retain a share of profits until the tenth year. Details of the phasing out of EDI's participation were to be negotiated with FINCO and the appropriate government officials.

Status of the Project

Phase I of the venture consisted of the commitment of EDI funds to the proposed project and a reconnaissance trip to Sri Lanka. The trip's aims were to ascertain the likelihood of obtaining necessary government approvals and to structure the joint venture with a Sri Lankan company. Discussions were held with a prospective commercial customer that expressed strong interest in charcoal purchases. EDI retained the services of a Sri Lankan law firm and an accounting firm to help obtain the necessary government approvals.

As a result of the trip, EDI investigated several ancillary projects, including export marketing of teak wall panels and parquet floors, pure coconut oil soap, handwoven cotton textiles, and a variety of spices in bulk and gift packages. These proposed projects could increase early cash flow, develop working relationships with key Sri Lankans, and increase EDI's impact in Sri Lanka.

Phase II would be a planning and feasibility study with the possibility of a cost-sharing arrangement with OPIC. If a project resulted, the study's cost would be capitalized as part of the overall project cost. If OPIC agreed to participate in the feasibility study and EDI decided to drop the project after the study, OPIC would reimburse EDI the lesser of $50,000 or up to 75% of the eligible costs of Phase II.

The objectives for the study would include (1) approval of the joint venture by the Foreign Investment Advisory Committee; (2) incorporation of the venture in Sri Lanka; (3) commitment of Sri Lankan equity capital; (4) a cooperation agreement with the Mahaweli Development

Board; (5) repatriation approval for profits, capital, interests, and fees; (6) tax relief for 5–10 years; (7) sales contracts with major customers; (8) a contract for the supply of wood; (9) land-lease agreements; (10) shipping agreements with commercial carriers; (11) a license to do business in Sri Lanka and other government approvals; and (12) a management plan including key personnel.

Phase II would be conducted during December 1979 and early 1980 with a budget of about $25,000. At its end another assessment would be made about continuing with the project.

Phase III was the production and sale of charcoal over eight years. This would require the initial fabrication of 50 portable metal kilns by a subsidiary of FINCO at a capital cost of $50,000. The plan was to acquire 300 portable kilns for a total capital cost of $300,000.

Funds available for this phase would amount to $363,000 cash at the outset to cover initial capital costs, startup expenses, working capital, and contingencies. Additional capital would be internally generated as a positive cash flow materialized.

Management and Organization

EDI was incorporated in Delaware and had 1,000 shares of authorized common stock. EDI's stock was subject to certain transfer restrictions. Resale required EDI approval; current stockholders had a right of first refusal. Since EDI's stock was exempt from SEC registration, stock had either to be sold pursuant to another exemption from registration or to be registered.

EDI's stock had been issued in compliance with the provisions of Section 1244 of the Internal Revenue Code, which permitted deduction of corporate stock losses from ordinary income if the stock complied with Section 1244's provisions when the loss was deducted. Normally, a stock investment loss was not deductible and was subject to special "capital-loss limitations" under the IRS Code. But if EDI's stock qualified under Section 1244 when the loss was deducted, an EDI investor was able to deduct a stock loss of up to $50,000 per year ($100,000 on a joint return) from personal income. Both the first and second offerings were exempt from Securities and Exchange Commission registration under Rule 240 and from the Securities Act of 1933.

The initial EDI participants in the proposed venture would be Keiley, president of EDI, and Nihal Goonewardene. Keiley, a former Navy officer, earned a Harvard MBA in 1967 and had founded a small consulting firm providing advisory services in management, economics, and environment with special emphasis on developing countries. Previously he had worked for Corning Glass Works as a market specialist, for the mayor of New York directing hospital renovations, and for the Smithsonian Institute providing policy guidance for land use. Goonewardene was Sri Lankan, educated in the United States in international law and diplomacy. He was a senior staff member of a U.S. consulting firm providing advisory services to developing countries.

Keiley and Goonewardene had just returned from a successful three-week reconnaissance trip to Sri Lanka. Earlier in 1979 Keiley spent two months in Sri Lanka preparing an economic analysis for USAID on a fuel wood and reforestation program. Additional EDI participants included Wesley Copeland and Marcia Wiss. Copeland, a chemist formerly associated with the U.S. National Academy of Sciences, had extensive experience in intermediate technology in developing countries. Wiss was an attorney specializing in international business with the developing countries.

Of critical importance would be the selection of the management team in Sri Lanka. It was expected that suitable candidates could be identified with the aid of the joint-venture partner and other contacts. This management team would be backed up by the chief executives of the joint venture partners, by appropriate legal and accounting services, and by Keiley, Goonewardene, and others. One consultant to the project would be William Bollinger, VP of Native Plants Inc. and the forest ecologist who designed Sri Lanka's Reforestation and Fuel Development Program.

With OPIC approval, EDI planned to purchase insurance covering political risks due to currency inconvertibility, war, revolution, insurrection, and expropriation. OPIC had not yet given assurances that this insurance would be available.

CONVERSATION WITH EDI CORPORATE OFFICIAL

A few days after reading the prospectus, Barrett spoke with Keiley about the EDI concept and the specific charcoal investment. Wiss, corporate secretary and legal counsel, joined them.

Genesis of the Ideas

Keiley spoke at length on several aspects he considered pertinent to the investment:

> I guess the whole thing started three years ago when I was enticed by a friend to cut and split some wood for him. Later that evening we got

to talking and discovered we were both interested in overseas development.

I had husbanded a longtime interest in working in the developing world ever since graduating from the Business School. Then, in March 1979, this wood-chopping friend linked me up with the possibility of providing economic input for an AID mission directed at a fuel wood and reforestation program in Sri Lanka. The thing stalked my path. A number of factors came together and pointed me in that direction. It was almost eerie.

I realized this clearing and reforestation program was going to produce considerable wood waste and represented an attractive business opportunity. When we finished the project and I left Sri Lanka, I went hiking for two weeks in the Lake District of the U.K. and mulled over the charcoal option. Was it commercially viable? Was the technology acceptable? I wondered why nobody had done something like this.

From August through December I sought out everything I could learn on charcoal technology. I spoke with people at AID and the World Bank and cleaned out their libraries. I became one of the best-informed people in D.C. on charcoal production technology. It seemed interesting from all aspects: biomass conversion, petroleum substitution, appropriate technology, and profitability.

I took the idea around to several people in business firms, offered it to them, but it fell between the cracks. They all thought it was a good idea. Finally, when I spoke to two close friends, they said it was a good idea, that somebody should do it, and that they'd be willing to invest in it. They suggested it was both logical and sensible that I start a corporation. It would fill a gap to mobilize capital, technology, and management for small-scale enterprises.

So I put together an initial investment proposal. In mid to late September an acquaintance suggested I should contact Marcia. I called her and we agreed to meet for lunch.

Reactions of Marcia Wiss

Barrett asked Wiss what she had thought of the idea.

My first reaction was: Why Sri Lanka? I wanted to know what Steve knew about the technology and Sri Lanka. In a more general way I was interested in the concept. I had worked for OPIC for five years and had seen many overseas projects, some well-conceived, most ill-conceived. There was a tendency for some entrepreneurs, especially small businessmen, to look for "quick in, quick out" projects. Steve's was the type of project I'd hoped to see at OPIC: dual goals—both profit and development.

I sensed this project was different. I respected the opinion of the person who suggested Steve get in touch with me, and I sensed truthfulness in Steve. So I agreed to work on the legal aspects. Steve wanted to keep everything simple—no razzle-dazzle corporate structures.

We also decided that the dual philosophy was sound business and was especially appropriate to the Third World. It's the only way to succeed in the long haul: build constituencies and a management team that wants to work for you.

Financing

Keiley continued on other aspects of the proposal:

I didn't want investors piggy-backing on my cash or relying on my judgment alone. I agreed to commit my time but not my cash. I wanted involvement from investors; I didn't just want their money. I told each potential investor to evaluate the project on the merits.

The net result is that our investors are very active. Two have gone to Sri Lanka on our behalf. This is an opportunity for them to put their money where their conscience is and to develop a corporate vehicle for ventures beyond Sri Lanka.

Originally we were going to offer shares at $168 and to sell all available equity, but some advised us that if things panned out we could raise twice as much. So we turned down some who wanted to invest in the first offering. So now on this offer the price is $600.

Main Concerns

Barrett asked Keiley what his main concerns were:

Our greatest concern is probably the availability of wood. There are still going to be waste forest products, but we may have to integrate backwards and contract for clearing. We have serious limitations in that we're a small fry. We hope to benefit from the reforestation program, the clearing, and the waste, but we have no clout if there are delays and inefficiencies. Even if market demand is there, the government through ill-conceived decisions could thwart us. We must rely on the fact that they realize we're providing a useful service to the country. After all, this concept has major implications for energy self-sufficiency.

CONVERSATIONS WITH ADDITIONAL INVESTORS

Barrett spoke with additional investors. *Jed Shilling and Jane Pratt* are a senior economist and a loan officer at the World Bank, husband and wife, and social friends of Keiley.

Reasons for Participation

Steve came to us knowing about the clear-cutting of wood and knowing that nobody knew what to do with it. Steve is very strong ecologically and has an infectious enthusiasm. He took a month to cost out the figures and talk to people. He wondered why no one else would take it. We both felt it was the type of thing we'd like to see more of. It was small-scale, development-oriented, appropriate technology, manageable, and nontrivial. I guess we just believed in it and Steve.

If the project didn't go, we would be disappointed in a professional sense but would have no regrets about our participation. We felt it imporant to pursue this experiment to see whether such a project could succeed, as we had often argued on a theoretical level. And this particular project looked like it had as good a chance as any, perhaps better.

We knew charcoal technology existed. When we initially considered investing, we divided up obvious areas of research. We found the original project basically sound and have been assiduous about researching subsequent variations. We are especially concerned about the contractual relation with TPI, the British firm. If that doesn't work we'd find someone else.

The big problem is that we may be making the wrong assumption about how the Sri Lankan partners and agents will react, but we have counseled Steve on possible snags based on our past experience in developing countries.

All in all, the project has about a 50-50 chance of meeting Steve's projections. If the supply side is tied down, I'd say 80–90% chance of success. Steve's overall projections are probably a little optimistic.

Bob Wieczerowski (investment counselor; he had not yet invested), was a lawyer by training who had worked for thirteen years at HEW and Becker and four years as U.S. executive director of the World Bank. He represented about 20 sophisticated investors and specialized in small, high-risk business.

Categories. I have four basic categories of investment. The first I call Opus #1. I expect companies in that category to triple value within 35 years with an even chance of 50% loss on the investment. The second is Adventure, as in a sailing voyage. Here I expect the investment to increase tenfold in five years and consider an equal chance of 100% loss of investment. The third I call Cloud Category, because clouds are where the angels live. Here there are psychological benefits. You're lucky if you just get your money back, but you're glad you did it. The fourth is Samaritan: You're guaranteed to lose your money, but the psychological benefits are high. I'll leave it up to you to decide where this investment falls, but I'll tell you I didn't put it in either the first or second category.

I screen my investments very carefully; I decided that if an investment is to be fun it should be labeled as such. I've never lost a substantial amount of money for any investor, and I know the distinction between a philosophy and religious fervor. I won't lead people into risks they can't afford.

In the investment proposal Steve brought me, some information was inadequate and might have led to misunderstanding. For example, he made no provision for taxes. I've seen million-dollar projects thought out by layers of professionals go down the tube. This project may make money, but it was hard to conceive it would without more institutional backup.

I define success as continuity, durability, and profitability. Just saying "I tried to do a good thing" won't get you into heaven. By the way, I haven't yet decided that I'm not going to invest in this.

INTERVIEWS WITH THE BOARD OF DIRECTORS

Wes Pickard, economist, investor in EDI, and member of the board:

I invested because I'm convinced energy prices will go crazy worldwide and because I believe in Steve. I'm in this 60% for business reasons, 35% for developmental reasons, and 5% for social. This will stumble along for ten years or so and eventually make some big money.

Brenda Eddy, vice president of a private development firm, former business professor at Georgetown University, and member of the board:

Steve came to me and was very direct. He said he wanted my advice and participation. To me it seemed obvious; I didn't know why it was not done all over. Steve pulled together pieces from lots of areas that I work in: business development and international marketing. I haven't invested yet but I probably will, and business will be only 20% of my motivation. I'm convinced international development must find some way to be self-sufficient. The governments of the developed world can't afford to provide assistance to LDCs forever.

There has to be an income-generating base. The problem is, American businessmen don't think in development terms and development professionals don't think in business terms. Here Steve found a strong local partner in FINCO and a country that is receptive to capitalism.

* * * * *

Having reviewed the EDI investment proposal and heard various opinions, Barrett pondered his own decision of whether to invest in EDI. He was intrigued by the concept but felt anxious about some aspects of the proposal. Before deciding, therefore, he thought it would be useful to specify the proposal's key strengths and weaknesses. He also wondered whether any risks could be lowered by modifying the project's design.

ENTERPRISE DEVELOPMENT INC.

Exhibit 1

External Trade

(In million rupees)

Item	1971	1972	1973	1974	1975	1976	1977	1978†	1979					
									Jan.	Feb.	Mar.	Apr.	May	Jun.
Exports(1)	1,947	2,009*	2,617*	3,472	3,933	4,815	6,638	13,206	1,106	1,060	1,232	1,143	989	1,266
Major exports	1,731	1,693	1,998	2,495	2,983	3,372	4,769	9,394	749	659	769	610	610	825
Tea	1,144	1,162	1,261	1,360	1,932	2,100	3,503	6,401	463	486	520	395	414	488
Rubber	307	265	592	738	654	890	931	2,021	214	113	187	144	112	248
Coconut products(2)	280	266	145	397	397	382	335	972	72	60	62	71	84	89
Other exports(3)	216	316	619	977	950	1,443	1,869	3,812	367	401	463	533	379	441
Cinnamon	28	30	38	59	39	70	73	161	6	9	6	6	25	8
Cocoa	6	5	6	11	8	13	39	50	3	5	3	3	5	5
Other minor agricultural products	79	82	123	173	121	148	266	447	49	58	85	71	53	79
Textiles	7	7	51	26	25	70	120	479	54	56	83	114	65	86
Petroleum products	20	16	134	350	353	510	597	927	66	70	104	93	160	108
Other industrial products	22	28	39	134	300	442	500	1,017	113	95	100	92	57	82
Precious stones		12	141	109	180	261	298	626	66	41	38	37	11	32

Imports(4)	1,986	2,064	2,715	4,554	5,251	4,645	6,007	14,662	1,593	1,684	1,973	1,811	1,777	1,799
Consumer goods	1,113	1,069	1,424	2,138	2,651	1,689	2,534	5,593	—	—	—	—	—	—
Intermediate goods	411	502	815	1,920	1,888	2,259	2,648	5,591	—	—	—	—	—	—
Investment goods	419	438	452	457	653	641	746	3,367	—	—	—	—	—	—
Other imports	43	55	25	39	59	54	79	110	—	—	—	—	—	—
Balance of trade	39	−55	−98	−1,082	−1,318	170	631	−1,456	−486	−653	−728	−731	−746	−533
Export indices (1967 = 100)														
Price index	117	118	137	213	199	239	382	698	—	—	—	—	—	—
Volume index	99	97	98	85	102	97	89	95	—	—	—	—	—	—
Import indices (1967 = 100)														
Price index	150	158	209	370	433	383	471	877	—	—	—	—	—	—
Volume index	90	88	79	56	69	75	97	132	—	—	—	—	—	—
Terms of trade(5)	78	75	65	58	46	62	81	80	—	—	—	—	—	—

†Provisional.

*Including value of bunkers.

(1) At f.o.b. prices

(2) Copra, oil, desiccated coconut and fresh nuts.

(3) Includes re-exports.

(4) At c.i.f. prices.

(5) Terms of trade = $\dfrac{\text{Export price index}}{\text{Import price index}} \times 100$.

SOURCES: Customs, Sri Lanka, Ceylon Petroleum Corporation, and Central Bank of Ceylon.

ENTERPRISE DEVELOPMENT INC.

Exhibit 2

Government Finance

(In million rupees)

Item	1973	1974	1975	1976	1977	1978	1979 Approved Estimates
1.0 Government receipts	4,046	4,787	5,083	5,739	6,686	11,633	11,431
1.1 Income tax	700	599	770	935	936	1,102	1,152
1.2 Business turnover tax	565	635	680	749	711	1,143	1,175
1.3 Receipts from sale of FEECs	674	964	1,055	1,073	1,157	329	—
1.4 Import duties	222	277	336	476	518	1,469	1,475
1.5 Export duties	386	660	430	421	620	4,236	4,500
1.6 Selective sales tax	408	750	831	918	1,407	1,884	1,700
1.7 Profits from sale of arrack	220	—	—	—	—	—	—
1.8 Receipts from gross trading enterprises	351	434	454	483	483	524	631
1.9 Others	520	469	527	683	854	946	798
1.9.1 Interests & dividends from corporations & public institutions	(108)	(106)	(137)	(217)	(363)	(141)	(197)
2.0 Government payments	5,038	5,821	7,187	8,653	8,813	17,710	18,087
2.1 Current payments	3,799	4,565	5,265	5,602	6,172	10,521	10,992
2.1.1 Purchase of goods and services	1,900	2,273	2,500	2,760	3,087	4,036	4,504
2.1.1.1 Administration	579	830	903	909	998	1,668	1,723
2.1.1.2 Social services	856	912	1,021	1,223	1,367	1,561	1,818
2.1.1.3 Economic services	166	165	165	194	212	241	345
2.1.1.4 Gross payments of trading enterprises	292	356	394	422	500	555	607
2.1.1.5 Intragovernmental payments	7	11	16	12	10	10	10

2.1.2	Transfer payments	1,896	2,291	2,765	2,842	3,085	6,485	6,488
2.1.2.1	Subsidies	757	1,046	1,362	1,091	1,168	2,760	2,846
2.1.2.1.1	Gross food subsidy	(701)	(952)	(1,230)	(938)	(1,043)	(2,163)	(2,333)
2.1.2.2	Interest on public debt	514	580	699	840	1,013	1,368	1,653
2.1.2.3	Pensions	270	292	331	378	414	457	496
2.1.2.4	To public corporations	166	164	134	129	146	1,076	789
2.1.2.5	Others	189	209	238	404	343	825	704
2.2	Capital payments	1,161	1,245	1,987	2,676	2,194	5,416	7,295
2.2.1	Acquisition, construction and maintenance of real assets	611	730	1,073	1,430	1,122	2,173	4,159
2.2.2	Capital transfers	445	402	806	1,023	937	2,190	2,616
2.2.2.1	Public corporations	(384)	(378)	(770)	(963)	(868)	(2,060)	(2,563)
2.2.3	Acquisition of financial assets	105	113	108	223	135	1,053	520
2.3	Net payment of advance account corporations	78	12	−65	375	447	1,773	−200
3.0	Net cash surplus (+)/deficit (−)	−992	−1,035	−2,103	−2,914	−2,127	−6,047	−4,970
4.0	Financing the deficit							
4.1	Net cash receipts or payments	929	996	2,073	2,947	2,618	5,989	4,970
4.2	Domestic nonmarket borrowing and repayments	243	−54	379	485	505	404	—
4.3	Domestic market borrowing and repayments	508	671	980	1,505	858	1,710	1,235
4.4	Foreign finance	179	378	714	957	1,255	3,875	3,737
4.5	Changes in cash balances	−63	−39	−31	33	492	−58	2
5.0	Public debt outstanding (net)	10,281	11,027	12,960	15,621	22,434	27,746	—
5.1	Domestic	7,530	8,143	9,255	10,653	11,841	13,163	—
5.1.1	Treasury bills	2,250	2,250	2,350	2,700	2,500	2,635	—
5.2	Foreign	2,751	2,884	3,705	4,968	10,594	14,582	—

1.2 Includes bank debt tax from 1970–71.

1.6 Duty on country liquor, tobacco tax, tea tax, betting tax and lottery tax.

1.8 Namely railway, broadcasting, electricity, post and telecommunication services and Port Commission.

4.1 Resulting from loan operations and grants.

4.2 Includes sundry loans.

SOURCE: Central Bank of Ceylon.

Exhibit 3
"Score One for Capitalism"[a]

By *Time* Correspondent Ross H. Munro, June 25, 1979

Its tea off, Sri Lanka gets teed off at socialist controls. Around the world, the siren song of socialism appears to be losing its lure. Countries as diverse as Britain and France, Peru and Algeria are moving away from the creed of nationalization and toward freer market economics. None has shifted quite so far, so quickly, as Sri Lanka, the verdant island nation off the coast of India that the world still knows as Ceylon.

Sri Lanka is awakening from a long socialist slumber. The severe shortages of such necessities as cloth, soap and matches that bedeviled consumers just two years ago have disappeared. Sarong-clad peasants fire bricks in newly made kilns alongside their coconut groves and paddy fields. The hotels are overbooked with foreign businessmen eager to add to the growing flood of investment from overseas. Since it overwhelmed the leftist regime of Mrs. Srimayo Bandaranaike in the 1977 national elections, the government of President Junius Jayawardene has been chipping away at one of the most complicated and burdensome combinations of restrictive regulation and high taxation ever concocted by 20th century socialists.

The new government has eliminated a multitude of licenses and permits, cut back price controls, reduced import duties and trimmed taxes on business profits and agricultural exports. Private managers have been put in charge of money-losing state corporations, and the government has reduced the free and subsidized rice and flour distributions that ate up more than 30% of the previous regime's annual budget. Foreign investment is now running at about $40 million a year, 13 times the level seen in the last year of the former government. Sri Lanka, in short, is experiencing creeping capitalism. Says Jayawardene, a lawyer: "The developing world is now giving up controls. Not only us. They've found it does not pay."

It has taken more than 30 years for Sri Lanka to find that out. After gaining independence from Britain in 1948, the country set up a welfare state that paid tangible dividends. Because of its free medical and educational programs, Sri Lanka today has one of the highest life expectancy and adult literacy rates in the developing world. But from the 1950s onward, socialist governments imposed increasingly stiff taxes on business to finance a maze of nationalized enterprises and a complex web of regulations that controlled everything from trade to foreign exchange.

In the early 1970s, the government seized the tea plantations that long generated about half the nation's export earnings. The result was a disaster. The plantations became run down as reinvestment was cut back, periodic replanting was stopped, and fertilizers were not applied. Production of Sri Lanka's three major exports (tea, rubber and coconut) plunged. Foreign investment dropped, and price and import controls created such shortages that city dwellers lined up to buy the simplest necessities.

[a]Reprinted with permission from *Time,* June 25, 1979, p. 62.

At the same time, private companies were paying as much as 90% of their profits in direct and indirect taxes. A bloated civil service, 420,000 strong, was required for an island population of 14.5 million. Recalls Rajah Maharaja, a leading businessman: "Many civil servants indulged in vindictive interference."

The then socialist government of the Sri Lanka Freedom Party (in coalition with the Communists and Trotskyists) was so discredited by 1977 that Jayawardene entered the election campaign daring to say nice things about foreign investment. When opponents condemned him as the "high priest of capitalism," Jayawardene blithely replied: "Let the robber barons come." Though his United National Party won that election by a landslide and last month again sent his political opponents down to defeat in local elections, he must still tread cautiously. The lifting of controls and the doubling of economic growth to 6%, together with higher oil prices, have sent inflation soaring to 17% or more. In a country where the per capita income remains below $200, rising prices particularly hurt those who have yet to benefit fully from the economic surge. While the high level of education will help future industrial growth, it creates problems at a time when adult unemployment is substantial.

The government's success will be determined largely by two key undertakings:

- As part of an assault on unemployment, Sri Lanka plans to build five major dams and reservoirs over the next six years. The $1.2 billion project, more than half financed by foreign aid, will employ 225,000 workers and add greatly to electricity generation and farm irrigation.
- As part of its open-door policy toward foreign investment, Sri Lanka has established a free-trade zone north of Colombo, where investors can be granted exemption from import duties and taxes.

Despite problems over lack of paved roads, running water and communications, six factories have already been set up and more are abuilding. Some will make work gloves, tea bags and latex rubber threads, but most will produce garments for the U.S. market. Indeed, many companies have been attracted because the U.S. does not yet impose import quotas on Sri Lankan garments. Typically, Jeffrey Bogatin, owner of a New York-based garment business, was attracted by wage costs of 73 cents an hour and a five-year tax holiday. Says he: "I'm shocked that there is not more of a rush by industry to this place. The people are educated and eager to work. This country is on the way up."

Exhibit 4
FINCO Group Description

HISTORICAL DATA

In 1943 N. E. Weerasooria, a leading lawyer and a queen's counsel for Sri Lanka, and a few others formed one of the earliest indigenous investment and trading companies, called Ceylon Investors Ltd. (CIL). (Sri Lanka was called Ceylon until 1973.) By 1960 CIL operations had grown too large for one company; the FINCO Group evolved from CIL to operate those interests.

The FINCO Group is an amalgamation of about 15 Sri Lankan corporations engaged in merchant banking, trading and distribution, manufacturing and proc-essing industries, tourism and transport, consultancy and management services, shipping agency work, plantation and livestock farms, and real estate and con-struction.

The FINCO Group is managed and operated by FINCO Ltd., the real decision-making body of the group. Each group company, however, has its own indepen-dent directorate, but some of the directors interlock. The group employs a total permanent staff of about 1,200, of which 175 are office employees, 25 sales personnel, and about 1,000 factory employees.

The group has over 30,000 square feet of office space in Colombo's city center and also operates branch offices in the capitals of the central, northern, and southern regions of Sri Lanka. The main office is equipped with all modern communication facilities, including telexes. The group has its own warehouse within the Colombo City area, enjoys bonded facilities with the principal banks, and is a Sri Lanka government-approved "credit agency." FINCO maintains close ties with several Sri Lanka banks and has its main account with the Commercial Bank of Ceylon Ltd.

The group turnover for the year ending March 31, 1979, was around US$13 million. Fixed assets as of that date were US$3 million, and the profit after taxes was over US$600,000.

The FINCO Group has been engaged in international transactions for several years and has established connections with many overseas companies, both in trading and in joint-venture manufacturing businesses in Sri Lanka.

Exhibit 5
Terms of Agreement

Whereas FINCO and EDI have agreed to collaborate to set up a joint venture to produce and market wood charcoal in Sri Lanka, it is agreed:

1. That FINCO will take steps to float a limited liability company (hereinafter referred to as the Company) to carry on the business of producing and marketing wood charcoal in Sri Lanka.

2. That FINCO will endeavour to obtain the approval of the Foreign Investment Advisory Committee (FIAC) for the project so as to enable EDI to hold 49% of the shares of the Company and FINCO and its associates to hold the balance 51% of the shares.

3. That EDI will invest up to a maximum of US$60,000 in this venture. The final capital costs, etc., however, to be agreed between the parties when the project is finalized. EDI and FINCO to be represented on the Board of Directors of the Company but the Chairman of the Board to be from FINCO. FINCO will be entitled to the management of the Company and EDI will provide whatever foreign technical assistance as may be necessary for the Company.

Industrias del Maiz S.A.

In March 1979 Emilio Magyar, new divisional vice president of the Peru-based von Rheineck Group, was perplexed by the continuing difficulties experienced by the group's cornstarch plant in Quito, Ecuador. Unlike most of the group's new enterprises during the 1970s, the plant had suffered continued losses for the past four years. Although beginning to break even, it was carrying forward a loss on its books of one million sucres. Magyar had been head of the group's Peruvian corn-products operation since its foundation. What was particularly frustrating was that the Peruvian plant had become the group's most profitable industrial enterprise while its Ecuadorian "copy" was floundering.

His first assignment as head of the group's new corporate industrial division was to tackle the Ecuadorian problem. Having been with the group for 15 years, Magyar was greatly respected by the group's head, J. Z. von Rheineck, and had been given considerable latitude in developing strategy. He decided to review the Peruvian strategy and operations to ascertain why the group was successful there, and then compare this with performance in Ecuador.

BACKGROUND

R. O. von Rheineck, a Swiss immigrant, founded the von Rheineck Group in 1922 as a small trading company in Lima. Beginning with sales commissions, the company grew slowly to include imports and exports. In the 1930s a subsidiary commercial company was founded in Ecuador. Slow, solid growth marked the company's first 30 years as a trading company. Then in 1956, with the opening of the group's first joint venture (a pharmaceutical lab in partnership with a French multinational pharmaceutical company), it started manufacturing operations. This industrial joint venture policy proved vitally important in providing the group with goods for distribution and, later, financial strength. The lab was followed

This case was prepared by Antonio Custer, MBA '79, and Associate Professor James E. Austin as the basis for class discussion rather than to illustrate either effective of ineffective handling of an administrative situation. Abridged with permission.

in 1961 by a shirt factory (in partnership with an American company) and in 1964 by the cornstarch plant in Peru.

By 1979 the group had 18 plants working or under construction in six countries in Latin America. These produced pharmaceuticals, corn products, garments, adhesives, paper products, chemical specialties, flavors and essences, and plastic and aluminum containers. Most were majority-owned joint ventures, whose minority partner was a foreign company providing necessary technology. The group's commercial side, with companies in four Latin American countries, accounted for $85 million of the group's $135 million revenues, but the industrial division was growing rapidly.

The group's industrial diversification strategy used these criteria: development of industries represented by the commercial companies; low capital investment; use of commercial company staff; and the expectation that each would quickly become self-sufficient. Some ventures were thus undercapitalized, but most soon turned handsome profits. The Peruvian cornstarch plant was a joint venture with the American company that supplied the group's Peruvian commercial company with glucose imports. By 1979 Industrias del Maiz S.A. Indemsa became the group's most important industrial venture with sales of soles 904 million (US$6 million) and profits of soles 107 million (US$668,000).

As head of the group, chairman and CEO of Indemsa, and CEO of the group's commercial company (Indemsa's sole distributor), J. R. von Rheineck maintained very close contact with Magyar, Indemsa's boss. This allowed for quick decisions on all matters. Magyar thought this rapport was critical to the success of his Peruvian operation. Furthermore, relations with the government, both directly and if needed through the von Rheineck Group, were excellent.

THE CORN PRODUCTS OPERATION IN PERU

Production

Output. In 1979 over 90% of the corn products in Peru was dominated by Industrias del Maiz S.A. The Indemsa plant had not increased its work force by more than 10% in its fifteen years, yet during this time sales more than tripled in real terms (and rose twenty times in money terms). Production reached the limit of installed capacity by the end of 1978 (65 tons of corn ground per day); plant expansion under way was expected to increase grind capacity to 90 tons by July 1979 and 120 tons in July 1980. Despite high local corn prices, the plant was internationally competitive in cost efficiency, yield recovery, capacity use, and flexibility to diversify product lines quickly. Had the plant been allowed to import foreign corn at international prices, its starch prices would have competed with the lowest in the world (*Exhibit 1*).

Indemsa operated in 1978 at 107% of rated capacity and during early 1979 at 108%. Of each corn kernel 70% was dry substance, from which Indemsa recovered 66.5% or 95% of the available starch in Peruvian corn. U.S. producers had a 68% starch recovery rate or 97.8% of the available starch. Production downtime for the Peruvian plant was 36 days in 1978.

By early 1970 Indemsa produced flavored corn table syrups (maple, molasses, etc.), potato and camote starch, and corn oil for direct sale to consumers (through retailers); it produced regular, industrial, oxidized, and modified corn starches for the food, textile, and paper industries; dextrins for adhesives; syrup; caramel coloring; grits for breweries; hominy for animal feed; germ for the food industry; and glucose, all for industrial use. The by-products in starch production were as shown in the accompanying diagram.

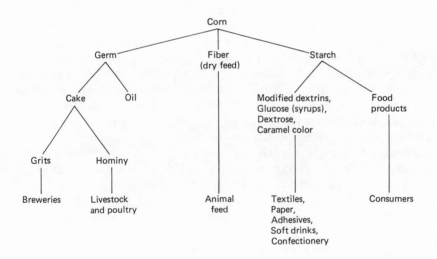

Indemsa also began to extract starch from potatoes and camotes. The newer potato and camote starch subplants were built on a new dual-process principle by which these crops harvested at complementary times could keep the subplants busy year-round. Moreover, starch from potatoes and camotes was virtually interchangeable. (But 14 kilos of camotes were needed to produce 1 kilo of starch, as compared to 10 kilos of potatoes, owing to the camote's higher water content.) Because of shortages caused by the Agrarian Reform, these subplants were producing at only 20–25% of capacity.[1]

The plant itself, including offices, storage area, complete machine shop, and the potato, camote, and yucca starch subplants, covered 250,000 square feet.

Technology. The technology used to develop Indemsa had been supplied by the original joint-venture partner, Union Starch & Refining Co. of the United States, which was later bought by Miles Laboratories, the current partner. Miles supplied most of the necessary process technology, particularly for the current plant expansion and for Indemsa's diversification into dextrins, potato starch, camote starch, and modified glucose production.

The plant had developed a high degree of in-house technological capability for maintenance and custom machinery development. This was mainly due to (1) the plant's running 24 hours a day and not being able to afford shutdowns for repairs, and, more important (2) the lack of skilled outside technicians who could handle the large, intricate, custom precision jobs required. All Indemsa workers, especially the maintenance mechanic staff, were trained in-house. Workers at first had been trained in all aspects of their jobs, down to essentials of personal hygiene.

Work Force. In 1979 relations between plant management and employees were excellent. At a time when 90% of Peruvian industry was working at 40% capacity (utilization) and underemployment and unemployment were rife, Indemsa was working around the clock. Indemsa had begun one of Peru's first worker-dividend distribution plans. Government legislation required companies to distribute a set percentage of profits to workers as bonuses in cash or stock. Moreover, the productivity of Indemsa's 180 workers was sustaining profits despite Peru's dire financial straits and allowing regular employee raises far above the industrial average. Finally, by early 1979 Indemsa had provided nearly 70% of its workers with home purchase or construction loans.

Location. Although the availability of an ample supply of relatively cheap unskilled labor had been one of the prime factors in choosing plant location, several other criteria were equally important: frontage on the major east–west highway from Lima into the Andes; proximity (10 miles) to Lima and most major industrial and retail customers; abundance of light, power, and water supply; and location at the center of a circle, with a radius of 110 miles, that included all suppliers of corn to the plant. Finally, and very important, the plant was close to RORSA, the group's

---

[1]Since the Agrarian Reform began in 1969, virtually all large Peruvian agricultural estates (haciendas) had been expropriated and divided into farmer-owned (but not farmer-run) cooperatives of up to 1,000 hectares. Private agriculture had farms of 5–80 hectares; many small farmers in the jungle held 1–10 hectares.

main Peruvian commercial company, which in the early years provided Indemsa with staff, contact with decision-makers, and even office space. Other criteria included Lima's better living conditions and the availability of a more competent middle management.

Procurement

Although corn was also grown in the north and the jungle, Peru's largest concentration of corn producers was within a 200-mile radius of Lima. This region normally provided amply for Indemsa's needs. Peru had produced about 0.5 million tons of corn in 1978 and in each of the four preceding years. From a 450,000-ton deficit that had to be covered by imports in 1974, Peru expected to import only 125,000 tons in 1979. Demand for industrial uses was around 200,000 tons. When Indemsa's plant expansion would be completed in 1980, the 40,000–45,000-ton annual capacity would represent 6–7% of the national market.

Corn was available in Peru year-round. Two crops occurred during the year: the small winter crop (July, August, September); and the big summer crop (January, February, March). Indemsa was the only large national buyer that purchased year-round. It guaranteed to purchase farmers' crops at the price prevailing at harvest time. But medium- or long-term contracts had not been successful with farmers, who generally failed to respect the contractual terms.

Indemsa purchased exclusively through middlemen. Corn was received in kernels "placed in plant." Each bushel thus delivered cost in Peru anywhere between US$3.30 and $4.80.[2] Indemsa used only national corn, although the government imported about one-third of Peru's industrial corn requirement (65,000 tons, or over half the corn imported) and sold it to industry at premium prices. The government set annual minimum guaranteed price levels for farmers, which usually fluctuated upward 15–20% during the year. Indemsa bought the best quality at the best price at the end of each harvest. Its high quality standards required more modern methods from farmers, so it helped them with those.[3] The government, moreover, imported 55% of the corn required by the feed-products industry.

In its early years Indemsa cut costs drastically by never storing more than 2% of annual corn requirements—as Magyar put it, "by walking the tightrope." Nevertheless, since the considerable turmoil caused by the

---

[2] In May 1979 a bushel of corn in the U.S. futures market was priced at US$3.00.

[3] Indemsa sent representatives to corn-growing regions to promote corn production. It also helped fund the national corn research program, which sought high-lysine corn and new corn varieties more suited to Peru's varied geographic/climatic conditions.

Agrarian Reform and the consequent decline in agricultural production in Peru (to the point that corn and potatoes, both native crops, had to be imported), Indemsa at times had to buy as much as US$1 million worth of corn at a time (equal to three to four months' supply). Corn prices, moreover, rose 75% during the early 1970s.

Marketing

The estimated Peruvian demand for starch was 7,700 tons in 1979, with an estimated 50% growth over the following five years. Glucose consumption was expected to rise 45% over the same period. Indemsa was planning to enter the national hard candy market (estimated to use 1,800 tons of glucose), which had been dominated by government-subsidized local sugar until 1978. In the mid-1970s glucose cost 300% more than sugar; by 1979 sugar prices rose to where glucose cost only 25% more. This removal of the sugar subsidy was part of the IMF-designed fiscal changes made during 1978 that abolished all subsidies on consumer staples, allowing them to find their own supply/demand-set level. Almost overnight gas rose 67%, cooking oil 125%, and flour 3%. Sugar's price rise also opened the possibility of selling glucose to Peru's breweries; in 1979 Indemsa was exporting glucose to Ecuadorian breweries.[4] Rising wheat prices also opened the avenue for the sale of starch to breweries for use instead of wheat. The cookie industry presented another 1,000-ton market for starch in 1978.

These market changes increased the need for the planned capacity increase, which would also provide greater flexibility for product diversification. In early 1979 Indemsa was forecasting a 67% real growth rate in sales over the following five years.

Indemsa's introduction of national cornstarch was slow and painstaking. Industrial buyers had been used to the whiter (but in no way superior) imported starch. Consumers preferred camote and potato starches when making many traditional desserts, and the confectioner (cookies, etc.) industry had used flour. But by 1979, years of carefully and successfully developed experiments led to an important use of cornstarch in even the cookie industry, and consumers were used to mixing cornstarch and camote starch in preparing desserts. Only in certain desserts did consumers still use potato starch. Indemsa was also successful in persuading textile mills to replace imported carboxymethyl cellulose (CMC) with cornstarch.

In early 1979, 1 kilo of cornstarch cost 120 soles in Peru; a kilo of

[4]Glucose exports to Ecuador had risen dramatically, from 100 tons in 1977 to 1,950 tons in 1978, and were expected to rise 92% over the next five years.

camote starch cost 160 soles. Potato starch was initially produced to replace imports of potato starch for human consumption. Peru's middle and lower classes were the main consumers of camote and potato starches, which were among the products Indemsa placed in consumer packs and sold directly to stores and at farm product fairs. Both national and international distribution of all Indemsa products was handled by the industrial sales division of RORSA (Peru), the group's trading company, under an exclusive distributorship agreement. Physical distribution was done by Indemsa's fleet of special trucks and its own personnel.

Indemsa negotiations with the government (mainly through RORSA) eventually obtained for Indemsa partial tariff protection. In 1969 the revolutionary government totally closed imports of goods produced in "adequate" supply within Peru. Although this helped Indemsa achieve its 1979 monopoly position within the Peruvian market, it also prohibited Indemsa's access to the world corn market.

GOVERNMENT POLICIES IN PERU

The leftist military takeover in Peru in 1968 radically changed private industry's status with government. New "social property" ownership industries (based roughly on cooperative lines and ranging from public transportation to some of the industrial sectors nationalized by the government) were emphasized. More incentive was given to the highly visible expropriated sectors, such as farm cooperatives, fishing, petroleum, and eventually mining.

Industrial Policy

At the beginning of the 1968 revolution, a policy of import substitution industrialization (ISI) in effect forbade imports of any products or capital goods already produced in Peru or that might compete with them. Few other incentives were offered. There were support prices for corn, potatoes, and camote; only EPSA (a government agency) could commercialize grain imported into the country.

The government also regulated investment closely: Any diversification, reduction, or expansion of plant required direct authorization by the Ministry of Industry. Foreign investment was restricted, depending on the sector, to between 25% and 49% ownership. Foreign investors could repatriate profits only up to a total of 33% of their net paid-in capital. ITINTEC, the government's technological bureau, was in charge of approving all technology imports.

Indemsa (following the group's strategy of developing less-visible industries) was a second-priority industry, defined as: support industry, food, and agro-industry. As such, 54.7% of its gross profits could be reinvested tax-free in any second-priority industry. This also meant that throughout the 1970s Indemsa-Peru was free from government price controls on its products. The corporate income tax in Indemsa's bracket (top) was 40%.

Indemsa received a 50% reduction of the existing (varying) duty on imported inputs and a 60% reduction on capital goods imports. Furthermore, only corn products that Indemsa did not have the capacity to supply could be imported (with a prior letter of consent by Indemsa to the potential importer, at Indemsa's leisure).

The drive for nationalization and national self-sufficiency was undertaken so suddenly and was so ill-administered that by 1975–76 President Velasco had been ousted by his own minister of finance. The latter then tried to rescue the economy without shelving some of the more radical tenets of the revolution. The only major changes in industry were that the 50% cooperative ownership was reduced to 33% and previously nontransferable stock could be bought and sold freely.

Trade Policy

In early 1979 the government finally confirmed its plan to promote nontraditional exports such as glucose, through the following measures:

- Exempt from all export duties and taxes (these ranged between 6% and 22%)
- To benefit from a more flexible certificate of tax reimbursement, in some cases providing additional reimbursement, than that currently received
- Materials and goods used as inputs for these goods to be tax-exempt
- Establishment of the industrial classification for export industries (this required an industry to reach 40% export of production in ten years)
- Exemptions from duties and taxes for export industries
- Government promotion of the establishment of the export consortium to foster a strong, direct, and effective relationship between manufacturers and exporters
- Establishment of warehouses in free trade zones abroad to ease export distribution
  - Install such zones also within Peru
  - Establish export marketing offices abroad
  - Guarantee competitive international prices for domestic tradi-

tional raw materials used in manufacture of nontraditional export products.

- Promotional freight and tariff rates
- Establish permanent financing for nontraditional exports

Already in 1978 Indemsa benefited from a 28% tax subsidy on glucose exports to Ecuador. Ecuador had no such incentive system.

Monetary Policy

Inflation began to take off in 1977. Peru's lack of reserves caused it to default on its external debt. Its currency was devalued four times (from US$1 = 70 soles in early 1977 to 130 soles by year end, to 135 soles by early 1978 and 195 soles by the end of 1978). In 1978 inflation had been 85–90%; two years earlier it had been 15–20%.

By the end of 1978 the strict exchange controls of the past eight years began to be eased to stimulate trade. But the government's economic mismanagement caused spiraling inflation and extremely tight credit due to unrealistically low—but rapidly rising—interest rates that put commerce and industry in a desperate money crunch. On one side, creditors required dollar payments while the sol slipped rapidly. On the other, some clients were unable to pay rising prices and collections were getting very difficult. By December, with inflation for the year at 85%, the official bank rate was still around 53%.

THE CORNSTARCH INDUSTRY IN ECUADOR

Entry into Ecuador

After the von Rheineck Group's success with Indemsa-Peru, and since the Andean Pact (a trade agreement among Andean nations to stimulate free trade) did not seem ready to take corn products off Ecuador's exceptions list, the group had begun by the early 1970s to consider building a cornstarch plant in Ecuador.

Whereas in Peru glucose (for which cornstarch must first be produced) was the desired output, in Ecuador the group initially sought to produce only starch. Because of Ecuador's slow bureaucratic process for starting a new company, the group had purchased a small, old-fashioned, failing yucca starch plant (one of four then operating in Ecuador), essentially for its documentation, licenses, and land (located on the outskirts of Quito). Its purchase obviated nearly a year and a half of bureaucratic paperwork to obtain incorporation. With this head start over other starch producers that were only beginning to consider cornstarch production (the least expensive of starches in price to consumers but also perhaps the most expensive in capital investment for production), the group felt it would be in a favorable position to obtain a strong market share.

Thus, with little prior study[5] and relying on its Peruvian success, Indemsa built a small cornstarch plant on the site of the yucca starch plant for an investment of about US$500,000.

Production

Output. Indemsa-Ecuador began operating at the end of 1974. In 1979 it was producing at its original installed capacity of 15 tons ground per day; it could have been pushed to 18 without expansion. This represented an estimated 5,000 tons of corn ground per year (50 weeks, 24 hours per day). The plant and warehouse covered about 15,000 square feet and stood on 80,000 square feet of land. As corn wet-milling plants go, it was a very small, simple, yet complete starch-producing operation.

There were two main reasons for building a plant producing only starch. The first was to minimize the size of the investment. Consistent with the group's strategy of "planting a seed," nurturing it, and then letting it pay its own way as soon as possible, the plant was spartanly built. It may even have been undercapitalized (despite more than $1 million in assets), in both cash to assemble a good management group and warehousing and repair facilities. (This later translated into poor preventive and corrective maintenance and further production trouble.) The second reason was Indemsa-Peru's strong low-cost producer position in glucose (*Exhibit 2*). Exporting nearly at cost and making a profit on by-products, the Peruvian company had 100% of the Ecuadorian glucose market. Ecuadorian ISI legislation forbade imports of goods already produced in the country (unless these were used as inputs for export goods). Hence, by a strong marketing effort from Peru and by refraining from building a glucose-processing plant, the group stimulated Indemsa-Peru's export sales while obviating a step in the development of the Ecuadorian plant that it could not have coped with until the early 1980s.

Four and a half years after coming onstream, in February 1979, Indemsa-Ecuador still produced only cornstarch, feed, and germ. An expansion and diversification plan had been instituted which would soon allow for the production of modified starch and corn oil.

Location. The plant's location was, in 1979, more than ever a point of

[5]Ecuador offered in 1974 an oil-boom economy with an Industrial Promotion Law far more complete than Peru's and no legislation restricting repatriation of profits. The group also believed it offered a much more stable investment climate.

concern. It was located a day's truck drive from both suppliers and by far the largest segment of its potential customers—Guayaquil. In Quito only the textile mills constituted sizable industrial customers. If the plant later entered consumer sales, then Quito would provide a market (albeit second to Guayaquil) for consumer-packed cornstarch.

Technology. A Mexican affiliate of Miles Laboratories gave technological assistance for construction, engineering, and maintenance. Other production expertise and some of the machinery came from Indemsa-Peru. Almost every piece of equipment made to order in Ecuador arrived far behind schedule, did not meet specifications, and had to be modified.

The small plant size created inefficiencies due to having machinery with varying throughput capacities, where the minimum capacity of certain machines was double the overall plant capacity. As a result, Indemsa-Ecuador could not achieve better than a 61% yield or 86–87% of the starch available in Ecuadorian corn.

Work Force. Although unskilled labor was abundant near the plant, training was not as rigorous as in Peru, a result of several years of management problems and the tight budget. This in turn meant shoddy maintenance and accelerated plant deterioration. In 1977–78 there were labor unrest and attempts by leftist agitators to organize the plant's 50 workers.

During the last half of 1978, labor relations improved markedly thanks to radical restructuring of the work force and management. Nearly half the blue-collar workers were fired; other middle management changes were made. Nevertheless, middle management was weak and insufficiently prepared, and trained technicians were lacking both in the plant and generally in Ecuador.

Procurement

Ecuador's large corn-growing regions in the Northwest and South were relatively near Guayaquil. The one major annual crop, between May and June, was insufficient to meet Ecuador's needs; the government had to import corn through the state grain storage and marketing institution (ENAC). Ecuador's corn consumption in tons in 1974–77 was between 218,000 and 275,000, or roughly one-third of Peru's.

Farming in Ecuador was worse off than in Peru. Most farms were small and hardly able to subsist. A few big (over 1,000 hectares) farms planted soybeans, corn, or other high-return crops. Unlike Peru's, Ecuador's soil was generally very poor as a result of insufficient use of fertilizers. Little certified seed was used, and most farms depended on rain (unlike Peru, where most corn farms had cheap irrigation year-round). Finally, Ecuadorian harvesting costs, not spread out over a cooperative as in most cases in Peru, were higher than in Peru.

Indemsa-Ecuador purchased its corn once a year and stored it for later use.[6] This need to purchase at least an eight-month supply of corn burdened Indemsa-Ecuador's already strained resources. Moreover, the plant's location made it more vulnerable to shortages, for not all required stock was stored in the plant. This lack of storage capacity had become critical by early 1979. Some small quantities of "sierra" corn were available in the Quito region during the "winter" harvest, but this had a high water content, unsuitable for making low-water starch. Prices of corn in Ecuador fluctuated between US$4.00 and $4.30 per bushel. Procurement was through agents of large farms or other intermediaries and, when necessary, from ENAC.

The supply of yucca came mainly from the mountains near Quito, which was why the older starch producers had concentrated there. The main corn-growing regions in Ecuador, however, were near the coast.

Marketing

The Ecuadorian market was different from the Peruvian in several ways. First, Ecuadorians preferred yucca starch (closest to potato starch in its overall characteristics). Second, industries using starch could import all cornstarch duty free when it was used as an input for export production. Consequently, Indemsa-Ecuador was virtually alone in the industrial segment of the Ecuadorian cornstarch market. Nevertheless, each prospective client had to be shown repeatedly that Indemsa's starch was equal in quality to imported varieties. Moreover, there was only one sizable textile mill in Ecuador, which produced cotton threads and denim for export and was thus still allowed to import CMC to the detriment of starch producers. But this was a small problem compared with trying to sell to the major users, cardboard banana-box plants, which could consume Indemsa's entire current output. But they were allowed to purchase imported starch at two-thirds Indemsa's price because they produced for export. If all their business could be secured, it would have meant a plant expansion that would allow for the installation of a refinery for corn oil.

Three plants (Cartonera, Procarsa, and Macarsa) dominated the market. With annual production of 100,000 tons of containerboard, Cartonera was the largest such plant in the world. Nearly all of the plants' output was used to produce cardboard boxes for banana export. These plants sourced their 4,000 tons of cornstarch from around the world and

[6]In late 1978 Indemsa-Ecuador was searching out the big farmers to reserve the corn to be bought at harvest time, although Indemsa would receive the corn at its Quito warehouse at any time and readjust prices according to quality. These prices might vary as much a 25–30% during the harvest season. Hedging against this high fluctuation was difficult under Ecuador's rather restrictive conditions.

ended up purchasing mainly from Argentina, because of lower prices and shipping costs.

Although the plants were receptive to local starch purchase, until 1975 (when Indemsa came on-stream) there was no local cornstarch production. A tentative yearlong contract with a local yucca-starch producer came to naught in the early 1970s.

When cornstarch production began in 1975, Argentine starch sold for half the price of local starch. The main factor in the huge price differential was the price of corn. In an efficient cornstarch operation corn cost is at least 70% of the total production cost. In Ecuador, where corn was an important consumer staple, the starch plant had to compete with the population for available corn, thus raising the price. Furthermore, the government had instituted corn support prices. In Argentina, where corn was used mainly for feed and not human consumption, the price was much lower.

Cartonera built a large warehouse in the early 1970s and received semiannual shipments of starch from Argentina. This satisfied the containerboard producers' four major sourcing criteria: packaging, quality, price, and delivery.

As Indemsa came on-stream, delivery problems and quality-approval stalling by containerboard manufacturers meant that cardboard mills were able to continue to resist pressure to buy part of their supply of cornstarch nationally. In 1973 government price controls on boxes began to be applied, as the first nationalistic ideological shifts resulting from the 1971 coup began to be felt. The Industrial Development Law was the result of this same ideological push. It explicitly allowed containerboard plants to source from overseas. Moreover, price controls on boxes (protecting the banana export industry) would require that the plants shrink their margins if they were to buy more expensive national cornstarch. Other industrial cornstarch users were small compared with the containerboard factories: textile mills (250 tons), paper mills (150 tons), and pharmaceutical labs (150 tons). There was practically no consumer market for cornstarch, and three of the four main industrial consumers (containerboard plants, paper mills, and pharmaceuticals) were located in Guayaquil on the coast, a day's drive by truck from Quito. The nonexport industrial segments could be considered more "captive." Yet their opposition to paying at least a 150% premium in price, no matter how good the quality, would take years to overcome.

Ecuador's food industry (in this case, confectionery, etc.) had not yet been educated about the benefits of cornstarch and did not use it. The plant planned to concentrate on the cookie, cracker, and bread-producing market segments, with eventually a more vigorous marketing attack on the wholesaling segments and perhaps development of a proprietary brand name.

Indemsa kept a price list, with each client having a particular negotiable price according to agreed-upon conditions. Sales for 1978 were US$1.2 million; 1979 sales were expected to be $1.6 million.

In the retail consumer market, two other producers (two of the three other plants that began producing cornstarch after Indemsa) sold under their brand names to the public through stores. Indemsa did not enter the market with its own brand mainly because it lacked the financial resources for competitive advertising, demonstrations, etc. Indemsa was unable to pay even a 1% commission to RORSA-Ecuador on sales, so thin had their margins become (*Exhibits 3* and *4*). Instead, their starch was sold directly to consumers through Fleischmann's Ecuadorian subsidiary (Royal brand), with RORSA-Ecuador acting as middleman. This combination was highly successful: In just two years a 55% share of the urban market for starch was obtained, while increasing the total market size by 20%. Corn oil was refined by subcontractors and sold under other brand names in stores and supermarkets throughout Ecuador.

GOVERNMENT POLICIES IN ECUADOR

The armed forces had been in power, except for a single coup d'état, since 1971. Not very stable politically, Ecuador nevertheless had had a more centrist, investment-reassuring military than Peru in the ten years since 1968. In April 1979 presidential elections were to be held. In the summer 1978 primaries, a leftist had emerged as the strongest single contender. The two centrist candidates would presumably unite.

By 1979 the earlier oil boom had slowed somewhat; its profits had not been optimally allocated to ensure continued accelerated growth. Although by 1979 the Ecuadorian economy was again steadying, it had not reaped the full benefits of its bonanza (*Exhibit 5*).

Ecuador had import-substituting industrialization policies that included import controls within and without the Andean Pact countries since the early 1970s. Official prices existed for corn and all agricultural goods. ENAC acted as middleman in distributing agricultural products and importing them where shortages existed.

This and other agencies were beginning to aid farmers with planning crops and using yield-increasing methods of farming to cover these deficits nationally. Unfortunately, the same tariff protection providing Indemsa with a captive market also forced it to buy national corn at prices far above the world market. By early 1979 there was a tendency to lower the tariff barriers, still protecting local industry but requiring it to reduce its cost structure to be more competitive internationally, as the Andean market opened up the doors between pact countries.

STRATEGY CONSIDERATIONS

As a final step in his comparative review of Indemsa's Peruvian and Ecuadorian operations, Magyar examined their profit and loss statements (*Exhibit 6*). Their stark contrast only heightened his original frustration, and he pondered possible explanations. The low return made him wonder whether it made sense to try to continue in Ecuador when the group had so many other, more profitable operations elsewhere. If Indemsa were to stay in Ecuador, the critical areas requiring closest review were plant location, procurement, and marketing, especially to the containerboard industry.

Exhibit 1

Percentage Cost Breakdown for Starch and Glucose, 1978
(Indemsa Peru and Ecuador)

| | Regular Starch | | Glucose, |
	Peru	Ecuador	Peru
Labor	4.3%	5.1%	2.9%
Raw material (corn)	79.2	81.0	74.2
Materials (pkg., etc.)	2.2	1.9	7.2
Steam	0.5	1.8	3.8
Electric power	4.2	5.4	0.7
Subtotal	90.4%	95.2%	88.8%
PLUS:			
Indirect costs (depreciation, control, production supervision, maintenance, warehouse)	9.6	4.8	11.2
Total	100.0%	100.0%	100.0%

1 lb. of starch = 119 Peruvian soles.

Exhibit 2

Domestic and International Starch Prices
(US$ per ton)

Product	Indemsa (Peru)	Indemsa (Ecuador)	Delmaiz (Colombia)
Regular Starch			
Domestic sales	$350–740	$535–815	$600–685
Export sales	260–280	—	—
Cost of imported starch (landed cost)	—	225–260	350–400
Yellow Corn			
Domestic purchase price	160–185	165–215	170–190
Cost of imported corn (landed cost)	140–150	135–150	—

INDUSTRIAS DEL MAIZ S.A.

Exhibit 3
Indemsa-Ecuador Balance Sheet: October 1978
(000s of Ecuadorian sucres)

Assets		Liabilities	
Cash	410.6	Accounts payable	1,593.0
Accounts receivable	4,578.0	Provisions for loss	304.0
Inventory	10,785.0	Short-term loans	13,030.0
Deferred taxes	1,193.0		
Investments	2,574.5	Current liabilities	14,927.0
		Long-term debt	6,088.0
Current assets	19,541.1		
Fixed assets	9,531.1[a]	Sharenolders' equity	10,076.0
Goodwill	303.0	(Less) accumulated	
		loss	(1,176.0)
Total assets	29,375.2	Total liabilities	29,375.0

US$1 = 26.5 sucres.

[a]Including land at book value of 530,000 sucres has a current market value of 3,710,000 sucres.

123

Exhibit 4

Indemsa-Ecuador: Profit and Loss, 1976–78

(1978 estimated; 000s of sucres) [a]

	Estimated 1978	1977	1976
Net sales	31,615	28,697	20,126
Cost of goods sold	24,975	24,060	15,762
Gross margin (plant)	6,640	4,637	4,364
Salary, general and administrative	5,545	4,260	4,296
Operating profit	1,095	375	68
Other income	—	85	38
Amortized loss	502	230	—
Gross profit	593	230	30
Less:			
15% employee participation	89	35	5
Profit before taxes	504	195	25
Tax	116	45	6
Profit after taxes	388	150	19
Accumulated loss carried forward	502	1,004	1,234

[a]Average exchange rate of US$1 = 26 sucres.

INDUSTRIAS DEL MAIZ S.A.

Exhibit 5

Ecuador: Statistics
(selected data)

	1965	1970	1971	1972	1973	1974	1975	1976
Population (millions)								
Total	5.1	6.0	6.2	6.4	6.6	6.8	7.1	7.3
Economically active	1.6	1.9	2.0	2.1	2.1	2.2	7.3	2.4
GNP (millions US$)								
Total	1,101	1,245	1,602	1,854	2,588	3,683	4,275	4,807
Per capita	218	293	260	291	392	539	605	658
Gross fixed capital formation (mln. US$)								
Total	131	272	367	352	447	668	933	963
% GNP	12	16	23	19	17	18	22	20
Disposable national income (mln. US$)								
Consumption by residents	932	1,479	1,314	1,472	1,897	2,691	3,380	3,626
Savings by residents	94	132	163	201	421	592	556	793
Total	1,076	1,611	1,477	1,673	2,318	3,283	3,936	4,419
GNP by economic activity (mln. US$)								
Industrial	958	1,483	1,381	1,599	2,244	3,234	3,743	4,252
Agricultural	338	477	421	467	615	804	982	1,071
Manufacturer	169	286	249	306	398	512	655	780
Government services	84	165	143	167	205	299	350	395
Industrial production index (1970=100)								
General index	56	100	112	122	145	158	174	191
Food	70	100	108	111	119	128	140	157
Textiles	52	100	127	138	142	151	151	157
Paper	75	100	107	112	109	109	126	120

(Continued on next page)

125

Exhibit 5
Ecuador: Statistics (*continued*)
(*selected data*)

	1965	1970	1971	1972	1973	1974	1975	1976
Consumer price index (Quito: 1970=100)								
Total	79	100	NA	NA	132	163	188	208
Food	74	100	NA	NA	142	188	223	245
Housing	86	100	NA	NA	121	139	154	172
Clothing	82	100	NA	NA	128	155	183	206
Balance of payments (million US$)								
I. Merchandise f.o.b.	26	032	NA	NA	187	350	7	235
II. Services	−51	−115	NA	NA	−207	−343	−274	−278
III. Transfers	7	17	NA	NA	27	31	32	41
Balance on current account (I–III)	−14	−130	NA	NA	7	38	−235	−2
IV. Long-term capital	19	110	NA	NA	77	105	200	295
Basic balance (I–IV)	1	−20	NA	NA	−84	143	−35	293
V. SDRs	—	4	NA	NA	—	—	—	—
VI. Short-term capital	−1	16	NA	NA	88	−114	68	−346
VII. Errors and omissions	—	—	NA	NA	4	−29	−33	53
International trade (million US$)								
Exports f.o.b.	132	190	NA	NA	532	1,123	891	1,127
Imports c.i.f.	165	274	NA	NA	297	678	943	993
Balance	−33	−84	NA	NA	135	445	−46	134
Principal exports								
Banana	50	83	NA	NA	74	127	140	137
Cocoa	19	22	NA	NA	26	103	42	32
Coffee	35	50	NA	NA	65	68	64	205
Crude petroleum	2	1	NA	NA	282	693	516	565
Imports by groups								
Consumer goods	31	36	NA	NA	64	102	103	99
Raw materials and intermediates	73	137	NA	NA	174	310	375	446

Capital goods and transportation equipment	46	82	NA	NA	148	235	448	438
Fuel and lubricants	14	18	NA	NA	11	30	14	1
Others	1	1	NA	NA	0	1	3	3
External debt (million US$)								
Total (as of December)	121	241	NA	NA	380	410	513	731
Public sector	120	229	NA	NA	361	303	365	540
Private sector	1	12	NA	NA	19	107	148	191
Public finance-central government								
Current income	105	148	NA	NA	327	452	504	604
Current and capital expenditures	136	210	NA	NA	336	474	492	690
Deficit(−)/Surplus(+)	−31	−62	NA	NA	−9	−22	+12	−86
Current income (million US$)								
Sources: Income tax	15	22	NA	NA	72	119	125	191
Production and sales tax	18	23	NA	NA	61	77	93	107
Import duties	44	62	NA	NA	118	143	165	165
Export tax	13	20	NA	NA	51	73	51	51
Expenditures								
Education	24	40	NA	NA	92	105	133	175
Public works	17	31	NA	NA	60	70	67	91
Monetary systems (Summary)								
I. Net international assets	—	53	NA	NA	222	327	249	448
International monetary reserve	—	55	NA	NA	226	339	246	434
II. Internal credit	—	437	NA	NA	560	687	969	1,308
Net central government	—	86	NA	NA	46	16	−20	13
Net remainder-public sector	—	13	NA	NA	−55	−71	−59	−98
Private sector	—	301	NA	NA	458	658	888	1,161
Nonclassified net assets	—	63	NA	NA	111	84	160	232

SOURCE: Banco Central del Ecuador, 1977, *Datos Estadísticos.*

Exhibit 6
Percentage Comparison of Profit and Loss
Statements for Peru and Ecuador, 1978

	Peru	*Ecuador*
Gross sales	100.0%	100.0%
Less discounts	13.5	3.7
Net sales	86.5%	96.3%
Less:		
Cost of goods sold	57.6	80.7
Salary, general and administrative	11.3	10.2
Financial costs	3.5	3.9
	72.4	94.8
Gross margin	14.1	1.5
Less:		
Reserve-losses	—	0.7
Taxes	5.4	0.2
Worker participation	1.2	0.1
	6.6	1.0
Net profit	7.5%	0.5%

3

Managing the Business–Government Nexus

In developing countries, governments are major actors in the business environment. The scope and impact of their actions are so great that we consider government to be a "mega-force." Governments tend to take such an active involvement in the economies because of a desire to accelerate the development process and a belief that the imperfections that exist in Third World markets impede the efficient and effective functioning of private market forces. The high government involvement is also often motivated by a desire to increase political power and control. Thus, business success is dependent to a significant degree on managers' abilities to understand and interact with government.

KEY ISSUES

The seven cases in this chapter focus on three critical aspects of the business–government interface: understanding the managerial significance of government policies and actions, negotiating with government, and handling the uncertainties and demands arising from changing political environments.

Understanding the Mega-Force

A prerequisite to dealing effectively with the government is understanding how its actions shape the competitive environment and the specific operations of the firm. The EAF provides guidance for this task through

129

the Public Policy Impact Chain discussed in Chapter 1 and presented there in Figure 1.2. Managers can trace the actual or possible effects of national strategies and their corresponding policies on the structure and competitive dynamics at the industry level and, still further, on the specific functional areas of the firm. Government's impact often comes through its role as a gatekeeper, whereby it affects firms' access to resources and markets. For example, LDC governments' use of import quotas, industrial licensing, credit and foreign-exchange allocations, and domestic content requirements can cause barriers to entry, affect the intensity of competition, and create competitive advantages and disadvantages for different firms. Government policies regarding trade tariffs, price controls, wage and benefit levels, interest rates, subsidies, and taxes affect corporate costs and profits. The bargaining power relationships between buyers and suppliers can be fundamentally altered.

The opening case of this chapter provides an opportunity to explore the experience of one major multinational, John Deere, in dealing with the multiple effects of the Mexican government's policies and actions. The case clearly reveals the pervasive impact of the government on the business environment. The "Background Note on Mexico," which follows the Deere case, provides descriptive data on the country and the government up to 1979, the year Deere management faced a major expansion decision that hinged on the government's tractor industry policy. The Mexican mega-force is indeed a powerful one. The chapter's other cases provide additional country windows for viewing governments' roles and business–government relations.

Negotiating with Governments

Some of the most strategic aspects of the business–government relationship involve bargaining.[1] It is clear that the government, as a mega-force, has many "resources" important to companies. In turn, businesses provide resources important to government's economic development and political goals: capital, technology, management, employment, markets, and infrastructure. Negotiations with government are likely to be more successful where the needs and resources of the two sides are congruent. Assessing and searching for the points of congruency become central to the bargaining process. This process often involves many political and economic actors affected by the issues under negotiation. Consequently, it is useful to create a "political map" that identifies the different groups' interests and power.[2] Understanding the government's perspective and needs is essential to formulating effective bargaining strategies.

The second case in this chapter, "Mexico and the Microcomputers," examines the bargaining situation facing IBM and the Mexican govern-

ment. IBM wanted to expand its operations in Mexico to produce microcomputers but did not wish to comply with the government's Mexicanization policy requiring significant local ownership. The government's Office of Foreign Investment faced the decision of authorizing or rejecting
IBM's proposal, which had generated intense debate among various political groups and segments of the information processing industry. Political
mapping and assessing goal congruency are highly relevant to the analysis. The chapter's third case, "Dow Indonesia," shifts the context to the
other side of the world and presents another bargaining situation. The
government of Indonesia has to evaluate Dow's proposal for a major
investment. This proposal can be evaluated by applying the technique of
Economic Cost Benefit Analysis to determine quantitatively whether the
investment would make a positive economic contribution to the country.[3]
The fourth case provides a different perspective on business–government
relations. "State Timber Corporation of Sri Lanka" presents the situation
of a state-owned enterprise (SOE) confronting a series of problems arising
from its government's actions. The case is another illustration of the
mega-force effects discussed above. It poses the additional issue of how
the corporation is going to bargain with the government, which is also its
owner. From the government's perspective, lurking in the background is
the option of privatizing this SOE.

    One of the ethically perplexing situations that managers sometimes
find themselves in when dealing with governments concerns bribery payments. As a basis for discussing this topic, we have included a minicase
which sets forth a series of such situations.

Coping with Political Change

Developing country political environments are often fraught with instability. Political processes and institutions are not sufficiently developed to
permit orderly and periodic regime changes and power transfers. Shifts
are often abrupt and sometimes violent. This can cause major alterations
in national strategies or specific policies. The prevailing "rules of the
game" for business may get tossed out, to be followed by a period of great
uncertainty as new officials experiment in search of new rules. Political
change may also lead to a major exodus of government officials, which
can dismantle a company's network of government contacts and relationships. Given the prevalence of patronage politics, this widespread turnover in government functionaries often occurs even when the regime
change is part of an orderly electoral process.

    The last two cases in the chapter give the reader the chance to explore
the challenges facing businesses operating in an environment that un-
dergoes major political change. In 1979 an armed revolution overthrew

Nicaragua's autocratic regime, and the new revolutionary government began instituting major political, economic, and social changes. The "Standard Fruit in Nicaragua" case describes the demands and difficulties faced by this multinational banana exporter in living through the armed struggle and in dealing with the revolutionary government and a dramatically changed business environment. The "Pandol Brothers, Inc." case provides a sequel to the Standard Fruit case and examines how a small, entrepreneurially oriented U.S. produce importer was able to work with the government to develop a business opportunity emerging from the tumultuous political situation.

CASE STUDY QUESTIONS

John Deere Mexico

1. How have the Mexican government's development strategy, policies, and actions affected Deere's operation?
2. What recommendations would you make to Deere regarding how it deals with the government and what strategy to pursue in Mexico?

Mexico and the Microcomputers

1. Why did IBM's proposal create such controversy?
2. What factors should the government consider in weighing the proposal?
3. What should the government do? What should IBM do?

Dow Indonesia

1. How should the government evaluate the Dow proposal?
2. Is it good for the country and the company?
3. What are the critical assumptions in the analysis?

State Timber Corporation of Sri Lanka

1. What are the causes of STC's performance problems?
2. What actions should Kenneth take and why?
3. Should the government privatize STC?

Bribery and Extortion

1. What ethical and operating considerations are relevant to the decisions on how to handle these situations?
2. What action would you recommend?

Standard Fruit in Nicaragua

1. Which variables in the business environment were changed by the revolution?
2. How did that affect Standard's operation?
3. What is your evaluation of the actions Standard took during the insurrection and afterward?
4. What should Standard do? What should the government do?

Pandol Brothers, Inc.

1. How effective was Pandol in dealing with the revolutionary government? Why?
2. What should Pandol do? What should the government do?

NOTES

1. For a further discussion of strategies and analytical techniques for managing the business-government relationship, see James E. Austin, *Managing in Developing Countries* (New York: Free Press, 1990), Chapter 6.
2. *Ibid.,* for a further elaboration of the political mapping and bargaining process.
3. For an explanation of the Economic Cost Benefit Methodology, see *ibid.,* Chapter 6, pp. 156–65 and Appendix D.

John Deere, S.A. (Mexico)

As he stepped inside from the searing Mexican midday sun, Reinaldo Richardson, managing director of John Deere, S.A., concentrated on the problem he was facing: He needed to decide soon whether to recommend going ahead with plans for doubling John Deere's Mexican tractor capacity, but the profitability of that decision would be highly influenced by the government's new policy for Mexican tractor production, which was about to be announced. Time was running out; the expansion had to get under way in November to be on the schedule presented to the government. Months had passed since the Mexican government had announced its intention to define a new policy. Now it was Monday, August 20, 1979, and Richardson was expecting a phone call from Mexico City that he hoped would end the lingering uncertainty under which the Mexican tractor industry had operated for nearly the past two decades.

DEERE & COMPANY

In 1979 Deere & Company[1] was the undisputed world leader in farm equipment sales, with an estimated market share of 27% of world volume of the ten largest manufacturers. 1978 sales were more than U.S.$4 billion, and its share of the U.S. market was estimated at 32%.

Deere's success in the United States was due to a strategy that emphasized a strong, independent, loyal dealer network; a well-designed, reliable product; and a move to higher horsepower appropriate for larger farms.

Deere & Company's Operations in Mexico

Deere tractors had been sold in Mexico since the early 1900s through independent dealers who imported them directly.[2] In 1955 Deere & Co.

---

[1] For more background on the company, see "Deere & Company: U.S. Farm Equipment Division" (4-578-083).

[2] See John Deere de Mexico, S.A. de C.V. (9-313-239), 1968.

This case was written by Jo Froman, Associates Fellow, under the supervision of Professor Ray A. Goldberg, as a basis for class discussion rather than to illustrate either effective or ineffective handling of an administrative situation. Abridged with permission.

set up a sales branch in Mexico to gain wider dealer distribution and to provide closer supervision and better service to dealers handling its products. By 1956 the company had decided for two reasons to build a factory in Monterrey, Mexico, to manufacture implements and assemble tractors. First, small implement manufacturers were springing up, and the Mexican government had a policy of refusing import permits for locally available implements. Second, the Mexican government was pressuring the automotive industry to increase the percentage of Mexican content of automobiles. By exhibiting willingness to cooperate with the government's objective by initiating the assembly of tractors in Mexico using locally produced components insofar as possible, Deere felt that the possible future requirement to manufacture tractors in Mexico could be avoided or deferred.

Deere's Monterrey plant began assembling tractors in 1958; in 1966 the plant was enlarged for local production.

The Mexican company's marketing emphasized a strong, independent, and well-supported dealer network. By 1979, 57 dealers ran 66 sales outlets throughout the country. John Deere, S.A. provided training to help dealers and mechanics stay up to date on the features, repair, and maintenance of John Deere products.

In 1979 John Deere, S.A. manufactured three basic lines of products: tractors and implements for local sale and forage equipment for export. Four models of tractors were produced: 60 horsepower (h.p.), 71 h.p., 100 h.p., and 125 h.p. The last was the most powerful tractor manufactured in Mexico. The implements included four types of disk plows, eight harrows, one planter, and a variety of cultivating implements. For export, five types of forage-cutting machines were produced; 90% of these went to the United States, but exports also went to more than 17 countries, including Australia, France, the Philippines, Venezuela, Bolivia, Ecuador, and Guatemala. Unit sales were roughly 70% for tractors and 30% for implements.

In 1978 John Deere, S.A. earned $52.8 million (Mexican pesos)[3] on sales of $1.2 billion; 1979 estimates were $91 million after-tax profits on sales of $1.8 billion. A financial summary is in *Exhibit 1*. Profitability was constrained both by an official price ceiling on tractors and by the lack of sufficient production capacity to keep up with increases in the demand for tractors as well as by government regulations requiring a minimum of 60% local content for production.

John Deere, S.A.'s profitability was very much dependent on its ability to import and sell farm equipment and machinery, including tractors, of

---

[3]All figures in the case are Mexican pesos ($) unless otherwise stated. In 1978 the Mexican peso was worth about U.S.$.04.

models and power ranges not produced locally. In general, the importation of equipment that did not compete with local production was unrestricted. The government's price ceiling applied only to tractors and not to implements. In unit terms, Deere's imports were about 15% of its domestic sales, but margins on imports were far higher. Besides combines and other machinery, the company imported roughly 70% of its repair parts.

THE MEXICAN TRACTOR INDUSTRY

Growth in the Mexican tractor market was a function of a large number of variables, including general economic development of the country, population growth and demographics, the value of crop production, the mechanization of agriculture, and many others, but the largest single influence was government policy. The Mexican government affected the tractor market directly in two ways: It was the largest customer for tractors, purchasing 40% of tractors sold, and it controlled the Rural Credit Bank (under the secretary of the treasury), which often was the only source of financing available to most of the customers buying the other 60%. Indirectly, the government influenced the tractor supply through incentives or disincentives to the Mexican tractor industry. Government price ceilings, import restrictions, tariffs, local content requirements, and compensatory export requirements[4] directly affected the profitability of local production, which in turn affected the availability of local supply. In 1969, 5,000 tractors were sold. A decade later national production capacity was about 12,000 units, and demand was estimated at 18,000 units. This deficit was due partly to a single order from the Mexican government for 5,000 new tractors, an order for which the industry was unprepared. The market was expected to grow 6% to 8% over the next twenty years. But these projections were made before the government announced its large new order.

Demand was shifting to higher horsepowers. From 1971 through 1976 tractors of 60–70 h.p. increased their share from 41% to 66%, and the 90–125 h.p. rose from 0% to 12%; those under 60 h.p. dropped from 58% to 22%.

The four companies manufacturing tractors in Mexico in 1979 and their respective unit market share were: John Deere, S.A. (17%), Interna-

---

[4]Under the compensatory export requirement, automobile manufacturers were required to export products equivalent to "x"% of goods imported. In 1977 the ratio was set at 1:1 for the automobile industry. While the tractor industry was regulated under the same decree, the compensatory export requirement had never been enforced for tractors, but could conceivably be applied at any time.

tional Harvester Mexico, S.A. (10%), Ford Motor Company, S.A. (27%), and Massey-Ferguson de Mexico, S.A. (45%). Massey dominated the lower-h.p. segment; Deere accounted for 40% of over-100-h.p. sales.

The four companies formed the Tractor Industry Association, a subgroup of AMIA, the Mexican Automobile Industry Association. One major role of the industry association was to defend the interests of Mexican tractor producers in relation to government policy. The government preferred to meet jointly with the industry rather than deal with each company case by case. This had not always been true; before the association was formed, each company had accumulated its unique history of government relations.

MEXICAN GOVERNMENT POLICY

In 1979 the Mexican tractor industry was still waiting for a policy that would clearly define the "rules of the game" for tractor production. For the previous two decades, the companies had faced a confusing array of government policies and regulations that were subject to change without notice and that were applied unevenly across the industry.

Early History: The 1960s

As early as 1960–61, the Mexican government had begun to make its goal known for the manufacture of tractors in Mexico. While there was no national policy *per se,* government officials had revealed three goals through public statements and private conversations with tractor manufacturers and importers:

- The manufacture of tractors in Mexico in the minimum practical time with the maximum possible percentge of Mexican content
- Substantial participation of Mexican capital in these manufacturing operations, preferably a majority interest
- Prices of tractors manufactured in Mexico comparable to those of imported tractors

Representatives of the tractor companies voiced several objections to the proposed goals. The Mexican tractor market was limited in volume and spread over a wide range of horsepower sizes. At the same time, costs of manufacturing equipment were high, inflexible, and justifiable only in high-volume production. Local manufacture was inhibited by the lack of auxiliary industries in Mexico to provide components and raw materials. Those raw materials and components available locally were more expensive than imported components. With both high-cost components and low-volume production, it would be impossible, they argued, to price Mexican-produced tractors to be competitive with imported tractors, which were produced in high volume with lower input costs. The prospect of low profitability made it unlikely that Mexican capital would be attracted to a tractor industry operating under such constraints as the government proposed.

In August 1961 the Ministry of Industry and Commerce called a meeting of all tractor manufacturers and importers to advise them formally of the government's desire for local manufacture of tractors. At that time Deere was the only company assembling tractors in Mexico. The government requested proposals for setting up tractor manufacturing operations in Mexico and specified the points that would be taken into account in considering the proposals, including participation of Mexican capital and degree of local manufacturing content proposed. Deere did not submit a proposal at that time but continued to study the potential for local manufacture.

Finally, in August 1962, after continual urging by Mexican officials, Deere submitted a proposal for local manufacture of two tractor models, of about 40 h.p. and 50 h.p. The proposal called for a gradual increase in locally purchased parts, reaching 40% after four years and 60% after eight years, and for the sale of 40% of Deere's capital stock to Mexican investors as soon as financial results and market conditions favored such a sale. Deere proposed an investment of U.S.$3.8 million for expansion of its facilities.

This proposal mentioned the assumptions and conditions on which it was based:

1. The objective was to manufacture tractors for sale at prices comparable to imported U.S. tractors.
2. The prices of Mexican components would be maintained at comparable levels to U.S. imports.
3. To maintain a required annual production volume of 3,500 units, imports of all tractors up to 62 h.p. would be restricted.
4. Components, raw materials, manufacturing equipment, etc., that had to be imported would enter duty-free.
5. Similar tax concessions to those allowed under the Law for the Development of New and Necessary Industries would be granted from the project's beginning.

The proposal was discussed by government officials, but no action was taken. In August 1963 the Ministry of Industry and Commerce convened another meeting at which the tractor manufacturers were told that the government planned to move ahead with tractor production in Mexico. Additionally,

- Proposals were required to be submitted by September 30, 1963, and to provide for reaching 60% local content within two years, that is, by November 1, 1965.
- Of the companies submitting proposals, only two would be selected to manufacture in Mexico.
- Manufacturing equipment, materials, and parts needed for the program would be imported free of duty.
- Tractor imports would be phased out, and the border would then be closed to competing units.
- Tractors to be manufactured would be in the 35–65 h.p. range.
- Retail prices were to be no more than 10% over current Mexican retail prices.

In considering its response to this invitation, Deere was encouraged by projections of moderate growth in the Mexican market. By restricting local manufacturers to two companies and by closing the border to competing units, the government would virtually ensure a 50% market share to each company within the 35–65 h.p. range, which was then the most popular in the local market. Furthermore, Deere already had a sizable investment in the Monterrey plant. The choice not to manufacture tractors locally would probably mean the eventual phasing out of the Mexican operation.

Deere submitted a proposal, as did several other manufacturers. In November 1963 a proposal submitted by International Harvester was approved. Later, in March 1964, Deere was selected as the second manufacturer. Deere began construction immediately at its Monterrey plant for the facilities needed to manufacture tractors with 60% Mexican content. The expansion called for an investment of about U.S.$4.6 million.

During construction of these facilities, a new administration took charge of the Mexican government, and certain policies initiated or promised under the previous administration were no longer adhered to. Imports of tractors by two major competitive manufacturers continued to be approved almost without restriction, and the government approved barter importations of tractors not previously sold in Mexico. To remain competitive with these relatively low-cost imports, Deere found that it could not charge even the maximum prices permitted by the government. Transportation to Mexico added about 10% to the cost of imports, and Mexican import duties on completed tractors added about 5% more. With unit production costs in Monterrey running 30% to 50% higher than in Deere's North American or European plants, the company was in a severe cost-price squeeze, and profits proved elusive.

In mid-1965 the Mexican government announced that it was consider-ing the approval of four additional tractor manufacturers. After two of these proposals were withdrawn, the government accepted a proposal from Massey-Ferguson in February 1966. The fourth manufacturer, Ford Motor Company, was approved in November 1967.

In August 1966 John Deere, S.A. received an official communication from the Mexican Ministry of Industry and Commerce that established new conditions for the tractor industry. Under these new conditions,

- Maximum prices were established for the tractors that Deere manu-factured at a level about 125% of the list prices of comparable trac-tors f.o.b. Deere Dubuque tractor plant in the United States.
- Within two months, 51% of the company's common stock was to be Mexican-owned. Mexican ownership was defined as ownership by Mexican nationals or by Mexican-controlled institutions.

To comply with the second condition, the company worked out an arrangement whereby it retained 49% of the common stock; 17% was taken by a private Mexican bank, Banamex; 8% was sold on the stock exchange; and the remaining 26% was held in escrow until market condi-tions allowed its sale. In 1979 this ownership structure was still un-changed. But Deere was the only company of the four that had sold a substantial portion of its stock in an attempt to satisfy the government's condition.[5]

Recent History: The 1970s

By the end of the 1960s the participants in the Mexican tractor industry were all in place. Some regulations and conditions had been established, but no single set of rules governing the industry was clearly defined and evenly applied. Many rules "on the books" were not enforced, but in the words of one tractor executive, "You never knew when someone might decide to enforce one of the forgotten rules."

This uncertainty lingered through the early and mid-1970s. In fact, it increased during the Echeverría administration (1970–76), when the Min-istry of Industry and Commerce was split into two separate ministries: Industry, which looked after industrial policy, and Commerce, which looked after price controls and import permits for machines and parts. Now, not only was there no single policy for the manufacture of tractors, but the industry no longer dealt with a single ministry.

In 1977, shortly after the arrival of Richardson at John Deere, S.A., the

[5]After 1973, 51% Mexican ownership was made compulsory, but the law was not applied retroactively to companies incorporated in Mexico before 1973.

government announced its Automotive Manufacturing Decree, which regulated the manufacture of automobiles, trucks, buses and, for the first time, tractors. This decree established degrees of local content for specific products, rather than an across-the-board average of 60%, and required that all imports be compensated with exports of equal value (dollar for dollar, or peso for peso).

The members of the tractor industry association were not satisfied with this decree, because they felt it ignored two fundamental differences between the government's historical treatment of tractors and automobiles: First, automobiles were exempt from price controls, unlike buses, trucks, and tractors, and prices had more than kept pace with costs. Second, the border was closed to all automobiles not produced within Mexico, so that any imports by the auto industry were likely to be on a small scale—repair parts or components rather than finished cars. Meanwhile, the border was not closed to tractors, for farmers could obtain permits to import "used" tractors, and federal and state agencies could bring in new tractors under permits. The scale of such imports was unknown, but records showed that in 1978, 800 tractor import permits were granted to the State of Mexico alone. For the farm equipment manufacturers, the automotive decree raised as many questions as it answered. They imported expensive specialized machinery not produced locally, such as combines worth U.S.$40,000–$50,000. Did the decree require that imports like those be compensated dollar for dollar with exports? It would hardly be possible, given that most exports consisted of small equipment, components, and repair parts. Would this mean that manufacturers could no longer import combines and large tractors? If not, the companies' profitability, which was currently highly dependent on these sales rather than local production, would be severely affected. The tractor industry was left with a decree that included them, made demands on them, but did not make clear the regulations as they applied to tractors. The industry petitioned the government repeatedly to clarify its position on tractors.

In the meantime, the manufacturers tried to resolve the problem of price. Because of the government's ceiling, tractor prices had not kept up with increases in input costs. Price increases were granted only on the basis of audited company invoices for component costs. John Deere had petitioned the government for a weighted-average price increase of 14.5% in December 1978, based on November 1978 cost figures. In April 1979 a 7% weighted-average increase was granted, with another 7% increase granted in July. Between January 1979 and August, there were major increases in the costs of steel, tires, and tubes, so the company found it necessary to petition for another increase in August. In general, granted price increases applied to all manufacturers, with some adjustments for differences in model and horsepower of their products.

John Deere recognized that the issue of price could not be divorced from other government policies, such as the government's own demand for tractors, its agricultural policy, its tax laws, and its industrial policy. Thus it was encouraged when an interministerial commission was formed in April 1978 to study the problems of the tractor industry. Deere felt this showed that the government had come to recognize the need for a comprehensive policy.

The Government's Tractor Order

In July 1978 the Ministry of Agriculture and the Rural Credit Bank began to discuss very ambitious plans for increasing the acreage under cultivation in Mexico. Initially they suggested that 15,000 tractors be purchased in the next year to accomplish those plans. Then as talk continued, the number of tractors was adjusted downward, first to 10,000 then to 5,000. By November 1978 the government had determined that the tractors were to be of higher horsepowers, making Deere the only possible local supplier. In fact, Deere was unable to supply more than a minimal part of the order from local production. The capacity of all Mexican manufacturers was already strained by meeting the normal demand that they had anticipated in their production planning.

When it was revealed that the Mexican government was planning to import 5,000 tractors, there was considerable agitation in the local press against government officials. Why, it was asked, did the government need to import so many tractors when there was a national tractor industry? These questions were then asked of the industry. When the secretary of industrial development asked why the local industry was unable to supply this order, the industry's reply was that (1) production could not be increased because the government's policies rendered it unprofitable, and (2) the industry had to know government plans for such large purchases in advance to allow sufficient lead time for production planning. In response, the secretary promised to assist the industry by asking the Agriculture Ministry and Rural Credit Bank to announce their plans for direct purchases for the future. He also promised that the "rules of the game" for tractor manufacture in Mexico would be established before Christmas.

In answer to the secretary, the Ministry of Agriculture announced that direct purchases would amount to 5,000 tractors each year through 1982. As one tractor company executive explained, 5,000 new tractors implied the need for 8,000 to 10,000 trained operators as well as large increments of fuel, repair parts, service, and implements. No one had thought about tractor implements in the original projections, and the country was experiencing a shortage of the steel used in their manufacture. While it was highly unlikely that the government would go through with the total projected purchases, the effect of its large order had been beneficial insofar as it called the government's attention to the problems of Mexican tractor producers.

Deere had received slightly less than one-fourth of the government's order and had arranged to supply 1,125 tractors from its plant in Argentina. Financing for the purchase had been arranged through the Argentine National Bank, which provided credit as an export incentive for its domestic manufacturers. The government of Mexico had required full financing for its tractor purchase.

John Deere's Plan for Expansion

Anticipating a large increase in tractor demand due to the government's agricultural development plans, Richardson submitted a plan for a US$8-million expansion of plant capacity to John Deere, S.A.'s Mexican board and Deere & Company management in Moline in August 1978. The plan called for an expansion of effective production capacity for tractors from 2,100 units to 4,200 units by the end of 1982. Now, in August 1979, he had to decide whether to recommend going ahead with the planned expansion, which Deere's management had reviewed favorably.

Christmas 1978 had come and gone without a further definition of the government's tractor policy. On May 7, 1979, the subsecretary of industrial development, Nathan Warman, had called another roundtable with the tractor industry to explain that the problem was proving more complex than anticipated.

It appeared that price increases could not be used as incentives to the tractor industry as they had for automobile manufacture. For one thing, automobile buyers were not a political group, whereas tractor buyers could and did exert influence on the government through the powerful National Confederation of *Campesinos* (farmer's union). Government's willingness to allow price rises was limited by the political reality of a large rural, agricultural population. Another inhibitor of prices was the proximity of the U.S. border. An awareness of U.S. list prices and product design features prevented the local market from going too far out of line. As long as import permits could be obtained for used tractors, the local industry had to remain competitive in price and design with tractors that could be purchased in the United States and driven "used" across the border into Mexico.

In lieu of price increases, the industry suggested that the government allow policy changes that would lead to lower unit production costs, such as reduction of the local content requirement for tractors and exemption from the compensating exports requirement imposed on automobile producers. Warman ended the May 7 meeting by requesting that each manufacturer submit, within thirty days, a plan for expansion of production capacity, including a proposal for local content and other incentives.

John Deere submitted its proposal on June 8 (*Exhibit 2*). In essence, the company proposed an expansion of both tractor and implement production and a reduction in the required local content for tractor manufacture. On July 25 Richardson sent another letter to Warman reminding him of the proposal and requesting a response so that the expansion could proceed on schedule. On Friday, August 10, Richardson received a letter confirming John Deere's offer and summoning him to a meeting in Mexico City on Monday, August 13. Richardson expected that the government would put forth its own proposal at that time. During the Monday meeting, each member of the tractor association made a presentation of its plans. At the end, Warman indicated that the government would announce its own decision soon.

Now it was August 20, and the company had been summoned to another meeting in Mexico City. This time Richardson had been unable to attend and had sent a representative. He had begun to doubt that the government would, in fact, define its policy in time for his company's expansion plans to proceed according to the schedule submitted to the government. Without government assurance that local content requirements would be reduced, he wondered whether the expansion ought to go ahead at all.

John Deere, S.A.'s Decision

For the expansion to proceed in November, Richardson would have to make a final recommendation to the board within the next two weeks. To go ahead without a definitive tractor policy from the government would risk involving the company in an unprofitable venture. On the other hand, to delay the expansion might weaken the company's competitive position if the other tractor manufacturers went ahead. Right now, Deere could import tractors to supplement its production, but if other companies started to produce competing models locally, this option might be closed in the future. Currently, Deere had a competitive advantage in the higher horsepower ranges. Would delaying expansion plans risk losing that advantage?

Richardson thought about two recent developments that were bound to affect Deere's competitive environment. In one case, Allis-Chalmers had announced its intention to begin assembling combines in Mexico. The total market for combines was less than 700 machines a year, with 400 to 500 being the average. If Allis-Chalmers went ahead with this venture, it could ask the government to restrict the importation of combines or at least try to gain the establishment of quotas and duties on imported combines. Currently combines paid no duties, and their importation was limited only by demand. Richardson knew that such a development would not help Mexican farmers, because the locally produced combines would be more expensive. Nor would it create many jobs, since the market for combines was small. But, it would seriously affect the profitability of the three tractor companies (Ford excluded), who depended on imports of this nature to balance the low profitability of their Mexican production. These companies would be left with two options: depend on getting import permits, or set up local combine assembly themselves. Richardson estimated that it would require an investment of about 100 million pesos to set up local assembly.

In the other case, Richardson had heard that Massey-Ferguson was negotiating with Mexico's largest industrial holding company, Alfa Group of Monterrey, for the sale of its Mexican subsidiary. While the entry of Alfa Group into the tractor industry could introduce a powerful ally in industry–government negotiations, it would also introduce a strong competitor in the market.

With its new petroleum-based wealth, Mexico was expecting a positive balance of trade in 1980. There had recently been talk of Mexico's joining GATT, a move that would substantially reduce restrictions and levies on external trade. Despite Mexico's heavy emphasis on industrial development, agriculture was still considered a high priority. In his 1976 inaugural address, President López Portillo stressed its importance in stating that Mexico's "first goal is to feed our people." In listing the country's priorities for investment, he had placed agriculture and livestock first.

The environment for tractor production in Mexico was clearly changing. If even a small part of the government's plan for expanding acreage came to fruition, the demand for tractors would take off again. The government seemed newly receptive to providing incentives to the local tractor industry. Mexico still had a large agricultural base. The current trend in farming was toward larger-scale collective or cooperative ventures, which the government was encouraging. With its traditional competitive strength in high-power, high-productivity equipment, John Deere's market position would benefit greatly if it was prepared to meet the new demand for larger tractors that the government was helping to create. John Deere had survived for over two decades in an environment of uncertainty and had made a substantial investment in the Mexican facilities. Did it make sense now, in this changing environment, to dramatically increase the investment? As he waited for the phone to ring, Richardson began to analyze John Deere's options.

Exhibit 1

Financial Summary for John Deere, S.A. for 1976–78

(Mexican pesos)

	1978	1977	1976
Net sales	$1,184,556,081	$758,590,796	$624,608,071
Net profit (loss) plus revaluation surplus realized	52,877,830	58,164,558	(47,748,498)
Profit to sales ratio	4.46%	7.67%	(7.64%)
Net profit (loss) plus revaluation surplus realized per share	$44.06	$48.47	($39.79)
Total assets	$569,463,439	$474,562,014	$351,606,613
Net working capital	$186,675,889	$142,744,317	$79,892,411
Current ratio	2.2 to 1	2.0 to 1	1.3 to 1
Long-term debt	$12,500,000	—	—
Owners equity and revaluation surplus	$394,682,454	$327,253,755	$111,854,077
Book value per share[a]	$328.90	$272.71	$93.21

[a]1.2 million shares outstanding

SOURCE: *John Deere, S.A., Informe Annual 1978* (1978 annual report; casewriter translation).

Exhibit 2
John Deere's Expansion Plan, June 1979

8 June 1979

Dr. Nathan Warman
Subsecretary of Industrial Development
Ministry of Industrial Resources and Development
Insurgentes Sur 552
Mexico, D. F.

Dear Dr. Warman,

We remind you of the meeting which we, the producers of agricultural tractors, held with you this past May 7th, and in which you solicited a reply to your suggestion that we increase our production, taking into consideration that we would be permitted to diminish our degree of local manufacturing content and would benefit from a price to the Mexican public higher than that of the country of origin—these being tax incentives created by you within the National Plan of Industrial Development.

Concerning this request, we wish to inform you that John Deere, S.A. has developed a plan for expansion which will permit us to double our production, that is, move from 2,100 units currently produced to 4,200 annual units by the end of our plan.

The first stage foresees additional production of 500 tractors, the second of 700, and the third of 900, which will permit us to double our production. In Annex 1, the above can be seen, as well as dates programmed to begin and complete each stage.

The degree of local content of each model we manufacture in accordance with the Component-Cost formula, would be the following:

Model	*Degree of Local Content*
2535	50%
2735	50%
4235	40%
4435	40%

To carry out this expansion, our investment will be between 185 and 200 million pesos, as can be seen from Annexes 2, 3, 4, 5, 6, and 7.

During the first stage, the investment will be minimal, basically because of the very long lead-time we are subjected to by our machinery suppliers and of the lapse required for the construction of new buildings which will permit us to increase our production.

For the second stage, our investment will be 61 million pesos, which will be applied to the purchase of new machine tools, materials handling equipment, a more appropriate finished goods warehouse, etc., which will permit us to reach a production of 3,300 tractors.

In the third stage, the investment will increase to 126 million pesos destined for the construction of a new building for assembly of tractors; a new system for painting; expansion of the product engineering workshop, and the administrative offices, and of employee parking facilities; purchase of machine tools, equipment for thermal treatment and materials handling; which will permit an increase in production capacity to 4,200 tractors.

It should be added that our production of agricultural implements will also show an increase from our current production of 5,000 tons to 6,250 tons with our plan for expansion. (See Annex 8.)

In relation to the creation of new jobs, we have estimated that during the first stage we will employ 100 persons, 150 during the second and 150 during the third; in other words, the investment will lead to 400 new jobs, to be added to the 1,043 persons currently working in our company.

We consider that the investment plan which we are submitting for your consideration today is a reflection of what our company can accomplish to assist in the industrialization of the country, substituting for imports of agricultural equipment and generating new employment.

We take advantage of the opportunity to convey warm regards and look forward to your esteemed commentary regarding our plan.

cc. Dr. Ernesto Marcos
Director of Industrial Development
Hermosillo #26
Mexico, D. F.

Ing. Juan Wolffer
Subdirector of the Automotive and
Transportation Industry
Hermosillo #26
Mexico, D. F.

SOURCE: John Deere, S.A. (casewriter's translation from original Spanish).

Background Note on Mexico

This note provides a brief political, social, and economic description of Mexico up to 1979 as a supplement to case studies about companies operating in Mexico.

POLITICAL BACKGROUND

Out of the bloody Mexican revolution of 1910–19 emerged the Partido Revolucionario Institucional (PRI), which has won all the presidential elections and controls all branches of the federal government. Opposition parties have been very weak. Immense power is vested in the presidency relative to the legislature and the judiciary. The PRI members encompass a wide range of political ideologies.

The government's role and bureaucracy are extensive: 18 ministries, more than 500 state-owned enterprises, and about 350 official commissions and trusts. The policy-making process has been viewed as "the exclusive prerogative of a small elite and is characterized by limited informational inputs, behind-the-scenes bargaining and accommodation, and low levels of public discussion and debate."[1] The bureaucracy is very powerful and is organized into personal alliances and networks based on a patron–client relationship. Superiors can offer jobs and promotion to subordinates who give their loyalty, obedience, and effort. With each six-year presidential change there is a tremendous turnover among all top officials and middle-level bureaucrats, as the new president and his team appoint their networks to run the bureaucracies. Some of the bureaucrats exit public service, but most move to new bureaucracies along with their "patron."

SOCIAL BACKGROUND

Organized labor played an important role in the revolution and thus gained social respect and political importance within the PRI. Struggle

[1]Merilee S. Grindle, "Bureaucracy and Public Policy in Mexico," Ph.D. dissertation, MIT, October 1975, p. 23.

Unless otherwise cited, statistics in this note have been drawn from the Harvard Business School note "Mexico: Development Strategies and Performance," 379-173, rev. 4/86, by Lokhi Banerji and James E. Austin.

151

over land ownership was a fundamental cause of the Mexican revolution and led to major agrarian reform.

As of 1979 about 65% of Mexico's 69 million people lived in urban areas with almost half of these being in Mexico City.[2] Population was growing at 3% annually. Nutritional deficiencies were considered extensive, particularly among low-income rural dwellers. Infant mortality rate was 50 per 1,000 (as against 11 in the United States).[3] The literacy rate was about 90% for men and women.[4]

ECONOMIC BACKGROUND

Additional oil discoveries since 1974 made Mexico a net energy exporter, with oil accounting for 85% of total exports by the late 1970s. The country was also rich with many other minerals.

Only 16% of the land was arable for agriculture, which occupied 40% of the labor force. Modern, larger farms occupied about 20% of the arable land but produced 53% of the national production. The remainder of the farms were small, often subsistence level, private plots or *ejidos,* land given by the government for which the peasants had lifetime usage rights but could not sell. Agricultural output grew significantly until the late 1960s, then did not keep pace with demand, leaving Mexico with the need to import about 20% of its food supply in the late 1970s. The government estimated in 1979 that existing trends would mean that by 1985 half of the country's oil revenues would have to be spent on food imports.

The industrial sector amounted to about 35% of GNP and was a major source of growth stimulated by the expanding domestic market created by the government's import substitution industrialization strategy. Industrial growth, however, had not been able to keep pace with the growing labor force, and unemployment continued to rise in the late 1970s. About 90% of manufacturing was done by small and medium-size firms, which were relatively inefficient and internationally noncompetitive. Direct foreign investment was encouraged but highly regulated by the government. DFI supplied about 5% of national investment in 1979.

The country's historical economic stability deteriorated during the presidency of Luis Echeverría of the mid-1970s, resulting in surging inflation, growing fiscal and trade deficits, and a 52% devaluation of the peso. President José López Portillo instituted austerity measures upon assum-

---

[2]*World Development Report 1985* (New York: Oxford University Press for the World Bank, 1985), p. 217.

[3]*Ibid.,* p. 219.

[4]*State of the World's Children 1987* (New York: UNICEF, 1987), p. 91.

ing office in 1977. By 1978 inflation had been reduced to 17%, public and private investment increased significantly, and GNP grew 6%. The budget deficit fell as a share of GNP. The trade balance improved, but capital inflows rose. Foreign debt service absorbed 66% of the country's exports.

The government was indicating a shift in national strategy toward export orientation and a loosening on import controls. By mid-1979 investment proposals from foreign companies were at an all-time high.

Exhibits 1–4 provide economic indicators for 1970–79.

BACKGROUND NOTE ON MEXICO

Exhibit 1

Balance of Payments

(Millions of US$; minus is a debit)

	Echeverría							López Portillo		
	1970	1971	1972	1973	1974	1975	1976	1977	1978	1979
1 Current account balance	−1,068	−835	−916	−1,415	−2,876	−4,042	−3,409	−1,854	−3,171	−5,459
2 Merchandise: exports f.o.b.	1,348	1,409	1,717	2,141	2,999	3,007	3,475	4,604	6,246	9,301
3 Merchandise: imports f.o.b.	−2,236	−2,158	−2,610	−3,656	−5,791	−6,278	−5,771	−5,625	−7,992	−12,131
4 Trade balance (2+3)	−888	−749	−894	−1,515	−2,791	−3,272	−2,295	−1,021	−1,745	−2,830
5 Other goods, serv. & inc.: cred.	1,587	1,762	2,100	2,699	3,369	3,352	3,728	3,608	5,178	6,702
6 Other goods, serv. & inc.: deb.	−1,822	−1,906	−2,187	−2,673	−3,574	−4,263	−4,996	−4,610	−6,797	−9,556
7 Other goods, serv. & inc.: net	−235	−143	−87	26	−206	−911	−1,269	−1,003	−1,618	−2,854
8 Private unrequited transfers	48	50	54	66	100	114	129	153	104	131
9 Official unrequited transfers	7	7	10	8	22	26	27	16	88	94
10 Capital other than reserves, nie	845	892	840	2,004	3,428	5,449	5,545	2,473	3,700	5,144
11 Net errors and omissions	244	79	265	−435	−472	−1,229	−3,041	51	−97	597
12 Total (1+10+11)	21	135	189	154	80	177	−904	669	432	282
13 Counterpart items	53	62	34	14	−37	−58	−90	7	23	114
14 Total (12+13)	75	197	223	168	43	119	−994	676	455	396
15 Liab. const. fgn. author. reserves	—	—	—	—	—	−7	312	−292	−1	—
16 Total change in reserves	−75	−197	−223	−168	−43	−112	682	−384	−455	−396

BACKGROUND NOTE ON MEXICO

Exhibit 2

International Transactions
(Billions of pesos)

International Transactions	Echeverría							López Portillo		
	1970	1971	1972	1973	1974	1975	1976	1977	1978	1979
Exports	17.54	18.84	21.24	28.27	37.34	36.30	53.52	102.05	135.65	204.86
Petroleum	.48	.39	.27	.31	1.54	5.75	8.40	23.23	41.42	89.32
Crude petroleum	—	—	—	—	.47	5.44	8.40	22.31	40.66	86.43
Cotton	1.55	1.50	1.85	2.07	2.27	2.18	4.37	4.40	7.03	7.90
Coffee	1.08	1.01	1.07	1.96	1.93	2.31	5.20	10.35	8.80	12.40
Shrimp	.79	.86	.98	1.26	1.46	1.48	2.54	4.20	3.44	8.21
Imports, c.i.f.	30.76	28.13	33.98	47.67	75.71	82.13	90.90	132.99	172.03	275.65
Imports, f.o.b.	29.30	26.79	32.36	45.40	72.10	78.22	86.41	126.41	163.53	262.52
Volume of exports (1980 = 100)										
Crude petroleum	—	—	—	—	1.2	13.2	14.8	25.1	45.2	65.8
Cotton	125	97	119	104	97	90	83	81	117	123
Coffee	65	73	74	103	93	110	127	83	89	136
Shrimp	84.1	90.7	96.3	91.0	83.4	91.1	91.5	98.7	93.8	97.4
Unit value of exports										
Crude petroleum	—	—	—	—	18.7	19.3	26.5	41.4	41.9	61.2
Cotton	17.2	21.4	21.5	27.5	32.4	33.4	72.6	74.8	83.2	88.5
Coffee	16.2	13.5	14.1	18.5	20.2	20.4	39.8	121.6	96.9	88.7
Shrimp	11.7	11.9	12.7	17.3	21.8	20.4	34.7	53.2	45.9	105.4

BACKGROUND NOTE ON MEXICO

Exhibit 3
Industrial Production
(1980 = 100)

			Echeverría					López Portillo		
	1970	*1971*	*1972*	*1973*	*1974*	*1975*	*1976*	*1977*	*1978*	*1979*
Manufacturing production	50.8	51.9	57.1	62.9	67.5	70.7	72.6	75.1	82.6	91.1
Mining production	53.5	55.0	60.3	65.8	70.3	73.2	75.2	77.9	84.9	92.8
Crude petroleum	63.6	61.5	64.3	68.5	75.8	71.7	75.9	76.5	78.1	81.8
	35.4	36.3	38.5	39.0	44.7	49.7	54.4	61.7	71.0	81.4

BACKGROUND NOTE ON MEXICO

Exhibit 4

Government Finance and National Accounts

	1970	1971	*Echeverría* 1972	1973	1974	1975	1976	*López Portillo* 1977	1978	1979
Government Finance (billions of pesos: year ending December 31)										
Deficit (−) or surplus	−6.1	−4.2	−17.0	−27.5	−34.3	−53.6	−64.1	−61.1	−62.7	−101.9
Revenue	42.5	47.5	58.2	69.5	95.3	133.4	168.6	240.7	322.8	438.6
Grants received	—	—	.2	.3	.2	.4	.4	.3	.4	.5
Expenditure	48.6	51.7	63.3	88.1	123.9	161.6	211.6	285.5	367.5	505.2
Lending minus repayments	—	—	8.2	9.3	5.9	25.8	21.5	16.7	18.4	35.8
Financing										
Net borrowing: Domestic	5.0	5.0	13.5	25.1	27.9	40.3	50.5	54.7	64.6	103.3
Foreign	2.0	.3	2.6	3.3	11.6	15.5	25.3	10.3	6.9	−7.1
Use of cash balances	−1.0	−1.2	1.0	−.9	−5.7	−2.2	−11.7	−3.9	−8.8	5.7
Debt: Domestic	58.8	58.9	74.6	99.1	127.3	177.3	282.4			
Foreign	12.3	12.6	13.9	17.7	29.6	40.4	90.3			

(Continued on next page)

157

BACKGROUND NOTE ON MEXICO

Exhibit 4

Government Finance and National Accounts (*Continued*)

	Echeverría							López Portillo		
	1970	*1971*	*1972*	*1973*	*1974*	*1975*	*1976*	*1977*	*1978*	*1979*
National Accounts (*billions of pesos*)										
Exports	34.4	37.4	45.5	58.1	75.7	75.8	116.4	190.8	244.7	343.3
Government consumption	32.2	37.3	48.7	63.4	82.3	113.5	150.9	199.0	255.2	334.3
Gross fixed capital formation	88.7	88.1	107.1	133.3	178.9	235.6	288.4	363.3	492.4	718.5
Increase in stocks	12.3	11.1	7.6	14.4	29.7	25.0	17.2	59.1	59.2	77.6
Private consumption	319.5	358.8	405.6	487.0	628.3	755.9	933.4	1,226.1	1,543.8	1,975.9
Less: Imports	−42.9	−42.7	−49.8	−65.4	−95.2	−105.8	−135.3	−189.0	−258.0	−382.0
Gross Domestic product	444.3	490.0	564.7	690.9	899.7	1,100.1	1,371.0	1,849.3	2,337.4	3,067.5
Less: Net factor payments abroad	−5.6	−6.5	−7.4	−10.0	−15.0	−17.9	−29.0	−43.0	−52.5	−77.1
Gross National Expenditure = GNP	438.7	463.5	557.3	680.9	884.7	1,082.1	1,342.0	1,806.3	2,784.9	2,990.4
Gross Dom. Prod. 1980 prices	2,256.9	2,350.8	2,550.5	2,764.8	2,934.0	3,098.5	3,279.6	3,340.8	3,616.7	3,947.9
Population (millions)	50.7	52.5	54.3	56.2	58.1	60.2	62.3	64.6	65.4	67.4
GDP per capita 1980 (000)	44.5	44.8	47.0	49.2	50.5	51.5	51.8	51.7	55.3	58.6

SOURCE: *International Finance Statistics, 1985*, pp. 450–51.

Mexico and the Microcomputers

In March 1984 Mario Espinosa de los Reyes, chief adviser to the under-secretary of foreign investments at the Ministry of Commerce, was in his office reading two documents. IBM de Mexico S.A. had presented to the Board of Foreign Investments a proposal to manufacture their system 56 (the IBM PC XT) in Mexico and a study of the potential market demand for it. The plant was to be in El Salto, Jalisco, very near to Hewlett-Packard's plant. The project was part what IBM called the "office of the future," which included parallel products such as a typewriter that could be used as a printer.

IBM had been in Mexico for a long time. It was the dominant firm in the minicomputer and mainframe markets, with shares of 36% and 49% in these two markets. Its total assets in Mexico were valued at $180 million. IBM carried its full product line in Mexico except for some very large mainframes and the PCs. It had also been successfully manufacturing and exporting its system 36 minicomputer.

It seemed likely that the proposal would be controversial because it departed from prevailing norms in the industry. To promote the computer industry, the Ministry of Commerce started a program in 1979 to produce microcomputers, minicomputers, and printers. The microcomputer market was reserved for firms with a majority of Mexican ownership. All existing firms were registered within this program, although it had never been officially ratified through signing and publishing. To be published, the program had to be endorsed by the ministers of finance, programming and budget, commerce, communications and transportation, and energy and mines, some of whom opposed an existing draft of the bill because it had several legal and economic flaws. Therefore, although everybody knew the program and many firms were working under its rules, it was technically nonexistent. A test case was necessary to establish what actual rules governed the computer industry.

IBM refused to enter the Mexican microcomputer market under the existing program begun by the Ministry of Commerce. IBM required 100% ownership rather than a minority position in a joint venture. For IBM 100% ownership was important for several reasons:

This case was prepared by Allen Sangines Krause under the supervision of Professor James E. Austin and Assistant Professor Dennis Encarnation as the basis for classroom discussion rather than to illustrate either effective of ineffective handling of an administrative problem. Abridged with permission.

1. The plant in Mexico would be devoted mainly to exports. Because IBM could supply these markets through other wholly owned plants, the investment made no sense to IBM without full ownership.

2. Creating a joint venture for microcomputers would create a conflict among IBM Corporation, IBM de Mexico (the current minicomputer manufacturer), and the new company. Transfer pricing difficulties and problems in dividing the export markets among different IBM plants were expected.

3. Creating a joint venture in Mexico could jeopardize IBM's position in other countries. In 1978 IBM withdrew from India rather than create a joint venture with 60% owned by the government.

IBM declared that it was very interested in Mexico if it could maintain three basic IBM principles:

1. Maintaining its standard of excellence
2. Obeying the laws of the country in which it does business
3. Participating in all markets with its full product line whenever possible with 100% ownership

Many within the Ministry of Commerce's Foreign Investment Office were concerned that Mexico was losing the race among new semi-industrialized countries for supremacy in the electronics industry. They believed Mexico needed huge foreign investment in export-oriented assembly plants that would create and pull the whole components industry behind it. The IBM project seemed perfect for this strategy. Big Blue would demand huge amounts of cables, connectors, capacitors, diodes, resistors, and a full range of other electronic components.

Within the Ministry of Commerce, the undersecretary for industrial promotion and his team had a very different perspective. They emphasized the fairness issue raised by changing the program's rules about foreign investment after other multinationals such as Apple and Hewlett-Packard had entered the market in minority joint ventures. They also stressed the dependency issue if IBM entered the market: Big Blue could easily move into a monopoly position, and it would then be impossible to develop a truly Mexican computer industry. They would allow IBM into the market only if it brought something really new to the industry, for example, a plant to produce locally high-tech components such as integrated circuits and the latest generation of printed boards.

One further complication was that IBM's proposal, for reasons of industrial secrecy, omitted some information needed for complete economic evaluation. Hence, the political aspects might receive even more attention.

IBM's First Proposal

The proposal IBM submitted in March 1984 consisted of a letter explaining the project, a demand projection for 1984–90, and the figures of this project (see *Exhibit 1*). IBM circulated its proposal widely among government officials, and it soon leaked to the press. By August 1984, after several rounds of negotiations at the Ministry of Commerce, IBM determined that the chances for approval of its project were slim, and it decided to present an improved version to the Board of Foreign Investments. The new proposal was virtually identical with the first, except that it called for more purchases of local components, which would have a positive effect on the net foreign-exchange balance. It also included two new offers:

1. An undetermined number of scholarships for technical training in the United States
2. Creation of an international office to export local components to other IBM plants abroad

IBM threatened that if the project were not promptly accepted, it would build the plant in Argentina.

The Electronics Industry in Mexico

Mexico did not have a full computer-manufacturing industry; the existing firms bought integrated circuits and all high-tech components abroad and then assembled computers with rudimentary processes (screwdriver technology). Some companies did not even do this. They bought computers in the United States, disassembled them, and then rebuilt them in Mexico. This happened because often a finished product sold for less than the kit. (See *Exhibit 2* for local vs. imported content.)

By August 1984, 25 companies were registered at the Ministry of Commerce as computer builders, but only 17 were active. Of the 17, four were multinational enterprises in joint ventures: Apple, Burroughs, Hewlett-Packard, and Honeywell. Burroughs and Honeywell had their products registered as mini- rather than microcomputers. Among the smaller companies, several were producing IBM clones; the rest mostly produced more expensive multiuser computers or IBM-incompatible PCs.

Industry Environment

Competitors' Market Shares. The Mexican microcomputer industry changed significantly as new firms entered. During its initial stages, the industry was very fragmented with many very small firms. By the end of 1984, the Mexican PC industry was still more fragmented than its American counter-part (see *Exhibit 3*).

Cost Structure and Barriers to Entry. The microcomputer assembly industry was characterized by a learning curve and economies of scale. Small companies in the market for some time had developed special abilities to produce on a small scale and to supply particular niches. A learning curve can create important barriers to entry for a large company that achieves a large market share.

By 1984 Altos, Columbia, Micron, LNW, Onix, and Cromemco had gained some industrial experience. Average costs would decline until a company reached a production rate of 20,000 computers a year. Therefore, the only possible strategies to survive were either to export to increase market size or to focus on special niches where product sold at higher prices.

The existing firms had few fixed costs, mainly in real estate. This low level of sunk costs made the industry volatile; the major loss in shutting down was the achieved industrial experience, and even this could be saved by becoming the distributor for a large company. By 1984 none of the existing firms had invested significantly in the industry, because of financial constraints and uncertainty about new entrants.

Employment. Each firm employed between 10 and 15 workers, all paid the minimum wage. Labor costs were negligible. Assembly on a larger scale became very capital-intensive, so labor costs were not crucial at any production level.

Research and Development. Although existing firms received their technologies from foreign enterprises (usually based in the United States), not all sold computers under a well-known trademark. The Ministry of Commerce required that local producers allocate at least 5% of total sales to R&D expenditures. In 1984 total R&D expenditures by all firms in Mexico were $2.6 million. This was extremely low compared to R&D expenditures by U.S. firms: In 1984 IBM had $2.5 billion invested in R&D, and even very small companies like Altos Computer Systems had an outlay of almost $5 million. In Mexico IBM proposed to invest 6% of local sales in R&D.

Pricing Policy. Trade barriers, the small number of producers, and the homogeneity of the two dominant strategic groups (multiuser computers and PC clones) resulted in prices in Mexico that were much higher than comparable U.S. prices during 1982 and 1983 (*Exhibit 4*). By the end of 1983, pressure from both the main buyer, the Ministry of Programming and Budget, and new entrants had pushed prices down. Since the entry of Apple and Columbia, price and advertising wars had become common among PC producers. Data on imports and exports of microcomputers are in *Exhibit 5*.

Buyer Demand and Concentration. Several industry market analysts, as well as IBM, estimated that the total domestic demand for the next five years would be between 300,000 to 500,000 computers. The undersecretary of industrial promotion considered this a gross overestimate and put the figure closer to 150,000. The Foreign Investment Office thought the industry estimates more or less accurate.

Buyers of microcomputers differed fundamentally from buyers in most Mexican industries. Government's share of total demand was around 85% (including the federal and local governments, government-owned firms, schools, and social security system, communications, and the banking system). The Ministry of Programming and Budget authorized and reviewed all public purchases of computers. The Law of Purchases for the Public Administration stated that the ministry's objective should be to buy at the lowest possible price. Since the ministry also managed budgetary expenditures, its interest was to achieve the automation of the Mexican government at the lowest cost. It was thus reluctant to subsidize producers through government purchases.

Suppliers. Mexican suppliers of so-called passive components (cables, diodes, capacitors, resistors) were rather numerous and well organized; they wanted the industry to develop faster because they had enough capacity to provide it with these components.

Some local producers of microcomputers were also buying printers, keyboards, video monitors, and cabinets in Mexico. The small scale of production often resulted in high costs and low quality. For example, cabinets were usually made of fiberglass or aluminum rather than plastic, which was cheaper only on a very large scale.

In contrast, none of the high-tech components (the integrated circuits, most printed boards and hard disks) were produced locally. Development of a full computer industry was impossible without these parts, which were at the core of the high-tech industry.

The Mounting Controversy

The National Development Plan, the official government program of President de la Madrid, proposed "rationalizing the level and dispersal of the foreign trade protection policy," using tariffs for consumption goods and licenses for intermediate inputs and capital goods. The plan provided some very broad guidelines for foreign investment.

The plan placed particular emphasis on the development of the electronics industry. "The sectors to receive special attention are microcomputers, telecommunication systems, and electronic devices with specific applications to health care and education." Nevertheless, the specific policies and goals for these industries were not given. They were to appear in a program for industrial promotion and foreign trade that was not published until July 1984. This program, ambiguous in itself, had a collection of subprograms, one of which dealt with the computer industry. And this subprogram, which was never officially ratified or published, just rephrased the 1979 document.

As soon as IBM presented its proposal, the local producers of micro-computers organized a lobbying association, AMFABI, to oppose IBM. They tried to get support from the undersecretary of industrial promotion and his team and decided to talk not independently but only as a group to government officials. AMFABI representatives met with Espinosa de los Reyes several times. The interviews were not always very friendly. Espinosa told them they were not investing at all, and they blamed him and his boss for the uncertainty of the industry environment. AMFABI published several ads in major newspapers. They argued:

1. It was unfair to accept IBM under rules different from those imposed on everybody else. AMFABI companies had complied with the existing program and expected the government to do the same.

2. IBM's demand figures were grossly overestimated. If IBM were allowed to produce the quantities announced in the proposal, Big Blue would gain monopoly power by crowding out existing producers, i.e., predatory practices.

3. AMFABI's member firms were able to grow and export; IBM was not needed to develop the internal market.

Furthermore, in a letter to President de la Madrid, AMFABI called for the immediate ratification of the existing program and for its enforcement, excluding majority foreign ownership from the microcomputer industry.

The controversy intensified, and by October 1984 it reached Congress. The Communist Party (PSUM) and two socialist parties (PST and PPS) officially asked the Congress to oppose the IBM proposal. They pointed out that the proposal did not satisfy legal requirements and that the government would lose credibility if it neglected the unpublished but existing regulations. They also accused the undersecretary of foreign investment of denying Mexico the possibility of having its own electronics industry, of giving away the right to a foreign monopoly. A representative of the government's party (PRI) defended the undersecretary, but the PSUM member counterattacked. "The efficiency arguments are not valid, they are false; the arguments of modernity are not valid, they are false; it is the arguments about R&D, production, of developing our own technology in an area considered strategic that we should listen to." He added: "Leaving electronics in the hands of a multinational is a danger for the sovereignty of the nation." Another representative stated, "We don't want to be a slave of the United States. It is ludicrous to have somebody from the PRI citing South Korea, Singapore, or Taiwan as examples. Yes, they are exporters, but they are also slaves of the United States. How can a representative, a Mexican, say such a thing? What should we expect next? To become one more star in the flag of the United States?"

Newspapers indicated that the quarrel extended throughout the government. At the Ministry of Commerce the division was clear-cut. The undersecretary of industrial promotion was against the IBM proposal while the undersecretary of foreign investment favored the project. Nobody was sure where the minister stood. People in charge of purchasing computers at the Ministry of Programming and Budget were interested in obtaining the lowest possible prices. They prepared an internal report on the industry that reportedly favored the entry of IBM but also called for further negotiations to get a better deal from IBM. The Bank of Mexico was also interested in the IBM project since the inflow of foreign exchange derived from it was very attractive. Yet those favoring the project were not communicating among themselves. Most people within the government, regardless of their views about the project, were reluctant to talk to anybody at IBM. Nevertheless, IBM kept pressing them through its manager for government relations.

The project was so widely circulated that it soon surfaced in the press. A well-known financial columnist published several unsolicited and possibly harmful pro-IBM articles in the major local newspaper. At the same time, IBM organized local producers of discrete components and spare parts to lobby for it. The sales office added to the proposal was meant to gain the support of these producers.

The Foreign Investment Office

The Minister of Commerce and Industry chaired the Board of Foreign Investment. The members of the board were the ministers of the interior, foreign affairs, finance, energy and mines, programming and budget, and labor (see *Exhibit 6*).

It was not certain what the various ministers' positions were. Meanwhile, pressure was mounting from the Undersecretariat for Industrial Promotion to reject the proposal. IBM was not being very helpful. The information it had provided was too limited; and rather than offer anything to make the plan more attractive, it was clearly waiting for a counterproposal. IBM had adopted a passive role with the government ("You tell us what else you want," it had said to Espinosa) and a very active role in public relations. Everybody was talking about the project. Articles in the *New York Times* and the *Wall Street Journal* announcing IBM's entry into Mexico were promptly disavowed by the government.

In January 1985 Espinosa knew that the case would be going to the board in a matter of days. He saw this event as the turning point in Mexico's industrial policy.

MEXICO AND THE MICROCOMPUTERS

Exhibit 1
The First Proposal

	1984	1985	1986	1987	1988	1989	1985–89
Total investment U.S.$[a]	0.5	4.6	0.9	0.3	0.3	—	6.6
Total production (units)	—	80,000	110,000	133,000	158,000	182,000	663,000
Exports (units)	—	77,000	104,000	122,000	144,000	165,000	612,000
Exports U.S.$	—	67.3	90.7	106.2	124.4	140.2	528.8
Purchases of local components U.S.$	—	11.1	15.3	18.5	22.0	25.3	92.2
Percentage of domestic components used	—	35	51	51	51	51	—
Direct employments in IBM (yearly average)	19	55	73.5	78	84.5	90.5	400.5
Indirect employment with suppliers	—	54	78	94	107	113	446
Other indirect employment	6	22.7	470.5	789.5	974.0	1,183.0	3,650.5
Net foreign exchange balance U.S.$	—	—	—	—	—	—	80–100

[a] All U.S.$ figures in millions.

Exhibit 2

Selected Computer Producers' Component Sources

Firm	Local Components[a]	Imported Components[b]
Apple	Cables, passive components, keyboard	Integrated circuits, video, cabinet
Burroughs	Resistors, cables	All rest
Computex	Passive components, power source, printed circuits, $5\frac{1}{4}''$ disks	All active components, keyboard, cabinet, hard disks
Televideo	Keyboard, cabinet, cables	Active components, plastic cabinets, some keyboards
LNW	Printed circuits, cabinet, keyboard, power source	Active components, hard disks
Ransom	Videos, power source, passive components	Active components, hard disks, cabinet, keyboard
Micromex	Cabinet, power source, cables	Active components, printed circuits, keyboard
Actos	Cabinet, metallic structures, cables, floppy disks, passive components	Active components, hard disks, magnetic tape

[a]Microcomputer producers with local content between 40% and 65% include Franklin, Altos, Cromemco, LNW, and Micron; others projected to reach these levels include Apple, Hewlett-Packard, Televideo, and Columbia.

[b]As of 1985, no manufacturer had yet complied with its export and foreign exchange compensation commitments made to the government.

Exhibit 3
Seller Concentration[a]
(January–June 1985)

		Market Shares
(20.1%)	PC Compatibles	
	Columbia	27.2%
	Hewlett-Packard	18.1
	Corona	16.3
	Electron	12.3
	Televideo	11.2
	Micron	9.1
	Others	5.8
(9.0%)	Other PCs	Market Shares
	Apple	58.2%
	Electron	11.9
	Cromemco	11.6
	Datum-ICL	9.3
	Franklin	3.1
	CICSA	2.3
	Others	3.5
(66.9%)	Home Computers	Market Shares
	Commodore	63.7%
	Sinclair	28.7
	Datum-BBC	7.6
(3.6%)	Multiuser Systems	Market Shares
	Burroughs	34.9%
	Ind. Electromecanicas del Norte	14.1
	Infosistemas	10.1
	Mohawk-Hero	8.1
	Altos	6.1
	Cromemco	5.5
	Others	19.7
	Shares of Total Revenues	
	Commodore	13.0%
	Columbia	10.8
	Hewlett-Packard	10.5
	Apple	8.0
	Corona	7.8
	Burroughs	6.8
	Electron	6.5
	Televideo	6.4
	Alpha Micro/Sinclair	6.0
	Micron	5.1
	Cromemco	4.0
	Others	15.3

[a]Among local producers.

Exhibit 4
Prices

Firm	Configuration	Prices $		Mark-up over U.S. Price (%)
		U.S.	Mexico	
Apple	Apple IIc-I	1,544	2,045	32%
	-II	3,200	5,574	74
Burroughs	B21-13	—	4,400	—
	B21-65	—	13,750	—
Columbia	1600 VP	2,495	2,495	0
	1600 4B	4,600	4,600	0
Corona	PC-1	2,195	2,985	36
	HD+	4,095	5,964	46
Hewlett-Packard	HP-150-I	3,995	6,020	51
	-II	6,450	10,355	61
Televideo	128 KB	2,595	3,341	29
	256 KB	4,495	5,609	25

Exhibit 5
International Trade
Imports of Microcomputers to Mexico
(Thousands of 1984 dollars)

1979	7,859.0
1980	5,351.0
1981	4,841.0
1982	3,475.0
1983	2,349.0
1984	2,326.0

Exports of Microcomputers from Mexico
(Thousands of dollars)

Firm	Amount
Apple	12,000 (1984)
Franklin	1,700 (1983)
	600 (1984)
Cromemco	4,000 (1983)
	6,000 (1984)
Altos	700 (1984)

Exhibit 6 Partial Organizational Chart

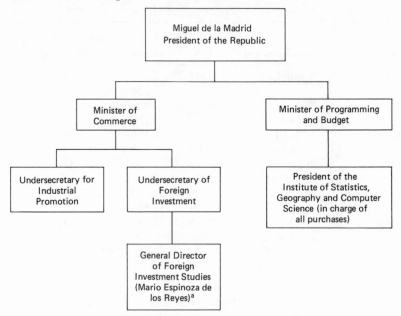

[a]Appointed general director as of February 1985.

Dow Indonesia

In early February 1977, Colin Goodchild, the manager of Dow Chemical's Indonesia office, was preparing for the next meeting with Indonesian government officials to discuss Dow's new proposal for a $700-million petrochemical project based on gas from the Arun gas fields in northern Sumatra. Mr. Goodchild was expecting Mr. Walker, from Dow's regional office in Hong Kong, to arrive within the next twenty-four hours to join in the discussions. Walker was eager to see some tangible progress in the negotiations, which had been going on for several years.

PREVIOUS DISCUSSIONS

Discussions for Dow participation in a petrochemical facility in Indonesia had begun in 1975 with Pertamina, the state oil company.[1] As originally conceived, the project would have been a joint venture, probably 50–50, between Dow and Pertamina, and had become known as the Aceh petrochemical project. The plant, to be located in Aceh Province between Banda Aceh and the Arun gas fields on the north of Sumatra island, would produce a range of petrochemicals from ethane, which would be extracted by Pertamina or a joint venture from the natural gas feeding a liquification plant operated by Pertamina. By 1977 liquified natural gas (LNG) was being sold to Japan and would also be sold to the United States, if U.S. permission was ever granted. The gas was supplied by Mobil Oil from the Arun gas fields, which it operated under a production-sharing agreement. The original plans for the LNG project called for a six-train facility, but in 1976 the plans were changed considerably as Pertamina fell into financial difficulties. It had run up more than $1 billion in short-term debts to foreign lenders. It had borrowed heavily to finance its expansion into a wide range of activities, including fertilizer plants, a steel plant, and

---

[1]This procedure was unusual. Negotiations for foreign investments in manufacturing were generally handled by BKPM, an investment coordinating board. Pertamina handled petroleum negotiations but had also been responsible for negotiating some other large projects.

This case was prepared as the basis for class discussion rather than to illustrate either effective or ineffective handling of an administrative situation. Written by Brizio Biondi-Morra, Research Assistant, under the supervision of Professor James E. Austin and Louis T. Wells, Jr., and Assistant Professor Dennis J. Encarnation. Abridged with permission.

a host of smaller businesses. Even with higher revenues from increased oil prices, in 1976 Pertamina was unable to meet its debt obligations. The government stepped in to assume its debts and thereby get increased control of Pertamina, which in the past had been called a "state within a state." Unfinished projects like the steel mill and the Aceh petrochemical plant were taken out of the control of Pertamina and put in the hands of J. B. Sumarlin, minister of state for administrative reform and vice chairman of BAPPENAS, the national planning agency.

Plans for expanding the current three trains of the LNG facility were set aside. Sumarlin also mentioned to Dow the possibility of a "Contract of Work," rather than a joint venture, for the Aceh petrochemical project. This was a form of contract common in Indonesia for nonoil mineral projects. Under most such arrangements, the foreign firm provided all funds and operated the project. As a result of these changes and a scaling down of the forecast of market growth in Indonesia, Dow was now considering a smaller petrochemical plant than originally planned.

THE NEW PROPOSAL

Dow's new proposal (*Appendix*) was contained in a feasibility study it made in January 1977. It proposed that the government of Indonesia grant Dow a "Contract of Work" to manufacture petrochemicals based on the Arun gas/liquids feedstock. Under the auspices of this "Contract of Work," Dow would be given approval to form a "Dow Venture" company using some 21,000 barrels a day of ethane to manufacture 600 million pounds a year of ethylene, 300,000 million of low-density polyethylene (LDPE), 150,000 million of high-density polyethylene (HDPE), and 500,000 million of vinyl chloride monomers (VCM). Under this new proposal the government and Dow would have to support the project with their respective resources to ensure the project's success. The government would sell the project ethane[2] and fuel gas and provide local know-how and protection from import competition. In turn, Dow would be responsible for the petrochemical technology, training, market development expertise, key expatriate staff, and financial resources. Dow would also have exclusive rights to import LDPE, HDPE, and VCM into Indonesia from the day of signing of the "Contract of Work" until about five years after startup.

According to Dow, the proposal was guided by four principles:

1. Profitable production of petrochemical products required by industry

[2]The casewriter estimated that each pound of ethane extracted from Arun gas would reduce the export value of the gas by $0.045.

2. Large-scale production with advanced technology to maximize manufacturing economies
3. Long-term raw material sources to permit extensive growth
4. Provision of stable sources of petrochemical products for Indonesia with excess product available for export by Dow

EXPECTED PERFORMANCE

The financing scheme Dow recommended was based on a projected balance sheet (*Exhibit 1*) and income statement (*Exhibit 2*) that resulted from a joint study by Dow Chemical Pacific and the First National City Bank project finance group. The figures were based on the assumptions that Dow would be responsible for raising funds and that the project would carry the interest burden.

The project's size was such that the products were destined largely for the Indonesian domestic market, which was currently supplied with imported petrochemicals. Forecasts assumed that tariffs and other taxes on imports would remain at least at their current level of 24%.

In its proposal, Dow noted three project characteristics thought to be extremely important. First, the project was heavily capital-intensive. Second, the manufacturing cost of the Dow Venture's product had a high fixed-cost element. And finally, the Dow venture would produce satisfactory returns only when sales levels enabled its plants to operate near capacity. Because of the project's reduced size, the resulting ethylene scale penalty, and the proportionally high cost of infrastructure, Dow's proposal asserted that the project offered only marginal returns to the company.

Losses during the initial period of production were considered unavoidable in a project of such magnitude and complexity. Once the project's plants were operating at capacity, however, the Dow venture was expected to generate sufficient cash to service the debt and yield an after-tax profit. Startup of the main facilities was phased over one year. Supporting services and the infrastructure for the complex would be in place in mid-1981, but some plants they were designed to serve would not be on-stream until the second half of 1982. The ethylene plant, representing a $150-million investment, would operate at capacity only when the plants consuming ethylene did likewise.

Dow believed that sufficient market existed for the venture's products so that most plants would be close to capacity operation within two years of startup. The existence of surplus funds and the ability to borrow short-term was thought to provide sufficient "cushion" for the project to meet long-term loan commitments during any short-term downturn in operating revenue.

Dow's feasibility study provided financial data but did not present returns on investment or discounted cash flows, since the Indonesian government and Dow would have their own standards for measuring economic viability. The casewriter prepared a cash flow of the project, presented in *Exhibit 3,* using Dow's numbers and several assumptions. The casewriter also estimated profits that Dow might earn from production and the exclusive rights to import LDPE, HDPE, and VCM in the early years. These estimates are in *Exhibit 4.*

The Ethylene Industry[3]

In 1977 the petrochemical industry was a major business in the Western countries and Japan. With total sales of over $300 billion, the industry accounted for about one-third of manufacturing investment in the United States, Europe, and Japan. But most producers were experiencing problems of overcapacity.

Most basic petrochemical products were derived from ethylene and its byproducts, which in turn were the main raw materials for making all major commodity plastics like LDPE, HDPE, and VCM. Together with ethylene, these plastics accounted for over half the output of the world's petrochemical industry.

During the 1970s many U.S. petrochemical producers barely covered their cost of capital. In Europe an assortment of state-owned and private companies fought over small increments of the market, earning huge losses in the process. In Japan a dozen giants, helped into the industry by the government, were also losing money and struggling for positions in a market half the size of European and U.S. markets. And in the Middle East, oil-producing countries' forward integration plans were likely to complicate an already difficult situation.

Many of the industry's current problems could be traced to its recent history. Although plastics based on phenol and vinyl had been made in the 1920s and 1930s, production of ethylene and the commodity plastics did not take off until the 1950s. Fueled by economic growth and cheap supplies of oil, these plastics rapidly replaced paper, wood, leather, metals, and other materials in many applications. But the world oil crisis of the early 1970s dramatically slowed this expansion. Raw material and energy costs skyrocketed, demand stagnated, and new, often heavily subsidized producers entered the market. As the plants commissioned in the 1960s and early 1970s came on-stream, it became clear that production capacity in most areas far exceeded demand.

Various studies estimated the oversupply of petrochemicals in 1977 at

---

[3]Description based partly on "Note on the Ethylene and Commodity Plastics Industries" (385-066), Harvard Business School.

about 20% above demand. It was usually believed that industrialized nations were exporting HDPE and LDPE at prices equal to 70% of their domestic prices, and that these products had been available in 1977 in Southeast Asia at "dumping" prices.

Forecasts made in a few of these studies predicted that the current oversupply would cease around 1985, after which a balanced situation was expected to prevail until 1987. From 1987 onward, supply according to these reports would be tight, and prices would increase substantially with incremental changes in demand. Since the demand for ethylene-based products was estimated to increase at about 8% per year worldwide, these studies concluded that the 20% excess capacity would be filled quite rapidly.

But other indications were pointing to a scenario of protracted over-supply beyond 1985. In Southeast Asia, for example, there were indications that a group of Japanese companies was considering the construction of a 660-million-lb.-per-year ethylene plant in Singapore, which was already the third-largest refinery center in the world and was well positioned to compete with the Aceh petrochemical project. Additional large projects could alter the validity of the optimistic long-term forecasts.

PROJECT BENEFITS TO INDONESIA

Indonesia, an archipelago comprising five main islands and thousands of smaller ones, is a mountainous region with a land area of 735,000 square miles, almost three times the size of Texas. In 1977 its population was estimated at more than 130 million, making it the world's fifth most populous country. Although 90% of Indonesians were Moslem, in the most populous island, Java, beliefs tended to include elements of Hinduism and animism from earlier days. About 60% of its 51 million labor force was employed in agriculture, forestry, and fishing; the country had an estimated 2%–10% rate of unemployment. Petroleum exports accounted for some two-thirds of Indonesia's export earnings and two-thirds of all government revenues. Far behind petroleum products, agricultural commodities were the next most important export. Indonesia's freely convertible currency, the rupiah, was considered by several economists to be overvalued by at least 20% vis-à-vis the dollar, with the official exchange rate set at Rp. 415 to the dollar.

Indonesia's president was General Suharto, who had taken power from President Sukarno in 1965. Although some ministries were headed by military officers, several important economic ministries, including BAPPENAS and the Ministry of Finance, were headed by technocrats who had been drawn from the economics faculty of the University of Indonesia. The Ministry of Industry and some other ministries were headed by people with engineering training.

According to Dow, the benefits of this Aceh Petrochemical Project to Indonesia were manifold and encompassed foreign-exchange savings and earnings, value added to hydrocarbons in Indonesia, employment, education, and local business opportunities. The project would be located in a province noted for its strict Moslem beliefs and with a history of efforts to break away from Indonesia. Dow felt the rewards to the Indonesian people, the government of Indonesia, and Dow were such that the project had to be considered a top priority of the government.

Dow estimated that ten years after the startup of the first plants the project would have saved Indonesia a cumulative net foreign-exchange sum of US$1.45 billion. Dow calculated this by adding the total capital spent in Indonesia, earnings from export sales, and the c.i.f. value of petrochemicals sold domestically, assuming they would otherwise have been imported. From this total were then subtracted the imported raw materials, the f.o.b. value of Indonesian raw materials consumed by the project, the principal and interest repayments on loans, and the dividends paid to Dow.

Dow also pointed out that at full capacity the chemical complex proposed in Aceh would add an annual value of US$190 million to the hydrocarbons used as feedstock and fuel. This was consistent with the government's stated policy of upgrading energy resources to petrochemicals rather than selling energy in its less-refined state as was currently being done by Indonesia.

Dow also estimated employment that would be generated by the proposed project. During peak construction about 3,800 people would be employed at the plant site. Permanent employees were expected to number 1,600.[4] Employment was also expected to be created as a result of local business opportunities in servicing the needs of the complex. But Dow claimed that the most significant effect on employment would be in the plastics fabrication and chemical consuming industry in Indonesia. Dow estimated that 50,000 jobs would be created in downstream sectors.

Dow also explained that Indonesia would gain technology for operating the plants. This technology would be passed on to Indonesians by training them in Indonesia and in Dow's U.S. and European operations before startup. Similarly, personnel would be trained in Dow's laboratories to learn technical applications and laboratory techniques. Additional skills would be acquired by instrument and electrical technicians, fitters, welders, mechanics, and carpenters. Dow was certain that some of the people and skills employed during construction would be used in other projects in Indonesia. And it expected many additional skills to develop in the downstream plastics-fabricating and chemical-consuming industries.

[4]Casewriters later assumed that wages would equal approximately US$1,000 per worker per year.

APPENDIX
EXCERPTS FROM DOW PROPOSAL

Introduction

Major changes have occurred in Indonesia that have had a significant effect on the Aceh project economics. These changes have resulted in a reduced project scope and a forecast lower growth rate of the Indonesian domestic markets.

There has also been a significant downturn in world economic conditions such that the growth rate in the chemical industry has slowed. This has affected the potential export markets and the rate of new investment in the industry.

In Dow's view the project economics and financial performance are marginal at best, and some additional incentives are necessary for the project to proceed.

The economics presented in this study have incorporated assumptions that have a high element of risk, not the least of which is the required Indonesian market growth. Before any negotiations proceed, Dow would request a response from the Government of Indonesia (GOI) on the following "Dow Proposal."

The "Dow Proposal" would be incorporated into a "Contract of Work" to be negotiated between Dow and the GOI for petrochemical manufacture based on the Arun gas/liquids feedstock.

As part of this "Contract of Work" Dow would request that a two-year period be allowed to evaluate the Arun gas reserves, negotiate the essential elements of the project, and implement a market-building program in Indonesia.

Only when this total project package is completed could Dow expect to obtain a commitment from financing institutions that would allow the project to be financed under the necessary conditions to proceed.

The Dow Proposal

  A. The GOI form a company to extract ethane from the natural gas feed to the liquid natural gas (LNG) facility.
  B. Dow be given approval to form a "Dow Venture" Company/Companies to manufacture ethylene, LDPE, HDPE, vinyl chloride, power/steam as an initial phase of a petrochemical project and as a later phase ethylene dichloride, chlorine, caustic soda, ethyl benzene, styrene monomer, polystyrene, and additional ethylene and power/steam.

C. The "Dow Venture" would have the right to manufacture these products, select equity partners, determine financing sources, and market products in Indonesia and for export.

D. Ethane and fuel gas must be sold by the GOI to the "Dow Venture" at prices such that the venture can be economically competitive.

E. The GOI approve the project and identify it as a high priority of the government.

F. Confirm that the benefits currently available to foreign investors will be available to this project, and specifically that all capital goods, equipment, and raw materials may be imported free of all customs duties and taxes.

G. Develop a way to extend the period of foreign investment licenses beyond the 30 years maximum period now permitted.

H. Dow will require OPIC or similar insurance on its investment.

I. Dow needs sufficient access to data validating the deliverability of ethane and fuel gas from the Arun field.

J. Confirm that the existing levels of tariff and border-crossing taxes will remain effective for products manufactured in the complex and that necessary steps will be taken to protect the investment from import substitute products.

K. Allow Dow exclusivity in the Indonesian market for LDPE, HDPE, and vinyl chloride from the day of signing the "Contract of Work" until the commercial debt is repaid, which is estimated to be five years after startup.

L. Grant Dow the right to manage the "Dow Venture" for the life of the project.

M. Dow would require that a utility company be established to operate the ethylene and power/steam plants as well as the town site infrastructure. This utility company would operate at 15% return on total cost before taxes (ROTCBT) on a long-term basis.

N. Dow would request that to nullify the effects of possible rupiah devaluation the assets of the "Dow Venture" be in U.S. dollar accounting and that pricing to the Indonesian market be on a U.S. dollar basis.

O. The project would require the establishment of a substantial polyvinyl chloride (PVC) industry. To this end, the GOI and Dow would work together to identify suitable PVC producers to develop and invest in the Indonesian market.

P. The GOI would make every effort to have this project recognized as an Association of South East Asian Nations (ASEAN) project and have access to ASEAN markets.

DOW INDONESIA

Exhibit 1
Dow Venture Pro Forma Balance Sheet
(Millions of $)

	1981[a]	1982	1983	1984	1985	1986	1987	1988	1989	1990	1991
Assets											
Cash	1.0	1.1	1.6	1.7	1.9	1.9	2.0	2.0	2.0	2.0	2.0
Inventory	5.4	21.0	27.1	29.1	30.6	31.4	31.4	31.4	31.4	31.4	31.4
Accounts receivable	13.8	39.4	49.0	54.0	57.0	58.4	57.5	57.5	56.7	56.9	54.6
Total current assets	20.2	61.5	77.7	84.8	89.5	91.7	90.9	90.9	90.1	90.3	88.0
Total fixed assets	653.1	614.6	565.3	516.0	466.7	417.5	368.2	318.9	269.6	220.3	174.7
Short-term investment	6.4	18.1	24.2	28.9	37.4	36.7	78.2	112.7	146.6	171.8	208.8
Total assets	679.7	694.2	667.4	629.7	593.6	545.9	537.3	522.5	506.3	482.4	471.5
Liabilities & equity											
Short-term loan	—	—	—	—	—	—	—	—	—	—	—
Long-term loan	480.0	500.0	450.0	369.2	268.4	164.6	131.6	98.6	65.6	30.0	—
Accounts payable	3.9	12.1	20.9	22.9	24.5	25.3	25.3	25.3	25.3	25.3	25.3
Tax liability	—	—	—	—	—	—	31.5	49.1	53.9	56.2	61.7
Equity	248.1	250.0	250.0	250.0	250.0	250.0	250.0	250.0	250.0	250.0	250.0
Retained surplus	−52.3	−67.9	−53.5	−12.4	50.7	106.0	95.3	99.5	111.5	120.9	134.5
Total liab. & equity	679.7	694.2	667.4	629.7	593.6	545.9	537.3	522.5	506.3	482.4	471.5

[a]One-half year.

179

DOW INDONESIA

Exhibit 2

Dow Venture Pro Forma Statement of Income

(Millions of $)

	1981[a]	1982	1983	1984	1985	1986	1987	1988	1989	1990	1991
Net sales[b]	27.8	226.6	315.6	348.5	371.7	383.8	388.8	395.3	401.1	402.1	404.6
Cost of good sold[c]	27.0	109.1	146.3	154.7	161.4	164.5	164.5	164.5	164.5	164.5	164.5
Depreciation	18.3	44.8	49.3	49.3	49.3	49.3	49.3	49.3	49.3	49.3	45.6
Gross profit	-17.5	72.7	120.0	144.5	161.0	170.0	175.0	181.5	187.3	188.3	194.5
Royalty[d]	0.8	6.8	9.5	10.4	11.2	11.5	11.7	11.9	12.0	12.1	12.1
Selling expenses[e]	4.2	21.1	28.3	31.1	33.4	34.7	35.6	36.5	37.6	38.1	38.9
General administrative expenses[f]	14.0	14.8	17.5	17.1	18.6	19.6	20.5	21.4	22.3	24.1	24.3
Operating profit	-36.5	30.0	64.7	85.3	97.8	104.2	107.2	111.7	115.4	114.0	119.2
Interest income	3.5	2.1	2.3	2.9	3.6	4.1	6.3	10.5	14.3	17.5	20.9
Interest expense[g]	19.3	47.7	52.6	47.1	38.3	27.6	16.5	13.2	9.9	6.6	3.0
Income before tax	-52.3	-15.6	14.4	41.6	63.1	80.7	97.0	109.0	119.8	124.9	137.1
Tax[h]	—	—	—	—	—	—	35.1	49.1	53.9	56.2	61.7
Income after tax	-52.3	-15.6	14.4	41.6	63.1	80.7	61.9	60.0	65.9	68.7	75.4
Earned surplus beginning	—	-52.3	-67.9	-53.5	-11.8	50.7	106.6	95.9	100.1	112.1	121.5
Total earned surplus	-52.3	-67.9	-53.5	-11.8	51.3	132.0	168.5	155.9	166.0	180.8	196.9
Dividend[d]	—	—	—	—	—	25.4	72.6	55.8	53.9	59.3	61.8
Earned surplus end	-52.3	-67.9	-53.5	-11.8	51.3	106.6	95.9	100.1	112.1	121.5	135.1

[a] Half-year only.

[b] Domestic sales volume (million lbs.)											
LDPE, tub. process	40	101	112	120	130	140	150	150	150	150	150
LDPE, auto. process	—	60	65	75	84	96	109	135	150	150	150
HDPE	20	106	117	129	141	150	150	150	150	150	150
VCM	—	83	182	200	220	242	266	293	322	322	322
Export sales volume (million lbs.)											
LDPE, tub. process	—	25	27	30	20	10	—	—	—	—	—
LDPE, auto. process	—	40	44	48	66	54	41	15	—	—	—
HDPE	—	14	18	21	9	—	—	—	—	—	—
VCM	—	105	230	250	260	258	234	207	178	178	178
Domestic prices ($/lb.)											
LDPE	0.467	0.520	0.520	0.520	0.520	0.520	0.520	0.520	0.520	0.520	0.520
HDPE	0.455	0.507	0.507	0.507	0.507	0.507	0.507	0.507	0.507	0.507	0.507
VCM	—	0.362	0.362	0.362	0.362	0.362	0.362	0.362	0.362	0.362	0.362
Export prices f.o.b. Indonesia ($/lb.)											
LDPE		0.367	0.367	0.367	0.367	0.367	0.367	0.367	0.367	0.367	0.367
HDPE		0.357	0.357	0.357	0.357	0.357	0.357	0.357	0.357	0.357	0.357
VCM		0.286	0.286	0.286	0.286	0.286	0.286	0.286	0.286	0.286	0.286
[c] Imported content of CGS (CIF, $ million)	3.5	44.7	76.5	82.9	88.2	91.0	91.0	91.0	91.0	91.0	91.0
Domestic ethane used at pro-forma cost of $0.038/lb. ($ million)	1.5	16.3	23.7	25.8	28.2	29.6	29.6	29.6	29.6	29.6	29.6

[d] Royalties and dividends are subject to a 20% local withholding tax.

[e] 60% local expenses; 40% to be paid abroad, probably to another part of the Dow enterprise.

[f] 90% local expenses; 10% foreign exchange cost.

[g] Interest and debt repayment go entirely abroad.

[h] The general Indonesian tax rate for corporate income was 45%. Foreign investors were usually granted two years of tax holidays. Investors could apply for an extra year for projects located on islands other than Java, another year for projects with large capital investment, and still another year for significant foreign exchange earnings or savings. High-priority projects could receive an additional year of tax holiday. Contracts of work had, in most cases, governed mining projects. Under recent contracts of work, mining activities had not received tax holidays. Rather, they had been subject to tax rates of 35% to 40% for the first ten years, and rates of 42% to 48% thereafter, with the rates varying by mineral. Such investors had been allowed tax credits in the amount of 8% of the investment outlay.

DOW INDONESIA

Exhibit 3

Cash Flow to Project
($ millions, year-end)

	1977	1978	1979	1980	1981	1982	1983	1984	1985	1986	1987	1988	1989	1990	1991
Sources:															
Borrowing		69.0	180.0	165.0	66.0	20.0									
Income after tax					(52.3)	(15.6)	14.4	41.7	63.1	80.7	61.9	59.9	65.9	68.7	75.4
Depreciation					18.3	44.8	49.3	49.3	49.3	49.3	49.3	49.3	49.3	49.3	45.6
Uses:															
Fixed investment	34.0	106.0	216.0	235.0	80.4	6.3									
Net working capital					16.3	33.1	7.4	5.1	3.1	1.4	35.9	14.0	5.6	2.1	7.8
Debt repayment							50.0	80.0	100.8	103.8	33.0	33.0	33.0	35.6	30.0

Notes: For 1977–80, Dow's additional cash investment equaled the difference between fixed investment and borrowing. In 1981 that investment was $71.1 million, bringing the company's equity in the project up to $248.1 million (see *Exhibit 1*). In 1982 that equity grew to $250 million again (see *Exhibit 1*), reflecting one final cash investment of $1.9 million.

182

Exhibit 4
Profit (Contribution) from Imports
($ millions)

	1978	1979	1980	1981	1982	1983
Indonesian market size[a]	186	207	230	256	284	316
Local production	0	0	0	28	227	316
Value of imports	186	207	230	228	57	0
Contribution at 25% on import exclusivity[b]	46	51	57	57	15	0
NPV at 20% = 140.2						

[a]Calculated by taking Dow's assumption of market size for 1983 and reducing the market by 10% each earlier year.

[b]Contribution to Dow's fixed costs was estimated as 25% of the CIF sales prices. This is considered conservative, given Dow's international operating margin of greater than 30% and the excess capacity in world petrochemical plants at the time.

SOURCE: Casewriter's calculations.

State Timber Corporation of Sri Lanka

On March 1, 1979, 45-year-old Kenneth Abeywickrama left his job as marketing manager of one of the largest multinationals in Sri Lanka to become board chairman of the troubled State Timber Corporation (STC), a company wholly owned by the government of Sri Lanka. In 1977 and 1978, STC experienced a big fall in the volume of timber extracted from Sri Lanka's forests, its operations plunged into the red, and its labor–management relations were increasingly strained.

None of these negative features deterred Abeywickrama from starting his new job with enthusiasm and optimism. The big salary cut he took to become STC's chairman did not bother him too much, because he had independent sources of income. STC represented an exciting challenge:

> I just couldn't understand how STC was making losses when, on the one hand, it had monopoly rights for timber extraction and, on the other hand, it faced a market with an insatiable demand. I felt STC was sitting on top of a gold mine and didn't know it! So I wanted to get in there and turn the company around!

As Abeywickrama tried to "turn the company around," he met many problems. Some concerned bottlenecks in the supply of raw materials, stemming mainly from major changes in government's forestry policies. Others were in marketing and internal organization.

POLITICAL BACKGROUND

Sri Lanka (formerly Ceylon) is a tropical island of 16.3 million acres; in 1979 it had 14.5 million people. It was politically stable with a government chosen democratically in freely contested elections. The two dominant political parties were the Sri Lanka Freedom Party (SLFP), led by S. Bandaranaike, and the United National Party (UNP), led by J. R. Jayewardene. The former leaned left of center; the latter, right of center. Power oscillated between the two parties: The UNP ruled in 1965–70, the SLFP in 1970–77 (with Communist and Trotskyite support), and the UNP

This case was prepared by Ravi Ramamurti, under the supervision of Professor James E. Austin, as the basis for class discussion rather than to illustrate either effective or ineffective handling of an administrative situation. Abridged with permission.

again in 1977–79. To some, the UNP majority in Parliament in 1977 was discomforting: It held 142 of the 168 seats, leaving only 8 for the SLFP and 18 for all other parties.

The central theme of the UNP's platform was to free the Sri Lankan economy from excessive controls and regulations and to rely more on market mechanisms. Therefore, numerous subsidies were withdrawn, budget deficts were to be reduced, and foreign investment was promoted. Several import and export controls were relaxed. State enterprises were encouraged to stand on their own, to charge market prices, and to compete with imports and the private sector. State ownership grew from 28 enterprises in 1957 to 156 in 1978, operating in almost every economic sector and accounting for about 12% of the country's total GNP. The government was not prepared to bail out continuously unprofitable state enterprises. There was also talk of "privatizing" some state enterprises by opening all or part of their equity to private investors. After three years of UNP rule, the large state-owned businesses were still largely intact.

THE BIRTH OF STC

STC was created in 1968 as an autonomous corporation to take over from the Forest Department the extraction, processing, and sale of timber in Sri Lanka. With its bureaucratic structure and processes, the Forest Department was thought to be unable to meet growing demand, which was outpacing the department's deliveries by 35%. A more flexible and commercial organization was deemed necessary.

Most of the Forest Department's extraction had been in easily accessible forests; its technology was traditional and labor-intensive. STC was expected to use modern, mechanized methods and to build roads for access to forest interiors. According to one observer, an unstated reason for creating STC was to get around the annual budget allocation exercises the department had to go through to finance extraction operations. Unlike the Forest Department, STC could be self-supporting and would not have automatically to give the Treasury any surpluses it made. STC stated its purposes as:

1. Extraction of timber from forests; conversion of such timber into sawn timber and finished products; sale of logs, sawn timber, and finished products; and construction of forest roads for the above purposes
2. Acquisition, construction, and operation of logging units, sawmills, impregnation and preservation plants, seasoning and drying kilns, and other necessary equipment and installations

3. Operation of timber and firewood sales depots
4. Manufacture and marketing of any byproducts from timber

STC derived its monopoly rights for timber extraction from Forest Department orders releasing specific forest areas for exploitation by STC from time to time.

About 700 senior staff from the Forest Department (forest officers, accountants, clerks, etc.) were transferred to STC in 1968. Additional staff were hired by a selection committee headed by the company chairman with the consent of the board of directors. By the end of its first year, STC's total staff numbered 1,229 and by 1979 1,582, 90% of whom were clerical and laborers.

STC also took over two large sawmills and nine mobile ones owned by the Forest Department and a third large sawmill owned by the River Valleys Development Board. It also supervised the operations of eight sawmills (mostly old and worn out) run by private operators for the department. STC also took over from the Forest Department two plants for impregnating and seasoning timber and 62 sales depots.

STC'S OPERATIONS

STC's core operations remained relatively unchanged between 1968 and 1978. The key steps were felling timber, moving it to a sales depot or processing unit, and selling the timber or processed product.

Almost 90% of the felling was done by private contractors paid per piece, who usually used elephants and hired labor to fell the marked trees, drag and load them into trucks, and deliver them to a sawmill, impregnation/seasoning plant, or sales depot. Contractors were supervised by a few regional managers and their staff, who moved from one felling site to another in STC jeeps.

In the early 1970s, in keeping with its original goals, STC ventured into a couple of mechanical logging operations, the most important of which was the Sinharaja Project. Carried out with Canadian assistance, it unfortunately ran into several problems and was finally abandoned. Thus, before 1978 most logging was done by traditional methods.

In 1978 STC had three giant sawmills, ten lumber harvesters, and ten small, privately owned sawmills. Frequent equipment breakdowns and inadequate sawmilling capacity prevented STC from selling more than 30–40% of its output as sawn timber; the rest was sold as logs. In STC's impregnation and seasoning plants, sawn timber, crossties for the railways, and transmission and telegraph poles were chemically treated to increase strength and durability. Up to 1978 STC carried out no other "value-adding" operations on timber extracted from forests.

Most of STC's major institutional customers were other state-owned agencies or companies, such as Railways, Post and Telegraphs; the Building Materials Corporation; and the Plywoods Corporation. This last purchased peeler logs from STC for manufacturing plywood; it was the only other company in Sri Lanka that extracted timber on its own. STC's recent sales were distributed among its customers about as follows: state-owned enterprises and government departments 40%; private house builders 40%; timber traders 13%; and others 7%.

STC-produced timber was classed in four descending grades: luxury, special, Class I, and Class II. There were also products such as firewood, railway ties, and poles. All prices were set by the Prices Commission, an agency controlled by the Finance Ministry. STC paid the Treasury a royalty of 10% of its sales for rights to exploit the state forests. This amount went into the general pool of the Treasury and was not automatically reallocated to the Forest Department for its reforestation programs.

ORGANIZATIONAL LINKS WITH THE GOVERNMENT

Although STC was supposed to be autonomous, it was formally and informally linked with various government departments. These links were quite different from the ones Abeywickrama had seen in the private sector. The government organization STC depended upon was the ministry that directly supervised its operations: Agriculture and Lands up to 1979, and Lands and Land Development after 1979.

One of the supervising minister's most important powers was that of appointing members to STC's five-member board. The minister was free to appoint anyone (except senators or members of Parliament) who "appears to the minister to have had experience of and shown capacity in industrial, administrative, commercial, financial, or legal matters, applied sciences, or the organization of workers." The terms and conditions of appointment of the STC chairman were decided by the supervising minister in consultation with the Ministry of Finance. Generally, directors were appointed for three years, although the law allowed the supervising minister "if he thinks it expedient to do so, [to] remove a director, other than the managing director, from office."

In its first 11 years (1968–79), STC had six different CEOs. (*Exhibit 1* gives details of their background, tenure in office, and reasons for departure.) Turnover of other board directors was fairly rapid. None of the changes stemmed from within the company; rather, changes in the supervising minister led to changes in the board. According to one STC manager, the great insecurity of a director-level appointment made it an unattractive job for internal managers, even if they had a chance to be appointed to the board in the first place. Thus, most directors on STC's board were civil servants from different governmental departments, chief executives of other state-owned enterprises with substantial interdependence with STC, private businessmen, or lawyers.

STC also depended on the supervising ministry for approval of a variety of decisions. Price increases approved by the supervising ministry were then sent to the Finance Ministry (Prices Commission) for approval. The same procedure was involved in making investments, raising equity capital or debt (which had come only from the government and not from capital markets), creating subsidiaries, or making major purchases. In all cases, the supervising ministry was important because of its approvals and the lobbying it had to do for STC's proposals with other ministries involved in those decisions.

The Finance Act of 1971 limited the power of boards of public corporations to make financial decisions. The UNP government liberalized these limits considerably, but financial controls were still fairly strong. For instance, in purchase decisions the board had the final say only for tenders of value up to Rs.2 million (Rs.18 = US$1); tenders of value of Rs.2–5 million required approval by a Tender Committee involving the ministry; and all tenders above Rs.5 million required cabinet approval. Similar restrictions existed for investments, whether funded from the corporation's internal resources or through government budgetary support. On some matters, such as raising a corporation's equity capital, formal approval of Parliament was necessary.

The supervising ministry also audited STC's accounts, and these were discussed in Parliament, which could question any of its activities.

TOP MANAGEMENT CHANGES IN 1979

STC's difficult years were 1977 and 1978: It had two different chairmen, timber production and sales fell sharply, and STC plunged into the red after years of marginally profitable operations. (See *Exhibits 2 and 3* for trends in STC's production, sales, and profitability.)

In September 1978 responsibility for supervising STC was transferred to the newly created Ministry of Lands and Land Development, headed by Gamini Dissanayake, a 37-year-old lawyer who had been a member of Parliament and successful politician for many years. As of June 1981, Dissanayake was also responsible for the prestigious multibillion-dollar Mahaveli Development Project.

Dissanayake explained his views on the role of pubic enterprises in broad social and political systems:

A public-sector company exists because the social, political milieu in the country requires that particular industry or sector to be in public hands. For example, in Sri Lanka it is inconceivable that the operations of the Forest Department or the Timber Corporation could be in private hands. If they were, there would be no forests left in this country! As long as relevant social and political factors are kept in mind by public-sector managers, a private-sector approach to management is something I would very much encourage on their part. Political objectives, in a broad sense, are finally achieved by a good system of management.

Dissanayake was not very pleased with STC's results in 1977 and 1978 or with the increasing strains in labor–management relations in STC in early 1979. In March 1979 he obtained the resignations of the entire STC board including the chairman, who had been appointed less than a year earlier. He explained his reasons for such drastic changes:

My ideas about what the STC should be and how it should be run perhaps differ from those of the previous minister. Also, there are differences in individual contacts, friendships, and social lines open to a minister that can be used to attract people to join the public sector. For instance, a minister from a university would try to attract people from university circles to a public-sector job, whereas a minister with a different background would probably look elsewhere. Ministers are of all types. Even within the same party, they vary from ultraconservative to ultraliberal, from dynamic to lethargic, and so on. Each has his own strengths and his own base, from which he will draw the people who will work with him.

Unfortunately, in the past in Sri Lanka, state corporations have been used to cater to a very basic political need, that is, employment. The STC was no exception to that. Previous governments never regarded the capacity for management as a basic qualification for people at the helm. However, most of my corporations, and STC in particular, have been lucky to get good people from the private sector and the administrative services to head their operations.

It was in this process that Abeywickrama became STC's chairman. The minister picked the board members, but Abeywickrama was informed of the minister's choices. The new board had no civil servants other than the conservator of forests, an *ex officio* member. It included two attorneys (one a member of the UNP; and a local politician from a Colombo suburb heavily populated with carpenters).

The minister explained why he selected Kenneth Abeywickrama:

Kenneth was known to me socially. I knew he was doing an outstanding job in Lever Brothers, where he increased exports from Rs.3 million to Rs.21 or 22 million. I knew of his army and university background. I persuaded him that a stint in the public sector would do him good. To make up for the financial loss he would suffer, I pointed out that he would have a very challenging job.

Abeywickrama explained his own reasons for coming to STC in 1979:

Several of us in Lever Brothers were approached by the government to take up public-sector jobs. I came to STC because the minister persuaded me to come. I knew him from before. I felt that the UNP, with its commitment to free enterprise and individual liberties, should be acquitted. Mind you, I am not a member of the UNP, though I agree with its basic approach and philosophy. Sri Lanka . . . has had little or negative growth under socialist parties. STC appealed to me because I couldn't understand how with a monopoly over timber extraction you could make a loss. . . . Of course, coming to STC has meant a big drop in my income. . . . I don't depend on this job for my livelihood; I have other sources of income. If I didn't, I wouldn't be able to take the risk!

In March 1979 Abeywickrama found STC in considerable difficulty, with questionable long-term prospects and considerable uncertainty regarding its role in the Sri Lankan economy. There were bottlenecks in the supply of timber; pricing and marketing practices were hurting both STC and its customers; and organizational problems were limiting STC's ability to exploit even the available opportunities.

SUPPLY BOTTLENECKS

Government's Forestry Policy

In August 1977, soon after coming to power, the UNP totally banned tree felling in state forests. For STC, engaged exclusively in timber operations, this was a threat to its very survival. The main purpose of this drastic action was to arrest the alarming trend of deforestation in Sri Lanka. In 1956, 44% of Sri Lanka (7.2 million acres) was covered with forests; by 1976 this proportion was halved. There were signs that the significant decrease in forest area was causing climatic and other problems for Sri Lanka.

Three factors contributed to this steady reduction in forest cover. First, STC had stepped up the rate of timber extraction. Second was widespread illicit felling. Influential private contractors stealthily exploited "free" forests to reap huge profits. Illicit fellers sometimes used sawyers in the forests; many had their own lorries, tractors, and elephants. The volume of illicit felling was thought to be about 270,000 cubic meters a year. The third factor was "chena cultivation," which involved tree slashing and burning by villagers, who used the cleared area for cultivation. With large increases in rural population, chena cultivation became so extensive that in many areas the forest had no time to regenerate and became denuded. If all these trends were allowed to continue freely, long-term forestry in Sri Lanka could be in crisis.

The rapid exploitation of state forests, both legal and illegal, was supposed to be compensated for by the Forest Department's reforestation programs. But shortages of resources and manpower seem to have made the department's efforts to arrest deforestation relatively insignificant. The Forest Department fell under the jurisdiction of the Ministry of Lands and Land Development. Ever since it shed timber extraction operations to STC in 1968, the department had only two main functions: regulating the exploitation of state forests and maintaining their health through a variety of programs, including reforestation. Its regulatory tasks were outlined in the Forest Ordinance, which among other things empowered it to release state forests for exploitation and to act against offenders of the Forest Ordinance. The department had little success in preventing illegal exploitation of state forests and convicting offenders. With its total staff of only 1,350 and an annual budget of some Rs.30 million, the department had been able to reforest only limited areas. In 1980 it planted an exceptional extent of 30,000 acres of forests, but about 175,000 acres were deforested every year. To get around this problem, it launched tree-planting campaigns involving schools, hospitals, and the public at large. Although as many as 750,000 plants were distributed under these campaigns, no one knew how many survived to become trees. In response to the grave deforestation situation, the government imposed in August 1977 a total ban on felling.

STC was one of the main victims of the felling ban. According to one executive, STC "agitated and convinced the Forest Department that a certain amount of selective felling is not only necessary but highly desirable to preserve the health of forests." The government was caught in the contradictions between the new forestry policy and other developmental goals. The massive construction program the UNP government had promoted since 1977 required large quantities of timber and timber products. The huge Mahaveli Development Project, a pet project of the UNP, called for clear-felling of some 650,000 acres over many years. This alone would have eliminated 18% of the existing forest cover.

During 1978 the following modifications to the August 1977 forest policy were announced:

1. Felling would be allowed in Dry Zone forests in only those areas to be cleared for developmental programs such as the Mahaveli Project (which called for clear-felling 75,000 acres over 1980–82, to yield about 215,000 cubic meters of timber).

2. In Wet Zone forests, "selective felling" of hardwood and peeler logs would be permitted. Selective felling meant that only mature or dying trees could be cut. On average, these conditions would permit about 30–35 trees to be felled per acre in a Wet Zone forest.

3. Clear-felling of Wet Zone forests to obtain timber would not be permitted. In line with this, the controversial Sinharaja Project would be abandoned. Sinharaja was one of Sri Lanka's few "virgin forests"; it had not been exploited for centuries and therefore had great scientific value. But in 1970 the government approved a project to extract about 85,000 cubic meters of timber a year from this forest for ten years using mechanized logging techniques and helped by a Canadian company. After the SLFP's victory in 1970, the Sinharaja Project underwent in 1971 a detailed inquiry by a government committee into its technical, economic, and environmental viability. For three years thereafter, the project continued as a pilot scheme, operating on a much smaller scale than originally envisaged. Even so, it yielded 15,300 cubic meters of timber valued at Rs.7.3 million in 1974. After 1974 the quantity of timber extracted from Sinharaja fell; in 1977 only 5,000 cubic meters of timber valued at Rs.2.4 million was extracted. The Sinharaja Project generated an accounting loss of Rs.5.1 million in 1976. Much of the machinery acquired for the project was underused. The project's debts continued to affect STC's financial results adversely in 1977 and 1978. With the abandonment of the project in 1978, the facilities and loans STC acquired for Sinharaja were a liability.

4. STC would supply peeler logs to the Plywoods Corporation only till June 1978. After that, the Plywoods Corporation was to make its own arrangements to import the peeler logs it needed.

5. Finally, the UNP government moved to enhance the powers of Forest Department officers to arrest offenders of forest regulations. The Forest Ordinance was suitably amended in 1979; penalties for offenses were raised. The allocation of resources for reforestation programs was stepped up, though still far short of required amounts. The government sought aid from the World Bank, the Asian Development Bank, U.S. AID, and other donor agencies to strengthen its forestry programs.

Not all developments in 1977 and 1978 were unfavorable for STC in their effect on its supply of raw materials. A cyclone hit eastern Sri Lanka in November 1978, damaging trees, plantations, and buildings. Almost 80,000 cubic meters of teak were damaged over 20,000 acres; STC was allowed to salvage as much of this teak as possible. The UNP government also allowed timber imports by STC and other independent importers in 1978. Imports had earlier been virtually zero. But imported timber was much more expensive than domestic timber, often double in price. Although other organizations besides STC were allowed to import timber and did so, STC was poised to be the single largest importer. It was unclear how imported timber would be priced and how imports would affect STC's ongoing operations.

The Problem with Private Subcontractors

The real rate paid to STC's private subcontractors who extracted and transported forest timber had declined over the years. This was due partly to the government's control of STC's sales prices, which thus limited what STC was willing to pay its private subcontractors. By 1978 many private subcontractors found working for STC unprofitable and turned to other growth sectors such as construction. (The rates paid subcontractors in June 1978 ranged from Rs.185 per cubic meter [Class III logs] to Rs.247 per cubic meter [Class I logs]. The rates for sawmilling were Rs.103–137 per cubic meter.) This was becoming an important obstacle to quickly exploiting even the limited areas available for felling in 1977 and 1978. According to one STC executive, private contractors found other ways to work profitably for STC; some carried off inferior "unwanted timber" generated during extraction. Such timber had a significant market value, but STC officers overlooked this practice to compensate contractors for the low rates they were officially paid.

MARKETING PROBLEMS

Excess Demand

Demand for timber exceeded supply throughout STC's life. Although STC substantially increased production between 1968 and 1977, demand rose even faster. The gap was estimated at around 30–40% of supply. After 1977 demand for timber products rose at an accelerated pace because of the construction boom. The government launched a plan to construct 153,000 new houses over five years as part of a socioeconomic development plan. President Jayewardene declared that the government "shall stimulate construction in all sectors and ensure, both through institutional means and individual assistance schemes, that a family shall possess its own house." The importance attached to construction was reflected in the fact that responsibility for local government, housing, construction, and highways rested with the prime minister himself.

Since STC was not able to meet the entire domestic demand, a rationing system was used. STC issued permits to those with government-approved construction plans. The system bred a black market for timber in which prices were 50–70% higher than those charged by STC, especially for superior grades of timber. Price controls, permit systems, and the shortage in timber supply did not help STC acquire a good reputation or a healthy relationship with its customers. With the sharp fall in timber supply in 1977 and 1978, these relations worsened further.

Price Controls

STC's prices were controlled by the Prices Commission, which used a cost-plus method. According to Abeywickrama, "We have not been charging the consumer enough. STC's prices have been half the price of timber sold in the open market. There should not be such a large gap. Maybe our prices should be 20% lower than those of private traders, because our service may not be as good. But they should not be lower than that." The company obtained a price increase in 1973, but of only Rs.1 per cubic foot of timber. In February 1974 STC applied for a 10% price increase, which was eventually approved in November 1974. At the same time STC stepped up the rates paid to its contractors by 20%. In April 1978 STC's attempt to raise prices ran into a political storm. The president ordered that price increases be suspended until he issued a directive on the subject. The president's office eventually but reluctantly approved the price increase in May 1978. (The STC's prices as of July 1976 and May 1978 are set out in *Exhibit 4.*)

ORGANIZATIONAL PROBLEMS

Abeywickrama entered the STC while labor–management relations were quite strained. The immediate cause was an incident involving the previous chairman that occurred soon after the cyclone of November 1978. The cyclone damaged the homes and property of some STC employees working in the affected areas. The chairman's response to this crisis was apparently viewed by the employees as too little too late. Visiting one of the affected locations some days later, he was surrounded by disgruntled workers, locked in a room, and allegedly assaulted. The chairman later launched proceedings against the employees involved. This further strained management–union relations, as the following extract from the minutes of the December 1978 board meeting shows:

> At the request of the five trade unions, the board agreed to meet representatives of these trade unions to discuss steps to be taken to grant relief to those corporation employees affected by the cyclone. Representatives were given an opportunity to meet the board. However, the representatives did not discuss relief measures but made the following demands:

(a) That the corporation should withdraw all action which the corporation has taken or intends taking against employees at Minneriya mill who had been involved in an incident when the chairman visited Minneriya on 29 November 1978. (They did not deny the incidents.)

(b) They also wanted the decision of the management conveyed back to them the same day.

After discussion, the unions were informed that the matter had already been referred to the ministry, and as such the management was unable to grant their request. Thereafter, the union representatives left the board meeting.

This incident, among other things, seems to have led to the previous chairman's departure. Abeywickrama had to take up from where his predecessor had left matters. The leading STC union owed allegiance to the ruling party. Other minority unions were affiliated with the SLFP and the Communist Party.

Apart from the immediate crises, Abeywickrama was also concerned about longer-term issues such as the quality of STC's management. Decision-making was centralized; the organization was somewhat apathetic; and important management control systems were not even in place. Regional managers came to the poorly organized head office for approval on minor matters. "I was really surprised," Abeywickrama said, to illustrate the point, "to find a whole bunch of overtime applications on my table on the first day I came to work. Can you imagine what it means when the chairman of a corporation has to waste his time signing overtime applications!"

But he felt quite positive about the innate quality of the STC's senior managers. Bright and well educated, most were former forest officers in the Forest Department. In his view, the only problem was that they had not been given opportunities to exercise their managerial abilities and therefore lacked a certain training and vision.

At lower levels in the organization, especially with workers at STC's sales depots and felling sites, he found a serious mismatch between the company's needs and the capabilities and training of the available people. Many employees had been thrust on the company by members of Parliament. In earlier years MPs would officially take turns nominating individuals to fill vacancies in public corporations at these levels. The UNP government replaced this practice with a new scheme in which all MPs, including members of the opposition, were periodically given 1,000 forms each for nominating individuals to be placed in a job bank. Public corporations were free to use whatever additional criteria they desired but could select people only from the job bank to fill their vacancies. Of course, this procedure was not applicable for selections at the executive level.

As Abeywickrama pondered problems confronting STC in March 1979, he realized his desk was full of matters that needed immediate attention. He wondered how he could reverse STC's decline.

STATE TIMBER CORPORATION OF SRI LANKA

Exhibit 1

Chairmen of STC from 1968 to 1979

Name	Approximate Age on Assuming Office	Period as Chairman	Background	Reasons for Leaving
P. H. Wickramasinghe	59 yrs.	1968–1971	Former civil servant who retired as chief valuer.	Resigned following change in ruling party.
B. I. Palipane	58 yrs.	1971 (9 months)	Attorney. Lost Parliament election in 1970. Landlord. May have been related to supervising minister.	Removed by minister along with rest of the board.
W. R. H. Perera	55 yrs.	1971– mid-1977	Conservator of forests. Was earlier on the board. Part-time chairman.	Resigned soon after change in ruling party.
M. A. Herman	48 yrs.	mid-1977– Jan. 1978	Planter and businessman. Appointed by Minister for Agriculture and Lands.	Resigned because he did not like the STC job. Returned to own business.
P. Aluvihare	58 yrs.	Jan. 1978– Feb. 1979	Former divisional revenue officer and planter. Member of UNP.	Asked to resign by Minister of Lands & Land Development soon after labor troubles increased.
K. L. Abeywickrama	45 yrs.	March 1979 onward	Former marketing manager, Levers (Ceylon) Ltd.	

STATE TIMBER CORPORATION OF SRI LANKA

Exhibit 2
Product Sales: 1968–78

Category		1968ᵃ	1969	1970	1971	1972	1973	1974	1975	1976	1977	1978
Logs	Rs. (million)	3.6	8.9	9.2	6.7	13.5	16.9	20.4	21.0	22.9	17.0	22.2
	m³ (000)	21.4	94.9	94.2	64.2	101.5	109.7	118.1	101.2	100.2	74.5	71.8
Sawn timber	Rs. (M)	2.5	5.7	8.4	6.8	9.3	10.2	9.5	12.6	13.7	10.8	7.8
	m³ (000)	6.1	18.7	20.7	12.9	20.7	20.4	18.3	22.6	23.4	17.3	11.5
Sleepers (ties)	Rs. (M)	0.9	2.2	3.2	3.2	3.0	6.7	3.2	5.9	7.9	1.6	2.9
	Nos. (000)	25.3	86.4	18.1	71.6	114.8	118.7	92.6	116.6	118.2	42.7	2.0
Transmission poles	Rs. (M)	0.5	0.8	0.6	0.3	0.5	1.5	2.1	2.7	3.6	2.7	1.8
	Nos. (000)	4.0	15.9	15.2	1.7	15.7	12.2	21.3	19.1	18.2	14.1	8.0
Firewood	Rs. (M)	0.3	1.5	1.4	1.2	2.0	1.7	2.1	2.8	2.6	2.5	2.9
	m³ (000)	23.4	95.6	93.6	65.8	118.5	104.5	98.1	137.6	137.8	73.7	21.7
Others	Rs. (M)	0.4	—	1.8	1.3	2.1	2.1	2.1	2.3	4.9	2.2	1.9
Total	Rs. (M)	8.2	19.1	24.6	19.5	30.4	39.1	39.4	47.3	55.6	36.8	39.5

ᵃFigures include production for much less than twelve months since STC was created in the course of the year.

Note: The inflation rate in Sri Lanka (as measured by consumer prices in Colombo) was around 7% in the 1970s. The consumer price index rose from 100 in 1969 to 193 in 1979, i.e., prices roughly doubled in the ten years. But in 1978 and 1979 prices increased by about 15% a year.

SOURCE: STC.

STATE TIMBER CORPORATION OF SRI LANKA

Exhibit 3

Profit and Loss Statements: 1968–78

Item	Year[a]										
	1968[b]	1969	1970	1971[c]	1972	1973	1974	1975	1976	1977	1978
Sales and other operating revenue	8.2	19.9	24.6	19.5	30.4	39.1	39.4	52.8	57.9	38.0	40.0
Cost of sales including royalty and business turnover tax[d]	NA	NA	13.4	11.8	18.4	28.1	29.4	NA	41.7	32.7	29.3
Gross profit	2.6	NA	11.2	7.7	12.0	11.0	10.0	NA	16.2	5.3	10.7
Selling and administrative expenses	3.2	NA	9.3	7.1	11.1	4.5	4.7	NA	11.3	11.8	14.5
Net profit (loss) before tax	(0.6)	(0.4)	1.9	0.6	0.9	6.5	5.3	1.6	4.9[e]	(6.5)[e]	(3.8)[e]
Tax	—	—	—	—	—	—	—	1.0	—	—	—
Net profit (loss) after tax	(0.6)	(0.4)	1.9	0.6	0.9	6.5	5.3	0.6	4.9[e]	(6.5)[e]	(3.8)[e]

[a]Accounting year is from April to March up through 1971 and follows the calendar year from 1972 on.

[b]Figures include production for much less than twelve months since STC was created in the course of the year.

[c]Results are for nine months only, i.e., April–December 1971.

[d]Royalty paid to Forest Department is 10% of sales.

[e]These results include losses from Sinharaja Project. For example, this contributed a *loss* of 5.1 million in 1976.

SOURCE: STC.

Exhibit 4
Sale Prices of Timber: July 1976 and May 1978

		July 1976	*May 1978*
Logs (Rs. per cubic meter)			
Special	1.5 m	909	1,509
	1.2 m	604	1,098
	1.0 m	532	755
Luxury over	1.4 m	2,006	2,401
	below 0.8 m	333	607
Class I	1.5 m and over	370	617
	under 1.5 m	333	563
Class II	1.5 m and over	274	518
	under 1.5 m	257	490
Sleepers (Rs. per piece)		74	98
Transmission poles (Rs. per piece)		165	215
Firewood (Rs. per ton)		96	120
Peeler logs (Rs. per cubic meter)		218	343
Sawn timber (Rs. per cubic meter)			
Scantlings (0.2 m and	— Special	1,166	1,722
over in length)	— Class I	799	1,159
	— Class II	501	796
Planks (0.25 m and over	— Special	1,372	1,948
in width)	— Class I	851	1,303
	— Class II	559	885

SOURCE: STC.

Bribery and Extortion
in International Business

The following caselets have been disguised, but reflect actual events.

1. *Pay the General.* You are in charge of trying to secure a contract for the sale of U.S. telecommunications equipment worth abot $40 million to the communications and transport ministry of a Latin American country with a military government. European firms are also eager for the contract. Quality differences in the products of the various suppliers are not important. A local accountant, who has helped you with government negotiating in the past, suggests to you that the company might receive the contract if it were willing to deposit $2 million in the Swiss bank account of the general in charge of the ministry.

2. *Hire the Speaker.* You are responsible for negotiating with an African government the terms under which your company would build and operate a battery plant in the country. You have U.S. counsel and know a local law firm with two Harvard-trained principals. However, other Americans who have successful investments in the country suggest that you hire the local Speaker of the House, who is a lawyer, to help represent you in the negotiations. You are aware that the House must eventually approve the agreement you negotiate.

3. *Hire the Vice President's Brother.* Your U.S. company has a major petroleum investment in a non-Arab oil country. All foreign investors have been notified that their contracts (covering taxes, royalties, and so on) will be reviewed in the light of events in other countries.

A lawyer, who is the brother of the vice president, offers his services to your firm in the upcoming renegotiations. The proposed fees are about 25% higher than those that might be asked by a U.S. law firm.

4. *The Luggage Clerk.* You are the U.S. manager of a local subsidiary in a developing country. As you are leaving the country for a brief visit to headquarters, the clerk at the counter for the local airline you are using points out that you have overweight luggage. (This was no surprise to you, since you are carrying home Christmas presents for your and your wife's families, but you know some international airlines have dropped the weight limit or would simply overlook the small amount of excess weight.) You ask the charge and hear that it is $75. When you look hesitant, the clerk suggests that $5 might actually take care of the matter.

5. *The Immigration Officials.* You have just been put in charge of a U.S.

These examples were prepared by Professor Louis T. Wells, Jr. as the basis of class discussion. Abridged with permission.

subsidiary in a developing country and have discovered that the previous manager has been paying $40 to immigration officials each time the residence permit of U.S. employees has been extended. There is no official basis for the charge and it has been paid each time in cash. You are told other foreign companies and even private U.S. foundations pay similar fees.

6. *The Tax Collector.* You are vice president for international operations of a U.S. company. One of your new managers of a rapidly expanding subsidiary in a developing country reports the following experience: A tax collector visited the firm with a bill for the firm's annual income tax. Although the bill seemed a bit high, based on the accounts earlier submitted to the government, the manager told the collector that he would authorize a check to the Treasury. The collector pointed out that the total due could be discussed and he was sure that some less costly arrangement could be worked out. The manager replied that he preferred to accept the Treasury's calculation and had a check made out. Two weeks later, the manager receives a registered letter from the collector saying that an error had been made and the company owed about 35% more. A bill was enclosed, but the letter mentioned that the tax collector would be happy to discuss the matter further.

7. *Rule Evasion.* You are on a consulting trip to a Latin American country and discover a very fine suit in a smart downtown shop. You ask about the price and discover that it is 9,000 pesos. The clerk explains that that would be $75, if you will pay in dollars. You realize that it is $300 at the official rate of exchange that you encountered at the airport and at banks.

8. *Ransom.* The American manager of one of your Latin American subsidiaries has been kidnapped by a leftist political group. You are informed that he will be released unharmed if you will have your company run an ad in the local newspaper presenting the group's criticism of the government in power, if you will provide $100,000 of food for distribution to the poor and pay $1 million in ransom to the group. You discover that the ransom payment would be illegal in the country.

Standard Fruit Company in Nicaragua

In late November 1980 Bob Fisher, senior vice president and general manager of banana operations for Castle & Cooke, was reviewing with other top management the future strategy of Nicaragua's banana production and export business. The Nicaraguan operations had a tumultuous ten-year history. Production was in a hostile agronomic climate where two previous attempts to produce bananas had failed; it had faced volcanic eruptions, earthquakes, rapid inflation, and, most recently, a successful armed revolution. The task facing Fisher and Castle & Cooke was to reach a mutually satisfactory agreement with the new government, headed by the socialist-oriented Sandinistas who had spearheaded the revolution.

INDUSTRY CONTEXT

Standard Fruit Company

The Standard Fruit Company started in 1899 when a small New Orleans partnership began importing bananas from Honduras. By 1904 it owned plantations and had received concessions from Honduras to build more than 300 kilometers of railroads and to open river mouths to transport bananas more efficiently. Standard expanded into Nicaragua in 1922, Mexico in 1923, Panama in 1926, and Haiti in 1934. Disease, world depression, civil strife, and outright expropriation in Mexico led to the demise of all four new operations by the mid-1940s.

While Honduras remained the base of its operations, Standard began to buy fruit from independent Ecuadorian growers in 1950 and established banana farms in Costa Rica in the mid-1950s. Acquired by Castle & Cooke in the late 1960s, Standard began to expand rapidly. It reestablished Nicaraguan operations in 1970, formed a Colombian division in 1976, expanded its Ecuadorian division, and introduced Dole-label bananas in 1972. By 1973 Standard Fruit had become the North American market leader, with close to a 40% share. In 1980 it supplied over 20% of

This case was prepared by Janice Honigberg and Professor James E. Austin as the basis for class discussion rather than to illustrate either effective or ineffective handling of an administrative situation. Abridged with permission.

the European market with fruit from Costa Rica, Colombia, and Ecuador; its Philippine operation served a growing share of the Japanese market.

Standard Fruit was vertically integrated from production through processing, distribution, and marketing. It shipped bananas in 25 to 30 owned or leased refrigerated ships. Results of the banana operations were erratic: Operating losses were incurred in 1974, 1978, and 1979, yet Standard was the largest single contributor to Castle & Cooke's earnings in 1973, 1975, 1976, and 1980. Besides Dole bananas, Castle & Cooke produced and marketed Dole pineapple and fresh mushrooms, Bumble Bee and Royal Alaskan seafoods, and Bud of California lettuce, celery, and cauliflower. Food operations made up over 80% of its corporate revenues (*Exhibit 1*).

Industry Structure

One of the earliest plants to be cultivated, the banana probably originated in southeast Asia but now grows in the humid tropics throughout the world. Spanish missionaries first brought it to the New World in the 16th century. Latin America, led by Ecuador, Costa Rica, Honduras, Colombia, and Panama, supplied most of the bananas sold on world markets (see *Exhibit 2* for 1979 production and trade).

The modern history of the Latin American banana industry began in the late 1890s with the exploits of the North American sea captains, railroad barons, and adventurers who formed the United Fruit Company in 1899. Through company-owned plantations and regular shipments in its own vessels, United commercialized bananas in the United States and Europe.

United Fruit dominated the industry for 50 years, supplying 75–80% of its markets. But in the 1960s United's share had fallen to less than 50% because of aggressive competitors and restraint orders in U.S. antitrust suits. Standard's share rose rapidly thereafter through expansion of its production sourcing in Nicaragua, Ecuador, and Colombia. In 1968 the Del Monte Corporation, to avoid acquisition by United, became the industry's newest entrant and third major competitor. Del Monte doubled its production in 1972 when a federal antitrust suit forced United to sell its competitor 58,000 acres of plantation lands in Guatemala. Del Monte held a 13% market share in 1980. (*Exhibit 3* describes the location and organization of the banana companies' sources of supply.)

Factors Affecting Production

The banana plant springs from a parent root into a 12-foot stalk topped by spreading leaves; about 12 healthy leaves are required to produce a marketable stem of bananas. A flowering stem emerges through the center of these leaves, producing a stem of about 200 bananas weighing up to 100 pounds. Cut down when the stem is harvested, the plant is replaced by a shoot that has been allowed to grow and is timed to blossom shortly after the "grandmother" stalk has been cut. Each banana plant has a nine-to ten-month growing cycle.

Several natural hazards threaten this fragile plant and its fruit. Drought, chill, floods from hurricanes or seasonal rains, and insects easily damage the fruit. The mature plant is tall, topheavy, and highly vulnerable to blowdown from windstorms. Winds as low as 20 miles per hour can tear the leaves, stunting the bananas' growth, and steadily batter the leaves against the maturing stem, scarring the fruit. Bananas are susceptible to diseases such as Sigatoka that necessitate efficient, costly spraying.

Production and Distribution Process

Bananas' delicacy and perishability present unique demands in cultivation and handling. Sophisticated drainage, irrigation, and flood-control systems must be installed. Good agricultural practices are crucial; banana farms take months, even years, to recover from improper land preparation, weeding, pruning, fertilization, and fumigation. As the "fingers" of fruit begin to mature, the entire stem is enclosed in specially treated plastic bags to guard against insects and birds and to protect it from bruising. Although bananas are harvested hard and green, they easily incur damage which does not appear until they ripen.

Because a maximum of three to four weeks may elapse between harvesting and consumption, harvesting must be precisely timed to meet shipping schedules and fluctuating seasonal demand. Once cut, the stems are transported to packing sheds on the farm. There the fruit is cut into "hands" of 10–12 bananas, bathed in cool water, selected according to strict specifications of length, shape, appearance, and maturity, and packed in 40-pound cardboard boxes. These travel by rail or truck to the port of origin, where they are loaded onto refrigerated ships. At the port of entry, the fruit is transferred to refrigerated trucks. The importer usually sells its bananas to one of 900 jobber-ripeners or supermarket divisions. The fruit is brought to optimum ripeness for distribution to retailers in special atmosphere-controlled ripening rooms.

In an industry where oversupply is common, margins low, and transportation costs enormous, shipping economies are crucial to profitability. Filling the banana ships to capacity requires extensive land for cultivation, which in turn necessitates a large, dependable labor supply and major capital investment in infrastructure. Moreover, the importance of capacity utilization of the ships reinforces the need for an efficient, well-coordinated, integrated production–marketing chain.

NICARAGUA

Located north of Costa Rica and south of Honduras, Nicaragua is the largest Central American republic; with 148,000 square kilometers, it is about the same size as England and Wales. Mountainous upland in its center divides the Atlantic from the Pacific lowlands. The Pacific coastal region had over 20 active volcanoes, whose ash enriched the soil in agriculturally active Léon and Chinandega.

In 1979 Nicaragua's population was 2.65 million. Population density was only 18 persons per square kilometer, compared to 44 in Costa Rica and 157 in El Salvador. But over 90% lived in the country's western half. The sparsely populated Atlantic region, a British protectorate in 1780–1885, was settled in the 18th century by colonies of Jamaicans, who mixed to some extent with the indigenous Misquito Indians. In contrast, western Nicaraguans are almost all mestizos, a mixture of Spanish and Indian.

In 1979, 30% of all Nicaraguans were economically active; of those, almost 44% were engaged in agriculture, down from 51% in 1970. Per capita GNP declined from a high of US$970 in 1977 to $540 in 1979. Average life expectancy was 50 years; about half were illiterate.

Before the 1979 revolution, Nicaragua's economic wealth was heavily concentrated in the ruling elite. Particularly visible were the extensive land and agroindustrial holdings of the Somozas, who had held political power for more than four decades.

Nicaraguan history had been marked by turbulence, foreign intervention, and despotism since its independence in 1838. In 1855 William Walker from Tennessee sailed for Nicaragua with 56 mercenaries and made himself president in 1856, but he was routed in 1857 by a coalition of Central American republics backed by Cornelius Vanderbilt. At the turn of the century the United States sent marines to ensure the installation of a pro-U.S. president and to safeguard U.S. economic interests. Hundreds, sometimes thousands, of marines were stationed in Nicaragua until 1933. During the last five years of occupation, nationalists under General César Augusto Sandino waged guerrilla war against both the marines and the presidents they protected. Unable to defeat Sandino's guerrillas, the marines supported a negotiated peace settlement. After the marines' withdrawal, General Anastasio Somoza, commander of the U.S.-trained Nicaraguan National Guard, seized power. The Somozas (Anastasio, then his sons, Luis and Anastasio) dominated Nicaragua until 1979, gathering much of its wealth into family coffers.

Nicaragua experienced overall steady economic growth in the decades before 1980. But because agriculture made up about 25% of GDP and over 70% of all exports, Nicaragua's growth rate often fluctuated with variations in its agricultural production and world commodity prices (*Exhibit 4*). Inflation was low until the 1972 earthquake in Managua, after which prices rose precipitously.

Although over half of Nicaragua's total land was virgin forest and only 12% of its arable land was used for crops, the Nicaraguan economy was predominantly agricultural. In the 1970s the chief crops were cotton, sugar, maize, bananas, coffee, rice, and beans. Exports of cotton, coffee, and sugar made up over 55% of the total value of exports; bananas were 11%. Cotton and sugar production were heavily concentrated in the northern Pacific region; over 40% of cotton acreage and 55% of sugar acreage were in the Department of Chinandega, where Standard Fruit established its banana operations.

STANDARD FRUIT'S INVOLVEMENT IN NICARAGUA

Initial Entry

Standard Fruit established its first Nicaraguan banana operations on the Atlantic coast in 1922. In return for a government concession of 50,000 acres, Standard invested more than $13 million in fixed assets, including more than 80 miles of railroad development, a wharf, port, hospital, worker housing, and offices. During its lifetime, Standard Fruit was the largest American enterprise ever established in Nicaragua; by 1932 bananas accounted for 49% of Nicaragua's exports.

Production peaked in 1929 at 4.2 million stems, or 810 million boxes. The Depression lowered banana prices, forcing Standard to cut production and lay off several hundred Nicaraguan workers. The layoffs and attendant worker unrest helped make Standrd Fruit the prime target for General Sandino. His forces assaulted Standard's operations in April 1931, setting fire to every building except workers' houses and killing at least 18 Standard employees. When other attacks followed in 1932 and both Sigatoka and Panama disease spread in the plantations, Standard began to abandon Nicaragua. But a contract with the Nicaraguan government obligated Standard to maintain the wharf and port facilities until 1970.

Competitors' Involvement in Nicaragua

In 1960 United Fruit signed a five-year purchase contract with independent growers around the city of Chinandega. After five years the contract was not renegotiated. Among other problems, fierce winds had reduced the quantity and quality of the banana harvest, causing huge losses for growers and underuse of United's shipping capacity.

When United Fruit ended operations in Chinandega, INFONAC, the National Development Institute, tried to continue the grower program. Although it solicited technical assistance from abroad to sustain the banana industry and diversify Nicaragua's agricultural production, INFONAC was forced to abandon the operations in 1967. Continued poor production had made shipping economies impossible and sunk growers further into debt.

Standard's Reentry into Nicaragua

Entry Rationale. INFONAC invited Standard to reenter the Nicaraguan banana industry in 1967. At first Standard was uninterested, but by 1969 it decided to renew its participation for several reasons. It needed to supplement its Ecuadorian production with a new Pacific Coast source to supply its rapidly expanding business on the U.S. West Coast. Nicaragua was geographically close to that market, and its Pacific Coast soils were among the finest available for bananas. Standard Fruit also felt that it already had a good relationship with the Nicaraguan government, which it thought particularly stable.

Corporate management was certain that Standard would succeed where United Fruit and INFONAC had failed. They were confident that yields would increase with superior irrigation systems and a shorter-stalked, heartier variety of banana. Standard also felt it had an advantage with its previous experience in Nicaragua, the unique structure of the new organization, and the quality of its management group.

Government Incentives. In negotiating Standard's entry into Chinandega, the Nicaraguan government gave Standard what one manager called a normal package of incentives for foreign investment, including duty-free imports and partial exemption from municipal taxes. In turn, Standard returned its remaining Atlantic Coast properties to the government and agreed to pay a 12¢ tax on every exported 40-pound box of bananas. Standard was also required to share its profits with Nicaragua, remitting 30% of the income earned from the sale of Nicaraguan bananas in the United States.

Although the government was very interested in having Standard develop the banana industry, negotiations were often difficult. It took four years of almost weekly meetings with the Port Authority to reach an agreement on rates, and two years with the electric company. One manager asserted that one reason for the delays was the fact that Standard refused to pay any bribes to public officials.

Grower Arrangements

The history of the Chinandega banana industry greatly affected the structure of Standard's new operation. Like United Fruit earlier, Standard Fruit wanted to base its organization on independent grower landowners, not company plantations. But the original growers had had such bad experiences in the 1960s that they refused to participate; Standard was forced to find an entirely new group of producers. To counter the negative attitudes toward bananas among Chinandega's landowners, Standard paid its growers a land rental competitive with rentals of land for cotton production. Standard reasoned that rental fees would be an important source of income for the growers during preproduction and early production phases of the program and would add to their profitability once banana cultivation was under way.

Standard Fruit formed uniform limited partnerships with each of its growers: The landowner held an 80% share and Standard held the rest. The partnerships' terms stipulated that Standard Fruit was to secure sources of financing for the heavy investment in infrastructure and would guarantee the partnerships' loans. Until debts were paid off (five to seven years later), Standard was given majority voting rights in the partnership. Standard specified the schedules, methods, and material inputs necessary for proper irrigation, fertilization, pest control, planting, growing, and harvesting. The company had to provide free technical assistance in all areas of banana production and processing.

The fruit purchase contract was also fundamental to the structure of the Nicaragua division. Standard Fruit guaranteed the partnership a fixed price per box of bananas meeting export-quality specifications; the contracted price (f.o.b. the Port of Corinto) was periodically renegotiated to allow for inflationary increases in high-use inputs. The partner agreed to sell exportable bananas exclusively to Standard Fruit. But fruit not meeting Standard's rigid specifications for export would belong to the growers, who could sell it domestically.

Standard formed partnerships with 13 growers around the city of Chinandega. Varying from 200 to 800 acres, the farms averaged about 450 acres and were 15–60 kilometers from the port of Corinto. Standard chose geographically separated farms to diversify the agronomic risks of banana production. Although it had made soil surveys around Chinandega, it was uncertain which soil types would yield the finest fruit. Standard also wanted to minimize the damage caused by one particular location's disease, heavy winds, or shortage of water.

Operations

After these negotiations, Standard Fruit's partnerships began to operate. In 1970 and 1971 each partnership built its own packing plant, cableways, and roads, and installed irrigation and drainage systems. Once the land was planted, production was slowly scaled up; Standard's first shipment of Nicaraguan bananas sailed for California in May 1972.

Organization. Standard Fruit of Nicaragua had about 100 employees, including three or four American managers. In practice, the organization paralleled the partnerships: Its main function was to support the farms. It did research, made recommendations on all aspects of operations, coordinated shipping and production schedules, and purchased inputs (boxes, insecticides, fertilizers) in bulk for all farms. It also trained farm managers and regularly sent its agricultural supervisors to the farms to audit and assist in the agricultural practices. It maintained the farms' accounting books in the central administrative office.

Labor Relations. Although Standard counseled growers on labor policies and efficiency guidelines, it was never directly involved in labor negotiations. In other countries, wages on banana farms tended to be higher than for other crops. Standard had a continuing dialogue with the growers about wages. The growers, who were often also cotton and coffee farmers, did not wish to disrupt those wage structures. Consequently, banana wages tended to be on a par with other crops.

Each farm had its own manager (named by and reporting to the board) and up to 500 workers (paid piece rate). Soon after banana production began, several unions vied for control of the farms' workers. In 1973, after months of labor agitation, the whole work force joined one union, which negotiated with the growers until the revolution.

Social Services. The partnerships invested only minimally in worker housing in the first years of operation, improving existing housing of cotton workers only slightly and building basic structures where necessary. The growers did not want to risk further investment in infrastructure, especially given the short-lived United Fruit and INFONAC operations. They also felt that permanent worker housing was unnecessary because workers preferred to live in the city. As the banana program progressed, however, growers realized the importance of better worker housing to attract and maintain a permanent, on-site work force. In 1975 the partnerships began a five-year, $2 million program financed by Standard to provide most banana workers with the best housing in the area. Free housing decreased worker turnover and the need for busing from towns.

As housing was improved and more workers came to the farms, the partnerships set up schools. By the time of the revolution in 1979, every farm provided educational programs and medical services for its workers and their children. Each farm had a small infirmary. One full-time nurse rotated among the farms; doctors periodically visited them. A physician was always on call in Chinandega. In the first labor contract, malaria and typhoid (endemic to the area) were included as coverable diseases. The company also helped some nearby towns to set up chlorination systems.

Performance: Prerevolution

Problems: Agronomics. According to Dave DeLorenzo, vice president of production for Latin America, "we had a lot of problems that we really didn't expect, making the operation far more difficult to manage than we anticipated." Standard Fruit quickly learned that Chinandega was a very inhospitable area in which to grow a good-quality banana. Because it almost never rained between November and May, Standard depended on irrigation more in Nicaragua than in any other country in which it operated. Tremendous effort was needed to have adequate irrigation throughout the dry season: Running water was scarce, yet the plants needed irrigation day and night, at least 3 inches a week.

Strong winds dried out already parched land, distorted the circles of the irrigating pistols (causing some plants to get inadequate irrigation), sometimes knocked down entire plants, and often shook the plants, deleafing them and bruising their fruit. Wind turned the Chinandega area into a veritable dust bowl. The dust scraped, bruised, and stunted the bananas.

Variations in wind strength and soil type made some banana-growing areas far better than others. Standard abandoned two marginal farms in poor growing areas in the mid-1970s, but replaced them with four others by 1979. Several marginal producers remained.

Problems: Costs. Unexpected costs made the operation's early years especially difficult. After the 1972 earthquake in Managua, the government imposed a 10¢-a-box export tax for two years to speed the city's recovery. The earthquake also induced a wave of inflation, which reduced overall profitability and tore the partnerships' cost structures apart. Standard stabilized the partnerships' costs and reduced the need to continually renegotiate its f.o.b. price by absorbing the added costs of the inputs most affected by inflation (boxes, Sigatoka control, insecticides, and petroleum-based inputs such as fertilizers).

Problems: Labor Supply. Worker turnover was enormous. Despite competitive wages and monetary incentives to remain on the payroll for more than a year, by 1978 more than 15,000 workers had been employed in 3,500 permanent jobs. The partnerships had incurred massive training costs and, more important, faced an unreliable labor supply.

These difficulties were due to several factors. First, seasonal employment during the cotton harvest had been dominant in the Chinandega area for decades. Because the labor market was extremely tight during the cotton harvest and competitive wages were geared to seasonal employment, workers often left banana farms to harvest cotton. Unlike banana operations, entire families could work in the cotton harvest, thus earning more. Second, workers preferred the life-style of seasonal employment. After experiencing full-time work with bananas, many chose to return to three months of intensive labor followed by nine months of subsistence farming. Third, the workers' living in town rather than on the farm made for a more transient work force.

Results. Despite its problems, by the mid-1970s Standard Fruit of Nicaragua had produced about 6 million boxes of quality fruit for export each year (*Exhibit 5*). The division was also quite profitable, given Nicaragua's proximity to the West Coast market and its competitive cost and quality compared with Ecuador. Moreover, the West Coast was a stable market. Standard and United each held half the market; total weekly shipments rarely fluctuated as in more competitive, oversupplied markets. Banana production gained greater acceptance among Chinandega landowners when most associate growers benefited during the program's first years of operation. The growers profited from banana production, land rental, and the sale of nonexportable fruit on the local market. The value of their land also increased because of the partnerships' investments in infrastructure. Although differences occasionally arose between Standard and the growers, management felt that these were always resolved in mutually satisfactory ways and that relations with growers were excellent.

The partnerships contributed to the economy. Locally, they provided permanent employment for 3,500 workers and housing, education, and health-care facilities. The social infrastructure was helping to reduce worker turnover. Banana production also had multiplier effects by stimulating Chinandega's transportation, construction, and manufacturing industries. Nationally, Standard supplied needed foreign exchange and paid both income and export taxes. Banana production helped Nicaragua diversify its agricultural base and promote exports of nontraditional crops.

REVOLUTION

Civil War

The Nicaraguan Revolution resulted from deep-seated popular dissatisfaction with Somoza's repressive regime and his failure to ameliorate the nation's social and economic ills. The murder of opposition leader Pedro Joaquín Chamorro in January 1978 sparked widespread resentment that soon escalated into civil war. A coalition of businessmen, clergy, intellectuals, and labor, representing every party on the political spectrum, united behind the leftist Sandinista National Liberation Front (FSLN) to oust Somoza and establish a democratic government.

In Chinandega, months of demonstrations and small-scale civilian insurrection culminated in a Sandinista offensive on September 9, 1978. The rebels captured the city, but the National Guard fought back; when they recaptured Chinandega on September 18, hundreds had been killed, thousands wounded, and much of the city destroyed. After 18 months of riots, general strikes, and fighting between the National Guard and civilians led by Sandinista guerrillas, President Somoza was overthrown on July 10, 1979.

Standard's Situation During the Revolution

Although Standard Fruit of Nicaragua did not have an intelligence network with either the government or the Sandinistas, its management foresaw the conflict, sensing the intensifying opposition to Somoza. Once civil war was under way, Standard received a tremendous amount of information through its everyday associations with growers, workers, service businesses, and government agencies. Its strategy was to remain neutral and maintain good relations with both factions; it felt involvement would be presumptuous. Moreover, it could not risk taking a position in the war given Nicaragua's uncertain political future. In about mid-1978 management's policy was that it would not do anything that would be seen as either defection or cooperation. Management thought it could survive if there was a change in governments. "The scenario of a new totalitarian regime was remote." The company also decided to fulfill an agreement made in 1977 to invest in a new banana farm in 1978 despite mounting problems caused by the turmoil.

Standard Fruit of Nicaragua took several other steps. Families of expatriate employees were evacuated before the Chinandega offensive began. Standard was determined to maintain the payroll to preserve some degree of worker loyalty. When cash was unavailable in Chinandega, it chartered planes to fly its workers' cash payments in from Managua. During the siege of Chinandega, Standard sent truckloads of bananas into town and dropped them on street corners to help with food shortages. It never cut back on farm inputs and practices during the revolution. Maintaining the farms was difficult because of the severe disruption of transport and supply systems. Some inputs (plastic bags) were barged into Corinto to avoid blockaded roads. Disease control, particularly of Black Sigatoka, proved very difficult; this disease arrived in June 1979 and spread due to lack of spraying.

Standard began to decentralize in mid-1978. Accounting, purchasing, and engineering were shifted to the farms to make them as self-sufficient as possible. A radio system using codes enabled the farms and central office to maintain communications. Strict discipline was not always possible: One employee's joke over the radio about troop movements caused the workers in one packing plant to rush home.

National strikes were one of the initial problems. Banana production by its nature could not be stopped, but sometimes Standard's central offices would close down during strikes. According to DeLorenzo, "There was consent from both sides to continue operations. Everybody was understanding."

The revolution greatly affected Standard's operations. Although its farms and facilities were unharmed, the division was forced to import boxes at 10¢ a box from Costa Rica when the St. Regis Box manufacturing plant was razed. This plant, in which Standard held a 14% interest, had been Nicaragua's sole source of banana boxes. More seriously, unrest caused a loss of 559,000 boxes in 1978 and 1,350,000 boxes in 1979. The company suffered two prolonged shutdowns in September 1978 during the siege of Chinandega and in June and July 1979 during the final offensive. The September 1978 Chinandega offensive paralyzed exports for more than a month.

During the rest of the revolution, Standard generally lost 15–20% of production through deficient agricultural practices and worker inefficiency. Although few workers fought, there were high expectations for the outcome of the revolution and great confusion over who owned the farms and what duties workers had. The conflict also engendered some fear and anxiety, making efficiency impossible.

Standard substituted its lost Nicaraguan production with bananas from Ecuador and never considered shutting down its Nicaraguan operations. DeLorenzo explained:

> We must run our business through hurricanes, volcanoes, and every other sort of natural and political disruption. Short-term disruptions are not uncommon; we are accustomed to shifting our fleets to export from different producing areas. While we were out of production in Nicaragua, we never missed a shipment to our markets. We simply replaced the production with Ecuador volumes. So we avoided losing the market, our share of the market, or our customers.

POST-REVOLUTION

By the time of Somoza's ouster in July 1979, more than 30,000 people had been killed and the Nicaraguan economy was at a standstill. GDP declined almost 35% in 1979; inflation rose more than 60%. Commerce and industry were virtually destroyed: Damage to commerce and services was estimated at $270 million; industry, $200 million; and infrastructure, $78 million. External public-sector debt had increased over 50% to constitute 50.7% of GDP. Recovery to 1978 levels was not expected until 1982.

Agriculture, too, suffered extensive damage during the war, declining about 12% in 1979. There were severe shortages of food for domestic consumption; few crops were exported. Soon after the revolution, the government formed INRA, the Institute for National Agrarian Reform. INRA's first action was to expropriate all assets belonging to Somoza and his associates. The government thus became Nicaragua's largest landowner, with 60% of its arable land and over 40% of the GNP.

Somoza was immediately replaced by a five-member Junta of both Marxists and moderates, a cabinet, and the nine-member Sandinista Directorate composed of the most influential revolutionary leaders. The Junta was from the private sector and the guerrilla movement and reflected the broad coalition that had supported Somoza's ouster. In May 1980 a 47-member Sandinista-dominated Council of State was formed to plan an election timetable and revise the constitution and legal system. The relationship between these political bodies was unclear to Standard, other outsiders, and even to many government officials. But most agreed that ultimate political authority rested with the FSLN directorate.

The absence of a single leader with total recognized authority sometimes clouded the direction of government policy. But government's commitment to reconstruction and reform within a mixed economy was clear. In the short term, the government needed the private sector to rebuild the economy. Yet the long-term future of the private sector, and foreign enterprise in particular, was less clear, despite several Sandinista leaders' statements about the desirability of maintaining a mixed economy and a pluralistic society. Many businessmen felt that if the Sandinistas consolidated their power and gained the necessary managerial, technological, and financial resources, the private sector's economic role would eventually be phased out. This concern manifested itself politically when the private sector's representative on the Junta formed an independent political party and later left the Junta. This party was strongly opposed by the Sandinistas and created considerable political tension.

STANDARD FRUIT AND THE REVOLUTIONARY GOVERNMENT

Initial Positions

The Nicaraguan banana industry interested many people in the new government, who thought banana production to be extremely important economically because it was one of the few crops exported after the revolution and was nonseasonal, unlike other crops. Also, Standard's program was highly visible, with concentrated production and heavy investment in infrastructure, and provided employment in an underemployed area. Finally, many in the government had strongly negative ideas about the activities of multinational banana companies in Central America.

Government officials voiced several major concerns, including the economics of Standard's marginal producers, implications of the program's organizational structure, and the company's long-term commitment to Nicaragua. The government also questioned the production workers' living and working conditions and the extent to which Standard had transferred managerial skills to native Nicaraguans. They wondered if Nicaragua received the best price for its bananas and if the fruit should be marketed to other socialist countries through barter arrangements. They speculated that another multinational or the government could produce bananas more efficiently and market them more effectively than Stanard.

One of the government's gravest concerns was Standard's previous relationship with Somoza. There was considerable suspicion that Standard had colluded with Somoza: In 1974 every Central American country except Nicaragua levied an export tax to improve their foreign-exchange earnings and dollar participation in the industry. South American countries did not follow the Central American example: Both Ecuador and Colombia continued to offer subsidized incentives for the industry's expansion in their countries.

The Nicaraguan government's position stressed three points: (1) The fruit was the country's, not the company's; (2) they wanted to do whatever was best for the country; and (3) the revolution intended to honor previous laws and contracts, assuming they coincided with the political, social, and economic goals of the revolution.

Standard's first move after the revolution was to restore order in the farms. Within ten days bananas were once again flowing northward. Standard's ships returned with badly needed medical supplies, which were donated to the government.

The second move was to make formal visits to the government officials. DeLorenzo described the company's approach:

> We wanted to learn their expectations and explain to them what the banana industry was about. We believed they would probably want to nationalize the industry; a banana company was an obvious target. We talked to all the main political bodies: the Junta, the Sandinistas, the lay ministers, and vice ministers.
>
> We repeated the same message: (1) Banana cultivation and export

was not the same as cotton, sugar, and coffee; it could be lost forever by impetuous decisions. (2) We believed that Standard was the best company for Nicaragua; we welcomed any study and urged them to talk to other participants in the industry. (3) Our operations were open to their scrutiny; we asked only that we be allowed to respond to their internal or external findings. (4) The industry could not be simplified; it is extremely complex. It was of utmost importance that the government study and understand the business in all its facets as quickly as possible.

July 1979–March 1980

During the months after the revolution, the Nicaraguan government explored its banana business. Hundreds of officials from many ministries interviewed Standard managers, who were more than willing to explain the industry. Standard conducted frequent tours of its facilities to prove that its operation was well-run and completely managed by Nicaraguans since the revolution and to show skeptics the quality of worker housing, education, and health care. Government auditors also examined company records. Government representatives visited the United States to study the market and talked with Standard's competitors and the governments of other banana-exporting countries. Even the competitors came through the Standard farms. DeLorenzo described this period:

> It was a time of great flurry, swaggering, and confusion. We decided to sit back and remain calm because we believed that Standard was in the best position to serve the Nicaraguan banana industry. If the situation was to be resolved by a logical decision, we would win. If it was resolved by a political decision, we'd be out anyway. We simply strove to keep the channels of communication open. We wanted to avoid unilateral action by the government.

The government eventually invited bids from Standard and several other banana marketers, including United Fruit, Del Monte, and COMUNBANA, the marketing arm of the Union of Latin American Banana Exporting Countries (UPEB), which Nicaragua had joined. Standard refused to bid, stating that its operation was competitive and that it would not bid for its own produce. Standard also argued against shipping Nicaraguan bananas to Eastern Europe, as some officials proposed. Nicaraguan fruit was very delicate because of difficult growing conditions and was unlikely to survive an eighteen-day journey to Poland in place of a five-day trip to Long Beach. But Standard would cooperate in any experiment provided that shipments were arranged in advance. Standard also insisted that the partnerships avoid participating in inevitable losses by receiving payment before shipment. The company pointed out to the government that each shipload represented a $750,000 risk; it would be a very expensive experiment. Once Standard even received "cut orders" via telex from COMUNBANA for an East European shipment that never materialized. The company did not proceed with any such shipments.

In November 1979 the government created the Ministry of Foreign Commerce to control all agricultural trade. By law, only its Bananic subsidiary was allowed to export bananas. In principle this constituted a breach of Standard's contracts; in practice Bananic made no effort to purchase, export, or sell Standard's fruit. The agency's directors, whose familiarity with the banana industry had come mainly from discussions with Standard, required only that the company formally apply for an export license before each shipment. The government did impose a $.50-a-box tax on banana exports.

Although Standard operated under what it thought a debilitating degree of uncertainty, it continued normal production during all the months of discussion and expropriation threats. Its business had nevertheless steadily deteriorated since the revolution. Black Sigatoka had caused extensive damage to most farms. The partnerships had to apply a much more expensive fungicide to control the outbreak.

An increasingly difficult labor situation also reduced farm productivity. Revolutionary rhetoric and heightened expectations of the revolution's benefits had changed the workers' traditional concepts of ownership and responsibility. Under new labor rules workers could force an unpopular foreman to resign. Standard found the labor authorities in Chinandega deaf to its appeals and simply could not control the situation. DeLorenzo explained that the net effect was "a grave lack of discipline on the farms: supervisors realize they are risking their jobs simply by trying to do their job. Management effectiveness is cut down drastically as a result. Supervisors are nominally selected by the management of the farms but are effectively selected by labor." One farm was being run by a workers' committee.

The financial condition of the partnerships declined with the farms' productivity (*Exhibit 5*). Standard steadily financed their growing indebtedness. Several farms were better left abandoned, but such a solution did not seem politically feasible.

To make matters worse, the dynamics of the West Coast market had changed dramatically. Del Monte had entered the market in 1978, upsetting both its stability and its profitability. Lower market share and depressed banana prices negatively affected the economics of Standard's Nicaraguan operations, particularly given the 50¢-a-box export tax, which amounted to a $3 million annual burden.

NEGOTIATIONS

Nine months after the revolution, the government expressed its intention of entering into a long-term relationship with Standard Fruit of Nicaragua. DeLorenzo summarized Standard's position in the negotiations:

We made it very clear that we were willing to cooperate, to set up any structures compatible with the revolution. But we could not have unilateral breaking of contracts or an environment in which all rules could be changed at any time; we could not break any legal contracts binding on the company and that bound our associates to us. It's a volatile business, and we have too big an investment in it. We require a highly disciplined, effective operation; uncertainty is our worst enemy. We also made it clear that time was working against us. We were increasingly concerned about the deteriorating economics of the Nicaraguan operation and of our ability to turn it around, given the environment.

In April 1980 Standard began negotiating terms of the agreement with the Ministry of Foreign Commerce and Bananic. The government chose to negotiate first with Standard rather than the growers. Many in the new government viewed the growers, as larger landowners, with some disdain, although most had supported Somoza's ouster. The growers' position was the same as before the revolution: They wanted no government intervention in their industry.

After 18 months of continual negotiations, each side better understood the position and needs of the other. Unfortunately, the company still thought the future uncertain. The division's efficiency and cost competitiveness had disappeared, and management's ability to turn production around was unsure, given the continued tumultuous labor situation on the farms and the confusion and tension of the many changes in institutions and attitudes of the ongoing revolution.

Company management faced a difficult set of facts:

1. Nicaragua had lost its cost competitiveness with Ecuador. The fruit could be easily replaced at an equal or lower cost.

2. Maintaining discipline and efficiency in a revolutionary atmosphere might be impossible. The company's task was aggravated by the lack of definition of the Nicaraguan government. Without the Sandinistas' open support, it was doubtful Standard's management could operate effectively. If it were ever to sign new long-term contracts with the government, Standard wondered whether it could deliver the technical assistance required to produce a high-quality product at competitive productiveness.

Yet experience gained in Nicaragua could prove invaluable to a company operating in many volatile parts of the world.

3. The government and the company had come a long way in understanding each other, except in the most basic area of economics. The company still felt that the government poorly understood the industry's economics and had unrealistic aspirations for what the industry could do for the country.

4. The company felt very strongly that the Nicaraguan growers' property and contractual rights had to be protected, but thought the government little interested in recognizing or protecting those rights. This would undoubtedly cause tension and problems.

5. Castle & Cooke faced a writeoff of up to $10 million should it withdraw from Nicaragua. Only $3 million was covered by OPIC risk insurance against expropriation.

6. A company withdrawal would probably disrupt competition in the West Coast banana market. The Nicaraguan government might either export fruit directly or make a favorable deal with a Standard competitor. Standard's withdrawal might shock the government to the precarious reality of the position and force them to offer a third party advantages that Standard would never be able to realize through negotiations. West Coast losses from competition with surplus fruit were projected to be more than $2 million before markets normalized and volumes returned to earlier levels.

7. Standard's managers were acutely aware that their responsibilities were multiple and that their actions were being scrutinized by many interested parties: shareholders of Castle & Cooke, the Nicaraguan employees, partners and friends, other friendly governments in the area, foreign banana producers and partners, other multinationals in Nicaragua, and even the State Department. By December 1980 Standard management faced a decision whether to stay in Nicaragua. Negotiations might continue forever at the present rate; the company obviously could not continue the present operation much longer. Standard had to determine under what conditions and set of economics it could remain in Nicaragua and under what conditions it might end its operations there. In either case it had to convince the government of the seriousness of their situation and the need for a timely resolution.

By December 1980 several points of possible agreement had been delineated for final evaluation by the company and the government:

1. The sale to the government of Standard's 20% interest in all partnerships

2. Standard's right to buy and export Nicaraguan bananas at an agreed-on price

3. The government's option to sell bananas to nontraditional markets with advance specification of volume and shipping dates

4. The maintenance of growers' contracts by Standard, including land rental, land use, and technical assistance

5. State participation in engineering, production management, and materials purchasing and importing

6. The partnerships' right to nonexportable fruit

Fisher and DeLorenzo had to evaluate these terms and make recommendations to the Castle & Cooke board of directors about the company's continued involvement in Nicaragua.

STANDARD FRUIT COMPANY IN NICARAGUA

Exhibit 1

Summary of Operations: Castle & Cooke
Selected Financial Data
(Dollars in millions except per-share amounts)

	1980 Amt.	1980 Pct.	1979 Amt.	1979 Pct.	1978 Amt.	1978 Pct.	1977 Amt.	1977 Pct.	1976 Amt.	1976 Pct.
Revenues										
Fresh foods	$878	51%	$745	48%	$596	46%	$402	40%	$356	42%
Processed foods	654	37	572	37	516	40	416	42	339	41
Real estate	50	3	94	6	65	5	71	7	49	6
Other activities	152	9	145	9	124	9	110	11	92	11
	$1,734	100%	$1,556	100%	$1,301	100%	$999	100%	$836	100%
Operating earnings										
Fresh foods	38	36	(6)	(7)	4	4	20	21	24	29
Processed foods	39	37	47	54	66	64	52	53	46	56
Real estate	12	11	24	28	17	17	14	14	4	5
Other activities	17	16	22	25	15	15	12	12	8	10
	$106	100%	$87	100%	$102	100%	$98	100%	$82	100%
Less interest and other costs	54		43		31		24		16	
Income taxes	20		13		23		28		25	

Income from continuing operations	$ 32	$ 31	$ 48	$ 46	$ 41
Discontinued operations	—	—	—	(1)	(3)
Net income	$ 32	$ 31	$ 48	$ 45	$ 38
Earnings per share—primary income from continuing operations	$ 1.12	$ 1.19	$ 1.90	$1.91	$1.69
Net income	1.12	1.19	1.90	1.86	1.58
Total assets	$1,264	$1,174	$1,022	$817	$725
Working capital	354	302	292	237	191
Current ratio	2.0	1.9	2.3	2.3	2.1
Long-term debt obligations	$ 346	$ 329	$ 312	$229	$179
Redeemable preferred stock	35	—	—	—	—
Cash dividends paid per common share	.80	.76	.69	.62	.57

Note: Prior year amounts have been reclassified to conform to the 1980 presentation.

SOURCE: Castle and Cooke Annual Report.

225

Exhibit 2
World Banana Production and Trade
(000 metric tons)

	1979 Production	*Exports*[a]	*Imports*[a]
World	39,129	7,140[b]	7,004
Developing	38,403	6,899	757
Latin America	19,320	5,512	311
Brazil	6,424	128	—
Ecuador	2,391	1,386	—
Mexico	1,929	20	—
Honduras	1,300	887	—
Colombia	1,300	633	—
Costa Rica	1,078	1,012	—
Panama	1,000	600	—
Guatemala	560	267	—
Nicaragua	160	110	33
Far East	12,603	929	69
India	4,000	—	—
Indonesia	2,905	—	—
Philippines	2,430	860	—
Thailand	2,082	20	—
Africa	4,214	321	42
Other (Near East, centrally planned)	2,265	136	635
Developed	727	241	5,946[b]
Europe	432	43	2,462
Australia/New Zealand	141	—	35
North America	2	197[b]	2,659
Other developed	152	1	790

[a]Totals may not tally because of recategorization.

[b]Includes reexports.

SOURCES: *FAO Trade Yearbook* 33 (1979), pp. 154–55, and *FAO Production Yearbook* 33 (1979), pp. 179–80.

STANDARD FRUIT COMPANY OF NICARAGUA

Exhibit 3
Banana Suppliers and Arrangements

	Honduras	Nicaragua	Costa Rica	Colombia	Ecuador	Guatemala	Panama	Philippines
Standard Fruit	• Company plantation • Co-op purchases • Government purchases	• Joint venture	• Company and independent planters	• Purchase contracts	• Contract and spot purchases			• Independent planters
United Fruit	• Company plantation		• Company and independents	• Company plantation • Independent planters	• Purchase contracts		• Company plantation, independent planters	• Independent planters
Del Monte			• Company and purchase contracts		• Spot purchases	• Company plantation and independents		• Independent planters
Others				• Spot purchases	• Spot purchases			

227

STANDARD FRUIT COMPANY IN NICARAGUA

Exhibit 4

Nicaraguan Balance of Payments

($ millions)

	1974	1975	1976	1977	1978	1979	1980[a]
Principal exports							
Cotton	135.9	95.6	130.6	150.6	140.9	135.7	30.3
Coffee	46.1	48.1	119.4	198.8	199.6	158.5	165.7
Sugar	12.3	42.6	52.8	27.8	19.6	19.6	20.5
Meat	21.9	27.0	37.6	37.3	67.7	93.5	58.6
Other	164.7	162.0	201.5	222.3	218.1	159.3	175.5
Total	380.9	375.3	541.9	636.8	645.9	566.6	450.6
Principal imports							
Consumer goods	126.0	121.9	145.1	181.4	148.0	101.3	257.8
Raw material and inter-mediate goods	309.7	265.8	262.9	362.5	301.1	202.2	487.6
Fuel	8.3	9.6	11.1	25.0	31.2	10.2	26.0

Capital goods	115.0	119.0	112.8	192.8	113.4	46.2	109.8
Other	2.8	.6	.2	.3	.2	.3	6.1
Total	561.8	516.9	532.1	762.0	593.9	360.2	887.3
Total trade balance	−160.6	−107.3	56.8	−68.0	92.0	227.2	−352.5
Services balance	−111.6	−93.5	−105.7	−125.2	−127.1	−138.6	−115.3
Net transfers	15.5	16.7	10.2	11.2	9.4	91.6	81.0
Current account	−256.7	−184.1	−38.7	−182.0	−25.7	180.2	−386.8
Net capital movement[b]							
Private	58.1	44.5	26.8	−67.1	−239.9[c]	−269.4	−104.5[c]
Official	173.4	112.2	65.3	196.4	49.3	123.7	281.1
Errors and omissions	−13.7	−4.3	−13.7	−3.9	—	−9.5	—
Change in reserves[d]	38.9	31.7	−39.7	56.6	216.3	−25.0	210.2

[a]Preliminary.

[b]Debt service on outstanding external loans was 12.1% of exports in 1975 and 18.0% in 1980.

[c]Includes errors and omissions.

[d]A negative sign indicates an increase in reserves; positive a decrease.

SOURCE: Instituto Nacional de Estadisticas y Censos, *Indicadores Socio-Economicos 1970–1980*, July 1981, Managua.

STANDARD FRUIT COMPANY IN NICARAGUA

Exhibit 5
Banana Production

Farms	1977 Boxes/Acre	1977 Total (000)	1978 Boxes/Acre	1978 Total (000)	1979 Boxes/Acre	1979 Total (000)	1980 Boxes/Acre	1980 Total (000)
Colonia	925	740	915	732	835	668	585	468
La Concha	931	219	1,069	251	757	178	562	132
Adelita	1,073	789	901	667	841	618	736	541
Magdalena	1,149	678	1,040	614	871	514	764	451
San Lucas	1,059	556	1,007	529	1,179	619	818	429
Santiago del Norte	1,394	279	1,154	231	995	199	1,054	211
El Rosario	1,143	229	1,144	229	900	180	943	189
Buena Esperanza	1,103	552	1,026	513	849	424	647	324
La Joya	1,263	410	1,214	395	949	308	1,008	328
Maria Pilar	1,152	445	1,104	475	942	405	900	387
Aguilar	781	582	673	501	670	499	686	511
Engracia	892	326	1,460	533	1,247	455	1,179	430
Tierra Final	—	—	882	542	1,334	820	1,100	677
Patagonia	—	—	—	—	653	170	1,072	279
Luz Celeste	—	—	—	—	710	160	1,040	334
Average yield and total boxes	1,072	5,805	1,045	6,212	915	6,217	873	5,691

Pandol Brothers, Inc. and Nicaragua

As he gazed at the Pacific Ocean from the Port of Los Angeles's Berth 199, Jack Pandol, president of Pandol Brothers, smiled. A few months earlier he had successfully negotiated with the Nicaraguan government a three-year extension of a marketing agreement that had made Pandol Brothers the exclusive importer of Nicaraguan bananas in the U.S. market. It was now August 6, 1984, and just like every other Monday since Pandol's Nicaraguan banana business had started, one of Reefer Express Line's refrigerated vessels was pulling into port with a load of about 80,000 boxes of bananas.

Jack thought that at least this time he did not have to worry about losing the cargo and ship, for the departing port of Corinto on the Nicaraguan Pacific Coast had recently been cleared of mines that counterrevolutionaries had put around its harbor. Pandol and the Nicaraguans also appeared to have survived the initial battle with the Big Three (Standard, United, and Del Monte) banana competitors; buyers now recognized Pandol as a reliable independent banana supplier. Yet the quality and quantity of recent fruit shipments had been poor, and second-grade, Cream-labeled bananas had been found in top-graded Three Brothers boxes, causing customer complaints. Jack was expecting the director of Bananic, the Nicaraguan state banana-trading company, to visit in a few days. He felt the time was right to sit down with his own people and review the challenges and strategy for the years ahead.

THE COMPANY

Pandol Brothers, Inc. was a family business.[1] Jack's parents had invested $56,000 in a farm in 1941, which Jack and his brothers pyramided into a trading empire. By the mid-1980s Jack and Matt oversaw a family business that:

[1]Description based on the article "How Jack Pandol Turned the Farm into an Export Empire," by Marcia Zarley Taylor, *Farm Journal Extra*, March 1984; used with permission of publisher.

Brizio Biondi-Morra and Professor James Austin prepared this case as the basis for class discussion rather than to illustrate either effective or ineffective handling of an administrative situation. Abridged with permission.

- Controlled interests in companies with annual sales of $200 million, more than $125 million of which were in farm products
- Farmed more than 6,000 acres of specialty crops: citrus, grapes, kiwis, apples, oriental pears, and some grain
- Employed more than 1,000 people
- Packed and shipped 100 kinds of fruit, vegetables, and nuts produced by the Pandols and neighboring growers in the San Joaquin Valley
- Traded with buyers from 30 countries, including China, Western Europe, Central America, and the Middle East
- Owned subsidiaries such as agricultural chemical plants, styrofoam manufacturing, a radio business, agricultural hardware stores, irrigation companies, and fish-processing plants
- Made several hundred thousand dollars a year by "playing the float" on their bank accounts (One agricultural banker said the Pandols' money management skills were "almost as good as Bank of America's.")

Jack served as president and sales coordinator of Pandol Brothers, the family's marketing arm. Matt and Jack, Jr., handled field operations on the Pandol & Sons farm. Two others—Jack's younger son Jim and Matt's son John—spent eight months a year as salesmen in the home office, then headed south to Chile during California's winter to supervise shipments to the United States. In 1983 the Pandols, acting as commission agents, sold on the two coasts 1.7 million packages of Chilean grapes, apples, peaches, and plums. A fourth Pandol, Louis, acted as the company's accountant and computer programmer.

Being a family firm was an advantage in competitive export markets, Jack contended. "Much of our trade is sealed on our word or a handshake. In the Orient, it would be an insult to send an employee to negotiate. Sending a family member is a sign of respect." "A lot of our export business comes because we are proficient shoppers," added Jim, the liaison for traders in Latin America. "We are somebody that a customer half the world away knows he can trust to represent his interest."

In trading, Pandol often overcame the foreign-exchange shortages of LDCs by bartering, for example, California apples for South American bananas. In 1983 Pandol's import-export business handled tens of millions of dollars in barter trade. "If your customers are countries that cannot afford to pay, you have to be creative," said Jack, who served as trade adviser on fruits and vegetables to the U.S. Department of Agriculture's Foreign Agricultural Service.

Pandol described himself as a farmer, even though his operation was the size of a Midwest cooperative. He preferred casual dress and said he loved his crops like his own children.

STARTING THE BANANA OPERATIONS

Pandol's first exposure to bananas occurred in 1977. Dr. Alfredo Oranges, former minister of agriculture of Panama, had become the president of COMUNBANA, a new marketing company formed by UPEB, the Union of Banana Exporting Countries. (Founded in 1974 after OPEC's success, UPEB's eight members were Colombia, Costa Rica, the Dominican Republic, Ecuador, Guatemala, Honduras, Nicaragua, and Panama.)

Dr. Oranges's task was to develop new banana export channels with consuming countries; he was looking for an American importer who had ties to the soil, a feeling for farm growers, a large enough marketing network to be able to distribute bananas west of the Rockies, and plenty of courage. Jack was introduced to him in Panama, and they met there several times. Together they visited Nicaragua, where Dr. Oranges introduced Jack to the Nicaraguan minister of foreign trade, Dr. Alejandro Martínez. Nicaragua was discussing with Standard (a subsidiary of Castle & Cooke) the future of its banana operations, and wanted to prepare contingency plans in case negotiations with Standard broke off. (See the previous case, "Standard Fruit Company in Nicaragua.") The Nicaraguans felt they could sell bananas also to the Soviet Union or other socialist countries. They would also see what COMUNBANA could do for them, although they did not seem excited about using COMUNBANA as a market intermediary. Pandol told them that selling to socialist countries was not feasible, for those markets were too far away, the logistical constraints—particularly shipping—would remove vital flexibility, and any experimenting would be expensive and risky.

As negotiations between Standard and Nicaragua continued, Jack explored other COMUNBANA countries. Eventually he started importing bananas from the Dominican Republic to the East Coast. But product quality was poor, and quantities were always too low. The Dominican ranch manager could not deliver on his promises, his company soon went bankrupt, and he was jailed for embezzlement, leaving Pandol with $500,000 in worthless credits.

In 1981 Jack was approached by Ron Elder, who for years had run several Castle & Cooke divisions and was founding a company to export palletized bananas from Ecuador to the West Coast under the Equapak label. The economics of palletized transportation appeared impressive on paper in an industry where containerization was the only major innovation since the 40-lb. box in the 1960s. But the idea proved to be ahead of its time: Ships were unable to control to temperature of fruit in cartons located in the core of the pallet, and Equapak lost 30,000 boxes of overripe bananas in an initial shipment. Even worse, the next year was a bad one: Rains ruined thousands of acres of bananas, including Equapak's. By

October 1982 Equapak advised the Pandols that it was no longer coming to the West Coast. Just then, when Jack Pandol was wondering what to do with his recently established banana sales organization, the Nicaraguan opportunity presented itself.

THE NICARAGUAN VENTURE

Nicaragua's first experience with banana exports went back to Standard Fruit's involvement on the Atlantic Coast during the years 1922–32. This first operation ended for a number of reasons, among them the Great Depression, General Sandino's repeated assaults on plantations, and the spread of plant diseases. A second brief experience in the early 1960s was United Fruit's unsuccessful participation on the Pacific Coast near Chinandega. The government's development agency also tried its hand, unsuccessfully, at banana production and export. In 1969 Standard replaced United Fruit on the Pacific.

Ten years later a revolution deposed President Somoza. A few months after assuming power, the new government created Bananic, a state-owned enterprise with exclusive trading rights on Nicaraguan bananas, and began negotiating with Standard Fruit. By December 1980 the two parties were deadlocked. Nicaragua felt it necessary to create Embanac, another state-owned enterprise, to which administration of the banana plantations had to be transferred from local farm owners and Standard Fruit. Standard felt that both Bananic and Embanac constituted a breach of Standard's contracts.

On December 22, 1980, Standard suspended all banana shipments from Nicaragua. In trade circles it was reported that Standard did this partly because it believed Nicaragua would be unable to market its own fruit directly. Nicaragua was determined to show Standard it could not be intimidated. While Junta member Dr. Arturo Cruz and Agriculture Minister Comandante Jaime Wheelock went to San Francisco to negotiate at Standard's headquarters, the minister of foreign trade, Martínez, arranged for Jack Pandol to meet the Nicaraguan delegation to discuss possible assistance. Jack brought with him his sales manager, Darrell Fulmer, and comptroller, Odgen Keisel.

The Nicaraguans asked Jack and his team to market three ships of bananas on the West Coast starting the following week. "I told them," said Darrell, "that I did not think they should try to market all three ships but that they might get away with one and make some money because the market was fairly firm. If they tried to sell all three the following week and to dump 129,000 boxes on the market, they would get buried and lose a lot of money."

Pandol did sell a ship of 120,000 boxes at a price $1.50 per box above the best promises of other independent distributors. Pandol agreed to a flat fee of $25,000 on the deal but had yet to recover $180,000 in outstanding receivable from buyers. But the Nicaraguans were delighted. On January 11, 1981, a few days after the first shipment's sales and after having reached a new tentative agreement with the Nicaraguan government, Standard resumed operations in Nicaragua.

During the next 22 months Standard continued to export, but it faced rising costs, a world banana glut, and what it said was Nicaragua's failure to sign and fulfill the tentative agreement reached in San Francisco. On October 24, 1982, Standard Fruit announced it was ending all operations in Nicaragua. The Nicarguan government turned once more to Pandol. "We all met at the Sheraton in Miami," said Jack, "and wrote a bunch of numbers on a napkin. They said, 'We want you. Are you willing?' We told them what we could do, and we said, 'Fine let's go.' That was the beginning, based on a handshake."

Pandol Brothers was to act as Bananic's agent, selling bananas on consignment for a flat commission, set at first 35¢ per box. Three months later it dropped to 25¢ per box and then rose to 30¢. Nicaragua would give no guarantee on volume but would grant Pandol exclusivity for the U.S. market. Nicaragua's responsibility would be production and shipping; Pandol's would start at the "tailgate," when boxes were loaded in the truck at the pier. Nicaragua would always own the fruit: Embanac from the farm to the port of Corinto and Bananic from then on. Pandol was to sell to the best of its ability; invoice under the Pandol name; use Pandol's Three Brothers label; collect from customers; take the commission out; pay on Bananic's behalf all ocean freight, insurance, wharfage, stevedoring, and truck-loading charges; and send the balance of the proceeds to Bananic. Pandol assumed responsibility for all credit risks and uncollected invoices. "If we sell to an idiot or a thief," said Jack, "that's our problem."

MARKET ENTRY

"Competition was very upset, naturally," commented Jack. "They said we would destroy the market, so they tried to destroy us instead. The rumor was that someone buying from us couldn't buy from others. We hired a young man who had previously worked with Castle & Cooke. He said that at their sales meetings half the time had been spent talking about 'where those Pandol brothers were going next.' "

"Finally, at one of the trade conventions I met the head man of one of the majors and said I didn't really appreciate the comments about Pandol being made in the trade and the assertions that we didn't have a contract with the Nicaraguans. He looked at me kind of friendly and said 'We didn't say that about you; we don't buy that.' We insisted and a little later he came back to me and said that I was right and that he had just passed the word that there were to be no more bad comments about Pandol. And from then on, everything stopped."

Ron Elder, now working for Pandol, commented: "What competition said, you know; what they actually did is harder to prove. They probably brought in more volume to depress prices momentarily and to discourage us. You have to overcome the adversity put in your path by the competition and put your reputation on the line."

Jack remarked: "We try to be nonpolitical. They keep asking us 'Are you a communist? Are you helping a communist government?' Our position is that we are fruit people, marketers; I am a grower. We feel food has to be produced. We don't believe in boycotting it for the good of somebody. We believe that politics belong to the politicians. Our instructions to our salespeople were 'Don't badmouth the competitors; keep it low key.' It looks like all hell is breaking loose in Nicaragua, so we don't put the country of origin on the labels because we don't want to stir people up. The U.S. government has never bothered us. We checked with them and asked if there were any objections, and they said no. I served on the California Board of Agriculture for four years under Reagan when he was governor. I got to know him quite well. Don't try to push him. He doesn't push. But if you are a reasonable man, he is a reasonable man."

THE MARKETING EXPERIENCE

The first four or five shipments of bananas to California were sold unmarked, but the quality turned out to be excellent. The word got around after the first two ships, and Pandol started getting more customers on the books and receiving better prices for the product.

Selling bananas on the West Coast was a one-week operation done hundreds of times over, and all by telephone. You received the product on Monday, made a first round of calls on Tuesday, started quoting your product around Wednesday, and Friday morning everything happened. Salespeople therefore had to know by Friday morning what was going on in the market, on whom they could depend, to whom they were counting on to sell, how much, and what kind of target price to look for from each customer. There were only 130 potential customers on the West Coast. You could default on your word only once; reputation was a key element in these weekly negotiations.

Six people handled Pandol's banana sales. Their three-room office in Long Beach was located a few minutes from Los Angeles's harbor. Elder headed the office and had 17 years of experience marketing fresh fruit. Helping him were Dave Guzi; port people who also oversaw operations such as unloading and deliveries; Ron's son Todd; and Myrna Melm, who handled the information, paper flow, and invoicing. All paperwork was done at the Delano office.

For banana sales, North America was divided into three areas: the West Coast, Gulf market, and the East Coast. Transportation costs were the main factor defining the boundary between regions. Beyond a certain distance from a port of entry, one could not compete with other areas with closer supply sources; Los Angeles, New Orleans, and Miami were the main ports of entry.

During the summer the West Coast received about half a million boxes a week or about 20 million pounds of bananas. During the winter volume rose to 600,000 boxes a week. Of these, Dole (Standard) supplied 180,000–220,000 boxes, Chiquita (United) 190,000–210,000, Del Monte 70,000–120,000, Pandol an average of 70,000, and few independents about 25,000 a week. Dole and Del Monte came almost exclusively from Ecuador; Chiquita was supplied by Panama and Costa Rica.[2]

Quality varied throughout the year because of climatic variations. Nicaragua had its dry season during the winter, which for Pandol was the most difficult part of the year. But Ecuador was at its best during winter, for it is their summer. Chiquita was probably the most consistent. It had better agricultural practices and also three sources of supply, which gave it flexibility that nobody else enjoyed.

Traditional channels of banana distribution had changed in the previous decade. More and more chain stores, representing about 60% of retail sales, were building banana-ripening rooms, thus doing on their own what jobbers and wholesalers had done exclusively (*Exhibit 1*).

If a firm had excellent quality or the best in the market at a given time, probably most of its sales went to chain stores, for they usually bought on a nonspeculative basis. When jobbers and wholesalers saw the market falling, they bought light on Friday and waited to deal on rollers (weekly unsold portions of a shipment) the next Monday and Tuesday. But chain-store buyers had many different items to buy and did the best deal they could on Friday.

This is why prices varied among customers. Price per box usually fluctuated between $5 and $10, plus 93¢ each for handling and fuel surcharge, plus freight to the customer's warehouse. In Los Angeles, for example, it amounted to about $1.23 over the f.o.b. price. Markups at retail then varied according to store policy and product mixes, including advertis-

---

[2]In late 1984 the Costa Rican subsidiary of United Brands was engaged in intense negotiations with the government of Costa Rica regarding the closure or sale of United's banana production estates there.

ing, with typical retail prices ranging between 30¢ and 40¢ per pound. Demand was dictated mainly by the supply and by availability of other products competing with bananas. The U.S. winter saw the least competition from other fruit.

Pandol and Bananic developed a weekly reporting system. Bananic telexed weekly shipment reports to Pandol. To facilitate discharging operations and help reduce costs, the reports specified the boat's expected arrival time in Los Angeles and its contents by product type, quantity, and precise location inside the ship. Bananic also sent weekly quality reports assessing current and expected production and specifying product characteristics by farm of origin.

In turn, Pandol sent weekly market reports on the selling situation, listing estimated market size, market shares, prevailing competitor prices, and Pandol's actual sales by customer, volume, and price. Pandol also sent its own weekly quality reports, on which Bananic was to take proper action. Guzi flew down to Nicaragua periodically to meet his telex counterparts and see Embanac's production firsthand. Others of the Pandol group also went to help on irrigation, cartons, fertilizer, etc.

In May–July 1984 poor irrigation significantly reduced banana quality, and the usual volume was halved to about 40,000 boxes per vessel. Pandol lost several customers as a result. Only with the start of the rainy season in Nicaragua was production returning to normal. But lost customers could not be recaptured as quickly.

1983 had been a good year. Pandol sold more than 4 million boxes of bananas, representing more than $1 million in commissions and about $30 million in sales for Bananic. In 1984 expected sales were about 5 million boxes or $40 million, with about $1.5 million in commissions. Shiploads had varied from 25,000 boxes to 110,000 (*Exhibit 2*).

Although Bananic's costs per box during the previous 20 months had ranged from $3.50 to $7.00 because of fluctuating volumes, total costs had remained stable in 1983 and had decreased in 1984. After subtracting from banana-sale revenues Pandol's commission and all ocean freight, insurance, wharfage, stevedoring, and truck-loading charges, Bananic's gross profit had always been positive.

"Dr. Martínez is very pleased," summarized Jack. "And I have never found a more agreeable arrangement. These are people I can work with. Two years ago, when I first met Wheelock (minister of agriculture), we talked for an hour and a half. He wanted to know what my thoughts were, no politics, only the problem at hand, how to do bananas better, what I thought about the future, what my suggestions were. Last year in July I had another meeting with him, and with Miguel D'Escoto (minister of foreign affairs); Martínez; Junta leader Daniel Ortega; and Commander Tirado (representing the labor organizations). This was when U.S. Navy fleets were coming toward Nicaragua; they were quite nervous. We talked for a couple of hours. They asked if I needed anything, if I had any suggestions. Whatever I asked, it was done. I said, 'If you need a water pump or a fungicide for the plantations, you need it now. You cannot have Embanac go through central planning and have some bureaucrat in Managua wait one week or six months to decide whether it is a priority.' So the directive came right from the junta: Embanac was authorized to do its own purchasing abroad."

INPUT SUPPLY OPERATIONS

When Standard pulled out of the plantations, the means of input supply (of parts, fertilizers, and pesticides) became tenuous. Nicaragua started to buy with letters of credit through purchasing agents, but it was very slow. Sometimes they were buying materials in Central America through traditional channels of supply for bananas that were centered in the Atlantic. While they had empty banana ships returning to Nicaragua, they had no one at the other end to coordinate purchasing and loading of the merchandise.

One time Embanac bought $250,000 of chemicals from Diamond Shamrock. The letter of credit was held up for weeks on such technicalities as the port of entry (specified by Embanac as Managua) having no access to the ocean. The bankers required the amendment of several forms which would have taken weeks, but Embanac needed the chemical right away. Diamond Shamrock asked Jack to guarantee the payment. Jack did, but said he would ask Bananic to reimburse him from the proceeds. He also asked Diamond Shamrock for a 5% discount, since he was paying cash. It accepted, and Jack then split it between Bananic and Pandol.

This was the principle by which Panagua was created in September 1983: a 50–50 corporate venture between Pandol and Nicaragua. Panagua would buy with cash from banana sales or with Pandol's credit in place of letters of credit. This would allow more rapid purchases with some leverage with the suppliers, since the credit was good. Panagua would retain a 4% commission on average, half to go to Nicaragua through its share ownership. Its 50% of the shares would be technically owned by a Nicaraguan trading company with operations in the United States. Nicaragua had three members on the Panagua board of directors; Pandol's three were Jack and Matt Pandol and Kiesel, Pandol's comptroller.

In 1984 the company bought about $10 million worth of banana cartons, fungicides, pesticides, irrigation supplies, plastic bags, files, welding equipment, etc. Sales could double in 1985 and grow much higher if Panagua could also act as fertilizer supplier for ENIA, the Nicaraguan state buyer of fertilizers and pesticides. "If we were to buy urea for ENIA," explained Larry Miller, Pandol's man responsible for running Panagua, "we could arrange purchase directly from Alaskan refineries. Though our margin might be only 1%, dollar volume would be in the tens of millions. But right now things are very slow because money is very tight for the Nicaraguans. But they may have a good year in cotton, and we could supply them with cotton harvesters, worth millions of dollars, with arrangements that they do not know how to make."

Larry pointed out some difficulties. To do these transactions, Pandol would have to cut a lot of red tape inside the government. Also, since all imports used foreign currency, the Foreign Currency Council had to approve each one, with all the delay and uncertainty that centralization implied. To avoid this, Bananic was the only state company authorized with Embanac to do its own purchasing abroad.

> Dr. Martínez is aware of the benefits for Nicaragua of this arrangement and often tells us the general needs of the ministry. We looked at 50 trucks for coffee, searched for refrigerated meat trucks, quoted fishing boats—all this representing millions of dollars, but Panagua's problem is that we lack lower-level ministry contacts to get needs specified in more detail and to determine the real priority of their desires. These searches could also take a lot of time and money at the expense of other activities for Panagua and Embanac, so getting a clear signal about what is wanted, the specifications, and the priority for the material is crucial.
>
> Another problem is that the players change so frequently in Nicaragua they don't have time to build expertise. For example, I don't think they appreciate how product's availability fluctuates with the seasons; there is also the sensitive area of the extent to which they need to secure financing. They remarked to me that they finally looked at new cotton harvesters because they were trying to get IMF or World Bank money and could get it only on new equipment. Or perhaps John Deere chose to finance them when new machines were not being sold. The problem is that we don't know for sure. Another problem is that most people at the Ministry of Foreign Trade and the Ministry of Agriculture don't know what Panagua is.
>
> One source of tension used to be the fact that until Panagua came along Embanac was the Nicaraguan trading company's best customer, but after a few months of our existence this trading company (our 50% stock owner) didn't get any more orders from Embanac. So we had to arrange a subcontract for some of our sales so they could get the commission needed to sustain their overhead.

Larry also explained the purchasing procedures:

> We negotiate a purchase as Pandol Brothers. When we agree on the price, we issue a Panagua purchase order, and Panagua takes title to

the goods and invoices Embanac. Panagua never writes purchase orders higher than what Pandol has in banana receivables, so we are always covered. If we have a big purchase coming up, Pandol holds payment of banana shipments to Bananic so we have enough for Panagua. In the end, Panagua pays its suppliers with Pandol's money, but Pandol gets its money from Bananic's banana sales. Technically we invoice Embanac, but actually Bananic is paid directly by Embanac. All Panagua does is keep its commissions.

Our invoices to Embanac are mailed to the U.S. office of the Nicaraguan trading company with an overnight delivery service; within two days of their reception, they are sent to Managua. But it sometimes takes more than three days to reach Embanac. Thus, the ship may arrive at Corinto before the invoice; it cannot be unloaded without the papers. To save time we invoice the approximate amount we think will be loaded on the ship. We hire a gang of labor at the Los Angeles pier for eight hours. After the bananas are discharged, the gang loads as much of Panagua's merchandise as they can within eight hours and leaves the rest for the next ship. We then telex Nicaragua what happened.

Sometimes we do not know what we actually loaded, because the ship arrived late and we could not hold it longer, since it has to be back the following Monday for banana sales. So we rush in anything we can grab and telex what we think is on the ship. We operate on a tremendous amount of trust and cooperation. I know they trust me because I know the kind of things they order. If they didn't trust me they would ask for a quote first, and the purchasing process would be three times as long.

PANADOL'S EVALUATION

Jack offered some final reflections on the operation:

Some newspaper articles criticized me for saying that the Nicaraguans were easy to work with and that their word is good. They said I had complimented a communist government. To us, they are neither communist nor capitalist. This is a commercial operation; I am not involved with them in politics. We try to do a professional job. Unfortunately, they have a lot of problems due to the war, and pressures have caused some problems at times with production. They would like to modernize the equipment. We think we can make a big improvement in drip irrigation and we know they want it.

They are very tense because of the relationship between Nicaragua and the U.S. government. For example, they could save 50¢ a box or about $2.5 million a year in shipping costs if they unloaded at Port

Hueneme near Santa Barbara, but they just wouldn't discuss it because there is a naval base there. That shows how sensitive they are about not antagonizing the U.S. government.

After one boat and then one year of selling bananas, they have signed an exclusive sales agreement for three years. Our commission is 28¢ per box in the first year, 30¢ during the second, and 32¢ in the third. If I steal, they can sue me and I could have problems, but if I simply do a poor job and sell bananas more cheaply than I should, there is nothing they could do about it. If they give the exclusive arrangement to somebody else, I can stop every single box that comes into the United States and take my commission on it without doing any other work. Yet they are willing to trust us.

I think the future will be better because they now recognize some of the faults, such as lack of water during their summer. We can help them remedy the irrigation problems and related quantity and quality problems. The government must decide whether they want to make that investment, because it is a bit expensive, but the net savings will be good for them. Early this summer they could probably have received a dollar more per box with irrigation and avoided the dead freight that is killing them. Since their contract with the shipping line guarantees minimum payload of 80,000 boxes per week, when they bring 40,000 in a vessel shipping costs per box jump from $1.75 to $3.50, and they lose $1.75 in freight plus $1.00 in lost revenues due to poor quality. We are talking about millions of dollars. This new irrigation on all 7,000 acres would cost $6 or $7 million, which they could pay back in a couple of years.

When we signed the new three-year contract, I told Martínez: "We are married now, for three years. Whatever I do to hurt you, you must believe that I am hurting myself. Whatever I do to help you, I do it to help myself. And vice versa." Our philosophy has always been: "Don't get nervous about competition. Just concentrate on performing well and getting customer satisfaction and repeat orders. Our goal is to do a top job for Bananic and to get another contract in 1987."

Exhibit 1 Banana Distribution Channels—West Coast

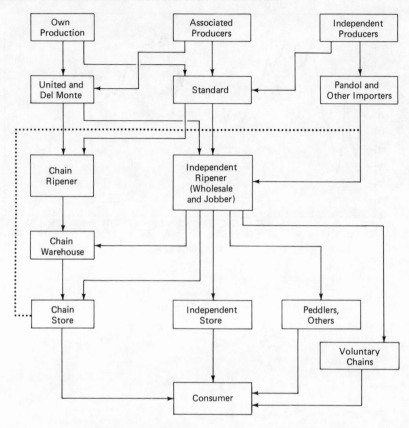

——— Traditional Channels (1960-1975)

········· New Channels (1975-1985)

Exhibit 2 Bananic Shipments, November 10, 1982 to July 16, 1984

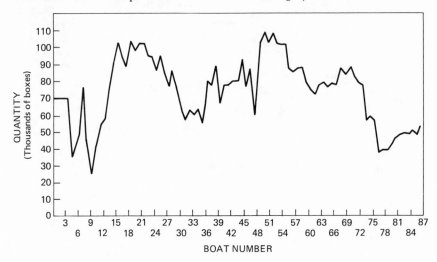

4

Production

The developing countries present demanding production environments. Input supplies that are taken for granted in more developed countries are often unreliable or deficient. For example, power failures are
common, local suppliers may lack the capability to produce up to required quality standards, imported materials may not be available because of foreign-exchange shortages or import restrictions. Production
operations in LDCs generally depend on technologies imported from the
more developed countries, and those technologies were not developed
with the LDC environmental constraints in mind. Therefore, a central
task in establishing and operating production systems in LDCs is managing the technology.

KEY ISSUES

The five cases in this chapter focus on technology and operations management issues. These include choosing the appropriate technology,
transferring it to the LDC, and operating it.[1]

Technology Choice

Choosing a production technology for the LDC production operation
involves a process of achieving a fit between the technology and key
aspects in the business setting. The key variables affecting the choice
include: relative factor costs (primarily labor versus capital so as to decide
among more or less labor-intensive options); market requirements (quality and quantity); technical constraints (such as for handling chemical
processes or hazardous or heavy materials, or for achieving physical accuracy); input scarcities (skilled labor, materials, energy, or equipment); and
competitive factors (such as rivals' actions or intensity and basis of compe-

tition). The chapter's first case, "Leather Industry in India," presents a proposed project to accelerate the production and export of India's leather goods. At issue are two basic technological alternatives, one being more labor-intensive and the other capital-intensive.

Technology Transfer

There are multiple mechanisms for transferring technology: FDI, licensing, technical services and training, equipment imports, and public information sources such as journals and conferences. By transmitting technical information, companies aim to increase human skills and knowledge. The more complex the technology, the greater are the skill and knowledge requirements. Through the transfer process, companies and countries can move up the "technological capability ladder," whereby their abilities increase from adopting technology, to adapting it to local conditions, to enhancing it through innovations, and on to creating new technologies. The second and third cases in the chapter provide an opportunity to examine several aspects of technology transfer. "Packages Limited" is a successful Pakistani producer of various packaging materials. The case first allows us to examine the technology transfer process from Sweden that enabled Packages to begin operations in Pakistan. Next, it presents us with a project proposal whereby Packages, having moved up the technological capability ladder, would be the transferer of its technology to a new joint venture in Zambia. In the "Thai Polyester Fiber" case we can analyze the multitude of problems encountered by two French firms involved in constructing and installing a $50-million polyester polymerization and filature plant in Thailand, in a joint venture with a major local business group.

Operations Management

Choosing and transferring technologies is only part of the production journey. The managers have to make the technologies work. This involves instituting and operating the management systems for inventories, quality control, scheduling, and logistics. Cutting across these tasks is the need to organize operations and manage personnel, which become more complicated in multinationals because of cross-cultural issues. The "Evans Food Corp." case presents the evolution of a Puerto Rican–based plastic container and bottling facility. It explores how the company dealt with cultural and other operations management issues in mounting a high-performing production system. The "Rio Bravo Electricos" case deals with General Motors' new Packard Electric Plant located on the Mexican border. At issue is how to organize the production units in the plant to achieve flexibility and efficiency in a way compatible with concerns of the local workforce.

CASE STUDY QUESTIONS

Leather Industry in India

1. What are the critical problems facing the leather industry's goal of increasing exports?
2. What are the strengths and weaknesses of the small-scale option and the integrated complex option?
3. Which alternative would you recommend?

Packages Limited

1. What were the key factors in the transfer of technology that enabled Packages to be started?
2. What are the most critical considerations for Packages' participation in the Zambian project?
3. What would you recommend to Packages' management?

Thai Polyester Fiber

1. How serious were the problems encountered in establishing the factory in Thailand?
2. Why did they occur? Could they have been avoided?
3. What should the French companies do? What should the Thai partner do?

Evans Food Corp.

1. What were the key factors that contributed to the strong productivity performance of the Puerto Rican operations?
2. What problems does instituting a Just-In-Time and new inventory management system cause?
3. What should the company do?

Rio Bravo Electricos, General Motors Corp.

1. Why did GM set up the Rio Bravo operations?
2. Why did it organize the production system in the way it did?
3. Should it change the existing structure and procedures? Why or why not?

NOTE

1. For an extended analysis of technology management issues, see James E. Austin, *Managing in Developing Countries* (New York: Free Press, 1990), Chapter 8.

Leather Industry in India

In 1978 the State Trading Corporation of the Government of India (GOI) was reviewing a strategy and program to accelerate development of India's leather industry. It was felt that Indian footwear and leather goods could obtain a part of the lucrative Western export market, provided leather quality and product design were improved. Outside experts had made two proposals to do this. The first involved setting up a few large integrated complexes; the second emphasized small-scale industries. The State Trading Corporation (STC), a public sector enterprise, would sponsor either alternative.

THE STATE TRADING CORPORATION

STC was incorporated as a fully owned public sector company in 1956 with paid-up capital of Rs.10 million. There were definite advantages for India and its business community to having trade in certain commodities and countries channeled through a centralized agency having government backing. STC's main purposes were to (1) overcome difficulties in expanding India's foreign trade, particularly with Eastern European and other communist countries; (2) explore new markets for traditional exports and develop new export products; (3) undertake import and internal distribution of scarce commodities to stabilize their prices; (4) arrange for bulk imports of commodities where demand exceeded internal supply; and (5) supplement private trading.

In its early years, STC found it difficult to clarify its objectives and scope of activities. GOI allotted specific commodities and areas to STC for only certain types of trading operations; it gave specific instructions for every detail of these operations. This hindered managerial development and the initiative of its officials. STC had seven commodity divisions (Agricultural Products, Chemical Products, Leather Products, Consumer Products, Engineering Products, Railway Equipment, and Export Assistance to Small Industries) and three service divisions (Administrative,

This case was prepared by Professor James E. Austin as a basis for class discussion rather than to illustrate either effective or ineffective handling of an administrative situation. Abridged with permission.

Finance and Accounts, and Economics). The product divisions handled
all work concerning their products. Coordination in different areas (e.g.,
experience in negotiating with country or customer, interdependence of
products in two or more product groups) was via notes, memoranda, and
frequent meetings between senior officers. The setup was identical in
each product division: A general manager was assisted by divisional managers, joint divisional managers, deputy divisional managers, and assistant divisional managers. All issues went through this hierarchy. A
full-time chairman and the directors (often nominated by different ministries) were the principal officers of STC.

In the late 1960s GOI appointed a committee to review the working of
STC; it recommended structural reorganization, more delegation of authority, and reevaluation of relationship boundaries between STC and
the ministries. Some of these recommendations were implemented. STC
officials well understood that it was not a department of GOI and did not
enjoy special privileges. But as GOI held its entire capital, it was account-
able to Parliament and administratively controlled by the Ministry of
Commerce.

Export Promotion by STC

As a *marketing agency,* STC had tried over the years to introduce new items
of Indian manufacture in world markets. Possible new markets included
Hungary and the USSR for woolen fabrics, textiles, tea, coffee, and leather
goods; Turkey and the German Democratic Republic for sewing machines, cycles, fans, and other appliances; Bulgaria, Poland, and Czechoslovakia for warm clothes and winter shoes; and North Korea for
chemicals. STC also tried to export items difficult to move because of the
disparity between domestic and international prices; it did this even at a
loss to earn foreign exchange on these commodities.

STC also provided *technical assistance* to small- and medium-scale industries to develop their export potential. For some years it promoted export
aid for small industries, which fostered direct business relationships in
export marketing between small Indian manufacturers and foreign importers and helped manufacturers explore markets, price products, design packaging, prepare sales literature, and establish credit facilities. A
large variety of products manufactured by small-scale industries was thus
made acceptable to overseas buyers.

In 1978 STC maintained foreign offices and regional ones in major
Indian cities. Its trading activities had expanded rapidly during previous
years; in 1975–76 about 17% of Indian exports were channeled through
STC. GOI named STC the conduit agency for several commodities, including semifinished leather and footwear.

DESCRIPTION OF THE LEATHER INDUSTRY

There were six steps in leather processing: (1) flaying—the dead animal's skin is removed; (2) tanning—the hide is cleaned and cured; (3) finishing—the tanned leather is trimmed and its surface prepared for a particular type of end product; (4) designing—product styles are developed to meet market needs and appropriate patterns are cut; (5) making—the finished leather is converted following the patterns into a semifinished or finished product; (6) marketing—the product is distributed in local or international markets.

Raw Material Processing

India boasted one of the world's largest livestock populations: About 12.5% of world livestock is there. But annual recovery rates for cow and buffalo hides were low (about 11% and 16%) because of low recovery rates from fallen animals and lack of meat-processing industries. Cattle were kept for their milk and dung but not eaten, owing to religious restrictions. Raw animal hides were considered "unclean" and were not touched by high-caste members; flaying was done by persons outside the social hierarchy. Recovery rates for goat and sheep skins were higher and closer to world averages of about 60% and 42%. Indian goat and sheep skins were of high quality, though smaller than in other countries; buffalo hides were coarse and water absorbent; cowhides were mostly from fallen animals and of inferior quality due to old age, disease, and poor flaying. Working usually in pairs, flayers moved from village to village. No state accounted for more than 12% of total flayings.

Hides passed through several layers of the traditional system of middlemen; flayers received no differential price for higher-quality hides. Because the animals were evenly distributed over the country, while most tanneries were in Calcutta and Madras, hides were transported long distances. Thus, a substantial deterioration in quality due to putrefaction in a hot and humid climate led to a loss in value of about 15–20%.

The leather industry was regionally dispersed. Tanning and leather-finishing were around Calcutta (east) and Madras (south). Manufacturing operations were at Agra (central) for footwear; Calcutta, Bombay (west), and Madras for leather goods; Meerut and Jullundur (north) for sports goods; and at Kanpur (central) for harnesses and boots. Transporting finished leather to production centers was costly, unreliable, and hindered by inadequate, time-consuming, long-distance communication, preventing proper coordination between suppliers and users.

About 96.8 million hides from all sources would be available for flaying in 1978–79. Total tanning capacity was about 120 million hides per year.

Calcutta accounted for 30% of this with 6 large and 200 small tanneries; Madras accounted for 60% with 5 large and more than 400 small tanneries. Twenty-three large plants (combined capacity: 41 million hides) produced most finished leather; government policy encouraged establishment of additional finishing capacity. By the end of 1978, total annual finishing capacity was expected to reach 50 million hides, about 50% of those annually available.

An industry analyst said of the problem of obtaining quality processed leather:

> Flayers often find their carcasses as abandoned, fallen animals that might have been dead for quite a few days. With no organized meat-packing industry, there is almost no coordination between leather users and their sources. Flayers dry, dehair, and treat the hides with simple preservatives and sell to middlemen in bulk. Wastage is large, as much as 50% due to flaying damage. There are very few mechanized tanning units. Most tanning is done at small tanneries that lack finishing equipment. Finishing is the most capital-intensive of the three processes; a finishing unit of the minimum economic size to produce export-quality finished leather would require an investment of Rs.1 million. Existing tanneries and finishing units lack equipment; as a result the finished leather is consistently of poor quality. Of course, the few large, fully integrated manufacturers (including Bata company) don't have this problem, but most small-scale manufacturers do.

The Finished Product: Footwear

The footwear industry annually produced about 200 million shoes and uppers (the top part of the shoe, excluding the sole), of which about 10 million were exported. Agra produced about 80% of all shoes and exported 1.5 million parts. Medium- and large-scale manufacturers elsewhere produced the remaining 20% and exported about 8.5 million pairs.

Agra had 3,000 footwear units, all small-scale, employing 50,000 craftsmen and 40,000 family members. A 1975 survey placed these units in three categories:

1. *Organized units.* Partially mechanized, they produced about 100 pairs a day and employed 50–100 workers. Of 359 such units, 25 were mechanized and produced for export mostly through STC, 275 were partially mechanized and produced less than 100 pairs a day mostly for export, and 59 manufactured on government orders for large-scale local distributors

and producers. (Large-scale shoe manufacturers subcontracted most of their production to small units.)

2. *Namewallas.* The 547 of these informal groups shared common equipment and produced 50–100 pairs a day with 20–40 workers, filling local orders or selling through agents.

3. *Family units.* These produced 20–50 pairs a day of mostly low-quality footwear and employed 5–10 workers. They numbered about 2,000.

With mostly manual operating methods and a few simple machines for stitching, cutting, and so on, capacity was a fluid concept. Capacity utilization dropped to 30% in the rainy season, when unemployment could rise to half the labor force. Only about 10% of the requirements of leather and other inputs (eyelets, laces, rubber sheets, etc.) were met by local production in Agra. The five Agra tanneries could supply only a small part of the required leather. Much leather came from Calcutta and Madras and was unsuitable for high-quality footwear. Because of long distances and unreliable transportation, delivery schedules and exact specifications were difficult to meet.

Faced with middlemen who bought at the lowest possible price without their own financial resources, small-scale units had neither ability nor incentive to use good-quality leather for high-quality shoes. Even the organized sector tended not to plough profits back into business; it had not modernized or grown in the previous ten years. Thus, the industry was not optimally adapted to the exigencies of export production in quantity, quality, and uniformity.

STC played a significant role in organizing production at Agra and marketing its shoes. It allocated export orders to 300 Agra units. In addition, some merchant exporters procured shoes from the small-scale units for supply to STC. Most of the shoes went to countries in Eastern Europe, but uppers were increasingly exported to the West.

The Finished Product: Leather Goods

India produced leather goods for consumers (travel kits, wallets, purses, gloves, harnesses) and industries. Like footwear, this sector had a few large manufacturers and a large number of tiny units. Total annual production was about Rs.200–300 million ($1 = about Rs.9), of which about a quarter was exported.

Calcutta produced about 80% of the leather goods and a higher percentage of total exports. About 150 organized units used decentralized production methods: 10,000 employees mostly working at home in small subcontracting groups. Other areas of concentration included Bombay,

Meerut, and Kanpur. Most units used manual methods; the units outside Calcutta were very small, and few of them had exporting experience.

THE EXPORT OF LEATHER GOODS FROM INDIA

In 1972 GOI began a plan to shift exports from semiprocessed leather to finished leather and leather goods during the Fourth Plan. Policy measures included: a quota system gradually reducing export of semifinished leather; and export duty on semifinished leather; and subsidies for export of finished leather and leather products. GOI later introduced additional incentives for exporters of finished leather and leather products: duty drawbacks (whereby an exporter was refunded duties paid on imported materials and machinery used to manufacture the exports), import replenishment licenses (whereby an importer was allowed to import certain kinds of goods equal to 10% of the value of goods exported), cash compensatory support (whereby GOI paid an exporter a sum of money equal to 5–10% of the value of goods exported), and air-freight subsidies. As a result of these policies, semifinished leather exports fell from Rs.1.9 billion in 1974 to Rs.380 million in 1978, while finished leather exports rose from Rs.6 million to Rs.1.5 billion, and leather footwear from Rs.180 million to Rs.1.5 billion.

The Export Markets

India's footwear export of about 10 million pairs per year in 1978 represented only about 1% of world trade volume. Exports to Eastern Europe were about 4 million pairs; the rest went to North America and Western Europe. Men's conventional shoes and shoe uppers were exported mainly to Eastern Europe; sandals and cowboy boot uppers were the major items for Western markets.

STC, State Leather Development Corporations, and the Central Leather Research Institute gave technical, financial, and marketing assistance to small-scale entrepreneurs. STC's assistance program to small-scale producers mainly in footwear was to develop exports. But most of STC's exports were in barter trade agreements to East European countries, where quality standards were less rigid and prices were lower than in the West. The growth potential of Indian exports to these markets appeared small.

Larger producers motivated by GOI's export incentives appeared prepared in 1978 to increase their small export volume to the promising

Western markets. Several footwear and components plants (one with production capacity of 800,000 pairs a year) and a number of plants making consumer leather goods were being established in the private sector for export production.

Footwear consumption in Western OECD countries was growing at about 2% per year or 50 million pairs yearly. Use of footwear with leather uppers increased at a lower rate than use of other footwear, but in 1975 leather seemed back in favor, partly because of the steep price rise of petroleum-derived plastics. The annual increase in leather footwear was 15 million pairs. Footwear production in most OECD countries except Italy was declining. STC officials were particularly interested in the relevance to India of Italy's export experience (see the *Appendix*). Imports from non-OECD countries, mainly Latin America and East Asia, were also rising rapidly. Imports of footwear with leather uppers from non-OECD countries rose from 74 million pairs in 1973 to 89 million pairs in 1974. Footwear prices appeared to increase at a rate exceeding the average consumer price rises in OECD countries. Imports, where cheaper, perhaps had a competitive advantage over domestic production.

Some industry observers believed it advisable for newcomers to this market to concentrate on medium- and high-priced products since the rapid, continuing increase in rubber, plastic, or canvas substitutes seemed to affect only the low-price market, where competition from other exporting LDCs was more pressing. Over the years India had been slow to use synthetic fibers in soles and linings in footwear.

One market test tentatively concluded that the quality of Indian finished leather was not yet acceptable in discriminating Western markets. Nonetheless, demand for handmade shoes was strong, provided good finished leather could be produced; long-term prospects were good for the export of leather uppers. In 1978 India had a price edge on competitors for its export of leather garments; some importers were impressed with the leather and workmanship but critical of design, fit, sizes, and late deliveries. Demand was strong for handbags, travel goods, and small leather goods, provided the quality and finish of "furniture" (locks, hinges, zippers, handles) were improved. There was much demand for footballs, particularly in high-quality markets. Prospects for sandals, slippers, harnesses, saddlery, and industrial gloves were good, and Indian quality standards in 1978 for these goods were acceptable.

In recent years STC had established programs of technical and financial assistance to small-scale producers channeling exports through STC. Apart from acquiring bulk export orders, this assistance included providing raw materials, quality control, and post-shipment credit. Furthermore, small-scale industries (SSIs) were provided with samples, designs, and access to a test laboratory at STC headquarters.

PROJECT PROPOSALS FOR THE LEATHER INDUSTRY

Outside consultants had recently suggested two different proposals to GOI to strengthen the leather commodity system for exports: (1) to establish six large, integrated complexes to produce footwear and leather goods for export; or (2) to develop the small-scale sector. The STC was to be the implementing agency in either case.

Integrated Production Complexes

Six integrated production complexes for footwear and leather goods manufacture would be set up at Agra, Jullundur, Bombay, Calcutta, Kanput, and Madras. Raw material supply (mainly semifinished leather) was not a factor determining these locations, because transport of semifinished leather was cheap (about 1% of value). The main requisite for a location was availability of suitable traditional labor with low mobility.

A production complex would consist of different production modules covering each stage from finishing to designing and making. Thus problems of the quality of raw material and finished product would be solved. Each module would be a production unit of an administratively and technically optimal size. This size would be determined using the experience of the West's capital-intensive methods and the mass-production technologies in labor-abundant Asia. (Details of Agra's production complex are given in *Exhibit 1;* a summary of the impact of all six complexes is in *Exhibit 2.*)

Production components. The Agra production complex would specialize in manufacturing high-quality men's shoes and shoe uppers. A materials flow chart for the complex is in *Exhibit 3.* The units making up the integrated complex were:

1. A light leather finishing plant for processing semifinished goat and buffalo calf leather
2. A tannery to produce sole and inside leather from cowhides to be fully absorbed in the local production complex
3. A plant producing a million pairs each of soles, heels, and inner soles
4. A plant producing 2 million pairs of goat and buffalo-calf uppers a year. The plant would have modern equipment to obtain necessary product standardization and quality and save raw material during cutting, but no automated equipment would be used merely to economize on labor.
5. A plant to manufacture a million pairs of men's shoes from uppers

and soles made in the complex. The shoes would be hand-lasted and hand-sewn. An attached shoe-finishing unit would have equipment for cleaning and finishing shoes before packaging.

6. A factory producing 50,000 pairs of lasts of high-impact polystyrene for use in the complex and for sale in the domestic market. (Lasts are models of a human foot on which boots or shoes are shaped or repaired.) The requirement for lasts in the complex would depend on the number of models produced, frequency of model change, and type of production process; demand for lasts in India was high and would easily absorb excess production.

7. Ancillary units serving the needs of other complexes: a laboratory and testing installation, a pattern-making and pattern-grading unit, a knife-making plant

8. Buildings and common facilities on 32 acres, which would include some room for expansion

Complexes suggested for Bombay, Calcutta, Jullundur, Kanpur, and Madras would have similar facilities and output, except for product lines specific to certain places.

Organization. Experts suggested that each complex be an established corporation. STC (as agent of GOI) and private investors could hold shares and own the corporation in proportion to their equity participation. Each corporation would lease production facilities to participating private investors.

STC's Leather Division would prepare feasibility studies for the six complexes and design and establish them. STC would select participating entrepreneurs, provide key management, and establish efficient operations. It would later exercise control as a large shareholder, but private investors would become ever more responsible for overall operations. STC would be responsible for initial detailed marketing investigation and later for all marketing. The Leather Division already marketed current exports, but this would have to be systematized, especially market research and strategy planning.

Each complex would have its own board of directors; representation and voting power on the board would be determined by equity participation. The board would be responsible for selection and control of participating entrepreneurs. The board would also establish regulations for profit-sharing, transfer-pricing, and standard costing. Management of a complex would be responsible for daily operations, production planning, site administration, raw material purchasing, training, and quality control.

All production would be managed by private entrepreneurs and lessees, whose main function would be operating specific production lines. Basically, two categories of entrepreneurs were required. One would operate small units producing, say, shoe uppers/footballs. Recruited from the small-scale sector, they would be qualified craftsmen with a moderate degree of managerial capability. Their financial burden would be rather light, for their equity financing requirements were small. The second kind of entrepreneur, for leather tanning and finishing units, would be experienced in operating a plant of comparable size and able to finance an appropriate part of the total investment involved.

Each complex's profit would be shared among the participants, STC, and private investors, in proportion to equity shares held. The transfer-pricing problem would be dealt with in each complex. A start could be made with standard costs for determining transfer prices, which would be reviewed periodically. As capacities of the production units in the complexes were balanced, regulations would have to be developed to control unplanned external sales and purchases of intermediate products, which would disrupt production and marketing.

Finance. The consolidated capital investment was estimated at US$80.1 million (see *Exhibit 4*). Consultants believed that the project's debt-equity ratio should not be higher than 60:40. Initially STC would acquire most of the share capital, financing more than 50% of project cost. Share capital could later be transferred from STC to private entrepreneurs, perhaps reducing STC's participation to under 50% of capital. Each entrepreneur's financial participation would be related to the size of the plant leased and operated. Financial requirements for the participants would be:

	Amount (US$ million)			Percent of Total Cost
	Equity	*Debt*	*Total*	
STC	28	—	28	35%
Entrepreneurs	4	3	7	9%
Banks (Central Govt.)	—	45	45	56%
Total	32	48	80	100%

Economic aspects. No detailed financial or economic analysis of the project had been performed by 1978; a comparison of estimated unit production cost and f.o.b. prices, however, indicated that the project would be economically viable (see *Exhibit 5*). A prefeasibility analysis estimated a 15% internal rate of return after taxes, with a positive cash flow from the second year on. Total gross annual export earnings at full capacity production were estimated at US$60 million in 1976 prices. Foreign-exchange operating costs would be US$18 million, giving annual net foreign-exchange earnings of more than US$40 million.

Small-Scale Industries

The second proposal was to develop certain small-scale leather industries for exports. Footwear production would be at Agra; other leather goods would be at Calcutta. This was to take advantage of the strengths of the region's SSIs in different product lines.

Quality finished leather was important. Rather than depend on existing production channels for this, STC was to own and manage leather-finishing facilities at Agra and Calcutta, after entering into technical contracts with foreign firms to gain know-how. Locating these facilities near manufacturers would expedite orders for specific sizes, colors, and widths.

Finishing was the only stage of the raw material system to require capital-intensive methods. An SSI producing finished leather of export quality would require investment of $6.8 million for each footwear and leather-goods component. Thus, total investment in finished leather capacity would be $13.6 million, and total employment generated would be about 700. Capital-intensive finishing facilities would also help improve tanning quality. STC would establish contracts with small-scale tanners, provided they selectively modernized their equipment and processing and chose hides more carefully.

Manufacturing. The suggested strategy was:

1. Select the best organized SSIs in Agra with at least 15 workers, reliable management, competent craftsmen, positive experience exporting and/or filling regular domestic orders, and at least partially mechanized (At first, units would be chosen from the 300 SSIs already exporting through STC; later units would be from another 900 SSIs with over 15 workers. Coverage would be gradually increased over four years.)
2. Provide financial and technical assistance to participating SSIs on selective improvements in equipment and technology
3. Develop a tight STC marketing organization to get large export orders, distribute them among associated SSIs, forecast fashion trends, adapt designs, collect and ship shoes, and supervise quality control and delivery
4. Improve quality of raw materials used by participating SSIs

Exhibit 6 indicates the gradual growth in SSIs covered by the footwear part of this project and the impact on production, employment, and exports over four years.

For an SSI producing 200 pairs a day, interest and depreciation charges would be US$5,000 a year; raw material costs would be about US$3 per pair of shoes. The average wage for a skilled laborer in the footwear industry was about US$100 a month.

The leather goods part of the project had a strategy parallel to that described for footwear. The projected SSI participation and the impact on production, employment, and exports are in *Exhibit 7*.

Organization. STC's responsibility for overall management and coordination of the project's footwear and leather goods parts would include (1) obtaining export orders; (2) contracting with SSIs; (3) (assuming that State Leather Development Corporations and/or STC provided technical assistance on processes and equipment), bulk raw-material purchasing and resale and organizing common service facilities; and (4) arranging bank financing for the SSIs. STC would own and manage the leather-finishing facilities.

Finance. Total investment would be about US$61 million for four years. Projected investment by components and product lines is in *Exhibit 8*.

THE STRATEGY REVIEW

In delineating its strategy, STC management decided to review carefully the implications of the industry's structure and the demands of the export market. It was particularly concerned about weighing the pros and cons of the two proposals with their alternative technologies.

APPENDIX
LEATHER INDUSTRY IN INDIA

ITALIAN FOOTWEAR EXPORT INDUSTRY

Italy had a large base of highly skilled footwear and leather-goods craftsmen organized in small-scale production units. It had become the major exporter of medium- and high-quality leather footwear by building on this SSI base: Over 95% of all footwear firms had fewer than 20. About 7,245 units with 125,000 workers produced 365 million pairs of shoes annually, 75% with leather uppers. In leather footwear, the average production unit had 18 workers each producing 10 pairs daily. Most units were involved in exports; over 65% of all shoes manufactured in Italy were exported.

Family units were predominant. Much of Italy's production of shoes and leather goods was based on centralized cutting, with decentralized networks of SSIs assembling shoes, sold under a single brand. Some networks had as many as 500 decentralized subcontracting units.

LEATHER INDUSTRY IN INDIA

Exhibit 1

Agra Integrated Complex

Production Unit	Capital Cost (US$ 000s)			Annual Production	No. of Shifts	Employment	Investment per Job (US$)
	LC	FE	Total				
Lasts making	143	199	342	50,000 pairs	1	56	6,100
Sole leather tanning	1,809	2,754	4,563	1,000 tons	2	117	39,000
Leather finishing	3,970	4,136	8,106	8 million sq. ft. of skins and hides	2	351	23,000
Soles and heels	212	305	517	1 million pairs	2	69	7,500
Upper making	2,003	602	2,605	2 million pairs	2	423	6,200
Shoemaking	910	9	919	1 million pairs	2	766	1,200
Shoe finishing	2,429	89	2,518	1 million pairs	2	84	30,000
Operations totals	11,476	8,094	19,570			1,866	10,500
Common facilities and offices	1,960	—	1,960			187	—
Land (32 acres)	192	—	192				
Land development	320	—	320				
Total complex	13,948	8,094	22,042			2,053	10,700

Exhibit 2
Summary for the Six Complexes

| | Capital Cost (US$ 000s) | | | | Investment per Job |
	Local	Foreign	Total	Employment	(US $)
Agra	13,948	8,094	22,042	2,053	10,700
Bombay	7,564	4,374	11,938	1,299	9,200
Calcutta	6,234	3,986	10,220	805	12,700
Jullundar	7,419	4,273	11,692	1,034	11,300
Kanpur	7,713	4,364	12,077	1,368	8,800
Madras	7,564	4,374	11,938	1,299	9,200
	50,442	29,465	79,907	7,858	

Output	
Men's shoes	1 million pairs
Shoe uppers	2,250,000 pairs
Slippers	750,000 pairs
Sandals	750,000 pairs
Travel goods	150,000
Handbags	625,000
Small leather goods	2,500,000
Leather garments	150,000
Industrial gloves	1,250,000
Footballs	125,000
Saddlery and harness	1,200 sets

Exhibit 3 Agra Materials Flow Chart

Materials Flow Chart

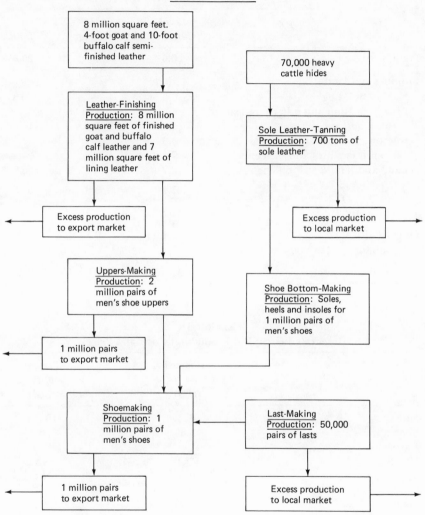

Exhibit 4
Total Capital Costs for Integrated Complex (all units)
(US$ million)

	Local Currency	Foreign Exchange	Total
Equipment	6.6	14.0	20.6
Building and land			
Factory building	6.3	—	6.3
Price escalation and other physical contingencies	5.6	5.8	11.4
Interest cost during construction	3.9	4.0	7.9
Common facilities and offices	7.1	—	7.1
Land and land development	2.2	—	2.2
Total	25.1	9.8	34.9
Working capital	17.7	5.3	23.0
Organizational costs (training)	1.1	0.5	1.6
Total costs	50.5	29.6	80.1

Exhibit 5
Integrated Complex: Production Costs and Prices

	Estimated Production Cost (US$)	Present f.o.b. Price (US$)
Shoes	8	15–18
Shoe uppers	3.60	6
Garments	47	45–50
Handbags	7	NA
Travel goods	9	NA
Sandals and slippers	5	6–7
Footballs	5.4	6–7
Harness and saddlery	90	120
Small leather goods	1.1	NA

NA = not available.

Exhibit 6

Projected Participation by SSIs in Agra in Footware Export Scheme

	Year 1	*Year 2*	*Year 3*	*Year 4*
No. units[a]	100	180	320	450
No. workers[b]	2,500	4,680	8,640	12,600
No. shoes/worker/per day[c]	5	6	7	8
Annual shoe production (million pairs)	3.1	7.0	15.1	25.2
Annual incremental exports (mil. pairs)	1	3	7	10
Export earnings (US$ million)	4.5	15.0	38.5	60.0
Incremental employment[d]	1,000	1,300	2,900	3,800
Total employment creation by yr. 4				9,000
No. extension workers[e]	6	10	18	28
Exports as % OECD market	0.1%	0.3%	0.7%	1.0%
Exports as % of India's present exports	10%	35%	60%	80%

[a]At first many units would be selected from 300 SSIs with some experience exporting through STC; in 1978 these units exported 1.5 million pairs of shoes and uppers or an average of 5,000 pairs per unit a year. The project would expand production of export-quality shoes by participating units to at least half of a larger production base, e.g., in year 1 an average of 31,500 pairs per participating SSI, since average employment would move to 25 workers and average daily shoe production from 3.5 to at least 5 pairs per worker; in later years productivity and employment would be expected to increase to an average of 8 pairs a day in year 4.

[b]Average number of workers was to increase from 20 workers in 1978 in organized units to 25 in year 1 and to 30 in year 3. Some SSIs would also turn out orders, expanding considerably their on-site production capacity.

[c]Detailed cost comparisons are needed to determine at what productivity level labor-intensive Indian SSIs are competitive with OECD and Latin American competitors in the medium- to high-quality market.

[d]Incremental employment based on the expansion of participating units; in addition to expanding employment, the project would include significant income increases among the 12,600 participating workers.

[e]Extension workers would provide assistance in the areas of management and organization.

Exhibit 7

Projected Participation by Organized SSIs and Groups
in Leather-Goods Export Scheme

	Year 1	Year 2	Year 3	Year 4
No. participating SSI units:[a] total	40	55	87	134
in Calcutta	20	35	45	60
in Kanpur	10	20	18	30
in Meerut	—	—	14	24
in Bombay	—	—	10	20
No. workers	1,600	2,310	3,697	6,030
Production				
Small leather goods				
No. items/worker (daily)	20	24	28	40
Average no. workers/SSI unit	45	48	50	45
Annual production (million items)[b]	5.7	11.1	18.3	36.2
Annual production (US$ millions)[c]	8.5	13.8	30.9	61.8
Exports (million items)	1.7	2.7	7.3	16.3
Exports ($ millions)	2.9	4.9	13.9	30.0
Incremental export earnings	1.6	3.0	8.0	20.0
Incremental employment	350	450	835	1,235
Handbags				
No. items/worker (daily)	4	5	6	8
Average no. workers/SSI unit	33	34	35	32
Annual production (million bags)	0.8	1.0	2.4	4.8
Annual production (US$ millions)[d]	6.6	8.9	23.0	51.1
Exports (million bags)	0.34	0.36	1.0	2.6
Exports ($ millions)	3.4	3.6	10.6	31.7
Incremental export earnings (US$ millions)	2.0	2.0	8.0	25.0
Incremental employment	350	430	600	980
Total				
Value production ($ millions)	15.1	22.7	53.9	112.9
Value exports	6.3	8.5	24.5	61.7

[a]One SSI unit in leather goods may consist of a single unit of about 30–40 workers (economic size for autonomous SSI) or larger associations of smaller producers with joint investments or reciprocal arrangements for bottleneck investments. In both cases, fixed investment would be US$25,000–50,000 depending upon equipment vs. manual choices. Decentralized units would tend to be more labor-intensive, with painting and other operations more likely to be done manually.

[b]About 60% of SSIs' workers would be in small leather goods, about 40% in handbags.

[c]Estimate $1 item cost, $1.40 selling price, and $1.70 for exports (factory price).

[d]Local factory sale price at $8, factory price for exports $10; export as percentage expected to develop as with small leather goods: 30%, 35%, 45%, and 55%.

Exhibit 8
Capital Cost for Small-Scale Industry Project
(US$ millions)

	Local	*Foreign*	*Total*
Footwear component			
Equipment			
Modernization	3.60	2.20	5.80
Upgrading facilities	0.30	—	0.30
Subtotal	3.90	2.20	6.10
Buildings	0.62	0.26	0.88
Working capital	10.20	1.80	12.00
Organization			
Salaries, STC Exports Division	0.30	1.20	1.50
Technical assistance, etc.	0.20	—	0.20
Subtotal	0.50	1.20	1.70
Total	15.22	5.46	20.68
Leather-goods component			
Equipment (single units and cottage units)	4.50	5.40	9.90
Buildings	0.30	—	0.30
Working Capital			
Single units	7.30	0.90	8.20
Cottage units	2.90	0.40	3.30
Subtotal	10.2	1.30	11.5
Organization			
STC leather-goods unit	0.10	—	0.10
Technical assistance	0.20	—	0.20
Subtotal	0.30	—	0.30
Total	15.30	6.70	22.00
Finishing/tanning facility	Local Currency		
Equipment	10.20		
Buildings	8.00		
Total	18.20		

Packages Limited

In September 1974 Babar Ali, managing director, and Tariq Hamid, general manager, of Packages Limited (Pakistan) were considering a new, somewhat bold twist to their overseas activities. Packages was by no means a mature multinational. It had neither an overseas network of manufacturing and sales subsidiaries nor an export business large enough to warrant an international division. In existence for some five years, Packages' foreign business included a small, steady flow of exports to the Middle East and a couple of management contracts in Indonesia and Tanzania. To date, the firm had no foreign direct investment to its credit. Nevertheless, the combination of Packages' part-Swedish heritage and Babar Ali, the colorful, well-known Pakistani at its helm, gave it the makings of a potentially tough competitor. Ali founded the company in 1956 and had only recently relinquished daily operating control to take on the chairmanship of Pakistan's state-owned National Fertilizer Corporation.

At the urging of the International Finance Corporation (IFC) of the World Bank, E. G. Kasonde, a Zambian entrepreneur and chairman of Century Holdings Limited (Zambia), invited Packages to set up a joint venture to manufacture packaging materials in Zambia. Kasonde had originally asked the IFC to finance a paper mill. The IFC recommended the packaging industry instead and Packages as a potential collaborator. Century Holdings was a relatively large Zambia-based conglomerate with interests in a variety of industries such as textiles, construction, and transportation. But it had no prior experience in the manufacture of either paper and board or packaging materials.

Although Ali and Hamid were interested in diversifying their geographic base and investing in longer-term projects abroad, the decision involved important strategic and other considerations. For a company somewhat dependent on short-term fees and exports for its foreign earnings, the Zambian venture represented a shift to equity and longer-term returns. For a company devoid of the capital resources common to large Western-based multinationals, its equity share would depend mainly on the value placed on its technical and manpower skills. Furthermore, it

This case was prepared by Carlos Cordeiro, Research Assistant, under the direction of Professor Louis T. Wells, Jr. as the basis for class discussion rather than to illustrate either effective or ineffective handling of an administrative situation. Abridged with permission.

required Packages to commit its valuable human resources to a project outside the confines of Lahore and the home country. And for any company just eighteen years in existence and from a developing country, the decision might mark a major turning point in its own evolution.

COMPANY HISTORY

Packages Limited was founded in 1956 in Lahore, Pakistan. Ali, twenty-eight at the time, was a striving entrepreneur from one of Pakistan's leading families, which have been major forces in commerce and industry since the British took over the country more than a century ago. The Ali family had been associated with many businesses. They operated Ford's only auto-assembly plant in Pakistan until its nationalization by the Bhutto government in 1973 and had participated with Lever Brothers (Pakistan) in a joint venture since 1945. The group's Wazir Ali Industries had been a dominant force in the vegetable oil and soap industries since independence in 1947. And they were also involved in the textile and razor blade industries.

On a visit to Sweden in 1954, Ali had approached A. B. Akerlund & Rausing, a leading Swedish packaging firm, on the possibility of its joining him in Pakistan to manufacture an assortment of packaging materials. It had been recommended to him by the Pakistan Tobacco Company (PTC), a subsidiary of the British American Tobacco Company (BAT) in Pakistan, as a reliable firm eager to expand its overseas business. Ali's original objective was to secure a relatively safe, cheap local source of paper, cardboard, cellophane, and plastic film packaging for the family group, particularly the razor blade business. Like PTC, the Ali group was almost entirely dependent on foreign sources for its packaging needs. It took almost two years for the Pakistani government to grant permission for the proposed venture; construction of the plant began in late 1956.

At the outset, the Swedes were offered 22.69% equity participation, the remaining 77.31% going to the Ali family. The Swedish share was given in exchange for technical and managerial assistance and for the imported European machinery required for startup. A contract for continued technical assistance (for solving technical problems and for manpower training) gave the Swedes an additional $35,000 for each year through 1976. A total of 22 Swedes stayed on during the first three years of operation. By 1974 Akerlund & Rausing's share was down to 14%, its equity position diluted by new shares issued to raise fresh capital since 1965. *Exhibit 1* lists the company's major shareholdings.

On most accounts, Packages fared extremely well (see *Exhibit 2*). By 1960 an additional shift was added, and in 1964 output volume was double that in 1957. While PTC accounted for some 80% of Packages' business in its first year of operation, by 1974 that figure had been reduced to 12%. Total sales had grown by 15% annually since 1968; by 1974 sales were at Rs.150 million.[1] And none of the original 22 Swedes were still in Pakistan, since local Pakistanis had been trained over the years.

According to several managers at Packages, much of this early success could be attributed to Ali himself. A good administrator, he developed a very paternalistic and loyal organization. As was typical in Pakistan, senior managers were all home-grown. The practice was to hire young college graduates intent on making permanent careers at Packages. Some 90% of these new hires had never worked for another company. Evidence of this recruiting policy may be seen in the company's managerial hierarchy. Both Hamid and the deputy general manager, Javed Aslam, had been hired directly from Lahore University and had worked their way up to their current positions. Besides providing his employees ample opportunities within the firm, Ali regularly sent managers to Sweden for three months of training. While abroad the managers were given on-the-job training and also had a chance to broaden their skills.

In 1965 Packages went public because of financial pressures from expansion. It raised Rs.6 million from the general public and state sources. The IFC also took a 13% equity share for Rs.4 million. In 1965 the Ali family maintained some 47% of the company's common stock; by 1974 its share was just under 30%. Soon after the firm went public, it integrated backward by constructing its own pulp, paper, and board mill.

PRODUCT LINE AND TECHNOLOGY

By 1974 Packages offered a broad line of packaging products and operated its own paper mill. The Packaging Division produced a variety of offset and flexo printed cartons, wrappers, and labels from cardboard, paper, cellophane, and plastic film, and transport and corrugated containers and boxes. Production was beginning on the Tetrapak line, paper containers specially made for milk and soft drink manufacturers. *Exhibit 3* gives the firm's organizational structure with a breakdown of the 3,000 employees by department.

Besides these packaging materials, which were all custom-made by order, Packages had diversified into a number of standard items like notebooks, file covers, duplicating paper, and stationery. But these items had not grown to become major sources of revenue, and the department was considered more of a "neglected baby."

[1]One rupee (Rs.) = US$0.13.

The Paper and Board Divison encompassed the company's paper and board mill. Out of a monthly output of 2,000 tons, some 1,900 tons were consumed by the Packaging Division. The facility was constructed in 1968 with the help of Swedish technology and personnel. Before construction of the mill, Packages relied on two sources for most of its paper and board requirements: East Pakistan (now Bangladesh) and imports. Operating at over 90% of capacity since 1969, the mill's tonnage had been slightly more than the total paper and board needs of the Packaging Division.

Packages' mill's installed capacity of 24,000 tons a year gave it about a third of the market supply. Total industry capacity in Pakistan for paper and board conversion in 1974 was 90,000 tons; an additional 50,000 tons were imported. Half of this combined total (70,000 tons) went to the packaging industry; the rest went mainly to newsprint producers and book publishers. Packages' mill was by far the largest of its kind in Pakistan. Packages was the only firm in the packaging industry to have integrated backward and was certainly the largest manufacturer of its line of packaging materials.

To a large extent, the core technology used in the packaging business was transplanted from Sweden to Pakistan. Nevertheless, three important distinctions can be drawn about the Pakistani operation. First, the overall degree of sophistication and the level of automation at the Pakistani plant were considerably below that in Sweden. Some processes normally handled mechanically in Sweden were changed to manual operations for Pakistan. For example, stripping involved the removal of unwanted portions of the original sheet of cardboard (after tracing the dimensions of the specified cartons). It was done by cutting and creasing machines in Sweden, but by hand at Packages.

Second, Packages put much effort over the years making machinery locally in the company's foundries and machine shop, which had originally been established to make spare parts. Machines like the small printing presses and the slitting, gumming, and coating machines were not simply copied; their designs were modified to make them more flexible. The short runs (relative to the scale of operation of a typical European plant) or most orders produced by Packages meant that there were significant returns to reducing the machines' setup time.

Third, a task-oriented research group was organized to "find" locally available materials as substitutes for many imported inputs. Consequently, outside dependence for materials like adhesives, lacquers, and refined linseed oil was reduced. Using crude local oils, the research team was able to match the required specifications. In another instance, alumina was being imported despite the availability of bauxite in Pakistan. A facility was built to manufacture alum using sulfuric acid and bauxite. Since the firm also relied heavily on imported plastic glues, techniques were evolved to improve the quality of locally available animal glues and to produce plastic adhesives. Simultaneously, local suppliers were helped to improve their needed ingredients such as soapstone, chalk, and sodium silicate.

Perhaps the main difference between Packages' plant in Lahore and an analogous one in Europe or the United States was the extent of specialization. In American plants operations were much larger and less integrated. A typical U.S. plant would specialize in corrugated board manufacturing; facilities for designing and printing work would be left to the user or an intermediary. In Europe, and to an extent in the United States, packaging machinery manufacturers were beginning to supply machinery directly to the users of packaging materials. A cigarette manufacturer would probably make its own packages and cartons.

The packaging industry changed constantly over the years. In the 1950s packaging of paper and board was at its prime. The 1960s saw the shift to plastics and combinations of paperboard and plastics. The continued exchange of ideas and the overseas training programs for Packages' employees helped keep the Pakistanis from lagging far behind the European state of the art.

In 1974 Packages' plant used two basic printing technologies: the offset and flexographic processes. These technologies were different in two important respects. In the flexographic line, packaging material was transferred to and from a reel; in offset the product was always in flat, sheet form. Offset was in some ways better suited for printing cardboard; the flexographic process was better for labels, cellophane, wrapping paper, and polyethylene bags. The two processes differed also in their relative sophistication and hence their cost. The offset system was considerably more sophisticated, automatically controlled, and hence more costly, but the print quality was also better. In 1974 eight of the fourteen printing machines at Packages were of the offset variety.

About 55% of the Packaging Division's revenues came from sales of offset-printed cartons, such as cigarette and medicine cartons. After the sheets were fed into the offset printing machines, they generally required two or three days to dry. The sheets were then cut and creased and the cartons stripped from the sheet boards. Folding and gluing were the final steps.

In the flexographic system, the packaging material was in reel form at the end of the printing process. From there a variety of processes could follow depending on the characteristics of the order. For example, the material could be waxed, waterproofed (bituminizing), or polyethylene laminated. Finally, the reels were cut to the required size via slitting or sheeting.

Recently Packages had averaged more than 2,500 orders a year. Orders varied by size (1,000 boxes to 100,000 cartons), type (shipping boxes or consumer packaging), and printing process. The planning department played a central role in production scheduling. Typically, an order was booked by the marketing department. Planning personnel informed the salesmen about workload and available capacity in the plant. Updated weekly, a production planning chart kept track of all booked orders. Consequently, jobs were processed according to required deliveries, and the machines were kept close to full operating capacity. This system was described as one in which the "job would wait for the machine"; the opposite was never to happen. A job card was completed for each order so that sourcing needed inks and other materials did not delay production. This planning function was considered so vital to the success of the company that the department's responsibility did not finish until the order was actually dispatched from the factory.

INTERNATIONAL OPERATIONS

Packages' marketing people were responsible for its firm's first foray into foreign markets. Exports of offset-printed cartons and corrugated boxes to the Middle East dated back to 1969 and constituted most of the export shipments. Typically, a marketing person would leave for a specific country with no firm orders in hand. He would return with signed orders for shipments of varying quantities. These revenues had averaged $500,000 annually since 1970.

The first major international activity of another sort came in May 1971, when Packages was invited to sign a management contract in Indonesia. P. T. Guru (Indonesia), a Norwegian–Indonesian joint venture, had experienced operating problems since its inception in 1968. A Norwegian shipping company (one of three sets of partners, which included a Norwegian entrepreneur and a group of Indonesians) that had provided some $6 million in capital above its initial allocation turned to Akerlund & Rausing in Sweden for help. The Swedes, in turn, suggested that P. T. Guru contact representatives of Packages, given their experience in managing a successful operation in a developing country.

Although it was not until August of that year that a three-year contract was agreed upon, Ali had eight Packages engineers and managers flown to Jakarta within a week of the request. Packages' staff saw this as a goodwill gesture. Working 16- to 18-hour days, the Pakistanis were able to put the plant in operating condition within three months by August 1971. In the following three years Packages employees continued to advise the venture about more than just operating. Guru's marketing strategy was revamped in 1972–73.

At the end of the contract, Ali turned down an offer for a continued agreement with limited authority and asked instead for an all-or-nothing deal. He was not inclined to share operating responsibilities with the Norwegians. No compromise was reached: The Norwegians held fast to their preference for only a technical contract. Although the experience was relatively short, the success increased the confidence of Packages staff and encouraged them to consider further expansion overseas.

The next opportunity came while the Indonesian story was unfolding. In Tanzania, Kibo Paper Industries had been in operation since 1965, making only corrugated boxes. Founded by an Indian immigrant as a private company, the firm was nationalized in 1970 by the Tanzanian government, which then hired a Britisher as a general manager. But the situation soon deteriorated. Packages was called in to help set matters right in June 1971.

Kibo had an operating loss of $40,000 for the six months ending in June 1971, on sales of $110,000. Ali had high regard for the people in Tanzania but thought they were unable to coordinate their affairs. The agreement with Kibo called for a five-year management contract. Unlike the issue that surfaced in Indonesia, Packages in this instance was given full reign of the Kibo operation.

Both the general manager and the production manager were replaced by Packages' men. For the next six months, sales were at $190,000 and a profit of $600 was achieved. In 1972 a marketing man and an engineer were added to the Packages team. Operations continued to strengthen. The client list was expanded, and overall coordination of marketing, scheduling, and production greatly improved.

A second shift of Packages personnel came on in 1973. In 1974 a production line for manufacturing multiwall cement bags was added. Some of the new equipment for the expansion was supplied by Packages' workshop in Lahore; the more sophisticated machines were imported from West Germany and the United Kingdom. Total capacity in 1974 was equivalent to about half that of the Lahore plant. At that time the Packages team advised Kibo to integrate backward into papermaking. With some 7,000–8,000 tons of wastepaper available for recycling, a mill that could use this supply was proposed and approved later in 1974.

ZAMBIAN JOINT VENTURE PROPOSAL

Emanuel Kasonde of Century Holdings Limited (Zambia) was an entrepreneur who had woven an intricate network of contacts in and out of government. For a number of years he had served the government in several senior positions. He also began Century Holdings, whose name says much about Kasonde's intentions. His objective was to amass a group of 100 different businesses. Early in 1974 he approached the International Finance Corporation for advice on constructing a paper and board mill in Zambia. Most of the country's paper and board requirements were imported because of the rather small, fragmented, inefficient local mills. Although there were opportunities for new entrants to the business, the IFC cautioned Kasonde and, instead, suggested that he research the possibility of entry into the packaging industry. The IFC also recommended that Kasonde contact Packages in Pakistan as potential collaborators. Packages had had several dealings with the IFC by 1974, starting with equity participation in Packages in 1965.

In response to Kasonde's invitation, Tanwir Ahmad and Munawar Malik left for Lusaka in June 1974. Malik's background was in production. Ahmad had marketing experience and was serving as general manager for Kibo Industries in Tanzania. Their study covered supply and demand, the joint venture's scope, and infrastructural problems.

1. Supply and Demand in Zambia

The study identified the following seven main product/market segments for Zambia's packaging industry: multiwall sacks for cement, sugar, and fertilizer producers; corrugated boxes, flat bags, gumtapes, polyethylene bags; offset printed cartons, wrappers, and labels; flexo-printed aluminum foil; and both waxed and plain polyethylene paper. Local manufacturers produced all but the flexographic printed packaging materials, which were imported at a cost of about $3 million in 1974.

Five major Zambian-based firms were involved in packaging in 1974. The largest, Monterey Printing & Packaging Ltd., manufactured offset-printed cartons, corrugated containers, paper bags, and multiwall sacks. They had dominant shares in the markets for multiwall sacks and corrugated boxes. In both lines their installed capacity exceeded local demand by several hundred tons annually. Nevertheless, the company had plans to expand these businesses. In the market for offset-printed products, Monterey and International Cartons & Packaging Ltd. held dominant shares. Here, again, industry capacity (4,300 tons) exceeded local demand by 800 tons.

Flat bags were produced by four smaller paper converters, which combined had a total of 13 paper-converting machines. In this instance, local demand also lagged installed capacity. A small amount of pregummed tape (100 tons) was imported by two other firms (IMCO and Wiggenstead), which then printed and cut the rolls to smaller widths. They were the only suppliers of gumtape in Zambia.

Six firms manufactured polyethylene bags. In most cases, the film and printing quality was poor because of lack of sophistication in the machinery being used. Much equipment was purchased secondhand, and maintenance was generally inadequate. The problem was compounded by unusually high local demand; bag manufacturers, in a sense, were able to "get away" with less than acceptable quality.

In the market for flexo-printed packaging materials, some 18 identifiable firms imported their needs from Scandinavian and other West European countries. These firms were mainly producers of consumer goods like sweets and biscuits and of perishable foods like pork and cold meats. *Exhibit 4* itemizes the flexo packaging materials imported by these Zambian firms. Although these materials varied, the bulk of demand was for printed wax paper and cellophane reels and bags. Smaller amounts of laminated bags, printed poly-parchment paper, and foil paper lined with wax were also imported. Demand for these materials was expected to increase by 10% annually, a growth like that expected for the total market for packaging materials.

2. Scope of Project

In 1974 none of the major packaging companies in Zambia had made public any plans to diversify into the flexo-printed packaging business. The preliminary study by Ahmad and Malik suggested that existing manufacturers of packaging materials had enough capacity to meet the country's demand for rigid packaging (such as offset-printed cartons, corrugated boxes, etc.), but there were no good facilities for flexible packaging. Packages thus suggested setting up facilities for flexible packaging. Because of the small and varied requirements of the consumer-products industry in Zambia, producers faced difficulties in getting their orders accepted abroad. Thus, users of flexible packaging were keen to buy their requirements locally. The proposed flexible packaging plant would import most raw material in bulk and then print and convert it according to the needs of local customers, thus saving foreign exchange in Zambia and providing a more reliable source of flexible packaging materials.

Since the essential equipment needed for polyethylene bag-making was the same as that for flexographic packaging, the report recommended that the venture also produce polyethylene bags. In that case, only two additional machines would have to be purchased, a film extruder and a bag-making machine. Kasonde, however, favored setting up a plant to produce corrugated boxes and offset printed cartons. His concern was that the relatively poor printing quality of the flexographic process might hinder the venture's long-term success.

The recommendation that flexographic packaging and polyethylene bags were the only feasible packaging ventures for Zambia in 1974 was based on two lines of thinking. First, both Ahmad and Malik thought that the demand for flexographic products in Zambia was a function of the total output of consumer goods industries. Thus, a market for cigarette cartons depended on the presence of a local cigarette manufacturer. The report noted that should the Zambian government further restrict the import of such items as biscuits, sweets, and toffees (this was considered likely), then local producers of these items, who were operating at 50–70% of installed capacity, would register sharp rises in demand for their products. Consequently, demand for flexographic-printed materials would rise above the current 700 tons a year. The Packages venture could then conceivably capture a large share of this expanded market. Even if this market did not expand beyond the forecasted growth of 10% a year, the present market itself justified the presence of a local plant.

Entry into the polyethylene bag market was seen more as providing a higher-quality product to a rapidly growing segment of the packaging market. Furthermore, the competitors were small and without the resources of a Century Holdings–Packages-sponsored joint venture. The report did note that entry into any other market segment of the packaging industry would be likely to result in competitors' fighting to defend their present positions.

The report recommended that Packages join with Century Holdings in setting up the plant for flexographic-printed packaging products in Ndola, Zambia. Ndola was chosen because of its proximity to many of the potential customers who had facilities in the area.

3. Investment Needs

A 700-ton flexographic-printed packaging facility would require the following basic equipment:

Machines	Quantity
Flexographic printing machine	2
Waxing machine	1
Slitting machine	2
Sheeting machine	1
Guillotine	1
Camera	1
Stereo equipment	1 set

A few of these machines (such as the slitting, sheeting, and guillotine) could be made in and exported from Pakistan; the rest would be purchased in Europe. On that issue, Packages' purchasing experience and its contacts in Western Europe would be helpful in both the advisory and negotiating phases. In fact, Packages had kept careful records on available equipment, as well as the firm's experience with maintenance and also obtaining spare parts and service.

The cost of the project was estimated as follows:

	Kwachas (000s)
Machinery & equipment	430
Building & land	200
Preconstruction expenses (clearing, planning, etc.)	72
Working capital	613
Other	25
	1,340

About one-third of this total would have to be paid for in a hard foreign currency (about U.S.$1.5 = k1.0). The rest could be procured locally with Zambian kwachas. The bulk of "hard currency" payments would be for select machinery and equipment available only in Europe. Because of the foreign currency requirements, the project would be dependent on an IFC ten-year loan equivalent to k455,000. The balance would be funded by capital from Century Holdings (k200,000) and a variety of domestic bank loans (overdrafts) totaling k685,000. See *Exhibit 5* for details.

The plant would operate at 50% capacity in its first year of operation, tentatively set for 1976, and at close to 100% thereafter. Installed capacity would include wax paper (300 tons), cellophane (400 tons), and polyethylene bags (200 tons). *Exhibit 6* gives projected sales figures. The forecast assumes an annual increase of 10%, which would match expected raw material price hikes. Price control by the government was not expected.

To support such an operation, k613,000 was estimated as working capital requirements for the first year, rising to k1,605,000 by year five. About 50% of the capital would go toward the purchase of raw materials such as paper, cellophane, polyethylene, inks, waxes, and foil. *Exhibit 7* details the projected raw material requirements. All materials would have to be imported via Dar es Salaam and then transported by truck to Ndola. A government import license and a reliable transportation company were thus critical to the successful operation of the proposed venture. The Pakistanis did not anticipate being able to source these materials locally for several years.

Finally, operation of the plant would require between five and ten relatively senior Packages employees to be posted in Zambia. These men would hold positions like general manager, plant manager, marketing manager, and a variety of technical functions. The study remarked on the lack of sufficient technical and managerial resources available locally, although it was hoped that Zambian nationals could be trained to fill these slots in the long run.

SKETCHING A CONTRACT

Besides the project's heavy reliance on the World Bank for financing, the government of Zambia for an import license, and Packages for managerial and technical support, Babar Ali and his staff were bothered by a number of other unresolved issues. Perhaps the most troublesome was Packages' overall level of participation in the proposed joint venture. The Pakistanis would prefer a flat fee of about $100,000 for startup and some lesser amount thereafter for a fixed period of time. In exchange, Packages would render both technical and managerial services. The IFC, on the other hand, favored their taking an equity share in the venture. Moreover, the IFC implied that the ten-year loan might hinge upon Packages' accepting an equity deal. But since the Pakistan government restricted the outflow of capital from Pakistan, Packages would not be able to contribute any cash.

Consequently, Kasonde proposed a two-tier formula to meet the wishes of both the IFC and Packages. The first part involved a consultancy contract spanning the startup phase, during which Packages would provide:

1. Details of feasibility report of the proposed venture
2. Planning, designing, and engineering the project, i.e., factory layout plans, etc.
3. Assisting in selection and purchase of machinery
4. Supervising implementation project
5. Recruiting specialist staff

In return, Packages would receive 25,000 shares (3% common stock) of k1/share par value and payment of all expenses (travel and living) associated with the Packages personnel assigned to the project.

The second part involved a technical advisory and management services contract wherein Packages would provide:

1. Technical services and specialized know-how
2. Management personnel:
   a. seven major positions (general manager, plant manager, marketing manager, chief engineer, chief accountant, and two technicians)
   b. semiannual visits to Ndola by senior management in Lahore
3. Series of monthly operating reports
4. Train local employees
5. Use of Packages' name and secret processes

In return, Packages would receive a minimum payment of k35,000 per year (before withholding taxes) or a percentage of net profit before taxes as follows: 10% of profits up to k350,000, 7.5% of profits of k350,000–500,000, and 5% of profits over k500,000. But in the first year of operation the k35,000 would be made in the form of 35,000 common shares, bringing Packages' total equity position in the venture to 7%. In years two through five the venture should guarantee that the net amount payable to Packages after deduction of all withholding taxes would not be less than the equivalent of $38,750. (The Zambian withholding taxes was 25% at the time.)

Another issue involved obtaining permission from the Zambian government to repatriate Packages' annual management fee. Although the Zambian government was not expected to object to Packages' 7% holding in the joint venture (Century Holdings would have about 51% at all times), Ali was unsure of its attitude toward repatriating the fee. Packages thought that the foreign-exchange savings resulting from the reduction in imports of flexographic packaging in Zambia would support its case for repatriation of the fees. This saving was estimated at k3.8 million over the first five years of the venture.

Another concern, although not directly related to the contract, involved the venture's tax status with the Zambian government. An assumption built into the pro forma income statements (*Exhibit 8*) was that the project would be free of income tax for the first five years of operation. The Zambian law specifically awarded tax holidays to "pioneer" companies, that is, early businesses operating in areas of national importance. It was not clear whether the packaging industry, as developed as it was, would be granted such status.

Finally, Ali had to concern himself with the manpower requirements as proposed in the contract. All seven of Packages' men would take on instrumental roles in the venture's operation. One of these people, typically the general manager of the venture, would represent Packages on the five-man board.

At the time, there were eight men on "loan" to Kibo in Tanzania. That number was expected to grow to 21 when the paper mill came on-stream in 1975. Packages' managers were happy to work overseas. But there were some problems. For one, it required sending the "best" men abroad. Replacements had to be found for their jobs in Lahore without a loss or slowdown in work performance. Ali wondered at what point in this process the value of overseas benefits would be outweighed by the loss in resources at home. For another, sending people abroad meant risking possible defections. Although Packages had yet to lose an employee overseas, competitors and local ventures had tried to hire away technicians and engineers.

To minimize these downside human resources risks, Packages had instituted guidelines for sending employees abroad. First, as a prerequisite, the employee must have spent at least ten years with the company in Lahore and at some point have undergone training in Sweden. This would rule out the less "loyal" employees and simultaneously set a minimum level of technical expertise. The guidelines also suggested that only "top" men in their respective functions be selected. As such, highly experienced engineers would be preferred over others in the "middle" of the hierarchy. But this also translated to a greater loss if the man should leave the employ of Packages.

Salaries were on a par with other expatriates working in similar jobs. One expected to be able to save more while working abroad. A small housing allowance, special tax exemptions, and a 25% gratuity (only at the culmination of the service) were added incentives. Men were also permitted certain import benefits like a car and refrigerator. Each man was abroad for no more than two years and was accompanied by family only when the time abroad was more than eleven months.

Ali and Hamid had to decide whether to participate in the packaging project in Zambia and, if so, how to deal with the various risks in transferring the technology and implementing this new international venture.

PACKAGES LIMITED

Exhibit 1
Shareholdings
(Rs. in 000s)

	1957		1964		1965		1970		1971	
	Amount	*%*	*Amount*	*%*	*Amount*	*%*	*Amount*	*%*	*Amount*	*%*
Ali family	Rs.3,966	77.31	6,181	72.72	14,606	47.12	13,117	34.76	11,284	26.85
Foreign investors										
Akerlund & Rausing (Sweden)	1,164	22.69	2,319	27.28	6,319	20.38	7,583	20.08	5,781	13.76
IFC/Citibank	—	—	—	—	4,000	12.9	4,200	11.12	4,620	10.99
Local Investors										
State-owned/controlled institutions	—	—	—	—	2,050	6.62	7,611	20.16	16,513	39.29
General public and private institutions	—	—	—	—	4,025	12.98	5,239	13.88	3,828	9.11
Total	Rs.5,130	100%	8,500	100%	31,000	100%	37,750	100%	42,025	100%
Comments	Initial capitalization		Bonus shares		Public issue		Bonus shares 1:5		Bonus shares 1:10	

283

Exhibit 2
Seven-Year Summary
(Rs. 000s)

Year	Sales	Fixed Assets	Equity	Profit Before Tax[a]	Dividend
1968	55,755	95,504	45,187	2,164	1,860
1969	57,324	97,433	46,926	2,219	-0-
1970	79,682	100,868	47,663	12,450	3,775
1971	76,689	109,877	47,513	8,476	3,760
1972	94,152	143,912	46,304	8,363	3,782
1973	118,602	147,534	49,765	15,451	6,304
1974	149,234	150,076	52,746	29,643	8,825

[a]Approximately 50% corporate income tax.

PACKAGES LIMITED

Exhibit 3 Organizational Structure - 1974

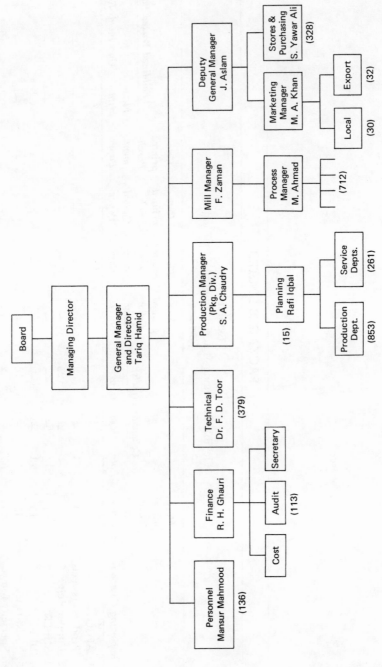

PACKAGES LIMITED

Exhibit 4

Flexible Packaging Materials Imported by Zambia, 1974

(Metric tons)

Importing Company	Flexo-printed Waxed Paper (reels)	Cellophane (reels)			Flexo-printed Cello: Bag/Sheets	Flexo-printed Laminate Bags	Roto-printed Poly Coated Paper	Roto-printed Parchment Paper	Foil-lined Waxed Paper		Remarks
		Roto	Flexo	Unprinted					Flexo-printed	Unprinted	
1. AFCO Products (sweets)	30	15	—	—	—	—	—	—	—	—	—
2. Copper Belt "	15	—	25	25	—	—	—	—	—	—	—
3. SUPER "	24	—	24	—	—	—	—	—	—	—	—
4. DUZI "	15	23	—	—	—	—	—	—	—	—	—
5. MANSHA "	45	—	—	10	—	—	—	—	—	—	—
6. Specialty foods	25	50	—	2	16 (2 ply bags)	5	—	—	29	15	—
7. Family biscuits	—	—	—	50	—	—	—	—	—	—	—

									Poly-laminated aluminum foil paper bags
8. Sunrise biscuits	—	20	—	20	—	—	—	—	—
9. Protons biscuits	—	—	—	20	—	—	—	—	—
10. Liberty biscuits	—	—	—	20	—	—	—	—	—
11. SUPA LOAF	60	—	—	—	18 (sheets)	—	—	—	—
12. PORK products	—	—	—	—	—	10	—	—	—
13. Cold storage board	—	—	—	—	6 (sheets)	—	—	—	—
14. Lusaka cold storage	—	—	—	—	2 (sheets)	—	—	—	—
15. LYONS Brooke Bond	—	—	5[a]	—	—	—	—	—	—
16. REFINED OIL	30[a]	—	—	—	—	—	—	15[b]	—
17. LBZ	—	—	—	—	—	—	—	5[a]	—
18. COLGATE	—	—	15	—	—	15	20	—	15
Total	244	108	49	147	42	15	20	20	15

[a] Unprinted.
[b] With punch.

287

Exhibit 5

Estimated Cost of the Project and Sources of Finance

(in thousand kwachas)

	Foreign Currency	Local Currency	Total
Estimated Cost			
Machinery and equipment	425	—	425
Laboratory equipment	5	—	5
Customs duty	—	Free	Free
Clearing, handling, and inland transportation	—	30	30
Erection expenses	—	7	7
Motor vehicles	—	10	10
Building (covered area 18,000 sq. ft. approx.)	—	144	144
Land (5 acres)	—	30	30
Furniture, fixtures, and one air conditioner of 7 tons capacity	—	26	26
Planning and setting-up fee	25	—	25
Contingencies 10%	—	25	25
	455	272	727
Working capital	—	613	613
	455	885	1,340
Sources of Finance			
I.F.C. loan	455	—	455
Capital by the sponsors	—	200	200
Development Bank of Zambia-O.D.	—	685	685
	455	885	1,340

Exhibit 6
Projected Sales

	First Year	Second Year	Third Year	Fourth Year	Fifth Year
Sales in tons					
Waxed wrappers	150	300	300	300	300
Printed cellophane	200	400	400	400	400
Printed poly film	100	200	200	200	200
Sales value (in thousand kwachas)					
Waxed wrappers	225	495	545	600	660
Printed cellophane	550	1,210	1,331	1,464	1,611
Printed poly film	225	495	545	600	660
	1,000	2,200	2,421	2,664	2,931
Less: Provision for any rebates to be given for quantity, etc. @ 1%	10	22	24	27	29
Net sales	990	2,178	2,397	2,637	2,902
Prices taken during the 1st year					
Waxed wrappers	k1,500/ton				
Printed cellophane	k2,750/ton				
Printed poly film	k2,250/ton				

Exhibit 7
Projected Raw Material Requirements

	First Year	*Second Year*	*Third Year*	*Fourth Year*	*Fifth Year*
Requirements in tons (including 10% process waste)					
Toffee paper	105	210	210	210	210
Cellophane	225	450	450	450	450
Polyethylene	110	220	220	220	220
Inks	25	50	50	50	50
Waxes	52	105	105	105	105
Aluminum foil	8	15	15	15	15
Others	2	3	3	3	3
Value of Raw Materials (in thousand kwachas)					
Toffee paper	65	143	158	173	191
Cellophane	365	803	883	971	1,068
Polyethylene	137	301	331	364	400
Inks	71	155	171	188	206
Waxes	30	66	72	80	88
Aluminum foil	8	17	19	20	22
Others	2	3	4	4	4
	678	1,488	1,638	1,800	1,979

Exhibit 8
Projected Income for Joint Venture
(In thousand kwachas)

	First Year	Second Year	Third Year	Fourth Year	Fifth Year
Sales	990	2,178	2,397	2,637	2,902
Cost of sales					
Raw materials	678	1,488	1,638	1,800	1,979
Wages & salaries	105	124	130	136	143
Fuel and electricity	4	9	10	11	12
Repairs & maintenance	6	12	13	14	16
Other expenses	17	34	37	41	45
Depreciation	63	63	68	71	74
Audit fee	3	3	3	3	3
Management fee (to Packages)	35	35	40	46	49
Variation in finished goods inventory	—	(6)	(7)	(7)	(8)
	911	1,762	1,932	2,115	2,313
Trading profit/(loss)	79	416	465	522	589
Less: Interest on bank overdraft (domestic loans)	72	50	12	—	—
Long-term borrowing	46	41	36	32	27
	118	91	48	32	27
Profit (loss) before tax	(39)	325	417	501	562
Taxation	Exempt	Exempt	Exempt	Exempt	Exempt
Profit (loss) after tax	(39)	325	417	490	562
Profit (loss) brought forward from previous year	—	(39)	246	623	1,073
Available for appropriation	(39)	286	663	1,113	1,635
Appropriations					
Retained earnings	—	246	623	1,073	1,595
Dividend	—	40	40	40	40

Thai Polyester Fiber (B)

In March 1975 Monsieur Luc Laurent, director of International Development for Chimie du Sud, was waiting in a Parisian café for friends to arrive. He had arranged to meet his friends and business associates, M. Jean-Pierre Batier, construction manager for the Chimie du Sud Textile Division (CST), and Mlle. Denise Lebec, installation engineer for the ARCT (Ateliers Roannais de Construction Textile).

In 1967 the ARCT and CST had agreed to share reciprocal rights to sell or supply each other's products, proprietary equipment, patents, and designs. M. Batier and Mlle. Lebec were to fly in from Bangkok, where they were working together on the construction and installation of the Thai Polyester Fiber Plant (TPF), a 1-billion-baht[1] polyester polymerization and filature factory.[2] TPF was the joint venture between CST and the Yipsoon Group, a family-owned textile conglomerate based in Thailand, which owned or operated more than 50% of the Thai textile industry. (CST held 48% of the stock in the joint venture, valued at 125 million baht; the Yipsoon Group held the other 52%, valued at 135 million baht.)

The next day M. Laurent and M. Batier were to meet with the Executive Board of CST to map out future worldwide textile strategy. In 1972 the textile industry was plagued with skyrocketing raw material prices, labor strikes, stagnant demand, and cutthroat price competition.

The problems were particulary severe in France, where Chimie du Sud expected tonnage sales to drop 18% and revenues to fall 20% for the second year in a row. The CST management was eager to learn about developments at TPF. As the first large French investment in Thailand, CST's most recent substantial capital commitment, and the first plant to use Chimie du Sud's newly patented revolutionary polymerization process, TPF was viewed as a flagship project and a critical test of the Textile Division's ability to transfer technology effectively and profitably.

M. Laurent was concerned because the plant construction, begun in December 1973, was behind schedule. He knew that some conflicts had arisen between the management of the Yipsoon Group and the engineers

[1]The 1975 exchange rate was 20.35 Thai baht per 4.49 French francs per U.S. dollar.

[2]See Appendix 1 for a summary of the polymerization and filature process.

This case (Case B) was originally prepared by Elizabeth Fouraker under the supervision of Associate Professor Philippe Lasserre. It was edited by Research Assistant Alvin G. Wint, for use at Harvard Business School as the basis for class discussion rather than to illustrate either effective or ineffective handling of an administrative situation. Abridged with permission. See Chapter 7 for Case C.

Copyright © 1980 Euro-Asia-Centre–INSEAD.

of CST and the ARCT. He did not want to assign blame; rather, he wanted to investigate the problem so that he and the CST board could provide M. Batier and Mlle. Lebec with any corporate support and advice they might need.

After M. Batier and Mlle. Lebec arrived at the café, they discussed the TPF situation:

M. LAURENT: You have been very busy during the past year, haven't you, M. Batier?

M. BATIER: Yes, I've logged more than 200,000 kilometers in the air, flying to and from Bangkok to oversee the construction.

M. LAURENT: Would you review the construction time-frame for me?

M. BATIER: During October and November of 1973, I started interviewing Bangkok civil engineering firms. As you know, one requirement of the technology transfer agreement was that we use Thai subcontractors, suppliers, and labor whenever possible. The firm I chose was really the only one big enough to do the job. Meanwhile, I was studying the plans because I had been in Brazil during the initial work on the technical specifications and cost estimates. They are sketchy and I'm still involved in firming up materials and specifications and supplying detail. Cost estimates were too low in every dimension: labor, supervision, equipment, and supplies.

M. LAURENT: When did you begin to realize that cost estimates were too low?

M. BATIER: When we started site preparation in December, we realized that local labor requires more strict supervision than we are accustomed to giving in less developed countries such as Brazil. Local subcontractors require more on-site and specific technical guidance and assistance than was provided for in the agreement. I had to adjust our service cost estimates upwards by 20%. We have maintained 40 to 50 French engineers on-site, some with their families, since January 1974. We estimate that completion of the factory will require 28 to 32 months, six of which will entail detailed finishing and waterproofing of the reinforced concrete floors, walls, and ceilings. The finishing stage is labor-intensive and will require technical supervision as well.

MLLE. LEBEC: We started with four engineers on-site in 1973, and we are increasing our component as the building becomes ready for installation of the ARCT machinery.

M. BATIER: You know, Luc, we initially planned that ARCT would install most of their basic structural equipment and wiring during construction, but that program has not worked out very well.

M. LAURENT: Why is that?

MLLE LEBEC: Bangkok is in a wet climate; the best of the three sites proposed by the Yipsoon Group is a rice paddy 40 kilometers outside the city. This site is only 80 centimeters above sea level and is extremely marshy. The humidity is such that any ferrous equipment put in place there rusts within weeks. Our instruments jam and stick from the dampness, and fungus and mold grow on everything. We are going to have to replace almost half of the material and equipment that have already been shipped to Bangkok. This includes more than 100 of our 1.8-meter staple drawing creels, which cost us 500 francs each to build in France.

M. LAURENT: How will you protect the materials in the future?

MLLE. LEBEC: We will wait until the construction and waterproof treatment are complete and the climatizing and dehumidifying plant is in operation before we risk shipping the sensitive and expensive equipment such as the extruders or the draw-twisters. We are working on ways of packaging and sealing the less expensive materials and bulky items which need to be in position before the buildings are completed.

M. LAURENT: What are the other causes of the construction delay?

M. BATIER: Site preparation and the laying of the foundation was a more involved process than we had expected. Because of the swampy terrain, 3,000 pilings, each 20 meters long, were sunk for the foundation. We imported 22,000 square meters of structural material such as rigid steel girders, with some delivery delays.

M. LAURENT: Aren't we committed to buying material in Thailand whenever possible?

M. BATIER: Yes, but the materials available in Thailand are not adequately standardized, are not of consistent quality, and are often not built to metric specifications. M. Yipsoon Praboon protested my materials invoices as violations of the contract. I don't see how you thought we could honor that contract, Luc. The infrastructure isn't big enough or sophisticated enough to meet our needs. I'm finding myself in an increasingly poor bargaining position with the Yipsoon Group. M. Yipsoon Praboon is a very sophisticated bargainer. He says he wants the benefits of the technology transfer to accrue to as many local engineering, contracting, and supply firms as possible, and is imposing the choice of local contractors, in some cases against my judgment.

M. LAURENT: You have a Singapore firm for welding the pilings and girders, don't you?

M. BATIER: Yes, and I haven't been happy with the results. I knew the welders should have been controlling and monitoring their work with X-ray photographic machines, but the Singapore subcontractor didn't have the experience or the equipment. M. Yipsoon Praboon insisted that we stay with that firm, and with the scarcity of welders, we were lucky to have them. Toward the end of the welding stage, we lost a lot of them to the Emirates, where they were paid three to four times more than in Thailand. Spot-testing told me that 30% of the welded seals and joints were defective, and I'm afraid we haven't corrected all of them. Extremely strict supervision of the local labor is required. The workmen don't seem to have any notion of maintaining quality. As far as I can tell, the workmen seem to think that it is better, more natural, to perform a repetitive task in a slightly different fashion each time. The problems are aggravated by the fact that virtually none of the Thai workers, supervisors, or technicians speaks French. We are having trouble finding translators; we don't have enough; and the ones we have are Thai–English translators.

MLLE. LEBEC: The Thai vocabulary is very small, and there are hundreds of words which cannot be translated into Thai. Long or metaphorical phrases must be used to get across simple concepts. For example, when I was demonstrating the operation of the spinning capstans to some Thai technicians, the translator told me that the thumb is called "the mother of the hand."

M. BATIER: We were frequently having what appeared to be theological disputes until we discovered that the translators were saying that procedures were "natural" in Thai, when we had said they were "rational" in French. Apparently "natural" was the closest translation they could achieve, but it is a concept critical to the Thai forms of Buddhism, and had fundamentally religious overtones.

MLLE. LEBEC: Sometimes I get the impression that the Thai people think we worship our machinery the way they worship their enormous reclining Buddhas. For example, we showed a team of technicians how to clean and lubricate the dredging pumps and they can do it expertly. But they do not seem to believe that it is necessary to do it even when there are no French watching. I wonder whether they think we require it of them for purely ritualistic reasons.

M. BATIER: They are a puzzling people. The work force is remarkably adroit, skillful, cunning, and clever, but seldom consistent. They entrust the serious jobs and the heavy labor to their women. Rice cultivation and harvest is the high-status work; industrial jobs are low-status work, relegated to women. You can ask the construction teams Monday, Tuesday, and Wednesday if they like their work, if they are content with their tasks and their supervisors, and if the food and housing we give them are satisfactory, and they will all say yes; yet, they will all be out on strike on Thursday.

M. LAURENT: That reminds me of the age-old story of the visitor going from Bangkok to Chiang Mai, 900 kilometers to the north. When he came to one of the ancient capitals about halfway between the two cities, he got lost in the marketplace and started back along the road by which he had arrived. Not feeling entirely certain of his direction, he

asked a local inhabitant, "Is this the way to Chiang Mai?" The villager
saw that the visitor was travelling in the wrong direction, but he could
not bear to imply that such a grand and wealthy person could be wrong,
so he replied, "Certainly, sir." The visitor continued in the southerly
direction, but was still somewhat doubtful, so he asked again and received the same answer. To verify this, he asked a second, "How far is
it?" "Very far" was the answer. Tell me about the strikes.

MLLE. LEBEC: It begins and ends with rice. In 1972 and 1973, the government was trying to reduce the trade deficit created by the import of
automobiles, machinery, and oil. They allocated an unusually high
proportion of the Thai rice yield to export. Domestic prices doubled.
There were severe droughts and floods in some regions of Thailand in
1974, but, due partly to the success of the high-yield hybrid strains, the
total crop was 13.8 million tons, 1.8 million tons in excess of the domestic demand. But wholesale rice prices have risen 135% since 1972. A
Thai wage earner spends, on average, 40% of his income on food,
mostly rice. Rice production is beginning to look like a profitable
business and Bangkok entrepreneurs are buying the rich rice paddy
land in the North Central area and hiring or driving out families who
have farmed their own land there for centuries. Due to the bad weather
in 1974, 4 million farming families are in debt, owing a total of 16
billion baht. These families are sending their children into the city for
the first time to earn the interest on the loans. They are among the
70,000 textile workers employed at 600 factories. During 1974, these
factories were facing exponential increases in raw material costs, 24%
inflation in operating costs, and stagnant world demand. Taiwan and
Japanese textile dealers were speculating in the Thai market by hoard-
ing and dumping. Thai textile inventories were backing up, so manufacturers, with the advice of the Board of Investment, decided to cut
production by an aggregate 25%. Fearing layoffs and pay cuts, textile
workers went on strike. They demanded an increase in the minimum
wage from 12 baht to 20 baht per day, severance pay, strike pay, measures insuring greater employment security, and more power for employment associations. Joined by students they denounced illegal
employment practices, the exploitation of cheap labor, and "the American, Japanese, and Taiwanese imperialists who invested in Thailand
with the cooperation of the ruling class and the tyrants to exploit and
make us slaves." They won their strike demands but the real income of
the average industrial worker, in terms of rice-buying power, is still
lower than in 1972.

M. LAURENT: You said inventories were rising. What is the textile inventory situation now?

MLLE. LEBEC: At the beginning of this year, unsold thread inventory in
Thailand totaled 12,500 tons, at a value of 145 million francs, and stocks

of woven fabrics were as high as 55 million square meters, with a value of 210 million francs. Many of the industrial textile projects which were accorded privileges, protection, or aid by the Bangkok Board of Investment have canceled or postponed construction. With the end of the war in Vietnam, Thailand will probably close off its borders, and will lose all its sales to Laos, Cambodia, and Vietnam, which have until now absorbed about 20% of Thai textile production.

M. BATIER: The regional political situation is explosive and unstable. The long tail of Thailand that runs south down the Malay peninsula is populated predominately by Muslim separatists. Their movement has few supporters in Bangkok. Unfortunately for regional relations, the movement has many supporters in Malaysia. No major roads connect the south with Bangkok, and Bangkok officials are unenthusiastic about committing public funds to roadbuilding. Roadbuilding efforts in the mountainous, isolated Northeast, funded by foreign aid (which is no longer forthcoming) were sabotaged by Burmese insurgents working with about 5,000 Nationalist Chinese irregulars. The politicians who thought that communications with the rural areas would reduce terrorists' activity and help to stabilize Thai politics have given way to the isolationists who argue that Bangkok is safer with few roads connecting it to the bases of the border and mountain guerrillas. Meanwhile, racial tensions in Bangkok are very high. Violent rioting broke out in Chinatown in July and lasted for three days. It was apparently triggered by the arrest of a Chinese taxicab driver, who refused to pay the Thai policemen the appropriate bribe to avoid going to jail. Thai attitudes toward Chinese, who represent about 10% of the total Thai population, but 38% of Bangkokians, are complex, but largely resentful and hostile. Most large-scale successful Thai entrepreneurs are of Chinese ethnic origin. At the same time, most of the compelling communist guerrilla leaders are also of Chinese origin, even in the Muslim-dominated South.

M. LAURENT: What does M. Yipsoon think about the racial relations?

M. BATIER: That is a sensitive matter; I haven't discussed it with him. Communications are not going very well with M. Yipsoon, or with his six sons who are in charge of the various operational divisions of the Yipsoon Group. Apparently it is M. Yipsoon's practice to "inspect factories" every morning at 5:00. He makes the rounds of all the Yipsoon Group plants, examining a different one each day at dawn. He had been coming to the TPF site with increasing frequency, giving instructions to the Thai supervisors and subcontractors. Thus, even on the rare occasions when I am certain they have understood my instructions, I know there is a good chance that they won't carry them out, because M. Yipsoon has given, or will give, opposing instructions.

MLLE. LEBEC: The subcontractors know that we are only going to be there another 12 to 16 months, but they hope to have many jobs with the Yipsoon Group in the future.

M. BATIER: At the time of the strikes and the race rioting I tried to suggest to M. Yipsoon that it might not be safe for him to wander around the construction site unaccompanied, but he didn't answer. I was told that he is carrying a revolver and that he doesn't go out without one or two bodyguards.

M. LAURENT: I understand you have had some conflicts with the Yipsoon Group over architects, as well.

M. BATIER: The first one we had was recommended by M. Yipsoon as "the most sensitive, artistic, and brilliant local architect." However, he didn't seem to understand the principles of reinforced concrete foundations. He didn't seem to realize the weight of the equipment that would eventually be installed. The specifications he drew up were much too vague, allowing for wide ranges of materials to be used in any given application, and allowing construction supervisors to "exercise their discretion" in finishing techniques. We had to get rid of him. We now have a part-time local architect who specializes in reinforced concrete, and a team working in France. This is another factor contributing to the delay in construction. Plant plans are now being drawn up while construction is under way. This is not an ideal operating situation; we are often stuck twiddling our thumbs and waiting for air delivery of technical drawings and equipment specifications from France. However, it may be a good situation from our point of view, because it keeps large portions of the plans out of the hands of our partners, who could interfere with construction even more effectively if they had them. Actually though, I've wondered if the Yipsoon Group engineered the brouhaha over the shower room.

M. LAURENT: What was the outcry over the shower room?

M. BATIER: Apparently, we put the shower room over the "axis of the arrival of the beneficent spirits." Someone started a rumor about it; the Thais got all excited, and we had to pull out the plumbing in haste and replace it on "the axis of the arrival of the malevolent spirits." No one on my team is an expert in Buddhism, so we just had to do what the Yipsoon people, acting as moderators, told us to do. We are also having a little trouble with our esteemed colleagues, the ARCTs, who are demanding higher fees for their construction services.

MLLE. LEBEC: We have had to make a lot of changes in our construction plans, because the original specifications supplied by Chimie du Sud didn't include adjustments for heat and humidity control, durability, and lack of sensitivity in the polymerization process equipment, automatic lubrication of machinery, and standby electrical generating equipment. Also, Chimie du Sud should pay at least part of the cost of the water damage inflicted on our proprietary equipment, which was shipped in and placed on-site according to the original schedule drawn up by Chimie du Sud.

APPENDIX 1
THE THAI POLYESTER FIBER PLANT:
SUMMARY OF THE POLYMERIZATION
AND FILATURE PROCESS

The Thai Polyester Fiber plant, built on a 135-nai plot on the Phaholyothin highway outside Bangkok, was to incorporate the newest, most advanced chemical technology in the continuous polymerization process, with 200 meters of automatic and semi-automatic staple fiber drawing lines, thread extruders, draw-twisters, and texturizers. The spinning equipment provided by the ARCT was not very modern. Dutch and British firms revolutionized spinning equipment design in 1972, with water jet spinning machines and looms. The new type of equipment spun fibers and filaments at a much higher speed. The TPF plant's production costs per kilogram spun might not be competitive with those of the newest European or Japanese textile plants.

The TPF plant would be registered with a capacity of 5 tons of polyester staple fiber and 2 tons of filament thread per day. All of the staple fiber would be sold locally, while market analysts expected that 30% of thread production would be sold overseas to traditional markets in Hong Kong, Taiwan, Malaysia, and Indonesia. The Yipsoon Group's spinning, weaving, and finishing firms were expected to absorb the bulk of the plant's product. It was partly for this reason that M. Damien of Banque Française du Commerce Extérieur, who organized the very favorable market feasibility and technical feasibility studies of 1972, felt that a secure market was assured. The majority of Thailand's textile exports were in the form of undyed woven fabrics, which went to finishing and dyeing firms in Southeast Asia, Europe, and the United States. The developed markets were imposing import quotas in order to protect their high-wage textile employment. There were some indications at regional trade fairs that China might be a possible direct market for TPF's products in the future.

The major raw materials required in the TPF process were ethylene glycol and dimethyl terephthalate (DMT), petrochemical derivatives whose world market prices increased by more than 100% during the 1973 oil crisis. DMT was selling for 4,000–6,000 baht per metric ton in 1975. The chemical process produced a viscous polyester substance and a by-product of methanol. Methanol, a psychotropic poison, had no current commercial application in Thailand. The production of 1 kilogram of polyester textile and 350 grams of methanol required 1,090 grams of DMT combined with 380 grams of ethylene glycol. Polyester fiber sold for 20 baht per kilogram in the 1975 domestic Thai market. Thread sold for 30% to 40% more; texturized, elasticized thread was the most expensive product produced in the TPF plant.

The following is a highly simplified summary of the plant's equipment and processes.

Ethylene glycol is heated and mixed with catalytic agents. The viscous mass is then pumped to a transisterifioation autoclave, where it reacts with nearly three times its volume of DMT (dimethyl terephthalate). The resulting monomer suspension is then pumped through a filter to a highly pressurized condensation autoclave where polymerization occurs at 190 to 260 centrigrade. The methanol by-product is then automatically removed, condensed, and stored. At this stage, CST's proprietary chemical process is complete, and the basic polyester substance is ready for the ARCT process of either:

1. Simple filature, which, through an automated continuous production line, produces bales of fibers, or

2. Densification and spinning, which, through a similar production line, produces bobbins of threads

In the fiber process, the substance passes directly into a set of measuring pumps, which distribute it in even amounts to batteries of filament spinning systems. In a filament spinning system, a monitored stream of molten polyester is forced through a cylindrical filter packed with sand. It then passes through a metal alloy screen with a diameter of 10 centimeters and more than 1,000 holes. The tiny threads which emerge are solidified into a continuous mesh by the cold air dryer. Next, the spinning and winding machines loop the mesh around a series of cylinders revolving at 1,000 meters per minute. The mesh becomes condensed and elongated into something like a thread. However, this condensed mesh does not have the molecular characteristics required of polyester material. To give the flexible but resilient and wrinkle-proof performance of polyester fibers, the long chain polymers must be oriented around the fiber axis in such a way as to allow temporary slippage between polymers, but they must be elastically bonded so that permanent slippage will not occur.

To create such an alignment in the polymers, the mesh is delivered from the filament spinning system into the fiber drawing lines, a series of spinning rollers in heated enclosures. The roller that accepts the mesh rotates at 300 meters per minute. The mesh passes around it and is delivered to a pulling roller, which turns at 900 meters per minute. This controlled and heated stretching process elongates the mesh up to 4 to 5 times its original length, and aligns the polymers. The polyester fiber that is produced is then drawn through gears and cogs, which crimp it, and delivered to a chopper, which turns it into fiber fuzz. The fine, colorless, curly elastic fuzz is then packed into bales.

Evans Food Corporation

At the annual strategic planning meeting of the Evans Food Corporation's Condiment Division in November 1986, the idea of transforming each of the division's facilities into a "world-class manufacturing" (WCM) operation was discussed. Corporate management at Evans (a highly decentralized company) typically set broad-based strategic direction for the company and then gave general managers significant latitude in determining how to implement change in each of their operations. Such was to be the case for WCM.

John Williams, general manager of the division's Cayey, Puerto Rico plant, wondered what WCM would mean for his operation. The Cayey plant already had a reputation for a "can-do" attitude, i.e., for being able to produce top-quality, low-cost products, quickly introduce new ones, or adjust to swings in production volumes. Employees at the plant tended to view problems as "opportunities to learn." Product costs had held constant since 1982, despite increases in wages and materials. The operation had also already embarked upon total quality control and just-in-time inventory programs and had taken steps to be self-sufficient from the division's headquarters staff. But Williams was known for never passing up an opportunity to make his operation even better. He had been general manager since the plant was built twelve years earlier and was approaching retirement; he had only a couple of years left to complete his legacy.

COMPANY BACKGROUND

Founded in the early 1900s, the Evans Food Corporation was a multinational manufacturer of food and consumer products. By the mid-1950s, it had three manufacturing sites (California, Michigan, and Pennsylvania), each producing the entire line of products for its market area. In the 1970s, the corporation decided to decentralize and form individual businesses, each responsible for marketing and manufacturing its own prod-

This case was prepared as a basis for class discussion by Research Associate Sabra B. Goldstein and Assistant Professor Janice Klein rather than to illustrate either effective or ineffective handling of an administrative situation. Abridged with permission.

ucts; one outcome was the creation of the Evans Condiment Division, headquartered in Philadelphia.

Once the new division was formed, division management began looking for a location for the first condiment facility. Puerto Rico was given top consideration because of a special tax law (Section 936 of the Internal Revenue Code) that allowed tax exemptions for fifteen years on income earned by U.S. firms on the island. The island's wages were also significantly lower than in the States, and a 35% unemployment rate provided an abundant supply of trainable workers. After investigating the experiences of other U.S. companies that owned facilities on the island, many of which had been there since the early 1960s, Evans purchased a new plant site at Cayey, Puerto Rico, in the summer of 1974.

The person chosen to oversee the new plant's construction resigned from the company in late 1974; he and his family did not like Puerto Rico, felt it would be too expensive to live there, and did not trust Hispanics. Williams, the group engineering manager at Evans's Pennsylvania facility, was asked to take over the assignment. Having worked for Evans since 1967, he was a natural candidate to head the project; he had a degree in mechanical engineering and had previous assignments in maintenance, production, and quality. This was his first assignment outside the continental United States. He was initially expected to stay in Puerto Rico for only three years and then return to the States to build the division's second plant. Although the second facility was later built in North Carolina, Williams chose to stay on as general manager of the Cayey operation.

Plant Startup and Expansion

Ground was broken on November 4, 1974, and construction of the Cayey facility began shortly thereafter. The plant was to produce two high-volume products (ketchup and mustard), but the building was sized to accommodate a doubling in the products' volume, and 50% more capacity was added to the warehouse because of concerns about receiving and shipping raw materials and finished goods to and from the island. The engineers designing the facility were reluctant to use any high technology in the plant, at least initially, for fear that the island would lack technical expertise. Their mottos for designing the operation were "nothing new" and "dazzle them with simplicity." Construction did prove difficult, especially because of language barriers. Although the engineers assigned to the project took a Berlitz course in Spanish, they were unable to communicate directly with the construction workers and had to convey their instructions through the supervisor, who acted as interpreter. The technical expertise of the outside contractors doing the construction and equipment installation was also less than optimal. As one engineer recalled,

"One of the contractors showed up with a hammer and pliers to install the equipment. We found we had to go to the local Sears store to buy them the needed tools and a box to put them in. We also had trouble finding standard nuts and bolts. We, therefore, had to make sure everything was specified and sent in from the States."

In September 1975 production began in a corner of the plant while the rest of the facility was completed. The first operation was a semi-automated liquid-filling line for filling 12-, 16-, and 20-ounce plastic ketchup bottles. The line automatically filled the bottles, screwed on caps, and glued labels on the front and back of the bottles. The only manual labor needed (13 packers) was for loading and unloading bottles on the conveyor belt. There were also a line operator and a utility person to monitor the line operation and clear jams, a machine cleaner, and a full-time mechanic assigned to keep the line running. The initial 17 employees were selected from a group of 2,700 applicants.

In early 1976 the mustard-filling line was added, and later that year plastic molding equipment was installed that enabled the plant to produce its own bottles and caps. As a result of its outstanding performance, additional work was reassigned to the Cayey operation over the years. In June 1982 the operation also began producing contract bottles for other Evans operations and in 1984 added a filling line for steak and barbecue sauces. As a result, the operation grew to include three filling lines, 13 extrusion and one injection blow machines, and four decorating lines.[1]

Evolution of the Plant's Culture

When Williams moved to Puerto Rico, the Evans Corporation was extremely busy reorganizing in the United States, which allowed Williams much latitude in shaping the plant's policies and procedures. In addition, although the division engineering staff laid out the initial plant specifications and oversaw much of the construction, Williams could recommend modifications in the physical layout. In so doing, he incorporated what he called his "no walls" philosophy. He explained:

> "No walls" is the basic concept I had for building and managing the Cayey plant. Why "no walls"? Basically, walls prevent or hinder verbal and visual contact between people. Walls are of many kinds: physical—solid walls in the factory or office area; functional walls are invisible ones that separate people by departmental responsibilities; class walls separate people such as exempt, nonexempt, salary, and

---

[1]An overhead conveyor, added in December 1985, took bottles directly from the molding machine to the decorating line, where labels were sealed onto the surface. This eliminated the labeling operation on the filling line.

nonexempt wage; community walls separate a factory from the people in the community; regulation walls, or complicated policies, also separate people.

We have as few physical walls as possible in our plant and still meet the necessary insurance requirements. We do things together: We are Cayey, not accounting or manufacturing. We try to prevent "oneupmanship" here.

We also try to minimize functional walls by sharing annual action plans with all employees, participating equally in company activities such as sports, and picnics, and so on. Furthermore, we break down walls to the community by participating in projects to improve Cayey. For instance, we have a work-study program with the local high school, we contribute money to various schools, and we work with the Salvation Army here.

The "no walls" philosophy that Williams espoused took some time to develop. When the plant first began operating, the senior staff was a mixture of "continentals" (mainland U.S. managers) and "locals" (Puerto Ricans), which caused some friction. Besides Williams (the only remaining continental in the facility), the first controller (who stayed through June 1978) and the first two quality-assurance managers (through 1979) were continentals. José Rodriguez, the Cayey engineering and maintenance manager and one of the first locals hired, recalled the early days:

At first we had a lot of problems between people (mainly continentals versus locals) and with the sophisticated equipment, but we said to ourselves, "We have to make it work, so we have to work together." John [Williams] had a lot of experience in maintenance and often wanted to do things his way, which wasn't exactly as we would have done here on the island. It took a few years for John to learn the culture.

Part of the difficulty between locals and continentals stemmed from cultural differences. For instance, the continentals would "yell and scream" at one another and at the locals during production meetings and then act like best friends afterward, as was typical in many U.S. manufacturing operations; the Puerto Ricans did not understand this "inconsistent" behavior. Moreover, the locals felt they were looked down upon by continental managers at the plant and by personnel from corporate headquarters, who they believed were prejudiced toward Puerto Ricans. The problems were exacerbated by the management style of Williams's first division manager (through 1980), who was said to enjoy "managing by conflict." He sent division staff members to the facility every two to three weeks to critique the operation; Cayey managers noted that he then used the information to pit one employee against another. This destroyed harmony at the staff level and trust throughout the plant and between Cayey and Philadelphia; everyone had to prove they could do the job. This disturbed the locals because to them the Puerto Rican culture nur-tured a family atmosphere and a pride in their work. But tension between the continentals and locals led the locals to band together to prove to the Evans Corporation that they could do the job and that the plant could be a success, thus preserving jobs for the island.[2]

Williams, too, was at first unaccustomed to Puerto Rican culture. For instance, during the first few years of operation, he closed the facility for Christmas on December 25 but not for Three King's Day on January 6, a bigger family day than Christmas. The locals were apprehensive at first about telling Williams that most Puerto Rican businesses closed also for Three King's Day, but when they finally did, he quickly changed the policy. As one manager explained, "It was a major turning point when the staff felt free to tell John, 'You're not making any sense.' Somehow, John changed his signals, which allowed the locals to do that." Indeed, Williams did change as he learned more about the local culture, and within a few years he gained a reputation as a demanding but fair manager. As one Cayey manager described him:

> John is viewed as a strong but flexible leader. He is sometimes autocratic, sometimes paternalistic, and sometimes participative. He projects responsibility and is tough but fair. You always know exactly where you stand with him. He's known to be aggressive and very demanding because he wants to get things done. If he's upset about something that's not done right, he gets cold. The people up in Philadelphia refer to him as the "little emperor."
>
> But people respect him. He analyzes things before saying yes or no. One staff member calls it the "wars of silence," describing the way John thinks before he responds. He's a good sensor of information. He identifies problems, then he calls the staff together and says, "Here's something I've heard. What are you going to do about it?" He lets the staff work out an action plan, but he follows up to make sure it was accomplished.

Although Williams learned to read Spanish quite well, he was not as adept at speaking the language. But this did not stop him from addressing the entire work force in Spanish every quarter to update them on the state of the business and other important matters. For those who had difficulty understanding him, his speech was also posted in Spanish on the plant's bulletin boards. Many employees viewed Williams's attempts to speak in

---

[2]Many U.S. firms, especially in textiles and electronics, had begun moving out of Puerto Rico, which led to fears of job loss.

Spanish and his "open-door policy" (whereby anyone in the plant could come to Williams to discuss something) as indications of his desire to be viewed as one of the Cayey family. But as one wage employee commented, "A few guys use the open-door policy but not often, especially since supervisors get upset if they go directly to Williams." But his knowing everyone's name and attempting to treat people like equals were appreciated.

Managers in Philadelphia also recognized the respect that Williams received from the Cayey work force: "John instilled a 'can-do' attitude within the operation. He's always been very autocratic, but I think the people in Puerto Rico deal well with that style." "They [plant personnel] respect John an awful lot. He's a reasonably autocratic ruler, though he'll tell you he's the renaissance man of team-building."

THE CAYEY ORGANIZATION

During the startup years, the organization looked much like other Evans operations, but in the plant's third year, when the plant manager was promoted, Williams chose not to replace him and instead had all staff members report directly to himself. The current organization, as shown in *Exhibit 1*, therefore had one less management layer than its sister plants. In 1982, when the liquids department manager departed, that position was also eliminated, thereby having the first-line supervisors report directly to the manufacturing manager.

By 1987 Williams's staff was working as a cohesive team: If one staff member, for example, was out of the plant, others would cover for him or her even if it were not their area of expertise. Whenever Williams suspected the staff was not working together, he would call a staff meeting, close the door, and tell them to settle their problems among themselves. Moreover, the staff worked closely whenever Williams was away from the facility since he delegated responsibility to each on a rotating basis, thus never creating a second-in-command. This approach was successful since the staff, several of whom had worked their way up in the organization, had been together for many years. Williams also rotated staff members between functions for their development and was known for supporting women and minorities. For example, in 1985 Evelyn Gonzales moved from the quality-assurance role to become manufacturing manager, thereby opening up the opportunity for Nilsa Chavez to be promoted to quality-assurance manager; both women had started as laboratory supervisors.

The plant experienced relatively little turnover and absenteeism except for the first few years. As Williams's first manager noted, "It was hard to find good people who could also get along with John. It wasn't all his fault, though; he just has high standards. For example, he went through five personnel managers in the first couple years." Turnover in the plastics department, due to rotating shifts and the need to work weekends and holidays, was also a problem. At first only engineers were hired for supervisory positions, but they soon became disenchanted with rotating shifts (in the plastics department) and having to remain in entry-level positions. In late 1977 the plant changed to promoting people internally, which helped to eliminate turnover and gave local wage employees an opportunity to grow within the company. Training became a way of life; anyone wanting additional training or further education was encouraged to take courses. As one manager noted, "The training is there and resources (both money and people) are available, so there is no need or reason to fail."

Evans quickly became known as one of the best companies to work for on the island. Although wages were average for the island, they were higher than any other plant in the Cayey vicinity. Fringe benefits were also superior to those of other companies; Evans also supplied all employees with uniforms and safety shoes. The Cayey facility, on 26 acres and comprising 130,000 square feet of floor space, looked more like a corporate office than a factory. The outside area was beautifully landscaped; the interior was decorated with plants and artwork (chosen by Williams's wife, an artist). The plant's housekeeping was immaculate, which helped eliminate accidents or injuries and contributed to its outstanding safety record. (It had gone 2,829,272 hours [more than seven years] without a lost time accident until August 1987, when a gardener cut his arm with a machete.) Housekeeping had been an area of central importance since the plant first opened; Williams felt it helped create a positive attitude at the facility. Maintenance was also strongly emphasized; $200,000, or up to 10% of the 1986 engineering budget, was dedicated to maintenance of the plant and equipment.

As the plant expanded, new unskilled wage employees were hired by word of mouth; skilled wage employees (mainly skilled trades) and salaried employees were in shorter supply and were often recruited through local newspapers or the local employment bureau. Potential recruits went through a rigorous interview process during which they were exposed to the plant culture and screened for "fit." Although supervisors (especially of wage employees) had the authority to reject possible hires, the employee relations department made a final review of all wage employee candidates, as did Williams for all salaried personnel.

Once the hiring decision was made, new employees attended a formal orientation program. Wage employees received two weeks of orientation, which involved background on the company and its philosophy, a tour of the entire facility, and a day and a half discussing safety and security. All salaried employees (exempt and nonexempt) spent their first week on the job meeting with every manager in the facility to learn what each did and how each area functioned. Throughout the entire orientation the values and performance expectations of the plant were continually reiterated so that new employees understood that the company was there to make money, but through its people. As one manager noted, "We stress that we are safety-oriented, people-oriented, task-oriented, and profit-oriented, and in that order." During their 90-day probation, new employees were subjected to monthly performance evaluations, and if their performance were judged inadequate, they were terminated. This was also true for permanent employees, who were removed from their jobs and when necessary terminated if they did not perform.

Performance achievement was emphasized at every level. Each senior staff member negotiated departmental goals and target dates for attaining them with Williams. Each week Williams would then meet one-on-one with his managers of manufacturing, quality assurance, engineering, and personnel (monthly with his controller) to review their progress against the targets. Most of the weekly meeting was spent discussing "follow-up" items; Williams kept a file on each staff member, which he used to keep track of the issues discussed at the weekly meeting and the actions that managers promised would be taken to solve problems. As one staff member commented, "You don't always know what follow-up questions he'll ask, so you have to be prepared for just about anything."

Williams ensured that key plant goals, i.e., planning values (quantity of output per a 7.5 hour shift) and waste figures (percentage of raw material cost lost), were always attained by setting the manufacturing department's goal at 102% of what was committed to division headquarters. (The division expected an annual 5% productivity growth.) In turn, Gonzales, the manufacturing manager, set her supervisors' goals at 105% of that commitment. The supervisors' performances against goals were recorded each shift on large posters in the plastics and liquids departments. Figures below the production goal were in red; figures equal or greater were in black. If production levels fell below the goal, supervisors would meet with operators to find out why. Line operators were also measured against output and waste goals, and results were reflected in their performance evaluations. Because output and waste levels were posted, there was intense competition between shifts and across lines. As one operator explained, "Everyone looks at the board, so there's competition between supervisors. They want to be on top, and we do too. Everyone wants to be on top." But preventive maintenance was strongly adhered to, despite the push for output. For instance, each time a mold was changed for a bottle size changeover, it was sent to a mold shop for preventive maintenance; the first and last bottles made from each mold were compared for wear. And during the annual shutdown, all molding and filling equipment was completely torn down, with every part checked for wear and lubrication.

Communications and teamwork were further strengthened in daily meetings held at 8:30 A.M., where the entire senior staff down to the first-line supervisors met to review the prior day's production. The meetings lasted two to three hours, and people complained that they were frustrating and ineffective. But once production was smoothly running, the meetings were shortened to fifteen to twenty minutes. As one supervisor stated, "Because of the daily meeting, production problems are solved within twenty-four hours."

For the first two years, Williams had participated in the meetings, which were held in English for his benefit. But language difficulties bogged down the discussions, so he stopped attending. Instead, he began meeting three times a week with the managers of manufacturing, engineering, and materials to get a summary of what occurred at the meetings and to check the status of production goals. Supervisors also held brief weekly meetings with their work groups to review production results and any other topics of interest.

PLANT IMPROVEMENT PROGRAMS

Through reassigning work to the Cayey facility (because of its low production costs especially in contract manufacturing), the Condiment Division was able to lower its total cost of goods from 40% to 35% of sales between 1980 and 1985. But bringing work in-house decreased Cayey's productivity (sales per employee of manpower), a key corporate measurement. As a result, over the past five years the local management had embarked upon a number of programs to improve the overall efficiency of the operation; it prided itself on typically being the first among other Evans plants in instituting many of these efforts.

Organizational Development. In response to a corporate program on improved productivity, a Work Climate Diagnosis was conducted at the plant in May 1982 by a Puerto Rican consulting firm. The survey had shown that plant employees felt communication could be improved, middle managers and first-line supervisors did not feel a part of management, and the wage employees wanted more involvement. In response, first-line supervisors and middle managers were brought into the annual plant planning and goal-setting process, the plant staff participated in a number of team-building exercises,[3] and team circles (quality circles) were formed. The latter was a total plant effort: All exempt personnel attended

---

[3]Team-building exercises were common within Evans. Beginning in 1982, the senior staff from Cayey and its sister plant in North Carolina met in Philadelphia for three days of team-building. This became an annual event in 1985. In addition, every year the divisional engineering staff met for two days for the same purpose.

a three-day training program, and two staff members (the manufacturing manager and the personnel manager) became circle facilitators in late 1983. There were several early successes, particularly in the warehouse and maintenance areas, where employees were involved in a rearrangement of the work areas, but by mid-1986 most of the circle activities were in remission. This was due mainly to the introduction of a new quality program (see below), which many employees viewed as superseding the team circle effort. After the teams had worked through their initial ideas, many of which were implemented by the technical support group, they generally felt there were no other problems to tackle.

Quality Improvement Program (QIP). In October 1985 Williams and his staff attended a week of training at Phil Crosby's Quality College in Florida. Soon thereafter, corporate began sending people to the college and decided to institute a formal QIP program. All employees (exempt and nonexempt) participated in the training, and managers were assigned to subcommittees to address Crosby's 14-step improvement process.[4] One of the first ideas stemming from the subcommittees was a "supplier day," designed to get local suppliers involved in the quality process. The first "supplier day," held in May 1987, involved representatives from every level within the plant, including wage employees.

Inventory Reductions. Over the previous five years, the plant's inventory levels had been drastically reduced, partly because of the elimination of warehouse space to make room for additional production equipment. In 1982, 7,500 square feet (of a total of about 80,000 square feet) were eliminated from the warehouse to make room for a new decorating line because a building expansion plan had been abandoned in anticipation of changes in the IRS's special tax law. In the fall of 1985 the warehouse manager relinquished an additional 17,500 square feet to allow for expansion of the plastics department. During the construction, the warehouse had to give up even more space; it was then found that the plastics area needed 300 square feet more for an additional machine. Finally, in 1986 the warehouse had to provide 700 square feet for the relocation of a battery charger. In total, more than 26,000 square feet of warehouse space had been given away during a period when new products had been brought into the plant and production levels had continually increased.

In early 1983 division management felt too many dollars were tied up in inventory (materials represented 70% of the product cost; direct labor less than 5%) and instructed the operation to reduce inventory. Concerns over shipping delays from the States and the reliability of local suppliers, caused the plant typically to carry as much as $3.5–$4.2 million worth of inventory on a monthly basis (three months' worth of most raw materials

---

[4]See the "Signetics (D)" case (#8-683-603) for details on Crosby's quality improvement program.

plus up to six weeks' worth of agricultural ingredients and plastic bottles); also, up to 2,025 trailer loads of finished goods could be outside the plant at any time, with each trailer accounting for $70,000–$90,000.

By increasing the number of on-island suppliers and gaining confidence in their ability to meet requirements, the operation was able to reduce much of the raw materials inventory to three weeks. The plant also began shipping finished goods "under impound" to Evans's warehouses in the States. Import regulations required that any product being brought into the country be held for seven days before being inspected for contamination. Since the Cayey operation had never had a contamination problem, and shipping to the States took seven days, division management decided to ship product in locked containers to be inspected upon receipt at the warehouse, thereby eliminating a week of inventory. By 1987 inventory within the Cayey plant was reduced to $2.2 million on average per month.

To facilitate inventory reductions, division management decided in June 1986 to transfer additional purchasing responsibility to the Cayey operation. This was to be done in phases. In the first phase, the plant absorbed an additional 10% of purchasing, which entailed close to 15 items equaling $2 million per year. Then in February 1987 the division purchasing manager told the materials manager that he could begin buying some of the agricultural commodities (basic ingredients) and chemicals, though the majority of commodities and chemicals continued to be purchased through Philadelphia. By May the plant was purchasing 48% of all its needed materials, an equivalent to $10 million out of its total yearly purchasing costs of $21 million. The plant's goal was to bring all purchasing in-house by 1988. But a recent reorganization of the division staff, splitting management responsibilities for operations and materials, threatened to reverse this trend.

CURRENT CHALLENGES

Besides the newly added goal of becoming a world-class manufacturing operation, the Cayey operation was introducing just-in-time inventory, increased automation on the filling lines, and new computerized process controls in the molding department.

Just-in-Time (JIT) Inventory. At the November 1985 strategic planning meeting, the division materials manager suggested that the division investigate JIT. The Cayey operation was considered the pioneer because it had already instituted "production to stock" (whereby daily production would be loaded onto trucks and shipped out within one day) in first quarter 1985, concurrent with the contraction of the warehouse and the ability to

ship under impound. But the division push prompted Williams to in-
struct his materials operation to investigate further the reliability of their
vendors to move toward "ship to production," which meant that incom-
ing raw materials would be used within one week of receipt. Although it
had been taboo within the plant to shut a line down for lack of materials,
the plant proceeded to introduce "ship to production" in early 1986. This
led to four line shutdowns in 1986, in three cases because local vendors
could not meet their requirements; one $2\frac{1}{2}$-day shutdown was due to the
lack of an ingredient obtained from Europe. The warehouse manager
commented:

> When you're using inventory, everybody is more lax. They go home
> and sleep well at night. With JIT there's more pressure. You need
> better organization and communication, especially with suppliers.
>   We are an island away from the States, and ocean transportation
> takes 57 days' transit time. Sixty percent of our suppliers are in the
> States or overseas. They have only four sailings a week, and if we don't
> take advantage of those four sailings, we can be shut down. Sometimes
> you have to airlift some materials, and that means eight times higher
> costs than by ocean. Before JIT, nothing came by air; now we airlift
> chemicals and labels. In the last eight or nine months when we've
> been using JIT, every week or every other week we bring something by
> air. It's not poor planning. It's just that the supplier is also trying to
> adjust to JIT.

In September 1986 the division commissioned a large consulting firm
to investigate further opportunities for inventory reductions. Its recommendation for the Cayey facility was to move to a monthly schedule,
which would mean that all models and sizes would be run three or four
times per month. (There was also talk of going to a bimonthly schedule.)
This implied a drastic increase in changeovers; at the time, each product
typically was run once a month.

Technically, the plant had not been designed for the flexibility needed
to meet such a schedule. Although the filling department was running at
a load capacity of 45%–50% based on a five-day, three-shift operation,
there were dedicated lines for each of its major products. This meant that
lines could be modified relatively quickly for bottle size changes, but
product changeovers on any particular line were practically impossible
because they required a total flushing of the lines from mixing to filling.[5]

---

[5]The third filling line, added in 1980, was designed to allow a bit more flexibility, since it was
used for both steak and barbecue sauces. Steak sauce was run for eight or nine continuous
months, and then the line was converted to barbecue sauce for the following three to four
months.

Because the plant had been designed to make long runs on high-volume products, piping had been totally welded shut during installation.

Bottle size changeovers were more technical than the operators' regular job; they required altering machine settings for labeling and cap components and then synchronizing the entire line. This meant that typically only maintenance personnel were occupied during changeovers, leaving operators idle. Synchronization alone could take up to an hour.

The plastics department had greater flexibility, but its changeovers were more complicated. There a changeover entailed changing the molds for different bottle sizes; 25 different bottle sizes were produced for internal use, plus 20 others for contractors. Changing from a small bottle size to a larger one took eight hours; the reverse took four. Each time a changeover to a different product (three for internal use and five for contract work) occurred, the resin had to be adjusted for different bottle compositions.

Plans were under way to train operators and packers to help the mechanics during changeover. But local management did not foresee any resistance from either operators or mechanics; the only concern was a perceived lack of mechanical ability among the packers.

The inefficiencies and lost time associated with changeovers also raised concern about the operation's ability to meet and exceed production goals. (See *Exhibit 2* for a summary of production statistics.) Several managers worried that wage employees might receive the wrong message if told to stop producing once the day's production quota had been met; they thought work force morale would suffer, which would weaken the plant's "can-do" attitude. The competition set up between lines and shifts had yielded continual productivity gains. But since sales had not increased, the practice of continually surpassing planning values eventually reduced volumes in subsequent production runs.

Reduced levels of work-in-process inventory would also complicate production planning and material ordering, particularly balancing production between plastics and liquids; liquids could fill bottles three times faster than plastics could mold containers. As one supervisor remarked:

> The biggest problem is how are we going to deal with the planning value while using JIT concepts? Now we're encouraged to beat the planning value. With JIT we are not encouraged to beat it. When you beat the planning value, you use up inventory faster than it is scheduled. We now order raw materials, or produce bottles for liquids, based on 110% of planning values, but sometimes the line beats their planning values by 30%. We also won't be able to react to emergency sales as quickly because raw materials won't be available.

Automation of the Filling Lines. Since island labor rates were so low relative to the States and the initial engineering plans had emphasized simple equipment, little new technology had been installed in the Cayey facility. Although equipment existed to load bottles automatically onto the line and package the finished products, packers at the front of the line pulled empty bottles out of a chute and set them upright on the conveyor belt, while packers at the end of the line manually packed filled bottles in cartons and sealed them for transfer to the warehouse. But Williams was concerned that the plant was not keeping pace with new technology and saw automation as a way to reduce costs further. As a result, new equipment eliminating packers at both ends was on order for one filling line. Although division engineering personnel were satisfied that local personnel had the technical expertise to maintain the new equipment, one local manager noted, "People are the only things that are truly flexible. Increased automation reduces flexibility; you have more complicated changeovers and more equipment to break down. I'm worried that we are reducing flexibility when it should be increased for just-in-time."

In total, the new equipment would replace 12–13 packers per shift, but if it proved successful, it would probably be added to the other filling lines, thus displacing additional employees. To help ease the introduction of new equipment into the plant, a line operator, mechanic, QA technician, and production supervisor were scheduled to visit the vendor in Minnesota to see the equipment and make recommendations for any needed modifications to its design.

The displaced packers, among the most senior employees within the facility, would be able to displace people in the plastics department. This concerned the plastics department because of the training required. Whereas packers on the filling line needed only six to ten months to reach proficiency, packers in the plastic department required two to three years of training to become proficient with the molding machines, where, for example, defect identification was more difficult and the pace more demanding. Nonetheless, the jobs in both areas were considered equal relative to pay. (Senior packers also preferred the liquids department to avoid working the rotating shifts in the plastics area.) Another concern was the effect of laying off short-service employees (those bumped out of plastics) on the rest of the work force. Except for 12 employees who had been laid off in 1976 (for alleged union activities), the permanent work force had never experienced work force reductions; seasonal fluctuations in volume were covered by a temporary third shift in the liquids department (typically seven to eight months each year).

Computerized Process Controls. In 1986 the plant purchased its own System 36 IBM mainframe computer and began developing tailor-made systems to fit Cayey's needs. The plant's three-member information systems staff had already created a receiving-shipping-inventory system specifically for the warehouse and was designing an in-house system to track costs and schedules in a JIT environment. To update the facility's technology further, key staff members, supported by the local information systems people and division engineering personnel, were evaluating a system for in-line process controls.

This proposed system could monitor process variables, the better to control deviations from the "centerline" (i.e., when variables exceeded the acceptable limits for optimum processing) on the molding equipment and to provide automatic statistical process control (SPC) charts at 27 terminals throughout the plant. The QA area already had a quasi-SPC system in place, but no charting was done in the production areas. Some staff members felt SPC was too technical for supervisors or operators. The computer would eliminate the need for them to get directly involved. Local management assumed that wage employees would be very accepting of the new system because it would bring improvements to the plant, but an engineer from Philadelphia questioned whether there would be total acceptance of the technology, noting, "They [Cayey personnel] tend to make the absolute best out of what they currently have versus stepping up to the next plateau."

BECOMING WORLD CLASS

Williams, though proud of Cayey's success, still felt improvements could be implemented. He had been reading about world class manufacturing (WCM) techniques[6] and was excited about the possibility of applying them at the plant. Williams commented on his view of WCM and what it would mean at the Cayey operation:

> WCM means I can compete on price with anyone in the world and still have the amenities we have now. We also have to get total employee involvement. We have to take the opportunity to let wage employees direct their operations more. We have to eliminate the supervisory ranks more and move toward more multiskilled workers.

The plant had already taken steps to broaden the wage employees' tasks by assigning them jobs that had previously been done by QA technicians. While operators assumed many of the simple quality checks, QA technicians still took samples of bottles from each of the molding machines four times per shift and checked them for various attributes, e.g., torque, height, and thickness. The QA supervisor noted:

> A year from now, maybe two years, the operators will be doing the QA job. Everyone will be involved in quality. We will also look for more

[6]See Richard J. Schonberger, *World Class Manufacturing* (New York: Free Press, 1986).

responsibility for the QA technicians. They'll do more auditing instead of being like a policeman in front of the operators. Transferring some of our QA jobs to the operator is a matter of survival.

Attitudes in the plant were indeed positive. But as one manager warned:

You have to be aggressive and innovative and open-minded, but there are too many things going on. We set goals and try to achieve them, but then the direction changes. For example, we had the QIP program, but now JIT is getting more attention. We're always being asked to cut expenses here and there; I've already heard the quality program is going to be cut down. Those types of management decisions are not healthy.

We at the plant know the goals and objectives and what we want to do with the plant. But corporate seems lost. They change their minds from one day to another. Quality, JIT, team circles—they spend so much money on all these things, they end up cutting into the operation.

Williams was concerned over the rate of change in the operation and wanted to ensure that the operation would be settled and ready to hand over to a successor within eighteen months. He noted, "I want to make sure the changes become a way of life; I don't want our efforts to fade away after I retire."

EVANS FOOD CORPORATION

Exhibit 1 Cayey Organization Chart (1986)

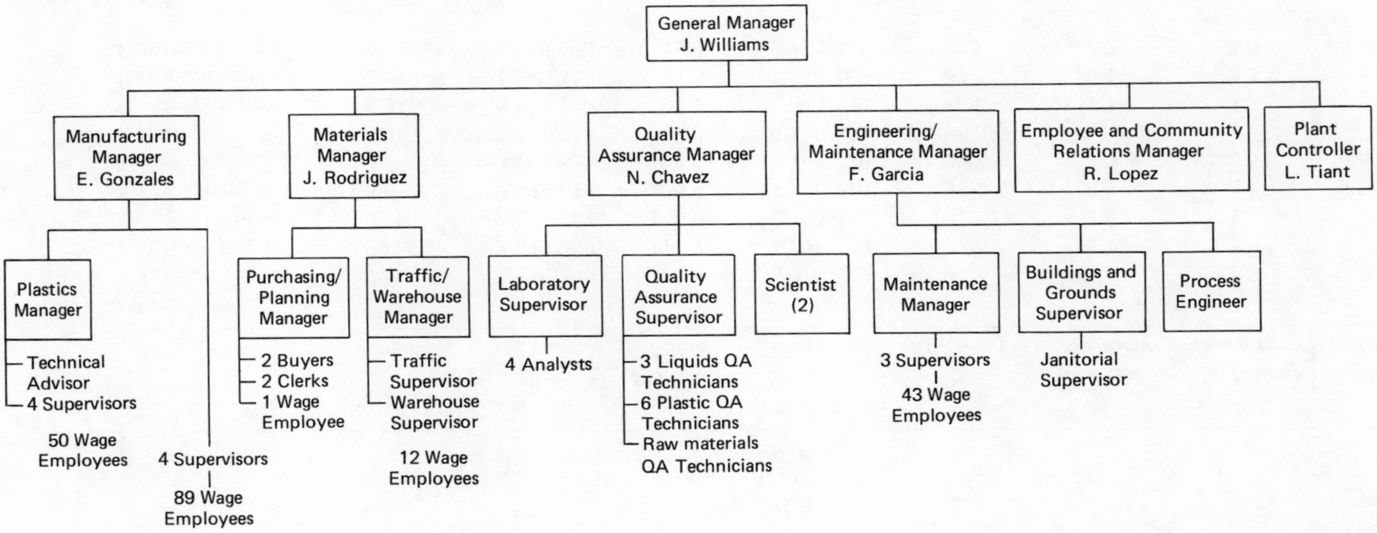

General Manager
J. Williams

- Manufacturing Manager
E. Gonzales
- Materials Manager
J. Rodriguez
- Quality Assurance Manager
N. Chavez
- Engineering/Maintenance Manager
F. Garcia
- Employee and Community Relations Manager
R. Lopez
- Plant Controller
L. Tiant

Manufacturing Manager — E. Gonzales
- Plastics Manager
  - Technical Advisor
  - 4 Supervisors
    - 50 Wage Employees
- 4 Supervisors
  - 89 Wage Employees

Materials Manager — J. Rodriguez
- Purchasing/Planning Manager
  - 2 Buyers
  - 2 Clerks
  - 1 Wage Employee
- Traffic/Warehouse Manager
  - Traffic Supervisor
  - Warehouse Supervisor
    - 12 Wage Employees

Quality Assurance Manager — N. Chavez
- Laboratory Supervisor
  - 4 Analysts
- Quality Assurance Supervisor
  - 3 Liquids QA Technicians
  - 6 Plastic QA Technicians
  - Raw materials QA Technicians
- Scientist (2)

Engineering/Maintenance Manager — F. Garcia
- Maintenance Manager
  - 3 Supervisors
  - 43 Wage Employees
- Buildings and Grounds Supervisor
  - Janitorial Supervisor
- Process Engineer

319

EVANS FOOD CORPORATION

Exhibit 2
Production Statistics
(3d quarter, 1986)

	Actual	Plan	% Planning Value	Theoretical	% Efficiency	% Machine Downtime	% Other Downtime	Shift Run
Plastics								
Contract bottle	9,723,486	7,373,706	131.8	9,013,922	107.8	3.5	2.8	1,016.9
Contract bottle	2,994,705	2,643,939	113.2	3,208,676	93.3	2.1	1.9	271.5
Contract bottle	2,643,730	2,260,124	116.9	2,465,680	107.2	2.5	1.6	292.7
Steak sauce	11,539,552	10,594,842	108.9	11,996,740	96.1	3.0	2.1	1,022.9
Mustard	6,457,514	6,184,815	104.4	7,153,228	90.2	3.3	2.0	615.3
Ketchup	8,070,721	7,961,034	101.3	9,166,931	88.0	3.3	2.5	789.5
Contract bottle	556,555	569,120	97.7	644,589	86.3	1.1	1.2	71.1
Barbeque sauce	1,628,144	1,942,316	83.8	1,978,462	82.2	5.1	8.3	117.6
Contract bottle	3,511,325	3,546,590	99.0	3,923,265	89.5	2.7	3.0	366.6
Liquids								
Ketchup	550,474	534,348	103.0	790,522	69.6	5.1	1.3	120.8
Mustard	534,246	519,099	102.9	740,149	72.1	3.9	3.2	124.8
Steak sauce	215,059	186,665	115.2	307,005	70.0	4.8	1.0	58.7
Barbeque sauce	74,763	68,754	108.7	112,888	66.2	4.1	1.2	20.6
	1,374,542	1,308,866	105.0	1,950,564	70.4	4.5	2.0	325.2

Rio Bravo Electricos,
General Motors Corporation

Despite the car's air conditioner, Alfonso Vazquez perspired impatiently in the line of cars waiting to pass through customs back into El Paso, Texas, from Rio Bravo, Mexico. He was in a hurry to buy transparencies in El Paso, for they were not readily available in Rio Bravo. The phones had not been working again, so he had not been able to find out when the office supplies store would close. Tomorrow he was to make a presentation on his study of the centralization of the capital-intensive lead preparation area of the plant. He would make his recommendations to the Latin American operations staff of the Packard Electric Division of General Motors Corporation.

This was August 1981, the summer after Vazquez's first year of the MBA program at a well-known Eastern business school. Previously he had worked for three years in engineering at General Motors. In the summer of 1981 he was assigned to operations for the first time, studying the manufacturing process and organization at the one-year-old plant in Rio Bravo. His fluency in Spanish and his desire to work in operations had been key in this assignment. He was anxious to do well.

GENERAL MOTORS' STRATEGY FOR THE 1980s

Despite lagging auto sales in the early 1980s, GM had strengths that other automakers did not: a larger volume of sales over which to spread research and new product development, and practically no long-term debt. Based on these, GM's strategy for the 1980s was to continue to produce a full line, to improve quality, and to fund and develop new products and manufacturing techniques. Quoting from the *1981 General Motors Public Interest Report:*

> General Motors has embarked upon an aggressive program to
> redesign nearly all its cars and most of the plants that produce them
> in the first half of the decade.

This case was prepared by Professor Roy D. Shapiro as the basis for class discussion rather than to illustrate either effective or ineffective handling of an administrative situation. Abridged with permission.

Copyright © 1990 by the President and Fellows of Harvard College. Harvard Business School case #690-041.

PACKARD ELECTRIC DIVISION, GENERAL MOTORS

Packard Electric Division was one of the major component divisions within General Motors, supplying electrical systems including wiring harnesses (bundles of electrical cables with connectors designed to be readily inserted into the automobile during assembly), connectors, electronic modules, and wiring expertise to the numerous domestic car divisions and foreign GM subsidiaries as well as a small number of nonallied customers. Packard's main function was to supply harnesses in high volumes at just the right times to supply the largest manufacturing process in the world, General Motors' automobile assembly system. It was highly integrated vertically, making complete wiring systems from raw copper cathode and train carloads of raw plastic. For example, Packard *daily* processed 100,000 pounds of plastic resin, 133,000 pounds of copper, and 25 million feet of cable into some 29 million parts, which were shipped to some 3,630 different destinations each month. Based in Warren, Ohio, Packard had been expanding geographically during the 1970s to support a growing product line.

THE MEXICAN MAQUILAS

In Mexico, the word *maquila* (mah-KEE-lah) referred to the toll charged by small local mills for grinding corn into meal. In the late 1960s and 1970s, maquila began to be used to refer to the practice, sanctioned by the Mexican government, by which American firms were allowed to ship components into Mexico, add labor value, then ship the finished products back across the border. A small U.S. duty was charged on the value added in Mexico. American firms gained through the lower-cost Mexican labor; Mexico gained the inflow of foreign-exchange wages from the United States. Squeezed by rising labor costs, Packard saw the maquila as a way to save on labor-intensive aspects of their business.

The first maquila experiments ended badly when a few unscrupulous textile companies cheated the locals by not paying the promised wages, but by 1981 the maquila concept was well-regarded by parties on both sides of the border. Several major American corporations had new and modern plants in the El Paso–Rio Bravo area. Because of shipping expenses and the cost of training, usually only labor-intensive operations were moved to Mexico. This implied that firms used machinery as efficiently as possible.

PLANT ORGANIZATION: CENTRALIZED OR MODULAR?

Two Packard plants were in the area: Rio Bravo Electricos (RBE), built in 1980, and Conductores Y Componentes Electricos, a three-year-old plant. Both plants were extremely successful by all measures: costs, delivery (despite shipping distances), and quality. RBE had the highest quality index of all North American Packard plants. Both plants had a "module" organization that was also reflected in the plant layout.

The module system was a way to break a plant up into more manageable units within the same building. Rio Bravo had three modules, with a fourth about to be added in vacant plant space.

RBE's organization consisted of a plant manager (Gary Richardson, the only American at RBE other than Vazquez) and, for each module, a module manager, a general supervisor on day shift, and three first-level supervisors on each shift. One of these supervisors ran the lead preparation area (lead prep), and the other two a final assembly area each. *Exhibit 1* shows the existing organization, *Exhibit 2* the proposed centralized organization, and *Exhibit 3* how the modular organization was reflected in plant layout.

Vazquez had been assigned to RBE to work for Richardson during the summer, as an "outside consultant" providing an objective analysis. Richard was one of Packard's most successful young managers. He had worked with both centralized and decentralized plants in Ohio and felt that lead prep should be centralized to save on expensive machinery. He asked Vazquez to make his own study, including an analysis of the relevant cost differences.

During his first week at RBE, Vazquez was invited to a staff meeting where centralization was to be discussed. He found that several managers had strong and divergent opinions, one way or the other, but John Wilson, the director of Latin American operations, wanted more facts before he would commit himself. Richardson made the best arguments for centralizing lead prep, emphasizing that the main reason for coming to Mexico was to reduce costs. Leonardo Ortiz, the manager of the Conductores plant, argued well for the module system. He had developed within that system and emphasized that it fostered teamwork. He also pointed to both plants' very successful record.

Ortiz and others who supported retaining modularity at RBE argued that the organization was able to respond quickly in a crisis because problems within the module had to travel only one organizational level (from supervisor to general supervisor) for integration. Although each module produced slightly different products, the risk of upsetting the entire plant during a process breakdown would be less since it would be confined to a single area. As an added benefit, having three independent units, each of which incorporated the *entire* process, made it possible to train three managers quickly for the job of plant manager. Richardson's goal was to replace himself with a local as soon as possible. (Conductores Y Componentes was already run by a Mexican.)

Richardson and others who thought a centralized plant would be more appropriate argued that despite these advantages, there were several inefficiencies in the modular organization, especially in lead prep, the capital-intensive part of the process. Dividing the plant would clearly increase in-process inventories. The actual cost of this increase was not known. Furthermore, certain leads common to all final assembly areas could be made on the same machine with the same setup. Therefore, the module system required more machine capacity, since time was taken for duplicate setups. Finally, every time the number of machines was calculated for another module, one had to round up to the nearest whole machine.

Near the end of the meeting, Wilson noted that Vazquez had remained silent and asked him for his thoughts. Quickly remembering what he had learned in Organizational Behavior, Vazquez jokingly suggested that he had spent almost a week at RBE and was therefore an expert. He would be glad to comment. Everyone laughed, realizing that they would have to wait for the MBA to commit himself.

PRODUCTION AT THE RIO BRAVO PLANT

Packard plants were designed to run two shifts, holding the third shift as reserve capacity. As a component supplier of parts that had low relative value in the automobile (as compared to the body, engine, drive train, etc.), RBE always had to meet the delivery needs of the car divisions. Similarly, high quality was considered to be essential, since once the wiring was installed and covered with interior finishing, it was hard to service. A defective harness would hold up the entire car at the assembly plant until it could be repaired or replaced.

Lead Preparation

RBE's inputs consisted of large spools of cable, plastic connectors, spools of terminals on headers designed for automatic or semi-automatic application, molding compounds for special connectors that had to be molded onto cables, and miscellaneous components such as splice clips, electrical tape, solder, and plastic conduits. The lead prep area prepared, cut, and partly or fully terminated cables that were sent to final assembly, where they were inserted into connectors and bundled into complete wiring harnesses. At lead prep large molding machines molded special connectors onto certain cables. Certain operations, such as splicing or soldering, were shared by both lead prep and final assembly. Each of the three operations (cutting, pressing, and molding) is elaborated on below.

Large spools of cable first had to be cut to various specified lengths on high-volume automatic cutters. Some cut the cable and automatically pressed on terminals at one or both ends of the cable after stripping the ends. These cutters, while automatic, required careful adjustment during setup according to the cable gauge (conductor diameter), specified length, and terminal types to be applied.

Cutters were unique in the process since *all* cables had to pass through them on their way to any other operation. As a result, "lots" were first created at cutters, since cut cables went into large plastic bins, each bin containing the quantity cut during one setup of the cutter. This quantity remained intact until it was delivered to final assembly. A cutter processed 4,000 leads during one setup. If those leads had to have a connector molded onto them, the molder would then also run 4,000 leads on a setup. Cutter lot size was based on yearly inventory carrying cost per lead of $0.01, cutter running capacity of 2,000 cut leads per hour (as opposed to *effective* capacity, which would be less because of the half-hour setup incurred when changing lead types), and average lead consumption by downstream processes within each module (presses, molders, or paced final assembly lines) of 100 leads of *each* type per hour. Cutters were the only fully automatic machines in the process. One operator could run three machines at once. The total direct cost (including tooling, maintenance, labor, and depreciation) for a cutter was $5,000 annually.

Presses were machines that pressed terminals onto the stripped ends of cut cables. The total direct cost for a press was $4,000 annually. Presses were operated by one person, who positioned the cable end in the machine and then stepped on a foot switch to apply the terminal. This operation required good dexterity and eye-hand coordination and a knowledge of the right method. Operators were also responsible for detecting when the machine was damaging the terminal or wire, something that required experience and a good eye. Most press operators were women.

The other major area of lead prep consisted of molders. Each molding machine had one operator and was semi-automatic. A cable with a terminal already applied was inserted into the machine, and a connector was molded around it. Many molders at RBE were old and required frequent service. These machines, because of temperature controls and electronics, were the most expensive and the slowest. Only a few types of cables required molding. The total direct cost for a molder was $7,000 annually.

Certain cables had to pass through all three operations before assembly; others went straight from cutters to final assembly.

Component Shortages

Logistics was somewhat complicated by two factors: (1) the large distance between RBE's El Paso warehouse (shared by Conductores) and Ohio, where components were made, and (2) poor communications across the border. The former could not be changed, and the latter resulted less from the language barrier (the Americans spoke Spanish rather well, and the Mexicans were taking English classes at the plant) than from a very poor local telephone system. Sometimes it was impossible to call across the border, and on several occasions the phones were shut down altogether.

When supervisors recognized that supplies of a part were inadequate, they usually contacted either the module's general supervisor or the materials general supervisor. If the part was not in receiving, the materials general supervisor would immediately order the part from the warehouse in El Paso, assuming the phones worked, or drive thirty minutes to ask for it personally. Even then, the part could be held up in Mexican customs for several days.

An alternative was to check with other modules to see if they had the part, which was often the case. Finally, they could also check with Conductores. Despite these alternatives, shortages sometimes occurred. There was some animosity between the materials general supervisor and the El Paso warehouse, each suspecting that the other was somehow at fault when a shortage occurred.

Maintenance Problems

Vazquez talked to several lead prep supervisors. Their chief complaint was bad support from the maintenance men ("técnicos"). Técnicos were responsible for machine setups as well as repairs. The reporting relationship was under study at the time. Técnicos reported to a maintenance general supervisor. They considered themselves elite because they had received more training than operators. Part of their workday was still spent on training.

Supervisors complained that tecnicos were sometimes nowhere to be found when needed. Vazquez observed técnicos coming in late in the morning and reacting with little interest to supervisors' urgent requests for service.

THE LABOR CONTEXT

There were about 700 locally hired, unskilled hourly employees at RBE. The work force was very young, mostly between seventeen and twenty-two years old, with the average being about nineteen. Annual turnover and absenteeism were very high. Turnover exceeded 40% despite excellent working conditions in the new, modern plant. Because of the number of new plants in the area, workers would often switch to a new plant closer to home (almost none had cars). They typically came to work in vans run by one of the large Mexican unions, though neither RBE nor Conductores was unionized. Another cause of turnover, among the técnicos in particular, was the hiring away of trained workers by new plants paying just above the prevailing wage to get a base crew of skilled workers trained by the existing plants.

Absenteeism was high because many workers came from very poor homes, where they sometimes filled the roles of breadwinner, mother, and daughter all in one. If other family members became ill, the worker might be the only one who could care for them. Working in an industrial environment was also a completely new experience for many; they did not understand the impact that their absence might have on the work group. This, too, made the supervisor's job difficult.

A TYPICAL SUPERVISOR'S DAY

As his electronic watch awakened him at 4 A.M., Vazquez asked himself how anyone could do this every day. He had arranged to spend an entire day with the lead prep supervisor in Module 1, and he wanted to arrive before the shift started at 6 A.M.

When he walked into the plant at 5:30, the supervisor, Eugenio Batista, greeted him. Batista, surprised that Vazquez would come in so early, enthusiastically began to show him the ropes.

Numerous things had to be done before the shift began. The molders had to be turned on so they would be warm when the operators arrived. Batista had to review the notebook used to communicate with the other shift's supervisor. It contained such information as what setups certain machines had had, which machines were down, which components were low, or whether final assembly needed emergency runs of any particular cables.

At 5:40, one of several "utilities" arrived. These were skilled operators who helped the supervisor with material and information flows. They rarely operated machines but spent their time seeing that operators did not run out of components. This utility was responsible for leaving "cut cards" on each cutter telling the operators what, and how many, cables to cut. The supervisor checked these cards before allowing the utility to distribute them. During the day, the utilities often came to the supervisor with problems requiring his assistance, such as getting a técnico to work on a machine or obtaining a component that could not be located.

By 6 A.M. the machines were running. Batista had to shift several opera-tors around to compensate for absences. Mondays were particularly bad. At 6:15 the cutter técnico appeared in the area, and Batista already had work for him. Several times final assembly utilities came to Batista re-questing emergency runs of certain cables. These runs were needed occa-sionally because the cable inventory report (which was updated on a chart halfway through the shift by production control personnel) was not cur-rent enough, especially at the beginning of the shift, or because a batch had been found to be defective by QC inspectors or final assemblies. Batista reacted quickly to these requests, and new cables were started very soon.

By 3 P.M., the end of the shift, Vazquez was exhausted. The supervisor had spent the entire day on his feet, handling one crisis after another. Vazquez wondered how centralizing lead prep would affect Batista's job. Batista said he liked the module system and would not like a centralized area.

THE QUANTITATIVE ANALYSIS

Vazquez realized he had to calculate a dollar amount that would represent the savings possible by centralizing lead prep (as a result of eliminating current duplicate setups). He found that only cutters seemed to be run-ning significant numbers of lead types that were common across modules. Combining these types in a centralized area would allow longer runs between setups, increasing effective capacity.

He also wondered what effect, if any, centralization would have on lot size and therefore on total plant inventory. After some thought, he was convinced that the often-seen square root relationship applied here. Thus, he could easily determine the optimal inventory level or lot size for multiple locations as a function of the optimal level for a single site, or vice versa. For example, centralization would double the demand on lead prep for Class B lead types (see *Exhibit 4*), and thus the optimal lot size would increase by a factor equal to the square root of two. Similarly, since the demand in a centralized environment for Class C lead types would be triple the demand previously faced by any module's lead prep area, the optimal lot size would increase by 73%.[1]

---

[1]Since $\sqrt{3} = 1.73$.

RIO BRAVO ELECTRICOS, GENERAL MOTORS CORPORATION

Exhibit 1 Present Modular Organization

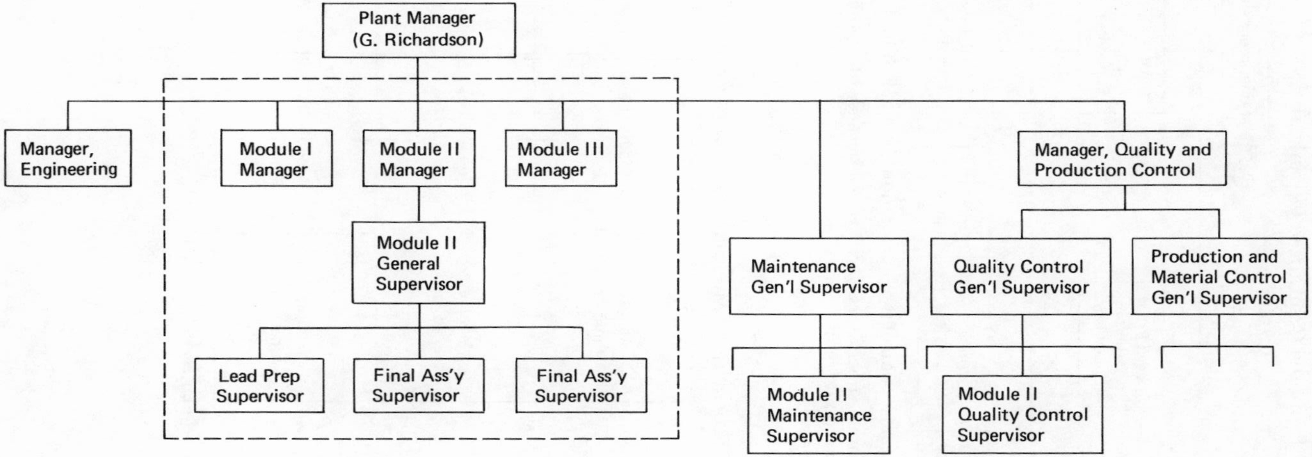

Exhibit 2 Proposed Centralized Organization[a]

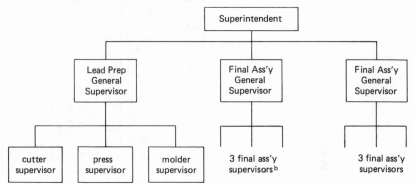

[a]to replace that section of the organization chart of Exhibit 1 enclosed by dotted lines

[b]Three separate supervisors were needed because of a policy that limited the number of workers who could report to one supervisor.

Exhibit 3 Schematic of Modular Plant Layout

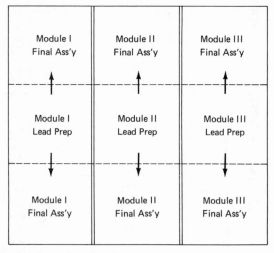

Arrows represent directions of product flow.

Exhibit 4
Commonality of Cutter Lead Types Across Modules

	Number of Types per Module		
	Mod I	*Mod II*	*Mod III*
Class A			
(lead types unique to each module)	70	50	100
Class B[a]			
(lead types common to all modules)	50 ----------------------- 50		
Class C			
(lead types common to all modules)	30 ----------------------- 30 ----------------------- 30		

[a]I.e., 50 of the lead types cut in module I are also cut in module II, with duplicate setups.

5

Marketing

Marketing in developing countries faces many special challenges be-cause of the distinctive environment. Developing country demographics are fundamentally different from those in developed countries. The LDCs' population growth rate is four times higher. Their age structure is predominantly young; about 40% of the population is under fifteen, almost twice the share in the older-aged developed countries. About 65% of the people live in rural areas and 35% in cities, which is almost the mirror opposite of the developed countries. However, the developing countries are urbanizing very rapidly and creating the world's largest cities, Mexico City with 18 million topping the list. Developing country markets are also hindered by deficiencies in infrastructure, information, and institutions. In response to those deficiencies and to the social impor-tance and political salience of marketing activities, governments often actively intervene in the markets.

KEY ISSUES

The four cases in this chapter focus on several important issues emerging from the distinctive marketing environment in developing countries. These include the nature and significance of government interventions, infrastructural and organizational problems in the distribution channels, and the use of advertising and promotional techniques, including "social marketing."[1] Chapter 8 contains cases that deal with export marketing from LDCs to other countries.

Government Interventions

As we saw in Chapter Three, the Mega-Force of government actions has a pervasive influence on the business environment. In the marketing area, government policies can affect many aspects of the marketing mix—for example, price controls; media and advertising regulations; product standards for safety, health, or packaging; and transportation rates and routes. The first case in this chapter, "Sabritas," examines the experience of a highly successful Mexican snack food subsidiary of a multinational corporation. Its continued success, however, is being threatened by the possibility of price controls and restrictions on advertising what some government officials considered "junk foods."

Distribution

In mounting distribution systems, developing country marketers often confront inadequacies in physical infrastructure and services such as transportation and storage. Market information on supply, demand, prices, and preferences is frequently scarce or inaccurate, thereby impeding the efficient functioning of marketplace forces and actors. Many marketing channels are excessively long and highly fragmented, with power sometimes concentrated in a small number of distributors. The management of Sabritas had to figure out how to adapt the supermarket-based distribution system used by its parent in the United States to Mexico City's food retail structure, dominated by thousands of small corner stores. "Milkpak," the chapter's second case, presents a project developed by Packages Ltd., the Pakistani packaging company discussed in the previous chapter. Packages was attempting to mount a sterilized milk processing plant that would employ its underutilized Tetra Pak packaging machines. The success of this project depended greatly on the company's ability to make major changes in the traditional milk distribution system.

Advertising and Promotion

Advertising levels in developing countries are about one-third of those in developed countries because of lower incomes, less developed and diffused communication infrastructure, and lower literacy. Although radio ownership is more widespread, television advertising captures a larger share of the LDC advertising expenditures. But LDCs tend to rely more on radio advertising than the developed countries, which in turn make heaviest use of print media. Three of the chapter's cases allow us to examine advertising and promotion activities from quite distinct perspectives. Sabritas, as a marketer of an impulse consumer good in a large urban area, makes intensive use of advertising, particularly television and radio. It plays a key role in the marketing mix, and an emerging local competitor is using larger advertising as the cutting edge of its market penetration strategy. The chapter's third case, on infant formula marketing by Nestlé and other MNCs reveals some adverse social consequences of aggressive advertising and promotion. It raises issues related to the appropriateness of these marketing techniques, given the socioeconomic conditions of low-income consumers who are enticed to buy the products but often not able to use them safely. The resultant international controversy and boycott reveal the political sensitivity of marketing in developing countries. In contrast, the final case in the chapter, "Population Services, Inc.," deals with the use of modern promotional techniques as part of a "social marketing" program to distribute contraceptives in Bangladesh to assist the government with its national population program.

CASE STUDY QUESTIONS

Sabritas

1. How successful has Sabritas been? Why?
2. How important are the government's actions to the company's future success?
3. How serious is the competitive threat from Barcel?
4. What should management do to deal with the government and Barcel?

Milkpak

1. What are the major impediments facing Packages as it attempts to mount the Milkpak operation?
2. What are the implications of the Milkpak operation for the traditional milk distribution system?
3. What recommendations would you make to management regarding the design and operation of its marketing system?

Nestlé Alimentana S.A.—Infant Formula

1. Why did the prevailing infant formula marketing practices draw criticism?
2. What is your evaluation of the ways in which Nestlé and other companies responded to the criticism?
3. What guidelines would you recommend for marketing infant formula or other products in developing countries?

Population Services, Inc.

1. What were the critical components of the social marketing program?
2. How successful has it been?
3. Why did it encounter problems?
4. What actions do you recommend to management and government?

NOTE

1. For an extended discussion of marketing issues, see James E. Austin, *Managing in Developing Countries* (New York: Free Press, 1990), Chapter 9.

Sabritas

John Warner, president of Sabritas, S.A. de C.V., was proud of its achievements. Since its reorganization in 1967 as a wholly owned subsidiary of PepsiCo Inc., sales volume had increased from $600,000 to an expected figure of nearly $200 million in 1981, with a 30% dollar volume increase in 1980. Dollar sales had grown at an average rate of 54% per year, even after a nearly 50% devaluation of the Mexican peso in 1976. Operating profits had grown equally spectacularly, and Sabritas was a valuable contributor to its parent, PepsiCo International Foods Division (see *Exhibits 1–3*).

As the main supplier to the Mexican snack food market, Sabritas manufactured and distributed a line of flavored snacks, including potato chips and corn- and wheat-based items in a variety of sizes and shapes. Plans for the 1980s were ambitious: A 100% capacity expansion program involving construction of a fourth and fifth plant and more than 4,000 new jobs was to be completed by 1985. Inaugurated on November 15, 1980, in the northern city of Saltillo, a third plant increased Sabritas capacity by 30% and provided 300 more jobs. Revenues were projected to expand 25% a year; Sabritas was to maintain its operating profit margin of 14.5%. With this expansion program, it expected to maintain its dominant market share, its position as one of Mexico's top private firms, and its ability to contribute substantially to its parent company.

Despite its past performance, Sabritas management faced difficult problems. Warner and his executive team were concerned about the company's ability to continue to meet home office expectations, given tendencies in the Mexican business environment. Four areas—expansion and government regulations, raw material supplies, consumerism, and company organization and management development—appeared critical to the design and implementation of a successful corporate strategy during the 1980s.

EXPANSION AND GOVERNMENT RELATIONS

As a wholly owned subsidiary of a multinational, Sabritas had to negotiate its expansion plans with the Mexican government. Under Mexican law,

This case was prepared by Kenneth Hoadley and Professor James Austin as the basis for class discussion rather than to illustrate either effective or ineffective handling of an administrative situation. Abridged with permission.

companies established after 1973 that were less than 51% Mexican-owned were required to negotiate their conditions of entry into Mexico with the government. While opposed to granting entry to companies not majority-owned by Mexicans, the government did make exceptions when foreign companies offered to provide jobs in outlying parts of the country or areas of high unemployment, contribute significantly toward generating export earnings, or in some other way help meet specific goals of the government's Global Development Plan. Companies in Mexico before the foreign investment law was passed that had not "Mexicanized" were allowed to continue operations but were limited in expanding into new markets or product lines, and even in growth of existing product lines when such growth involved physical expansion, for building permits required government negotiations that were guided by the government's overall development plan.

During negotiations for a permit to construct the plant in Saltillo, Sabritas committed itself to the generation of new jobs in a developing area and to a balance of payments surplus in its own operations (excluding dividend payments sent abroad) by 1982. Management was concerned about designing a strategy to comply with this commitment. Doing so via exports would be limited by the presence of another PepsiCo affiliate (Frito-Lay) in the United States with a similar product line, and by the restraints Mexican law imposed on Sabritas in expanding into new product lines. Management was also concerned about negotiations for future plant expansion; it sought to develop growth alternatives attractive to the Mexican government.

Raw Material Supplies

Supply constraints were a second problem. Manufacturing companies (Mexican and foreign) were not allowed to invest in agricultural production, and Sabritas's need for raw materials was growing faster than its sources of supply. A potato seed improvement program and a producer financing scheme had helped eliminate a major bottleneck in potato chips (Sabritas's leading product), but other needs ranging from cooking oil to packaging materials would also have to be filled. This supply problem was compounded by Mexico's stagnating agriculture and government programs to focus production on meeting Mexico's basic food needs and away from nonessential consumption.

Consumerism

A government-encouraged consumerism campaign had singled out "transnational junk food companies" as its favorite target; Sabritas management felt that criticism had been inflammatory and unfair. While the attacks had not hurt sales, they might have adverse effects on government policy-makers whose approval was needed for company expansion plans or on policies affecting raw material supplies.

Company Organization and Management Development

Finally, internal issues about company organization and management development concerned Warner and his senior executives. During the 1980s Sabritas expected to double its volume every five years; by the end of the decade it would be a half-billion-dollar company. While over the years it had successfully brought in highly qualified young Mexican executives with management training, its organization and top management remained largely unchanged. Although this gave continuity, future plans required greater attention to both the organization and preparation of local managers for top positions, and more middle-management jobs. A key objective here was to preserve Sabritas's flexibility and creativity while ensuring sound management in an expanding organization.

COMPANY BACKGROUND

Sabritas's history began in 1947 in the kitchen of Pedro Marcos, who prepared snack foods that he sold to street vendors for distribution on bicycles. He soon bought a small van and began direct distribution to retailers. In the 1950s he launched the Sabritas brand of potato chips; within ten years he was a leader in snack food, with a 25% share of the Mexico City market. In 1966 PepsiCo Inc. acquired a modest manufacturing facility and the strong Sabritas brand from Marcos. In 1967 PepsiCo installed Warner as president and CEO of the new company. A graduate of the University of Minnesota Engineering School and Michigan State University with a master's degree from the Thunderbird Graduate School of International Management in Arizona (where he developed his ability to speak Spanish), Warner began his international business career with Pepsi-Cola International in Mexico. As a regional sales manager, he developed many of Pepsi's franchises in Mexico in the early 1950s. Later posts in Pepsi-Cola included regional manager positions in Venezuela and the Caribbean; director of marketing for Latin America in Lima, Peru; division vice president for the Far East in Sydney, Australia; international marketing vice president at New York corporate headquarters; and division vice president for the Western United States. Upon becoming CEO he renamed the company Sabritas, S.A. de C.V. and inaugurated the most modern food-processing factory in Latin America. The first factory, with the world's largest potato-processing volume, was built in the Federal

District (Mexico City); a second was built in 1972 in Guadalajara, Mexico's second largest city.

By 1980 Sabritas had become the dominant factor in Mexican snack food and one of Mexico's major agribusinesses. It purchased 10% of the nation's commercial potatoes; its distribution network reached 260,000 retail sales locations in 300 cities throughout the country via 3,300 delivery trucks.[1] Half its 6,000 employees were salesmen, who made on average 500,000 deliveries per week, visiting each point of retail sales twice a week. Direct delivery routes were serviced from 120 company-managed warehouses throughout Mexico. Total delivery routes serviced by Sabritas salesmen grew from 50 in 1968 and 990 in 1975 to 3,000 by the end of 1980. In the Federal District, with 27% of total sales, 580 route salesmen visited 60,000 retail outlets three times a week.

Since the beginning, Sabritas policy was to service retail sales outlets directly (the "store-door direct-delivery system") and never to use independent distributors or jobbers. Management felt that this emphasis on direct distribution reflected its main competitive strength. In the words of Warner:

> Anyone can manufacture a good potato chip. Our success lies in mass merchandising a quality product. This involves having a superior product to start with, and independent tests confirm that our products are the quality leaders in Mexico. But it also means timely deliveries to ensure freshness, superior service to our dealers to ensure their loyalty, an efficient national network to achieve volume, and strong advertising and promotion to maintain our product in the public's eye. We are first of all a distribution and merchandising company, although we back up our sales efforts with product quality.

Besides plain potato chips (sold in individual and family-size bags), Sabritas's 1980 product line included potato chips with a chili flavor, "ruffled" potato chips; fried corn chips with various flavors, Cheetos, three kinds of popcorn, four of roasted peanuts, fried and flavored wheat chips, and fried pork rinds (*chicharrones*—a traditional Mexican snack). (*Exhibit 4* presents a sales history of the major product lines.) While potato chips, plain fried corn chips (Fritos), Cheetos, and fried wheat chips were the biggest-volume items, many smaller-volume items were seen as important to Sabritas's marketing strategy as defense brands against the competition.

By the early 1970s Sabritas had achieved nationwide distribution and a

[1]Supermarket sales were only 6% of total volume and less than 1% of sales locations. (Mexico had about 150 supermarkets in early 1980.) The other 94% came mainly from small miscellaneous or "Mom and Pop" stores, kiosks, schools, factories, stadiums, and entertainment centers. Sabritas was the single largest private buyer of trucks per year (650 in 1980).

dominant share of the Mexican snack market, with the remainder divided among many local or regional brands. At the time of PepsiCo Inc.'s acquisition, both Kellogg and Del Monte had entered the Mexican snack market. In 1968 each company had a 25% share of market, but they both left snacks when their share dropped below 10%. During recent years, however, one competitor emerged as a threat to Sabritas. Bimbo, Mexico's largest (and wholly Mexican-owned) producer and distributor of baked goods (with 7,000 direct delivery routes and estimated 1980 sales of $550 million), acquired Kellogg's snack manufacturing facilities. Bimbo's Barcel subsidiary entered the snack market in 1978 with a strategy based on the existing Bimbo presence in most sales locations, an image closely resembling Sabritas's, and an advertising budget double that of Sabritas in 1979 (even while Barcel's sales were less than a third of Sabritas's). Barcel's strategy pursued market share at the expense of short-term profit and resulted in a proliferation of competing snacks and a rapidly expanding distribution network. (Like Sabritas, Barcel used the direct "store-door" sales system and presented its products at each sales location on a large display rack refilled on each visit by the route salesman.) As an example of its market penetration strategy, Barcel increased its routes in 1980 by 300, as against Sabritas's increase of 500 routes. Barcel sales per route/week in 1980 were about $800; Sabritas averaged $1,300 per route/week. (In the United States the comparable figure was $4,000.) By late 1980 Barcel won most of the market share held by regional and local brands and was poised to compete head-on with Sabritas.

Marketing Strategy

Two concepts were the base of the company's marketing strategy: the image of happiness and the "small bags into many stores," direct, store-door sales system (rather than wholesalers, jobbers, and warehouse deliveries).

An image of happiness while eating Sabritas products was conveyed via the smiling-face logo (*Exhibit 5*), happy colors, and advertising context. The desired image was one of happy people having good times together and enjoying Sabritas products. Backing up that image was the idea that today's population was young and on the move, eating snacks when there was no time for formal sitdown meals. This marketing concept was the result of Pepsi-Cola's many years of experience in the soft-drink market outside the United States—a mass-marketing system that sold and advertised individual brands, rather than the unbranded, commodity-type selling that U.S. snack marketers employed in the 1940s and 1950s.

Potato chips and other snacks were traditionally sold in the United States in large bags and through normal food-distribution channels. But

Sabritas distribution was patterned after that of soft drinks and allowed for immediate consumption by the purchaser either "on premise" or "on the move." "Small bags into small stores" meant that both product presentation (individual 1–1.5-ounce bags selling for 15–22¢ each) and point of sale (thousands of sales points convenient to the individual purchaser) could maximize the snack's ease of purchase and consumption and thus complement its fast-paced, active life-style image.

The objective of Sabritas's marketing strategy for the early 1980s was to maintain market share and operating profit margins in an expanding market. It sought to build volume in its traditional product lines—especially in its exclusive brand items such as Cheetos—while keeping the competition (Barcel) at bay by focusing its defense on products competing with Barcel's line. This strategy was implemented via policies governing new products, advertising and promotion, pricing, and distribution.

One objective of the *new products policy* was to protect the traditional product line from Barcel through competitive attack or defense. Another was to develop unexplored areas of the Mexican snack industry with totally new product lines aimed at new segments or at satisfying changing consumer demands. With nonbasic foods under attack both in Mexico and abroad, Sabritas and PepsiCo Inc. felt that diversification into more nutritious items might offer new opportunities and protection against a "junk food" image—an image Sabritas management felt was based on misinformation about the existing product line. (*Exhibits* 7 and 8 contain information on Sabritas products and compares them to other nutritious foods.)

Mexico's agriculture had not kept up with overall economic and population growth. Thus, food and feed grains, edible oil grains, and sugar were imported at nearly a million tons a month by the end of 1980. (In 1973 Mexico had been a net exporter of both grain and sugar.) National concern over such staggering imports and over the plight of the rural poor led to a program sponsored by the Office of the President to improve the national diet, reduce imports, and increase rural incomes. The SAM (*Sistema Alimentario Mexicano,* or Mexican Food System) program began by assessing Mexico's food needs and worked back to measures required to meet those needs. In several diagnostic studies that were part of SAM, multinational agribusinesses were criticized for diverting food or food-production resources from SAM's objectives and doing little to alleviate hunger, raise small farmer incomes, or reduce food imports. Sabritas and other multinational food companies felt strongly that only a partial picture had been presented and that government studies had ignored the fact that these companies created thousands of jobs and supported tens of thousands of people, brought capital and technology into Mexico, and provided sure markets for agricultural production. Sabritas contended that far from detracting from people's nutrition, it

actually contributed to it by providing nutritious foods, hygienically prepared and packaged, affordable, and readily accessible.

In late 1980 the recently created New Products Division was studying a
variety of new products, including nutritional snacks, nutritionally forti-
fied versions of the traditional product line, complementary product
lines (such as cocktail dips), and line extensions of existing products.
Management sought to balance its future overall product line between
those of proven strength, those with high competitive potential, and
image-building "nutrition" items. Company resources limited the total
number of new products that might be offered; decisions had to be based
on overall corporate strategy, including financial goals and future tendencies within and for the industry.

Advertising and promotion had earlier been important in Sabritas's marketing, although a recent law prohibiting promotions aimed at children
had reduced its promotions during 1980. (Plastic toys in bags of Sabritas
products, earlier a highly successful promotion, was now outlawed.) Advertising, especially on TV (in the six major markets), was the major
marketing activity. Brand recognition was also developed via Sabritas's
logo and brightly colored packages and delivery vans.

Public-relations programs were begun in the early 1970s to reinforce the
image of the products and the company. Scholarship programs for Mexican students with the University of North Carolina and Michigan State
University were created, and social responsibility projects were launched
with the American Chamber of Commerce. As a large industrial employer, Sabritas strove to maintain good labor relations, and workers were
given opportunities to advance.

Production and Raw Material Supplies

With the opening of the Saltillo plant, Sabritas had the capacity to meet its
sales requirements through 1983. (All products except the peanut line,
accounting for only 4% of sales, were produced in its three plants.)
Production technology in all three relied on methods developed in other
U.S. PepsiCo affiliates; most major machinery items were imported. The
process was more labor-intensive in Mexico than in the United States,
with an average investment of $10,900 per worker, as against about
$18,000 in Frito-Lay.

Besides machinery, some of Sabritas's raw materials had to be imported, including cornmeal (for Cheetos), pork-rind pellets (for *chicharrones*), and occasionally corn for corn chips. While corn was also
produced in Mexico, supply channels and quality requirements often
made local sourcing difficult. Import permits for these products were all
but impossible to obtain, however, and arrangements for delivery of

desired quantities and qualities were a major manufacturing problem. Through its R&D department, Sabritas was experimenting with contracts with local producers, but this involved locating both reliable producers and varieties (mainly of corn) that satisfied processing criteria and adapted to Mexican growing conditions. Government controls over distribution and seed development made company efforts difficult.

Cooking oil, another major input, was also difficult to obtain in the required quantity and quality. While sesame oil was produced in Mexico in sufficient quantity, government export promotion and differential pricing frequently caused domestic scarcities. Sabritas then had to use other varieties of oils that altered taste and product shelf life.

Since potatoes were one of its biggest purchases, and since both supply and quality varied widely, Sabritas tried for several years to improve varieties and to ensure quality supplies through a producer-financing scheme. The Potato Improvement Center, an independent organization financed by Sabritas, worked on seed improvement via varietal selection. With government approval it operated a 1,600-acre experimental farm. Under a potato partnership program, Sabritas gave improved seed stock (which comprised about half of potato production costs) to selected producers, who agreed to repay the seed with a percentage of the harvest and to sell the remainder (if it met quality standards) to the company at a predetermined price.

While management felt this program was generally successful (in 1980 participating producers provided 60% of Sabritas's potatoes), the seed improvement program was costly and did not produce seed stock clearly superior to that commercially available. Furthermore, several extension services offered to participating producers were felt to be superfluous and were dropped in 1980.

Management believed that continuing agricultural research was necessary but that future efforts might take fuller advantage of commercial expertise and offer producers only what they might not get elsewhere. Above all, management felt that coordination among seed suppliers, financial institutions, producers, and Sabritas was needed to ensure its raw material supplies. As an example of this newer strategy, efforts to ensure corn supplies involved identifying those seed companies that had developed or were able to develop varieties meeting Sabritas's quality requirements, rather than trying to develop varieties itself. The company then encouraged contracted growers to use these varieties.

Company Organization

During Sabritas's formative years, it had been run by a small group of senior executives. Besides Warner there was John Waid, general manager.

A native of West Virginia and a graduate of the University of Virginia, Waid received an MBA in 1961 from Harvard Business School before joining the IBM sales department. A series of positions with Colgate-Palmolive, ending with the job of treasurer for Colgate-Palmolive in Mexico, gave Waid a command of Spanish and management experience in Venezuela and Mexico in the operation and financial management of a marketing-oriented company operating in a developing country.

Warner brought Waid into the organization shortly after becoming president to complement his own marketing background with a strong operations and financial management background. The two have worked as a team to manage Sabritas since its earliest years. William Dunckell, a MexPepsi executive, was named senior VP and built up the western Mexican market. Mexicans held several key management positions: a financial officer, a sales manager, and a plant manager. Top management thought of themselves more as entrepreneurs than as corporate bureaucrats. Building the distribution system, a company image, and a recognized brand name were tasks that required creativity, flexibility, and a willingness to do what had to be done, without rigidity in formal planning and control systems, specific job definitions, organizational charts, or human-resource development programs. In the late 1970s several bilingual Mexicans were appointed to significant positions; all were in their early thirties and had MBAs. They were identified as future leaders and merged into the management team of what was then considered the most successful growth company in Mexico.

One result of the management style that had developed over the years was the "two-hat syndrome." Key executives often performed two (or more) jobs and reported to two or more executives. This was thought quite appropriate when corporate goals were geared to maximum growth, market development, and product innovation. But when annual growth rates might have peaked, when market share had to be defended rather than built, and when yearly financial results were important and highly dependent on efficient cost control, a "tighter" system would perhaps be more appropriate.

In 1981 it was not clear at Sabritas that growth rates had peaked or that a change from aggressive entrepreneurship to steady corporate management was required or even an issue. But Sabritas's growth was making the two-hat syndrome impossible by placing too much of a burden on too few people. Yet "hats" could not be reassigned unless management resources were developed.

To plan for future management needs, Sabritas commissioned an international consulting firm to study its organizational requirements and suggest changes. The study recommended that the company: (1) decentralize operations by creating four geographic zones, each with its own regional director and functional staff; and (2) create several new corporate staff positions and departments to coordinate national aspects of the business. Concurrent with the study, Warner was asked to present a long-range management succession program for the 1980s and beyond to his immediate superior, Jack Kickham, president of PepsiCo International Foods Division (all non-U.S. PepsiCo food subsidiaries). Warner developed and sent to Dallas division headquarters a management development plan with career paths for each of Sabritas's top fifty managers.

While both management and the corporate parent initially accepted the reorganization recommendations, neither was entirely satisfied. PepsiCo Inc. later decided to give Sabritas up to two years to reorganize itself again along functional lines, following the pattern of other PepsiCo affiliates. One motive behind this second reorganization was to ensure tighter management control over costs, inventories, and financial reporting as Sabritas entered a probable period of lower growth and more competition. A critical tradeoff involved training future top management. Broad training would be easier to attain under the decentralized divisional structure than under the functional structure, but tighter controls would be more easily achieved under the latter.

Financial Management and Results

With direct investment of $1.25 million in 1972 and a dividend policy that left about 50% of net earnings in the company each year, PepsiCo's equity at the end of 1979 totaled nearly $22 million of Sabritas's $44 million total assets.[2] Financial policy traditionally included substantial debts; at the end of 1980, 75% of the $19 million debt was with foreign (non-Mexican) banks. Nearly all debt was dollar-denominated. (Mexican peso debt carried a 10-point premium over U.S. bank rates in late 1980. The peso-to-dollar exchange rate had stood at about 22:1 since 1977.)

The 15–18% differential between Mexican and U.S. inflation rates, coupled with record high U.S. inflation, created many problems for Sabritas's financial management, ranging from maintenance of operating profit margins to concern over its net exposure to devaluation. Although the high cost of debt and the resulting need for tight cash management concerned PepsiCo Inc.'s treasury department, the NOPAT performance measuring system removed concerns about interest charges. NOPAT (net operating profit after taxes) was designed to reflect Sabritas's contribution to its stockholders independent of technical service payments (2% of sales) or interest charges, both responsibilities of other areas of PepsiCo.

---

[2]The $1.25 million investment in capital stock was to be increased by $4 million (from retained earnings) in 1981. This increase was part of the agreement negotiated with the Mexican government that preceded construction of the Saltillo plant.

Sabritas maintained profit margins by keeping price increases ahead of inflation. No Sabritas products in 1980 were subject to price controls, which were applicable only to "basic products" or products considered to be essential to the public. While this obviously benefited the company, controls were possible with Sabritas's new products in nutrition, or if price controls were generalized over all parts of the food industry because of even higher inflation.

Concern over devaluation did not present serious operating problems. All company fixed assets were carried at dollar acquisition cost and revalued in Mexican pesos as parity rates changed. Peso-denominated financial assets and product inventories were balanced with peso-denominated debt. (A computer routine at PepsiCo's treasury office warned Sabritas management whenever net exposure became dangerously big.)

While local management was not directly responsible for interest payments, current assets on the periodic balance sheets were closely watched, and management was encouraged to maintain strict control over inventories and receivables.

Relations with the Mexican Government

When PepsiCo purchased Sabritas in 1966, government–business relationships in Mexico were not very different from those at home. The peso was stable and freely convertible; foreign investment was welcomed with few if any governmental conditions. In this climate, PepsiCo by 1973 had invested $1,250,000 in Sabritas's capital stock, and Sabritas's $10.5 million asset base was financed by the capital stock, retained earnings, and a 38% debt load.

In 1973 the Mexican government passed the Foreign Investment Act, severely limiting the freedom of action of companies not majority-owned by Mexicans. As a wholly owned subsidiary of a foreign company, Sabritas found itself unable to get permission to construct additional warehouses in several cities. A temporary solution was to create a separate Mexicanized distribution company. Later, when an investment package involving the construction of the Saltillo plant was negotiated, Sabritas was permitted to take over operation of the warehouses earlier operated by the distribution company.

The Balance-of-Payments Problem

In those same negotiations, Sabritas agreed to generate a balance-of-payments surplus in its own operations (excluding dividend payments) by 1982. (While oil exports promised to help Mexico's balance of payments over the long term, it still had deficits in its current account and sought to reduce imports while promoting exports.) Compliance with this agreement would probably involve a combination of reduced imports of goods and services, exports of some traditional product lines, and exports of nontraditional Sabritas products.

In this last category were sporting goods. Since Wilson Sporting Goods was another PepsiCo affiliate in the United States and since most sporting goods available in Mexico were imported, the government encouraged Sabritas to enter this field to serve the local market and to generate export earnings. In 1980 Sabritas set up a sporting goods division in Mexico with the idea of importing partially finished goods, finishing them locally, and reexporting them to the United States. Early results were less than encouraging: While Sabritas saw a potential for generating up to $1 million in net foreign-exchange earnings, doing so cost it an average of 30% on the sales of these items and a total loss of $60,000 in 1980. Although these losses might eventually be reduced, the sporting goods export scheme would probably never be profitable, although it would help with the balance of payments.

On the other hand, if it reduced the import content of its sporting goods products and began to sell to the Mexican market while continuing to export enough to cover foreign-exchange costs, it could tap a market that would probably grow as fast in the 1980s as the snack food market had in the 1970s. (Management estimated the sporting goods market in Mexico in 1980 at about $50 million, half of which was imported, with another $50 million of goods entering the country when Mexican residents returned with items purchased abroad.)

Sabritas's other export alternative was supplying Frito-Lay with products made in Mexico. One product offered immediate export potential. The Sabritones line consisted of a wheat-based, chili-flavored item resembling deep-fried pork rinds or *chicharrones*. Sabritas had developed this item and considered it nearly the "perfect" snack in view of its production characteristics and long shelf life, and because its raw materials did not change seasonally in price and could be stored for a long time. Not available in the United States, Sabritones were thought to have tremendous sales potential to the Mexican-Americans of the U.S. border states. (They had already become very popular as a Mexican snack, with sales being almost 20% of the total snack market.)

A Frito-Lay decision to purchase products from Sabritas (which in reality would be a Frito-Lay decision to locate a plant in Mexico, because Frito-Lay Inc. was one of PepsiCo's major operating divisions, as were the Pepsi-Cola Company and PepsiCo Foods International, Sabritas's parent) would be based on the cost of production; the plant would probably be located in the U.S.-Mexican border free zone to facilitate use of U.S.-sourced raw materials. Given the size of Frito-Lay requirements and the economies of scale of highly automated production technologies, the benefits to Frito-Lay of locating a plant in Mexico were not all that obvious. Sabritas would have to devise a plan to make a Mexican plant attractive to Frito-Lay if it hoped to use exports to Frito-Lay to balance its payments. *Exhibit 6* presents Sabritas's 1980 balance of payments and various alternatives for meeting the payments surplus commitment by 1982.

Permits for Future Plant Expansion

Even while Sabritas sought to meet the conditions agreed on to construct the Saltillo plant, it began to plan for future expansion and for the negotiations preceding the construction of the next plant. With Saltillo in operation, capacity planning indicated the need for a second plant in the Mexico City area to serve the growing market in south Mexico. Also considered were facilities required by any new food product lines with high nutritional value for mass distribution throughout the system.

Sabritas thought construction near the Federal District plant would probably be the easiest way to increase capacity, but that plant was in Mexico City's twenty-year-old industrial zone, and the government did not encourage further expansion there. But a low-income residential area outside the Federal District on the highway to Puebla had developed into a city of about two million in 1980. Nezahualcoyotl suffered from all the social and economic ills of a city of unskilled migrants from the country-side looking for work. Unemployment was estimated at 35%.

Sabritas reasoned that new plant construction providing employment for Nezahualcoyotl's residents might be well received by state government authorities and that such authorities might convince the national government to grant necessary building permits. Management had approached the governor of the State of Mexico[3] with the idea and hoped that he would formally invite Sabritas to construct a factory within the state. With this invitation, Sabritas then planned to approach federal officials.

If Frito-Lay decided to purchase finished products from Sabritas, a fifth Sabritas plant would have to be built. Since this plant's product would be exclusively for export, no impediments to obtaining building permits were expected. Of course this export-oriented facility would not really benefit Sabritas itself, which would still need to increase capacity again for the Mexican market within the next few years.

A final problem with the Mexican government had to do with other PepsiCo Inc. subsidiaries operating in Mexico. Although each of PepsiCo

[3]The United Mexican States consisted of 32 states and the Federal District. Each state was governed by an elected governor and a state legislature, although the federal government retained considerable power through fiscal authority and the prominent and pervasive role of the major political party in Mexican politics and government.

Inc.'s operations in Mexico (Pepsi-Cola Mexicana–operated bottling plants, Wilson Sporting Goods distributor, Pizza Hut, North American Van Lines franchises, Lee Way shipping agents, and Taco Bell [projected]) reported to a separate corporate division, each completely autonomous in its operations, the Mexican government expected all divisions of the same corporate entity to behave in a coordinated manner. Thus, regulatory problems at, say, the Pepsi-Cola plant in Mexico might have the effect of holding up a Sabritas expansion permit.

STRATEGIC PLANNING FOR THE EIGHTIES

As Sabritas ended the first year of the new decade, it became apparent to its management and its division head, Kickham, that many policy issues in different areas of the company were related to each other and to its basic business strategy. During the 1970s the business strategy had been quite clear: a rapid expansion of the Mexican snack market and maintaining a dominant market share through creative merchandising techniques emphasizing the Sabritas brand image and the "small bags into small stores," store-door, direct-delivery system.

But Barcel's competitive threat, the Mexican government's increasing pressure to contribute to its development objectives for permission to pursue company objectives, the not always friendly climate toward multinational food companies (especially those marketing nonessential food items), and increasing difficulty in obtaining needed quantity and quality of raw materials all suggested that the next years would require new policies to deal with new problems. Sabritas management asked in late 1980 whether the policy decisions it would shortly be making in new products, advertising, plant expansion, raw material sourcing, company finance, and organizational design would require a change in Sabritas's basic business strategy to deal more effectively with Mexico of the 1980s.

SABRITAS

Exhibit 1

Summary of Key Performance Indicators

Year	Sales $000	Sales % change	Contributory Income[a] $000	Contributory Income % change	NOPAT[b] $000	NOPAT % change	Contributory Income % of Sales	Average Asset Base[c]	Return on Assets Employed Income	Return on Assets Employed NOPAT
1968	1,824	67	(170)	—			—			
1969	4,003	119	329	—			8	1,710	19.2	
1970	6,648	66	594	81			9	2,645	22.5	
1971	9,988	50	1,060	78			11	4,278	24.8	
1972	15,700	57	1,992	88			13	5,782	34.5	
1973	21,217	35	2,750	38			13	7,561	36.4	
1974	32,008	51	3,490	27			11	11,944	29.2	
1975	48,045	50	5,837	67			12	14,162	41.2	
1976	56,686	18	7,924	36	4,608		14	15,215	52.1	30.3
1977	58,853	4	6,557	(17)	3,886	(16)	11	21,024	31.2	18.5
1978	83,243	41	8,639	32	4,917	27	10	26,441	32.7	18.6
1979	127,456	53	17,156	99	9,430	92	13	29,885	57.4	31.6
1980[d]	161,845	27	19,881	16	12,265	30	12	47,360	42.0	25.9
1981[e]	197,207	22	23,688	19	15,050	28	12	55,953	42.3	26.9

[a]Contributory income = operating profit less interest, other expenses, and foreign exchange loss.

[b]NOPAT (net operating profit after taxes) = operating profit less other expenses and foreign exchange loss, less (total) taxes. NOPAT was initiated as a performance measure in 1976.

[c]Average asset base = net assets less accounts receivable from company affiliates less accounts payable, accrued taxes, and other payables (equals equity plus bank debt).

[d]Estimated

[e]Projected

SOURCE: Company records.

Exhibit 2
1979 Balance Sheet
(*December 31, 1979*)

Assets		*Liabilities and Equity*	
Cash	3,383,144	Notes and loans	
Net accounts receivable	4,805,788	payable	9,811,000
Net inventories	9,753,850	Accounts payable	5,167,292
Prepaid expenses and		Accrued taxes	3,218,547
other current assets	1,504,531	Other accrued	2,781,859
Total current		liabilities	
assets	19,447,313	Accounts payable:	
Noncurrent receivables	21,790	affiliates	343,174
Property, plant, and		Total current	
equipment	34,933,556	liabilities	21,321,872
Less accumulated		Other liabilities and	
depreciation	10,762,414	deferred credits	361,798
Net PP&E	24,171,142	Deferred income taxes	598,866
Goodwill	129,515	Total liabilities	22,282,536
Other assets	284,788	Equity	
		Capital stock	1,250,000
		Retained earnings	20,522,012
		Total equity	21,772,012
		Total liabilities and	
Total assets	44,054,548	equity	44,054,548

Exhibit 3
1979 Income Statement
(U.S. $)

Revenue	
Gross sales	127,455,895
Discounts and allowances	8,894,072
Total Revenue	118,561,823
Cost of sales	57,624,389
Operating expenses	
Selling and distribution	30,406,304
Advertising and marketing	6,690,157
General and administrative	5,756,832
Total Operating Expenses	42,853,293
Operating profit (loss)	18,084,141
Other income	27,695
Other expenses	2,494,850
Foreign-exchange gain (losses)	(41,427)
Net operating profit before taxes	15,575,559
Income tax provision on NOPAT	7,567,696
Net operating profit after taxes	8,007,863
Pretax interest expense (−)	870,312
Income tax expense on interest (+)	365,531
Net income (loss)	7,503,082

SOURCE: Company records.

SABRITAS

Exhibit 4
Small-Bag[a] Sales of Sabritas Products
(1,000 bags)

	1966	1967	1968	1969	1970	1971	1972	1973	1974	1975	1976	1977	1978	1979
Plain potato chips	2,645	3,219	7,438	22,258	42,489	56,991	81,827	78,679	80,278	94,360	105,455	112,263	111,239	138,159
Floured potato chips	—	—	—	—	—	—	—	—	—	—	—	—	28,994	110,190
Ruffled potato chips	—	—	—	—	—	—	5,393	28,357	28,034	27,476	35,483	36,738	43,771	49,726
Fritos	969	1,357	3,960	6,090	10,076	20,324	32,404	36,586	50,992	74,194	72,521	81,913	96,619	116,874
Doritos	—	—	3,141	8,590	11,351	20,043	29,870	31,806	42,983	56,355	56,247	57,338	62,242	109,827
Chicorrumais	2,246	1,884	1,465	1,054	3,165	6,234	12,683	18,091	23,582	27,925	30,001	30,234	36,411	50,008
Cheetos	—	—	—	—	—	—	—	—	—	—	9,601	40,106	65,878	113,598
Popcorn	—	—	—	—	—	—	—	—	—	—	4,893	39,807	43,555	52,732
Sabritones	2,261	3,054	3,844	11,514	18,998	23,741	34,105	35,816	45,464	70,445	79,065	90,020	98,387	132,805
Chicharrones	—	—	—	—	—	—	—	—	—	—	—	—	—	5,979

[a]Small bags accounted for about 87% of total sales revenue in 1980.

SOURCE: Company records.

354

Exhibit 5 Corporate Advertising Copy

"Where there are smiles, there's Sabritas"

Exhibit 6

Alternatives for Reaching Balance-of-Payments Equilibrium by 1982

(U.S.$ millions)

	1980	Strategic Alternatives for 1982		
		A[a]	*B*[b]	*C*[c]
Foreign currency payments				
Technical services	2.5	3.4	3.4	—
Machinery and equipment	1.5	.7	.3	.3
Interest	1.5	1.1	—	—
Spare parts	.2	.2	—	—
Total payments	5.7	5.4	3.7	0.3
Foreign currency receipts				
Sporting goods exports	.4	1.7	1.7	1.7
Snack foods exports	.1	1.2	1.2	1.2
Total receipts	.5	2.9	2.9	2.9
Net payments abroad	5.2	2.5	0.8	(2.6)

[a]Alternative A: Make no adjustment of policies governing foreign-exchange costs.

[b]Alternative B: (i) Reduce debt to non-Mexican banks to zero. (There had been a severe credit shortage for peso-borrowing funds in Mexico for many years. Mexican-owned firms were given priority for such loans for farming projects and highly essential industries.) (ii) Source new machinery and equipment and all spare parts from Mexican suppliers (judged by engineering to be feasible by 1982).

[c]Alternative C: All of Alternative B plus elimination of technical service payments (or reduction to figure complementary to export earnings). In the past, PepsiCo Inc. had had excess foreign tax credits, making it prefer technical service payments to dividends.

SOURCE: Company records.

SABRITAS

Exhibit 7
Nutritional Information on Food Often Used as Snacks

	Potato Chips	Apple	Raisins	Banana	Orange	Carrot	Celery
Nutritional Information per Portion							
Quantity per portion	1 oz. = 28.35 gr	1 apple 5.3 oz. = 150 gr	1 package 1/2 oz. = 14.17 gr	1 banana 6.1 oz. = 173 gr	1 orange 6.3 oz. = 178 gr	1 carrot 1 oz. = 28.35 gr	1 stalk 1.4 oz. = 39.7 gr
Calories	160	80	40	100	60	12	8
Protein (grams)	2	0	0	1	1	0	0
Carbohydrates (grams)	14	20	11	26	16	3	2
Fat (grams)	10	1	0	0	0	0	0
Percent of U.S. Recommended Daily Allowance (RDA)							
Protein	2	2	*	*	2	*	*
Vitamin A	*	2	*	4	4	60	2
Vitamin C	10	10	*	20	110	2	6
Thiamine	2	2	*	4	8	*	*
Riboflavin	2	*	*	4	2	*	*
Niacin	4	*	*	4	2	*	*
Calcium	*	*	*	*	4	*	*
Iron	2	2	2	4	2	*	*
Vitamin E	20	*	—	2	—	*	*
Vitamin B6	10	2	2	40	4	2	*
Phosphorus	4	*	*	2	2	*	*
Magnesium	4	*	—	10	2	*	*
Copper	4	*	*	8	*	*	*
Pantothenic acid	1	*	*	4	4	*	*

*Contains less than 2% of the RDA.

Exhibit 8
Nutritional Information per Portion
(One portion = 1 ounce = 28.35 grams)

	Potato Chips[a]	Doritos[b]	Cheetos[c]
Calories	160	140	160
Protein (grams)	2	2	2
Carbohydrates (grams)	14	19	15
Fat (grams)	10	7	10
Percentage of calories from fat	59	42	57
Polyunsaturated (grams)	5	1	3
Saturated (grams)	2	1	2
Cholesterol (milligrams)	0	0	0
Sodium (milligrams)	260	185	260
Potassium (milligrams)	205	50	35
Percentage of U.S. RDA			
Protein	2	2	2
Vitamin A	*	*	2
Vitamin C	10	*	*
Thiamine	2	*	*
Riboflavin	2	*	2
Niacin	4	*	*
Calcium	*	2	*
Iron	2	2	*
Vitamin E	20	2	10
Vitamin B6	10	4	—
Phosphorus	4	4	2
Magnesium	4	4	2
Copper	15	8	4

[a]100 grams of potato chips contain 0 mg cholesterol, 925 mg sodium, and 720 mg potassium.

[b]100 grams of Doritos contain 0 mg cholesterol, 635 mg sodium, and 170 mg potassium.

[c]100 grams of Cheetos contain 10 mg cholesterol, 925 mg sodium, and 125 mg potassium.

*Contains less than 2% of the RDA.

SOURCE: Company records.

Milkpak

In April 1979 Syed Babar Ali, chairman of the Ali Group in Lahore, Pakistan, faced a decision that seemed to have critical implications for the future of one of the group's companies, Packages Limited: Should the group proceed with a large investment in a milk processing plant, an activity outside its main lines of business? The investment proposal had grown out of a need to find a use for packaging equipment that Packages had purchased in the 1960s. Attempts to develop a market for milk packaging material had led the company to experiment with a small milk processing facility in 1977. That experiment led to the proposal now confronting Mr. Ali.

PACKAGES LIMITED

Packages was founded in Lahore, Pakistan in 1956. Mr. Ali, twenty-eight years old at the time, was an entrepreneur from one of Pakistan's leading families which, since the British took over the country more than a century earlier, had been major forces in commerce and industry. The Ali family had been associated with a multitude of businesses. They had operated Ford's auto assembly plant in Pakistan until its nationalization by the Bhutto government in 1973. The group's Wazir Ali Industries had been a dominant force in the vegetable oil and soap industries since independence in 1947 until it was nationalized. Packages was involved in management consulting, computer services, and its main activities in manufacturing paper and packaging. Other family members were active in razor blade and textile manufacture. It also held an insurance company (the life insurance portion had been nationalized), which had holdings in the enterprises of the group.

Packages' origins could be traced to 1954. On a visit to Sweden that year, Mr. Ali had approached A. B. Akerlund & Rausing (A&R), a leading Swedish packaging firm, on the possibility of their joining him in Pakistan to manufacture an assortment of packaging materials. A&R had been

This case (Case A) was prepared by Professor Louis T. Wells, Harvard Graduate School of Business Administration, and Assistant Professor Ehsan-ul-Haque, Lahore Graduate School of Business Administration, as the basis for class discussion rather than to illustrate either effective or ineffective handling of an administrative situation. Abridged with permission.

recommended to him by the Pakistan Tobacco Company (PTC), a subsidiary of the British American Tobacco Co. in Pakistan, as a reliable firm eager to expand its overseas business. Mr. Ali's original objective was to secure a relatively safe and cheap local source of paper, cardboard, cellophane, and plastic film packaging for the family group, particularly for the razor blade business. Like PTC, the Ali Group depended almost entirely on foreign sources for its packaging needs. It took less than six months for the government to grant permission. However, plant construction started after two years because of various delays involved in acquiring land, arranging foreign exchange, and completing certain other formalities.

A&R received 22.69% equity in the venture for the imported European machinery it contributed, with the remainder in the Ali family. In addition, A&R signed a contract for continuing technical assistance. In 1965 the company went public. Soon it added its own pulp, paper, and board mill. By 1987 Packages' sales had reached Rs.241 million per year with after-tax profits of Rs.22 million.[1] To deal with the difficulty of obtaining imported parts, Packages built its own foundry and machine shop. Using its acquired skills, it began to modify machinery for the local environment and eventually to build some of its own machinery. Similarly, it developed in-house facilities for making rubber parts such as "o" rings, gaskets, and conveyor belt parts. It next provided technical assistance to paper machinery and packaging facilities in Indonesia, Tanzania, Zambia, and Nigeria. These overseas experiences, as well as participation in overseas management programs, added to the training of Packages' management.

HISTORY OF THE MILKPAK PROPOSAL

In a 1976 management committee meeting, soon after Syed Wajid Ali had become Packages' managing director, he asked for a report on the utilization of Packages' equipment. According to the producion manager, all equipment was being utilized at 80% of capacity or more, with one exception. The Tetra Laminator was running only occasionally; that machine was designed for making packaging material for long-life milk. "Are there no milk plants in Pakistan that can use this material?" asked Mr. Wajid Ali. "No sir," responded the production manager. The marketing manager corrected: "There is a milk plant which can use this paper, but it has been inoperative for five years." "Perhaps we should lease it," suggested Mr. Wajid Ali. He then requested his managers elaborate a proposal to develop a market for the Tetra Laminator's products.

[1] Exchange rate in 1979: Rs.10 = $1.00. All dollar figures in the case are U.S. dollars.

Packages had acquired the laminator in 1967 from Tetra Pak of Sweden, one of the Rausing Companies, for about $200,000. The Tetra Laminator had been developed to produce paper packaging that could be used for sterilized milk. Sterilization processes, based on direct injection of super-heated steam, had been developed in Switzerland and Denmark. When properly packaged, sterilized milk had a shelf life of at least three months, without refrigeration. The Swedish company had realized early on that sterilized milk was a potentially valuable product for developing countries. In Europe, milk was usually sold as pasteurized fresh milk. Often, pure-food laws were so strict that no ingredients, even steam, could be introduced in the processing of milk. Further, refrigeration equipment existed at the farm, in transportation to dairy processing plants, at the retail level, and in consumers' homes. Refrigeration assured that milk could be kept fresh until consumed. In contrast, in most developing countries such a chain of refrigeration did not exist. Thus, milk was generally delivered unpackaged from the farm to the consumer. Spoilage and adulteration were major problems. The Swedish innovators thought that consumers in developing countries would be willing to pay the additional cost of sterilization and accept the change in milk taste, if the packaging problems could be solved, in order to receive clean, fresh milk. It was to this end that the Tetra Laminator had been developed. The packages were shaped as tetrahedrons (a four-faced pyramid) and economized on packaging material. The tetrahedron packages were shipped in special plastic crates that would be made by Packages. The process could also be used for more conventional brick-shaped packages, which required more and heavier paper. The brick shape had the advantage of not requiring special cases for shipping and storage. The machine that Packages had acquired could produce packaging for up to 250,000 liters of milk per day (based on half-liter containers). For a relatively small additional investment, the capacity of the equipment could be at least doubled. Management estimated Rs.100 of sales would contribute roughly Rs.25 to overhead and profits, after accounting for the incremental costs of paper, labor, and power.

Packages' Tetra Laminator had never been used for its original purpose: A sterilized milk plant proposal at the time did not materialize. Although the machinery could have been used for making packaging for fruit juices and fruit drinks, potential users had difficulty obtaining Tetra Pak filling machines. Government regulations generally would not allow leasing of equipment from abroad; Tetra Pak would supply equipment only under lease. Although one filler was imported for fruit drinks, its user failed. Packages' Tetra Laminator was utilized to some extent for laminating packages for pharmaceutical and detergent products, but this use accounted for only a tiny fraction of its capacity.

THE EXPERIMENT

In response to the questions raised in the 1976 meeting, a proposal was developed for Packages to take a three-year lease on the unused "Milko" plant to test the market for sterilized milk in Pakistan. This plant, with capacity for 17,500 liters of milk per day, had been built in 1970 to package sterilized milk. The sterilizing equipment was Danish; the filling equipment was leased under special government permission from Tetra Pak of Sweden. But the owner, a military officer, had been stationed abroad before production started. Packages went ahead with its experiment in spite of failures of other milk processing plants in Pakistan. Since independence, some 14 plants had opened to pasteurize and package fresh milk. All except three very small government-owned plants had failed. Milko, however, was the only plant designed to produce sterilized milk.

One of the problems Packages' management had to face immediately was the high cost of the imported paper for which the Tetra Pak system was designed. Research personnel succeeded in developing a special paper that could be made locally. It was simpler than the imported paper, omitting the laminated aluminum foil that was used in Europe. This resulted in a reduced shelf life of the product, from three months to two weeks in the worst temperature conditions. The paper could be made in the existing paper and board plant of Packages, and foreseeable demand was well within the existing capacity.

Milko's new management, seconded from Packages, quickly found itself involved in efforts to assure regular sources of unadulterated, fresh milk. It eventually established two milk collection centers to receive milk, chill it, and ship it in tank trucks to the Milko sterilizing and filling plant. Milko ordered insulated stainless steel tanks that could be mounted on subcontractors' trucks. These subcontractors transported milk from the collection centers to the plant.

Milko's managers also decided to set up a sterilized-milk distributor. A manager in Packages was offered the distributorship and was kept on his Packages salary at the outset. When volume justified it, he was offered the opportunity of operating independently, on commission. The commission amounted to Rs.0.12 to Rs.0.14 per liter.

The distributor delivered milk to retail stores. Retailers paid in cash, which was remitted immediately to Packages. Packages thus had outstanding accounts receivable of less than three days. The retailer had a margin of Rs.0.25 to Rs.0.30 per liter.

The milk, all in half-liter containers, was priced at Rs.4 per liter in 1979, which was about 20% above equivalent unpackaged milk in Lahore. In spite of almost no advertising or sales promotion, sales reached the plant's capacity of 17,500 liters a day. Summary financial statements for Milko are shown in *Exhibit 1*.

Packages' management thought the Milko experiment had shown on a small scale that sterlized milk could be sold in Pakistan. If other investors would set up sterilized milk plants, the original problem of the underutilized Tetra Laminator would disappear. Further, increased sales of sterilized milk would increase the utilization of Packages' board plant. But new milk plants were not being built by others. Part of the problem, Mr. Ali surmised, was that the milk business was a low-status business in Pakistan. Entrepreneurs preferred projects with more cachet: steel, electronics, and so on. Industrialists who were risk-takers were not interested in small, lowly milk plants. Thus, management thought that Packages might have to provide its own market by establishing larger milk plants itself. Or else a successful larger plant might at least show the risk to be so low that other entrepreneurs would be attracted into the field.

TRADITIONAL MILK DISTRIBUTION

Lahore, Pakistan's second largest city after Karachi, with a population of 2.8 million people in 1978, illustrates the Pakistani supply, consumption, and distribution patterns for fluid milk in urban areas. Daily milk consumption averaged about 422,000 liters in 1978 and was expected to grow to 537,000 liters by 1983. Fresh milk was supplied from buffaloes kept in some 1,000 supplying villages within a 100-kilometer radius from the city.

Demand

Of the milk brought into Lahore, approximately one-third was drunk directly as milk; another third was used for making sweets, yogurt, or yogurt drinks (lassi); and the final third was used in tea. This contrasted with Karachi, where about half the milk sold was used in tea. A household survey for pasteurized packaged milk showed that some 80% of those surveyed preferred raw over pasteurized milk and that about half of those surveyed thought raw milk was more nutritious and were not aware of adulteration problems with raw milk.

Most households had no refrigeration. Thus, milk was bought daily. Almost invariably, milk was boiled in the home before it was drunk. Some of the cream (buffalo milk generally contains about 6% butterfat, as against 3.5% for cows) would be skimmed off during the process and used as a spread or for making butter or ghee.

The demand for milk was cyclical, being highest in the hot summer months of May, June, and July.

Milk and its derivatives were considered a source of physical strength by Punjabis, the natives of the province in which Lahore was located. They tended to look on the citizens of Karachi, on the southern coast, as weaklings who drank mostly tea.

Production

Almost all milk drunk in Lahore came from buffaloes. A single buffalo would produce roughly 1,200 liters per year. This flow, however, was not evenly spread over the year. The usual cycle in the Lahore area is shown in *Exhibit 2*. The cycle was the result of the timing of births of buffaloes in the region.

Distribution

In Lahore approximately 75% of milk was produced outside the city and passed through a multistage distribution system. The remaining 25% was produced in or near the city and was distributed directly by the farmer to the household.

Milk produced outside the city was sold to milkmen, who traveled the countryside on bicycles. Each milkman would generally carry on his bicycle two 40-liter cans. He would visit farmers early in the morning to collect that day's output. Each milkman might, on a regular basis, serve 15 or 20 farmers, located in one to three villages. Each village would be served by several milkmen. It was common for milkmen to give farmers cash advances when their buffaloes came into lactation, which started with the birth of a calf, peaked some 60 days later, and lasted about 280 days. Milk was then purchased over the lactation period against these advances. Accounts were kept by the milkmen, and prices were those generally prevailing in the area. Milkmen delivered to contractors, who iced the milk and trucked it into Lahore to retailers. Each contractor might be serviced by some 70 or 75 milkmen. Contractors paid milkmen in cash on a weekly basis.

Lahore had several thousand retailers served by contractors. Retail milk shops were scattered throughout the urban area. Retailers would pay cash to contractors on a weekly basis. Milk shops in Lahore had no refrigeration. As a result, milk had to be sold quickly. Most shops sold their milk early in the morning and closed by 10 A.M. Customers usually brought their own containers and milk was sold in quarter-, half-, or 1-liter amounts, or according to a traditional unit called "seer." Milk was usually not sold through other outlets. General grocery stores did not sell fresh vegetables, meat, or milk. The only refrigeration in grocery stores was usually supplied by producers of soft drinks or ice cream and was to be used solely for those items. A tiny volume of milk was sold through a few grocery stores in polyethylene packages. This milk, supplied from a small government-owned plant, was pasteurized and chilled at the plant, packaged, and delivered in insulated containers. It had to be sold quickly since it was not sterilized and no refrigeration was available.

Milk was also supplied by about 100,000 owners of buffaloes in the Lahore area. Most owned only one or two animals. The owners would milk their animals in the morning and deliver fresh milk directly to households.

Prices

A typical set of prices for milk produced outside the city might be as follows: Rs.2.50/liter to the farmer, Rs.3.00/liter to the milkman, Rs.4.00/liter to the contractor, and Rs.4.50 to Rs.5.00/liter at retail. On the other hand, high-quality undiluted milk delivered directly to households from buffaloes in the Lahore area might bring Rs.5.00 to Rs.6.00/liter. However, as dilution increased, prices decreased. In Karachi, milk prices were higher than in Lahore. If milk was being sold at Rs.4.50 to Rs.5.00/liter in Lahore, it might sell for Rs.6.00 to Rs.7.00/liter in Karachi.

Meeting the Cycles

Since supplies were lowest during the peak demand period, prices fluctuated. If prices were Rs.2.00 to Rs.2.25/liter to the farmer during January to April, they might rise to Rs.2.50/liter in May to July. Retail prices would remain stable, however, the difference being made up by dilution and by increased skimming of cream for butter or ghee.

Another source of milk during low production periods was imported powdered milk. Imports had increased from 34 million to 300 million liters a year (fluid milk equivalent) from 1975 to 1978. Powdered milk was very cheap in the world market, primarily because of excess production in the United States and the European Economic Community. The equivalent of one liter of milk, including butterfat, could be landed in Karachi in 1978 at about Rs.1.50 after payment of taxes and duties. This was, according to some calculations, only about two-thirds of its costs of production in the European community. In Lahore, the retail price of powdered whole milk was roughly the same as fresh milk. In Karachi, where retail milk prices were higher than in Lahore, powdered milk sold at about 25%

less than fresh milk. Powdered milk was better accepted by consumers in Karachi than in Lahore.

During periods of surplus milk production, milkmen refused to buy all output. There was virtually no capacity in Pakistan for converting surplus milk to powder.

THE MILKPAK PROPOSAL

The proposal was for a U.S.$9.0 million project to sterilize 100,000 liters per day of fresh milk. The new company would be called Milkpak, and the product would be marketed under the Milkpak trade name. The plant would be located about 50 kilometers northwest of Lahore. This would be far enough from the city to be near sources of low-cost milk, close enough to be attractive to managers, and in an industrial development area that would entitle the company to duty exemption on the import of machinery. Milk would be packaged in half-liter Tetra Paks for sale in Lahore, Karachi, and the Rawalpindi area. Tetra Pak of Sweden had agreed to sell filling equipment in Pakistan, a departure from its usual lease-only policy. Production would begin in January 1981.

The new enterprise would be financed from loans and equity as shown in *Exhibit 3. Exhibit 4* shows the planned utilization of these funds. Danish Turnkey Dairies (DTD) of Denmark, which had built the original Milko plant, would provide design, engineering, and technical services, and would assist in the procurement of all foreign machinery for the project. It would provide a dairy engineer and a dairy technologist. Tetra Pak would provide the services of a packaging engineer, and DANAGRO[2] would provide assistance in developing an extension program for small farmers. This would include efforts to upgrade the quality of livestock. All these services would be provided under technical service contracts, the details of which remained to be negotiated. Packages would, of course, provide the Tetra Pak packaging material.

Initially the project would include six milk collecting and chilling centers within 75 kilometers of the plant, to collect up to 60,000 liters of milk per day. The chilled milk would be trucked in insulated vehicles to the plant. In periods of plentiful milk supply, excess butterfat would be skimmed off at the plant to reduce the content from 6% to 3.5%. Surplus butterfat would be frozen. In periods of short supply, this butterfat would be combined with imported skimmed milk powder, water, and fresh milk. Powder would also be used as necessary to bring up the solids content of

[2]DANAGRO was the Danish service company offering agricultural extension services in Europe.

milk, since it tended to be diluted through the use of ice for chilling. Any excess butterfat would be used to produce butter. Eventually, four more collection centers would be added. Smoothing of the production process would enable the firm to guarantee to take all the milk that contracting farmers could produce. Further, to encourage the delivery of clean, un-adulterated milk, the project would pay farmers a little more than the going rate for milk. Farmers would, it was hoped, have an incentive to increase the yield from their buffaloes and expand the number of animals that they kept. The milkmen would receive a margin of Rs.0.60 rather than the usual Rs.0.50 per liter.

Skim milk powder was imported under an "open license policy," without customs duty or sales tax. Whole milk powder, in contrast, was subject to a 20% sales tax. The policy was under review by the government, and importers expected that skim milk powder would soon be subject to the sales tax, while a tariff would be added to the charges for whole milk powder. Consequently, the projections were based on the assumption of a 20% tax on milk powder for Milkpak. The plant would also require a stabilizer that would be imported at a cost of Rs.0.05/liter of milk.

The chairman of Milkpak would be Syed Babar Ali, who played a major role in the overall strategy of the Ali group. The managing director would be Mr. Walid Nazir, a forty-four-year-old chemical engineer, who had been a plant manager at Dawood Hercules Chemicals, Ltd., and was currently the managing director of a large public sector fertilizer company. The technical staff would be trained at Milko, Tetra Pak, and DTD.

Milkpak would market its products through independent distributors, some of which would be established by managers from Packages. They would sell the products to supermarkets (in Karachi), groceries, and bakeries. The commission would be Rs.0.10/liter for distributors and Rs.0.20/liter for retailers. This compared to an equivalent of Rs.0.14/liter for canned milk powder. The sterilized milk would be sold at retail at a premium of about 20% over the prices of fresh milk in milk stores.

Projected financial statements for Milkpak are shown in *Exhibits 5–7*.

Exhibit 1
Summary Income Statement for Milko
(first nine months of 1978; Rs.000s)

	January–September	*September*[a]
Sales	8,804	1,286
Less returns	341	45
Net sales	8,463	1,241
Cost of goods sold	8,406	1,148
Gross profit	57	93
Sales and administrative	573	54
Operating profit (loss)	(516)	39
Financial charges	—	—
Net profit	(516)	39

[a]By September 1978 the plant was operating at capacity.

Exhibit 2 Demand and Supply of Milk in Lahore Area
(over one year)

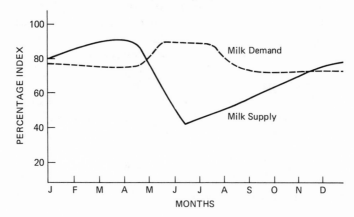

Exhibit 3
Sources of Investment for Milkpak
(In $000)

	Currency		
	Local	*Foreign*	*Total*
Equity			
Ali family	550		550
Packages, Ltd.	250		250
IGI[a]	200		200
Public offering	1,600		1,600
International Finance Corp.		200	200
Tetra Pak		300	300
DEG[b]		200	200
DTD[c]		100	100
IFU[d]		100	100
Total Equity	2,600	900	3,500
Long-term debt			
International Finance Corp.[e]		2,400	2,400
DEG[f]		800	800
IFU[g]		300	300
Rupee loans	1,675		1,675
Customs debentures	325		325
Total long-term debt	2,000	3,500	5,500
Total	4,600	4,400	9,000

[a]International General Insurance Company, a nonlife insurance company 99% owned by the Ali group.

[b]German Development Institute (Deutsche Gesellschaft fuer Wirtschaftliche Zusammenarbeit).

[c]Danish Turnkey Dairies, Ltd., Denmark.

[d]Industrialization Fund for Developing Countries, Denmark.

[e]Ten years, in dollars, with a two-year grace period, interest at $10\frac{3}{4}\%$.

[f]Same repayment schedule as IFC, in German marks, interest at 8%.

[g]Same repayment as IFC, in dollars, interest at 11%.

Exhibit 4
Utilization of Investment for Milkpak
($000)

	Foreign Currency	Local Currency	Total
Fixed assets	4,002	3,345	7,347
Other assets	386	1,267	1,653
Preoperating costs		381	381
Interest during construction	256	146	402
Pre-financial interest	130	90	220
Net working capital		650	650
Total	4,388	4,612	9,000

MILKPAK

Exhibit 5

Projected Income Statement for Milkpak
(Rs.000s)

	1981	1982	1983	1984	1985	1986	1987	1988	1989	1990
Production (000 liters)	15,300	34,000	34,000	34,000	34,000	34,000	34,000	34,000	34,000	34,000
Sales (000 liters)	14,940	33,760	34,000	34,000	34,000	34,000	34,000	34,000	34,000	34,000
Net sales (Rs.000)	52,888	119,510	120,400	120,400	120,400	120,400	120,400	120,400	120,400	120,400
Cost of materials										
Fresh milk	16,916	37,589	37,589	37,589	37,589	37,589	37,589	37,589	37,589	37,589
Milk powder and recodan	5,098	11,329	11,329	11,329	11,329	11,329	11,329	11,329	11,329	11,329
Chemicals	90	225	225	225	225	225	225	225	225	225
Total materials	22,104	49,143	49,143	49,143	49,143	49,143	49,143	49,143	49,143	49,143
Packaging material	9,771	21,712	21,712	21,712	21,712	21,712	21,712	21,712	21,712	21,712
Direct labor	342	536	536	536	536	536	536	536	536	536
Utilities & other expenses	1,065	1,477	1,581	1,584	1,558	1,558	1,558	1,558	1,558	1,558
Stores, repairs, & maintenance	1,532	2,106	2,698	3,310	3,841	3,841	3,841	3,841	3,841	3,841
Plant overheads & supplies	569	1,121	1,121	1,121	1,121	1,121	1,121	1,121	1,121	1,121
Transportation schedule	3,943	8,910	8,973	8,973	8,973	8,973	8,973	8,973	8,973	8,973
Depreciation	6,173	6,273	6,373	6,473	6,611	6,611	6,811	6,911	7,011	7,111
Closing stock variation	(1,001)	(514)	—	—	—	—	—	—	—	—
Cost of sales	44,498	90,764	92,137	92,852	93,495	93,595	93,695	93,795	93,895	93,995
Cost of extension services	2,043	2,965	2,214	2,510	2,484	2,484	2,484	2,484	2,484	2,484
Total Cost of Sales	46,541	93,729	94,351	95,362	95,979	96,079	96,179	96,279	96,379	96,479
Gross income	6,347	25,781	26,049	25,038	24,421	24,321	24,221	24,121	24,021	23,921

(continued on next page)

371

Exhibit 5
Projected Income Statement for Milkpak (*Continued*)

	1981	1982	1983	1984	1985	1986	1987	1988	1989	1990
Operating expense										
Administrative & selling expenses	3,878	4,689	4,230	4,250	4,227	4,227	4,227	4,227	4,227	4,227
Amortization of preoperating expenses	783	783	783	783	783	783	783	783	783	783
Total operating expense	4,661	5,472	5,013	5,033	5,010	5,010	5,010	5,010	5,010	5,010
Operating income	1,686	20,309	21,036	20,005	19,411	19,311	19,211	19,111	19,011	18,911
Nonoperating expenses										
Interest	5,887	5,651	4,787	3,847	2,939	2,117	1,299	479	79	50
Income before tax & workers funds	(4,201)	14,658	16,249	16,158	16,472	17,194	19,712	18,632	18,932	18,861
5% workers profit participation	—	733	812	808	824	960	896	932	947	943
2% workers welfare fund	—	—	295	359	377	392	417	490	454	460
Profit before tax	(4,201)	13,925	15,142	14,991	15,271	15,942	16,599	17,210	17,531	17,458
Income tax (current)	—	—	2,103	7,922	8,319	8,638	9,185	9,702	10,015	10,149
Net Income	(4,201)	13,925	13,039	7,069	6,952	7,304	7,414	7,508	7,516	7,309

MILKPAK

Exhibit 6

Projected Balance Sheets for Milkpak at Year Ending December 31

(Rs.000)

	1980	1981	1982	1983	1984	1985	1986	1987	1988	1989	1990
Current assets											
Cash	6,187	3,743	13,854	23,589	29,420	25,858	26,832	27,369	29,257	34,730	42,423
Inventories	3,338	6,528	9,960	9,960	9,960	9,960	9,960	9,960	9,960	9,960	9,960
Accounts receivable	—	3,457	5,765	5,765	5,765	5,765	5,765	5,765	5,765	5,765	5,765
Total current assets	9,525	13,728	29,579	39,314	45,145	41,583	42,557	43,094	44,982	50,455	58,148
Fixed assets and others											
Fixed assets and preoperating expenses	81,300	81,300	85,060	87,017	88,974	94,551	96,508	98,465	100,422	102,379	104,336
Accumulated depreciation & amortization	—	7,600	15,806	24,563	33,420	42,377	51,434	60,591	69,848	79,205	88,662
Net fixed and other assets	81,300	73,700	69,254	62,454	55,554	52,174	45,074	37,874	30,574	23,174	15,674
Total assets	90,825	87,428	98,833	101,768	100,699	93,757	87,631	80,968	75,556	73,629	73,822
Current liabilities											
Accounts payable	825	1,629	3,463	3,463	3,463	3,463	3,463	3,463	3,463	3,463	3,463
Dividends payable	—	—	3,500	5,250	6,125	6,125	7,000	7,000	7,000	7,000	7,000
Taxes payable	—	—	—	2,103	7,922	8,319	8,638	9,185	9,702	10,015	10,149
Current portion of l.t. debt	—	4,354	8,707	8,707	8,166	7,624	7,624	6,437	2,756	250	250
Total current liabilities	825	5,983	15,670	19,523	25,676	25,531	26,725	26,085	22,921	20,728	20,862

(continued on next page)

Exhibit 6

Projected Balance Sheets for Milkpak at Year Ending December 31 *(Continued)*

	1980	1981	1982	1983	1984	1985	1986	1987	1988	1989	1990
Long-term debt											
Deferred customs duties	3,250	2,708	1,625	542	—	—	—	—	—	—	—
ICP consortium	16,750	15,438	12,813	10,188	7,563	4,938	2,313	875	625	375	125
IFC loan	19,000	17,643	14,929	12,215	9,501	6,787	4,073	1,359	—	—	—
AMEX bank loan	5,000	4,643	3,929	3,215	2,501	1,787	1,073	359	—	—	—
IFU & DEG	11,000	10,214	8,643	7,072	5,501	3,930	2,359	788	—	—	—
Net long-term debt	55,000	50,646	41,939	33,232	25,066	17,442	9,818	3,381	625	375	125
Equity											
Ordinary shares outstanding	35,000	35,000	35,000	35,000	35,000	35,000	35,000	35,000	35,000	35,000	35,000
Retained earnings & reserves	—	(4,201)	6,224	14,013	14,957	15,784	16,088	16,502	17,010	17,526	17,835
Total equity	35,000	30,799	41,224	49,013	49,957	50,784	51,088	51,502	52,010	52,526	52,835
Total liabilities and equity	90,825	87,428	98,833	101,768	100,699	93,757	87,631	80,968	75,556	73,629	73,822

374

Exhibit 7
Sensitivity Analysis

Case 1: Reduction of assumed 20% price premium over regular milk to a 10% premium

Case 2: Increase in milk collection during the third year is only 75% of the expected increase. Thus, unit sales are reduced by about 15%.

Case 3: 10% increase in raw milk cost

	Net Income ($000)	*Return on Original Equity (%)*	*Debt Service Coverage (X)*
Projected	1,024	29.3	1.8
Case 1	234	6.7	1.2
Case 2	734	21.0	1.5
Case 3	851	24.3	1.6

SOURCE: Company calculations.

Nestlé Alimentana S.A.— Infant Formula

In October 1978 H. M. Holloway[1] became vice-president, infant and dietetic productions, of Nestlé Alimentana S.A., in Vevey, Switzerland, and assumed worldwide responsibility for coordinating the 1979 marketing plans for these product lines. Because of the political climate, he had been asked to give particular attention to the marketing programs for the company's line of infant formulas and to recommend whatever changes he deemed appropriate.

At the same time Holloway assumed his new position, the Nestlé Company, Inc., the wholly owned U.S. subsidiary of Nestlé S.A., was the target of a boycott. Since July 4, 1977, an organization called INFACT (Infant Formula Action Coalition) had been coordinating and promoting a consumer boycott of all products marketed by the U.S. company, because INFACT asserted Nestlé employed inappropriate marketing techniques in selling its infant formula products in less developed countries (LDCs). Because Nestlé S.A., the parent, was a Swiss company, Americans could bring little or no shareholder pressure to bear on the company's operations. Boycotting the products of the U.S. subsidiary was an attempt to exert economic pressure on the Swiss parent company by threatening the profitability of its second largest market.

Of particular concern to Nestlé's critics was the company's positioning, distribution, advertising, and promotion of its infant formulas in LDCs. Holloway would therefore have to give particular attention to these elements of the marketing mix in any recommendations he might make.

---

[1]Certain names have been disguised.

This case was prepared from published sources by Neil Harrison, Research Assistant, under the supervision of Associate Professor Claudine B. Malone, as a basis for class discussion rather than to illustrate either effective or ineffective handling of an administrative situation. Abridged with permission.

NESTLÉ ALIMENTANA S.A., COMPANY BACKGROUND

In 1977 Nestlé earned Swiss Fr.830 million on worldwide sales of Swiss Fr.20 billion,[2] ranking it 36th among the world's largest industrial companies, and the leader among food processors. About one-fifth of total sales were in LDCs. The company employed more than 140,000 people in more than 50 countries.

Nestlé's worldwide operations were managed by its regional and country managers, with staff support provided by various functional divisions located at the company headquarters in Switzerland (*Exhibit 1*). The individual country managers were allowed considerable autonomy in operating their subsidiaries. They submitted, and were evaluated against, annual budgets that were consolidated by the planning and functional support staffs in Vevey.

Country managers recommended marketing plans for their specific areas; there was no standardized marketing program (*Exhibit 2*). Coordinating marketing ideas and techniques among the different countries was done through the product staff in Vevey, who acted in an advisory capacity. A country manager could refuse to manufacture or market a particular product if it was believed the local market conditions were unfavorable.

As described in a 1975 *Harvard Business Review* article,[3] Nestlé guided its marketing planning by means of a set of instructions communicated to the subsidiaries in a loose-leaf marketing budget manual. Annual marketing planning started with each subsidiary preparing a general fact book for its home country and a product fact book for each major product the subsidiary sold. The general fact book provided a format for gathering information on factors that could affect the subsidiary's marketing, such as population composition and trends, economic climate, industry outlook, competition, and marketing legislation. The product fact book contained—again in standardized format—specific information about each product, such as its total market size and segments, market shares and trends, consumers' habits and attitudes.

Using the fact books as a starting point, subsidiary managers were then expected to propose both six-year and one-year marketing plans in an internationally uniform format. In addition to detailed figure work, the annual plan had an essential qualitative part. It not only explained the figure work but also discussed and justified actions planned for the com-

---

[2] In 1977 US\$ = 2.09 Swiss francs; Swiss franc = US\$ 0.478.

[3] Ralph Z. Sorenson and Ulrich E. Wiechmann, "How Multinationals View Marketing Standardization," *Harvard Business Review*, no. 75312, May–June 1975, p. 45.

ing year, identified critical success factors, spelled out responsibilities and deadlines for implementation, and established yardsticks for performance measurement.

THE INFANT FORMULA MARKET

Evolution

Infant formulas arose out of medical research conducted as early as 1920 into childhood disease and malnutrition. At that time development, clinical testing, and use of infant formulas were confined to hospitals and medical institutions.

Commercial development of infant formulas was begun by two types of companies: pharmaceutical companies and food companies experienced in milk products. By the late 1920s a number of large U.S. pharmaceutical companies, such as Ross Laboratories, Mead Johnson, and Wyeth Laboratories, manufactured and marketed infant formula in the United States. Each of these firms was later acquired by larger pharmaceutical companies.[4]

Food companies further stimulated the development of the infant formula market. Such companies as Borden and Nestlé had marketed sweetened and condensed milk since well before the turn of the century, and some mothers had fed these products to their babies. But when infant formulas were proved to be nutritionally better than condensed milk for the child, food companies began to develop new products to compete in this growing market. Nestlé developed and marketed its own infant formulas in the 1920s and Borden in the 1950s.

Until the end of World War II, U.S. sales of infant formulas were confined largely to hospitals and other medical institutions. After the war, the changing attitudes of the "modern" mother produced a receptive consumer market for infant formula. This and the baby boom provided a large U.S. market for infant formulas up to the late 1960s, when market saturation and a declining birthrate spurred the U.S. companies to expand abroad. Europe, other developed areas of the world, and LDCs presented attractive growth opportunities for the marketers of infant formulas.

---

[4]Wyeth Laboratories was acquired by American Home Products in the 1930s; Ross Laboratories by Abbott Laboratories in 1964; and Mead Johnson by Bristol-Myers in the late 1960s.

The "Nutrition Gap"

Medical research revealed that beyond a certain age, generally three to six months, a child's protein requirements could not be satisfied entirely by breast milk. During this critical period a child's rate of growth was greater than at any other time in its life, and even healthy mothers were unable to provide sufficient breast milk. Ordinary family foods were unsuitable for a baby's delicate digestive system much before eighteen to twenty-four months. Consequently, between the ages of six months and eighteen months children needed additional sources of protein to supplement breast milk. This deficiency was known as the "nutrition gap." In areas where mothers were likely to be undernourished, such as LDCs, this gap was found to be more pronounced and to develop at an earlier age. Infant formula, if affordable and if properly used, was one alternative food able to fill the nutrition gap and ease a transition to normal family foods.

Many critics of infant formula usage in LDCs argued that local foods administered by cup and spoon were a preferred weaning food because they were affordable and entailed less risk of contamination. Examples cited included rice- and maize-based cereals high in caloric density with 10–12% protein content. Where available and affordable, raw eggs could be added to these paps to increase the protein level further.

The Product

Infant formulas were composed of various formulations of processed foods based on cow's milk. While chemically similar to breast milk, they did not contain the antibodies and other immunological substances that were in mother's milk and that protected the newborn child from such diseases as measles, diarrhea, bronchitis, pneumonia, and other respiratory infections. But infant formulas were nutritionally superior to all other milk-based, commercially produced infant feeding alternatives, like powdered, evaporated, or condensed milk.[5] Sold in powdered form, infant formula had to be dissolved in water in exactly the correct proportions, and all nipples, bottles, and utensils had to be sterilized to avoid transferring harmful bacteria to the child.

It should be emphasized that bottle feeding did not necessarily mean that a child was receiving infant formula or any other milk-based alternative. In the rural areas of LDCs the bottle frequently contained various combinations of millet or rice, which, when mixed with water, produced a

[5]James E. Post and Edward Baer, "Analyzing Complex Policy Problems: The Social Performance of the International Infant Formula Industry," Lee E. Preston, ed., *Research in Corporate Social Performance and Policy*, volume 2 (Greenwich: JAI Press, 1980).

pap or gruel. Although high in carbohydrates and very filling, many of these paps and gruels were severely lacking in nutrition, especially protein.

Because a baby's stomach is so small, feedings are frequent and in small amounts. Depending on the baby's digestion and capacity, breast feeding can be desirable as often as every hour. Formula feeding tends to be required less frequently and more routinely, generally every three to four hours, thus giving mothers more uninterrupted time.

Market Size

One characteristic of this market was the absence of any "official" statistics on total world sales. Estimates of worldwide infant formula sales in 1975 ranged between $980 million and $1,090 million. Dr. James Post of Boston University, in testimony before the U.S. Congress in 1978, estimated world sales of infant formula at about $1.5 billion in 1977, with LDCs representing about $600 million. He forecast total world sales to reach $2 billion by 1980, an annual compound growth rate of 10%, and LDCs to account for 50%. Thus, sales to LDCs were expected to grow by about 19% per annum over the next three years, or about five times the rate of growth in non-LDCs.

Competition

In the early 1970s there were at least 15 major manufacturers of infant formula from the United States, Europe, and Japan. They tended to be either pharmaceutical companies, such as Abbott Laboratories, Bristol-Myers, and American Home Products, or packaged-food companies, such as Nestlé, Carnation, and Cow & Gate. Consistent with their basic business strategies, these two groups had traditionally adopted different strategies in the infant formula business.

The pharmaceutical companies used detail representatives to push infant formulas in much the same way they sold pharmaceuticals.[6] These representatives, usually women in LDCs, visited hospitals and clinics, promoting the benefits of their infant formulas to new mothers and medical staffs. They often left free samples of their products at various medical institutions. Once the new mother left the hospital or clinic, she could obtain more formula from retail stores or, in more rural areas, from the companies' traveling representatives or village "wholesalers," who

---

[6]James E. Post and Edward Baer, "Demarketing Infant Formula: Consumer Products in the Developing World," *Journal of Contemporary Business,* 7, no. 4: 17.

distributed products to isolated regions (often carrying merchandise on their heads).

In contrast, the packaged-food companies tended to rely on more traditional mass marketing techniques, particularly mass distribution and mass advertising via TV, radio, movie theater ads, print, and posters. They had also used promotions directed at the medical profession, such as providing free samples to hospitals and clinics.

Manufacturers employed both direct and indirect distribution systems. According to industry observers, most infant formula was distributed through local wholesalers to retail outlets, particularly in urban areas. In a number of LDCs of French colonial origin, such as the Ivory Coast, infant formula was supposed to be available only through pharmacists. But policing of formula distribution was very poor, and observers noted bottle, nipple, and product availability in many stores and markets in both urban and rural areas. Additional product was distributed through hospitals, clinics, and company representatives in rural areas. Although exact figures were not available, it was believed that a greater percentage of infant formula sales occurred in urban areas. In an attempt to increase sales, many distributors promoted infant formulas to broad segments of the population. Therefore, those exposed to the promotion were not only higher-income urban mothers, but also the poor and those in rural areas of LDCs who were only marginally able to afford the product.[7]

During the 1970s various sources indicated that worldwide sales were dominated by four major multinational manufacturers. Nestlé was thought to be the market leader, with between 35% and 45% market share. Dr. James Post's estimates of the sales of major multinationals are shown in the accompanying table.

	World Market	*LDC Market*
	($ millions)	
Nestlé	600	360+
Abbott Laboratories	222	20+
American Home Products	170	55+
Bristol-Myers	165	50+
4-firm total	1,157	485+

SOURCE: Dr. James E. Post, testimony before U.S. Congress (1978).

As early as the late 1950s, American pharmaceutical companies had expanded geographically to escape the more mature and slower-growing U.S. infant food market, and foreign sales were still providing significant

[7]James E. Post and S. Prakash Sethi, "Public Consequences of Private Action: The Marketing of Infant Formula in Less Developed Countries," *California Management Review*, 21, no. 4 (Summer 1979): 35.

sales growth during the 1970s. Bristol-Myers's subsidiary, Mead Johnson, was cited as enjoying a record year in 1974, largely due to increased foreign export sales of its infant formula Enfamil.[8] The Ross Laboratories division of Abbott Laboratories was believed to have experienced growth rates of 30% in 1974 and 1975 for its foreign sales of infant formula, as against 10–12% domestically.[9] In 1977 it was the largest U.S. manufacturer in the $300-million U.S. market for infant formula. Industry analysts estimated Wyeth Laboratories' foreign sales of infant formula to be $60 million in 1975, about twice the size of its American competitors' sales outside the United States.

In many cases infant formula was just one of a bundle of products that these manufacturers sold in LDCs. In certain LDCs, importer-distributors were restricted in the number of products they were allowed to import and then distribute and were therefore particularly interested in products with high volume potential or high unit margins. Infant formulas were thought to offer both high volume and high margin.

NESTLÉ'S INFANT FOODS AND DIETETIC PRODUCTS

Infant foods and dietetic products represented 7.3% of the company's total sales revenue in 1977 and had grown at an average rate of 5.4% a year over the previous six years. Infant foods and dietetic products included infant milks, liquid milk, follow-up milks, infant cereals, baby foods, and specialized milks. These products were sold in 45 markets around the world and were supplied by local production, imports, or both. Nestlé first entered the LDC markets in the 1920s, when it introduced a line of dairy products, including infant formula, in Brazil. Over the next fifty years, Nestlé expanded into about 20 additional LDCs. Over these years Nestlé had developed a broad line of infant formulas. Lactogen, based on cow's milk, was introduced in 1921. In 1927 Eledon was introduced specifically for children with digestive problems. A low-fat-content formula, Nestogen, was marketed in 1930, and Pelargon, an acidified formula for tropical areas, was developed in 1934.[10]

By 1978 Nestlé manufactured and marketed three broad categories of infant foods: "starter" formulas, "follow-up" formulas, and "weaning foods." They were marketed under different brand names in different

---

[8]Ann Crittenden, "Baby Formula Sales in Third World Criticized," *New York Times,* September 11, 1975.

[9]*Ibid.*

[10]James E. Post, hearing before the Subcommittee on Health and Scientific Research, United States Senate, May 23, 1978, p. 233.

areas of the world. Starter formulas were for children up to the age of four months and supplemented or replaced breast milk. Follow-up formulas were not patterned on breast milk but were intended to follow or supplement breast feeding after about four months. Weaning foods were cereal-based and supplemented the child's feeding once its dietary needs exceeded that supplied by milk alone. Nestlé positioned its infant formulas as supplements to breast milk or, in cases where the mother was incapable of breast-feeding, as a substitute for breast milk.

CHRONOLOGY OF A CONTROVERSY

During the late 1960s a number of health workers, nutritionists, and pediatricians became increasingly concerned over statistics suggesting that since World War II the incidence of breast feeding in LDCs had steadily declined, particularly in more affluent urban areas. Certain studies conducted in LDCs concluded that some correlation existed between declining breast-feeding and increasing illness among babies because of the absence of immunological elements in nonbreast-milk foods and because of greater potential bacterial infection of utensils and materials used in their preparation.

Compared to breast-feeding, artificial feeding, whether with infant formula or more "traditional" foods like paps and gruels, exposed the child to greater risk of bacterial infection. In the poorer areas of LDCs, water used for making food and cleaning utensils was often polluted. The relatively high cost of fuel (including animal dung) often resulted in the mother's preparing the child's food in a large batch, which was then stored, without refrigeration, for later use during the day. Utensils were frequently cleaned with cold rather than hot water. In such an environment, the child was in greater danger of contracting diarrheal infection and disease.

Recognizing these trends, the Protein Advisory Group (PAG) recommended a meeting among medical, governmental, and industrial representatives to discuss infant-feeding practices. Two meetings occurred: in Bogotá in 1970 and in Paris in 1972. As a result of these meetings, PAG issued "Statement #23: PAG Recommendations for the Promotion of Processed Protein Foods for Vulnerable Groups." The report concluded that breast milk was the best food for infants and, if in sufficient supply, would satisfy the needs of a child up to 4–6 months. In cases where breast-feeding was insufficient or impossible, the use of nutritional substitutes was encouraged.

Up to this point, the debate had been of a scientific nature. In 1973, however, the issue acquired a more "popular" appeal.[11] The August issue of *New Internationalist* contained an interview with two medical experts who believed that marketers of baby food had contributed to the incidence of diarrheal disease among infants in LDCs. Less than a year later, the journalist Mike Muller wrote an article called "The Baby Killer," which decried the promotions of infant formula manufacturers in LDCs as stimulating the trend away from breast-feeding.

The cause was then taken up by the Third World Action Group (an organization of young volunteers that disseminated information to schools on Swiss foreign-aid programs, based in Switzerland), which translated Muller's original article into German and singled out Nestlé by changing the title to "Nestlé Kills Babies." Though Nestlé successfully sued for defamation, the judge suggested the company reconsider its advertising practices:

> Hence, the need ensues for the Nestlé Company fundamentally to rethink its advertising practices in developing countries as concerns bottle feeding, for its advertising practice up to now can transform a life-saving product into one that is dangerous and life-destroying. If the complainant in future wants to be spared the accusation of immoral and unethical conduct, he will have to change its advertising practices.[12]

Marketing Techniques Criticized

By late 1974 increased public attention was focused on certain marketing techniques being used by infant formula manufacturers in LDCs.[13]

Mass Media Advertising. The use of mass media, such as posters in hospitals and clinics, billboards, loudspeaker vans, radio, TV, and magazines, was criticized. The advertising often carried the statement, "Breast feed your baby, but when you have to supplement, use Nestlé's Lactogen." It was felt that advertisements overemphasized infant formulas at the expense of breast-feeding, without differentiating situations in which using infant formula was unnecessary. Showing healthy-looking babies being fed infant formulas was thought to mislead mothers into thinking that healthy babies were "infant formula babies." Given a mother's natural anxiety to do best by her child, she was especially vulnerable to the advertising messages. A further criticism of mass media advertising was

[11]J. A. Sparks, "The Nestlé Controversy: Anatomy of a Boycott," Public Policy Education Fund Inc., April 1979, p. 1.

[12]Andy Chetley, *The Baby Killer Scandal, A War on Want: Investigation into the Promotion and Sales of Powdered Baby Milks in the Third World* (London: War on Want, 1978), p. 111.

[13]Post and Sethi, "Public Consequences of Private Action" p. 39.

that companies did not selectively target their advertising campaigns. Mothers who for various socioeconomic reasons were thought an inappropriate audience were also exposed to the mass advertising.

Informational Pamphlets on Infant Feeding. Distributed widely through hospital and clinics, informational booklets provided information on feeding babies and the conditions under which bottle feeding could be used. Critics asserted that the earlier booklets often omitted or downplayed any reference to breast-feeding while showing correct or incorrect ways to bottle feed. Nestlé used graphics extensively to overcome illiteracy barriers. The texts were translated into many languages and distributed throughout the world. (See *Exhibit 3* for poster text.) As with mass advertising, however, critics felt the booklets misled mothers into believing bottle feeding was equal or superior to mother's milk. Before the controversy, Nestlé advertising and literature had been produced for each country individually. In late 1974 Nestlé required all advertising to be authorized by Vevey before being used.

Free Samples. Hospitals and clinics were often supplied with free samples of infant formula and sometimes also free feeding utensils. Once the mother left the maternity ward she might also receive samples from company representatives. The concern about free samples was that once a mother bottle-fed her baby, she soon became physically unable to breast-feed because her milk supply diminished if it was not used. Critics believed mothers were thus "hooked" on bottle feeding from the beginning and consequently their natural abilities were reduced.

Particularly dangerous was the situation when a low-income mother returned home and continued to use infant formula even though the local sanitary conditions were unsuitable for its safe preparation. Furthermore, the relatively high cost of infant formula (estimated to be as much as 50% of a family's disposable income in poor areas of LDCs) forced some mothers to dilute the formula to make it last longer, thus causing the child to receive less nutrition than it needed.

Promotion Via the Medical Profession. Critics argued that the use of infant formula in hospitals and clinics led new mothers to believe that it was "correct" to feed their child infant formula and that it was the best way to give the child a healthy start to life. Doctors were aware of the potential benefits of infant formula and were therefore main targets, particularly of the pharmaceutical manufacturers.

"Milk" or "Mother-craft" Nurses. "Milk" nurses were company representatives, usually women, who promoted infant formula to the medical profession, hospitals and clinics, and expectant and actual mothers. They also gave free samples, booklets, and advice on infant feeding. Milk or mothercraft nurses differed from the normal detail representatives in their educational role. Besides performing the usual counseling tasks, these nurses were also expected to educate and counsel mothers on infant feeding.

Nestlé reportedly employed about 200 "nurses" worldwide,[14] which was a small fraction of its total detail force.

Their titles and the fact that they often wore white uniforms like nurses' uniforms were thought to lead mothers to associate infant formula closely with the medical profession. Although many "milk nurses" were medically trained, they were still paid employees of infant formula companies, and some received a sales bonus in addition to their basic salary. They visited mothers in isolated regions and often carried supplies of infant formula. Another criticism of milk nurses was that, by hiring these nurses, companies were effectively denying the country's health service of their scarce talents. Critics believed the milk nurses could be more fully productive by working in local health institutions rather than as company representatives.

The Formation of ICIFI

In 1975 the infant formula industry formed an association, the International Council of Infant Food Industries (ICIFI), to foster free exchange of information and cooperation with respect to infant nutrition. Apart from Ross Laboratories and Bristol-Myers, all the major formula manufacturers joined the organization. Ross Laboratories withdrew from the initial discussions because it felt the code of practice the association drew up was too weak; it later developed its own code, which prohibited consumer advertising. Additionally, any contacts with mothers were to be done only with the permission and guidance of health care professionals, and home visits were never allowed. Samples were given to health care personnel only at their request. No employees were to wear nurses uniforms or be compensated based on sales volume. The company also provided nonproduct-related materials and services to health care professionals to help them encourage breast-feeding, promote child nutrition and care, and improve sanitation. Abbott invited anyone to report any deviation from their code by employees.

The ICIFI ethics code recognized the nutritional superiority of breast milk. Consistent with this basic tenet, members were required to ensure that product labels and advertising claims supported breast milk as the first choice in feeding infants. Greater emphasis was to be placed on informing mothers about the correct way to prepare infant formula and of the dangers of diluting the formula or using polluted water. Milk nurses were to be professionally trained and wear an ICIFI emblem to identify them as company personnel. They were not to discourage moth-

[14]Sparks, "The Nestlé Controversy," p. 7.

ers from breast-feeding, they would contact mothers and provide free samples only via appropriate medical personnel, and their compensation would not be tied to sales volume.

Critics felt the ICIFI code did not go far enough to restrict the marketing practices of the infant-formula manufacturers in LDCs. The public outcry thus continued. In late 1976 a number of individuals and church and social welfare organizations joined with members of a study group at the Third World Institute of the Newman Center to form the Infant Formula Action Coalition (INFACT), based in Minneapolis, Minnesota. On July 4, 1977, INFACT called for an organized boycott of all Nestlé products in the United States. It then sent a brochure to organizations and individuals in the United States drawing attention to what it described as inappropriate marketing of infant formula in LDCs by Nestlé S.A. and requesting donations to support INFACT's activities. INFACT reportedly operated on an annual budget of $29,000.[15] It regularly distributed newsletters and reports and made available a film called *Bottle Babies*, to be shown at gatherings around the country. INFACT did not advocate total withdrawal of infant formula from LDCs, but rather the cessation of such practices as the use of "milk nurses," the distribution of free samples, promotion of formula through the medical profession, and the direct promotion of formula to consumers.

Nestlé responded by providing information on the role of infant formula, by producing a filmed response ("Feeding Babies: A Shared Responsibility"), by having company representatives speak to interested gatherings, and by continuing to work with medical, governmental, and industrial representatives. A company statement issued in February 1977 reiterated Nestlé's concern for infant feeding (*Exhibit 4*). It also indicated that Nestlé medical representatives would not wear official uniforms, that their salary would not be sales-related, and that they would not be allowed to sell infant formula to mothers.

On May 23, 1978, the U.S. Senate Subcommittee on Health and Scientific Research, chaired by Senator Kennedy, heard testimony by pediatricians, church organizations, INFACT, and infant-formula manufacturers (including Nestlé). The objective of the hearings was to "learn what the problems are in . . . the use of infant formula in developing nations; to explore the questions of responsibility for improving conditions; and for developing an understanding of those steps the Congress and the U.S. Government can take to make things better."[16]

In his concluding remarks, Senator Kennedy stated that postmarketing

---

[15]*Business Week,* April 23, 1979.

[16]United States Senate, Subcommittee on Health and Scientific Research, Committee on Human Resources, *The Marketing and Promotion of Infant Formula in Developing Nations,* May 23, 1978, p. 3.

surveillance by infant formula manufacturers of where their products end up and how they are actually used did not appear to be a primary consideration of the manufacturers.[17] He felt they tended to rely on the medical profession, the nurses, and the distribution networks in LDCs. Kennedy called for a meeting of the World Health Organization to continue the discussion of infant-feeding problems throughout the world. Members of ICIFI strongly supported this suggestion.

THE ENVIRONMENT FACING HOLLOWAY IN LATE 1978

By 1978 the volume of data on infant-feeding practices in LDCs had reached overwhelming proportions. Some studies showed a downward trend in breast-feeding, others showed an increase in infant morbidity and mortality, still others concluded that reversing the trend toward bottle feeding would alleviate malnutrition problems in LDCs. But the literature also included articles casting doubt on some of these conclusions or citing areas where these trends were not evident.

After surveying more than 350 published sources, one author concluded that to a large extent the apparent conflict in evidence was due to a lack of scientific method used in the various studies:

> There is a lack of understanding of scientific method. Only a comparatively small number of studies made use of proper methodology in sampling technique, research design, and in the handling of statistical data. Thus, it is often impossible to replicate the study or validate the results. Often the investigator is only interested in proving a point. Many studies are purely impressionistic. . . .
>
> Frequent errors occur in the analysis of data. The "mean" is often used without the standard deviation and the methodology is not described.[18]

Inconsistent definitions, poor statistical design and analysis, and the different objectives of individual researchers made comparison of apparently conflicting results difficult. For example, there was often no control of "other variables" or any "prestudy" and "poststudy" observations. Some studies were criticized on the grounds that the term "bottle feeding" was used without describing the contents of the bottle—formula, native gruels, cow's milk, etc. Similarly, when comparing breast versus bottle feeding, some studies failed to enumerate the incidence of mixed

---

[17]*Ibid.*, p. 151.

[18]Elisabeth Cole, "Breastfeeding: A Critique of the Literature," *The Lactation Review*, II, no. 3 (1977): 5.

feeding (using both breast and bottle). Also, studies were often conducted in isolated areas, such as a single village in one area of a country, without due recognition of specific environmental influences. Broad generalizations and comparisons were therefore extremely difficult. The article concluded that the relationship between infant health and feeding practices was not clear.

Numerous investigations concluded that any declining trend in breast-feeding resulted from a combination of factors, including the urbanization of LDCs and the problems of young mothers unable to breast-feed their babies while at work; the tendency for the breast to be increasingly viewed as a sex object, causing embarrassment of breast-feeding in public or fear of lack of appeal after breast-feeding; the status associated with bottle feeding because this was practiced by "modern" mothers in the developed countries; and the practices of MNCs in promoting infant formula and bottle feeding. But the relative influence of these factors was far from clear.

A more sensational allegation leveled at the infant-formula manufacturers was that promoting infant formula had caused a decline in breast-feeding and consequently an increase in infant malnutrition and death. The high cost of infant formula, poor sanitary conditions, and pervasive illiteracy in LDCs were thought to have resulted in misuse of the product leading to consequent malnutrition and disease.

Thus, in the fall of 1978 Holloway faced conflicting scientific evidence and a highly emotional and political environment. Even though Nestlé did not market infant formula in the United States, his recommendations regarding infant formula marketing elsewhere in the world could have significant implications for the American operation. Against this backdrop, Holloway would have to make marketing recommendations for the infant foods and dietetic products group in 1979. Specifically, he would have to address criticism of Nestlé's positioning, distribution, advertising, and promotion of infant formula in LDCs.

Exhibit 1 Organization Structure

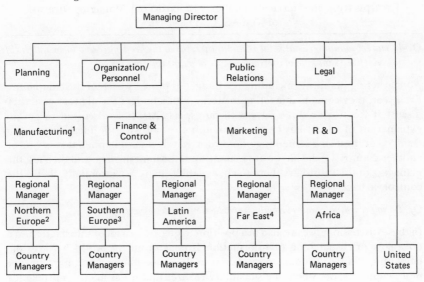

[1]Canadian operation reports to head of Manufacturing.

[2]Germany, U.K., Austria, Switzerland, Scandinavia.

[3]France, Spain, Italy.

[4]Includes Australia and New Zealand.

Marketing Division in Vevey, Switzerland

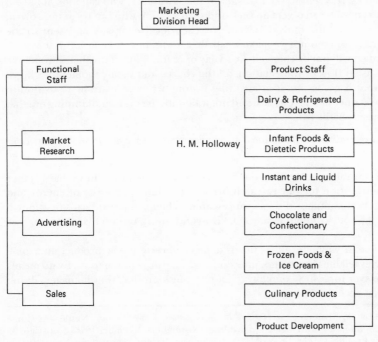

Exhibit 2
Excerpts from an Interview with Pierre Liotard-Vogt, Managing Director
of Nestlé S.A., 1968–1975

Q. *In market planning, what is the relationship between the head office and the managers of the subsidiaries? What kind of control does Nestlé maintain from Vevey?*

All marketing planning, including the budget, is done by each of the companies. Each year, they come to a meeting in Vevey with a budget for the year, and they discuss it for two or three days with our specialists. It is discussed to get an explanation of why it has been proposed, not at all with the idea of having it changed or imposing something of our own. Rarely does it happen that in one or another country we decide we are making an important mistake and then ask the managers of the subsidiary there to change their plans. So, essentially, that is the control we have.

Q. *Do you coordinate your marketing introductions in these meetings too?*

In these discussions, we are also in a position to give them a lot of information. We do a sort of dispatching of information from around the world because the launching of a new product may be done at the same time in three, four, five, or more countries. So, when one subsidiary realizes that it has made a mistake for such and such a reason, then of course we give that information to other subsidiaries. No country is exactly the same as another, but there are certain basic things that are true anywhere.

Q. *How much autonomy would that manager have in Brazil, say, compared with his counterpart at a U.S. multinational food company like General Foods or Kraftco?*

The budget of the subsidiary of an American company is usually made in the United States. It is sent to the manager of the subsidiary, who can look at it, who can discuss it, who can object on such and such a point, who can try to improve it. In our company, the budget is made by each local company and sent to the headquarters. Sometimes we make small alterations, but we can reckon that 95% of the budget will not be changed. Everyday operations are controlled abroad. We have the usual flow of information, all the charts, and at any moment we know exactly what is going on. So if anything is done wrong, we are in a position to intervene at once and give advice and not wait until the disaster of finding out that the business is badly run.

Q. *How decentralized are the decisions on whether to introduce a new product in particular areas?*

What we centralize at Vevey is the finance of the company, and we have rather high centralization for our research because it would be a waste of energy and money if every company did its own research. When a new product is developed, we offer it to our companies abroad. "Do you want it, or don't you want it?" we ask.

Of course, if we believe that this is a very interesting new product and some subsidiaries tell me they are not interested, we may urge initial trials. By no means would we ever force any company to launch a new product if its managers didn't think it was acceptable.

NESTLÉ ALIMENTANA S.A.—INFANT FORMULA

Exhibit 3
Text of Poster

1. The duty of a healthy mother is to feed her Baby if possible for the first six months of his life. Breast milk is the best food for your Baby.

2. Wash your breasts carefully with boiled water before and after each feed.

3. If bottle feeding is recommended, put the bottle, teat and cap into a pan of boiling water. Sterilize all utensils by leaving them to boil for 5 minutes, then drain.

4. Always wash your hands thoroughly before preparing the feed.

5. Pour the required amount of water which has been boiled and left to cool (about 40°C) into the bottle.

6. Add the indicated number of level scoops of powder.

7. Close the bottle with the stopper and cap.

8. Roll the bottle in your hands or shake it until all the powder has completely dissolved.

9. Fix the teat and screw the stopper securely, taking care not to touch the part which Baby puts in his mouth.

10. Check the temperature of the milk by letting a few drops fall onto the back of your hand. Never put the teat into your mouth.

11. This is the correct position for bottle feeding. Never let Baby drink his bottle unattended. Never keep what is left for the next feed.

12. At the end of the feed hold Baby upright for a moment so that he can bring up wind.

393

Exhibit 4
Nestlé Food Policy Statement, February 1978

Nestlé INFANT FOOD POLICY

INTRODUCTION

From its very earliest days, Nestlé has devoted particular attention to the subject of infant feeding. In close cooperation with leading clinicians, especially pediatricians, constant review and development of policy in this field takes place in line with the evolution of scientific knowledge.

In view of the increasing interest shown in these questions by medical and public opinion, Nestlé believes that it will be helpful to publish the essential elements of its infant food policy as summarized below.

BASIC PHILOSOPHY

Breast milk is the best food for babies during the first months of life, and Nestlé infant foods do not set out to compete with breast milk, but they are intended to:
supplement
breast milk (when breast milk alone is insufficient to cover the baby's needs);
follow-up
successful breast feeding;
replace
breast milk only when mothers cannot, or elect not to, breast feed.

PRODUCT DEFINITIONS

In line with the above philosophy, Nestlé manufactures and sells a wide range of infant foods designed for the above purposes. These fall into the following groups:
"Starter" milk formulae:
Intended to supplement or replace breast milk during the first few months of life. Most are modeled on the composition of breast milk and they include modern low-solute ("humanized") milks which are the product of many years of scientific research).
"Follow-up" milk formulae:
Principally intended to follow or supplement successful breast feeding from about the fourth month of life onwards. In order to provide an adequate safety-

(Continued on next page)

Exhibit 4
Nestlé Food Policy Statement, February 1978 *(Continued)*

margin in case of "formula-stretching" or the use of inadequate weaning foods, "follow-up" milks are not patterned after the composition of breast milk.

Weaning foods:

Based on cereals or other locally available food sources and designed to provide a valuable nutritional supplement from the moment the baby needs more than milk alone to cover his dietary needs.

Efforts are made to adapt products, packaging, distribution, and price to the needs of different social groups.

COMMUNICATION POLICY

Nestlé recognizes that even the best products will fail to produce satisfactory results if they are not prepared carefully in accordance with the instructions of the health services or the manufacturer.

Nestlé also believes it is the duty of manufacturers to present accurate and objective information about the quality of its infant feeding specialties to those capable of making informed judgments about their use, and to cooperate fully in education efforts aimed at preventing the misuse of these products.

HEALTH SERVICES

The health services are recognized as the main intermediary between the manufacturer and the mother. Assistance must therefore be given to the medical and paramedical professions, as well as to the health authorities in their work connected with nutrition and general health education.

This assistance is given by medical representatives (who may include qualified nurses, midwives, and dieticians) who have received specialized training in order to enable them to render a genuine service and give scientific and objective information on Nestlé product characteristics and utilization.

Advertising to the health services must be as informative as possible and no claims must be made which cannot be substantiated.

MOTHERS

Nestlé recognizes its obligation to cooperate with the health services in giving the fullest possible guidance to mothers in order to ensure that our products make the optimum contribution to child health. This is done in the following ways:

(Continued on next page)

Exhibit 4
Nestlé Food Policy Statement, February 1978 *(Continued)*

Superiority of breast feeding

This is to be clearly featured on all product labels, educational materials, and advertising for infant milks, with the use of our products defined in a supporting role.

Instructions/educational material

Detailed instructions are included on product labels. To facilitate understanding, supplementary details in the major vernacular languages together with step-by-step illustrations are supplied either together with the product or distributed separately through the health services.

Educational material must make clear reference to the precautions to be observed in use.

Mothers are recommended to seek the advice of the health services before giving any milk other than breast milk, as well as at all times when there is any doubt about the use of our products or about the health of the baby.

No suggestion is to be made that implies that the product concerned is in any way superior to breast milk, or that it should replace breast milk when breast feeding is possible.

COMMUNICATIONS

If media advertising is used for infant milks, the following conditions must be fulfilled:

- The general economic, cultural, and intellectual level of mothers in the audience addressed by the specific media used is such that they are in a position to take a responsible decision in consultation with a doctor, nurse, or health worker as to the form of infant feeding to be adopted.
- The message is predominantly educational, with clear emphasis on the importance of breast feeding as the preferred method of feeding during the first months of life.
- Use of the media concerned is approved by the local health authorities.

PROMOTION

Infant milk samples may only be given to mothers by official health personnel.

Nestlé will contribute to all efforts made towards controlling the distribution of samples both to avoid abuse, and to avoid samples reaching mothers who do not need them.

(Continued on next page)

Exhibit 4
Nestlé Food Policy Statement, February 1978 *(Continued)*

NESTLÉ PERSONNEL

As mentioned earlier, the main duty of Nestlé medical representatives is to assist the health services. In keeping with this concept, appropriately qualified personnel (e.g., nurses, dieticians, health educators) may assist in nutrition and health education work if requested to do so by the appropriate health authorities.

In order to avoid any possible confusion with public health service personnel, Nestlé personnel will not wear official uniforms even when their qualifications entitle them to do so.

In order to underline their educational function in accordance with the philosophy outlined earlier, the salary paid to Nestlé representatives is not related to sales and they are not permitted to sell our products to mothers.

SOURCE: Issued by the Infant and Dietetic Products Department, Nestlé Products Technical Assistance Co. Ltd., Switzerland, February 1978. Reproduced with permission.

Population Services International
The Social Marketing Project in Bangladesh

Population Services International (PSI) was a nonprofit agency founded in 1970 to help control the population explosion in many less-developed countries by disseminating family-planning information and products. In 1976 PSI concluded an agreement with the government of Bangladesh to carry out the Social Marketing Project (SMP), a program for marketing birth-control products through local retail outlets. SMP marketed two products: Raja brand condoms and Maya brand oral contraceptives.

Late in 1983 Philip Harvey (PSI's founder), Robert Ciszewski (PSI's executive director), and William Schellstede (project adviser for SMP) met at PSI headquarters to discuss 1984–86 marketing plans for SMP. They were concerned that while Raja sales had increased steadily over the past six years to 50.4 million pieces in 1983, Maya sales had declined from a high of 1.1 million cycles[1] in 1980 to 0.62 million in 1983. Both products had been promoted with similar marketing strategies. The approach was to reach consumers directly through an intensive mass media campaign backed by extensive product availability through Bangladesh's widely dispersed retail store network. Harvey explained the discrepancy in sales results:

> Our goal was to reach the largest number of people possible. We knew most of them were illiterate and did not have access to professional doctors or pharmacies. We built our entire program on two basic principles: motivate the consumer and motivate the trade. Many people were worried that our aggressive approach would desensitize a sensitive product category and take away the seriousness of family planning. On the contrary, we wanted to motivate the husband and wife to seriously and frankly discuss family planning with each other. What we achieved was a stunning success for Raja but a failure for Maya. People associate condoms with sex, but pills are associated with birth control; people think of a condom as an

[1]A cycle was a package of 28 pills.

This case was prepared by Assistant Professor V. Kasturi Rangan as the basis for class discussion rather than to illustrate either effective or ineffective handling of an administrative situation. Abridged with permission.

over-the-counter consumer product, while a pill is perceived as a powerful drug. If anything, our marketing approach should have helped Maya more than Raja.

POPULATION SERVICES INTERNATIONAL

Philip Harvey and Timothy Black were graduate students at the University of North Carolina's Public Health Program when they founded PSI in 1970. Harvey had earlier worked for CARE (a nonprofit American agency involved in relief and development) in India for five years. Black had practiced medicine in Australia and New Guinea, specializing in family planning and midwife training. PSI was set up as a nonprofit agency with the fundamental objective of "disseminating family-planning information and marketing birth-control products to people who needed to avert births but did not know where to seek the information or products."

Though their first project concerned the prevention of unwanted teenage pregnancies in the United States, the population explosion in the less developed countries (LDCs) was their prime motivation for founding PSI. Harvey reasoned that none of the poorer countries had enough medical personnel to treat the many diseases afflicting their people. He predicted that a diversion of these scarce resources to birth control would never work. Yet, "if contraceptive products like pills and condoms are made the leading vehicles of family planning," Harvey reasoned, "the entire society would be better off."

As a matter of policy, PSI was not involved in marketing clinical methods of birth control like intrauterine devices (IUDs) or male or female sterilization. PSI's managers described their business mission as follows:

> We are here to create the climate in which socially desirable products become part of the daily life of the marketplace. We would like to assure their distribution in efficient fashion so that their availability becomes routine and expected. The fundamental purpose is to facilitate the exchange between the buyer and seller so that the transaction is fruitful for both. The person who practices family planning with contraceptives purchased in a social marketing program is not a patient or client nor a recipient or acceptor. He or she is a consumer making a careful, prudent choice among many options available in the marketplace.

In 1973 PSI won a contract to initiate and implement a contraceptive marketing program in Sri Lanka. During the next five years, it received contracts to manage similar projects in Bangladesh and Mexico. For political reasons, PSI's involvement in the Mexican program was short-lived, but the Sri Lankan program was a tremendous success, especially in condom marketing. In 1976 Family Planning Association of Sri Lanka took over program management from PSI, leaving Bangladesh as PSI's only active program.

PSI was headquartered in Washington, D.C., and had a staff of six, including managerial personnel. Of the founders, Harvey continued as a board member. He did not involve himself in daily operations but was always active in strategy meetings. Black had resigned to set up a non-profit family-planning organization in Ireland. Ciszewski joined PSI as project adviser on the Bangladesh project and was now the executive director at headquarters, handling most of the daily affairs of the company. Ciszewski's successor in Bangladesh was fired for "poor sales performance" after a brief stint on the job. Schellstede was the current project adviser.

THE SOCIAL MARKETING PROJECT (SMP)

PSI completed an agreement with the government of Bangladesh in 1976 to carry out a program of family planning through social marketing. The objective was to use modern marketing techniques to sell subsidized contraceptives through commercial outlets. The agreement also defined the organizational structure and management process for SMP. Policy guidelines were to be provided by a project council consisting of a chairman and eight other members. The chairman was the secretary for health and population control for the Bangladesh government. The government nominated four more members to the council. Three council members were from PSI, USAID (U.S. Agency for International Development), and UNFPA (U.N. Fund for Population Activities). The ultimate authority and responsibility for implementation were given to a general manager, who was appointed by the project council upon nomination by PSI. The general manager was a Bangladeshi national and the ninth member of the council. He was responsible for implementing strategy through a national sales manager, who had a network of eight sales offices. In all, about 300 people reported to the general manager. *Exhibit 1* gives a brief overview of SMP's organizational structure.

The three key constituents for policy-making were the Bangladesh government, USAID, and PSI. A brief description of their roles follows.

Bangladesh Government

The Bangladesh government was involved in population control both directly, through its various programs, and indirectly, through projects like SMP. Bangladesh, with a land area of 55,598 square miles (about the size of Wisconsin), a population of about 100 million, and a per capita income of $120 a year, was one of the poorest countries in the world. With its GNP expected to grow at 3–4%, the government did not expect near-term improvement in its people's standard of living. Further, with an annual population growth rate of 2.4%, its population was expected to exceed that of the entire United States by the year 2025. Since the economic and social consequences of such a scenario were devastating, the government of Bangladesh set for itself the goal of achieving zero population growth by 1995. At the same time, since 85% of its population were conservative Muslims,[2] the government had to consider their religious sentiments. The government closely monitored all aspects of all family-planning programs. It reserved the right to restrict any aspect of any program it thought sensitive. The government's role, then, was to encourage and promote, but closely supervise, family-planning activity.

USAID

This American agency was involved in the social and economic development of many LDCs. USAID funded family-planning programs in many other LDCs. It funded almost all of SMP in Bangladesh. SMP revenues from contraceptive sales were $423,000, but the contraceptives' cost was $3.8 million and operating expenses in Bangladesh were $1.3 million plus a $417,000 service fee to PSI. USAID covered the resultant $5.1 million loss.

PSI

PSI was responsible mainly for devising marketing strategies, getting them approved by the project council, and implementing them through the general manager. Schellstede was located in Dacca (Bangladesh) and managed PSI's relationship with the project council and the general manager; Ciszewski managed the relationship with USAID in Washington. Both had had extensive management experience with LDC development projects before joining PSI. PSI's relationship with the Bangladesh government was excellent; very few foreign agencies enjoyed the respect and rapport PSI had achieved. Ciszewski had taken tremendous care to under-

[2]Muslims practiced the religion of Islam. Koran was their holy book. Though several Islamic scholars argued that Koran did not take a stand on family planning, many mullahs (holy priests) of Bangladesh believed family planning was against God's will.

stand, empathize, and work with the government bureaucracy. He described PSI's role:

It's difficult and trying at times. Phil, Bill, I, and our other colleagues
are in this for the fun of it. We get much personal fulfillment in being
able to promote a social good, but let me tell you managing this
project is awfully tricky. We don't control the project council or the
marketing organization, yet we are responsible for devising a strategy
and implementing it. We don't have any funds of our own. We are a
small team at PSI, and we barely survive year after year. Frankly, it's
not my salary that I worry about, it is the lack of funds for
implementing new strategy. It's amazing how long and hard we have
to lobby the members of the council and with USAID before we make
any headway. Luckily, the general manager is our nominee; we see eye
to eye on many issues. If we have an approved and implementable
strategy, we are pretty much able to execute it.

COUNTRY BACKGROUND

Bangladesh is a river delta located on the Bay of Bengal. The scarce
resources of this already poor country were further threatened by un-
abated population growth. The 20 million couples in the fertile age group
were the main targets of family-planning programs. Though family planning had the government's full backing, certain characteristics of the local
environment made it challenging for the SMP to design its marketing
strategy. Some of these factors were:

1. *Culture and attitudes.* Most of the country's people lived in villages;
only 9% lived in the cities. The literacy rate was about 27% among males
and 12% among females.

In a national survey, only 6% of the respondents cited religion as the
main reason for not adopting family-planning practices. Simple igno-
rance of birth-control methods and products was one reason for large
families; others were linked to family economics and culture. Bangladesh
did not have a system of social security or state pensions for its elderly;
parents therefore depended on their sons for future security. Epidemics
and natural calamities like monsoon floods and tidal waves claimed as
many as 100,000 lives each year, hence families thought it prudent to have
more than one son. Since daughters went away to their husbands' families
after marriage, parents could not rely on them for financial support in
their old age. On the contrary, the custom of providing a dowry (a sum of

money) to the bridegroom's parents at the wedding made it economically sensible to have at least as many sons as daughters.

In a survey conducted by SMP (see *Exhibit 2*), many individuals appeared to understand the economic benefits of a small family. But in personal interviews they expressed confusion about where to draw the line between personal welfare and social welfare. The SMP survey also revealed higher awareness of family planning among urban dwellers and certain differences in the perceptions of men and women.

2. *Buying–selling process.* Even though Bangladesh's economy was modeled on a central planning system, distribution and marketing were left entirely to the marketplace forces of supply and demand. An overwhelming bulk of life's necessities were bought and paid for in the market, and at prices the market demanded. About 20 tributaries of two major rivers crisscrossed the length and breadth of Bangladesh, making transportation and travel extremely difficult. As a consequence, an intense network of local retail outlets had developed. Most of Bangladesh's retail trade was owned by small-scale entrepreneurs. They were financed by their wholesalers but conducted their sales on strict cash terms. Working capital was a constant problem; most retailers preferred quick inventory turns to high margins.

In 1983 contraceptives were sold in Bangladesh through a network of 30,000 pharmacies, 40,000 general stores (about half of them grocery stores), and 30,000 "pan" stores.

Pharmacies were usually in urban areas. Typically 300–400 sq. ft. in area, they sold a wide assortment of pharmaceuticals, drugs, and indigenous medicinal preparations. Most items (including birth-control pills) did not require a doctor's prescription. The consumer usually went to the sales counter and asked for a product by name or described the general nature of the ailment. The salesperson would then suggest an appropriate product or brand. After the consumer had made a decision, the salesperson went to the store shelves to fill the order. Consumers were not allowed to select products off the shelves.

General stores were typically small, although larger ones existed in the cities. Most general stores were family-owned independent operations, not part of a chain. Not more than three or four individuals operated the store (including the owner). A typical store was about 400–500 sq. ft. in area and carried about 50–100 items. All product items were assembled, measured, and bagged by store personnel on order. As with the pharmacies, consumers were rarely, if ever, allowed into the shelf areas.

Pan stores were smaller versions of the general store, carrying soft drinks, cigarettes, aspirin, and other convenience items. In total, they carried about 25–30 product items. Most pan stores were small and in rural areas. One of the many fast-moving items sold by these stores was pan, an assortment of special spices and a specially prepared paste of calcium wrapped in a betel leaf. Among Bangladeshi men, consumption of pan was a habit as strong as, if not stronger than, drinking tea or smoking cigarettes. Other major sale items were cigarettes (often loose), aspirins, cookies, candy, local brands of soft drinks, and local newspapers.

Pan stores operated out of temporary enclosures at street corners or other busy locations. They were typically 20–40 sq. ft. in area and operated by one person, generally the owner, who sat behind the sales counter and deftly made pans to individual order, mixing and matching the right amount and variety of spices. Men gathered around pan stores to take a break from their routine. They exchanged news and information to the tunes blaring from a radio in the store. Pan stores were convenient socializing spots for men; women preferred to make and consume pan at home. Unlike pharmacies and general stores, pan stores were open until late at night.

3. *Medical care system.* Bangladesh was served by 125,000 doctors, only about 5,000 of whom had formal medical education. These 5,000 had graduate degrees in Western, or allopathic, medicine. Most doctors had excellent credentials, spoke fluent English, and practiced and lived in urban areas.

In addition to Western-trained physicians in cities, about 20,000 spiritual doctors practiced mainly in villages. Their care was quite unscientific but nonetheless valued by their patients. They wrote secret formulas, uttered special hymns, and claimed to invoke God's power in treating illnesses.

The rest of the country's 100,000 doctors were rural medical practitioners (RMPs), whose approach to medicine was a blend of modern and traditional methods. They were not trained in Western medicine and usually did not speak English, but they kept in touch with professional doctors and hospitals through a system of patient referrals. They had a working knowledge of common illnesses and drugs mainly through association with professional doctors whom they respected. RMPs dispensed either indigenous medications or allopathic drugs, depending on their diagnosis. They operated a few hours every day out of their offices; the rest of the time they made extensive house calls. An RMP participated in village community activities and was respected and regarded as friend, philosopher, and guide by many village people. RMPs did not charge a fee for consultation, but patients were expected to buy medications from them. Many carried a general assortment of medicines in a travel kit. Payment terms were flexible and generally included a number of installments, depending on the patient's financial capability.

Besides 125,000 doctors, there were about 25,000 field workers in Bangladesh, who disseminated information on family planning through hospitals, dispensaries, and shopping locations. They were educated and literate and were paid by the government or the social welfare agency employing them. They were not professional doctors, but they were well trained and motivated to communicate the social and economic benefits of family planning.

FAMILY-PLANNING ACTIVITY IN BANGLADESH

The government of Bangladesh coordinated all family planning. It had no financial involvement in any program except its own. Family-planning communication and products were delivered through four distinct programs.

1. The government used the country's *hospitals, clinics, and dispensaries* to promote family planning mainly through a network of nearly 20,000 field workers. The network was fairly evenly spread throughout the country. The social workers also distributed free condoms and contraceptive pills. The government received its supply of contraceptives as a donation from USAID. It provided incentives for the country's 5,000 trained doctors to perform clinical birth-control procedures. Cash incentives were also provided to the field workers and consumers. Every sterilization procedure or IUD insertion was fully subsidized by the government. The direct cost of a clinical procedure was estimated to be about $5, and the cost of incentives to field workers and reimbursement to consumers about $10.

2. Various *volunteer organizations* sponsored education and communication programs on family planning and birth control. These volunteer agencies involved about 5,000 field workers, who promoted family-planning themes and benefits and referred interested couples to the appropriate medical facilities. Some organizations procured contraceptives from government or private sources and distributed them free of cost.

3. A number of *privately held pharmaceutical firms* marketed their own brand of oral contraceptive pills. Some of them had licensing arrangements and collaborations with European and U.S. pharmaceutical firms. These companies sold their products mainly through the pharmacies. Their sales forces called on professional doctors and made systematic presentations on product benefits. Though prescriptions were not necessarily required to buy oral contraceptives, professional doctors wrote prescriptions or advised their clients to use specific brands.

4. The fourth program was *PSI's Social Marketing Project,* started in late 1977 to promote Raja brand of condoms and Maya brand of oral contraceptive pills.

MARKETING STRATEGY FOR RAJA AND MAYA

The name Raja was chosen for two reasons. First, "raja" in Bengali means "king" or "emperor." PSI's experience in Sri Lanka had indicated the need to create a positive, relaxed attitude for family planning. People did not respond well to messages highlighting the negative consequences of a large family. A king was associated with masculinity, bravery, and power. Raja therefore had a number of positive connotations. The other advantage of choosing the name Raja was its wide recognition. A popular pastime for men in Bangladesh was playing cards. Terms related to card games had high recognition among men; Bengali equivalents of king, queen, and jack were easily recognized. Moreover, the high level of illiteracy made it necessary to choose a brand name that could be understood pictorially. Raja fitted the requirements rather well. The only other widely distributed condom in the market was the Bangladesh government's Tahiti brand, which USAID donated to the government. A third brand, Sultan, was marketed by a private trader and was not widely distributed. Sultan means "king" in Arabic.

In Bengali "maya" means "magic," but the cultural translation was much more positive; people commonly interpreted Maya to mean beauty. Once again, the basic idea was to create a positive feeling and sense of optimism about the product. Maya was one of only two brands with a Bengali brand name.[3] The other important brands on the market were Ovastat, Lyndiol, Ovral, and Nordette. The Bangladesh government's pill, donated by USAID, had no brand name. In 1983 the total market for family-planning products was roughly divided as follows:

1. *Condoms* (million pieces)

a.	Raja	50.0
b.	Tahiti	25.0
c.	Sultan	5.0
d.	Durex	3.0
e.	Others	2.0
	Total	85.0

2. *Pills* (million cycles)

a.	Bangladesh government	3.0
b.	Ovastat	2.0
c.	Lyndiol, Ovral, and Nordette	2.0
d.	Maya	0.6
e.	Others	0.2
	Total	7.8

3. *IUDs*   75,000

4. *Sterilizations*   300,000

USAID purchased contraceptives on contract from North American manufacturers and shipped them to the port of Chittagong. The SMP

[3]The other brand was named Santi, meaning "peace." This pill was formulated by Dr. K. M. Hossain, who also owned a pharmaceutical factory. Dr. Hossain offered free consultations and advice on family planning and gave his clients a "100% guarantee" for his product. In its local market area, Santi had shown impressive growth in market share.

received contraceptives in bulk in an unpackaged, unlabeled form. It then transported them to a central warehouse at Dacca for repackaging and labeling. Both Raja and Maya were packed attractively, to get attention for the product and to add color and appearance to the retail store. Raja had three packaging formats: 3 pieces to a pack, 12 pieces to a pack, and 100 pieces to a pack. Pan stores generally bought the 100-piece pack and sold singles to customers. Maya was packed 28 pills to a cycle (21 birth-control pills and 7 iron tablets). The products then were sent to 7 subwarehouses for distribution to 22 wholesalers. The wholesalers sold to pharmacies, large general stores, and about 5,000 semiwholesalers or stockists. Semiwholesalers broke bulk and sold in smaller lots to pan stores and small general stores. Area sales managers were responsible for sales mainly to wholesalers; SMP's sales reps were responsible mainly for selling wholesaler's stocks to semiwholesalers. Some sales reps also sold to pharmacies and large general stores from wholesalers' stocks.

Wholesalers were either grain, cigarette, or pharmaceutical distributors. Semiwholesalers were more varied and included distributors of soap, tea, cookies, toothpaste, newspapers, and magazines. When the SMP program started in 1977, some wholesalers and semiwholesalers distributed contraceptives solely as a national duty, but over the years they discovered that the financial benefits were quite adequate and had willingly participated in the program ever since. Wholesalers and semiwholesalers generally achieved 10–12 inventory turns per year on Raja; the retailers achieved 5–8 turns. Inventory turns on Maya were 5–6 wholesale and 3–4 at the retail level. The price and margin structure for Raja and Maya are shown in the accompanying table.

	Raja *(pack of 3 pieces)*	*Maya* *(1 cycle)*
SMP's selling price	Tk.0.29	Tk.0.45
Wholesaler's selling price	Tk.0.31	Tk.0.49
Semiwholesaler's selling price	Tk.0.33	Tk.0.53
Suggested retail price	Tk.0.40	Tk.0.70

1 Takka = 4 cents.

SMP's prices for Raja and Maya had no relation to the cost structure for the products. USAID's purchase cost for a pack of Raja was about 1.25 Takkas and for a cycle of Maya, 3.5 Takkas. Over and above product costs, if other marketing costs were added the contraceptives were being sold at one-tenth their total cost.

USAID and other international donor agencies were willing to provide contraceptives entirely free to consumers, since they were already subsidizing the other nine-tenths, but PSI thought it important to charge a price mainly to convey a sense of value to the customer. Yet the prices had to be within the reach of most of the population. Reference points for pricing were provided by what consumers paid for a cup of tea, a box of matches, or a cigarette. SMP's prices provided adequate margins for the channel members, especially the retailer. A PSI manager commented, "By charging a price and providing a margin, we got 80,000 retailers to distribute the products. We could never have done it if the products were free."

One highlight of the strategy was the intensive communication support Raja and Maya received. PSI's approach was to skip all intermediate levels of influence, including doctors, and to go directly to the consumer. The basic approach was to create an atmosphere of fun and happiness. The themes of "happy marriage" and "confident choice of the prudent family" were repeatedly communicated through radio, press, billboards, and posters. Sales promoters with megaphones carried out street canvassing, boats carried advertisements on their sails, and Raja and Maya T-shirts were distributed.

With an average spending level of $400,000 per year, SMP was the second largest advertiser in Bangladesh. Raja and Maya received about equal amounts of advertising dollars. The media allocation for each product is shown in *Exhibit 3*.

PROBLEMS WITH MAYA

After years of intensive promotion, it was quite clear that Maya was not as well accepted in the market as Raja. *Exhibit 4* shows the trend of CYP[4] shares for Raja and Maya. Since 1978, almost all growth in the condom market had come from Raja, while Maya was losing ground both to the government's free distribution program and to private brands. Ciszewski, the architect of the successful Raja strategy, was known to be a pragmatic manager open to new ideas. Almost immediately after Schellstede had taken up his job, Ciszewski had suggested in a letter:

> In Bangladesh we know that 80% of all products, including products for women, are purchased by men. Our surveys show that women are more prone to personal influence than men [see *Exhibit 5*]. Bill, if you can think of a clever way to communicate to the man to buy Maya for his woman, we will be in great shape.

Six months later, Ciszewski wrote another letter:

[4]CYP or Couple of Years Protection was a notion used to compare and quantify the benefits of different contraceptive methods. Based on frequency studies in Bangladesh, it was estimated that 100 condoms offered one unit of CYP in Bangladesh; 13 cycles of oral pills were equivalent to one CYP. One IUD insertion was equivalent to 2.5 CYP, and one sterilization was equivalent to 7.75 CYP.

Bill, if you think we should discontinue Maya altogether and start from scratch with a new brand name, a new consumer segment, and a new communications program, don't hesitate to let me or Phil Harvey know. We are solidly behind you. We have had tremendous success with communication and distribution, but you can help us focus this strength for Maya.

Despite several such suggestions, Schellstede's responses from Bangladesh were lukewarm. "Either he disagrees with me totally or he is still learning his job," Ciszewski thought. Finally, after Schellstede had been on the job for nearly a year, Harvey decided to convene a strategy meeting in Washington. The purpose was to put together an action plan for improving Maya sales.

As the meeting got under way, the three PSI managers carefully pored through all the market data Schellstede had provided. Harvey spoke first:

It seems strange that Raja should be more successful than Maya. Look at what Raja has to compete with: essentially free goods. The Bangladesh government gives away its products free, while we charge a price for Raja, yet we get a dominant share. Maya, on the other hand, is behind Ovastat in market share—and Ovastat is priced ten times higher than Maya. Lyndiol, Ovral, and Nordette are priced five to seven times higher than Maya. I can't believe that consumers in a poor country would want to pay more for products that are available cheaper!

Ciszewski responded:

That may be the exact problem: We don't have the support of retailers for Maya. Other pills in the market give them sixteen times as much margin as Maya. We need to do something to motivate retailers better. There may be other problems with Maya, too. In informal conversations with many professional doctors, I was surprised to learn they thought Maya was a poor drug, though they were not able to pinpoint the exact reasons. When I told some of them that Maya was exactly Syntex's[5] Noriday, which in fact is stronger than Syntex's Normest, they were really surprised.

Maya's image problem was not restricted to professional doctors. Many RMPs also thought Maya was an inferior drug and many of them had advised their patients to discontinue Maya. An SMP field supervisor told this story in one of his field reports:

[5]Syntex was a U.S. pharmaceutical firm that sold its contraceptive pill, Noriday, to USAID. Other pills in the Bangladesh market, such as Ovastat, were roughly equivalent to Syntex's Normest. USAID supplied Noriday to the Bangladesh government and the SMP. While the Bangladesh government packed and sold the pill in its generic unbranded form, the SMP repackaged the pill as Maya.

I heard the other day about the mother of three children who went to Tayub Sahib (a respected RMP). The woman complained of backache and nausea. Tayub Sahib advised her to discontinue Maya. The woman replied that she was poor and could not buy English medicines, but she could obtain Maya free from the government dispensary. Tayub Sahib explained to her that what she was taking was not Maya, but the government pill that was somewhat better than Maya. All the same he advised her to discontinue the pill for 15 days and the woman politely replied that she would heed Tayub Sahib's advice and discontinue Maya.

Ciszewski was quite convinced that pricing, retail motivation, and image were important areas to be addressed in any new plans for Maya. With SMP's strengths and successes in mass media promotion with Raja, Ciszewski was quite confident of devising an effective Maya communication strategy. He proposed that the image problem be addressed by going directly to consumers with an effective communication strategy.

Though Schellstede agreed with the contents of the discussion, his analysis suggested a dramatically different action plan. He opened his files, pulled out some notes he had prepared and began to read:

One factor of possibly great importance has been not having someone trusted to recommend Maya and to hold the hands of the new customer through the first cycles when side effects are most common and most likely to cause discontinuation. This *someone* could possibly be the doctor. We have consciously not tried to develop medical channels because of funding limitations. Whether anybody likes it or not, the RMP is the person to whom our target group actually turns for medical help. We have good reason to believe that because neither we nor the government have enlisted their help, they are quite happy to have contraceptives to blame for the many ill-defined but real aches and pains of being poor, hungry, and sick. Given this background, our sales of 50,000 cycles a month is no mean achievement, regardless of what anybody says. We should accept the RMPs for what they are—medical entrepreneurs—and help them improve the service they offer by detailing them with our products.

Schellstede's proposal, which was a reversal of the successful Raja strategy, worried PSI's founder considerably. Harvey summarized his thoughts:

USAID evaluates us on cost effectiveness, so any strategy that increases our cost per CYP would be difficult to get approved. Moreover, we are a professional outfit, selling quality products for a social benefit. We should not as a matter of policy associate ourselves with untrained quacks.

Regardless of any decision that the three men might take, they would have to convince the project council of its usefulness. The council normally took a larger view of the project. Any additional costs would need justification, not merely in market share but in benefits to Bangladesh society. The council would need to know how many additional births would be averted[6] by the new program and how it would benefit the economy.

---

[6]The CYPs were multiplied by a factor of 0.25 to arrive at the number of births averted. The reduction was an adjustment for fertility rates.

Exhibit 1 Organization Chart for SMP

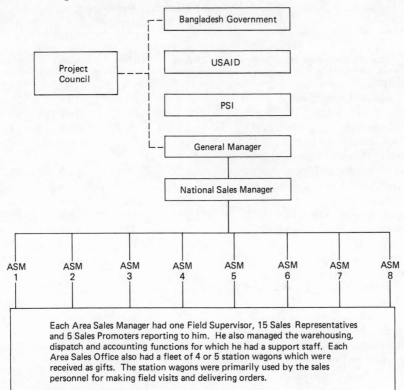

Each Area Sales Manager had one Field Supervisor, 15 Sales Representatives and 5 Sales Promoters reporting to him. He also managed the warehousing, dispatch and accounting functions for which he had a support staff. Each Area Sales Office also had a fleet of 4 or 5 station wagons which were received as gifts. The station wagons were primarily used by the sales personnel for making field visits and delivering orders.

Exhibit 2
Specific Family Planning Meanings Mentioned
by Participants in a SMP Survey

Specific Meanings Mentioned	Female		Male	
	Rural	Urban	Rural	Urban
Limit family size	48.9[a]	53.1	73.7	48.9
Have small/happy family	16.4	30.3	12.2	36.0
Stop having children	48.4	31.4	16.9	13.7
Two children are enough	2.7	5.7	8.5	15.8
Space childbirth	5.5	6.3	—	3.6
Preserve health of mother	20.1	21.7	3.3	2.2
Assure healthy children	2.7	1.1	4.2	5.0
Assure good health for mother and children	8.2	6.9	—	3.6
Assure good health for all	3.7	3.4	8.9	12.9
Assure food and clothing	58.0	57.1	32.9	38.8
Less poverty	21.5	19.4	33.3	43.2
Live within means	8.7	9.7	12.7	9.4
Saving for future	8.7	15.4	9.4	4.3
Avoid subdividing property among children	8.7	1.7	6.1	3.6
Peace and happiness in the family	48.4	48.6	35.7	40.3
Happier family life	4.1	6.9	0.5	—
Assure education for children	42.0	62.9	17.4	53.2
Rearing children properly	12.8	10.3	2.3	4.3
Number interviewed	219	175	213	139

[a]48.9% of the 219 interviewed mentioned that "limit family size" was one of the meanings they got out of family planning communication.

Exhibit 3
Allocation of Advertising Expenditures by Media,
1983

	Raja	Maya
Radio	18%	20%
Newspaper	35	25
Cinema[a]	10	3
Poster/signboard	13	16
Point of purchase	18	20
Mobile film unit	6	6
Television	—	10
Total	100%	100%

[a]Movies screened in cinema theaters in Bangladesh generally had about ten minutes of commercials at the start and another five minutes at halftime.

Exhibit 4

CYPs for Industry and SMP Products[a]

	Raja CYPs	Total Condom CYPs	Maya CYPs	Total Pill CYPs
1978	97,000	560,000	37,000	450,000
1979	173,000	330,000	78,500	370,000
1980	227,000	640,000	84,500	510,000
1981	316,000	590,000	54,000	480,000
1982	358,000	680,000	45,400	350,000
1983	504,000	850,000	47,800	620,000

[a]CYP, or Couple Years Protection was a notion used to compare and quantify the benefits of different contraceptive methods. Based on frequency studies in Bangladesh, it was estimated that 100 condoms offered one unit of CYP in Bangladesh; similarly 13 cycles of oral pills were equivalent to one CYP.

Exhibit 5

Sources of Messages on Family Planning

	Female		Male	
Mass Media Mentioned	Rural	Urban	Rural	Urban
Radio	85.5%[a]	83.7%	88.2%	85.9%
Television	5.3	49.0	14.1	50.0
Cinema	1.3	12.5	7.1	18.5
Newspaper	1.3	16.3	5.9	37.0
Poster/signboard	7.9	17.3	10.6	27.2
Family planning worker/public contact	31.6	10.6	23.3	4.3
Number interviewed	76	104	85	92

[a]85.5% of the 76 people interviewed were made aware of family planning messages through the radio.

6

Finance

The financial environments of developing countries are often tumultuous. Erupting inflation and drastic devaluations can wreak havoc on
business plans and operations. Furthermore, the international debt crisis
has aggravated the LDCs' chronic condition of capital scarcity and increased the financial stress for banks, borrowing companies, and countries.

KEY ISSUES

The cases in this chapter concern the managerial problems caused by
inflation and devaluation as well as some of the key issues emerging from
the debt crisis that face lenders and borrowers. In all instances the core
analytical task is the formulation of financial strategies to fit the tumultuous conditions of the developing countries.[1] This task, however, almost
always requires a broader reexamination of a company's overall strategy.

Inflation and Devaluation

Developing countries, of course, have no monopoly on inflation or devaluation, but the magnitude and volatility are much greater there. This
increases the uncertainty and complexity surrounding the financial management task. Inflation can cause decapitalization, tax bracket creep,
rising finance costs, and liquidity complications, and can require significant adjustments in business relationships. Devaluation poses three types
of foreign-exchange risks: transaction exposure (the value of a contract at
a fixed price in a foreign currency is altered); translation exposure (the
local currency value of subsidiary's assets and profits lose value when
translated into the parent company's currency in the consolidation of
financial statements); operating exposure (changes in the real rather than

417

nominal exchange rates alter a firm's costs, prices, and competitiveness). Inflation and devaluation can have positive and negative impacts on companies, depending on their nature and how they are handled, so they need to be viewed simultaneously as problems and opportunities.

To provide an opportunity for a more in-depth analysis of an environment caught in the throes of both rapid inflation and major devaluations, we present three company cases dealing with Mexico's financially chaotic environment at various points during the 1980s. The first case, "Electrohogar, S.A.," concerns a local distributor of electrical appliances that finds its past financial strategy rendered obsolete, and its survival threatened, by the emerging and accelerating inflation in early 1980s. The second case, "Compañía Telefónica Mexicana," deals with a U.S. telecommunications equipment subsidiary reeling from the impact of a major devaluation of the peso in 1982 and struggling to deal with the risk of further such shocks. The third case presents Colgate-Palmolive's effort to formulate a strategy, in late 1987, for dealing with both Mexico's hyperinflation and its devaluation.

Financial Institutions and Mechanisms

The emergence of the international debt crisis suffocated international bank lending to developing countries and left multinational banks with large loans of questionable worth. To understand the genesis of the Third World's trillion-dollar debt, one must examine the role of the international banks. The rapid expansion of lending in the 1970s was fueled by the pressures to recycle petrodollars and the attractive spreads on loans to the capital-hungry LDCs. Banks engaged aggressively in large syndicated country loans to LDC governments and institutions. The "Citibank in Zaïre" case presents the situation of one leading international bank wrestling with the problems of Third World lending. The EAF provides guidance in carrying out the country analysis relevant to this lending situation. By the early 1980s the full seriousness of the debt crisis had become apparent, and many approaches and mechanisms for dealing with it began to emerge. Debt-to-equity swaps are one example. These reduced the developing country loan burdens while providing an attractive source of local currency for investors. In our fifth case we return to the Mexican environment with "International Pharmaceuticals Inc.," as it considered, in 1986, the merits of using the swap mechanism to finance an expansion of its Mexican subsidiary.

The scarcity of international and local capital has intensified competition among banks for deposits. Technology is playing a major role in these competitive battles as banks speed along the modernization track. The final case describes how the "Thai Farmers Bank" makes a major investment in a computerized information system to overcome the competitive disadvantage caused by a rival's institution of an automatic teller system.

CASE STUDY QUESTIONS

Electrohogar, S.A.

1. How will the rising inflation affect the company?
2. What policies should management adopt to deal with this new environment?

Compañía Telefónica Mexicana (CTM)—ATM in Mexico

1. How seriously is the company affected by the devaluation?
2. What is your assessment of the actions it took?
3. What recommendations would you make for managing this risk in the future?

Colgate-Palmolive in Mexico

1. Where and how seriously is the inflation affecting the company?
2. What are the difficulties the company faces in dealing with these problems?
3. What actions do you recommend?

Citibank in Zaïre

1. Why did Citibank and others lend to Zaïre?
2. What are the strengths and weaknesses of Zaïre as a borrower in the future?
3. What is your assessment of Citibank's syndication strategy?
4. What further actions would you recommend that Citibank take to gain more banks' participation in the syndication?

International Pharmaceuticals Inc.

1. What are the pros and cons of the proposed debt-equity swap?
2. What should the company do?

3. How should governments deal with these swaps?

Thai Farmers Bank

1. Why did the bank lose competitive ground?
2. How important is computerization to its future?
3. How should the bank proceed with the ATM operation?

NOTE

1. For an extensive discussion of financial issues in developing countries, see James E. Austin, *Managing in Developing Countries* (New York: Free Press, 1990), Chapter 7.

Electrohogar, S.A.

At the end of February 1982, Dionisio González, general manager of Electrohogar, S.A., was asking himself what would be the impact on the finances of his firm of the series of events which had recently unfolded in the Mexican economy.

On the night of February 16 the Mexican government had announced that the Bank of Mexico (the central bank), was retiring from the foreign-exchange market and letting the peso float in accordance with the free play of supply and demand. This was the virtual equivalent of the currency's devaluation. In fact, with the government's withdrawal the exchange rate quickly rose from M$27.00 to M$38.50 per US$1.00. Many expected that the exchange rate would soon rise to M$50.00 and then descend to stabilize around M$45.00 to US$1.00.

Although the company did not have any foreign currency debts and the products it sold were all manufactured in Mexico, González thought that the devaluation would set off a new inflationary spiral, given the extreme "dollarization" of the Mexican economy.

González knew that although his suppliers manufactured locally, they used significant portions of imported inputs; furthermore, the government would seek a salary adjustment to leave the workers' purchasing power intact; and finally interest rates would continue their upward tendency.

In recent years the Mexican economy had been enjoying extraordinary growth, accompanied however by annual inflation rates varying between 25% and 30%. After the devaluation several experts were forecasting that the prices in the typical consumer basket of goods and services would be 60% higher than at the beginning of the year. Some economists foresaw "stagflation"—stagnation in the economy accompanied by high inflation rates.

ELECTROHOGAR, S.A.

Electrohogar is a distributing company for household electrical appliances and other household goods. Founded in 1962 by the brothers

This case was prepared by Dr. Carlos G. Sequeira, Professor, Finance Area of the Instituto Panamericano de Alta Dirección de Empresa, Mexico, D.F. (P)F-236. Abridged with permission.

Copyright IPADE, July 1982.

Dionisio and René González and other minority investors, it is located in the city of Monterrey in the state of Nuevo León.

Dionisio has been general manager since the beginning, while René is in charge of the Commercial Division, and Rafael Lara, CPA, of the Financial Division.

Electrohogar buys the products it sells from a large number of national appliance factories, which have been cutting back the credit terms to their clients. Payment terms are thirty days after delivery. Electrohogar was used to unilaterally extending the credit term of its suppliers, but they let the company know that henceforth the thirty-day payment period must be scrupulously adhered to or deliveries would be suspended. In addition, rumors persisted that soon the principal suppliers would demand advance payments to process orders. Electrohogar sold through stores in Monterrey and other important cities in the north. Its sales were normally level throughout the year, with slight rises in May, June, and December. Ten percent of its sales were for cash and 90% on credit. Until December 1981 credit had been eighteen months; it was reduced to twelve months since then.

The Commercial Division had prepared a 1982 sales forecast of M$713,000,000. This represented a 45% increase over 1981. René González explained:

> In reality we are considering an increase in real terms of 11% compared to last year. Nevertheless, when we incorporate the effect of inflation—the average rate of which we expect to be 30% on the price of our goods—we end up with a 45% increase in our budget.
>
> We believe that this expectation is not overly optimistic. We have recently opened a new store and we are giving a strong push to our sales in other Mexican cities.

Electrohogar, S.A., had a pricing mechanism based on applying on the average a 44% gross margin to its sales prices to the public.

Elaborating further, René González continued:

> I believe that we can manipulate adequately the mix of credit and cash sales as well as the payment term. What is difficult to change is the price of the product, because we could easily get shoved out of the market or run into problems with the government. Therefore, I believe that we cannot adjust our prices further than what the inflation rate would permit us.
>
> Nevertheless, if we are really aggressive, we could reach annual sales of M$785,000,000 with only an increase of M$7,500,000 in our sales costs. After all, the people prefer to buy today instead of tomorrow at higher prices.

C.P.A. Rafael Lara said:

We feel really concerned about the way profits dropped in 1981 [*Exhibit 1*]. In 1980 profits were almost M$40 million and we had finance costs of M$35 million. Last year, however, we had profits of M$16 million and we paid the banks M$90 million in financing costs. I feel that in some way the rules of the game have been changed. For some reason financial leveraging is not functioning; although we have no foreign currency debt, we end up working to benefit the bank.

We became more indebted to the banks; we were not able to increase the capital of the firm; and the interest rates have shot up. In 1980 we paid an average interest rate of 23% annually; in 1981 the average was 40% and our bankers have indicated that for 1982 the rates will be between 45% and 50% and that money will be very scarce; and all this even though they consider us an AAA client.

In addition, the opening of the new store has put considerable pressure on our finances. The company had to pay rental advances so that the real estate company could finish the facilities; this has obligated us to incur a sizable deferred asset. We hope it will be in the range of M$4.4 million by the end of 1982.

On the other hand, the shareholders may decide not to withdraw any dividends during 1982. I believe this would alleviate a little of the financial pressure.

The Finance Department had elaborated a 1982 budget that did not include financing costs but did include increases caused by inflation and salary adjustments. Sales and administrative costs were estimated at M$153.7 million for the year. Other income of M$30.8 million was expected. Income taxes and other deductions were estimated at a 50% rate. It was estimated that by year's end cash and bank deposits would satisfy the compensating balances demanded by the banks. These compensating balances were expected to be 12% of the outstanding bank debt.

"Other" current assets were to be reduced to zero, and fixed assets were expected to remain unchanged. The account "various creditors" would be reduced to M$10 million to reflect funds temporarily loaned by members of the shareholders' families.

OBSERVATIONS OF THE GENERAL MANAGER

Dionisio González did not hide his concern for the global situation of the firm:

I believe that René, as a man oriented toward sales, only sees the bright side. His estimates are too optimistic. What worries me a great deal are the high interest rates that banks are charging and the predictions of even higher rates and tight credit in the near future. This is of special concern because we work with a great deal of outside money.

I believe, based on my experience, that if we restrict credit and are hard on collections, and taking economic recession into account, our sales will remain constant, although falling 10% in real terms, in spite of geographic expansion and new points of sale.

In general, I believe that the parameters with which we had been working for years have changed. The usual way of doing business is no longer valid, at least not as valid as it used to be. There are so many things that have changed simultaneously that it is logical that our form of operating also has to change.

I believe that the most critical need in these moments is to know in which direction the target is located, because only in this direction will we have some chance of making a bullseye. If we direct our efforts in the opposite direction, we are certain to miss.

Exhibit 1

Balance Sheet as of December 31

(Million pesos)

	1980	*1981*
Assets		
Cash and bank accounts	14.1	24.0
Accounts receivable	318.8	316.7
Inventory	45.9	72.6
Other	3.0	—
Current assets	381.7	413.3
Fixed assets (net)	5.7	7.6
Deferred assets	7.6	9.3
Total	395.0	450.2
Liabilities		
Bank credit (short term)	123.5	198.0
Suppliers	59.6	52.3
Various Creditors	12.3	12.3
Others	16.1	11.8
Total	211.5	274.4
Capital		
Equity	130.0	130.0
Retained earnings reserve	53.5	45.8
Total	183.5	175.8

Income Statement, January 1–December 30

(Million pesos)

	1980	*1981*
Sales	420.6	492.8
Cost of sales	236.3	277.9
Operating costs:		
Sales & administrative	76.8	107.6
Financial	34.8	89.6
Total operating costs	111.6	197.2
Operating profit	72.7	17.8
Other income	4.2	14.3
Profit before taxes	76.9	32.1
Taxes (50%)	38.5	16.0
Net profits	38.4	16.1

Compañía Telefónica Mexicana S.A. (CTM)

On a cold day in March 1983, Carlos Peres, a slide presentation tucked firmly under his arm, walked briskly from the offices of the Telecommunications Division of American Telecommunications Industries (ATI) to the corporate headquarters building in White Plains, New York. While his shoes splattered the slush on the sidewalk, his mind raced over the cold facts summarized in his slides.

As general manager of Compañía Telefónica Mexicana (CTM), Peres prepared the presentation outlining options for ATI's Mexican subsidiary. The year before, caught in the midst of Mexico's debt and currency crisis, CTM had recorded a loss of more than $27 million and ended the year with a negative equity of more than $15 million. Today, Peres was meeting with ATI's Telecommunications Division president, Jim Gordon, to decide CTM's future. (See *Exhibit 1* for ATI's organization.) Was there a chance to rebuild, or would CTM have to close its doors forever? Although spring had officially arrived the week before, Peres found the days still too cold for comfort.

ATI

American Telecommunications Industries was born in the 1920s as the outgrowth of an investment in several small local telephone companies. Through internal growth and continuous acquisitions, ATI became one of the largest independent telephone operators in the United States.

After World War II, demand for telephone services exploded, and ATI found its growth hindered by limited equipment supply. In 1951 ATI acquired Associated Communications Inc., a major manufacturer of telecommunications and transmission equipment with manufacturing plants, sales agencies, and distribution outlets in Canada, Europe, Latin America, and the United States.

ATI's organization was divided into three groups: *Telephone Operations,*

This case was prepared by Tomás Kohn, under the supervision of Associate Professor Christopher Bartlett, as the basis for class discussion rather than to illustrate either effective or ineffective handling of an administrative situation. Abridged with permission.

which included all companies providing telephone services; *Telecommunications Products*, which included all domestic telephone equipment manufacturing plants; and *ATI International*, which comprised all overseas manufacturing and sales.

Having successfully assimilated the acquisitions of the 1950s, ATI felt ready and able to expand abroad. One executive recalled:

> When Larry Johnson became ATI's chief executive in 1963, he charged Dave Warren, president of ATI International, with the task of planting the ATI flag around the world. In the telecommunications field, Warren acquired companies in Germany, France, Spain, Mexico, Chile, Colombia, and Brazil.

ATI's international sales grew from insignificant amounts in the early 1960s to more than $1.4 billion in 1975 (see *Exhibits 2* and *3*). ATI's local executives were responsible for their operations; corporate controls consisted mainly of reviews of the subsidiaries' results relative to budgets. The European operations, the most important, were managed through ATI's French subsidiary in Marseilles. All the company's other foreign plants were in Latin America and were controlled by the Latin American Operations (LAO) headquarters in New York City.

THE TELECOMMUNICATIONS INDUSTRY

Some sixty years before ATI was established, Alexander Graham Bell, a Boston University professor, invented the telephone. Armed with extensive patents, he and his associates developed what was to become the American Telephone and Telegraph Co. (AT&T) and the Bell System of telephone-operating companies.

The industry always consisted of the basic segments characterizing it in 1983: the provision of *telephone operating services* and the supply of *telecommunications equipment* (TE). TE fell into three basic categories: main-exchange or switching, transmission, and terminal.

Switching equipment was used to route telephone calls from the calling to the called party. Switching equipment represented some 65% of all TE sales. The first automatic switch was invented in 1898 by Strowger. The crossbar switch, invented in Sweden in the 1930s, operated faster and with fewer problems than the Strowger, while requiring 40% less labor for assembly. Yet switching equipment manufacture remained highly labor-intensive. Even a modest assembly plant required several thousand workers. The development of semielectronic switches by Bell Laboratories in 1965 breathed new life into the industry.

Transmission equipment included coaxial cables, microwave transmitters, modems, etc. Innovations were almost continual; R&D efforts were not quite as large as in switching.

Terminal equipment (telephone handsets, PABXs, key systems,[1] and telex machines), was used directly by subscribers, who usually leased it from local operating companies. R&D costs were less than in switching or transmission. PABX technology, in fact, was usually a by-product of switching technology. Terminal equipment manufacture was highly labor-intensive.

A network consisted of an interconnected system of these three types of equipment. Central switching equipment accounted for some 40% of the total investment, including the required infrastructure. Switching and terminal equipment was manufactured to many national standards, creating serious problems for equipment interfacing. Transmission equipment was manufactured to only two standards, greatly simplifying the use of equipment from different suppliers in a network.

Until the deregulation wave of the 1980s, telephone services were either government-owned or government-controlled. In the United States and Canada, telecommunications services were operated by private regulated utilities; elsewhere these services were provided by government-controlled national post, telephone, and telegraph authorities (PTTs). Nearly all main-exchange switchgear, some 90% of transmission equipment, and around 75% of terminal equipment was sold to PTTs or the regulated utilities in North America.

Governments considered telecommunications a critical part of their infrastructure, vital to their national defense and economic development and a source of employment and technology. Traditionally, PTTs strongly preferred local suppliers; thus, by the 1930s most European countries, and by the 1960s most Latin American ones, had some local manufacture of TE. In 1982 North America represented 41.4% of the US$57.3-billion global communications market, Europe accounted for 26.7%, Japan 8.0%, the Middle East 10.0%, other LDCs 11.5%, and other OECD countries 1.6%. These shares were expected to remain rather stable through the 1980s with a small tendency for Europe and the United States to decrease in importance while all other regions increased. By 1987 the total TE market was expected to reach US$83 billion in 1982 dollars.

International trade in TE was limited except for transmission equipment, which was least affected by pressures for local manufacture. Its manufacture was not labor-intensive; unlike other equipment, many transmission projects had characteristics of a "one-shot deal." Turnkey

---

[1]*PABX*, or private automatic branch exchanges, were systems with a small switchboard that allowed institutions to operate their own internal telephone systems. *Key systems* were simpler systems used by smaller businesses with a few trunk lines and extensions but no switchboard.

transmission network projects were usually followed by equipment orders to maintain, expand, or upgrade the network.

About a dozen suppliers controlled most the world TE market. Industry concentration in individual countries was very high and varied by industry segment, being highest in central switching and lowest in transmission equipment. Western Electric in the United States produced some 20% of the world's equipment, followed by ITT (U.S.) 10%, Siemens (Germany) 8%, ATI (U.S.) 6%, and Ericsson (Sweden), GTE (U.S.), and NEC (Japan), each with about a 4% market share.

In addition to PTTs' preference for local equipment suppliers, the provision of up-to-date products, adequate price, financing, and after-sales service were all important criteria in awarding contracts. Interfacing switching equipment was always complicated, and the design and flexibility of a switch and the provision of local technical support were key. Thorough knowledge of the existing equipment in a telephone switching station, and of the demand patterns it served, were vital for successfully incorporating new equipment into such a station.

ATI IN MEXICO: THE BEGINNING

The merger with Associated in 1951 gave ATI a sales office in Mexico, which later became part of the ATI International organization. ATI's early business in Mexico consisted of TE imports, mainly from ATI's French plants. These imports were handled by Jerry Bono, who joined ATI in 1957 and was assigned to Mexico in 1959. In 1961 he was placed in charge of export sales to Latin America. In his New York City office, he became increasingly frustrated by the difficulty of breaking into the Mexican market, where ATI's sales remained below $1 million per year.

The Mexican Telecommunications Market and Industry

With 47 million inhabitants, Mexico in 1969 was the world's fourteenth most populous country. It was a federal republic whose chief of state, the president, was elected by direct vote to a nonrenewable six-year term. Since 1934 all of Mexico's presidential transitions had been peaceful and constitutional under the umbrella of the Partido Revolucionario Institucional (PRI), which ruled the country for almost forty years. Real GDP grew at about 6.5% per year between 1950 and 1970 (*Exhibit 4*). Industrial development, spurred by a policy of import substitution, was at the core of the country's growth. Direct foreign investment played an important role in that development and, although restricted, was generally welcomed.

Three government institutions played a key role in the Mexican tele-communications industry: Secretaría de Comercio y Fomento Industrial (SECOFIN), Secretaría de Communicaciones y Transportes (SCT), and Teléfonos de Mexico (TELMEX).

SECOFIN supervised local content requirements, which in the telecommunications industry stated that at least 35% of the materials in a finished product had to be manufactured in Mexico. If not in compliance, a manufacturer had to negotiate with SECOFIN a program to reach the desired levels. SECOFIN also established programs to increase the level of local content in products that already met minimum requirements. All products sold in the Mexican market had to be authorized by SECOFIN.

SCT regulated the industry. It licensed telephone and other telecommunications operators, specified standards, and approved the use of equipment. SCT itself provided some services such as leasing channels for TV transmissions.

TELMEX, the national telephone-operating company, was formed in the early 1950s to bring telephone operations into the hands of Mexican citizens. Originally the government was a minority shareholder, but by the 1980s it owned a majority of the company. TELMEX's CEO often stayed in that position for more than a decade.

Until TELMEX was formed, subsidiaries of ITT and L. M. Ericsson (LME) provided over 80% of the country's telephone services.[2] Both companies had started in the 1920s and operated networks that overlapped in Mexico City but were not interconnected. By buying out ITT's and LME's operations, TELMEX assumed control of most of Mexico's telephones and brought order to the chaotic situation by interconnecting the networks. Over the next thirty years TELMEX slowly acquired all other telephone operating companies in Mexico.

TELMEX did not retire old equipment; central exchanges were often a potpourri of switchgear from different eras. While ITT and LME continued to supply most of TELMEX's equipment needs, other vendors had difficulty getting orders because of problems with equipment interfacing. Furthermore, TELMEX's executives and technicians were often ex-LME or ITT employees, still loyal to their previous employers.

In the 1960s Mexico stepped up its emphasis on import substitutions. SECOFIN started to demand increased local content, and SCT made it difficult to use imported equipment. LME and ITT responded by establishing wholly owned manufacturing plants in Mexico. ITT's INDETEL opened in 1967 and LME's TELEINDUSTRIA in 1969. Both manufactured mainly switching equipment but also some telephones.

---

[2]ITT was a U.S.-based company with most of its telecommunications businesses outside the United States. LME was a privately held company based in Sweden. Over 75% of LME's business, which was mainly in telecommunications, was done outside its home country.

CTM

The Formation of CTM

Mexico's location and market characteristics made it an ideal place for LAO President John Buchanan to implement ATI's strategy of selective international expansion. It was in 1966, while Buchanan was searching for places to "plant the ATI flag," that Jerry Bono was deeply concerned about his inability to export into Mexico. Bono suggested it was time to manufacture in Mexico and that the best way to do so was to buy CTM.

CTM was a small TE company in the northern Mexico town of Saucillo. The owners of Comunicación Nacional (CN), a local telephone operating company, established CTM in 1936 to rebuild used telephone equipment for CN's use. After World War II CTM adapted war surplus equipment for CN's needs. CTM was managed by Roberto Torres, one of the original shareholders and a highly qualified technical man who dreamed of building CTM into a self-sufficient TE company. To do so, he entered into a licensing contract with ITT to manufacture equipment for TELMEX in the late 1960s.

With high hopes for the future, Torres started construction of a new plant. His dream was shattered when ITT built its own plant to manufacture an upgraded version of the equipment it had licensed to CTM. Roberto died that year, and his cousin Victor took over. With a new plant but no products, Victor sold 62% of the company to ATI, hoping to get an ATI agency agreement.

Jery Bono remarked:

> Government officials had suggested that if ATI had a presence in Mexico, possibly TELMEX and SCT would give us, on a most-favored basis, more import business. Buying CTM accomplished that. This was a reliable and quality-conscious supplier to TELMEX that also had a captive market in CN. But, basically, it was the only way we could get into Mexico.

CTM's Operation, 1967–78

Victor Torres was retained as CTM's managing director. CTM's sales, which had been below $.8 million per year in 1968, reached $17.2 million by 1978 (*Exhibit 5*). Felix Lamadrid, a grandson of one of the company's founders and a shareholder in the company, was named plant manager. Lamadrid said:

> In 1968 we had practically no work. Our first task was to find something to keep our 110 people occupied. This we did by getting

odd jobs either for the local market or by doing "maquila" (assembly) work for U.S. companies on a subcontract basis. At the same time Victor patiently worked on TELMEX. We could not go for the core businesses, which were in the hands of ITT and LME, but we pushed hard to get any incremental business that developed. It was a slow and steady process. One of our first successes was the sale to TELMEX of pay telephones designed with ATI's help.

Torres reported to Bono, who, in addition to ATI's export functions, was responsible for the Mexican operation. They met frequently to discuss CTM's operations. To support Torres, ATI marketing and technical personnel spent varying lengths of time in Mexico. ATI staff members assisted with cost accounting and annual reporting procedures. But the main link between ATI and CTM was Bono. He described his role as "taking ATI's products and fitting them to the Mexican market." Thus, CTM's operating plans were based on Bono's product and local-market knowledge. Implementation of the plans was mostly Torres's function. LAO executives received monthly financial reports to evaluate performance relative to the plans.

In 1973 a new foreign investment law required majority participation by Mexicans in the TE industry. ITT reduced its shareholding in INDETEL to 49% by 1977. LME also reduced its participation in its Mexican subsidiary, but TELEINDUSTRIA's importance as a TELMEX supplier, the high level of local content in its production, and the fact that it was exporting allowed LME to maintain 80% ownership. CTM had to be profitable to attract the new shareholders needed to reduce ATI's holdings to 49%. This caused ATI to postpone Mexicanization plans.

In 1976 the Mexican peso was devalued from 12.5 to 19.95 pesos per dollar. Although CTM had profits of $2.1 million in 1976, exchange losses of $2.3 million and translation losses of $1.0 million left the company with a net loss of $1.2 million. In the devaluation's aftermath, Victor Torres was replaced as managing director by Felix Lamadrid.

After 1978 Bono pushed for a new strategy based on the introduction of an advanced PABX system. This system (dubbed T-4), a version of a well-established design used by ATI in the United States, was modified by CTM's technical personnel to gain SCT's approval for direct sales to consumers. Before the T-4, CTM's products were based on designs from ATI's European operations; the T-4 was the first ATI product adapted for Mexico.

CTM pursued a two-pronged marketing approach aiming separately at the institutional market (mainly TELMEX) and the private or consumer market. Although the latter represented only 10% of the total market, in it CTM avoided direct competition with LME and ITT at TELMEX. Distribution channels were built and an intensive marketing effort was begun to reach potential T-4 customers. Over the next two years, CTM became the main PABX supplier in Mexico (*Exhibit 6*).

CTM's Mexicanization

By 1979 CTM had started to reap the benefits from its patient courting of TELMEX and its newly established distribution network. Timing had been right. The buildup of the distribution network coincided with the takeoff of the Mexican economy, spurred by fast-growing oil exports at ever-increasing prices.

In 1979 CTM's sales and profits reached record levels (*Exhibit 5*). Mexicanization became feasible. An internal memo from ATI Treasury described the company's Mexicanization objectives: "to overcome the political impediments that restricted the growth of the company; to elim-inate ATI's guarantees of CTM loans; and to provide a capital infusion and broaden the company's investor base."

An executive on ATI's legal staff described the change:

> Going to a minority position was a necessary evil to stay in the Mexican market. Although I strongly believe that joint ventures are doomed to failure, I had hopes for the Mexican joint venture because the partners who entered the business knew nothing about telecommunications, admitted this willingly, and said they trusted ATI with the company management.
>
> We have always looked for something in addition to money from our partners. Their contribution is their social, economic, and political standing in the country and their network of contacts. These contacts are vital for a company like ATI that follows strict guidelines precluding any questionable payments.

An LAO executive who didn't share the "necessary evil" view of Mexicanization observed: "We were not too happy with the way the com-pany had performed up to 1979, and among many of us there was the feeling, 'Let's go to a minority position and give it another try.' "

In January 1980 CTM increased its capital by 29%. New shares were sold to distinguished investors in Mexico City for Ps.46 million (about $1.9 million). ATI's share decreased from about 62% to 49%. Lamadrid was retained as managing director, and an executive committee was estab-lished to review the company's operations. As ATI's representative on the committee, Bono traveled monthly to Mexico. The other two committee members were the chairman and vice chairman of the board of directors, both Mexican nationals. Bono's opinion of ATI's change to a minority position was clear: "It was very positive, very positive indeed," he said.

CTM continued in 1980 and 1981 the growth that started in 1979. Sales and profits reached record levels; for the first time, employment surpassed 1,600 people. The optimism of CTM's executives matched the optimism that permeated the environment. U.S. and European bankers flocked to Mexico to extend credit to all takers, and Mexican President López Portillo spoke about "the management of wealth" as one of the country's problems.

ATI AFTER 1977

In 1977, while CTM was struggling with the effects of devaluation, ATI was wrestling with its own problems. In the aftermath of Watergate, ATI was one of more than 400 U.S. corporations to begin internal investigations of their own operations. The special audit committee established by the board reported that "payments found during the five-year period [1972–76] that appear to have been made to foreign officials were mostly made by ATI International [personnel]." ATI signed a consent agreement with the SEC.

The following year saw a major reorganization of the company in which all manufacturing and related marketing worldwide were reorganized into two divisions, each oriented toward a particular worldwide product field: TE and office equipment. The goal of each of these global businesses was to capitalize more effectively on the business growth opportunities in both domestic and international markets.

A highly placed executive in ATI's human resources department commented on the changes of 1977 and their effect on the ATI's international operations:

The sensitive payments issue was just before the reorganization. When the worldwide product businesses were formed—and I must stress that the payments disclosures did not dictate the reorganization—people from International were less likely to be put in charge of the worldwide businesses. The leadership of the worldwide businesses went to domestic people who had no involvement in the sensitive payments issue and, unfortunately, also had no idea of international operations. Some didn't even have passports!

When ATI International was an independent division of the company, there was vitality in international operations, but with the organization change that feeling dissipated. The international operations represented a small percentage of each product division's total business, so naturally the focus of attention went to the domestic business.

The business environment was also becoming more difficult. Many of ATI's European subsidiaries were suffering the consequences of an industry shakeout. The TE division sold its plants in Spain and Germany, where ATI was unable to break the hold on the switching market of ITT and Siemens, respectively. Nonetheless, the division's worldwide sales continued to increase (*Exhibit 7*).

In 1981 Daniel James, formerly a GTE vice president, became president of ATI. Within a year he had implemented a new strategic planning process, as a result of which the company acquired Dacom, a data communications network. In early 1983 ATI acquired SMI, a supplier of long-distance telephone services. These acquisitions represented responses to the upcoming deregulation of U.S. telecommunications and the growing links between the telecom and computer technologies.

INDUSTRY CHANGES AND THE CRISIS OF 1982

Changes in the Telecommunications Industry

The telecommunications industry was undergoing dramatic change during the late 1970s and early 1980s. The development of electronic switches reduced switching time, enabled telephone operating companies to automate all call control and billing procedures, reduced the space required to house central exchanges, and reduced equipment interfacing problems. Assembling an electronic switch also required less than 25% of the labor required to assemble a crossbar switch.

The advent of electronic switching increased the technological intensity of the industry. For example, ITT's cost of developing its System 12 digital switching equipment exceeded $1 billion. ATI spent more than $1.2 billion in R&D between 1979 and 1982, during which period its R&D expenses grew 17.8% per year. For the entire U.S. telecommunications industry, R&D expenses that in the mid-1970s averaged around 7.6% of sales jumped by 1981 to 9.6% of sales. At that level the telecommunications industry was more than three times as R&D-intensive as the average U.S. industry.

The change to digital technology also brought telecommunications into an overlap with the computer industry, while the role of the telephone in the "office of the future" created an overlap with the fast-developing office equipment industry. TE companies faced new competitive threats and expanded business opportunities as the boundaries of their industry shifted.

Digital technology also brought other changes. Prices declined, making it necessary to ship ever increasing numbers of units to absorb a fixed value of overhead (especially R&D) expenses. And employment in the industry was decreasing, despite increasing sales volumes, creating pressures to increase volumes further to avoid additional layoffs.

Regulatory changes were in full swing in the United States and were beginning to influence policy-makers in other countries. As of January 1, 1983, telephone operating companies were required to offer terminal equipment for sale to customers at unregulated prices. Deregulation, combined with the planned breakup of AT&T, profoundly changed the rules of the game in the industry:

- Western Electric, the previously captive suppliers to the Bell telephone system, would be free to enter the international market.
- The newly independent regional telephone operating companies would become potential customers for both U.S.-based and foreign-based equipment manufacturers.
- Telephone subscribers would be free to buy terminal equipment, from uniline telephones to large PABXs.
- Services such as long-distance telephone, data transmission, and packet switching would be offered by many suppliers, and private telecommunications networks would proliferate.

Mexico in 1982–83

By 1982 Mexico was the eleventh most populous country in the world, with 73.1 million inhabitants. Mexico City, the capital, was approaching a population of 17 million. Between 1978 and 1981, real growth in GDP, which had been running at an average of 6.3% per year during the previous twenty years, accelerated to 8%. While growth depended heavily on industrial development, the discovery of vast oil reserves provided impetus for the growth spurt of the late 1970s and was at the core of the optimism that permeated the economy.

But beneath the surface prosperity there were problems with agricultural production, unemployment, uneven income distribution, and widespread political corruption. During the 1970s and early 1980s growth and government expenditures were financed through deficit spending and foreign credits. In 1982, with the price of oil falling, interest rates on the foreign debt reaching unexpected levels, and inflation rising out of control, the economy came to an abrupt halt.

That year, GDP fell by 1.5%. The government of López Portillo devalued the peso and allowed the currency to float on February 18, 1982. To stem the massive capital flight, currency controls were established, the banking system was nationalized, a two-tier exchange system was established, and payments on all foreign debt were suspended. Finally, by

November 10, on the initiative of the IMF, the international financial community agreed to the necessary debt rescheduling. Mexico was forced to commit to severe reductions in government spending to reduce the public-sector deficit from 16.7% of GDP to 2.5% by 1985.

On December 1, 1982, López Portillo's term came to an end. Miguel de la Madrid Hurtado was inaugurated as President of a Mexico in crisis. With the pronouncement "Now we work!" de la Madrid set out to redirect the country's economy. To give himself breathing room he further deval-ued the peso. (During 1982 the peso devalued from 23.7 to 96.5 to the dollar.) He then embarked on a program to reduce government deficits, control inflation, and reestablish Mexico's international creditworthi-ness. Boosting exports was a key element to provide the foreign exchange needed for this purpose.

CTM's Operation During the Crisis

The 1982 devaluations caught CTM totally unprepared with most of its assets financed with short-term dollar-denominated debt (*Exhibit 8*). Clearly, CTM's management team needed reinforcing. Dietrich Her-mann, a soft-spoken but dynamic Swiss accountant, became CTM's new controller. Previously he had spent six years as controller of ATI's TE operations in France, where he had participated in the turnaround of that company in the late 1970s. Hermann described what he found when he arrived in Mexico in June 1982:

> Although the February devaluation had taken place, CTM's people were in an optimistic mood. (Because of different accounting treatment of exchange losses, devaluation looked very different to CTM and ATI.) The company had sold so much during the previous years that a pure marketing mentality permeated the organization. This mentality was behind the excessive inventories and accounts receivable. As an example, the company planned to sell 5,000 PABXs in 1982 when in 1981, which was already a record year, it had sold only 2,500. Not only were the inventories high, they were also unbalanced. Of course, the high inventories would not have been such a problem if they had not been financed with dollar debt. We could increase the sales price of the products, say by 100 percent, but the cost of the debt went up by 400 percent.
>
> The financial controls were poor and the information very rudimentary. CTM was essentially run like a family business, and the systems which were adequate to manage the one-man show of the mid- and late seventies could not handle the needs when sales exploded. Sure the required annual forms were filled out for ATI's use in the United States, but the information was not backed by the systems

needed to generate it. The forms were filled just to satisfy headquarters.

As the gravity of the situation became apparent, Carlos Peres, who was in charge of marketing for LAO, was sent to Mexico in July 1982 to assume responsibility for CTM's operation. By November, CTM executives had managed to establish one currency hedge for $6 million. Thirty million dollars of unhedged debt remained outstanding. Hermann commented on debt hedging:

> People may ask: "Why didn't we hedge more of the debt?" Well, let me tell you that it was not that simple. First, the cost of hedging was enormous. It cost us Ps.240 million to enter into the $6 million hedge, fixing the exchange rate at 48 Ps./$. Can you picture yourself adding Ps.240 million to the financial costs of your company based on the belief that there will be a devaluation? What if the devaluation didn't take place or it wasn't as large as you expected? The opinions were not unanimous in favor of the hedge. It took some time until we (CTM, ATI-LAO, and ATI-Corporate Treasury) all agreed to go ahead and hedge the debt. Second, once we decided to make the hedge, it wasn't so easy to implement. The whole country had the same idea at the same time. We made the first $6 million hedge. We had all the papers ready for an additional $7 million hedge and were in the midst of getting corporate approval when the November devaluation occurred.

CTM's Future

After the T-4 PABX was successfully introduced into the Mexican market, CTM's executives felt that an electronic version of the product would have wide appeal. The design was contracted to a consulting firm in the United States. The new system, dubbed the T-5, was almost ready for production when Peres took over CTM's management. He immediately realized this product's potential in the newly deregulated U.S. market, estimated at 1 million PABXs per annum. Peres estimated it was reasonable to expect ATI to capture some 10% of this market, and felt CTM would be an ideal source. In this way, ATI could enter the U.S. market immediately, benefiting from CTM's trained and low-cost labor, until demand in Mexico absorbed CTM's production capacity and ATI geared up its domestic T-5 manufacture. (See *Exhibit 9,* for projected costs.)

With the help of Jerry Bono, Carlos Peres brought the T-5 to ATI headquarters and began to sell it internally. Domestic ATI marketing personnel were excited. Questions lingered, however, about relying on an unknown plant just when ATI was about to make its debut in the deregulated U.S. market. Telecommunications manufacturing staff at ATI's headquarters questioned the reliability of a product developed by outsiders: "How in the world were they [CTM] going to come up with a decent product spending only $300,000 for its design when we had spent over $5 million and had not come up with a good product?" asked one executive. ATI Treasury questioned the wisdom of investing the additional sums needed to shore up CTM when enormous resources were required to prepare ATI for operation in the deregulated U.S. market. In the words of one staff manager, "CTM is a small marginal operation with little chance of becoming much more. It's the kind of company that can become a sinkhole for corporate resources and management time—and with a huge domestic market opening up and two acquisitions to absorb, we just can't afford such a distraction."

Carlos Peres and Dietrich Hermann were in White Plains preparing the presentation to Jim Gordon. They knew that although TELMEX had cut back its purchases for 1982 and 1983, the government had emphasized that telecommunications was a high-priority, and that TELMEX would have to have the resources needed to grow (*Exhibit 10*). They were also aware of persistent rumors circulating in Mexico about a government-backed plan to hedge and restructure all dollar-denominated debt.

Peres knew that for ATI to continue in Mexico involved a high degree of operating and financial risk. But he felt strongly that if CTM closed its doors, ATI would in effect be making a conscious decision to write off the Mexican TE market and perhaps the entire Latin American market. As he considered the options he was going to present to Jim Gordon (*Exhibit 11*), Carlos wondered which one made most sense for ATI.

Exhibit 1 ATI's Organization 1983

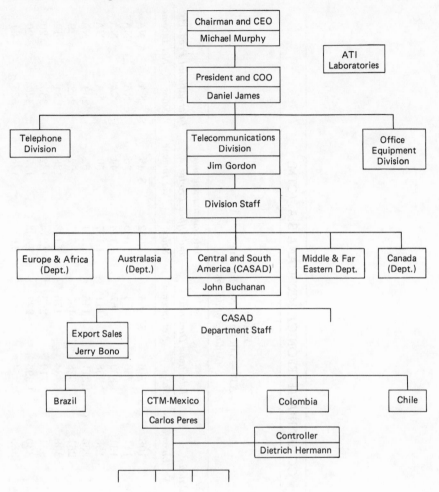

COMPAÑIA TELEFÓNICA MEXICANA S.A. (CTM)

Exhibit 2

ATI—Sales and Net Income

(Millions of dollars)

Year	Consolidated		Telephone Division		Telecommunications and Office Products[a]		International Products[b]	
	Sales	Net Income	Sales	Net Income	Sales	Net Income	Sales	Net Income
1960	$ 1,767	$ 108	$ 716	$ 63	$1,052	$ 45	$ NA	$ NA
1961	1,841	111	786	75	1,055	36	NA	NA
1962	1,992	131	869	87	1,124	44	NA	NA
1963	2,165	158	968	111	1,197	50	NA	NA
1964	2,661	206	1,211	146	1,451	62	209	NA
1965	3,054	251	1,328	162	1,727	92	242	9
1966	3,587	308	1,484	176	2,103	128	284	12
1967	3,933	321	1,719	203	2,214	132	335	20
1968	4,398	330	1,995	227	2,403	117	423	20
1969	4,893	353	2,264	243	2,630	128	525	21

1970	5,159	324	2,510	249	2,649	105	662	24
1971	5,832	399	2,889	305	2,943	137	749	23
1972	6,563	453	3,330	366	3,231	137	911	24
1973	7,610	516	3,801	423	3,807	197	1,206	39
1974	8,492	365	4,263	465	4,230	164	1,446	3
1975	8,922	548	4,781	531	4,142	111	1,554	(5)
1976	10,109	609	5,514	591	4,595	117	1,743	14
1977	11,505	758	6,165	704	5,340	147	1,980	29
1978	13,098	884	6,899	779	6,200	210	1,986	59
1979	14,937	918	7,830	813	7,107	192	2,226	53
1980	14,969	669	8,892	866	6,077	140	2,636	87
1981	16,539	1,037	10,311	1,074	6,228	20	3,045	134
1982	18,099	1,208	11,736	1,265	6,363	30	3,203	98

[a]Telecommunications and office products results *include* international products.

[b]International products include telephone directory services.

SOURCE: 1960–70 and 1980–82 ATI annual reports, financial statistics supplement.
1971–75, 1975 annual report.
1976–79, 1979 annual report, except for international data which are from:
- 1976–77, 1977 annual report
- 1978–79, 1979 annual report.

443

Exhibit 3
ATI Consolidated Balance Sheet[a]
(Millions of dollars)

As of December 31	1969	1976	1982
Assets			
Property, plant & equipment (net)			
Telephone operations	$ 7,694	$15,327	$25,751
Other operations	530	791	1,602
Total PP&E	8,824	16,118	27,353
Investments & other assets	327	555	842
Current assets	1,814	3,729	5,219
Total assets	$10,365	$20,402	$33,414
Liabilities and equity			
ATI common stock equity	$ 2,921	$ 4,703	$ 8,724
Minority interest in equity of subsidiaries	129	207	896
Preferred stock	422	1,536	1,116
Long-term debt	4,302	8,066	12,456
Reserves and deferred credits	224	1,938	4,877
Current liabilities	2,369	5,454	5,373
Total liabilities	$10,365	$20,402	$33,414

ATI Consolidation of Income
(Millions of dollars for the years ending Dec. 31)

	1969	1976	1982
Telephone Division			
Revenue	$2,264	$5,514	$11,736
Net income	243	591	1,265
Other operations			
Revenue	2,630	4,595	$ 6,363
Net income	128	117	30
Other corporate income (expenses) net	(18)	(99)	(87)
Net income applicable to common stock	353	609	1,208
Primary earnings per common share	$ 3.35	$ 4.94	$ 7.05

[a]Sums may not tally due to rounding.

COMPAÑIA TELEFÓNICA MEXICANA S.A. (CTM)

Exhibit 4
The Mexican Economy

	1955	1960	1965	1970	1975	1980	1981	1982
GDP (1980 prices)[a]	850.0	1.1	1.6	2.3	3.1	4.3	4.6	4.6
Population (millions)	31	36	43	51	60	69	71	73
GDP per capita (000 pesos)	27.4	31.8	37.6	44.3	51.6	62.0	65.0	63.1
Exchange rate Ps./$	12.5	12.5	12.5	12.5	12.5	23.3	26.2	96.5
GDP deflator (1980 = 100)	10.4	13.6	15.9	19.7	35.5	100.0	127.2	200.8
Implicit inflation rate[b]	—	5.5%	3.2%	4.4%	12.9%	23.0%	27.2%	57.9%
Imports as % of GDP	12.5%	9.5%	7.6%	6.9%	7.5%	10.5%	10.0%	7.8%
Exports as % of GDP	11.9%	9.1%	7.2%	6.6%	7.1%	10.0%	9.6%	7.4%
Trade balance, f.o.b. (MM$)	21	(354)	(352)	(888)	(3,272)	(2,310)	(3,329)	7,048
Government deficit (% of GNP)	—	—	—	1.4%	4.9%	3.2%	6.9%	16.7% (est.)
Indices of industrial production:								
Manufacturing	16.6	23.8	37.1	54.6	74.4	100.0	107.4	103.1
Mining	47.4	50.9	59.3	71.8	81.0	100.0	115.4	127.6
Crude petroleum production	13.0	22.1	26.7	35.4	49.7	100.0	113.1	139.1
All industrial production	16.5	23.8	39.3	49.0	69.2	100.0	108.8	106.7

[a]Billions of pesos.

[b]Implicit average annual inflation rate during the five previous years, except 1981 and 1982, based on GDP deflator.

445

Exhibit 5

CTM's Sales and Income

(Thousands of dollars)

Year	Sales	Net Income
1969	$ 2,241	$ 183
1970	3,542	219
1971	3,243	(452)
1972	5,982	380
1973	5,108	341
1974	8,057	719
1975	13,406	1,079
1976	15,962	(1,199)
1977	14,889	(63)
1978	17,166	(308)
1979	34,313	2,025
1980	45,188	3,543
1981	68,625	4,931
1982	43,688	(27,956)

SOURCE: CTM financial reports to ATI.

Exhibit 6

Major Competitors in the Mexican Telecommunications
Market by Business Segment—1980

	Terminal Equipment	Network Switching	Customer Switching	Transmission Equipment
ATI (CTM)	26.0%	1.0%	5.6%	9.0%
ITT	14.8	48.9	10.3	29.8
L. M. Ericsson	14.8	48.0	24.2	29.6
GTE	23.0	2.1	7.8	10.3
Siemens	NA	—	12.5	—
ROLM	NA	—	12.5	—
Digital	NA	—	14.6	—
Mitel	—	—	12.5	—
Iwatsu	12.0	—	—	—
NEC	NA	—	—	10.6
TELETRA	NA	—	—	10.7
Not specified	10.0	—	—	—

SOURCE: LAO Strategic Plan.

Exhibit 7
ATI Sales of Telecommunications Products
(Millions of dollars)

Year	Worldwide Sales	Domestic Sales[a]	International Sales	Intercompany Sales[b]
1973	$1,662	$ 995	$ 668	$ 870
1974	1,830	1,050	780	914
1975	1,878	930	948	800
1976	1,994	NA	NA	888
1977	2,307	NA	NA	1,055
1978	2,606	NA	NA	1,295
1979	3,078	1,680	1,398	1,515
1980	3,219	1,706	1,514	1,398
1981	3,299	2,304	995	1,409
1982	3,818	2,852	996	1,683

[a]Net of eliminations.

[b]Intercompany sales consist mostly of telecommunications products sold to ATI's telephone operating companies.

SOURCE: ATI annual reports, 1973–78.

COMPAÑIA TELEFÓNICA MEXICANA S.A. (CTM)

Exhibit 8
CTM's Financial Results

	U.S. Dollars (millions)[a]				Mexican Pesos (millions)[b]			
	1979	1980	1981	1982	1979	1980	1981	1982
Net sales	34.4	45.2	68.6	43.7	753	1,031	1,686	2,447
Less: Cost of goods sold	18.9	24.9	34.5	24.2	437	561	773	1,353
Gross Profit	15.5	20.3	34.1	19.5	317	470	913	1,094
Less: Expenses	11.4	13.5	21.0	16.5	216	296	624	1,247
Exchange loss (gain)	—	0.2	2.3	38.3	—	—	—	270
Operating profit (loss)	4.1	6.6	10.8	(35.3)	101	174	290	(435)
After-tax income (loss)	2.1	3.6	5.9	(33.9)	47	84	143	(323)
Less: Translation loss (gain)	—	—	0.9	(6.0)	NA	NA	NA	NA
Net income (loss)	2.1	3.6	5.0	(27.9)	47	84	143	(323)
Current assets	20.6	31.4	45.9	25.7	504	714	1,236	3,039
Net fixed assets	2.0	2.4	5.1	6.0	84	167	233	539
Other assets	—	—	—	—	5	44	111	1,402
Total	22.6	33.8	51.0	31.7	595	925	1,580	4,980
Current liabilities	18.2	24.5	36.8	45.5	452	599	1,101	4,539
Long-term liabilities	—	—	—	2.1	5	5	6	186
Equity	4.4	9.3	14.3	(15.9)	136	321	473	255
Total	22.6	33.8	51.1	31.7	593	925	1,580	4,980
Dollar-denominated debt as % of total liabilities	66%	69%	76%	99%				99%

[a]Dollar results are the figures ATI used in LAO headquarters for budget control, financial analysis, etc.

[b]Peso results are the figures CTM's shareholders receive annually. These figures are prepared according to Mexican accounting and are audited by an international auditing firm.

Exhibit 9
Cost Analysis for Manufacturing the T-5 PABX System[a]

	Cost Per Unit	Units	Total Cost
A. Switch			
Materials[b]	$155.5	—	$155.5
Direct labor (18 hours)[c]	10.3	—	10.3
Variable overhead	18.0	—	18.0
Shipping costs	6.3	—	6.3
	190.1		190.1
B. Handsets			
Materials[b]	30.0	×8	240.0
Direct labor (4 man-hours)[c]	2.3	×8	18.4
Variable overhead	3.9	×8	31.2
Shipping costs	1.2	×8	9.6
	37.4		299.2
Total system cost			$489.3

Minimum Hourly Salaries (pesos)

	1970	1980	1981	1982	1983[d]
Saucillo	3.16	17.50	21.25	28.13	45.63
Mexico City	4.0	20.4	26.2	35.0	56.9

[a]A PABX consists basically of a control board and a number of telephone handsets. The analysis that follows assumes a system consisting of one board and 8 handsets.

[b]About 25% of the materials were to be sourced locally in Mexico. The remaining 75% were to be imported.

[c]The above table gives the relevant hourly salaries for three locations in Mexico. The exchange rate of $1 = 120 pesos, which was estimated to apply to T-5 exports as of June 1983, was used to calculate direct labor costs.

[d]One industry observer estimated that U.S. wage rates for comparable work in 1983 would be $6–7 per hour. Rates would be considerably higher in unionized plants. But productivity in the United States could be 25–50% higher.

Exhibit 10 TELMEX Expansion Plans 1983–88

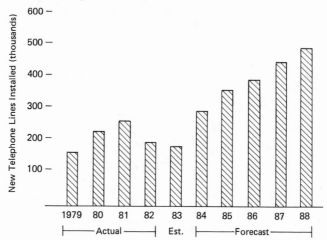

SOURCE: 5ta Reunión Anual de Planeación Corporativa en TELMEX, p. 148.

Note: An investment of about US$1,000 in 1982 dollars per new telephone line was a reasonable basis to estimate TELMEX's investment program.

Exhibit 11
Summary of Carlos Peres's Presentation to Jim Gordon

ATI had essentially two options regarding CTM:

1. Assume financial and managerial control of the company by capitalizing $9 million in intercompany debts[a]
2. Liquidate CTM

[a]There was a legal precedent for adopting Option 1. In a similar situation, Ericsson capitalized $20 million of intercompany debt and assumed 100% ownership and control of TELEINDUSTRIA.

OPTION 1

In addition to the $9 million capitalization, this option assumed that CTM would export the T-5 to ATI's U.S. operations. Based on these assumptions, the following forecast was presented:

CTM Income Forcast
(*Millions of dollars*)

	Actual	*Forecast*					
	1982	*1983*	*1984*	*1985*	*1986*	*1987*	*1988*
Revenues:							
in Mexico	41.3	23.1	29.6	30.9	33.9	38.0	43.4
intercompany	2.4	5.6	18.2	18.3	12.2	12.8	9.8
Total revenues	43.7	28.7	47.8	49.2	46.1	50.8	53.2
Net income in Mexico	(33.9)	(5.7)	4.1	6.3	5.0	5.7	6.6
Net translated income[b]	(27.9)	3.0	6.2	6.0	5.0	5.7	6.6

[b]Because CTM had a negative equity, the translated financial results showed a translation gain in 1982, 1983, and 1984. A small translation loss was planned for 1985.

OPTION 2

Since ATI had withdrawn its guarantees of CTM's loans when it reduced its shareholding to 49%, liquidating CTM would result in an after-tax loss of about $3 million if ATI simply wrote off its investment. If, to protect its corporate image and banking relations beyond the strictly legal requirements, ATI assumed 100% of CTM's financial obligations, the loss would be $16.1 million.

Colgate-Palmolive in Mexico

Colgate-Palmolive's (CP) worldwide market presence was built on the strength of its household and personal care products. Long known for its Colgate brand toothpaste and Palmolive brand soap, the company was a major global force in the packaged goods field and had in international reputation for excellence. CP's chairman and chief executive officer, Reuben Mark, believed that strengthening its current activities and selectively introducing new products would be the key to Colgate's continued growth in world markets.

CP sold its products in more than 100 countries and had manufacturing or distribution facilities in 54 countries. Its principal overseas manufacturing facilities were in Australia, Brazil, Canada, Colombia, France, Germany, Italy, Mexico, and the United Kingdom. CP operations were organized into seven subsidiaries: the United States, Mexico, France, Europe, Latin America, Asia-Pacific, and Africa and the Middle East. Excluding the parent operation in the United States, only two divisions, Mexico and France, were free-standing. Both were among CP's largest subsidiaries in sales and profits. CP's Mexican operating results were not combined with those of the Latin American division, and France's were not included with those of CP's European division. The president of the Mexican operation, Michael Tangney, reported directly to Senior Executive Vice President Roderick Turner in New York. Tangney was also an international vice president. All general managers of the subsidiaries were expected to recommend and then implement decisions about strategy and operating policy.

CP's Mexico subsidiary had responded remarkably well to the two oil price shocks in the 1970s. Its new product launches, particularly in powdered cleansers and hand dishwashing detergents, kept it healthy through the early 1980s. But changes in Mexico's economy since the beginning of its debt crisis in 1982 made Colgate-Mexico a special concern among CP's subsidiaries because of Mexico's relative inexperience in operating under hyperinflation. At the beginning of 1987, Mexico's annual inflation rate for 1987 was forecast to increase to 120%, and growth of the gross domestic product was expected to slow to 1% (*Exhibit 1*). In the year before the

Research Associate Julia Horn prepared this case under the supervision of Professor Michael G. Rukstad as the basis for class discussion rather than to illustrate either effective or ineffective handling of an administrative situation. Abridged with permission.

U.S. stock market crash on October 19, 1987, Mexico's stock market was the fastest growing in the world. But the decline of the U.S. stock market precipitated declines around the world; Mexico was no exception. Just five weeks after its all-time high on October 5, 1987, the Mexican stock market had lost 75% of its value.

On November 16–20, 1987, in the midst of continued fear of economic decline in Mexico, CP-Corporate and Colgate-Mexico management, including Turner and Tangney, conducted the annual budget meeting in Mexico City. See *Exhibits 2* and *3* for Colgate-Mexico's financial performance.

ECONOMIC AND POLITICAL BACKGROUND

Beginning in the 1940s and continuing through the 1960s, Mexico's economic policy was based largely on protectionism and import substitution. When President Echeverría took office in 1970, he addressed the problem of dependency on foreign capital by announcing an aggressive trade policy to limit imports and boost foreign-exchange earnings. He passed a restrictive new law on foreign investment. Inflation, largely nonexistent since 1950, began to climb. Meanwhile, exports dropped to such low levels that the deficit on the external current account more than tripled, from 3% of GDP in 1970 to 9.5% of GDP in 1976. In August 1976, only a few months before the end of Echeverría's term, the Bank of Mexico devalued the peso by 64.8%, the first devaluation since 1954.

In 1976 President López-Portillo took office just after the peso had lost over half its value and nearly $4 billion of capital had fled the country. At the beginning of his term, estimates of huge new oil finds were first made public. In the five years of oil price increases that followed, Mexico borrowed a total of $60 billion abroad against future oil revenues. "However, by 1981, during which one-third of the money was borrowed, the borrowing was not to finance investment; it was designed to prop up the country against the effects of a softening oil price, high interest rates abroad, and a world recession. Inflation was on the rise, anticipating the inevitable devaluation of the peso, and capital left the country."[1]

The first devaluation of the peso, by 45%, occurred in February 1982. By early August, after wage and price increases, a new flight of capital began. On August 5 the government restricted interest payments and vital imports to the current exchange rate of 49 pesos to the dollar, while an open market was in effect for all other transactions. The result was a second devaluation of the peso by 50% on that day. On August 13 the Mexican government announced it could no longer service its foreign

[1]*Economist,* September 5, 1987.

debt. After the announcement, the Federal Reserve Board and the International Monetary Fund encouraged public and private bankers to help, resulting in an aid package totaling $11 billion, including a ninety-day postponement of principal repayments.

After the onset of the debt crisis and nationalization of the banks in September 1982, President de la Madrid took office in December 1982. He was committed to a broad new economic policy to open Mexico's economy to world markets, roll back the extent of state ownership of resources, and move toward fiscal stability. After all of Mexico's $80 billion in debt repayments was rescheduled over twenty years in 1982, real GDP in 1983 contracted by 5.5% from the previous year, the worst decline in postwar years. In 1984 real GDP grew by 3.5% as the worldwide recession of 1981–82 came to an end and demand for Mexican exports increased by 8.4%. But by 1985 the flight of capital and the strain of servicing the $100-billion debt renewed pressure on public finances. In addition, Mexican oil, which sold for $26.70 a barrel in February 1986, collapsed to $8.60 by July 1986. The lower oil price reduced government revenues by more than 30% and forced new changes in the management of the Mexican economy.

De la Madrid's new trade policy was based on exposing Mexican businesses to competition from abroad and encouraging the growth of nonoil exports. (See *Exhibit 1* for the Mexican balance of trade.) In 1986 Mexico ratified membership in the General Agreement on Tariffs and Trade (GATT) and began to open up trading channels and to reduce protectionism. That year only 38% of the value of Mexico's exports was from oil and mining, down from 78% in 1982. Some state-owned industries, mainly energy, continued to be outside GATT rules, and Mexico still enjoyed some of GATT's concessions that protected developing countries. But Mexico was reducing both the level of its tariffs and the number of tariff rates. By the end of 1987, when the country's new duty law (written to abide by GATT rules) would come into effect, higher official prices for imported goods, used to calculate tariff levels, would be abolished.

COLGATE-PALMOLIVE'S CORPORATE STRATEGY

CP's corporate goals focused on increasing profitability and enhancing shareholder value. By 1991 the company hoped to reach and maintain a 15% return on capital. It had averaged 10.5% since 1984, when Mark first established the 15% goal. CP was also taking steps to achieve global low-cost producer status. Numerous new product introductions and product revitalizations were important to the company's overall growth and profitability. In 1985 alone, CP worldwide launched or revitalized 277 products.

In that same year Colgate-Palmolive began a strategic restructuring to increase profitability by concentrating on three core businesses: household and personal care, health care, and specialty marketing, made up of smaller businesses occupying distinct market niches. The largest, household and personal care, comprised 74% of total company sales and 56% of operating profit in 1986. Health care accounted for 20% of sales and 26% of operating profit, and specialty marketing accounted for 6% of sales and 18% of operating profit in 1986.

COLGATE'S MEXICAN STRATEGY

The main goal of Colgate-Mexico's strategic plan, common to all CP subsidiaries, was to improve market shares with high-quality products while working gradually to improve dollar profits and remittance. As Assistant Controller Morgan O'Brien summarized, "Our main financial charge is to achieve our budgeted profits while simultaneously building consumer franchises and brand loyalty." Profitable volume growth and protection of shareholder equity were basic goals. "In 1986," Tangney explained, "we even reduced tonnage growth because that growth was not predicted to be profitable." Colgate-Mexico's functional goals related to its broader strategy to be a cost-competitive producer of high-quality household and personal care products for the Mexican domestic market while continuing to be a good corporate citizen.

KEY OPERATING POLICIES
IN A HYPERINFLATIONARY ENVIRONMENT

Products

Colgate-Mexico produced 40 different products in 16 product categories. In comparison, there were 43 products in 13 categories in the United States. The subsidiary had dominant market shares of 70% to 90% in some products such as fine fabric detergents, fabric softeners, and dental creams. Beginning in the 1960s, the Mexican government imposed price controls on certain essential consumer goods, including soaps, laundry detergents, and dental creams. In 1986, 86% of Mexican households already used laundry detergents and 83% used dental creams, whereas 35% used liquid cleaners and 21% used scouring powders.

Though most of Colgate-Mexico's products were targeted to the basic needs of Mexico's 82 million consumers, some products such as fine fabric detergents and fabric softeners were aimed at high- and middle-income groups. The vice president of marketing and sales, Ken May, noted that certain products like bar soaps and some detergents were largely recession-proof. But all buyers were sensitive to price rises; in tough economic times, they often switched from more expensive shampoos and liquid floor cleaners to cheaper bar soaps to clean hair and powdered detergents to wash floors.

Marketing

May and the rest of the Marketing Department were responsible for at least staying even with inflation. "In the past two years," said May, "prices for all products have had to increase in response to faster increases in our cost structure due to growing inflation." Margins were forecast between 30% and 45% in 1987. In price-controlled categories, the government used a complicated formula based on documented cost increases so as to recover them when they accumulated to a 10% change. But during 1987 the government began to slow down the procedure for authorizing price increases and to grant only a fraction of the increase needed to offset the cost increase.

In 1987 Colgate-Mexico stopped shipping price-controlled products to clients until they accepted the approved selling price increases. Notably, government-run accounts, comprising as much as 30% of Colgate's volume, would refuse to accept a new purchase price until private sector retail accounts raised prices to the public. In noncontrolled product categories, Colgate's general policy was to allow customers one week to accept selling price increases. The stricter policy for selling price increases partially compensated for delays in price increase approvals.

For nonprice-controlled products, there was free-market pricing. Price increases were typically announced one week before they became effective. The percentage by which individual product prices rose varied from month to month. Product costing was based on replacement cost estimates and projections. This method, begun in 1985 (the company had been on LIFO accounting since 1982), was based on what the company expected to have to pay to restock inventory. Therefore, the marketing department had to keep in close contact with the purchasing department, which daily monitored prices for some 2,000 items of raw and packaging materials. These costs had to be projected into the next month. Colgate-Mexico's latest price increases before the November budget meeting were made on October 25, in response to the local inflation rate of 8.3% for the month of October. The nominal interest rate for October was 11.6% for thirty-day loans.

Another key function was managing customer credit. May's goal was to reduce accounts receivable from over thirty to under twenty-five days by offering stricter new credit and trading terms. Furthermore, May believed that a significant opportunity lay in accelerating the steps involved in recuperating invoice and collection documents from clients, especially the government. May thought this could save the company as much as $5 million of pretax income. He emphasized that incremental sales often came with a significant fall in margin: "Profitability can disappear quickly if we must purchase incremental or replacement raw and packing materials with borrowed money, only to sell to customers who will delay paying us by as much as thirty days beyond our stated terms."

Credit terms had historically been set by product category: Price-controlled categories were generally twenty-one days, noncontrolled household products between thirty and forty-five days, and personal-care products (with higher margins and slower in-store rotation), forty-five to sixty days. Government accounts generally demanded 10–15 days more than the private sector. With an average "days outstanding" of about thirty, CP was already the strictest among its competitors in selling terms. With almost 50% of sales in personal-care categories, CP stood in very good financial shape relative to its competitors. Although 90% of its business was in price-controlled categories, Procter & Gamble's receivables, by comparison, were estimated at twenty-five days. A local competitor, La Corona, ran about forty-five days, given its reliance on government distribution channels and its long-term policy of relying on promotions to the exclusion of all media advertising. Two personal-care product companies, Gillette and Chesebrough-Ponds, had standard credit terms of sixty days.

Colgate-Mexico hoped to generate $18 million (or 7%) of incremental sales by the end of 1988 on a wave of new-product introductions that would return at least a 20% contribution (margin minus advertising and promotion) while maintaining profitability into the 1990s. The new products ranged from what May termed "fast payback engines," such as a fresh-breath gel toothpaste, to those that were part of a portfolio expansion, such as a new line of colognes. In 1987 it estimated that new products would increase tonnage by 13,000 tons (4.7%) and add $10.4 million (4.5%) to total sales. By the end of 1988, new products could add 34,000 tons (13.3%) and $45.3 million (16%) to total sales. The marketing department had set minimum standards for new product launches, including net yearly sales of greater than $1 million, a contribution margin greater than $300,000 or 30% by the third year, and a five-month payback period. For new personal-care products, criteria included net sales exceeding $650,000 and a payback period of eight months. Flanker or side brands like Ajax Pine Cleaner, a flanker brand of Ajax, had to comprise at least 10% of main brand sales and offer a higher operating profit than the main brand and an eight-month payback period to be considered for introduction.

Competitors

Colgate-Mexico's largest competitor across all product categories was Procter & Gamble (P&G) which sold in 4 of Colgate's 16 product categories. (See *Exhibits 4* and *5*.) P&G had not followed CP's strategy in the 1970s of launching new products into nonprice-controlled categories of soap and detergents. P&G's Mexican subsidiary, established in 1948, operated two plants in Mexico City, one of which it acquired when it bought Richardson-Vicks in 1986. The Mexican subsidiary employed about 3,600 people, including Richardson-Vicks. In 1986 P&G in Mexico had about the same sales volume as Colgate-Mexico and was estimated to report a minor pretax loss (excluding Richardson-Vicks) due to price controls on soaps and detergents. P&G was the market leader in toilet soaps and detergents, with 45% and 49% market shares, respectively. Colgate was the leader in more than half the product categories in which it competed. May believed Colgate-Mexico's financial and marketing successes were because "many important new product launches were made in the 1970s, in the nonprice-controlled categories, where P&G was less aggressive in expanding its product lines."

Unilever, a potential competitor, was essentially inactive in Colgate's product categories in Mexico, but it was active in dental creams, fabric softeners, shampoos, and body cleaners in the United States and elsewhere and was thought to be the largest producer of detergents outside the United States. Unilever had a strong Mexican presence in foods and artificial flavors through its acquisition of five local companies, each with its own plant. The company had also acquired Chesebrough-Ponds in 1986, a U.S.-based manufacturer of personal-care products and toiletries (including lotions), with a plant in Mexico. Chesebrough-Ponds of Mexico had 1986 estimated sales of $36 million and pretax profits of $8 million. Unilever could become a direct competitor in Mexico in the next year or two. Because detergents, one of Unilever's leading product categories, were price-controlled in Mexico, Colgate's management had little concern over a new detergent entry from Unilever.

In four of Colgate-Mexico's markets, it faced a third competitor, La Corona, a local household-products company that produced soaps and detergents. La Corona had one plant in Mexico, employed about 2,600 people, and had 1986 sales of about $200 million and pretax profits of $20 million. Unilever had a licensing agreement with La Corona to market two of Unilever's soaps locally (Lux and Rexons), and some industry sources had speculated that Unilever would eventually buy La Corona, which was also competitive in two significant traditional Unilever products.

Distribution and Sales

Colgate-Mexico distributed its products through three main channels. *Food wholesalers* sold to both the small supermarket chains (which made up over half of Colgate-Mexico's business) and "mom and pop" stores that were not government clients. The food wholesalers typically paid Colgate quickly and on time. Another channel was the *national supermarket chains,* where five major clients represented the bulk of the business. *Government clients,* the largest of them CONASUPO, accounted for 12% of total sales. CONASUPO owned 25% of Mexico's supermarkets and controlled the movement of agricultural commodities in Mexico. Government clients typically extended credit terms the furthest. *Drug wholesalers* were a fourth, smaller channel. They distributed the products to drugstores around the country and accounted for about 10% of sales.

Colgate had its own distribution and sales force of 120 people. An estimated 100–150 trucks carried products out of the Mexico City factory each day. Sales force performance was evaluated by account, territory, and zone. Key accounts (customers like CONASUPO), represented 60–70% of the business. Salespeople typically visited key accounts once or twice a week. Nelson García-Mella, director of trade marketing, explained:

> The main traditional direct expenses of each retail account are salesmen, freight, promotional allowances, the shelf staff who arrange products on the shelf, and the push staff who demonstrate products to customers in the store. More important, however, is the "accounts receivable cost" or the financial cost of waiting for these accounts to pay us. The financing of accounts receivables is key in measuring if a given sale or order is profitable.

Purchasing and Production

The main function of Purchasing Director Michael Vander May and his staff of 25 was to obtain some 2,000 different chemicals and packaging materials necessary for Colgate's products. Of Colgate-Mexico's purchases in 1986 of $150 million in material, about $125 million were made locally, with the remainder imported. Raw materials made up 55% of the purchases, 35% were packaging materials, and 10% were essential oils (perfumes, flavors, and their components, imported mostly from international suppliers).

One of the department's packaging goals was reducing costs. The subsidiary had been negotiating to acquire a local bottle producer, Demi, which had sales of about $1 million, some to Colgate. Demi could produce almost 35% of Colgate's total bottle purchases. Colgate-Mexico's in-house packaging group had also developed lighter-weight, cheaper plastic bottles for liquid cleaners and fabric softeners, which were expected to reduce packaging costs.

Vander May worked closely with the Finance Department on price negotiations with suppliers, to monitor the effect on margins and determine the need for new selling prices. Vander May and the Purchasing Department met weekly to discuss ways to reduce costs. Supply contracts were typically for three months; when imported materials were involved, they were generally for one month because of possible exchange rate fluctuations. "All contracts were open to negotiation, and suppliers usually did not guarantee a price," Vander May added. Colgate often bundled credit terms with prices in the total package offered suppliers. The largest supplier, Pemex, the state-owned petroleum company, demanded payment in twenty-four hours on certain products.

Negotiations and purchasing contracts for imported and domestic materials were based on the less volatile government-controlled exchange rate rather than the free-market rate, which fluctuated daily. Many of the company's imported materials waited on the U.S. side of the border for import documentation needed to purchase controlled-rate dollars. The free market rate was used to purchase dollars for dividend remittances. The controlled rate was used to buy raw materials and pay royalties. The government estimated that 80% of all dollar-based transactions in Mexico occurred at the controlled rate.

Vander May explained purchasing options: "Though there is alternative sourcing, we are not as flexible as we would like. Many of the necessary materials have only a few suppliers. In the case of detergents, because the government owns many of the companies that supply the chemicals we use such as sodium sulfate, we have only one supplier. This makes negotiations somewhat difficult." But, Vander May explained, Colgate-Palmolive did have leverage. In addition to the option of using imported raw materials (which were not necessarily cheaper), Colgate-U.S.'s international purchasing department could help find the best alternative sourcing by combining its worldwide purchasing and competitively bidding on sources. Before Mexico's accession to GATT in 1986, import permits were required and were especially difficult to obtain when sourcing inputs for which local substitutes existed. In 1987 the country was reducing import duties, and permits were easier to obtain and were often not needed.

Of Colgate-Mexico's total product costs, 60% were input costs and just 3.5% were direct labor. Mexico's minimum wage of about $.44 an hour was among the world's lowest (as against $3.35 an hour in the United States). Colgate-Mexico was one of the largest employers in the country, employing 2,130 people directly and 5,000–6,000 people in all. David Stinson, vice president of manufacturing, said, "Because capital expenditures for equipment are almost nonexistent, we have to get more out of the equipment we have." In 1986 the company imported $3–$4 million of equipment for its only plant located in Mexico City. "The government understands that we have to import equipment. Some sophisticated equipment is just not available here," Stinson said.

Colgate's Mexico City plant had been built in 1948 and was relatively antiquated. Unlike new plants, it had much fully depreciated equipment. It employed batch production, not modern continuous flow production processes. It took 180 minutes to switch production from one type of dental cream to another. In total, the company produced about 1,100 tons per day and more than 200 tons per worker in 1986. Management believed that installing significant additional capacity or vertically integrating at the current site in Mexico was unlikely because of government restrictions on expansion.

Finance and Control

Being a wholly owned subsidiary of CP, Colgate-Mexico's main thrust was to develop strong brands by strengthening market share to grow profits gradually, to increase remittances, and to increase CP-shareholder value.

O'Brien explained the rationale for these objectives: "Maximizing market share in the long run allows us to slowly improve profits and remittances. Growing dollar remittances help fulfill CP's need for an adequate return on investment and provide a measure of protection against future devaluation."

Remittances were sent in the form of dividends and royalties; both were tax-deductible in Mexico and subject to withholding tax: royalties at 21% and dividends at 55%. Remittances were subject to a 46% U.S. tax for the parent, yet foreign taxes paid are available for credit.

Royalties were preferred over dividends for remittances because of the lower withholding tax. The Mexican government authorized Colgate-Mexico's royalty payments to CP under an agreement to transfer technology from CP to its subsidiary. In 1986 the company sought to change its technology agreement and increase royalty payments above 2% of sales, which had been in force for many years.

In two months CP's legal and research departments demonstrated the correctness of a move to the 5–7.5% rate paid by its other subsidiaries.

The documentation was presented to the Mexican Transfer of Technology Department. After a few months of review and negotiation, a new contract was signed increasing royalties to either 3% or 5%, depending upon the product.

The new contract also permitted monthly rather than quarterly remittances. The government typically granted royalty contracts for ten-year periods and often requested services to the Mexican economy in return. Such services included improving the local company's technology and balance of payments. Colgate offered to start a program to help Mexican Ph.D. candidates with scholarships. Colgate also became a supporter of the Mexican Development Foundation with, among others, a project to develop Mexican essential oils to substitute imports.

O'Brien noted that financial reporting requirements for subsidiaries of U.S. companies operating in Mexico were extremely complicated. The Mexican subsidiary had to comply with U.S., GAPP, Mexican tax, and corporate management reporting requirements. In 1984, under an IRS allowance, Colgate-U.S. began reporting Colgate-Mexico as a branch rather than a subsidiary for U.S. tax purposes. Foreign branch operations were regarded as part of the parent's own operation, and branch earnings were taxed the year they were earned, regardless of remittances. The benefit to CP was that a branch's foreign exchange translation losses could be written off against U.S. taxes owed for all CP's foreign operations. The result, while not reducing Mexican taxes, was a U.S. tax savings of millions of dollars after restatement of all tax years from inception in 1926.

Colgate-Mexico also had to comply with the financial accounting standards board (FASB) rule no. 52, which established uniform standards for translating foreign-currency-denominated financial statements into dollars for consolidation. FASB-52 required that all foreign currency revenue and expense items be translated at the rate in effect when those items were recognized. Foreign-exchange losses on monetary assets and liabilities were recognized as exchange rates changed. Furthermore, companies could translate the local currency used by a subsidiary (peso at Colgate-Mexico) to the functional currency used in the parent's main economic environment (U.S. dollars at CP).

In nonhyperinflationary countries, translation gains and losses bypassed the parent's income statement and were accumulated in a separate equity account on the parent's balance sheet, typically called "cumulative translation adjustment." In hyperinflationary countries (with cumulative inflation of 100% or more over three years), FASB-52 required that translation effects go directly to profit and loss. The balance sheet of a foreign entity was translated at the rate used to remit dividends. Thus, a subsidiary's profits in a hyperinflationary country were generally converted at the dividend rate as of the balance sheet date.

Colgate-Mexico's borrowing requirements to finance working capital were generally denominated in local currency. But in June 1987 the company entered into a dollar-denominated, six-month loan for $4 million. Athole Stewart, director of finance, explained: "There was a window period where dollar-denominated borrowing looked better because dollar interest rates were much cheaper." This loan was cheaper than local borrowings even including the cost of a controlled-rate hedge contract purchased to protect against devaluations.

Colgate typically borrowed from local banks, which offered better interest rates than the debt markets. The average "long-term" debt in Mexico was six months; and the typical loan was thirty days.

THE NOVEMBER BUDGET MEETING

When Tangney and other members of management reviewed the 1988 budget, they began with a framework of their expectations for the Mexican economic and political situation into early 1988. Though the economy continued to be depressed, they expected moderate 3% growth in demand for Colgate's main products into 1988. Colgate-Mexico had originally estimated an inflation rate of 80% for 1987 but had updated that estimate to 120%. The company also expected interest rates to increase because of a lack of liquidity, and as a government move to compensate for expected inflation and to prevent the likely outflow of capital that a devaluation could produce.

After the stock market crash on October 19, 1987, the Mexican government proposed a recovery plan under which it would participate with brokers to purchase and hold large volumes of stock to increase investor confidence. But just days before Colgate-Mexico's budget meeting, the Mexican government announced that it would not institute any recovery plan and that the year-to-date inflation of 109% had already surpassed the highest annual level in Mexican history. Those announcements, together with two days of sharp stock market declines on November 16 and 17, created a rush by investors to buy dollars. On November 18, after spending between $1 billion and $3 billion to buy pesos in the market (7% to 20% of reserves), the Bank of Mexico announced its decision to withdraw support for the free market pesos, resulting in a 32.8% devaluation in the free market rate. The controlled rate declined only slightly.

Estimates of 1987 inflation, set at 120% before the budget meeting, were raised to 160% at the conclusion of the meeting. The peso's daily devaluation had been governed mainly by the gap between Mexican and American inflation rates. At the end of October Colgate-Mexico had concluded that year-to-date devaluation had in fact not been sufficient to balance the inflation differential, but it had anticipated neither the precise timing nor the magnitude of the November devaluation.

In 1987, because the free and controlled exchange rates were essentially the same, Colgate transacted its business at one exchange rate. But because the free rate devaluation of 32.8% was larger than the controlled rate devaluation of 1.0%, the differential between the free and controlled exchange rates now posed new opportunities and problems for the company. At the end of the budget meeting, Colgate-Mexico management had to assess quickly what should be done, given the previous days' events.

COLGATE-PALMOLIVE IN MEXICO

Exhibit 1
The Mexican Economy

	1960	1970	1980	1981	1982	1983	1984	1985	1986	1987
GDP (1985 prices)	11.7	23.1	43.8	47.2	47	44.5	46.1	47.4	45.7	N/A
Population (millions)	36	51	69	71	73	75	77	78	80	81
GDP per capita (000 pesos, 1985 prices)	391	462	634	665	644	593	599	607	571	N/A
Exchange rate (ps./$)	12.5	12.5	23.3	26.2	96.5	143.9	192.6	371.7	923.5	2,209.7
GDP deflator (1985 = 100)	1.3	1.9	10.2	13	20.9	40.2	63.9	100	174	N/A
Implicit inflation rate (based on GDP deflator)	—	11.7%	34.2%	27.5%	60.8%	92.3%	59.0%	56.5%	74.0%	140.0% (est.)
Real manufacturing wage (1980–82 = 100)	—	69	94	99	100	77	72	72	70	66
Imports as % of GDP	14.6%	9.7%	13.0%	12.9%	10.3%	9.4%	9.6%	10.3%	12.6%	12.6%
Exports as % of GDP	17.0%	7.6%	10.7%	10.4%	15.3%	19.0%	17.4%	15.4%	17.2%	19.7%
Trade balance	(354)	(888)	(3.4)	(3.9)	6.8	13.8	12.9	8.4	4.6	8.4
Government deficit (% of GNP)	—	1.4%	3.1%	6.6%	15.7%	8.1%	7.5%	8.8%	13.9%	9.9% (est.)

SOURCE: All data based on the IMF's 1989 *Yearbook of International Financial Statistics*, pp. 512–15, except for the real manufacturing wage, which is based on *Indicadores Economicos*, published by the Bank of Mexico.

466

Exhibit 2
Colgate-Mexico—Balance Sheet
($000)

	1985	1986	1987
Cash and marketable securities	$ 8,336	$ 8,087	$ 950
Accounts receivable	12,774	14,728	23,006
Inventories	21,574	24,178	24,927
Total prepaid expenses	(2,464)	82	4,130
Total current assets	40,220	47,075	53,013
Total intercompany balances	(512)	13	4,403
Property, plant and equipment			
Land and buildings	1,940	1,940	1,940
Machinery and equipment	42,562	45,921	49,701
Total property, plant and equipment	44,502	47,861	51,641
Depreciation and amortization	19,535	22,531	25,182
Total property, plant and equipment (net)	24,967	25,330	26,459
Miscellaneous investments	4	1	1
Total assets	$64,679	$72,419	$83,876
Short-term debt	0	637	11,120
Long-term debt payable in one year	811	70	5
Accounts payable	9,248	14,576	12,094
Miscellaneous accruals	8,348	5,973	4,090
Total current liabilities	18,407	21,256	27,309
Long-term debt	1,247	18	0
Deferred liabilities	1,863	1,298	1,242
Common stock	26,533	8,409	8,409
Retained earnings	16,629	41,438	46,916
Total stockholders' equity	43,162	49,847	55,325
Total liabilities and stockholders' equity	$64,679	$72,419	$83,876

Exhibit 3
Colgate-Mexico—Income Statement
($000)

	1985	1986	1987
Sales	$217,205	$193,409	$229,474
Cost of sales	151,298	136,902	156,386
Gross profit	65,907	56,507	71,088
Media	9,583	5,817	6,468
Promotion	1,050	980	2,312
Total advertising	10,633	6,797	8,780
Total marketing and selling	4,287	3,614	4,151
Total freight and warehousing	13,095	11,075	11,285
General and administrative	20,546	13,952	26,342
Total operating expenses	47,561	35,438	50,558
Net profit before taxes	18,346	21,069	20,530
Total provision for taxes	11,331	9,908	11,553
Net profit after taxes	7,015	11,161	8,977

Exhibit 4
Consolidated Financial Data of Colgate-Palmolive, P&G, and Unilever
(In $ millions)

	1987	1986	1985	1984	1983
Colgate-Palmolive:					
Sales	5,647	4,985	4,524	4,985	4,855
Net income	54[a]	177	109	72	198
ROE (%)	6.2	18.8	15.7	11.7	14.9
ROC (%)	12.7	11.2	10.2	10.0	11.8
Total assets	3,228	2,846	2,814	2,568	2,664
Procter & Gamble:					
Sales	17,000	15,439	13,552	12,946	12,452
Net income	327	709	635	890	866
ROE (%)	7.5	12.6	12.3	18.4	38.8
ROC (%)	7.5	8.5	9.2	14.1	
Total assets	13,715	13,055	9,683	8,898	8,135
Unilever:					
Sales	29,790	25,368	24,205	18,670	19,410
Net income	1,361	982	748	583	559
ROE (%)	24.8	17.5	16.9	13.6	12.3
ROC (%)	12.2	10.2	9.2	8.6	8.8
Total assets	17,998	20,413	13,521	11,236	11,206

[a]Colgate-Palmolive undertook a major restructuring in 1987. The charge of that restructuring was $150 million after taxes.

SOURCE: Company annual reports.

COLGATE-PALMOLIVE IN MEXICO

Exhibit 5

Household and Personal-Care Products: Competitive Position in Mexico

	Five-Year Average Growth in Tons (1982–86)[b]	Percent of Colgate-Mexico's Sales in 1987	Competitors and Market Share[a]				
			Colgate-Mexico	Procter & Gamble	La Corona	Del Centro	Total
Price-controlled products:		67%	14/48%[c]				
Detergents	(3)	25%	3/22%	4/49%	3/27%		10/ 98%
Hand dishwashing products	6	9%	1/57%	1/42%	1/ 1%		3/100%
Laundry bar products	(9)	1%	3/ 3%	1/ 1%	2/55%		6/ 59%
Toilet soap	(0)	12%	6/32%	3/45%	3/13%		12/ 90%
Dental creams	9	20%	1/90%	1/ 8%			2/ 98%
Nonprice-controlled products:		33%	14/54%[c]				
Powder cleansers	(4)	2%	2/80%				2/ 83%
Liquid all-purpose cleaners	7	4%	2/18%	1/12%			3/ 30%
Fabric softeners	27	8%	1/90%	1/ 1%			2/ 98%
Fine fabric liquid detergents	6	4%	1/90%				1/ 98%
Shampoos	17	9%	3/22%	1/ 1%		3/18%	7/ 41%
Male hair preparations	(1)	1%	2/23%				2/ 23%
Toothbrushes	NA	1%	2/13%				2/ 13%
Baby line	4	3%	1/40%				1/ 40%
All other	NA	1%					

[a]Number of brands/share of market.

[b]Total growth in tons is over the four-year period 1982–86.

[c]An average weighted by the number of shares.

Citibank in Zaïre

Hamilton Meserve, vice president of Citibank, reviewed the latest participation figures in the bank's attempt to raise up to $250 million for the government of Zaïre. By January 1978, after six months' effort, the bank had raised only $149 million. Meserve reported the figure to Dr. Irving Friedman, senior vice president and senior adviser for international operations, who had been a top official in the International Monetary Fund and the World Bank. At Citibank Friedman had final approval authority for all foreign currency exposure. Because of the precedent-setting implication of the Zaïre loan, Friedman had been asked to supervise the project. Previously vice president for Africa, Meserve now worked for Friedman and was responsible for Africa and the Middle East. He commented on the Zaïre project: "We are really encountering severe resistance. The head of the Syndication Department even told me that we are holding a weak credit with little better than a 50-50 chance for a successful offering. He also pointed out to me with concern that the bank had never failed in any previous offering." Friedman was not willing to admit failure: "The stakes are very high with this loan. What's at issue is the whole principle of private bank lending to developing nations. We must get this message across."

Citibank was trying to avoid Zaïre's default on its external debt, which could have a domino effect on Third World lending. The debt at the end of 1975 was estimated to be $2.7 billion, including more than $800 million to private banks. In November 1976 Citibank agreed to make "best efforts" to raise $200–$250 million in new funds if Zaïre was able to reestablish its creditworthiness.

Citibank's substantial loan to Zaïre reflected its strategy of international expansion and increased emphasis on lending to LDCs. International commercial loans formed the main part of its loan portfolio (*Exhibit 1*); international earnings far surpassed domestic ones (*Exhibits 2* and *3*). At the end of 1977, Citibank had $30 billion in overseas loans, of which $11.3 billion were to non-oil-exporting LDCs and $3 billion to oil exporters (*Exhibit 4*).

This case was prepared by Ajit Thakur, MBA '78, under the direction of Associate Professor James E. Austin and Assistant Professor Philip A. Wellons as the basis for class discussion rather than to illustrate either effective or ineffective handling of an administrative situation. Abridged with permission.

The United States had strategic and economic interests in Zaïre: it bordered nine countries and was resource-rich. Gulf Oil was developing offshore oil production; output was expected to reach 1.5 million tons in 1976. About 95% of all U.S. cobalt needs were met with imports, and Zaïre supplied more than 75%. Zaïre also had significant copper reserves and hydroelectric potential being developed by U.S. companies and commercial banks. At the end of 1976 U.S. investment in Zaïre was estimated at $1 billion.

The events preceding Citibank's efforts to hold off Zaïre's default follow.

1973 AND 1974: STRUGGLING FOR NATIONHOOD

Political and Economic Developments

Zairianization. On November 30, 1973, President Mobutu Sese Seko proclaimed a set of measures directed toward Zaïre's economic independence. Plantations still in European hands were to be "Zairianized," as were foreign-owned retail and wholesale houses, construction firms, small factories, and farms. These enterprises were to be distributed to Zaïrians "with the means and the vocation."[1] (Greek, Portuguese, and Belgian businesses that had retained control over the above sectors since independence bore the brunt of Zairianization; most American companies were exempt, for they were covered by the Investment Code of 1969, established to give the private and public sectors incentives.) In the next months 1,500–2,000 foreign-owned enterprises were turned over to Zairians named by the state, who were usually already well off. Compensation over ten years was promised the former owners, but the government made no payments.

The November measures were disruptive to agriculture and commerce. The new owners of small trade and transport operations often liquidated the businesses out of lack of interest or business experience. Major parts of the country's distribution system were demolished. The national road system (largely maintained by Belgian plantation owners) suffered accordingly. Agricultural productivity declined further. The larger trading companies, influenced by the turn of events and the overvalued zaïre (Z1 = US$2 in 1974), turned most of their operations to importing.

---

[1]Crawford Young, "The Portuguese Coup and Zaïre's Southern African Policy," August 9, 1977, mimeo.

The measures became a political liability. The intellectual elite and the general public began openly to resent the "acquirers." The situation flagrantly contradicted the national party's slogan "Serve others, not yourself."[2] (After Mobutu came to power in November 1965, he outlawed all political parties and created a new one, the Mouvement Populaire de la Révolution [MPR].) On December 30, 1974, corrective measures were announced, including the nationalization of "large enterprises" to end abuses by the new owners. Enterprises with turnover of over Z1 million were entrusted to government representatives (délégués généraux). Enterprises under the Investment Code were still exempt. The government also asked "party cadres" to return to the state all businesses taken in their own name. The measures banned foreign bank accounts and property holdings and dismantled the effective but foreign-dominated religious educational network.

Zairianization and nationalization imposed heavy pressures on the banking system. Transitional difficulties and inexperienced management led Zairianized companies into liquidity shortage. They pressed for bank credit, and some state-owned enterprises accumulated excessive debt. Pressured to finance also the government deficit, the Bank of Zaïre abolished credit ceilings, introduced the rediscount system, and raised reserve requirements. This gave the banks more autonomy in operations while maintaining mandatory minimums for loans to priority sectors and Zairian-owned enterprises. But, the Bank of Zaïre also let the reserve ratio fall to 23% despite a 40% ratio requirement.

Mobutuism. To enhance this dominance at home and Zaïre's role in the Third World, Mobutu announced several important measures in July 1974: a new official doctrine and constitution, reorganization of the Political Bureau, and creation of a party school. The official doctrine, Mobutuism (the teachings, thoughts, and actions of Mobutu), was to be spread by high party officials. The measures gave Mobutu full, direct control of most of Zaïre's major institutions. Mobutu also attempted to integrate the military into MPR and tried to keep Zaïre in the forefront of efforts to resolve the Angolan crisis.

While these political reforms were being made, serious economic pressures due to international price instability and accelerated government spending were accumulating.

Price Increases. Increases in copper prices led to increased foreign-exchange earnings. Prices reached a high in December 1973 and ap-

---

[2]David J. Gould, "The Role of Dependent Public Administration in Underdevelopment and Its Impact on Decision-Making and Administrative Reform in Local Zairian Administration," *African Studies Association Paper* (presented at the Nineteenth Annual Meeting of the African Studies Association, Boston, November 1976), p. 23.

proached a record high in April 1974. (As copper prices increased, major copper users tried to develop substitutes, e.g., glass fiber for copper coaxial cable.) But Zaïre's balance on current account still remained in deficit (*Exhibit 5*). The 1973 deficit was $279.3 million. In 1974 it jumped to $471.7 million because of a sharp increase in import prices. Zaïre's oil bill increased from $36 million in 1972 to $140 million in 1974 as oil prices rose to $13.63 per barrel. Rising prices caused the food import bill to more than double from 1972 to 1974. Before independence, Zaïre had been a net food exporter.

Government Budgetary Expansion. Expenditures continued to surpass revenues in 1974. Budgetary receipts, largely from copper, rose to Z539 million in 1974 (*Exhibit 6*) but were offset by government current expenditures. Overspending and disregard of the budget were common in almost all departments. A complete breakdown of the budgetary control mechanism in 1974 made it impossible to restrict expenditure. Government investment expenditures also rose from $170 million in 1973 to $280 million in 1974. Investment was mainly in Kinshasa-Bas Zaïre and Shaba province (mining and mineral processing).

Citibank's Exposure

As Zaïre's financial needs grew, Citibank noted its huge mineral wealth and followed other private banks into the country. In 1971 Citicorp's chairman, Walter Wriston, had set a 15% annual earnings growth target for the next five years. With flat U.S. markets and wide margins in LDC lending, Citibank expanded abroad; by 1971 its branch network gave it an edge in competing for business from multinationals. Although several U.S. banks had arranged loans earlier, Citibank led in 1972. In the next two years, Citibank and its Paris and London affiliates helped arrange loans to Zaïre of $164 million (59% of all borrowing). Few banks at that time rigorously analyzed the risk of lending to countries. At first, Zaïre's low debt-service ratio, spreads of 1 ¾ % (when other LDCs paid 1% and lower), and IMF and World Bank assistance in framing economic policy made Zaïre attractive. Citibank opened an office in Kinshasa, becoming the second foreign bank with a branch in Zaïre. By the end of 1974 Citibank had outstanding loans of $18 million to Zaïre. In total, commercial banks had made $123 million in unguaranteed loans and $200 million in U.S. government-guaranteed loans to Zaïre. The U.S. Export-Import Bank (Ex-Im Bank; an agency of the U.S. government) held $200 million in loans to Zaïre. The U.S. State Department encouraged these loans.

1975 AND 1976: THE CRISIS YEARS

Balance of Payments

As Zaïre's balance of payments deteriorated, the government limited imports of merchandise and services, freely issued import licenses for essential items (food, pharmaceuticals, raw materials, and spare parts), and required Central Bank approval for nonessential items. It limited the number of importers of food and pharmaceuticals and suspended the transfer of salaries, rent, and revenues, except for the profits of enterprises under the Investment Code. Scarcity of foreign exchange led to a lack of spare parts and raw materials. Real GNP stagnated (*Exhibit 7*).

Copper export revenues deteriorated (*Exhibit 8*). Copper production declined from 471,000 tons in 1974 to 463,000 tons in 1975 and 410,000 tons in 1976 through lack of imported spare parts and motor fuel and the closing of the Benguela railway. The drop in copper prices aggravated the situation. The countries of CIPEC (Intergovernmental Council of Copper-Exporting Countries), of which Zaïre was a member, could not agree on copper prices because of varying production costs and cash needs.[3]

The Angolan civil war exacerbated the balance of payments deficit. As a November deadline for Angolan independence approached, there were bloody encounters between the Frente Nacional de Libertaçao de Angola (FNLA), which Mobutu favored, and the Movimento Popular de Libertaçao de Angola (MPLA)). As Portuguese authority collapsed, Russia sent the MPLA supplies and personnel, and the United States increased its support to the FNLA through Zaïre. Zaïre gave air logistical support and several thousand troops to the FNLA. But in November the influx of Soviet weapons increased, and the MPLA, supported by Cuban troops, routed the FNLA and Zairian forces. Early in 1976 the U.S. Congress prohibited further funds for military purposes in Angola.

Zaïre's involvement in the Angolan war was disastrous; its army was humiliated and its regime discredited. Chinese and North Korean ties diminished until Zaïre could expect no diplomatic or economic assistance from those countries and was, instead, more dependent on the West. But the biggest blow was loss of the Benguela railway, Zaïre's main export route to the coast (56.6% of all copper tonnage followed this route in 1974). Alternative routes through independent African territory either had limited capacity or were more costly and slower. In February 1976 Zaïre normalized relations with the MPLA. Interest payments as a percentage of GNP had risen from 0.5% in 1971 to 2.2% in 1974, and were

[3]*Business Week,* June 5, 1978, p. 69.

still rising. International reserves as a percentage of disbursed external public debt had fallen from 41.5% in 1971 to 3.5% in 1975.

Public Finance

During 1975 Zaïre's debt increased to about $1.7 billion from $1.3 billion in 1974. The government's ambitious development programs were partly responsible for the country's external debts. There were several huge construction projects. Phase two of the Inga Dam, estimated at $250 million, had doubled in cost; the Inga-Shaba high-tension power line experienced massive overruns on a $350-million estimate. The government also financed 12 multimillion-dollar cargo ships for the Zairian shipping line, DC-10s for Air Zaïre, an ambitious airport construction and improvement program, and a steel mill of dubious profitability. As revenues failed to cover these capital expenditures plus government's current expenditures, Zaïre increasingly turned to external financing from governments and private creditors.

The government introduced new measures in March 1975 to curb expenditures. Through quarterly budget allocation and a monthly treasury plan, the Finance Ministry would reduce expenditures. But the management of public finance was not improved: Budgeting procedures remained unchanged, policy was not coherent, and implementation was unsystematic and entirely flexible. Government departments continued to overrun budgets; the minister of finance continued to authorize expenditures outside his area of responsibility. A revenue shortfall occurred when Gécamines failed to meet its tax liability because of lower copper exports and higher wages.

Money supply in 1975 continued to rise. Foreign-exchange reserves absorbed most of the increase in credit to the economy. To restrict credit expansion to the private sector, the Bank of Zaïre raised the reserve requirement to 45% in June 1975. But by June 1976 the price index had jumped by 85%.

As Zaïre moved through crises, Mobutu strengthened his position by maintaining direct personal control of the military. He quelled a coup against him and expelled the U.S. ambassador in 1976, accusing him and the CIA of supporting the plot against him. Observers suggested it was a device to wrest greater support from the U.S. government.

Signs of Default

As Zaïre's financial crisis deepened, the country became unable to service its external debt. Interest payments slackened; many private (commercial) banks stopped receiving them altogether. By 1975, 98 banks worldwide held Zairian debts of about $887 million. Private banks from the United States, Europe, and Japan each held about a third of the total. The unguaranteed part of the debt was $500 million, of which U.S. banks held $162 million. About 10% of this was to be repaid or rolled over in the first half of 1976. Citibank and others asked about their loans but received no replies. "Normally, when a country is having payment problems, it contacts the banks a good six months before default," said one banker. "But Zaïre just wasn't talking."[4] Zaïre paid Belgian and French banks and others that were most insistent.

Zaïre fell behind also on payments due official lenders. By 1975 Zaïre owed foreign governments about $797 million, of which about $270 million in direct loans was held by the Ex-Im Bank and the U.S. Agency for International Development or had come through the U.S. commodity aid program.

HEADING OFF DEFAULT

In early 1975 the Zairian government asked Citibank's Friedman to bring it together with all private creditors. Fearing such a meeting might result in creditors' calling a default, he declined but recommended that Mobutu invite an IMF mission to negotiate a stabilization program and an IMF standby credit. Friedman believed that the solution lay in Mobutu's acceptance of the IMF's conditional loan.

The Stabilization Program

Despite Mobutu's declaration upon taking power in 1965 that the IMF would never again enter the country and impose restrictions, Zaïre adopted the IMF program in March 1976, purchasing $48 million in foreign exchange from the Fund under the enlarged first credit tranche. (Drawing on the first tranche is accompanied by the IMF's economic monitoring; compliance with IMF recommendations is not required, only the government's best effort. For later drawings compliance is mandatory and often involves exchange rate adjustments.) The program's main objectives were to limit growth of domestic demand, improve the balance of payments, and stimulate domestic production. Zaïre set up a stabilization committee to monitor implementation of this one-year program.

[4]Nancy Belliveau, "Heading Off Zaïre's Default," *Institutional Investor* (International Edition), March 1977, p. 23.

Budget and credit controls were instituted to dampen the growth of domestic demand. Budget restrictions were to hold expenditures at Z615 million by limiting wage increases to 20% and slashing capital expenditures to Z144 million. The current budget was Z471 million. Zaïre moved from only indirect credit controls back to credit ceilings (higher for priority sectors). Credit to a company with negative working capital required Central Bank authorization. Indirect control measures (interest rate structure and reserve requirements) also remained in force.

To improve the balance of payments, the government depreciated the zaïre, pegged it to Special Drawing Rights (SDR) (Z1 = SDR1 = $1.15 at the time), and introduced additional import controls. Through direct import controls, it allocated foreign exchange to enterprises and required a 10% deposit on export proceeds to safeguard debt service. Indirect controls usually required a 100% deposit from importers; food and pharmaceutical imports required only 50%; and raw materials and spare parts, no deposit. This control was not completely effective, however, since essential spare parts, raw materials, and pharmaceuticals remained scarce while food for wealthy consumers was abundant.

The government sought to stimulate productivity by increasing producer prices and the availability of imported raw materials and spare parts, and clarifying issues of the ownership and management of enterprises. It raised producer prices for coffee (74%), maize (60%), tea leaves (200%), palm fruit (100%), rice (50%), seed cotton (150%), and cattle (300%) and retail prices for petroleum products, water, electricity for homes, and some mass consumption products. Under "deradicalization" measures to encourage the return of foreign entrepreneurs, certain Zairianized businesses were entirely returned to former owners. In other cases, the government offered former owners 40% ownership. "Délégués généraux" were replaced by Europeans or retained only as members of mainly European management committees.[5]

Zaïre also announced that it would seek debt rescheduling from its creditors. The objectives were to (1) renegotiate outstanding loans to limit the debt-service ratio to 13%; (2) obtain loans for productive purposes and to aid the balance of payments; (3) cancel nonpriority loans; (4) reexamine medium-term investment policy; and (5) open a special account for servicing external debt.

Finally, helped by the World Bank, the government in September 1976 set up a Public Debt Management Office to help develop borrowing policies and to police debt servicing. It was directly responsible for recording and servicing all debt contracted or guaranteed by the government or by public corporations.

---

[5]Gould, "The Role," p. 24.

Enter the Paris Club

After the debt-rescheduling policy was set in the stabilization program, the Paris Club met in June 1976 to consider rescheduling Zaïre's official debt. (The World Bank had already refused to reschedule the debt and invoked an arrangement with Zaïre giving it preferred creditor status.) An informal group of government officials from major lending nations, the Club met whenever an LDC had trouble paying its debt to evaluate each request for debt rescheduling. The group for Zaïre included the United States, Canada, Japan, West Germany, France, Italy, Britain, Belgium, the Netherlands, Sweden, and Switzerland.

An April 1976 consolidation agreement between Zaïre and the Paris Club called for rescheduling 85% of principal and interest in arrears as of June 30, 1976, and 85% of principal payments due in the second half of 1976 and in 1977. Under the agreement, 85% of the debt owed or guaranteed by Zaïre in 1975–76 would be postponed for three years, then stretched over the next seven years. Although U.S. Treasury representatives wanted more information on Zaïre's finances and urged the imposition of conditions, the French, supported by the U.S. State Department, pushed unconditional rescheduling through in a day. The Paris agreement merely stated principles by which each creditor government would individually settle with Zaïre. Zaïre agreed to pay on July 1, 1976, the remaining 15% due from 1975 to June 1976 but then failed to make the payment. The agreement did not cover Zaïre's debt to private banks, although as usual Zaïre promised to adjust commercial debt "on a comparable basis."[6] About the Paris Club accord, Meserve commented, "This turned out to be our biggest albatross."

Enter the Private Banks

Zaïre was almost a year behind in payments to private banks before they did anything. Lacking experience in cooperating, they acted only at the Bank of England's prodding, which was prompted in turn by the Paris Club agreement. In London in June 1976, 13 agent banks representing 98 creditor banks in 13 different syndicates met to discuss Zaïre's default. Falling into three loose groups, one led by Citicorp, they accomplished nothing then or for the next four months. As one participant put it, "There was a great deal of vacillation among the banks about how to approach Zaïre. No one bank wanted to be singled out as the arm twister."[7]

[6] *Washington Post,* April 24, 1977, p. 22.

[7] Belliveau, "Heading Off," p. 23. All quotes in this section and the next are drawn from Belliveau, pp. 24–25.

In August 1976 Citibank sued the Ex-Im Bank and Manufacturers Hanover Trust, claiming they sought preferential treatment by Zaïre. The suit concerned a new $68-million loan the Ex-Im Bank made to finance additional costs of the Inga-Shaba electric power project. (Ex-Im Bank had loaned $120.2 million for this project in 1973, and private banks, about $200 million.) For the $68-million loan, Ex-Im Bank required that Zaïre set up an account abroad to receive foreign exchange from copper exports and to service new and old Ex-Im Bank loans for the project; to Citibank, this covenant amounted to preferential treatment. Citibank and ten other banks had loaned Zaïre $50 million in 1972 under an agreement requiring that no other external debt of Zaïre be treated more favorably than the $50-million loan. In October 1976 Ex-Im Bank withdrew its demands for the old loan and Citibank dropped its lawsuit.

The lawsuit made the bankers cooperate and request a meeting with Zairian officials. The banks also learned that if they did not contest the Ex-Im Bank convenants, Zaïre intended to treat its private debt on the same terms as its government debt.

Secret meetings in September 1976 between the 13 banks and Zairian officials led by Governor Sambwa of the Zaïre Central Bank were not fruitful. Trying to outdo a political rival (who had negotiated the rescheduling agreement with the Paris Club two months earlier), Governor Sambwa demanded that all private debt be rescheduled over fifteen years. His stance swayed most bankers toward rescheduling. "Everyone was resigned to a rescheduling or refinancing," recalled one banker. (Refinancing replaces current debt with a new loan; rescheduling stretches out maturities on existing loans.) "We felt we had to agree to the Paris Club approach because we could see no way of avoiding it." But Citibank refused rescheduling without more data on Zaïre's actual debt and economy. The government had no statistics on its actual debt to the banks. Friedman later recalled that "the difficulty was that the first knee-jerk reaction of the bankers was to reschedule. We said, 'Let's make Zaïre creditworthy and then let the banks individually decide what to do in the future.'" The banks did not reach agreement then with the Zairian government but did set up two subcommittees, one to review economic prospects and balance of payment statistics and the other to project Zaïre's external debt and debt-servicing requirements for the next seven to eight years.

Consensus eluded the bankers when they met again on October 5, 1976. They were concerned not so much about Zaïre's actual debt amount but about bunched maturities, 60% of which were due by the end of 1978. Morgan Guaranty Trust urged a five- or six-year refinancing of Zaïre's private debt with "a new loan of $225 million to retire the old debt." One banker thought refinancing was suggested "because it is legally simpler than a rescheduling and is viewed by some lenders as less damaging to a country's image." Most supported this view.

Citibank's Counterproposal

Believing that both refinancing and rescheduling should be avoided, Citibank suggested that major private lenders supply up to $300 million in short-term credit for purchase of equipment to revitalize Zaïre's productive capacity, but only after the country got current on its arrears and instituted fiscal reforms. Zaïre could then "use its scarce cash resources to continue paying us back and get their house in order. We wanted to keep the pressure on Zaïre and control the use of funds." Citibank dismissed refinancing because once it was agreed to, drawdowns would be virtually uncontrolled. The bankers "decided to give Citibank a chance to see if their solution would stick." But they were dubious and put refinancing to their syndicates for approval as a fallback position. One banker explained that the bankers' meeting had been very theoretical in nature, because no one knew what the Zairians would be responsive to.

Citibank was secretly working hard to get Zaïre to accept its plan. The bank got involved because inadequate solutions were being devised without its participation. "Perhaps we should not have taken such a strong lead," said Citibank's Costanzo. "But things were drifting. And we had to step in."

Events reached a climax at the banks' October 21 meeting in New York. Attending formally for the first time, Friedman said he had recently approached Governor Sambwa informally and persuaded him to accept Citibank's plan. Friedman's key argument to the governor was that Zaïre would eventually have to go to the private market for capital. Therefore, preserving Zaïre's creditworthiness was critical. Citibank would make its "best effort" to raise $250 million in short-term import credit if Zaïre paid its arrears and applied for the second and third IMF tranches. This disclosure angered the bankers, for at the October 5 meeting they had agreed not to present any proposals to the Zairians. "The bankers felt double-crossed by Friedman," recalled one banker. "He'd kept his colleagues busy working on one set of proposals while he went directly to the Zairians with another." Friedman answered that Governor Sambwa would be in New York the next day, and quick decisions needed to be made.

In less than a month, a Memorandum of Understanding (not legally binding) to reestablish Zaïre's creditworthiness in international financial markets was signed by the government and the 13 agent banks. Citibank had persuaded the Zairians to give up the demand for a fifteen-year rescheduling, and the other 12 agent banks to go along with the plan and not to call Zaïre into default. The agreement, signed in London on November 5, 1976, provided that Zaïre would (1) pay all outstanding interest (about $40 million) on its medium-term syndicated bank debt before the end of November; (2) begin negotiations with the IMF and become eligible to draw under the higher IMF tranches by April 1, 1977; (3) start making provision for the payment of arrears of principal (about $50 million) on its medium-term syndicated bank debt by the end of February; and (4) not suffer any "material adverse change" in its international credit standing.

Governor Sambwa insisted that the principal be paid into a special blocked account. This amount would be released to the banks when Citibank, as part of the understanding, produced written commitment for the $250 million in new *medium-term* credit on a "best efforts" basis.[8] The new credit would be phased in quarterly over a year to open dollar letters of credit (LCs) for essential imports. The six-month revolving LCs would be available for up to five years, conditional on Zaïre's continued compliance with the Memorandum of Understanding. Banks in Zaïre and in the syndicate would maintain standard correspondent relationships, but after all money was drawn upon, syndicate members would shift new debt among themselves based on each bank's commitment to the loan of $250 million. By the end of 1976 Zaïre began payments according to the November agreement: $4.5 million in back interest to Citibank and $46.5 million to other banks.

Citibank's Rationale

Citibank's proposal stemmed not from its own Zairian exposure but from the general role of private banks in development financing. About 80% of Citibank's loans to Zaïre were guaranteed through the Ex-Im Bank; only about $28 million were at stake in the negotiations. The main thing, according to Friedman, was that "as private lenders, our only view can be that we get paid and paid on time. We haven't figured out any other way to run a private bank." Speaking of rescheduling, he said that "it does not affect a country's creditworthiness."[9] Although it is often viewed as a positive method of development assistance, he said that setting a precedent of rescheduling debt for a government already in default could have undesirable ripple effects.

---

[8]Anthony B. Greayer and W. John N. Moore, "Zaïre Promises to Do Better," *Euromoney,* December 1976, p. 114.
[9]Belliveau, "Heading Off," p. 25.

Citibank's plan also reflected the bank's views on lending to developing countries. "There is a genuine feeling that this may be a new way to deal with the developing world."[10] "Sure, we could have rescheduled," said Costanzo, "but if we did that, Zaïre would lose access to the private [capital] markets for years. . . . And Zaïre needs private financing to develop its tremendous resources . . . today if a country loses access to the international capital markets, it loses its economic growth."[11] Under Citibank's plan, then, Zaïre would avoid an admission of bankruptcy. Friedman admitted the plan was a test of whether LDCs can manage private debt requirements. Meserve added that if Zaïre treated private debt like public, "it would blow Citibank right out of LDC lending because of the scrutiny of the comptroller of the currency and of shareholders. Our stock price had already dropped from $50 to $25, and the Street was telling us that LDC lending was dangerous."

Citibank believed it could help Zaïre back on its feet. Lacking good balance-of-payment statistics, it estimated Zaïre's trade surplus to be about $150 million. Gécamines, the Central Bank, and individuals each controlled about a third of the foreign exchange; there was sufficient foreign-exchange flow to repay debt if Zaïre's foreign exchange surrender and allocation system was shaken up enough. Friedman, therefore, felt that other banks had to be moved away from the approach of recouping losses.

Other Banks' Reactions

Despite negative reactions, the other banks ultimately agreed to the Citibank proposal. To some, the blocked account and the $250 million in medium-term financing appeared to be a disguised refinancing or rescheduling. "The bankers are lending out of one pocket and getting paid back in another," one banker said. "We won't know if the Citibank deal is a success for three or four months, and we may have lost valuable time in helping Zaïre with its problems. If Citi's plan is to succeed, there has to be a net increase in our exposure to Zaïre, and no one wants to do that right now." The syndicate chief of one major New York bank added that if some unsophisticated banks among the 98 did not cooperate and "major lenders refuse to make up the difference by increasing their own exposure to Zaïre, Citibank might well come up short of its $250 million." Said an-

[10]Paul Strauss and Christian Hemain, "The LDC Watch: How Bankers View the Trouble Spots," *Institutional Investor,* September 1977, p. 54.
[11]Belliveau, "Heading Off," p. 28.

other, "Every single bank in the world is hanging back, hoping someone else will step up." Some doubted that Zaïre would regain creditworthiness in the time suggested by Friedman. "The Zairois might feel they made all those sacrifices for nothing. They've been able to demonstrate to the world that they could successfully negotiate a deal whereby they are once again creditworthy. And if they are still unable to raise new money, they could turn out to be more intransigent negotiators the second time around. The best that could happen would be to go back to a straight refinancing."[12]

The IMF Role

Given Zaïre's problems, private banks wanted the IMF involved early in its financing and administration. They couldn't "see the commercial banking system alone continuing to increase its loans to LDCs at the same rate as they have in the past. We want the IMF to come in and do what we can no longer do because we don't have the lending power."[13] Others felt that early IMF intervention could have brought order into a messy situation. "It should have been the catalyst for bringing together the creditors, so that the rescheduling that the public sector creditors came up with made sense with what the private creditors came up with, instead of the way it actually turned out—all the debt negotiations being done piece-meal with the different parties." Private banks also wanted the IMF to give them current, complete data on member countries, perhaps even sharing country analyses with them.

The IMF did not agree with the banks on these issues. The IMF's involvement in a country was complicated. The IMF standby was voluntary; it was the country's decision to borrow in higher tranches. A staffer indicated that while early involvement was desirable, "when you've got a Mobutu who has political objectives, who wants to arm himself, he doesn't listen until he hasn't got the money." According to IMF's deputy managing director, "Countries have to face up to the realities of situations themselves. They've got to take political responsibility. What we can do is sit down and figure out a feasible program for them, but they've got to want it for it to be doable." The IMF found it could not cooperate as closely with the private banks regarding information on countries. Yet the private banks resisted lending without having information that they believed only the IMF could obtain.

[12]*Ibid.*, pp. 26–28.

[13]All quotes in this section are drawn from Cary Reich, "Why the IMF Shuns a 'Super' Role," *Institutional Investor*, September 1977, pp. 36, 39–40.

1977: ESTABLISHING CREDITWORTHINESS

In 1977 Zaïre began negotiations with the IMF to draw higher credit tranches. Having drawn the first tranche in November 1976, it conducted new negotiations as part of the November agreement with the private banks to get the new $250-million loan. At Mobutu's invitation, an IMF mission visited Zaïre in December 1976 and in February 1977.

In March Mobutu formally laid out the year's economic and financial programs in keeping with IMF's requirements, and the IMF agreed to a $52.2 million second tranche and partial third tranche from its standby arrangement and a $32.8 million loan. The programs' objectives were to improve the balance of payments and achieve internal financial self-discipline and domestic austerity.

Economic Programs and Political Events

Balance of Payments. Stricter foreign-exchange allocation and a change in the import portfolio were to increase the balance of payments. The planned deficit was Z55 million.[14] In March the government established a Foreign Exchange Committee, comprising OGEDEP, the Department of Finance, the new Department of Planning, and the Bank of Zaïre, to supervise foreign-exchange allocation and restrict governmental foreign-exchange demands for nonessentials. The government annulled the import deposit requirements of 1976 but planned to limit imports to essential consumer items, raw materials, and supplies.

Public Finance. The government planned to reduce the budget deficit by raising revenues and further curbing expenditures. Revenues were to be raised to Z674 million in 1977 through new taxes and increased exports of coffee and crude oil (at Z0.65/kg and Z4/barrel, respectively). Coffee was important in Zaïre's export portfolio; its prices had risen from $0.72/lb. in 1975 to $2.29/lb. in 1977. Excise taxes on some beverages were also raised. Expenditures were to be reduced to a total of Z834 million through a wage freeze, further slashing of nonpriority capital expenditures to Z158 million, and limitation of current expenditures.[15] Each government body was to work out quarterly budgets with the Department of Planning; all payment orders were to be authorized by the state commissioner for finance.

---

[14]*Quarterly Economic Review of Zaïre, Rwanda, Burundi* (hereafter *QER of Zaïre*), 3d quarter 1977, p. 9.

[15]*Ibid.*

New monetary and credit measures were to reduce inflation to 30% in 1977. Interest rates were to be liberalized to account for risk and inflation for nearly all credit applications; agricultural and small-business loans were to have a preferred rate. By centralizing all arrears, the Bank of Zaïre would tighten all banks' liquidity positions and thus limit bank credit to Z290 million.[16]

Political Situation. The new year saw Zaïre establish full diplomatic relations with Angola. Zaïre anticipated the reopening of the Benguela railway, ensuring faster, cheaper transportation of its copper. Since the railway's closing, Zaïre had lost copper sales of $80 million and incurred additional transportation expenses.[17]

In March, soon after the IMF's visit, Zaïre found itself fighting rebels occupying areas of Shaba province (formerly Katanga). The government forces and administration demonstrated their weaknesses. Claiming responsibility for the rebellion was the Congo National Liberation Front (FLNC), a revolutionary movement formed in 1975, "working closely with the masses to replace the Mobutu regime with a new social order."[18] Its leader, General Nathaniel M'Bumba, said, "We want new men, not old burnt-out rulers," adding that he would accept no mediation with the Mobutu government, "whose whole team will be liquidated." The FLNC did not wish to damage the copper installations.[19] (Concern about possible threats to copper supplies in Shaba had provoked a small rise in the London Metal Exchange's price for copper.)

A number of allies came to Mobutu's defense. The United States conducted an emergency airlift of military and medical supplies; France and Morocco sent troops. Toward the end of May, after less than three months, the insurgents were routed. Diplomatic sources said then that resolving the situation hinged partly on improving Zaïre's relations with Angola, or "this kind of incursion will happen again."[20]

On July 1, 1977, in a speech to MPR officials and the diplomatic corps, Mobutu announced a political reform and reorganization plan, and his own nomination as armed forces head. Admitting a crisis in Mobutuism, he said he intended to democratize the political structure, including the Office of the President. (But presidential elections were held in December; unopposed, Mobutu was reelected for another seven-year term.) He created a Ministry of Rural Development and a Court of Accounts for administrative control of governments and agencies.

---

[16]*QER of Zaïre,* 2d quarter 1977 and Annual Supplement 1977.

[17]*Ibid.,* 2d quarter 1977, p. 7.

[18]Galen Hull, "Internationalizing the Shaba Conflict," *African Report,* July–August 1977, p. 4.

[19]*Financial Times,* April 13, 1977, p. 7; *QER of Zaïre,* 2d quarter 1977, p. 6.

[20]*African Report,* July–August 1977, p. 30.

In August Mobutu further reshuffled his government, jailing several high-ranking military officers and dismissing Governor Sambwa, the bankers' access to Mobutu. Sambwa was replaced by the finance minister, who, at the Paris meeting, had won rescheduling concessions on the debt held by foreign governments.

National Recovery Plan. On November 26, 1977, Mobutu detailed a "national recovery plan." Economic management would be improved, productivity of basic foodstuff and agricultural exports (coffee, tea, cocoa, rubber, and wood) would be increased, rural living conditions improved, and employment created through labor-intensive industries.[21]

Mobutu also denounced widespread corruption. "Holding any slice of public power constitutes a veritable exchange instrument, convertible into illicit acquisition of money or other goods or the evasion of all sorts of obligations. . . . Our society risks losing its political character, to become one vast marketplace, ruled by the basest laws of traffic and exploitation."[22] The fiscal drain of corruption significantly impeded recovery. For example, soaring coffee prices in 1976 should have brought Z272 million in foreign exchange, but only Z80 million entered because of fraudulent trading transactions by firms related to the regime. The removal of Governor Sambwa was allegedly partly related to Central Bank efforts to stop these foreign-exchange diversions. A complicating factor was that several of Mobutu's relatives heading government agencies were above Mobutu in the tribal hierarchy.

With Zaïre's new plans and the IMF agreement, Citibank renewed its efforts to raise the additional capital. It had to decide which banks to approach and what arguments to use to persuade them to participate. *Exhibit 9* lists the current lenders' situation.

---

[21]*QER of Zaïre,* 1st quarter 1978, p. 5.

[22]Information in this paragraph is drawn from Crawford Young, "Zaïre: The Unending Crisis," *Foreign Affairs,* 57 (Fall 1978): 172, 174.

CITIBANK IN ZAÏRE

Exhibit 1

Citicorp: Loan Portfolio

(In millions of U.S. dollars)

	Loans Outstanding at Dec. 31, 1977	1977			1976		
		Average Loans	Net Loan Losses	Percent of Losses to Average Loans	Average Loans	Net Loan Losses	Percent of Losses to Average Loans
Commercial loans							
Real estate loans							
Domestic	$ 1,460	$ 1,774	$ 58	3.3%	$ 1,880	$ 65	3.5%
Overseas	1,321	1,325	41	3.1%	1,307	45	3.4%
REIT loans	416	475	18	3.8%	630	20	3.2%
Loans to major multinational corporations	7,752	7,290	—	—	6,557	—	—
Other commercial loans							
Domestic	8,595	7,988	48	.6%	8,460	28	.3%
Overseas[a]	19,197	17,037	35	.2%	13,548	65	.5%
Total commercial	$38,741	$35,889	$200	.6%	$32,382	$223	.7%
Consumer loans worldwide	6,711	5,256	56	1.1%	4,558	68[b]	1.5%
	$45,452	$41,145	$256	.6%	$36,940	$291	.8%

[a]Other commercial loans overseas include loans to the public sector.

[b]Consumer net loan losses in 1976 include approximately $16 million resulting from a change in consumer loan writeoff policy by certain Citicorp subsidiaries.

SOURCE: Citicorp 1977 Annual Report.

488

CITIBANK IN ZAÏRE

Exhibit 2

Citicorp: Operating Earnings After Tax[a]

(In millions of U.S. dollars)

	1977		1976		1975		1974		1973	
United States (excluding U.S. possessions)	$ 68	18%	$112	28%	$102	30%	$120	35%	$102	40%
Asia-Pacific	28	7%	42	10%	56	17%	47	15%	52	20%
Canada and Caribbean	44	12%	36	9%	44	12%	33	11%	27	11%
Europe	96	25%	91	22%	58	17%	58	19%	38	15%
South America	104	27%	81	20%	44	12%	29	9%	20	8%
South Asia, Middle East and Africa	41	11%	43	11%	44	12%	26	8%	16	6%
	$381	100%	$405	100%	$348	100%	$313	100%	$255	100%

[a]Income before securities gains (losses).

SOURCE: Citicorp 1977 Annual Report.

CITIBANK IN ZAÏRE

Exhibit 3

International Earnings Growth of Thirteen Major Banks, 1970–76
(In millions of U.S. dollars)

	1970	1976	% of Total Earnings	Compound Annual Growth Rate 1970–76	Growth 1974–75	Growth 1975–76
Citicorp	$ 58.0	$291.0	72.0	31.0%	26.2%	19.0%
Bank American Corp.	25.0E	134.0	40.0	32.0	66.3	8.0
Chase Manhattan Corp.	30.7	82.0	78.0	18.0	13.5	−19.0
Manuf. Hanover Corp.	11.4	80.0	56.0	39.0	12.7	19.0
J. P. Morgan & Co.	25.5	108.0	53.0	27.0	43.9	−6.0
Bankers Trust NY Corp.	7.8E	37.0	64.0	30.0	7.0	−8.0
Chemical NY Corp.	7.7	41.0	44.0	32.0	41.9	−7.0
First Chicago Corp.	1.2	16.0	17.0	54.0	1,096.7	−56.0
Continental Illinois Corp.	−.1	30.0	23.0	70.0	307.9	88.0
Charter New York Corp.	3.7E	25.0	58.0	38.0	6.4	−7.0
First National Boston Corp.	3.3	28.0	65.0	43.0	36.0	300.0
Wells Fargo & Co.	2.9	8.0	12.0	18.0	28.3	0
Security Pacific Corp.	.2	5.0	7.0	71.0	4.5	−44.0
Total	$177.3	$885.0	49.2	21.0	35.6%	3.9%

SOURCE: Philip Wellons, "The International Banking System and LDC Debt," HBS Case Services 1-378-244.

CITIBANK IN ZAÏRE

Exhibit 4
Citicorp: Overseas Loans at Year End 1977
(In millions of U.S. dollars)

By Domicile of Borrower[a]	Local Currency Loans	Guaranteed Foreign Currency Loans[b]	Other Foreign Currency Loans				Total Loans Overseas
			Due Within 1 Year	Due from 1 to 5 Years	Due after 5 Years	Total	
Industrialized countries	$ 9,777	$N.A.[c]	$1,551	$3,000	$1,019	$ 5,570	$15,347
Centrally planned economies	33	41	44	324	21	389	463
Oil exporters	1,184	329	758	527	191	1,476	2,989
Nonoil-exporting developing countries							
Higher income	2,138	499	2,127	3,314	771	6,212	8,849
Middle income	383	243	689	557	143	1,389	2,015
Lower income	233	94	40	53	1	94	421
	$13,748	$1,206	$5,209	$7,775	$2,146	$15,130	$30,084

[a]Developing countries are categorized using World Bank definitions (minimum of $500 per capita for higher-income countries and from $200 to $499 for middle-income countries). Countries with centrally planned economies, located principally in Eastern Europe, are not members of the World Bank but are grouped separately for information purposes.

[b]Foreign currency guaranteed loans are guaranteed by governments, government agencies, banks, or corporations whose principal domicile is in an industrialized country.

[c]Other foreign currency loans to borrowers domiciled in industrialized countries include more than $1.6 billion guaranteed by a third party.

SOURCE: Citicorp 1977 Annual Report.

Exhibit 5
Zaïre: Balance of Payments
(In millions of U.S. dollars)

	1971	1972	1973	1974	1975
Goods, services & transfers	124.8	−365.4	−279.3	−471.7	−599.5
Exports of merchandise, f.o.b.	696.9	690.3	1,038.3	1,520.7	863.4
Imports of merchandise, f.o.b.	−684.2	−752.1	−977.3	−1,439.3	−993.5
Exports of services	60.1	68.0	92.6	168.9	145.1
Imports of services	−318.2	−377.3	−459.7	−725.3	−668.5
Private unrequited trans. net	−75.0	−71.9	−82.6	−94.8	−62.8
Govt. unrequited trans. net	195.8	77.5	109.3	98.1	116.8
Long-term capital, n.i.e.	34.0	317.5	256.0	258.9	240.8
Direct investment	52.6	104.4	75.8	125.8	37.2
Other government	−42.5	82.1	181.2	168.6	119.4
Other	24.0	130.9	−1.1	−35.5	84.3
Short-term capital, n.i.e.	22.3	16.9	67.2	156.9	182.0
Deposit money banks	4.8	3.8	−9.7	−17.9	38.0
Other	17.5	13.1	76.9	174.9	144.0
Errors and omissions	6.4	13.1	7.6	3.8	44.1
Total	−62.1	−17.9	51.5	−52.0	−132.7
Allocation of SDRs	12.1	13.0	—	—	—
Monetization of gold	.4	.4	.4	−40.6	−10.2
Total	−49.5	−4.5	51.9	−92.6	−142.9
Reserves and related items	49.5	4.5	−51.9	92.6	142.9
Liabilities	1.6	37.7	−8.1	−.4	62.2
Assets	47.9	−33.2	−43.8	93.0	80.7

SOURCE: *International Financial Statistics,* December 1978, IMF, Washington, D.C., p. 410.

Exhibit 6
Zaïre: Government Finances
(In millions of Zaires)

	1971	1972	1973	1974	1975
Flow:					
Deficit (−) or surplus	−75.4	−81.9	−139.5	−326.7	−223.2
Revenue	295.3	305.5	376.7	538.6	431.9
Foreign grants received	34.7	38.7	51.6	53.9	55.4
Expenditure	405.4	426.1	567.8	919.2	710.5
Financing					
Borrowing: Domestic	32.5	31.1	32.3	211.0	118.4
Foreign	44.1	50.7	107.2	115.6	104.8
Stock:					
Foreign liability	1.93	21.85	23.73	33.19	65.87

SOURCE: *International Financial Statistics,* December 1978, IMF, Washington, D.C., p. 410.

CITIBANK IN ZAÏRE

Exhibit 7

Zaïre: National Accounts

(In millions of zaïres)

	1971	1972	1973	1974	1975	1976
Exports	373.7	377.5	561.7	817.2	514.3	932.9
Government consumption	280.6	261.1	306.7	419.6	437.6	528.9
Gross fixed capital formation	299.3	371.3	372.0	551.0	547.5	650.3
Increase in stocks	46.3	15.4	70.0	—	65.3	89.8
Private consumption	505.4	629.2	826.7	1,003.4	1,102.0	1,798.9
Less: imports	−467.3	−521.7	−645.5	−937.4	−737.3	−1,093.4
Gross domestic product	1,038.0	1,132.8	1,491.6	1,854.0	1,929.4	2,907.4
Less: net factor pymts. abroad	−55.5	−57.5	−75.2	−105.1	−74.4	−78.4
Gross nat'l expenditure = GNP	982.5	1,075.3	1,416.4	1,748.9	1,855.0	2,829.0
Nat'l income, market prices	900.0	971.3	1,285.8	1,594.3	1,661.2	2,189.8
Gross dom. prod. 1975 prices	1,801.1	1,807.0	1,955.2	2,052.8	1,929.4	1,846.6

SOURCE: *International Financial Statistics*, December 1978, IMF, Washington, D.C., p. 410.

CITIBANK IN ZAÏRE

Exhibit 8

Zaïre: International Transactions

	1971	1972	1973	1974	1975	1976	1977 I	1977 II	1977 III
Exports[a]	343.5	345.8	502.0	647.5	413.4	747.3	223.9	228.3	220.3
Copper	207.8	203.1	309.0	429.6	216.5	316.5	91.6	100.4	74.9
Cobalt	23.1	26.8	38.6	35.7	48.4	98.6	26.2	21.9	24.9
Diamonds	16.0	21.4	28.7	31.1	27.6	47.4	9.7	10.8	19.9
Coffee	24.6	28.0	36.3	30.2	27.1	103.1	43.7	45.2	49.7
Imports, c.i.f.	309.5	312.7	377.2	525.5	452.4	546.6	157.1	141.0	128.4
Imports, f.o.b.	262.3	265.0	327.7	455.8	392.0	471.2	135.4	121.6	110.7
Volume of exports[b]									
Copper	75	81	84	79	100	91	59	75	73
Coffee	122	123	112	133	100	179	170	128	47
Copper prices U.S.¢/lb.	NA	NA	80.7	93.2	56.0	63.6	65.5	62.2	54.5

[a]In millions of zaïres.

[b]With 1975 export volume indexed at 100.

SOURCE: *International Financial Statistics*, December 1978, IMF, Washington, D.C., pp. 410–11.

Exhibit 9
International Banks' Exposure by Home Country
(In million of U.S. dollars)

	Outstanding Since 1974	*Cumulative Projected Arrears*[a] *2/78*
Japan	120	44
U.S.	96	57
of which, Citibank	(18)	(12)
France	41	11
Britain	56	13
Canada	30	31
Belgium	15	10
Italy	11	5
Germany	8	2
Netherlands	1	1
Other Countries	3	1

[a]Based on the assumption that Zaïre continues to default in payments.

SOURCE: Citicorp.

International Pharmaceuticals Incorporated

John Smiley, assistant treasurer of International Pharmaceuticals Incorporated (IPI), sat in his Manhattan office after a meeting with representatives of the Morgan Guaranty Trust Company in September 1986. IPI had decided in January 1986 to expand the plant facility of La Compañía de Pildora S.A., a subsidiary based in Mexico City. Traditionally, IPI would have used intercompany trade credit to finance the project. But Morgan suggested that IPI might save as much as $1,580,000 on a $5,000,000 project if it financed the expansion through a debt-for-equity swap. The swap involved buying Mexican government external dollar debt at a discount, redeeming the debt at the Mexican Central Bank for pesos, and investing these pesos in the subsidiary.

As he thought about his decision, Smiley couldn't help recalling what Richard Huber, a group executive at Citibank, had said about these deals: "We think everybody ends up a winner. The country has its total foreign debt reduced. Investment funds are pumped into the economy. And the seller of the debt gets liquidity."[1] Smiley had to decide within the week which form of financing best fitted IPI's needs.

COMPANY BACKGROUND

International Pharmaceuticals Incorporated, founded in 1933, produced a wide array of pharmaceuticals and consumer household products. Incorporated in New York, IPI was the parent company of numerous subsidiaries that manufactured products in 39 countries for worldwide distribution and sale. The company had little leverage, a conservative corporate culture, and centralized financial management. IPI's success over the years was demonstrated in its recent financial statements (*Exhibit 1*).

The corporation was divided into ten domestic and four separate inter-

[1] *New York Times*, September 11, 1986, p. D5.

This case was prepared by Professor W. Carl Kester with the assistance of Richard P. Melnick as the basis for class discussion rather than to illustrate either effective or ineffective handling of an administrative situation. Abridged with permission.

national divisions. IPI had been in Mexico since 1951, where several of its divisions had subsidiaries. La Compañía de Pildora S.A. was a 100%-owned subsidiary that reported to the Rolan International Division. Based in Mexico City, La Compañía de Pildora manufactured oral contraceptives, nutritional products, and veterinary products, all for domestic consumption. Expected sales in 1986 were MP10 billion, or about $10 million.

THE LATIN AMERICAN DEBT PROBLEM

The debt-for-equity swap proposed by Morgan had its roots in the broader Latin American debt problem. This, in turn, had its origin in the 1973 oil shock. After the surge in oil prices, many OPEC nations deposited their dollar surpluses in Western money center banks. This influx of deposits made credit a borrower's market, prompting many major banks to turn to the less developed countries (LDCs) to increase profitability. Banks had lost few loans to the LDCs since the 1930s, loan spreads favored LDCs rather than developed countries, and new funds in the LDCs would support export-oriented growth that began in the 1960s. During the recovery from the 1973 shock, LDC exports rose to the point where, in 1978, current account deficits decreased in borrowing countries.

When the second oil shock hit in 1979, the situation was quite different. Billions of dollars flowed into Western banks, but by this time the LDCs already had multibillion-dollar debts. Most post-1979 borrowing was short term, which contributed substantially to subsequent LDC debt problems. Many LDC government officials believed inflation would increase commodity prices while decreasing real interest rates, thus lowering the cost of their dollar debt. To their dismay, the reverse scenario ensued. While inflation dropped, U.S. interest rates remained relatively high, attracting capital and driving up the dollar's value. Expensive dollar-denominated loans and low commodity prices drove the debt service ratios for average Latin American borrowers to 125% of exports in 1982. This scenario placed enormous pressures on the LDCs, and finally, in 1982, Mexico announced that it could not make its debt service payments.

By 1984 Latin American debt totaled $450 billion. About 15% of this was short-term trade financing, 30% was owed to governments or international organizations, and commercial banks held the remaining 55%. As the problem spread, banks began to search for solutions. Restructuring instead of rescheduling loans might give the LDCs enough flexibility to stimulate their exports. Some analysts recommended increased funding from the IMF or other international agencies, which would then allow a transfer of some debt from private to public sources.

EVOLUTION OF DEBT-FOR-EQUITY SWAPS

While banks searched for solutions to the LDC debt problem, an inter-bank swap market for LDC debt emerged in 1983 as one private-sector means of controlling exposure to LDC debt. Bankers Trust was one of the most active players in this market, executing 12 deals that year. In its largest deal, Bankers Trust traded $90 million in cash and $100 million in Brazilian debt for $190 million in Mexican debt from the Brazilian Banco Real. With this deal, illiquid sovereign credits of international banks began trading in a secondary market. Many incentives stimulated these transactions. One was to increase or decrease exposure to a particular country. Bankers Trust, for example, reduced loans to Brazil by $149 million and increased loans to Mexico by $235 million in the third quarter of 1983. Occasionally banks leveraged down their loans by swapping higher-quality public loans for private paper and cash. These deals also allowed banks to improve their balance sheets by trading up or consolidating positions without taking the write-downs on the loans that Congress and regulators demanded if the loans were actually sold. In addition to Latin American and American banks, Middle Eastern and European banks also put some loans up for swaps. (See *Exhibit 2* for major U.S. banks' exposure to Mexico.)

These deals raised banking, accounting, and regulatory questions. Perhaps the most important issue was valuation. The bank's loan portfolios were accounted for under the assumption that loans would mature at full face value. In 1983 the U.S. comptroller of the currency and the Federal Reserve Board decreed writeoffs for certain loans ranging from 10% to 75%. When a loan was sold or swapped, the difference between historical and market values had to be recorded as a gain or loss. Swaps posed a problem because it was difficult to value an exchange of, say, Chilean for Brazilian debt. If, for example, a bank sold 30% of its Mexican debt at a 20% discount, should that bank have to write down the remaining 70%? Such concerns discouraged banks from doing these deals on a larger scale. Moreover, the interbank swapping of loans only helped individual banks to optimize their portfolios; it did not reduce the overall exposure of the banking system as a whole to LDC debt, nor did it do much to solve the LDC debt problem itself.

A novel idea for tackling the LDC debt problem, and a precursor of the modern debt-for-equity swap, emerged when Congress passed the 1982 Export Trading Companies (ETC) Act. This act gave banks the ability to own equity in export trading companies that took title to goods for resale. Once a bank created an ETC, it could place its outstanding loans to an LDC company in the ETC at par value. In exchange, the ETC would be entitled to receive a percentage of the LDC company's exports, which the

ETC would sell in the United States and the international market. Principal would be repaid from profits from the sales. Yet, because of their complexity and bank inexperience with commodity trading, these deals were never very popular.

In 1983 the Brazilian government established a debt conversion plan in which $1.8 billion was converted into equity invested locally. This plan differed from later developments in other countries in that it was unofficial and only added capital to existing projects. No new projects were stimulated by the plan. By 1984 Brazil terminated this plan, reportedly because it was embarrassed to be dealing in its own debt, which was selling at a deep discount.[2]

THE MODERN DEBT-FOR-EQUITY SWAP PROGRAMS

Debt-for-equity swaps of the type proposed to Smiley were among the most popular deals in 1986. Chile's program appeared to be the most successful (based on the extent to which it was imitated by other LDCs), though Mexico's was the biggest. Mexico's first deal involved the Nissan Motor Company's purchase of $60 million worth of Mexican government debt for $40 million, resale of the debt to the Mexican central bank for $54 million worth of pesos, and the investment of the pesos in its Mexican subsidiary. These capitalization schemes seemed popular with everyone. From the debtor country's perspective, they retired hard currency debts at a discount while promoting local investment. Commercial banks could take some bad loans off their books, while investment banks or commercial banks could earn substantial fees (generally 1% of face value) acting as financial intermediaries in these deals. Multinationals liked them because they could increase their equity stake in the LDCs at greatly reduced cost.

LDC nationals who repatriated flight capital were another group that benefited from these swaps. Residents withdrew significant capital during the early 1980s, and this "flight capital" continued during the 1983–85 period of involuntary lending. Creditors hesitated to lend new funds until debtor nations stopped capital flight. If aggregate foreign assets of residents were repatriated and yielded 6%, the earnings would generate enough foreign exchange to pay the interest on one-third of total LDC external debt.[3] The discount these swaps provided enticed locals, particularly in Chile, to repatriate flight capital.

---

[2]*Institutional Investor,* February 1987, p. 180.

[3]*World Financial Markets,* Morgan Guaranty Trust Company of New York, September 1986, p. 6.

Given that discounts ranged from highs of 55% for Poland and 46% for Mexico to lows of 17% for Colombia and 10% for Romania, the basic plan underlying these deals was straightforward. A financial intermediary acting for a multinational bought LDC debt from a commercial bank (usually U.S. or European) at a discount, paying, say, $.65 on the dollar. After presenting the debt certificate to the LDC central bank for redemption, the intermediary would receive, say, $.85 worth of local currency for each dollar. The central bank, representing the LDC government, retired the debt. The intermediary then had to turn the money over to the multinational that would invest it in the local economy. Though the intermediary could use cash for the initial debt purchase, the intermediary usually started a chain of deals that involved swapping other foreign debt with banks from other countries. Thus, these swaps were seldom as simple and straightforward as they appeared on paper.

The Chilean Program

The rules governing swaps varied from one country to the next. Chile's conversion program was the most active because it had the fewest restrictions and the clearest regulations. By September 1986 Chile had executed 26 swaps totaling $280 million, and Finance Minister Buchi was aiming for $2 billion (10% of Chile's $21 billion debt), by 1987. Richard Huber, Citibank's group executive in charge of Latin American and equity financing, said, "The Chileans have essentially said, 'We don't care much about where the money comes from as long as we can create equity.' "[4] Chile placed a four-year deferral period on dividends for equity that had been converted from debt. After four years, dividends could still be remitted at only 25% of net profits.

The Mexican Program

As of September 1986, Mexico had executed 23 deals worth $300 million and expected to do $1.2 billion more in the next year. A major reason for Mexico's success was that the government dismantled many important obstacles to foreign investment. The regulation of the capitalization plan appeared in Clause 5.11 of the Agreement on the Restructure of the Foreign Debt (*Exhibit 3*). Whereas investors previously had to win approval from various ministries before they could start operating in Mexico, now approval from the ministry of Finance (Hacienda) was sufficient. Mexico usually redeemed debt at 60–70% of face value. The redemption

[4]*Institutional Investor*, February 1987, p. 180.

rate depended upon how the pesos were to be used and the difference between the free and controlled exchange rates (see *Exhibit 4*). The best redemption prices were given for new investments or capital expansions that created jobs and helped the trade balance. Analysts expressed some reservations about these swaps, because the approval process for each deal was often cumbersome and arbitrary.

Nobody saw debt-for-equity swaps as a panacea for the LDC debt problem. Optimists hoped the program could eliminate 15% of the global debt. Shearson Senior Vice President Bindert concluded, "If nearly $50 billion can be done through debt-equity over the next 10–15 years, which could happen if full-scale privatization programs take place, the debt mess could be that much easier."[5]

MEXICO AND THE CLIMATE FOR INVESTMENT

The Mexican peso was devalued in 1954 from MP8.65 to MP12.50 per U.S. dollar and remained at that level until 1976. A combination of confidential bank accounts and political stability in the 1960s maintained the solid peso and led to economic growth. Mexico avoided the currency crises of the early 1970s. At times, the IMF actually used the stable peso to support other major currencies.

Problems began shortly after the discovery of major oil deposits. In 1973 the Foreign Investment Law was passed, which restricted foreign investment and led to reductions in investment and economic expansion. Consumer prices rose 76% in 1970–75 as massive foreign borrowing kept the country solvent. In 1976 the peso was devalued by 43%, prompting capital flight. Mexico abandoned fiscal restraint in 1979 in an effort to expand production and create jobs. With the help of large foreign loans the economy expanded. But in 1981 inflation was out of control, the economy depended upon sagging oil prices, and in 1982 the deficit- and debt-ridden economy collapsed. Massive capital flight emptied the Mexican treasury's foreign-exchange coffers. International banks put together a $10 billion rescue package when Mexico declared a moratorium on foreign debt payments.

Despite Mexico's drastic austerity program and an 80% devaluation of the peso in 1982, the economy's problems continued. By 1986 the central problems facing Mexico were the declining oil industry, a foreign debt that grew from $15 billion to $96 billion in ten years, and rapid (2.5%), population growth. Oil sales, representing 70% of Mexico's export income, dropped by half because of falling oil prices. The devastating

[5]*Ibid.*

Mexico City earthquake of 1985 took 10,000 lives and left 150,000 more people umemployed. Data Resources Inc. said at the start of 1986 that conditions in Mexico "were somewhat similar to [those of] 1962. Now, as then, the foreign sector is in disarray, inflation has escalated rapidly, and the budget deficit has escalated to record levels."[6] Both inflation and interest rates were expected to reach 100% by the end of 1986. Though the peso fell from MP27 per dollar in January 1982 to MP250 per dollar in June 1985 the next twelve months saw it fall even further. By November 1985 the rate was MP500 to the dollar, and in June 1986 the peso fell 30% in six days until it stood at MP727.[7]

As a response to chronic devaluation, the government provided monetary investments that could be used as a hedge. Companies could keep their money in short-term Treasury Certificates (Cetes), which paid close to 100% interest by mid-1986. (See *Exhibits 5* and *6* for Cetes rates and other economic data for Mexico.) Another option was Federation Treasury Bills (Pagafes), created by the government in July 1986. These six-month instruments were denominated in dollars and yielded dollar interest, but were bought and redeemed in pesos using a controlled exchange rate (see *Exhibit 6*).

FINANCING LA COMPAÑÍA DE PILDORA'S PROJECT

By early 1986 La Compañía de Pildora's plant operated at capacity. With demand expected to grow, IPI had the choice of expanding its capacity in Mexico or allowing market share to erode. It eventually decided to expand its facility in Mexico City by building a new floor covering 2,500 square meters and renovating the main floor.

Smiley's responsibility was to determine the best way to finance the project. IPI's traditional means of financing subsidiaries was intercompany trade credit. La Compañía de Pildora would record its purchases as an account payable, and IPI would record the transaction as an account receivable. Although ostensibly short-term, the payable owed the parent could, in fact, remain outstanding until the subsidiary had enough cash to repay IPI. Other alternatives included intercompany dollar debt at prime plus 2% (prime in September 1986 was 7.5%), a revolving credit arrangement (from a foreign or local bank), and straight equity from the parent to be invested as required.

---

[6]*American Banker,* January 9, 1986, p. 2.

[7]The plunge occurred in the "free" exchange rate, which represented only 20% of Mexico's currency transactions. The regulated float rate, used for imports and exports, accounted for the other 80%. This rate was set by the central bank and stood at MP545.70.

As in any subsidiary financing, taxes were also a factor in Smiley's choice of financing methods. The prevailing tax rates were those shown in *Table 1*. Though profitable, La Compañía de Pildora had not remitted a dividend to its parent since 1982.

Table 1

Mexican corporate tax rate	42%
Mexican withholding tax rate on dividends	55%
Mexican withholding tax rate on intercompany loan interest	42%
Mexican withholding tax rate on bank loan interest	15%
Parent tax rate	46%

A Morgan representative recommended that IPI finance La Compañía de Pildora's expansion through a Mexican debt-for-equity swap. With the help of Morgan, La Compañía de Pildora would submit an application to Hacienda to finance the project through the swap. Upon approval of the application (which could be granted if Hacienda were satisfied with La Compañía de Pildora's profit and performance forecasts), IPI would have Morgan purchase $5,700,000 face value of Mexican government debt from a commercial bank at a discount of about 40%, or $3,420,000 net cost. La Compañía de Pildora would present the $5,700,000 debt certificates to the Mexican central bank for redemption at about 88% of the face value or $5,000,000 in pesos, converted at the free rate on that day. The discount the Mexican government offered depended upon the expected contribution of the project to the economy (*Exhibit 4*).

Since the proposed project spanned eighteen months (*Exhibit 7*), the government would set up a deposit for the subsidiary at the central bank. La Compañía de Pildora would submit receipts and pro formas allowing it to draw down the pesos as needed. To offset potential losses from devaluation, the central bank would pay a substantial interest rate on the funds in the account. Money in the account would earn either the Cetes (ie., T-bill) or the Pagafe (i.e., annualized dollar devaluation plus 4%) rate. Once La Compañía de Pildora received the peso payment from the central bank, La Compañía de Pildora had to issue "Qualified Capital Stock" to IPI. The restrictions on Qualified Capital Stock appear in *Exhibit 3*.[8]

---

[8]IPI had two accounting alternatives for this transaction. It could credit $3.42 million from cash, and debit $3.42 million to fixed assets. Or IPI could credit cash $3.42 million, debit fixed assets $5 million, and recognize a $1.58 million gain on the transaction. La Compañía de Pildora would debit $5 million from fixed assets and credit $5 million to Qualified Capital Stock.

Smiley sent a description of this swap to IPI's legal department. Ray Edwards, an IPI lawyer who had studied Latin American problems for twenty-five years, urged Smiley not to undertake the proposed deal. Edwards had two major concerns. First, he feared the Mexican government might renege on the deal. A new government that might not recognize debts of the previous administration could come to power at any time. He thought the program uncertain because it was implemented by an agency of the Mexican government rather than enacted through legislation. The second concern was the sheer complexity of the transaction. Besides IPI and Morgan, other parties such as a foreign creditor bank and a Mexican bank would have to be involved. Ultimately, as many as eight separate parties would have to be signatories to the swap. This complexity is reflected in the schematic shown in *Exhibit 8*.

THE DECISION

The debt-for-equity swap was attractive for many reasons, but especially because of the expected savings of more than a million dollars for IPI. Yet the legal department's concerns and other complicating factors gave Smiley food for thought. He had little time in which to weigh the conflicting advice and decide which financing method to use.

INTERNATIONAL PHARMACEUTICALS INCORPORATED

Exhibit 1

Recent Financial History

($ millions, except ratios and per share data)

	1980	1981	1982	1983	1984	1985
Sales	$2,532.3	$2,754.1	$3,054.7	$3,237.7	$2,990.3	$3,123.1
Operating margin	22.0%	23.1%	23.9%	24.8%	26.4%	26.7%
Depreciation	32.9	35.9	48.5	63.7	62.4	64.5
Net profit	297.3	331.5	386.7	418.1	437.2	478.1
Income tax rate	46.1%	47.4%	45.7%	44.8%	44.2%	40.8%
Common shares outstanding	155.54	155.07	155.86	155.87	152.00	150.89
Earnings per share	$1.91	$2.14	$2.48	$2.68	$2.88	$3.17
Dividends declared per share	1.13	1.27	1.43	1.60	1.76	1.93
Working capital	783.4	892.7	757.5	905.3	959.8	1,075.8
Long-term debt	0	0	0	0	0	0
Net worth	981.9	1,103.0	1,229.1	1,365.9	1,392.4	1,527.9
Net profit margin	11.7%	12.0%	12.7%	12.9%	14.6%	15.3%
% earned net worth	30.3	30.1	31.5	30.6	31.4	31.3
Dividend payout (%)	59.8	59.9	59.8	59.9	62.0	61.7

INTERNATIONAL PHARMACEUTICALS INCORPORATED

Exhibit 2

Major U.S. Banks' Exposure to Mexico in 1985
(Millions of dollars, except ratios)

Bank	Total Assets	Net Worth	Return on Net Worth	Total Loans to Mexico 1985	Mexican Loans/ Total Assets	Mexican Loans/ Net Worth
BankAmerica	118,541	4,547	(7.4%)	2,700	2.3%	59%
Bankers Trust	50,581	2,495	14.9	1,277	2.5	51
Chase Manhattan	87,685	3,795	14.9	1,700	1.9	45
Chemical Bank	56,990	2,820	13.8	1,500	2.6	53
Citicorp	173,597	7,765	12.9	2,800	1.6	36
Manufacturers Hanover	76,526	3,547	11.5	1,800	2.4	51
Morgan Guaranty	69,375	4,392	16.1	1,152	1.7	26

SOURCES: *New York Times*, July 23, 1986, p. D1, and bank annual reports.

Exhibit 3

From Agreement on the Restructure of Foreign Debt (Mexico)

SECTION 5.11.   Capitalization of Credits.   (a) General.   Subject to written agreement between the Obligor and any Bank and subject to all required Mexican governmental authorizations, including authorization by the Ministry of Finance and Public Credit, the National Commission on Foreign Investment and the Ministry of Foreign Relations of the United Mexican States, all or a portion of the Credits held by such Bank may be exchanged for Qualified Capital Stock. The Obligor and such Bank will promptly notify the Servicing Bank in writing of any such agreement that has been so authorized, which notice shall specify each Credit (or portion thereof) to be exchanged for such Qualified Capital Stock. Upon delivery of such Qualified Capital Stock by or on behalf of the Obligor to such Bank or its designee, (i) each Credit (or portion thereof) in respect of which such Qualified Capital Stock is delivered shall cease to be a "Credit" and "External Indebtedness" for all purposes of this Agreement and the Obligor shall have no further obligations in respect of any such Credit (or portion thereof) and (ii) the Obligor and such Bank shall deliver to the Servicing Bank a Correction Notice reducing the principal amount of each such Credit by the principal amount exchanged for such Qualified Capital Stock.

(b) **Qualified Capital Stock.**   For purposes of this Section, "Qualified Capital Stock" means capital stock of any Mexican public sector entity or Mexican private sector company (i) which is issued in registered, certificated form in the name of such Bank or a Person designated by such Bank which is not a Mexican Entity (as defined below), (ii) which is not transferable on the registration books of such public sector entity or private sector company before January 1, 1998 to any Mexican Entity and the certificate of which bears a legend with such restriction, (iii) which is not by its terms subject to redemption on a basis more favorable to such Bank or its designee than the amortization of the Credit or Credits exchanged for such capital stock, (iv) which is not entitled to guaranteed dividends payable irrespective of earnings and profits, except as expressly contemplated by Article 123 of the Ley General de Sociedades Mercantiles, and (v) which is not convertible into any instrument or security other than Qualified Capital Stock. As used herein, the term "Mexican Entity" means any Person who, in the case of an individual, is a resident of or, in the case of an entity, has its principal place of business in the United Mexican States.

SOURCE: *Operating Manual for Capitalization of Liabilities and Substitution of Public Debt by Investment,* published by the Mexican Ministry of Finance and Public Credit, and the National Commission of Foreign Investment.

Exhibit 4
Mexican Discounts for Debt/Equity Swaps

Category	Discount (%)	Conditions
0	0	Buy government corporations that Mexico wants to sell.
1	5	New corporations, expansions, or activities in which 80% of production is exported. Corporations located within certain locations. New firms with state-of-the-art technology.
2	8	New corporations or expansions where 50% of production is exported. Firms working in priority sectors of the economy and generating foreign exchange. Projects with national integration levels comparable to similar firms.
3	12	Firms with state-of-the-art technology. Projects at a late stage of development. New firms or product lines with at least 30% exports.
4	13	Buy corporation with balance of payments deficit. Corporation is self-sufficient in foreign exchange.
5	14	Project that improves the negative trade balance of a firm. Expansion reduces liabilities to domestic suppliers.
6	15	Incomplete capitalization or prepayment to FICORCA of local debt.
7	16	Full payment to FICORCA of local debt.
8	25	No foreign exchange generation.

INTERNATIONAL PHARMACEUTICALS INCORPORATED

Exhibit 5

Mexican Economic Data

(Billions of U.S. dollars, except ratios and indexes)

	1980	1981	1982	1983	1984	1985
GDP (1980 prices)	186.3	201.1	200.1	189.6	196.2	202.0
Wholesale price index	100.0	124.4	194.2	402.7	686.0	1,053.4
Consumer price index	100.0	127.9	203.3	410.2	679.0	1,071.2
Relative prices, Mexican/U.S.:						
WPI	1.00	1.16	1.74	3.57	5.94	9.17
CPI	1.00	1.16	1.74	3.39	5.38	8.21
Treasury bill rate	22.46%	30.77%	45.75%	59.19%	49.47%	63.36%
Exports	23.9	29.4	26.1	27.1	30.4	26.6
% oil and related	43.6%	49.5%	63.0%	59.0%	54.6%	55.7%
Imports	26.3	34.4	20.2	12.8	16.2	18.6
Trade balance	(2.4)	(5.0)	5.9	14.4	14.2	8.0
Total external debt	41.0	52.9	59.5	82.3	87.5	98.0
Debt service/exports	33.1%	34.8%	44.3%	43.7%	48.6%	54.7%
Exchange rates (MP/$):						
Controlled rate	23.26	26.23	96.48	143.93	192.56	371.70
Floating rate	n.a.	n.a.	149.25	161.35	209.97	450.75

SOURCES: *International Financial Statistics*, World Bank data, and *The Economist Quarterly Review of Mexico*.

Exhibit 6

Cetes and Pagafes Rates

(Annualized rates of return)

Month (1986)	Cetes Rate
January	73.80%
February	75.70
March	78.47
April	80.52
May	80.46
June	84.00
July	91.11
August	94.70
September	98.37

Pagafes[a]

Issue	Maturity Date	Annualized Yield[b]	Total Issued	Sold to Public
			(thousand dollars)	
8/21/86	2/19/87	8.64%	70,000	40,000
8/28/86	2/26/87	13.66	45,000	39,510
9/04/86	3/05/87	15.96	18,000	3,910
9/11/86	3/12/87	16.66	19,000	8,770
9/18/86	3/19/87	18.78	23,000	12,820
9/25/86	3/26/87	21.94	21,000	1,070

[a]The controlled exchange rate averaged MP665 for the month of August and ended at MP695.7. In the month of September, the controlled rate averaged MP725 and ended at MP751.6. The freely floating rate for August averaged MP682 and ended at MP714.5, and for September, averaged MP743 and ended at MP765.5.

[b]Annualized six-month yields on U.S. T-bills at each corresponding issue date are as follows:

Date	Yield
8/21/86	5.44%
8/28/86	5.32
9/04/86	5.26
9/11/86	5.43
9/18/86	5.43
9/25/86	5.34

INTERNATIONAL PHARMACEUTICALS INCORPORATED

Exhibit 7

La Compañía de Pildora S.A. Schedule of Planned Expenditures
Under Capitalization of Credit Program

	Project Cost U.S. Dollars	Pesos Equivalent at Estimated MP 900/$1.00	Paid Prior to Oct/1/86	Monthly Outlays[e]								
				Oct/86	Nov/86	Dec/86	Jan/87	Feb/87	Mar/87	Apr/87	May/87	Jun 87
Engineering & construction management[a]	154,000	138,600	20,000	—	—	—	27,600	2,600	27,600	2,600	24,400	2,600
Building construction[b]	1,409,500	1,268,550	34,000	—	450,000	35,000	35,000	35,000	155,500	35,000	35,000	35,000
Building equipment[c]	2,339,400	2,105,460	10,000	—	800,000	100,000	60,000	155,460	55,000	55,000	55,000	155,000
Manufacturing equipment[a]	1,097,100	987,390	—	—	—	—	—	—	329,390	329,000	329,000	—
Total project cost	5,000,000	4,500,000	64,000	—	1,250,000	135,000	122,600	193,060	567,540	421,400	443,400	192,600

	Monthly Outlays											
	Jul/87	Aug/87	Sept/87	Oct/87	Nov/87	Dec/87	Jan/88	Feb/88	Mar/88	Apr/88	May/88	Jun/88
Engineering & construction management[a]	2,600	2,600	2,600	2,600	2,600	2,600	2,600	2,600	2,600	2,600	2,600	2,600
Building construction[b]	35,000	35,000	35,000	35,000	35,000	35,000	35,000	35,000	35,000	35,000	35,000	34,000
Building equipment[c]	55,000	55,000	55,000	55,000	55,000	55,000	55,000	55,000	55,000	55,000	55,000	55,000
Manufacturing equipment[a]	—	—	—	—	—	—	—	—	—	—	—	—
Total project cost	92,600	92,600	92,600	92,600	92,600	92,600	92,600	92,600	92,600	92,600	92,600	91,600

[a]Fees for design and layout, drawings, and on-site management.

[b]Cost of physical construction, including demolition and land improvement.

[c]Air conditioning, electrical, water treatment, plumbing, and related building services.

[d]Pharmaceutical manufacturing equipment.

[e]The Schedule of Planned Expenditures includes allowances for estimated cost inflation during the construction period. The exchange rate of MP900/$1.00 represents the average expected rate at which dollars could be exchanged for pesos over the anticipated construction period.

Exhibit 8   Schematic Diagram of Debt-Equity Swap

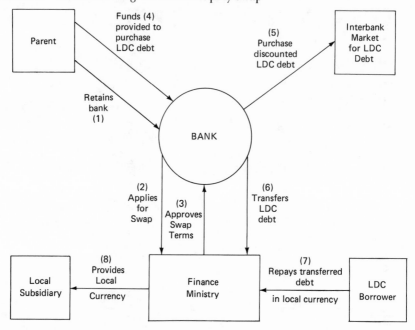

Thai Farmers Bank

In February 1984 Bancha Lamsam, chairman of Thai Farmers Bank (TFB), was speaking to Kaorop Nutchanart, the new senior vice president of the computer department:

I have just finished reviewing your assistant's report after her trip to Mexico. We must carefully evaluate her recommendation to cancel our September 1983 order for five distributed on-line computers in Bangkok and place a new one for a single high-powered mainframe at headquarters. According to Ms. Vanadurongvan, the centralized approach will better facilitate automating our branches. But this new order will complicate the implementation. I still want to see the first Bangkok branch go on-line by the year end, most of the others by the end of next year, and also 15–20 up-country branches. Siam Commercial Bank [SCB] already has on-line branches and over 50 automatic teller machines [ATMs] in Bangkok. Unless we catch up fast, they will capture a significant portion of our market share. You will have to manage a rapid turnaround. I know you can do it. You have my total commitment of the bank's resources for this project.

COMPANY BACKGROUND

By February 1984, with assets exceeding baht75 million,[1] TFB was the second largest commercial bank in Thailand with about 8,500 employees and 238 domestic and foreign branches. Domestic retail banking was its major business, in which it held 13% market share. TFB was organized by function (see *Exhibit 1*). In 1960 Bancha Lamsam's uncle, chairman of the family-owned TFB, died in an airplane crash, and Lamsam, thirty-seven years old and working for his family's insurance company, joined TFB as

[1]Baht23 = US$1.00 (1983).

Ajay S. Mookerjee prepared this case under the supervision of Professor James I. Cash with the support of the International Center for Information Technologies, Washington, D.C., as the basis for class discussion rather than to illustrate either effective or ineffective handling of an administrative situation. Abridged with permission.

chairman. TFB was then the 12th largest bank in Thailand. Mr. Bancha Lamsam:

> My top priority over the next two decades was to build a cadre of high-quality professional managers in the bank. I decided to develop people in the bank rather than shop around for people from outside. We gradually raised salary levels to match Bangkok Bank's [BB], to attract bright, young people. We also set up a scholarship to sponsor a few TFB employees each year for advanced degrees at U.S. schools. These students had to sign a bond to work two years at TFB for each year of schooling. Many of them are still with us. Today we have the most qualified people in the industry: Many of our managers have MBAs from Harvard, Wharton, Chicago, etc.

In the late 1960s and through the 1970s, Lamsam concentrated on building the number and quality of TFB branch banks, especially in up-country regions. Between 1967 and 1979 TFB established 113 of its 160 up-country branches. According to the president, Banyong Lamsam:

> Our early success was because we decided to be mainly a retail bank. Other banks did not aggressively pursue a retail strategy. Branch expansion was our early priority. Bank of Thailand [BOT], our central bank, closely regulates branch expansion, but we persistently submitted the maximum allowable number of applications for new branches.

As TFB started growing, one major constraint was capital, so the family began to raise capital from the stock market. By 1984 TFB was more interested in protecting market share than continuing aggressive growth. According to the chairman:

> We don't want our retail market share to go above 15% because BOT would force us to participate in a broader portfolio of loans. This would yield a higher percentage of bad loans. But Siam Commercial Bank's use of ATMs poses a significant threat to our current market share. We have already seen an increase in their retail deposits.
>
> By the end of 1983 it became clear that we had not made much progress in the use of computers. Our two major competitors already had on-line branch systems. SCB had installed over 30 ATMs in Bangkok. We had to rethink our computer strategy and prepare to make a major investment. We had just completed construction of our new B800 million headquarters building, so this was a good time to install the computer. I had to raise B2.6 billion additional capital from the stock market due to a BOT requirement, and that left enough money for the computer. The question was: What should we do?

COUNTRY AND INDUSTRY BACKGROUND

Officially named Siam until 1939, Thailand is the only Southeast Asian country that was never colonized. First united as a nation in 1238, Thailand has been governed by a constitutional monarchy since 1932. Bangkok, the capital, is a popular tourist attraction. In 1983 Thailand's population of about 50 million (growth rate of less than 2%) comprised Thai (80%), Chinese (10%), Malay (4%), Lao, Indian, and others (6%). Its area of 514,000 sq. km. (the size of France) is shaped like the head and trunk of an elephant and is bordered by Burma, Laos, Kampuchea, and Malaysia. Geographically, it has a mountainous north, a semiarid northeast plateau, fertile central and eastern plains, and a tropical southern isthmus. The society is basically agrarian, with around 75% of the population employed in farm production. Recently, rapid industrial development has taken place in the eastern seaboard region. Most political, commercial, financial, and industrial activity centers in Bangkok; its population of 6 million is 60 times that of the next largest city, Chiang Mai, in the far north.

The Thai economy improved in 1983 after several years of sluggish growth. The GDP grew 5.95%, as against 4.1% in 1982. Agriculture, manufacturing, and construction showed improved growth rates (see *Exhibits 2A, 2B,* and *2C* for economic indicators). In 1983 inflation (3.8%) was a record low for the 1971–83 period. But the trade deficit persisted at a high level (B90 billion), prompting authorities to impose several measures by early 1984, including control on the opening of letters of credit for nonoil imports and an 18% limit on commercial banks' credit expansion.

The Thai economy was expected to grow by 5.5% in 1984. The agricultural sector was expected to grow by 4.5% in 1984, and the nonagricultural sector only by 6.1% as a result of the restrictive credit policy.

In 1983 the Thai banking system, started only forty years earlier and originally dominated by foreign banks, began to mature. The First Banking Act (1962) curbed the spread of foreign banks by prohibiting expansion of their branches. The Second Banking Act (1979) reduced the concentration of the few large domestic banks by forcing them to dilute their shareholdings. The Thai banking industry was mainly retail and tightly regulated by BOT. Reduced inflation in 1983 induced a rapid increase in deposits, even though BOT lowered interest rates. Increased demand in credit was somewhat larger than the increase in deposits. This caused the surplus liquidity left from the end of 1982 to disappear. To attract more deposits, the major commercial banks were pressed to introduce services such as transferable certificates of deposits, ATMs, and on-line branch systems.

COMPETITION

In 1983 competition in Thailand's banking industry centered mostly on domestic retail accounts. Foreign banks, because of their limited number of branches, could not play any significant role. Sixteen domestic banks were incorporated, but of those only Bangkok Bank (BB), Thai Farmers Bank (TFB), and Siam Commercial Bank had dominant positions. BB, TFB, and SCB had deposits of about 36%, 13%, and 7%, respectively, of the total retail market (see *Exhibit 3*). Brief outlines of BB and SCB follow.

Bangkok Bank

In December 1983, with around 19,000 employees and 16 foreign branches, BB was the largest bank in Thailand and the only domestic Thai bank with significant international and wholesale operations. BB had led wholesale banking at least ten years before BOT ruled that all banks must extend credit to finance Thailand's industrial development. In 1983 a BOT ruling forced BB to play a major role in the nation's industrial growth.

The first bank to introduce computers in Thailand, BB had batch processing retail systems as early as 1970 and on-line systems for all its Bangkok branches by 1979. But according to an industry observer, BB was not considered an aggressive player in the retail market. They did not exploit the early lead with on-line systems, and SCB's introduction of ATMs in 1983 came as a rude shock. At that time BB's computer function depended on one key man, who was the only person who understood fully all systems; without him the department would be in trouble. Also, too much incompatibility was built into its architecture to allow it to introduce ATMs quickly.

Siam Commercial Bank

In December 1983 SCB was the fourth largest bank in Thailand with about 4,700 employees and four foreign branches. SCB had always been primarily a retail bank. From a leading position in the early 1960s, SCB slipped to fourth by the end of the 1970s. In 1983 SCB was executing a turnaround, begun four years earlier, with an aggressive strategy in the retail market. SCB's retail share had been slowly growing. Computers were central in SCB's retail strategy. By the end of 1982, 13 on-line systems were installed in its Bangkok branches; this grew to 54 by the end of 1983. Further, by the end of 1983 SCB had installed 32 ATMs in its Bangkok branches and some major shopping centers.

SCB's information systems department had a total staff of 130 well-qualified people. It had an all-IBM network of computers for the on-line interbranch deposit system, ATM system, and VISA/MasterCard credit card systems.

INFORMATION TECHNOLOGY ENVIRONMENT IN THAILAND

In February 1984 IT use in Thailand was emerging (*Exhibit 4*). About 12 private organizations had mainframes the size of IBM's 3000 series computers. Less than 35 organizations had an annual DP budget exceeding B200 million. IBM and CDC had fully staffed sales and support offices in Bangkok. Several distributors sold a range of computers manufactured by leading U.S., European, and Japanese companies. The availability of data communications equipment was limited, and the quality of telecommunications infrastructure was poor.

In 1984 there were no digital telecommunications lines; all switching was done using crossbar technology. The Telecommunication Organization of Thailand (TOT) provided local voice, data, and long-distance (domestic and international) voice services. The Communications Authority of Thailand (CAT) provided all long-distance data service. Waiting time to get leased lines could run up to two years. Many restrictions were imposed on attachments (especially modems) to the public network. The quality and reliability of leased lines were poor; some microwave long-distance lines were frequently subject to weather disruptions.

Thailand has been very successful in avoiding a "brain drain" of qualified systems people; it is quite common to find U.S.-trained MBAs or computer professionals working in Bangkok. TFB in particular had been successful in attracting and retaining qualified computer professionals: Turnover in its computer department in 1975–83 was less than 5% per year.

TFB COMPUTER DEPARTMENT HISTORY

TFB's computer department was established in 1975 and was headed until mid-1983 by an ex-salesman from Centronics.[2] Early systems installed were batch processing retail systems, using mainly Centronics equipment. According to Banthoon Lamsam, first VP of international banking:

> Between 1975 and 1982, our computer department was run by technicians; there was no tie-in with business strategy. The

[2]Disguised name of a major computer manufacturer.

department head almost had a personal vendetta against IBM, and he installed the earlier Centronics computers bought by the bank. In 1983 SCB came up with their ATM system, and that was a rude shock to us. We did not even have on-line systems. In fact, as late as 1982 stand-alone CT5900s were installed at 20 branches.

In mid-1983 Bancha Lamsam got involved in EDP planning. He set up a technology committee that he headed. Peat Marwick, retained as consultant, submitted a report recommending a total writeoff of more than B75 million in Centronics equipment and installing four IBM 4361s for major Bangkok branches, linked to an IBM 4381 at headquarters via leased lines, using mostly package software (*Exhibit 5*). Bancha Lamsam accepted their recommendation. Kaorop Nutchanart, an economics graduate with no training in computers but with twenty years of experience in the domestic banking department, was made head of the computer department. Ms. V. Vanadurongvan (diploma in programming from Michigan, with several years of EDP and accounting experience), Mr. S. Yodpinit (master's in computer science from Illinois, with several years' system experience), and the veteran computer programmers were key figures in the small (141) but well-qualified staff reporting to Nutchanart.

Key employees involved in the computerization but from outside the computer department were the technology committee members. At that time Banthoon Lamsam (Harvard MBA) was secretary, assisted by Somchai Wasantwisut (BS in computers, Thailand, and Harvard MBA), who succeeded him as secretary. The business development manager, Opaswongkarn (BS in computers, Thailand; MBA and PhD, Wharton), joined in mid-1985. In September 1983 an order was placed for four IBM 4361s and one IBM 4381. Bancha Lamsam described the environment:

> I set the end of 1984 as the deadline for installing the first ATM and on-line branch system. I knew my people were committed, especially after I had clearly demonstrated my personal involvement. I attended almost every meeting, most of which lasted several hours. But I was concerned about the adequacy of a number of people. We had to recruit many people quickly who had experience with data communications and on-line systems. Also, due to our radical shift to IBM systems, I was concerned that we might lose people.

On February 1, 1984, Ms. Vanadurongvan went on a field trip to Mexico to study the on-line branch and ATM system implemented at Banco Internacional (BI), the fourth largest bank in that country. BI then had 300 branches and 12,000 employees. The banking environment in Mexico was similar to Thailand's, and BI was similar in size to TFB. It was hoped that useful insights would come from her trip.

On her return she submitted a report to the chairman and the members of the technology committee, with the following observations and recommendations:

1. BI's computer department has a staff of 270, comprising 49 analysts, 39 programmers, and 182 operations personnel. Two things distinguished BI's from TFB's computer organization: the existence at BI of a separate communications unit, and a unit called the "help desk," set up to help tellers resolve operational problems with on-line branch systems. Staff recruitment for a telecommunications unit was recommended, as was setting up a help desk after the system became operational.

2. BI had been using a software product called SAFE for its on-line branch system, and another called FAATS for its ATM, and the results were satisfactory. In 1984, 55 of BI's 300 metropolitan branches were on-line, each with an average of 3–4 teller terminals and 1–3 ATMs. Using off-the-shelf software had reduced implementation time considerably.

3. Implementation of branch on-line systems was handled by assigning implementation teams of four people to different branches.

4. In the metropolitan area, BI was using a single IBM 4341 at its head office for all on-line branch systems. According to BI personnel, this was considered better than a network of lower-power computers. BI was concerned initially that the single computer approach might suffer from poor local telecommunications service of computer overload. BI's experience since 1978 indicated that telecommunications quality was not a crucial problem. Also, the on-line system did not overload as feared; the teller terminal response time at peak loads was 2–3 seconds per transaction, which was acceptable. The total system load in February 1984 averaged 45,000 transactions a day. At that time BI had planned to upgrade the mainframe to an IBM 3083.

Ms. Vanadurongvan's report recommended that TFB acquire a single IBM 3083 instead of the one IBM 4381 plus four IBM 4361s.

After review of this report, Nutchanart was asked to prepare a new proposal by the end of February 1984. The proposal suggested the following steps:

1. *Hardware:* A single IBM 3083 CPU at the Bangkok headquarters to serve all metropolitan branches and connecting to the three regional centers (see *Exhibit 6*).

2. *Software:* Continue with the plan to use SAFE and FAATS for branch on-line and ATM systems. Most software for other applications would have to be developed in-house.

3. *Implementation Schedule:*

	Total # of Branches[a]		
	1984	*1985*	*1986*
Bangkok	1	90	10
North	—	7	1
South	—	4	2
East	—	7	4

[a]All ATMs were planned for installation within branches (with 24-hour outside access). After SCB had installed a few off-premise ATMs, BOT ruled that all future ATMs installed by banks must be within their branches. Otherwise, it would be tantamount to branch expansion.

4. *Investment.* The expected investment needed was as follows (baht million):

	1984	*1985*	*1986*
Hardware	408	500	50
Software	3.7	20	25
Total	411.7	520	75

5. *People.* Recruitment of 70 additional people with experience in on-line and communications systems.

6. *Training.* The part-time training program to familiarize existing computer personnel with IBM equipment was started in January 1984. It was recommended that this program be continued until the end of March 1984.

7. *Applications.* The list of applications proposed on the new computer system was not changed. (See *Exhibit 7* for a detailed list of proposed applications.) The top-priority applications remained the on-line branch and ATM systems. Except for these two systems, software for most other systems would be developed in-house.

COMMENTS OF BRANCH AND ZONE MANAGERS

Line managers most directly affected by TFB's computerization proposal were the branch and zone managers. TFB's branches were divided into 30 zones (9 in Bangkok, and 21 up-country). Zone managers reported to branch administration at headquarters, headed by Nivat Phanayangkul. Comments from some of these people follow.

Wachrin Wamasuree, Manager, Patpong Branch

This was a medium-size metropolitan branch, with a total staff of 50 people. A stand-alone, batch-processing Centronics minicomputer was the sole computing equipment.

> Due to poor computing support our workload is intense. Our normal working day is from 8 A.M. to 8 P.M. I expect the new computer to ease our workload, so I welcome it. The present environment is vulnerable to errors, and I expect this to change with the on-line system. Further, SCB has a competitive advantage due to their computer, and this bothers me. My only concern about installing the on-line system is that my people have to be trained to use it accurately. My staff has an open mind and I know they will welcome the new system.

Somchai Trilerklith, Manager, Sukhumvit Cholburi Branch

Sukhumvit Cholburi was a large up-country branch with a total of 37 people. A stand-alone, batch-processing minicomputer was the sole computing support.

> My workload is very high. The normal working day is from 8 A.M. to 7 P.M. On month-ends and half-yearly closing, work goes on beyond midnight. Due to this, the morale of my employees is low. I am overjoyed that my branch will be the first up-country branch to be computerized, not only for TFB [but for all other banks as well]. My people are happy because they feel they would be actually able to see the sun!
>
> My major concern is that I don't know much about computers. One wrong keystroke can lead to a major error. Our zone manager did, however, organize a two-day computer literacy course taught by some local university professors, and that has helped. My staff's main concerns are that they may not be able to use the on-line system and also that the interface is in English, not Thai.

Cherng Liamtrakul, Manager, Zone 6

This zone was typical of the nine in Bangkok. It was housed in one of the branches. Cherng and two secretaries were the only people in the zone office. There was no computing support.

> My main function is data collection, reporting, and supervision of the branches. In the current environment, it is nearly impossible for me to get my work done. The on-line system will facilitate data gathering,

and the MIS applications that will follow will certainly improve the information flowing to my office from the branches. My only concern is that the implementation schedule is too tight.

Sutee Prathomvarl, Manager, Zone 25

This zone, in the eastern province, supervised nine branches, including the Sukhumvit Cholburi branch. This was also the intended site of the first regional computer center to be installed in 1985.

My workload is very high and the new system will reduce it. Therefore I am looking forward to the on-line branch systems in my zone and also the regional computer center. My major concern is that the implementation schedule is very tight, and I don't have enough people to achieve it.

Nivat Phanayangkul, Senior VP, Branch Administration

In February 1984 Nivat commented:

Today the average deposit or withdrawal time at the bank is nearly ten minutes. I expect that to go down to 1–2 minutes. Also, the on-line systems will ease the workload at the branches. My job is very difficult in the present environment. Since different branches have different computers, all stand-alone, each branch maintains a unique chart of accounts. It takes me over thirty days to consolidate this information at headquarters. I expect this situation to change. The only negative comments I've heard about the computer system concern the potential elimination or deskilling of jobs. But there have been very few of these.

SUMMARY

Bancha Lamsam addressed the technology committee:

We have reviewed the new proposal, and now we must decide. This is going to be a bold investment decision, and it requires top management support. I can assure you about my full support and involvement with this project. We need careful planning, preparation, and teamwork to meet our tight implementation goals. The key to our success is going to be unity from one and all.

THAI FARMERS BANK

Exhibit 1 Organization Chart

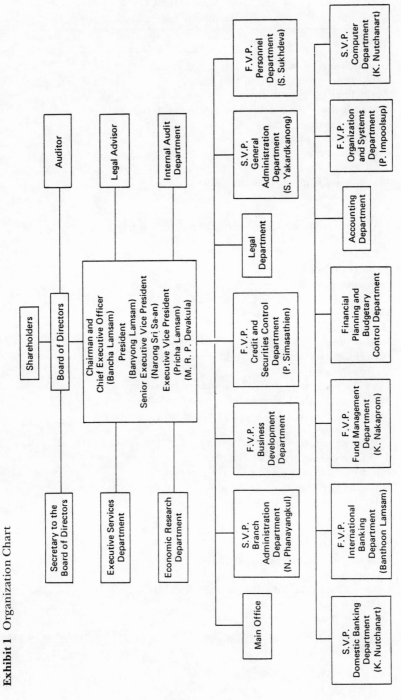

Exhibit 2A

Economic Indicators

	1983
GDP (billions of baht)	924.0
GDP (% growth rate p.a. in real terms)	5.9
Agriculture (% growth rate p.a. in real terms)	4.3
Nonagriculture (% growth rate p.a. in real terms)	6.7
Manufacturing	6.9
Mining and quarrying	−1.4
Construction	4.9
Others	6.5
Investment (% growth rate p.a. in real terms)	7.9
Private	7.2
Public	9.2
Public consumption (% growth rate p.a. in real terms)	5.5
Exports (billions of baht)	146.5
Growth rate (%)	−8.6
Imports (billions of baht)	236.6
Growth rate (%)	20.3
Trade balance (billions of baht)	−90.1
Current account (billions of baht)	−65.0
Government revenue[a]	136.6
Growth rate (%)	20.0
Government expenditures[b] (billions of baht)	165.1
Growth rate (%)	8.5
Government budget deficit[b] (billions of baht)	28.5
Money supply (M1) (December–December % change p.a.)	4.4
Money supply (M2) (December–December % change p.a.)	23.3
Prime rate (%), end of period	
Minimum lending rate (MLR)	16.5
Minimum overdraft rate (MOR)	16.5
Interbank rate (%), end of period	16.0
Discount rate (%), end of period	
1st tier	13.0
2d tier	14.5
Assets of commercial banks (billions of baht)	540.0
Growth rate (%)	25.2
Deposits of commercial banks (billions of baht)	407.6
Growth rate (%)	25.7
Loans of commercial banks (billions of baht)	401.6
Growth rate (%)	34.0
Loans/deposits ratio (%)	98.5

(continued on next page)

Exhibit 2A
Economic Indicators (*Continued*)

	1983
Borrowing of commercial banks (billions of baht)	64.6
Growth rate (%)	31.0
Number of commercial banks' branches	1,727
Banks incorporated in Thailand	1,704
Domestic	1,688
Overseas	19
Banks incorporated abroad	20
Net international reserves (million US$)	1,593.5
Growth rate (%)	−33.7
Inflation rate (%)	3.8
Exchange rate (baht/1 US$), end of period	23.00

[a]Forecast.

[b]Fiscal year.

SOURCE: Thai National Accounts Division, NESDB.

THAI FARMERS BANK

Exhibit 2B
Thai Economy 1983
Gross National Product by Industrial Origin

Line	1981 Millions of Baht	1981 As % of GDP	1982 Millions of Baht	1982 As % of GDP	1983 Millions of Baht	1983 As % of GDP
Agriculture	187,886	23.9	188,742	22.3	204,443	22.1
Crops	138,886	17.7	139,852	16.5	149,973	16.2
Livestock	24,727	3.1	23,608	2.8	28,840	3.1
Fisheries	13,183	1.7	14,150	1.7	14,466	1.6
Forestry	11,090	1.4	11,132	1.3	11,164	1.2
Mining and quarrying	13,373	1.7	14,807	1.7	16,480	1.8
Manufacturing	158,272	20.1	164,659	19.5	176,200	19.1
Construction	42,008	5.3	43,040	5.1	47,129	5.1
Electricity and water supply	10,743	1.4	14,454	1.7	16,319	1.8
Transportation and communication	57,281	7.3	63,133	7.5	73,708	8.0
Wholesale and retail trade	150,293	19.1	159,849	18.9	165,812	17.9
Banking, insurance & real estate	52,025	6.6	61,021	7.2	71,722	7.7
Ownership of dwellings	8,411	1.1	9,912	1.2	11,210	1.2
Public administration and defense	30,645	3.9	37,349	4.4	42,551	4.6
Services	75,229	9.6	89,170	10.5	98,680	10.7
Gross domestic product (GDP)	786,166	100.0	846,136	100.0	924,254	100.0
Plus: net income from abroad	−21,787	—	−26,376	—	−25,370	—
Gross national product (GNP)	764,379	—	819,760	—	898,884	—
Less: indirect taxes	79,879	—	83,904	—	100,947	—
Capital consumption allowances	59,259	—	65,649	—	73,386	—
National income	625,241	—	670,207	—	724,551	—
Per capita GNP (Baht)	16,096	—	16,906	—	18,174	—

SOURCE: Thai National Accounts Division, NESDB.

Exhibit 2C
Major Exports and Imports
(Millions of baht)

Line	1980	1981	1982	1983
A. Exports				
Food	59,338	80,038	86,371	73,755
Beverages and tobacco	1,393	1,758	2,599	1,860
Crude materials	19,095	16,722	15,134	16,288
Mineral fuels and lubricant	86	37	40	30
Animal and vegetable oils and fats	222	232	298	270
Chemicals	936	1,191	1,253	1,673
Manufactured goods	29,474	26,941	26,587	26,002
Machinery	7,618	7,662	8,293	8,356
Miscellaneous manufactured goods	8,467	11,731	13,404	14,756
Miscellaneous transactions and commodities	3,777	2,650	2,060	1,332
Reexports	2,791	4,039	3,689	2,150
Total	133,197	153,001	159,728	146,472
B. Imports				
Food	5,763	5,795	5,061	6,501
Beverages and tobacco	1,518	1,588	2,327	1,268
Crude materials	10,755	13,297	11,516	14,376
Mineral fuels and lubricant	58,733	65,100	60,765	57,065
Animal and vegetable oils and fats	1,458	903	438	781
Chemicals	22,352	26,761	24,848	31,804
Manufactured goods	28,152	34,512	30,597	39,034
Machinery	42,102	54,371	46,503	68,361
Miscellaneous manufactured goods	10,959	10,899	11,195	14,039
Miscellaneous transactions and commodities	5,894	3,520	3,346	3,345
Gold	0	0	20	35
Total	188,686[a]	216,746[a]	196,616[a]	236,609[a]

[a]Excluding imports of aircraft that have been taken account of in the balance of payments statistics for the actual month of imports.

THAI FARMERS BANK

Exhibit 3

Salient Indicators of Banks Incorporated in Thailand—As of December 31, 1983
(Millions of baht)

Bank	Assets		Deposits		Loans		Capital Funds		Domestic Branches	
	Amount	*Market Share (%)*	*Amount*	*Market Share (%)*	*Amount*	*Market Share (%)*	*Amount*	*Market Share (%)*	*Number*	*Market Share (%)*
Thai Farmers Bank, Ltd.	75,331	12.42	58,560	13.04	57,417	13.18	3,048	12.05	254	14.82
Bangkok Bank, Ltd.	217,648	35.89	159,968	35.63	169,850	39.00	8,162	32.28	292	17.04
Krung Thai Bank, Ltd.[a]	81,793	13.49	63,490	14.14	53,055	12.18	2,840	11.23	207	12.08
The Siam Commercial Bank, Ltd.	43,391	7.16	31,568	7.03	30,280	6.95	1,757	6.95	150	8.75
Bank of Ayudhya, Ltd.	28,442	4.69	21,641	4.82	19,845	4.56	1,440	5.70	146	8.52
The Bangkok Bank of Commerce, Ltd.	24,951	4.11	21,923	4.88	15,887	3.65	945	3.74	140	8.17
Bangkok Metropolitan Bank, Ltd.	28,391	4.68	18,130	4.04	19,376	4.45	1,086	4.30	94	5.48
The Siam City Bank, Ltd.	17,332	2.86	14,736	3.28	12,334	2.83	939	3.71	100	5.83
The Thai Military Bank, Ltd.	21,391	3.53	16,156	3.60	14,922	3.43	1,438	5.69	91	5.31
First Bangkok City Bank, Ltd.	19,438	3.21	11,182	2.49	12,124	2.78	1,053	4.16	51	2.98
The Bank of Asia, Ltd.	12,888	2.13	9,801	2.18	8,479	1.95	590	2.33	46	2.68
The Thai Danu Bank, Ltd.	5,958	.98	4,201	.94	4,473	1.03	467	1.85	19	1.11
The Laem Thong Bank, Ltd.	4,664	.77	2,305	.51	2,469	.57	242	.90	5	.29
Wang Lee Bank, Ltd.	3,714	.61	2,190	.49	2,516	.58	148	.59	12	.70
Total	606,384	100.00	448,957	100.00	435,384	100.00	25,284	100.00	1,714	100.00

[a]A public sector bank, consolidated from several failing banks, and not considered a serious competitor.

530

Salient Indicators of Banks Incorporated Abroad, as of December 31, 1983
(Millions of baht)

Bank	Assets		Deposits		Loans		Thai Branches	
	Amount	Market Share (%)	Amount	Market Share (%)	Amount	Market Share (%)	Number	Market Share (%)
The Chase Manhattan Bank NA	5,214	16.99	1,825	15.75	4,493	19.50	1	5
The Mitsui Bank, Ltd.	4,654	15.17	1,799	15.53	3,800	16.49	2	10
The Bank of Tokyo, Ltd.	4,091	13.33	1,344	11.60	3,119	13.53	1	5
Bank of America NT & SA	3,693	12.03	1,683	14.52	2,967	12.87	1	5
United Malayan Banking Corp., Bhd.	2,636	8.59	343	2.96	1,772	7.69	1	5
Bangu Indosuez	2,028	6.61	770	6.65	1,637	7.10	2	10
The Hong Kong & Shanghai Banking Corp.	1,688	5.50	1,172	10.11	1,210	5.25	2	10
European Asian Bank	1,600	5.21	360	3.11	1,320	5.73	1	5
Mercantile Bank, Ltd.	1,573	5.13	209	1.80	447	1.94	2	10
The Chartered Bank	1,518	4.95	1,060	9.15	986	4.28	3	15
Bharat Overseas Bank, Ltd.	742	2.42	377	3.25	555	2.41	1	5
The International Commercial Bank of China	560	1.82	228	1.97	444	1.92	1	5
Four Seas Communications Bank, Ltd.	373	1.22	239	2.06	108	0.47	1	5
The Bank of Canton, Ltd.	317	1.03	179	1.54	189	0.82	1	5
Total	30,687	100.00	11,586	100.00	23,045	100.00	20	100

531

Exhibit 4
Thailand's Information Systems Environment, February 1984

Item	*Number*	*Remarks*
1. Computer installations	371	About 12 private companies have mainframes equivalent in size to IBM 3000 series.
2. Computer & communication equipment manufacturers	None	Data General and Far East Computers expected to start production in 1985.
3. Sales offices of manufacturers	2	IBM: mainframes, office systems and PCs.
4. Computer distributors	96	IBM, Epson, Fujitsu, NEC, Apple, Philips, DEC, Sharp, Hitachi, IBM PC, CDC, Northern Telecom, Prime, Wang, Perkin-Elmer, NCR, HP, Honeywell, Sperry, Datapoint, Nixdorf, Burroughs, etc.
5. Data communication distributors	12 36	Control Data: mainframes and communications equipment. DEC-net, SNA, Paradyne, Modems, CDC, 255X, ODL-Lan, NCR (DSA), TRT data modems, Philips P 5000, and Dana Lan, Honeywell (DSA), General Datacom/Modem and Multipliers.
6. Peripherals distributors	36	Most major types available.
7. Systems consulants	18	Largest is Coopers & Lybrand (staff: 78); second largest is Siam Tech—40% equity held by White Group Ltd. (Staff: 30).
8. Data processing bureaus	8	—
9. Data preparation bureaus	2	—
10. Training services	3	—
11. Recruitment services	3	—

SOURCE: Asian Computer Directory.

Exhibit 5

PEAT MARWICK SUMMARY OF COMPUTERIZATION PROPOSAL

The original proposal submitted by Peat Marwick in mid-1983 proposed the following hardware configuration:

1. Write off all Centronics equipment
2. Install an IBM 4381 at the head office, using an IBM 3705 as communications controller to tie in with remote sites
3. Install seven IBM 4361s, four at major Bangkok branches and three at regional computer centers in the north, east, and south. All IBM 4361s were to connect to the head office 4381 (via the 3705), using modems and leased lines
4. Each branch should have 1–3 ATMs, and teller terminals controlled by an IBM 4701, all connecting to the nearest computer (4381 or 4361), using modems and leased lines.

The report also recommended using off-the-shelf application software (FAATS for ATMs and SAFE for the on-line branch systems). The report pointed out the necessity of recruiting at least 125 people in 1984, especially those experienced in on-line systems and data communications. The current staff included only 115 programmers, and of these around 75 had less than two years of work experience. Further, it was recommended that the staff be trained to familiarize them with an IBM environment.

Exhibit 6   Hardware Configuration—Revised Proposal, February 1984

1) Headquarters Computer Center

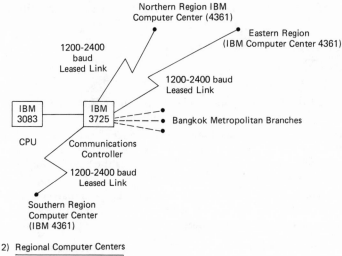

2) Regional Computer Centers

3) Branch Hardware

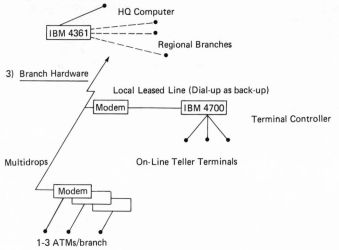

Exhibit 7
Key Applications in the Computerization Proposal

System	Application/Software
On-line	SAFE
ATM EFT	FAATS
Credit card	VISA/Master Card/TFB Card
Payment & collection	Company payroll/credit card supplier payment/utilities
Loans	Internally developed
Regional computer centers	East/North/South
Innovation products	• Telephone banking • Point of sale • Video banking • VISA authorization
Image building effort	• Computer park for children • Micro-lab: training for public • Videotex • School computer center
MIS	• Customer info system • Personnel info system • Stockholder system • Fund management • Accounting
International banking system	Internally developed

7

Organization

The organizational side of business can be viewed through many different windows, such as human resource management and organizational design and behavior. Of particular interest to our focus are cultural and cross-cultural factors affecting organizational structures and relationships.[1]

KEY ISSUES

The cases in this chapter can be viewed as dealing with human resource management and organizational issues surrounding two categories of relationships: employees and partners.

Employee Relationships

The first three cases concern the management tasks of selecting, promoting, and interacting with employees. In the first one we revisit Packages Limited (Chapter 4) and its new venture Milkpak (Chapter 5). The top management of Packages faced the task of choosing the management to head up the Milkpak operation. Underlying the deliberations is the fundamental issue frequently facing LDC businesses: to choose a family member or an outside professional manager. Another issue is the difficulty in using managers from government-owned enterprises to run a private company. Several cases in previous chapters deal with related personnel and organizational issues (e.g., Evans Food Corp. and Sabritas). The second case, "Turrialba Mining Company," concerns a multinational corporation and cross-cultural issues, but the focus is on union relationships and how political factors can shape the interaction with employees. The third case, "The Untouchable Water-Carrier," deals with the constraints that traditional social structures and relationships place on hiring and promotion decisions.

Partner Relationships

The final two cases deal with structuring and managing joint venture partnerships between developed and developing country firms. The first case rolls the clock forward on the Thai Polyester Fiber Co. presented in Chapter 4 as a startup situation. Now we examine the operating experience of this major French–Thai joint venture. The partner relationship was fraught with difficulties. Understanding their causes is the focal point for analysis. The next case, "Ashamu Holdings Ltd.," presents the strategic decision of a major Nigerian agribusiness conglomerate to use joint international ventures as its primary organizational form. This would constitute a radical departure from its previous strategy of associating only with well-known locals. The analytical task is to weigh the costs and benefits of this strategy and to figure out what actions are necessary to avoid the problems that plagued the French–Thai joint venture.

CASE STUDY QUESTIONS

Selecting a New Manager at Milkpak

1. What difficulties did using public sector employees cause?
2. What criteria should the selection process use?
3. What should Mr. Ali do?

Turrialba Mining Company

1. What is your assessment of the company's approach toward unionization?
2. What is your evaluation of the general manager's actions and attitudes?
3. Why did problems with the unions and government arise?
4. What should the company do?

The "Untouchable" Water-Carrier

1. Why did the bank manager make his specific appointment as water-carrier?

2. What are the consequences, and how should he handle them?

Thai Polyester Fiber (C)

1. What are the sources of the difficulties between the joint-venture partners?
2. How should they be dealt with?

Ashamu Holdings Limited

1. What is your assessment of Chief Ashamu's new strategy to rely heavily on outside joint-venture partners?
2. What guidelines would you recommend to him for managing such relationships?

NOTE

1. For additional material on related organizational issues, see James E. Austin, *Managing in Developing Countries* (New York: Free Press, 1990), Chapter 10.

Selecting a New Manager at Milkpak

"The problem with bringing public sector managers into the private sector is that they're more concerned with explaining why things went wrong than with making them go right," Syed Babar Ali reflected. Ali, chairman and managing director of Milkpak Limited, a Pakistani milk processing and distribution firm located in Lahore, was explaining his decision some three years earlier to fire the entire Milkpak management team that had been hired away from a major state-owned enterprise.

Now, in early 1986, Ali was contemplating a new change of management. He had reluctantly assumed the managing directorship of Milkpak in late 1982. Now, however, business pressures at Packages Limited, his major business holding, and other interests were demanding his complete attention. "My nephew Yawar has done a good job as commercial manager at Milkpak," he said, "and deserves consideration for promotion to managing director. But he's still young, and I'm concerned about perceptions of too much favoritism toward family members. One of my managers here at Packages is ideally suited for the job, but he's not very keen on being transferred to Milkpak."

SYED BABAR ALI

Ali was a member of one of Pakistan's most prominent commercial families. He and his brothers collectively owned companies in the textile and insurance industries in addition to Packages, which was engaged in manufacturing paper and packaging materials. The family had also operated Ford's Pakistani automobile assembly plant and owned a major vegetable oil and soap company prior to their nationalization in the early 1970s. Each of the Ali family's business enterprises was managed independently by the family member who held its managing directorship. In 1985, Packages' total revenue was 575 million rupees; this was about 50% of total group revenues.[1]

[1] The average Pakistani rupee–US$ exchange rate was 15.928 to 1 during 1985. For exchange rates in other years, see *Exhibit 1*.

This case was written by Eugene Salorio, Research Assistant, of the Harvard Business School under the supervision of Professor Louis T. Wells, Jr., of the Harvard Business School, as the basis for class discussion rather than to illustrate either effective or ineffective handling of an administrative situation. Names in this case have been disguised.

Ali was proud of his family's ability to combine the best elements of traditional Pakistani business practices with more modern, Western-oriented management methods. Packages regularly recruited management trainees from the top universities in Pakistan and was deeply concerned with the development of management skills. Ali himself had completed the Harvard Business School Advanced Management Program in 1973, at the age of forty-three, and had since sent several of Packages' senior managers to Harvard's executive courses. He had used Packages' joint ventures and management contracts with foreign investors to challenge Packages' young executives with greater responsibilities and autonomy. He was interested in further diversifying operations to provide additional opportunities to develop and test his executives. Ali felt that this concern with management training had enabled him to develop a well-trained group of professionals who understood Western management practices and worked well together, and on whom he could rely.

MILKPAK

Before Milkpak was formed in 1980 to supply sterilized milk to urban Pakistani markets, only fresh milk sold almost entirely through a traditional distribution system had been available. Adulteration and spoilage rates were high (see "Milkpak" in Chapter 5). Ali had calculated that a significant segment of the milk-consuming market would pay a premium for milk packaged in containers permitting an extended life without refrigeration, and distributed outside traditional channels.

These special containers could be produced by some of Packages' Swedish cardboard manufacturing equipment that was currently underutilized. Since none of the local milk processing companies was interested in using these containers, Ali had formed a joint venture among the Ali family (15.7%), Packages (7.1%), the Swedish supplier of technology (8.6%), the International Finance Corporation (5.7%), and several other investors to establish their own dairy processing company. As a means of assuring sufficient raw milk supplies to allow for high capacity utilization at the Milkpak plant, agricultural extension services were provided to local dairy farmers by a specialized Danish concern that had also made a small investment (2.9%) in the new company.

FORMATION OF THE ORIGINAL MANAGEMENT TEAM

"Once we'd made the decision to go ahead with Milkpak and lined up all the investors, my first task was to assemble a management team," Ali recalled. "I didn't want to use anyone from Packages because I needed them all there as we were in the process of a major capacity expansion."

"I'd been very impressed with the manager of a milk plant in Italy I'd visited while trying to decide whether to go ahead with Milkpak," he continued. "He was a chemical engineer trained in an oil refinery. He explained that the mechanical and pressure system used for this type of milk processing was very similar to that in some chemical plants. So it seemed logical to find someone locally with a similar background and put him in charge." Ali described his selection:

> I thought that Walid Nazir, a chemical engineer with whom I'd worked at the National Fertilizer Company [NFC], would be an excellent choice. When I was chairman of the NFC in the early 1970s, I brought him into the state-owned sector from a private fertilizer firm. He was later put in charge of one of the NFC's subsidiaries, and a number of people considered him as a potential future candidate for the NFC chairmanship. I thought that he was very competent and of the highest integrity. So I hired him as managing director of Milkpak and promised him complete operating autonomy, including the right to select his own management team. We did send a financial man from Packages, however, in order to provide some continuity since he had been involved in the Milkpak project since we first started our evaluation of the proposal. Given that this was a new enterprise, I wanted to make sure that Nazir had some equity in the company; he bought a number of shares in the initial public offering [49% of Milkpak's capital was raised in the public offering].

Mr. Nazir was sent abroad for a few months to study milk processing operations in several European countries. On his return, he selected six of his former colleagues at the NFC to serve as Milkpak's general managers and to run its personnel, transport, and production planning departments.

START OF OPERATIONS

After some delays in installing the equipment and setting up the plant, operations were initiated in October 1981. Capacity utilization during the first three months was very low, and Milkpak suffered a 1.7-million-rupee loss for the October–December quarter. "I attributed this at first to startup difficulties, but when the losses continued during the first six months of 1982, I put Nazir on notice that he had three months to turn the situation around," Ali stated. He continued:

> I became increasingly unhappy with the way Nazir and his team were

running the operation. Our standby generator went on the blink during the middle of that summer. You can imagine the disaster we would have had on our hands if our main power supply failed: All our milk products in process and our raw milk inventory would have been ruined. The plant manager called Nazir, who in turn informed me right after. When I called the plant manager a few days later to make sure everything was going smoothly, I was astounded to find that the generator still hadn't been fixed. When I asked him what he was doing about it, he merely responded that he had informed the managing director and assumed that the matter was settled.

Nazir claimed that some of his problems were caused by faulty communications and that the supply of leaky containers from Packages had led to large losses and marketing problems. I knew that there had been some problems at the start, but that Packages had quickly improved the quality of the containers.

By October, the plant was still operating at only about 45% of capacity and the accumulated loss for the first three quarters was well over 5 million rupees. I dismissed Nazir and the rest of this team. This caused quite a stir in Lahore. Some of Nazir's friends said that he had been sabotaged by several managers at Packages who were jealous of him. I can't accept this view, however. In any case, with the departure of Nazir I had no choice but to assume direct control. Although I couldn't really spare him from Packages, I also had to call on the assistance of that company's general manager, Mr. Tariq Hamid. Our first priority was to rehabilitate morale and change Milkpak's philosophy after a year of losses. For example, we sold off half of the company's 10 cars since we didn't need them. In fact, Milkpak had never needed them, but when I once brought this to Nazir's attention, his reply had been that the feasibility proposal had included plans for purchasing 10 cars so that was how many he had bought.

THE CHANGE IN MANAGEMENT

Ali continued:

We found that we didn't need to replace any of the seven employees I'd dismissed—they were redundant—and we eliminated the production planning department. The organization chart that they had developed was based on theory rather than on what the company needed. We found that by eliminating the top layer of management we were able to push decision-making down to lower levels while cutting overhead substantially, since Nazir's salary alone came to almost 1 million rupees. I decided to take a production man from

Packages and make him technical manager at Milkpak and appoint my nephew Yawar as commercial manager. He's the son of my eldest brother, and had done a good job in his seven years at Packages as a regional sales manager and as managing director of our operations in Zambia. I had great faith in him since he had a degree in chemical engineering and he received an MBA from the Stevens Institute of Technology in 1970. Plus, I wanted to make sure that the next generation in our family was not ignored in management positions, since this would have caused great resentment.

We made a small profit in November and December, even though we had to pay off the fired employees with three months' salary. And we made over 6 million rupees in 1983 (see *Exhibit 1*). In less than twelve months we got capacity utilization up over 65%, strengthened our milk collection network, developed a national distribution system, and introduced a few new products.

By the time we had accomplished this, both Tariq and I realized that we couldn't keep dividing our time between Packages and Milkpak and do both jobs effectively. Plus, we wasted a lot of time commuting. The milk plant was about 45 kilometers from Packages' office on a poor, heavily traveled road.

I've now decided that the time has come for Tariq and me to remove ourselves from operating decisions at Milkpak, although of course, we'll remain on the board, and I'll continue as chairman [see *Exhibits 2* and *3* for Milkpak's and Packages' directors]. We've provided the new managing director with four strong legs on which to stand: production, procurement, marketing, and finance. My older brother has recommended that we promote Yawar; he says that the time is right to have the next generation of our family begin to assume control of some of our enterprises. I guess there should be concerns about appointing a family member. Our family does, however, have substantial interests in this group of companies. They can hardly be expected to stay out of management.

On the other hand, I have a man here at Packages, Nawaz Khatak, who would be ideal for the post. He's got over twenty years' experience with Packages and recently completed the Program for Management Development at the Harvard Business School. I have complete trust and faith in him, and I think at this point that he would greatly benefit from running his own operation. But he's reluctant to take the post, since he says that the real action is here at Packages. He also recently had a heart operation and says that the constant travel to the plant would be hard on him.

"I've got to make a decision soon," Ali concluded. "Should I promote Yawar or try to induce Nawaz to take the job?"

Exhibit 1
Milkpak Five-Year Results
(*In thousand rupees*)

	1985	1984	1983	1982	1981 (2 months)
Sales	251,835	214,663	137,311	96,129	9,409
Cost of sales	223,486	185,175	114,743	85,894	9,987
Employees remuneration	9,330	8,330	5,768	5,723	1,254
Profit/(loss) before tax	5,725	8,926	6,059	(5,023)	(1,697)
Profit/(loss) after tax	4,122	4,391	6,059	(5,023)	(1,697)
Fixed assets—at cost	121,863	112,610	100,303	96,322	78,952
Accumulated depreciation	47,663	35,755	23,615	12,458	2,446
Long-term liabilities	24,474	34,108	38,518	45,202	46,489
Shareholder' equity	37,576	38,703	34,312	28,253	33,275
Paid-up capital	35,000	35,000	35,000	35,000	35,000
Share value rupees	10.74	11.06	9.80	8.07	9.51
No. of employees, permanent	210	205	168	158	163
Average annual foreign exchange rate (rupees per US$)	15.928	14.046	13.117	11.847	9.900

SOURCE: Milkpak Limited Annual Reports and IMF, *International Financial Statistics* (for exchange rates).

Exhibit 2
Milkpak's Board of Directors, 1985

Syed Babar Ali
Chairman and Managing Director

A. Jamil Nishtar
Chairman of the Pakistan Agricultural Development Bank

Tariq Hamid
General Manager, Packages

Carl Joergen Dan Jensen
Danish Turnkey Industries

Ch. Nazar Muhammad
Chairman, Servis Industries

Waldemar Kroders
German Development Institute

S. A. Samad

Imran Azim
Pakistan National Investment Trust

Exhibit 3
Packages' Board of Directors, 1985

Syed Wajid Ali
Chairman and Managing Director, Packages, Limited
  (elder brother of Syed Babar Ali)

A. Sami Quereshi
Chairman and Managing Director, Pakistan National Investment Trust[a]

Bror Anders Mansson
Akerlund & Rausing

Gad Rausing
Vice Chairman, Tetra Pak Group of Companies

I. H. Quarni
Managing Director, Pakistan National Investment Trust[a]

Qammaruddin Siddiqui
Chairman, State Life Insurance Corporation of Pakistan[a]

Riaz ul Hassan Ghauri
Chairman and Managing Director, International General Insurance Company
  of Pakistan, Limited[b]

Syed Mohammad Mohsin
Chairman and Managing Director, Mitchell's, Limited
  (brother-in-law of Syed Babar Ali)

Tariq Hamid
General Manager, Packages

Zaka Rahmatulla
Director, Treet Safety Razor Company, Limited[b]

Adviser: Syed Babar Ali

[a]State-owned enterprise.

[b]Part of the Ali Group.

Turrialba Mining Company

The Turrialba Mining Company,[1] a subsidiary of the Lincoln Mining and Manufacturing Company of New York City, was a large producer of iron ore and other minerals. It was the largest single employer in the country of Kurfana with a payroll of some 10,000 persons, most of whom worked in the mines or the "beneficiating" (concentrating) plant at Turrialba; the rest operated the company's port facilities at Santa Cruz and the railroad connecting the mines to the sea. All but the eight top managers were nationals of Kurfana. Since its founding in 1902, the company had been the target of much political debate and the scene of many conflicts. But its overriding importance to the Kurfana government had remained in that it accounted for 40% of the nation's foreign-exchange earnings. Despite Turrialba's history of contributions to Kurfana, extremist cries for nationalization of the company had become increasingly persistent.

The only other major U.S. company in the country, Chaco Oil Company, had exemplary labor relations. Nonetheless, it too had been the target of nationalization talk. One important difference between the situations facing the two companies was that Chaco's labor union strongly opposed nationalization of the oil industry. The home office managements of both companies were deeply concerned over recent events.

BACKGROUND

Kurfana was a country of 286,396 square miles with a population of 6.2 million. More than 70% of the population lived in the fertile central section of the country. From the earliest days of European settlement, this area had been the nucleus of Kurfana. Emigration from this area to the hot deserts of the east or the mountains of the west (Turrialba) had been largely a phenomenon of the last seventy-five years, when oil and minerals were discovered in these regions. Most of Kurfana's people were of a Spanish-Indian mixture. Spanish was the official language of the country.

[1]All names of companies, places, and persons are fictitious.

This case was prepared by George C. Lodge as a basis for class discussion rather than to illustrate either effective or ineffective handling of an administrative situation. Abridged with permission.

Copyright © 1990 by the President and Fellows of Harvard College. Harvard Business School case (Case A) #390-099.

Some 30% of the Kurfanese were illiterate. Although the country was a constitutional republic with executive, legislative, and judicial branches of government, political power had until recently remained, as in colonial times, highly concentrated among the large landowning and commercial interests, buttressed by military support. During most of this century, strong military regimes, usually coming to power through coups backed by the aristocracy, had ruled the country in summary fashion. But these governments had been at least outwardly responsive to popular will and had promulgated advanced social legislation, much of which had gone unobserved.

Kurfana's chief exports were cotton, sugar, iron ore, and oil. For many years government revenues had been heavily dependent upon taxes received from the mining and oil companies. The United States was Kurfana's chief trading partner. Manufacturing was rapidly expanding and ranked third in economic importance after mining and agriculture, accounting for 20% of national income.

Turrialba and Chaco were the two largest companies in Kurfana, representing total investments of $40 million and $25 million, respectively.

Kurfana's transportation system, like its population, was concentrated in the center of the country. River transport was of almost no importance, because the rivers were short and flowed rapidly. Rail connections were scanty except for two lines: one running north and south into neighboring countries, and the other east and west. The latter was constructed by Turrialba Mining in 1902 to carry ore from the mountains to the port city of San Juan.

POLITICAL AND LABOR SITUATION

The trade unions of Kurfana grew out of mutual aid societies that were organized as early as the middle of the nineteenth century. Their history was marked generally by strong government opposition and, in some cases, oppression. By 1903 Kurfana trade unions had a membership of about 40,000. The first federation of trade unions was organized in 1909 and was called the Federation of Kurfan Labor (FKO).[2] It quickly developed a strong Marxist orientation, listing among its aims "abolition of the capitalistic system with its unacceptable scheme of industrial and commercial organization which reduces most people to slavery." Among the early targets for union organization were railroad, port, and government workers and the employees of Turrialba and Chaco. Chaco anticipated

[2]*Exhibit 1* contains a list of political parties and organizations mentioned in this case.

the FKO drive and encouraged the growth of an independent union, which survived successfully. Turrialba, in a series of bitter, frequently violent conflicts, was able to avoid organization of its work force at the mines until 1959, although its railroad and port employees were included in the early drives of the FKO (later the NLF).

In 1921 FKO joined the Red Trade Union International and entered into a cooperative agreement with the Kurfan Communist Party. In 1928 the Federation had a membership of 100,000 out of a labor force estimated at 2.5 million.

The formation of the Socialist Party in Kurfana in 1933 further stimulated the organization of trade unions, and a socialist federation of trade unions was formed. With continued suppression by government and opposition from employers, the two labor movements merged in 1936 into the Kurfan Workers' Confederation (KWC), which played a major role in a "popular front" movement resulting in the election of President Francisco Aguilar. Its success in this election permanently established the Kurfan Labor Movement as an important political force.

The Socialist–Communist merger broke apart in 1940; the Socialists kept the name KWC, and the Communists called themselves the National Labor Federation (NLF).

The landed aristocracy and the army became apprehensive about the growing power of labor and in 1949 backed a coup led by General Guillermo Henli. Henli appealed to the socialist trade unions for support and promised widespread reform and liberal social legislation. The coup was successful, and although much of the promised legislation was passed, it was only partially enforced. As the years went by, General Henli became more and more oppressive and finally forced the labor movement to a standstill.

In 1956 General Henli was shot; with the country in chaos, a military junta took over with the promise of new elections. Once again the Kurfan labor movement united temporarily and succeeded in electing a prominent socialist intellectual, Jaime Arboles, as president.

In 1958 Arboles became concerned about the growing power of the Communist elements in the labor movement and outlawed the Communist Party. He sought the cooperation of Turrialba and Chaco in the formation of a government-sponsored KWC labor organization to counter Communist efforts, but in this he was largely unsuccessful. In 1959 Arboles announced his intention to nationalize foreign mining interests and instituted a tax reform program that alarmed the business elite. In September of that year his regime was overthrown in a coup led by his naval aide, Juan Delgado, who in turn became president.

Delgado inaugurated a regime of labor oppression, and many union leaders were forced into exile or prison. The Communist Party split itself and its trade union affiliate, the NLF, into two groups, one of which went underground with the KWC while the other cooperated with the Delgado regime and was allowed to operate. The effect of this was to encourage the growth of Communist-dominated labor organizations while anti-Communist leadership was prevented from acting.

During this period the number of unionized workers in Kurfana was scarcely more than in the 1930s. The KWC claimed to have 85,000 dues-paying members, and the NLF (Communist) claimed 40,000, the most important of whom were unquestionably the newly organized Turrialba mine workers. Several more thousand were organized in independent unions such as that of the Chaco Oil Co. Nevertheless, the vast majority of agricultural, industrial, and commercial workers were not organized in any union.

Delgado was popular with the business circles of Kurfana, including U.S. interests. He spoke English well and was the life of many a country club party. On his birthday Turrialba, together with other Kurfan companies, purchased several full-page advertisements in the three newspapers of Kurfana extolling his virtues.

The U.S. government was also pleased with the Delgado regime, which spoke out loudly and firmly in the United Nations and elsewhere against the evils of Communism and the USSR (from which Kurfana had withdrawn diplomatic recognition). The country welcomed U.S. military assistance and allowed certain key military installations to be located on Kurfan territory. In 1961 the U.S. Embassy awarded Delgado a medal for his great contribution to the cause of liberty in the world.

Meanwhile the KWC, led by Jorge Casita, a prominent Socialist and union organizer, had established a powerful underground movement with headquarters on an old hacienda in rural Kurfana. In rural exile, Casita was able during this period to organize substantial groups of sugar and other plantation workers who had not been unionized before. In July 1963 he called a general strike and sent armed bands into the capital city. The army, which had never entirely trusted Delgado because of his naval background, stayed in its quarters. The police joined Casita's troops and seized the presidential palace. Delgado barely escaped with his life in a U.S. Air Force jet.

A junta of young army officers friendly to Casita restored order. General elections were held, and Casita, the leader of the new Party of Revolutionary Development (PRD), was elected president by an overwhelming majority. Casita was determined to reform his country, give representation to all its people, pursue a vigorous program of land redistribution, place the country's substantial natural resources in Kurfan hands, and exploit them for the benefit of Kurfanese. While he did not feel that nationalization of Kurfana's mining interests would necessarily lead to increased efficiency and betterment of the economy, he believed that nationalization might well be necessary as a symbol of reform to give impetus to his new administration.

The Communists were discredited for their part in the Delgado regime, but those who had gone underground with the rest of the trade union movement managed to hold an edge of strength outside the KWC's ranks. While Casita had the overwhelming support of the people, his party, the PRD, did not control the National Assembly, which was divided into about a third PRD Socialist, a third Communist, and a third a loose coalition of conservative followers of the recently overthrown dictator, Delgado. As in many other Latin American countries, the Communists were divided between the more traditional Moscow types and the more violent Pekingistas, who advocated the way of Mao and Castro.

TURRIALBA MINING COMPANY BACKGROUND

A retired U.S. army engineer prospecting for gold in a mountainous and remote region of Turrialba in 1901 discovered rich iron ore deposits there. He persuaded Lincoln Mining and Manufacturing to develop the area's mining potential, and in 1903 the company sent three young mining engineers to start constructing preliminary facilities and exploring the mining site. General Tulio Sanches, who was ruling Kurfana at that time, gave his complete cooperation.

Turrialba developed rapidly. Housing was built for the engineering staff and supervisors and camps for the enlarging work force. Roads, schools, and hospitals were constructed. It was not long before a new town was born. Two mining operations were developed: a shaft mine into the side of the mountain and, more recently, an open pit mine 10 miles away. Both were serviced by a common beneficiating plant located about halfway between. Railroad connections had to be built between these facilities and Santa Cruz, 200 miles away, where the machinery and material required at Turrialba were unloaded from freighters and where, in turn, the ore was shipped out.

The Kurfan government was especially pleased by the company's railroad system, which provided transportation and access to vast reaches of the country for the first time. It was, therefore, most generous in the right of way it allowed the company through rich sugar country for its rail line to the coast. In 1927 Turrialba joined with a British consortium and, combining 10,000 acres of its right-of-way land with a tract purchased by the British firm, became a majority shareholder in a 20,000-acre sugar plantation. But it has had little to do with the management of the plantation.

Turrialba produced 65% of the iron ore used or distributed by Lincoln. The ore was valued highly because it was singularly free of impurities; in fact, it was ranked among the highest-quality ore in the world. Virtually all of Turrialba's ore was exported, most of it proceeding directly to the United States, although some was sold in Brazil. Even though the company now had to pay 60% of its gross profits to the Kurfan government, construction of a second open-pit mine was scheduled for 1966.

Turrialba's salary scales had traditionally been 10–15% higher than those of local industry. Blue-collar laborers received an average of $4 a day in 1964 plus housing and numerous other fringe benefits. Skilled and white-collar workers, who constituted about 15% of the work force, received an average of $6 a day plus benefits. Since its beginning the company had prided itself on its extensive contribution to the country's social and economic infrastructure. For sixty years it had maintained hospitals, schools, housing, and transportation facilities for its employees. Most of the company employees at the mines lived in three-story barracks, although some still used the smaller units that were part of the original camp construction. The company had virtually eliminated the diseases that were once the scourge of the region, and its workers enjoyed a considerably longer life span than the other citizens of Kurfana. In view of this history of beneficient activity on behalf of its work force and the community, the management found it perplexing to be so frequently confronted with labor relations problems.

Many disputes arose from jealousies and resentments among workers who felt that Turrialba had been discriminatory in the assignment of housing. The barracks and other housing were supposed to be maintained by the company, which was under continual attack for failing to provide adequate services. Turrialba felt that the workers were negligent and irresponsible and should be expected to take better care of their quarters.

Despite repeated attempts by the Communist NLF in the early years and later by the KWC, Turrialba consistently resisted efforts to organize the work force at the mines. It discouraged organization attempts in various ways, sometimes by discharging organizers, sometimes relegating them to poorer jobs or less desirable housing. The management reasoned that the workers were better off than any others in the nation; there was a long backlog of men who wanted to come to work in the mines (in fact selection of new workers was something of an embarrassment to the company); they and their families were well cared for; therefore, a union was not justified and would only be a disrupting obstacle to company–worker relationships. The company had a Kurfan industrial relations director in charge of each mine and the beneficiating plant, as well as the service and machinery shops and the railroad and port facilities. While there were no formal grievance procedures, Turrialba felt that the indus-

trial relations directors were able to understand and deal with the problems of their countrymen.

The first sustained and militant effort to organize the mine workers was
started by Ernesto Brava in the late 1940s. He lived with his wife and four
children in one of the smaller, more ramshackle houses. Although little
more than a shack, his house to him was a proud symbol of his station and
independence.

Brava came to the company as a miner in 1942 when he was twenty.
Extremely hard working, he managed to work his way up to a position as
a mine foreman. He took a correspondence course given over the radio at
night and taught himself to read and write. He read everything he could
get his hands on, and what he read strengthened his belief that communism was a fraud, promising pie-in-the-sky it could not provide. At the
same time he was convinced that revolutionary social reform was a necessity for Kurfana, and he believed the trade union movement, working for
the establishment of a socialist government, was the most effective engine
to produce this reform. He believed, however, that the labor movement
had relied too heavily on political ties and influence and that to achieve
real strength it must increase its economic bargaining power with individual companies. He therefore felt that organization of Turrialba's workers
was a patriotic duty of the highest order.

The company management regarded Brava as a dangerous radical. He
talked too much, and some felt that he was a Communist. But the company recognized his qualities as a foreman and, realizing he was a leader
among the workers, never dared to discharge him. In 1950, partly as a
device to resist his repeated attempts to organize the mine workers into a
KWC affiliate, the company encouraged the formation of the Turrialba
Association, through which it administered certain welfare and pension
activities. The association had no bargaining power, and no more than
10% of the work force ever joined the association at any one time. The
company repeated its argument that there was no need for a union as long
as the workers were receiving higher wages and more benefits than those
engaged in similar work in Kurfana. It also felt that if it were to allow
union organization, Communist extremists would almost certainly take
over the organization. The company was supported by the Henli regime.
On several occasions Brava sought an appointment with David G. Kendall, the general manager of Turrialba, to express his aims and objectives
but was denied a meeting.

Kendall had been general manager of the company for fifteen years. He
graduated first in his class at the University of Colorado and took a
graduate degree in mining engineering at MIT. He then joined Lincoln as
chief engineer at the mines, working his way up to the top job in 1947. He
rarely left Turrialba and was totally consumed by his work. He regarded
his task as the ultimate in mining engineering: running a large, modern

mine in the wilderness, having to overcome countless natural obstacles, making new machinery when it broke down, improving, inventing, and working with all his might. Sometimes he became agitated at the Kurfanese, who he felt did not really understand the meaning of "a good day's work," but he was a calm and well-balanced man and prided himself on his understanding and ability to get along.

He tried to keep the company outside of politics and to heed the advice laid down by New York headquarters in a policy statement:

> Lincoln Mining and Manufacturing has 22 operations around the world, most of them in developing countries undergoing rapid political and social change. It is essential to the best interests of the company and its stockholders that local managers keep themselves, their associates, and their operations free from involvement in the political affairs of each country. Managers should develop warm and friendly contacts with the business community and should be guided in their policies in general by the standards and traditions of that community. In view of the nature of our operations and because we are an American company, it will undoubtedly be necessary for us to provide greater community service and better wages and working conditions than may be customary. But we should endeavor to cause as little disruption to the existing order of things as possible. In general, managers should conduct themselves so as to protect the company investment and produce the best possible return to our stockholders.

Kendall did his best to observe this rule. Even if he did not have time, he made sure that his fellow U.S. management officials met regularly with the Kurfan business community. This was done informally at the country club and within the company's regular entertainment schedule in the capital city. While Turrialba's size and U.S. orientation made it unique in many ways, its labor and community policies were well within the Kurfanese norm, although slightly on the liberal side.

CURRENT SITUATION

Kendall reasoned that he was quite within the spirit of headquarters policy in opposing Brava's organizing efforts. The business community of the country was surely in sympathy with his position, as was the government, although the latter had sought company cooperation in strengthening a union that Henli's followers had formed to broaden his political base.

When the Arboles regime came to power in 1956, Brava received governmental encouragement to pursue his organizing efforts. But by this time strong Communist-financed leadership had moved into the mining areas.

Tulio Arias, one of the early leaders of the NLF, returned from a six-month trip to the USSR in 1957 and later moved into the small hotel at Turrialba with three organizers, equipped with two jeeps and a mimeograph machine. Arias appeared as almost the opposite of Brava. Fifty years old, urbane and cultivated, he spoke English well and seemed in all respects a quiet and soft-spoken gentleman.

One spring evening in 1958 he dropped in at Kendall's house, saying he had heard of the labor difficulties at Turrialba and was distressed by them. He said that ever since he had been a young man he had marveled at the ingenuity and genius that had developed the mines into a great resource of Kurfana. Kendall was impressed by him and thanked him for his visit. When he was told later by one of his industrial relations officers that Arias was a Communist and a longtime leader of the NLF, he found it hard to believe. He remembered the late 1920s, when the NLF had been trying to organize the mines, and saw little similarity between Arias and the dangerous radicals of those days.

In November 1958 Arias announced his intension to form the Turrialba Miners Union, to be affiliated with the NLF. He called for elections and for certification of the new union by the Arboles government. His careful, well-financed efforts paid off in widespread worker support. The small group remaining loyal to Brava continued sporadic organizing activities, now with the help of ORIT (the regional arm of the International Confederation of Free Trade Unions) and the International Mine Workers Federation (an international trade secretariat).

On Christmas Eve, 1958, fighting broke out between Brava's followers and company police. Arias and his supporters watched as five of Brava's men were killed. The fracas was soon over, and two days later Arias led a delegation to see Kendall, who was severely shaken by the events. Arias pointed out that his union could provide the company many benefits. He pledged the maintenance of labor peace, help in increasing worker productivity and improving mine discipline, help in meeting the problems of squatters around the town, and other actions which, together with his persuasive, sophisticated manners and his good English, convinced Kendall that he sincerely wanted to promote Turrialba's best interests. Kendall was impressed with Arias and realized that he represented a more powerful force than Brava. He was also mindful that over the years the small NLF unions of company railroad and port workers had not caused any trouble. While aware of the rumors of Arias's Communist connections, he could not believe that a man so highly motivated and intelligent could be a Communist. Kendall therefore placed no obstacle in the way of Arias's organization of the company's work force.

Disillusioned and bitter, Brava complained angrily to the minister of labor, the local representative of ORIT, and the labor attaché of the U.S.

Embassy. All were sympathetic. The labor attaché persuaded the ambassador to call Kendall in and try to persuade him to reconsider his action. The ambassador told Kendall that while the embassy did not have proof that Arias was a Communist, there were strong grounds for suspicion. Kendall replied that in his view Brava was more of a Communist than Arias and said that Arias was a better man than "the young rabble-rouser." He added that the NLF while "supposedly Communist" had been quite cooperative. He further stated that labor relations at the Turrialba mines were none of the ambassador's business. The ambassador noted that it was typical of Communist organizations to be cooperative until a command came from "higher authority" to "go into action." The labor attaché, acting on his own but with what he assumed to be the ambassador's approval, thereupon met with Brava and the ORIT and IMWF representatives to see what could be done to overthrow Arias and organize Turrialba's workers under Brava and the KWC. Upon hearing this, the company complained to the ambassador, who advised his labor attaché to go more slowly.

In the meantime, Kurfana's business community, the Army, the U.S. military advisers, and the U.S. Embassy were becoming ever more apprehensive about what appeared to be leftward tendencies of the Arboles regime and doubtful of the regime's ability to control increasing Communist activity. This concern heightened when Arboles, responding to what he considered irresistible popular pressure, advocated nationalization of the nation's mining industry and a new income tax law.

Kendall appealed to the embassy for help and wired his home office, requesting that the Lincoln management go to Washington and urge the secretary of state to act in such a way as to halt these movements by the Arboles regime. At the same time the Defense Department was becoming concerned over Arboles's talk of forcing the United States to abandon its small but important Kurfan military installations.

As United States pressure built, Arboles became bitterly resentful. He pressed his plans for nationalization and other similar measures forward with renewed vigor. On July 4, 1959, the army led a coup, and Juan Delgado became president of Kurfana. Arboles fled to Mexico.

Widely known as a personal enemy of Arboles, Arias was made minister of labor by Delgado, who saw this appointment as an opportunity to secure the political support of the left that he badly needed. Arias left one of his loyal lieutenants in charge of the Turrialba union, but the company was assured there would be no problems either from him or from the office of the minister of labor. Arias had secured passage of a law providing that only one union could represent the workers in any one plant. Ernesto Brava, who refused to stop his activities, was branded a troublemaker and forced underground, where he joined Jorge Casita and other KWC leaders. During this period they were financed by ORIT, largely with money from the American labor movement.

Juan Delgado ruled with an iron hand. Trade union activity was limited to only that which the above-ground NLF affiliates (including Turrialba) were allowed to carry out under Arias's watchful eye. Kendall became increasingly happy with his new labor relationship, which brought with it none of the trouble and difficulty he had foreseen accompanying a union organized by Brava. The union gradually took over many of the more distasteful tasks the company had to perform, such as supervision of the company town, initial interviewing, screening, and selection of workers for the mine, and even some of the more elementary training operations. The union and the company prospered.

The Alliance for Progress put the Delgado regime into something of a quandary. The Alliance requirement of land and tax reform and other measures designed to ensure social justice were quite inconsistent with the aims of many of the oligarchy supporting the regime. Communist and NLF underground leaders opposed the Alliance as a "fraud and a plot by the North American capitalists to screen their imperialistic designs behind appealing words." But it was important to Delgado that he maintain his friendship with the United States and a continuing flow of foreign aid and assistance. His supporters in the business community praised him loudly and urged both Turrialba and Chaco to do everything they could to support Delgado. So the two companies joined the business community in placing advertisements in the papers and extolling his virtues.

Popular resentment grew against the oppressive policies of the Delgado regime. There were widespread feelings that he was running the country for the benefit of U.S. interests, and he was also suspected of personal corruption.

Casita's KWC forces were joined by the Communists who had gone underground with the fall of Arboles, and in 1963 Casita led a general strike, overthrew the regime, and later became president. Despite a brief attempt to take over the revolutionary movement, Arias was discredited and forced to leave the country, more for his betrayal of the labor movement during the Delgado regime than because he was a Communist. While Casita's victory brought obvious new strength to the KWC and thus to Brava, the NLF through its principal affiliate, the Turrialba Miners Union, was strongly entrenched at Turrialba. The NLF represented the hard core of Communist strength in the country.

In late 1963 a Peking-trained Kurfan named Hector Santos took over the leadership of the Communist Party and, from this position, set the policy for the NLF. Santos's strategy was to oppose and defeat Casita's reform program in every way possible. His tactics were to:

1. Join the conservative forces in the Assembly to vote down reform measures, arguing that they didn't go far enough and were "frauds on the people"
2. Call periodic strikes at the Turrialba Mining Company, which sup-

plied 40% of Kurfana's foreign exchange, thereby bringing economic pressure to bear on the government while gaining useful opportunities to decry U.S. capitalist imperialism and demand nationalization of foreign firms

In the meantime, a new ambassador had come from the United States. His two main concerns in Kurfana were keeping the Casita revolution free of Communist influence and thwarting the almost inevitable push for nationalization of Turrialba and Chaco.

The New York office of Lincoln Mining and Manufacturing was perplexed and concerned at the situation in Kurfana. Santos's directed work stoppages had cut production by as much as 20%. Turrialba showed a slight loss in 1963, and 1964 promised to be worse.

The trying years had taken their toll on Kendall's health. He was no longer a young man, and he was not in the least disappointed at the suggestion from New York that a younger man be sent to assist him and perhaps gradually take over the operations. But some at headquarters argued that Turrialba's treasurer, a fifty-year-old native of Kurfana, should be Kendall's successor.

Exhibit 1
Political Parties and Labor Organizations in Order of Appearance

Federation of Kurfan Labor	FKO	Organized in 1909. Joined Red Trade Union International and entered into a cooperative agreement with the Kurfan Communist party in 1928.
Socialist Party		Formed in 1933.
Kurfan Workers Confederation	KWC	Formed by a merger of the FKO with the Socialist trade union in 1936. In 1940 the merger collapsed, and the Socialists kept the name KWC.
National Labor Federation	NLF	The Communist portion of the old KWC. Formed in 1940.
Party of Revolutionary Development	PRD	Formed under the leadership of Casita in 1963. Political orientation was Socialist.
Turrialba Association		A company union formed in 1950.
ORIT		Regional arm of the International Confederation of Free Trade Unions. Supported Brava.
International Mine Workers Federation	IMWF	An international trade secretariat.

The Case of the "Untouchable" Water-Carrier

It was seven o'clock in the morning, time for "Good and Great Thoughts" on the state-owned All India Radio. As he listened to the day's preacher quoting Mahatma Gandhi's railings against the pernicious custom of untouchability,[1] Sundara Raman's thoughts took on a hue of self-congratulation. After all, he had reason to be happy. Within six months after taking over as the manager of a medium-size, semiurban branch of the state-owned bank, he had appointed an "untouchable" to the job of water-carrier in the bank. It was the first time in the branch's five year history such an appointment had taken place. The opportunity arose when the previous water-carrier was promoted as a messenger. The appointment was a temporary one. But Raman felt that after a few months he would be able to make it permanent. Raman wondered how his staff would react to the appointment. After all, there had been other candidates, equally poor and badly in need of a job, but from upper and middle castes.

"Untouchability is a crime against humanity,"[2] intoned the voice from the radio. "Of course, it is," muttered Raman to himself. But he could not help recalling his accountant Jagan Mishra's misgivings when he told him of the appointment. Jagan Mishra was forty-five years old and had risen from the ranks, having joined the bank as a clerk more than twenty years before. He said: "Mr. Raman, you are new to North India. Here habits die hard. This appointment will not go down well with the staff. Untouchables are considered unclean. No upper caste person will be prepared to eat at the same table as the untouchable. Do you expect them to drink water from this person's hand?" Raman had brushed aside such objections saying that in his state in the South, where such customs prevailed before, things had changed in the last thirty years since independence.

---

[1]See Appendix A for the Preamble to the Constitution of India and Appendix B for a description of the caste system.

[2]Untouchability was not confined to India alone, as a March 9, 1983, headline of the *International Herald Tribune* proclaimed: "Untouchables in Japan Fighting Prejudice in Jobs and Marriage."

This case (Case A) was prepared by U. Srinivasa Rangan, Research Associate at IMEDE. The case is intended for classroom discussion and is not designed to illustrate either effective or ineffective handling of administrative situations. Abridged with permission.

Now there was no stigma attached to castes, particularly in urban areas. Surely things had changed here as well.

Just a couple of years before Raman's graduation from the university, with a first-class honors degree, the Indian government had taken over all the major banks in the country. The nationalization was justified by the political party in power as a necessary step toward achieving economic and social justice in a country of contrasting wealth and poverty. The extension of government control also meant that statutory rules relating to the reservation of jobs for the socially disadvantaged, low-caste people applied to these banks as well. The state control also meant that the job openings in the banks were filled by means of competitive examinations open to all. Government had also ordered a massive and rapid expansion of the banks into rural and semiurban areas in the name of helping the poor and economically disadvantaged farmers. Sundara Raman came from an upper-caste family in South India. Like other ambitious young men of his generation, Raman had taken the All India Competitive Examination in banking and had joined one of the large nationalized banks as a management trainee. After his training period of two years, when he had received high praise from his superiors for his conscientious and dedicated work, he had chosen to serve in the Small-Scale Industrial Finance sector of the bank. This decision surprised many of his colleagues, who felt he would have done well to choose one of the more glamorous postings like the Foreign Exchange Department, which held possibilities of an overseas assignment in the future. Raman had no regrets about his decision. He knew it would mean that for a long time to come he would have to serve in small-town branches. For a person who prided himself on his enlightened family background and who had often participated in college debates where he had consistently spoken on his vision of an egalitarian and progressive India, it was an opportunity "to serve the small man" and, as he put it, "to practice what he had preached."

Over the next three years, Raman had distinguished himself as a tireless worker. He had been promoted to manager within two years. He had already served short stints as a manager when his Head Office asked him whether he would be willing to go as branch manager to a slightly larger town branch in North India, a few hundred miles east of New Delhi. It was a challenging assignment, his boss said, in a poor and backward district. Raman, whose recent marriage had been arranged in traditional Hindu fashion, had agreed enthusiastically despite his wife's reservations about living more than 1,500 miles from their native town amid people who spoke a different language from theirs. For Raman it was an opportunity to live in another part of India and experience a different culture.

The first few months had been somewhat frustrating. Raman felt he could not expect the same kind of efficiency from his supervisors and clerks as he had come to expect from his subordinates in his earlier branches. The new branch, which had expanded its business rapidly in an area previously not served by a bank, had fallen on hard times. As with trends elsewhere in the country after nationalization, the customer service was believed to have fallen off steeply. But slowly things were improving. He believed he had established good working relationships with the staff.

Feeling confident that he could motivate his staff, Raman had agreed to a substantial increase in many aspects of the budget—deposits, loans, and profits—for the year, although another nationalized bank had recently opened a branch in the town. In his discussions with the regional manager in January he had conceded the need to keep staff costs down and increase profits. He knew that nationalization had come in for criticism on account of the poor profit performance of banks. The bank management had responded by insisting that their managers achieve budgeted profit goals. Further, in the future, performance reviews were to become the bases for promotions. Raman had also agreed to make more loans to the farmers in the surrounding areas in order to meet the bank's targets for the agricultural sector.

Raman believed he could also work well with the leader of the clerks' union. The union leader, Charan Singh, seemed a dedicated socialist. His conversations were often peppered with references to equality of workers and officers and working class solidarity. Charan Singh came from a highly respected landowning family in the village nearby. He was thirty years old and had joined the bank five years earlier, soon after graduating from a little-known college a few hundred miles to the east. Raman had come to like him. Unlike other union leaders, who often resorted to work stoppages and slogan-shouting at the slightest provocation, Singh seemed a man of sound common sense. It was widely believed that bank unions, with their membership assured of lifetime employment, had become more powerful than the management themselves. After nationalization the salaries and perquisites of staff had gone up substantially in relation to other sectors of the economy. For example, in rural India the salary of a bank messenger often exceeded that of a high school teacher. Raman was aware of the advantages of good working relationships with the unions. Although the office started only at ten o'clock, Raman was usually at his desk at nine. This day in April was no different. As he walked to his office, Raman could not but reflect on the hot and humid early summer weather. At the entrance of the bank building, the new water-carrier, Kishore Kumar, was polishing up his brass water pot. He looked happy in his new, neatly pressed and clean uniform. Raman had instructed him to bathe or take a shower in the morning before he came to the office and groom himself to give a good impression. Kumar seemed to have followed that advice. As he saw Raman, Kishore Kumar drew himself upright and politely wished him a good day. Raman nodded back and headed toward his room.

It was eleven o'clock. It was usually the busiest hour in the branch. Raman started out on his customary stroll through the bank. As he walked through the main banking hall, he could feel some inexplicable tension in the air. Everyone seemed to be busy. The messenger carrying the files dutifully nodded his head in salutation. But the usual smile on his face was not there. Raman wondered why. He saw Kishore standing near the large table of the accountant. He looked crestfallen. His water pot and the cups were on the floor next to him. The accountant looked sullen.

As he strode up to Jagan Mishra, Raman could tell something was wrong and that it had to do with the water-carrier. He was right. Mishra said in a low voice; "Mr. Raman, none of the staff wants to drink the water served by Kishore. Everyone wants to be allowed to go out to drink water in the neighboring restaurant. But how can I allow that with so many customers waiting to be served at the counter?" As Raman looked at Kishore Kumar, in whose sunken eyes large teardrops seemed to be welling up, he wondered what steps he should take next to deal with this sensitive and seemingly urgent issue.

APPENDIX A
THE CONSTITUTION OF INDIA

PREAMBLE

WE, THE PEOPLE OF INDIA, having solemnly resolved to constitute India into a SOVEREIGN DEMOCRATIC REPUBLIC and to secure to all its citizens:

JUSTICE, social, economic and political;

LIBERTY of thought, expression, belief, faith and worship;

EQUALITY of status and of opportunity;

and to promote among them all:

FRATERNITY assuring the dignity of the individual
and the unity of the Nation;

IN OUR CONSTITUENT ASSEMBLY this twenty-sixth day of November, 1949, do hereby ADOPT, ENACT AND GIVE TO OURSELVES THIS CONSTITUTION.

APPENDIX B
A SHORT NOTE ON INDIA AND THE CASTE SYSTEM

India, although a sovereign nation today, has always been called a subcontinent. This was not without reason; its size (seventh largest land mass in the world), its extremes of physical geography (ranging from permanently snowbound mountains in the North to the hot and humid tropical climes in the South), population (world's second largest at about 680 million), and multiplicity of religions (all major religions of the world are represented in India), languages (18 major languages and about 200 dialects), and castes (some 3,000-odd) make the appellation subcontinent an apt one, even in 1983.

The real binding force in the subcontinent was, however, the all-pervasive influence of Hinduism. Hinduism had frequently been compared to a great sponge which absorbs endlessly. In the early centuries of the Christian era, it almost totally absorbed Buddhism. Even today Moslem and Christian converts from Hinduism sometimes retain enough of their old customs to seek their marriage partners only within their original subcaste. And Sikhism has retained, in spite of the founder's intentions, the caste system of the Hindus. As is well known, Indian society is divided into castes, each of which is endogamous and into one of which a man or woman enters irrevocably at birth. Status and, to some extent, occupation are still largely determined by caste, and caste considerations enter greatly into politics; though the scene is a complex and rapidly shifting one in many regions.

An all-encompassing definition of the caste system and explanation of its durability are difficult if not impossible to achieve. The four classic castes of the Hindu scriptures, the Brahmin (priest), the Kshatriya (warrior), the Vaishya (trader), and the Sudra (cultivator or artisan), have constantly proliferated. Sometimes subcastes are linked with occupation, but often they are not. "It suggests," said one commentator, "a division of the inhabitants of England into families of Norman descent, Clerks in Holy Orders, positivists, ironmongers, vegetarians, communists, and Scotsmen." The best working description is probably the often quoted one: "A caste is a group of families whose members can marry with each other and eat in each other's company without believing themselves polluted." Avoiding pollution or undergoing ritual purification when pollution had occurred was (and is) a complicated and time-consuming business for the orthodox Hindu. The caste system also created the "Untouchables" whose touch was polluting to other castes. The "Untouchables" were often forced to live in colonies outside the village limits in unhygienic surroundings. It may be that the caste system made for stability and reduced tensions in a plural society, since everyone knew his place and could not greatly change it. By its sanctification of tradition it may also have provided some safeguard against arbitrary authority. But, over the years, the system had acquired considerable rigidity.

The rigidity of the caste system provoked reactions in India long before there was any Western influence. In part, Buddhism itself, originating in Northern India in the sixth century B.C., was such a reaction. But a thousand years later, although it had by then spread to other parts of Asia, it had virtually disappeared in India itself. Only in very recent times has there again been an increase in professing Buddhists in India, significantly a high proportion of them converts from the former "Untouchables." The advent of the British and their influence during the colonial period between 1727 and 1947 added pressures from within by reformist-minded Hindus. The latest and most famous of these reformers was Mahatma Gandhi. He was especially concerned about the depressed status of "Untouchables," who performed all the most menial functions. Significantly, in his moral crusade for the uplift of the "Untouchables," he argued not that the Hindu Scriptures were wrong but that they had been misinterpreted.

The reformist movements had had considerable success in abolishing the custom of untouchability. But the progress had been uneven; there were wide variations among different regions of India and between rural and urban sections. When India obtained its independence in 1947, the framers of the Indian Constitution took the opportunity to legislate against the custom. The Constitution rested on the notion of individual liberty as against the idea of group identity. The Preamble of the Constitution of India is the quintessence of the spirit of Indian law today. The Constitution abolished caste "untouchability" (now to be legally defined by courts) and forbade any other restriction on public facilities arising out of caste membership. Subsequent legislation against caste restrictions had proved generally influential at the urban temple or the crossroad coffee shop but not at the village well. It is worth mentioning here that the chief architect of the Indian Constitution was himself an Untouchable.

Independent India had also gone on to make special provisions for the "Untouchables" by stipulating job reservation quotas for them at every level of entry and promotion in the civil service and state-owned companies. There were also quotas for them in educational institutions and state and federal legislatures. While they had gone far in the direction of alleviating the grievances of the "Untouchables," there had been a backlash from the middle castes, particularly the landowning farmers, in recent days, because of this kind of "positive discrimination." In a poor country with few employment opportunities, this was believed to be inevitable, but it had exacerbated tension among the various castes. There were several press reports of violent clashes between different caste groups, particularly in North India.

Many observers now believe that the "Untouchables" problem, at the current stage, is akin to those of blacks in the United States, Indians in Central and South America, minority tribes in several African states, non-Moslem minorities in many Moslem countries, minority immigrants in many West European countries, the natives of Australia and New Zealand, and the descendants of Japan's former caste of Untouchables.

Thai Polyester Fiber (C)

A colorful supplement of the *Bangkok Post,* dated January 4, 1979, contained a speech by M. Yipsoon Patipong, joint managing director of Thai
Polyester Fiber Co. Ltd. (TPF) on the occasion of TPF's grand opening:

> It is indeed an auspicious day to have Thai Polyester Fiber Co. Ltd.
> officially opened. This is undoubtedly the result of much effort by
> many people. January 4, 1979, will also be the day when all bad
> rumors about TPF will be forgotten once and for all. This is the date
> when all shareholders, staff members, creditors, and everybody
> directly or indirectly involved with TPF can look forward to a bright
> future.
>
> On behalf of the management, we are very grateful to the Supreme
> Patriarch[1] to have his holy presence here for the opening ceremony.
> His holy presence will be a good omen forever for TPF. We are also
> indebted to our valuable customers, board of directors, shareholders,
> staff members, and workers for the cooperation they have rendered to
> the company. We are especially indebted to M. Patranaphong
> Sudrom, president of the Bangkok Bank; M. Yipsoon Praboon,
> president of the Yipsoon Group; and M. Claude Deloin, vice-
> president of Chimie du Sud S.A. Without them this project would
> have never survived the extremely difficult period TPF went through
> in 1977.

The Thai Polyester Fiber Company, a 1.6-billion-baht[2] polymerization
and filature enterprise, was founded in 1972 as a joint venture between
Chimie du Sud, one of the world's largest chemical conglomerates, and
the Yipsoon Group, a diversified textile company that owned or operated
more than 50% of the Thai textile industry. In 1979 the company had
sales of 800 million baht, profits of 9.6 million, debt of 1.2 billion, and an
equity of 400 million.

TPF incorporated the most advanced chemical technology in continu-

---

[1]Thailand's divine monarch is the head of the Buddhist hierarchy in Bangkok.

[2]The 1979 exchange rate was 20.40 Thai baht per 4.11 French francs per U.S. dollar.

This case was originally prepared by Elizabeth Fouraker, under the supervision of Associate
Professor Philippe Lasserre. It was edited by Research Assistant Alvin G. Wint, for use at the
Harvard Business School as the basis for class discussion rather than to illustrate either
effective or ineffective handling of an administrative situation. See Chapter 4 for Case B.

ous polymerization of polyester with a more conventional system of spinning, winding, and attenuating synthetic fibers and threads.

The Bangkok Bank lent 55% of the project costs and financed the working capital. The bank agreed to join the shareholders of the joint venture when they were invited by M. Yipsoon, an important customer and a member of the bank's board of directors. The Bangkok Bank had two directors on the TPF Executive Board of Directors. They reported directly to the board of directors of the Bangkok Bank. The Bangkok Bank held 9% of the joint venture's capital stock.

The initial period of operation, from 1975 to 1979, was fraught with problems resulting from stagnant demand, exponential increases in raw material costs, and management conflicts. The TPF Company lost hundreds of millions of baht during this period. In 1979 the market was improving (thanks, partly, to the recently instituted direct trade with China), and TPF management hoped to be able to pay its first dividends by 1984.

When conflicts between the partners over management style, technical problems, and purchasing agreements made by the Yipsoon Group became very severe, the president of the Bangkok Bank stepped in as a mediator.

Chimie du Sud appointed M. Jacques Villermon as a special delegate in Thailand in charge of monitoring the crisis. When operations started, M. Pagkol Prasarn, who was not a member of the Yipsoon family, was appointed as a joint managing director with M. Yipsoon Patipong. M. Pagkol reported to a special committee, the executive board of directors, which met every fifteen days.

At one time the Yipsoon Group had wanted to withdraw from the partnership and write off its losses, but the president of the Bangkok Bank persuaded it to stay and arranged for the capital to be increased from 260 million baht to 400 million baht. In 1978 M. Yipsoon Praboon, the dynamic entrepreneur who created the Thai partner firm, was asked to stay out of the management of TPF.

The Yipsoon Group's observations concerning the problems of the joint venture revolved around five major issues:

1. Despite the fact that the building was completed on schedule by the Thai engineering subcontractors, the Chimie du Sud Textile Division and Ateliers Roannais de Construction Textile engineers claimed that the building was not ready for equipment installation; thus the French did not succeed in getting the machinery in place until a year after the original startup date. Later, the French engineers admitted that the building had been ready but that they had not completed the assembly of the equipment in France. The French firm was not sufficiently familiar with the technology it sold to the joint venture.

2. The plant's technical performance was below standard. There were initial problems with the quality, consistency, and texture of the fibers and threads. The major problems took eight months to solve. Polyester fibers still tended to stick in the bales. The filament thread still tended to break during draw twisting, which resulted in poor quality. M. Yipsoon Patipong believed that the TPF firm had used inferior raw materials to control costs. The product was not acceptable, even in Thailand, where quality tolerances were greater than in the export markets. The French partners blamed the Yipsoon Group for failing to sell all the plant's products. The Yipsoon Group later agreed to buy the TPF products, despite continuing quality problems, in order to ensure the survival of TPF. Yipsoon management felt that it could obtain polyester thread and fiber of better quality at a lower price elsewhere, but purchased the TPF products because it had a large stake in the firm.

3. Operating costs were much too high because of the presence of 40 to 60 high-paid French technicians, some with their families. Salaries for this cadre totaled five times the sum of the salaries, housing, and food provided for the 800 Thai workers.

4. The French engineers and technicians were withholding knowledge from the Thai engineers. Although 99% of the work was done by Thais, a crucial 1% was controlled by the French. Chimie du Sud was withholding critical training in theory technology in order to remain indispensable to the plant's operation and in order to maintain a high level of involvement in the plant's activity. Information did not go through the right channels; the recently appointed joint managing director, M. Pagkol, did not report directly to the executive board of directors as he should, but to Chimie du Sud's special delegate, M. Jacques Villermon. (See *Exhibit 1* for the organization chart and formal lines of communication in TPF.)

5. M. Villermon was an engineer and had had no experience in Thailand. He was therefore manipulated by M. Pagkol.

The Chimie du Sud Textile Division's arguments were as follows:

a. The Thai partner sought the most recent technology, and insisted that the division supply the most advanced and complex continuous polymerization process available. The Yipsoon Group's other textile operations were all entirely traditional and conventional in design and technology. The Yipsoon Group management had no conceptual grasp of the kinds of problems that could arise in high-technology plant construction and operation.

b. Despite their engineers' lack of experience in high technology, the Yipsoon Group interfered with construction in violation of the joint venture agreements. The president of the group, M. Yipsoon Praboon, came to the plant early in the morning before the French engineers were at work, and gave instructions to the Thai supervisors and workers.

c. The Yipsoon Group insisted that the division use local engineers and suppliers during construction. However, the local firms and local labor were not sophisticated enough to handle the kinds of tasks required of them; they had to be supervised very closely, and much of the construction work had to be redone. The Yipsoon Group blamed factory performance problems on the division's designs and engineers. Those designs were not at fault. The problems arose because the Thai technicians did not have experience with the sensitive advanced equipment used by TPF. Training was also a very difficult problem. Even after they had completed operations training programs, conducted in Thai, the Thai technicians did not adjust or maintain the machinery properly. In response to the complaints of the Yipsoon Group, the division's engineering team was reduced to eleven, which was not enough to ensure that all of the equipment was kept in good working order.

d. The Yipsoon Group was inconsistent and irrational in its ideas of the managerial role and function of Chimie du Sud staff. It argued that M. Villermon, who was not a purchasing specialist, should attend to the details of local supply, purchasing, and inventory. Although the initial agreement was that the Yipsoon Group would manage local marketing, the Yipsoon Group now claimed that M. Villermon was the TPF director of sales and that he was responsible for local marketing details, and for deciding whether or not credit should be granted to local buyers. Textile selling in Thailand required numerous personal visits and factory inspection trips to evaluate customers' equipment and its compatibility with synthetic threads. In keeping with the joint venture agreement, M. Villermon was trying to train and develop Thai managers within the firm, and it was appropriate for him to delegate supply invoicing and sales visits to other managers. Yet the Yipsoon Group managers claimed that M. Villermon was not fulfilling his responsibilities.

See *Exhibit 2* for the account of the conflict recorded in the French press.

Exhibit 1 Organization Chart and Formal Lines of Communication in TPF

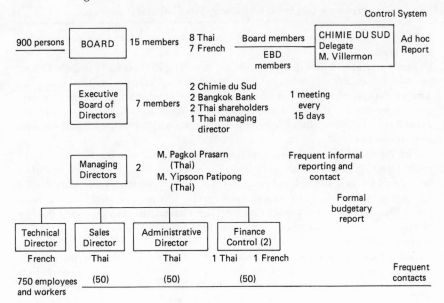

Exhibit 2
Problems of a French Settlement in Thailand:
An Unfortunate Experience
[From our correspondent in Southeast Asia]

Bangkok—Set up in Dec. 1972, just before the energy crisis and its disastrous consequences on the synthetic textiles industry, the French-Thai enterprise "Thai Polyester Fiber Co. Ltd" the most modern polyester factory in Southeast Asia, faced serious problems of production, financing, and outlets. Added to these difficulties were acute differences of opinion between the partners. Head winds finally brought the firm to the brink of bankruptcy in Sept. 1977. An increase of capital (140 million baht, or $4 million) required by the three Thai banks which provided short- and medium-term credits brought some respite. But, since the beginning of the factory in 1976, it has suffered losses estimated at over $4 million.

Initially, Chimie du Sud was supposed to set up the factory, at a total cost of $60 million. However, the French company took a 40% share in the firm, which was increased to 48% in 1976. The Thai partner, Yipsoon Textile Group, holds about 30%. The rest—i.e., 22%—is divided between the 3 banks of Bangkok. Right from the start, many conflicts emerged between partners. The delays in the building of the factory, which was the responsibility of the Thais, have directly influenced the

(Continued on next page)

Exhibit 2

Problems of a French Settlement in Thailand *(Continued)*

delivering of sophisticated material and technology—which was the responsibility of the French.

The material was stored in the open air, resulting in theft and spoilage. Consequently, some 12% of the material was not delivered at the scheduled time. The Thais complained, and added that certain elements were not in accordance with the agreement. So, the Thais are asking for $6 million damages. Obviously, the French refused, citing the government regulations which certified that the norms were respected.

The Yipsoon Group is also complaining about the fact that the factory's capacity is lower than previously expected. However, its subsidiaries are not able, because of the crisis, to sell the products. The factory, which has a capacity of 74 tons a day, is working at 40% capacity in certain sectors. The staff is also a cause of conflict. To reduce the production costs the Thai partner has proposed that the number of French technicians be reduced from 43 to 29. But the Chimie du Sud representatives indicated that such a policy, because of the lack of skilled Thai technicians, would work to the detriment of the factory's quality and functioning.

These numerous difficulties do not surprise everybody. Some groups now assert that the conflict was inevitable and that the French committed themselves in this affair quite thoughtlessly. Anyway, it is paradoxical, even in the business world which is always full of surprises, that the Thai partner is at the same time a direct competitor. The Yipsoon Group holds a share in the Teijin Polyester Co., a competitor, which serves the local market. Thus, Yipsoon, is playing a double game.

In a country where French investments are rare, the trial of Chimie du Sud appeared as a test. Those who know a lot about this affair may be hesitant to invest in this country, although the Thai government does its best to attract foreign capital which is urgently needed for the Thai economy.

SOURCE: Translated from "Les difficultés d'implantation française en Thaïlande—Une expérience malheureuse de Rhône-Poulenc,"*Le Monde,* January 11, 1978.

Ashamu Holdings Limited
Let the Goat Eat Salt

The Mercedes bounded violently over the rain-drenched mud road to Oke-Afa, Ashamu Holdings Limited's headquarters outside Lagos, Nigeria. As the driver skillfully avoided 2-foot-deep puddles, the Ashamu executive turned to the visitor and pointed to the construction 25 feet away. "When they have finished this bridge, this drive will take no time at all. We worked many years to get this bridge. It is slow progress, but it is progress nonetheless."

Despite the sometimes frustrating slowness with which efforts to build new things progressed in Nigeria, Chief E. O. Ashamu, chairman of the board, and his deputy, Gunter Stargardt, had in August 1980 just built something of their own. This was a proposal to alter radically the management system of Ashamu's agribusiness and other divisions through a series of international joint ventures. By seeking foreign partners to participate in "technical services agreements," Ashamu Holdings was changing its previous management strategy of vesting ultimate operating authority in Nigerian nationals, some of whom had known the chief and his associates for many years. The term "technical services agreement" understated the importance of many of the proposed partnerships, which included technical consultation, management contracts, and sizable financial commitments.

Ashamu Holdings had started this program several years earlier by signing agreements with foreign firms to collaborate in various business undertakings. The strategy was now about to undergo its most important test. In a short while Ashamu Holdings Limited was scheduled to sign an agreement with Interagra, a French company, which would commit over 20% of the Ashamu Holdings' assets to management under the new philosophy. Although both Chief Ashamu and Stargardt had worked hard to structure the proposal, they needed to make a final examination of this arrangement and the general philosophy underpinning it. More than any other decision Ashamu Holdings was likely to make in the next decade,

This case was prepared by Thomas Craig, Associates Fellow in Business Administration, under the direction of Professor Ray A. Goldberg, as a basis for class discussion rather than to illustrate either effective or ineffective handling of an administrative situation. Abridged with permission.

this would affect the fate of the company. Beyond the group's interest, the decision had significance for the overall direction of Nigeria's development effort.

BACKGROUND

Emmanuel Oyedele Ashamu, a chief's son and himself a chief, had apparently inherited the keen business instincts of his Yoruba ancestors. Respect for the land and its power and prestige was deeply ingrained; as he put it, "Land is the key to success." Since his first land acquisition in 1951, after his graduation from Pharmacy School in Western Nigeria, he continued to expand his holdings. By 1978 land and its products were still the foundation for his activities in agriculture, mining, real estate, and industry. In his view, such trade in industrial equipment, fertilizers, and food responded to the many needs of the people and government of Nigeria, where development projects were reshaping the economic, social, and political environment.

A devout Christian, fifty-year-old Chief Ashamu was the patriarch of a traditional extended family and close-knit community whose many members looked to him for guidance and solicited his support in alleviating the burdens of daily life. But even these responsibilities paled beside his role as head of E. O. Ashamu & Sons (Holdings) Limited and its numerous subsidiaries[1] (taken together, perhaps the largest privately held black African enterprise) and as leader of the companies' thousands of laborers, technicians, and managers. In the pattern of many Nigerian organizations, Chief Ashamu, as top man, was the only person in the complex of companies who knew the full details of its extensive landholdings and operations, but full decision-making responsibility was increasingly shared by the entire board. Efforts to integrate trusted and qualified managers into key roles had lately begun to show encouraging results, thus easing the pressures of operating several companies at once.

THE ASHAMU GROUP[2] OF COMPANIES

Originally formed in 1954, the group consisted of ten major companies with activities including large-scale farming, food processing, manufac-

---

[1]E. O. Ashamu & Sons (Holdings) Limited held 90% of equity of the subsidiaries. Chief Ashamu and his wife owned the remaining 10% of each company.

[2]E. O. Ashamu & Sons (Holdings) Limited will hereafter be referred to as Ashamu Holdings Limited, and the entire organization will be called, for convenience, the Ashamu Group.

turing, mining, shipping, real estate, transportation, and management and consultancy services. The group was also involved in general bulk supply and distribution covering plant and machinery, general goods, building materials, munitions and industrial explosives, chemicals, and pharmaceutical products. Each company was a self-motivated autonomous unit with separate management and operating budget. A good example was Nigerian Explosives and Plastics Company Ltd. (NEPCO), the largest firm with the broadest base and the highest annual turnover, handling for DuPont its industrial explosives and other products indispensable to construction and mining. The Group's pretax profits in 1977 were nearly $2.7 million on sales of just over $64 million. These profits and sales included $630,000 profit and nearly $20 million sales from the operations of the four companies forming the agribusiness complex: Agrotec Services, Oke-Afa Farms, Oyo Feeds, and Pioneer Farms; the last of the four posted the only net loss for 1977 of $289,000. (See *Exhibit 1* for sales mix.)

BACKGROUND ON THE NIGERIAN ECONOMY

In 1978 Nigeria was approaching a changeover to democratic civilian rule the following year, with a population fast approaching 100 million at an increase of over 3% a year (based on voter registration figures). Some 70% of the people still lived in rural areas even as migration to the cities reduced the farm labor force, thus raising the average age of the remaining small farmers. Demographically, the country was roughly divided into three major tribal regions: the predominantly Moslem Hausas in the north, the Ibo in the east, and the Yoruba in the west, all of whom were commerce-oriented.

While under British colonial administration, Nigeria had become an important exporter of agricultural commodities, including cocoa, coffee, peanuts, palm oil, and rubber. This lead position in agriculture had severely deteriorated in the 1970s, with less than half of Nigeria's 175 million acres of arable land in production in the late 1970s[3] and some 95% of agricultural production still taking place on small holdings of 3 acres or less. Fluctuating world commodity prices, rising rural wages, scarce farm credit, and crop failures helped explain why the nation's farmers had not prospered significantly during the last several years of turbulent development.

The apparent strategy of the former military head of state, Gowon (who

---

[3]Chief Ashamu estimated that no more than 1% of all arable land in Nigeria was being farmed commercially using large-scale mechanized methods.

held power from 1966 until his peaceful overthrow in 1975) was to finance development of the "growth" (manufacturing and petroleum) sectors with the earnings of the agricultural sector. Between 1960 and 1974
only 20% of governmental expenditures went into agriculture, yet that
sector contributed over 50% of total national output. Long-neglected
rural infrastructure suffered additional damage during a protracted civil
war between the central government and the seceding Ibo, which ended
in 1970. The resulting deterioration of paved roads and bridges, rural
electrification, manpower training, and water supplies helped explain
why agricultural output grew only 1.3% per year from 1972 to 1975.[4]

This would have been inadequate to feed the rapidly growing population properly even if incomes had remained steady. But the dramatic rise
in petroleum prices in the early 1970s brought new wealth to Nigeria, as it
became the United States' second largest oil supplier.

THE PETROLEUM ECONOMY

By 1977 revenues from Nigerian petroleum exports were exceeding $10
billion. The government embarked upon a number of large-scale development schemes to provide an economic base for the late 1980s, when oil
reserves were predicted to taper off. But the country's infrastructure was
able to absorb only part of the influx of materials; during 1975 more than
400 vessels were moored outside the major port of Lagos awaiting unloading. The boom increased urban incomes, which immediately caused increased demand for foodstuffs, especially poultry, meat, and dairy
products.

But hit by the civil war, the 1972–75 Sahelian drought, and chronic
inattention, agricultural output had not kept up with population growth.
Nigerian agricultural activity dropped from a 1970 share of 65% of GDP
to below 25% in 1977, exports of traditional products dropped, and
imports of wheat, rice, corn, and other agricultural products rose dramatically. Food prices and urban housing shortages helped push inflation
rates over 30%. Slower agricultural growth was perceived as one of the
main reasons why the GDP's rate of growth declined from an 8% yearly
average since 1973 to around 5% for 1977. Apparently the boom was
winding down. Pressures on the government to react grew stronger. In
company with heavy subsidies for key inputs (75% for fertilizer distributed through the states' Ministry of Agriculture to groups of small farm-

---

[4]Ironically, an effect of the increased emphasis on primary and higher education was the
general response of many young people to abandon the rural way of life in favor of
potentially better life-styles through white-collar jobs in the cities. The image of oneself as a
peasant farmer became less acceptable in a "land of plenty."

ers, for example) and the provision of improved seeds, pesticides, and tractor services, a newly promulgated government campaign to stimulate food production, Operation Feed the Nation (OFN), turned to student labor in 1976 as 25,000 young people spent their summer months in menial or clerical agricultural work.[5] But the expected surpluses in basic commodities failed to appear, leaving newly built "strategic-reserve" storage facilities empty as farmers sold their output to markets paying over double the government's minimum guaranteed price. The program achieved some success, however, in raising the public's sensitivity to the food problem.

CONTINUING GOVERNMENTAL INITIATIVES

Nigeria's efforts did result in increased agricultural production, with 1975–77 growth rates estimated by outside sources to have reached 2–3% per year. But this fell short of the development plan target of 4.8%, and the federal military government (FMG) decided that additional incentives and motivation were required. Five large-scale projects were planned, with World Bank support totaling US$262 million, as integrated packages of investments in rural infrastructure, agricultural support services, and inputs designed to affect 60,000–70,000 farmers each. FAO similarly had 53 development projects under way in all phases of agriculture, including livestock, forestry, and fisheries.

LARGE-SCALE MECHANIZED FARMING IN NIGERIA

Existing operations in Nigeria had had mixed results. One West German firm had recently given up, after several years of work on 10,000 acres, in the face of apparently overwhelming bureaucratic delays and obstacles. An American firm achieved significant results with heavy machinery and Kansas know-how on a 105,000-acre maize, soybean, and rice operation that excited much high-level governmental expectations. Foreign participation[6] in such highly visible schemes was quickly coming to be appreci-

---

[5]The failure of student involvement in OFN served mainly to dampen government hopes of inspiring young people to take up farming. The enormous gap between rural and urban living conditions was reinforced again, partly because of unclear government intentions and improperly coordinated program implementation.

[6]The Indigenization Decrees of 1972 and 1977 had placed a ceiling of 40% on foreign participation in integrated agricultural enterprise, the remaining 60% to be Nigerian-owned. In April 1978, as part of further efforts to stimulate agricultural production, the percentages were reversed. This was the first major occasion of the FMG's changing its policy in a shift away from "Nigerianization" of essential industries.

ated as one of the few promising avenues to greater food production, and efforts to facilitate such participation appeared more often on the government's agenda. Questions of land use raised by large-scale mechanized farming received widespread public and private concern.

THE NATIONAL BUDGET FOR 1978–79

In April 1978 the head of state, General Obasanjo, announced the FMG's national budget for the following year, agricultural development was to become a preferred sector. The country's international reserves had fallen to $3 billion, since oil revenues and disappointingly low agricultural exports had failed to keep up with Nigeria's growing foreign debt repayments. Inflation hovered above 30%, and none of the existing food programs managed to stem the tide of rural migration into overcrowded cities. To deal with these problems, General Obasanjo said:

> In recognition of the critical role of agriculture, especially food production, in the nation's economy, this administration has given the highest priority to agriculture by making direct investments in food and livestock production. Our efforts are beginning to bear fruit.

ASHAMU GROUP'S OPERATING RECORD

The Group had had a mixed record of successes and failures.[7] Most of the successes had been in nonagricultural subsidiaries. NEPCO had realized many of its operating and financial needs under the management of Jordan Wenberg, an American on "loan" from Du Pont. Du Pont, which supplied a substantial percentage of NEPCO's products, agreed to place Wenberg in charge of NEPCO. This became necessary to give NEPCO strength to face competition from European suppliers who backed their operations with large lines of credit. Rather than try to sell its products (mainly explosives and freon) through different channels, Du Pont agreed to work more closely with the Ashamu Group, which Du Pont believed was the most promising distributor in the long run. Du Pont granted a substantial line of credit to NEPCO and supported an application for a $3-million line of credit from the Ex-Im Bank. Other arrangements for credit from Nigerian banks were under way.

Part of the Group's new management philosophy required that each

---

[7]See Ashamu Holdings Limited, HBS case 4-578-188, for a complete background on the company.

company in the group (including NEPCO) be controlled by a managing director. The director was responsible to a company board of directors, which included two or more directors from the foreign managing company and the managing director. Each company maintained a link with the holding company through its board of directors.

Besides management changes, the Group revised its overall financial policy. Under the new system, intercompany cash transactions were not permissible; each company had to build its own financial base. Chief Ashamu viewed this as a critical difference between the new and old systems.

PHARCO, a pharmaceutical company, had also improved significantly over the past two years. It had a new technical service agreement with E. Merck A.G., a West German pharmaceutical company. The new managing director was Mr. Uflerbauemer. Merck had granted PHARCO a large line of credit and had guaranteed large Nigerian bank loans to PHARCO of more than N2 million. Sales and profits had increased by over 100% in the past two years.

The Group's other industrial operations were also operating satisfactorily. Igbetti Mining Industries (IMI) Limited's building materials division showed great promise, barring major supply interruptions. But IMI's mining division was threatened by compulsory purchase by the government, which was trying to expropriate Ashamu's mining assets.

Agrotec continued to build its reputation in technical consultation and as a supplier of farming inputs despite problems importing certain supplies. The Ashamu Group's agribusiness ventures had not done as well. Feed shortages and harsh fiscal measures by the FMG between 1977 and 1978 (which made it difficult to obtain working capital from the banks), were the two main reasons for the group's difficulties. While the government restricted imports of feed ingredients, Nigeria did not produce enough grain to supply its poultry and livestock industry properly. Oke-Afa Farms, Nigeria's largest poultry operation, was forced to cull much of its broiler and layer[8] flock because of feed shortages. The chief decided to curtail existing production and planned expansion until the government committed itself to permanently liberalizing feed import policies and guaranteeing a constant flow of funds to agribusiness.

Many problems plaguing poultry production also plagued field crop production. Although Pioneer Farms' maize farm at Okaka had shown great promise, Ashamu Holdings did not plant any corn in 1980. Plans were reversed because funds from the federal government's Agricultural Bank didn't come as promised and scheduled. Commercial banks with loans to Pioneer insisted that the farm expand to a large-scale commercial

[8]Broilers are chickens raised for eating; layers lay eggs.

operation. At its peak in 1978, the Okaka farm produced 58 bushels of corn per acre on 1,000 planted acres.[9] Of the available 10,000 acres, 3,000 had been stumped to prepare for cultivation. An additional total of 50,000 acres was available to Pioneer Farms for future expansion.

The management of Okaka eagerly anticipated the next crop year when, under a new technical agreement, it hoped the farm would be able to operate. The normal season for maize started in May with the rains and ended in September. Chief Ashamu hoped the government would legislate funding to support its promulgated policy of expanding domestic grain production. Local farmers at Okaka continued to plant and harvest corn and were still eager to participate in any proposed outgrower scheme organized by the Ashamu Group.

The Ashamu Group had been able to lay off many of the field hands and machinery operators employed by Pioneer Farms Limited. But managerial and clerical workers still remained on the payroll and spent most of their time on upkeep and maintenance of the company's physical assets. Management believed it would have no problem rehiring needed farm labor when the time arose.

Oyo Feeds, now under a management contract with Loxmann Cuxhaven, a German company, had endured uneventful years. With a dearth of feed ingredients and little livestock to feed, the company's sales and profitability had fallen considerably. Yet the long-term potential for the feed market in Nigeria was still excellent.

The company's operation would be greatly enhanced when the government finished construction of a navigable drainage canal across Ashamu property. The canal would allow Oyo Feeds to bring feedstuff by barge from Lagos's Tin Can Island Port directly to the feed-processing and storage center. Feed grains currently were handled by truck over 13 miles of congested roads.

Despite these temporary setbacks, the Ashamu Group continued to seek new possibilities in field crop and poultry production. The Group had gained the right to develop land for corn production in a northern state of Nigeria. There, the potential acreage that could be planted to corn was "virtually limitless" and reportedly of better quality than the land at Okaka or Ofe-Afa. The land was served by several transportation routes: railways, federal express roads, and an international airport that was to be built at Abuja, the new federal capital.

With access to such promising land resources, Ashamu was ready to redouble his efforts to produce primary grains. Pioneer Farms had dem-

---

[9]By comparison, the average U.S. yield for corn was over 100 bushels per acre in 1979–80. A good farm harvested 175 bushels per acre. Worldwide average production was about 40 bushels per acre between 1978 and 1979.

onstrated that corn could be produced in Nigeria at N90–120 per acre or N60–90 per ton (depending on yield).[10]

DEVELOPMENTS IN NIGERIA

The most important development in domestic Nigerian affairs since 1978 was the institution of civilian rule under a federal government. President Shagari, an intelligent, capable, well-respected man, had become the head of the government. His efforts to unify the 19 Nigerian states formed after the civil war were meeting with success despite regional squabbles and jousting for power over local affairs. Several major infrastructure projects, notably a highway system and port facilities, were at or near completion. Communication systems that previously were completely broken down were also improving, albeit slowly.

But the Nigerian economy had been jolted by the unexpected shortfall in oil revenue stemming from reduced worldwide demand. This shortfall underscored Nigeria's vulnerability as a one-commodity economy. Consequently, the government had renewed its commitment to self-sufficiency in basic economic sectors. Agriculture had once again been singled out as the first priority for development. The government planned to make available up to N4.5 billion in government agriculture loans in 1981 for large-scale farming. Many other benefits (tax advantages, investment credits, and licensing preferences), granted under the former military government were still in effect in 1980. The government guaranteed that farmers would receive N200 per ton for maize they produced.

THE TECHNICAL SERVICES AGREEMENTS

The Ashamu Group's new management philosophy was to be implemented through a series of technical services agreements with foreign partners. Most of the partner firms had broad experience in developing countries. Several agreements had been formalized by contracts, and partners were already managing affairs in Nigeria. The most important of these agreements, both completed and unsigned are listed here:

Oke-Afa Farms Ltd. Ashamu Holdings had signed an agreement with Lohmann Export GmbH., a German company, to assume all managerial and operating responsibility for the poultry division at Oke-Afa. The

---

[10]As of August 1980, N1 (naira) was worth US$1.80.

validation of this contract was conditional on a N2.5-million working capital loan from a Nigerian bank.

Oyo Feeds Company Ltd. The feed company had signed an agreement with Lohmann Tierernöehrung GmbH., another German company. A German employee had already assumed responsibility for technical and general management of the company.

NEPCO. As described above, NEPCO was now under the management of Jordan Wenberg through an agreement with Du Pont International S.A.

Nigerian Pipes and Tubes Ltd. This company was to be managed by Nile Investments of Nairobi, Kenya. The company had received more than $13 million of credit from the Australian Export Credit Bank and a U.S. bank after the management agreement was signed. Arrangements for working capital from local Nigerian banks were already completed. The company was to produce pipes and tubes from PVC.

PHARCO (Nigeria) Ltd. This company was the first to be taken over by a team of specialists working for E. Merck of Germany. The success of the Merck management team caused the Group to seek further outside management assistance in its other companies.

Asian African Containers (Nigeria) Ltd. A new venture born out of the marriage of Ashamu Group (which held 40% of the equity) and the Orient Overseas Container Line, Inc. (which held 60% of the equity), the company would "engage in ocean transport, shipping lines, terminal warehousing, and operations for direct clearing of cargo." Business was scheduled to begin in the near future pending completion of the Lagos Port.

Doumeng Projects

Agrotec Services Ltd. Ashamu had negotiated an arrangement with Interagra of the Doumeng conglomerate to "handle the importation, distribution, and service of agricultural equipment throughout Nigeria and the sales of turnkey projects for Interagra." It expected the Doumeng group to take equity participation in Agrotec in the near future.

Pioneer Farms Ltd. The technical services agreement for Pioneer Farms stipulated that Doumeng would undertake the development and management of Okaka Farms. The contract also stipulated that a German company named Fortschritt Landmaschinen Export/Import would join the effort to develop Ashamu's farmland.

Grain Silo Project. Ashamu had negotiated a contract with Doumeng to build and operate grain silos at Nigeria's Tin Can Island Port, where the Ashamu Group had been granted a valuable twenty-year lease over 6,000 square meters of dock space. The proposal called for a 50% division in ownership. Doumeng would arrange for 70–80% of the necessary export credit and would have complete control over technical and managerial matters.

Proposed and signed technical services agreements covered all but two of the Group's divisions. The proposed agreements with Doumeng affiliates affected 20% of Ashamu's assets and encompassed the most promising area for future growth, namely agribusiness. *Exhibit 2* presents a brief self-description of Doumeng's Interagra.

A DESCRIPTION OF THE NEW MANAGEMENT PHILOSOPHY FOR JOINT VENTURES

These agreements were an important departure from the previous management philosophy. The new philosophy was adopted largely because the Group felt it was falling short of its potential in agribusiness. A section of the Group's recent report follows:

> Ashamu has long realized that potential agribusiness development in Nigeria will involve considerable capital. The Federal Government of Nigeria shares very positively this belief, hence in the 1977 Nigerian Enterprises Promotion Decree, foreign participation in agribusiness of industrial dimension is permitted to reach 60% ownership. Substantial incentives are also guaranteed.
>
> Ashamu's effort is therefore being directed towards setting a very strong broad-based capital-intensive agribusiness. It is hoped that participation in such agribusiness in Nigeria will involve one or a consortium of several reputable international agribusiness interests. Ashamu is mounting considerable effort at securing understanding and participation of such international agribusiness companies. It is Ashamu's very strong view that such enterprise should be completely free of government participation while it should enjoy all government support as stipulated in the 1977 Nigerian Enterprises Promotion Decree.
>
> It appears that the potential for the agribusiness of E. O. Ashamu Group is not being exploited to the extent possible. Two problems appear to be limiting extension into operations that could be highly profitable to the Group and also make a significant contribution to Nigeria's producing its own foodstuffs. These factors are: (1) insufficient working capital, and (2) management capability for large-scale agriculture, poultry, and livestock operations.

Ashamu had carefully defined what it expected of an agribusiness partner like Doumeng in a joint venture. The report continued:

The partner would be responsible for providing working management and, where applicable, help for working capital for such items as (1) land clearing, fertilizer, seed or seedlings and all requirements for crop production; (2) refurnishing and restocking operations; (3) establishing a cattle and swine operation. This could include processing and marketing (wholesale); and (4) establishing fruit garden production (fresh produce such as lettuce, beans, peas, tomatoes, potatoes, carrots, etc.). This could lead to a future venture into frozen foods. Fruit garden operations could be on a wholesale produce type of venture.

Correspondingly, the group's contribution to the joint venture would be the following: (1) land; (2a) work force required for all operations, including laborers; (2b) Nigerian counterparts of management and executive grade; (3) staff required for making up payrolls, record-keeping, government reports, etc.; (4) contacts with federal and local government agencies; (5) facilities required for storing and processing crop, egg, poultry, swine, cattle, and truck (garden) production; (6) distribution; (7) buildings, machinery and equipment, livestock, and other means of production already available; and (8) finance and financial guarantees (wholly or partly, as agreed). It is stressed that the lead joint-venture partner will have full management control and supervision of all activities.

The group realized that implementing this new management philosophy entailed risks. On the subject of risk and participation the Group stated:

The chief feels strongly that by entrusting the assets, reputation, and future business prospects of the firm he has established to the hands of an external management team, he is demonstrating his absolute faith in that firm. The risk of fraud or mismanagement that he faces (at least in a theoretical sense) is very real, and he seeks some confidence that the managing firm is itself taking a risk in the venture in some way commensurate with the level of its commitment. As a confirmed capitalist, he is convinced that any individual or organization puts forth its best effort when its own earnings are somehow at stake. In the chief's view there are basically four ways in which this all-important commitment by the managing partner can be evidenced.

In summary, they are as follows (note that the alternatives are ranked in decreasing order by the strength of the commitment evidenced, and consequently, in decreasing order of preference from Chief Ashamu's point of view):

1. Direct investment by the managing partner in the involved Ashamu Group enterprise.
2. Guarantees by the managing partner of all loans, etc., from banks provided to the Ashamu operation under the managing partner's control.
3. All remuneration (including fees and expenses) payable to the managing partner to be determined as a percentage of income or revenue.
4. Guarantees of certain base-line production or earnings targets supported by escrow accounts or bank guarantees. (Note: if bank guarantee fees add significantly to the total fee package and are passed directly to the Ashamu Group company, the commitment evidenced through this mechanism is questionable.)

REFLECTIONS ON THE NEW STRATEGY

Chief Ashamu and Gunter Stargardt stressed that this new philosophy did not denote a change in Ashamu Holding Group's long-term objectives. Those objectives were to operate a profitable, partially integrated, well-financed multisector conglomerate under Nigerian management that served the country's development needs and the interests of its owners and employees. But the new philosophy did reflect a temporary digression on the road to those objectives.

The original Indigenization Decree of 1977 had, in a very short time, radically altered the management of most companies operating in Nigeria. The original decree required that all companies in Nigeria be at least 60% Nigerian owned (later changed to 40%) and that the companies had to transfer direction to Nigerian nationals. This caused many companies immediately to transfer executive management responsibility to Nigerians in middle and lower management positions. Few foreign-owned companies before the promulgation of the decree had sponsored programs to train local managers in modern techniques needed to operate a sophisticated enterprise successfully. Therefore, many top positions were filled with managers who were not yet duly experienced for the task given them. Besides personnel problems, many Nigerian businesses found that even twenty years after the end of colonialism they still needed much technical expertise, financing, and market access overseas that could be provided only through foreign partners. Although Nigeria had made huge strides toward self-sufficiency in the two decades since independence, the reality was that a mutually beneficial partnership between Nigerian companies, and foreign companies in which each partner shared risks and rewards, where each alternately was teacher and student, and where each brought its unique advantages to the company, was now the preferred system for doing business.

Ashamu Holdings had discovered it could significantly benefit from such partnerships. Many banks were willing to lend to local companies in partnership with well-known foreign partners when they might not lend to wholly indigenous companies, however efficient. This was especially true if the foreign partner had contributed equity. Such partnerships suggested to banks that the venture would have access to overseas technology, advanced management techniques, overseas markets, and overseas financing.[11]

Ashamu had also discovered that by bringing in foreign partners it could give its own Nigerian managers a first-rate management education more effectively and less expensively than by training them at academic institutions. The laws governing joint ventures with foreigners stipulated precisely that the partners must create and operate training programs for Nigerian employees geared eventually to putting them in control of operations. The expectation was that these managers, once proficiently trained and properly seasoned by high-level managerial experience, would then displace the foreign managers and operate the companies themselves. The new management strategy was thus a realistic detour on the road to realizing Ashamu's long-term corporate objectives.

Chief Ashamu, a realist, spoke with forethought about foreign collaboration. Like others, he believed that the country moved too quickly to implement its plan of putting Nigerian business under Nigerian management, to the detriment of the private sector. He recognized that Nigeria had come from a history of dependence on foreign resources and markets, and that foreign countries had refined the science of management beyond the level generally found locally. The momentum of past relationships with foreigners was too great to be reversed instantly by legislative fiat. Nor was it desirable to sever all relationships with foreign partners who generally were good for a business relationship.

For the chief, an old Yoruba proverb best summarized the rationale for promoting joint ventures with foreigners and seeking creative ways to allow them to participate in Nigerian business:

> In the days of our forefathers, salt was a valued possession. It was
> necessary for life. The goat was also a prized possession, the building
> block of a man's wealth. Yet sometimes the goat would, for its own

[11]Credit management was an important issue in Nigerian business. There had been a severe capital shortage in the country in the past. Only short-term capital was available, and even then only in limited amounts. Companies like Ashamu Holdings had been forced to finance long-term assets, such as land, with short-term debt. Only recently had banks begun to give longer-term loans (up to five years).

survival, eat salt when he had access to it. They had to either kill the goat to preserve the salt or devise a way to get him to eat less so they lost neither the goat nor too much of the salt.

Armed with this "If-you-can't-beat-'em-join-'em" attitude, the chief and his deputy had put together the new management strategy. The chief stressed as one of his selection criteria that foreign managers be employed by large, well-known multinationals. In this way, Ashamu believed he had recourse if things were not proceeding satisfactorily. Also, these firms were able to seize on opportunities quickly and act decisively. The multinationals also knew better than Ashamu who the capable managers were who could effectively operate in Nigeria. It was up to the foreign partner to design and implement a training program for second-tier Nigerian managers. Many of Ashamu's divisions operating under joint agreements had already hired some extremely bright and capable young Nigerians trained at the world's best schools.

In reflecting on the joint ventures, the chief said: "Management by Europeans is an inevitable phase we have to go through. But we are a modern company now. Nepotism is the old system; professionalism is the new system."

Organization

Exhibit 1
Sales and Profit Shares
(%)

Subsidiary	1977 Sales Share	1977 PBT[a] Share
Agrotec	14.3	17.4
Oke-Afa	8.9	17.6
Oyo Feeds	9.2	2.6
Pioneer Farms	.1	(11.7)
Ikeja Real Estate	8.7	33.2
IMI (Building)	5.7	.1
IMI (Mines)	3.9	(5.6)
NEPCO	31.9	22.9
PHARCO	12.9	16.3
New Age	4.4	7.2
Totals 1977	100.0	100.0

[a]PBT = Profit before tax.

SOURCE: Ashamu (Holdings) Ltd. company documents, esp. 1978 budget.

Exhibit 2

A Brief Summary of Interagra and Its Involvement in Nigeria
(based on a telex from Jean-Baptiste Doumeng)

Our group is composed of 337 French agricultural cooperatives and companies dealing with the development of markets and supply channels on the international level.

Interagra's turnover is about 2 billion dollars.

Our best abilities lie in the sales of commodities, cereals, vegetable oils, meat, butter, alcohols, wines, fruits, and vegetables.

With respect to equipment, we are building silos, cold storage facilities, milling plants, feedlots, fertilizer mixing units, and workshops for upkeeping agricultural equipment and tractors.

We operate in developing countries. In Nigeria we have an agreement with the Ashamu Group to manage and bring into cultivation many thousands of acres for the production of corn and other grains, rice, livestock, and other goods. We are also assisting on a port silo, a milling plant, industrial bakeries, a feedlot, and a poultry farm.

After we complete these initial projects, we hope to help develop a decentralized system for these activities.

We hope our experience will become a model insofar as it represents a new way for technology transfers between firms located in industrialized countries and producer organizations in developing countries. Because of its production and oil capacities, the Nigerian economy must be able to ensure the financing of such efforts for the development of agriculture. We hope, with the support of the Ashamu Group, to build an example for collaboration in Nigeria.

As chairman of the Economic Bureau of the International Cooperative Alliance of Agricultural Cooperatives (the largest international cooperative organization in the world), I am quite sure we will be able to ensure very positive results.

Best regards,

Jean-Baptiste Doumeng

Exporting from the Developing Countries

Exporting has become increasingly important for developing countries. For many, the imperative of servicing their large international debts has made earning foreign exchange through trade a top priority. During the 1980s the average share of LDC export earnings needed to cover external debt payments doubled to about 20%, and it was much higher in some countries. The traditional reliance of LDC exports on agricultural or mineral commodities causes great variability in their foreign-exchange earnings due to the large price fluctuations in international markets. Accordingly, there has been significant effort to diversify exports into manufactured goods and nontraditional agricultural products. Export diversification and expansion face many difficulties but also represent important business opportunities.

KEY ISSUES

The four cases in this chapter focus on three questions facing firms seeking to mount exporting operations from LDCs: What are the key barriers to be overcome? How can the government affect the exporting operation? What should the strategic focus be?

Barriers

Exporting is difficult. There are a multitude of new variables and impediments that emerge as soon as one enters the international arena. Often the initial barrier is lack of information about foreign markets' preferences, requirements, structure, and competitive dynamics. Each of the exporting companies in this chapter, Embraer in Brazil, Daidong in

595

Korea, the Cut Flower Industry in Colombia, and Merban in Indonesia, had to develop information conduits. The development of new industries for export requires acquiring and developing the requisite technologies to meet the export market requirements. This was a daunting and ambitious task for Embraer as it attempted to develop turboprop aircraft. For Daidong this meant having to meet the demanding technical standards of its Japanese clients. For the Colombian flower producers it meant introducing farming techniques far more sophisticated and rigorous than the traditional norm. Infrastructure deficiencies are another common impediment. For Colombia's pioneering flower exporters rapid air transport and refrigerated storage were critical to success, yet neither existed. Low costs are often essential to gaining entry into export markets, but new exporting firms may face higher costs due to dependence on high-priced imported or locally supplied inputs, or due to low volumes and lack of economies of scale. Lastly, market access may be hindered by restrictions imposed by importing governments, often in response to pressures from local companies adversely affected by the LDC exports. Both Embraer and the Colombian flower exporters encountered intense lobbying attacks from U.S. producers.

Government Actions

LDC governments can significantly affect the success of export operations. As was discussed in Chapter 3, the Public-Policy Impact Chain provides guidance in tracing through the effects of government policies and actions. Governments have placed higher priorities on exporting and are increasingly shifting from import-substituting to export-promoting strategies. Through financing, subsidies, taxes, and tariffs, governments can directly affect companies' costs and competitiveness. The cases allow us to compare the governments' roles and uses of these policy instruments in Brazil, Colombia, and Korea. Regulatory actions are another important area of government influence. Controls over imports and exports can be critical. The "Merban" case deals with the problems and opportunities surrounding the Indonesian government's requirements for countertrade, whereby imports were allowed only in exchange for exports. On a global basis countertrade may account for one-fifth of world commerce.

Exporting Strategies

Any exporting strategy has to be tailored to the specific circumstances of the company involved. The core, generic questions are where, what, and how to export. The choice of market is the critical starting point, because meeting market requirements dictates much of the rest of the strategy. Geography is one market variable. Proximity might create competitive transportation advantages, for example, Mexico over Taiwan for the U.S. market (see the Hitchiner case in Chapter 2 and the Rio Bravo Electricos case in Chapter 4). Market size becomes a magnet, as the United States was for Embraer and for the Colombian flower exporters and as Japan was for Daidong. The product characteristics may be driven by a quality strategy, a low-cost strategy, or a quality-cost combination that creates competitive advantage on a value basis. The path pursued will be influenced by the country's and company's possible sources of comparative advantage, e.g., low-cost labor, climate, or government policies. Deciding how to export involves, among other things, making the distribution arrangements in the importing country. This entails strategic choices between using existing distributors or setting up one's own channels, i.e., integrating forward. These were important issues facing Embraer and the flower exporters.

CASE STUDY QUESTIONS

Empresa Brasileira de Aeronáutica S.A.—Embraer

1. What barriers did Embraer face to developing its capacity to export?
2. How was it able to overcome these?
3. What should it do to penetrate the U.S. market?

The Cut Flower Industry in Colombia

1. What were the key factors that enabled this industry to export successfully to the United States?
2. What factors threaten its continued success?
3. What should Asocolflores do? What should the government do?

Daidong Mould and Injection Co.

1. Why was the company able to export successfully?
2. What should it do to ensure continued success?

Countertrade and Merban Corporation

1. Why does countertrade arise?
2. Why was Merban able to operate effectively in its Eastern Europe countertrade deals?
3. What should Merban do about the Indonesia opportunity?

Empresa Brasileira de Aeronáutica S.A.

Starting from scratch a few years ago, Brazil has emerged as the sixth leading aircraft producing nation in the world. And, as often happens when a developing country breaks into a new manufacturing market, the Brazilians are under fire from established competitors who have witnessed a sharp decline in their Brazilian sales.

Led by Cessna Aircraft Company, American makers of light aircraft have taken their case to the White House and are arguing that the Brazilians have not only set up insurmountable import barriers at home, but are on the verge of exporting more than a score of their planes to the United States.

New York Times, November 13, 1976.

At the center of the above controversy, on the Brazilian side, was Empresa Brasileira de Aeronáutica S.A. (Embraer), an enterprise promoted and partly owned by the Brazilian government. In 1978 this nine-year-old company was supplying almost 90% of all new aircraft registered in Brazil, and its most successful product was the Bandeirante, a twin-engine turboprop that had been developed by a team of Brazilian engineers. Since 1974 Embraer had also produced light single- and twin-engine planes under an industrial cooperation agreement with the Piper Aircraft Co. of the United States. With this development, the Brazilian market for civil aircraft (excluding large jets) was almost totally inaccessible to foreign suppliers, and the Cessna Aircraft Company was among the main losers. In addition, Embraer was meeting well over 50% of the Brazilian Air Force's requirements for military aircraft. Not content with dominating the large, protected domestic market, Embraer began in 1975 to sell several of its planes overseas, first to other Latin American countries, then to a few in Africa, and more recently to commuter operators in France, Britain, and Australia. In 1978 Embraer was knocking at the doors of the American market.

This case was prepared by Assistant Professor Ravi Ramamurti of Northeastern University with the assistance of Professor James E. Austin of the Harvard Business School. Field work for this case was made possible by a partial travel grant provided to Ravi Ramamurti in 1981 by the Committee on Latin American and Iberian Studies, Center for International Affairs, Harvard University. This case is intended as the basis for class discussion rather than to illustrate either effective or ineffective handling of an administrative situation. Abridged with permission.

Ozires Silva, the forty-seven-year-old president and director-superintendent of Embraer, was anxious that his company gain access to the $2-
billion American market, the largest in the world. A soft-spoken man,
Silva's personality and style belied the company's aggressive and determined efforts to become a world-class aircraft manufacturer. Formerly a
colonel in the Brazilian Air Force, he had played a critical role in formulating and implementing the plan that led to the development of the
Bandeirante within the Brazilian government's aeronautical research center in the late 1960s. And as Embraer's CEO since the company was
founded in 1969, he had been one of the main architects of its success.

Silva saw a lucrative market for the 18- to 21-seater Bandeirantes in the
United States, where the commuter airlines industry was expected to
boom after the recent deregulation of the airline industry. But a host of
technical, political, and managerial problems would have to be overcome
if Embraer and Brazil were to participate in those opportunities. At stake
was the business potential for both the Bandeirante and the larger 30-seat,
pressurized plane, the Brasilia, that was on the drawing board in
Embraer's design office, and for which the United States was expected to
be one of the main markets.

THE INTERNATIONAL GENERAL AVIATION INDUSTRY

The term "aircraft industry" normally brings to mind names like Boeing,
Lockheed, and McDonnell Douglas. Embraer does not belong to this
category of large jet aircraft manufacturers; rather, its activities predominantly match those of "general aviation manufacturers," who produce
smaller planes such as single-engine and multiengine aircraft, agricultural
planes, turboprops, and small jets for use by recreational flyers, business
executives, commuter airlines, farmers, and, to a smaller extent, defense
departments. In 1978 the unit price of these aircraft varied from as low as
$20,000 for a 2- or 4-seat recreational plane to more than $1 million for an
18- to 20-seat turboprop and almost $1.5 million for a business jet.

The "general aviation industry" has traditionally been concentrated in
the United States, with almost 90% of the "free world's" production
accounted for by 13 American firms. In 1978 Cessna, Piper, and Beech
accounted for about 75% of the total U.S. production. These long-
established firms were the only full-line producers of general aviation
aircraft in the United States; collectively, they exported about 30% of
their production, and all had extensive dealership networks overseas.
Only in recent years, under pressure from host governments, had Cessna
and Piper (but not Beech) begun local manufacturing or assembly operations in some foreign markets. The other U.S. firms typically concen-

trated on one or two general aviation lines: for example, Gates manufactured mainly business jets, and Sweringen (a subsidiary of Fairchild Industries) concentrated on turboprops.

The general aviation aircraft industry was characterized by fairly high
expenditures on R&D, averaging 5–6% of sales in the case of the American industry. Cessna, the largest of the American firms, spent around $40
million annually on R&D.

Outside the United States there were prominent manufacturers of gen-
eral aviation aircraft in such countries as Canada (de Havilland), France
(Aerospatiale), Britain (British Aerospace), Germany (Dornier, VFW-
Fokker), and Spain (CASA). The only developing countries with an air-
craft industry of any significance were Brazil, India, Indonesia, and
Taiwan. Of these, Brazil had achieved the greatest success in export sales.

Brazil, with an area greater than that of the continental United States
and composed of very difficult terrain, had turned out to have one of the
largest markets for general aviation aircraft outside the United States.
Embraer, the heart of the Brazilian aircraft industry, had sales of $104
million in 1978, of which $38 million was exported. For its most successful
product, the indigenously designed Bandeirante, Embraer's main competitors were Beech, Cessna, and Sweringen in the United States and de
Havilland of Canada.

THE BRAZILIAN AIRCRAFT INDUSTRY BEFORE EMBRAER

More than sixty years before Embraer was created and barely three years
after the first flight by the Wright brothers, a Brazilian, Santos Dumont,
had designed and flown the first self-propelled, heavier-than-air craft in
Paris. Brazilians are quick to point out that Santos Dumont's achievement
was more significant than that of the Wright brothers, whose plane took
off from a rooftop, not the ground, and whose feat was not witnessed by
photographers and journalists. Nonetheless, the Brazilian aircraft industry did not develop in any significant scale for many years after Santos
Dumont's successful flight, although many later Brazilians designed their
own versions of planes.

Given Brazil's size and difficult terrain, its government was keen to
develop a strong aircraft industry. It created an Aeronautics Ministry in
1941 and in 1946 the Aeronautical Technical Center (CTA) to sponsor
and undertake projects in the aircraft sector. In the same year, the government also created the Aeronautical Training Institute (ITA) as part of the
CTA, with the help of specialists from the Massachusetts Institute of
Technology, to train aeronautical engineers. By 1951 the first students
had graduated from ITA; the Ministry of Education did not officially

recognize them as qualified aeronautical engineers until 1958. Meanwhile, between 1941 and 1947 the government produced a series of military planes at a factory in Galeão.

From time to time, the Brazilian government also tried to attract experienced aeronautical engineers from Europe to come to work in Brazil with less experienced local designers. The most ambitious of such moves was made soon after World War II, when a number of highly experienced designers were out of work in Europe. After lengthy discussions and bureaucratic delays, the Brazilian government persuaded 50 specialists from Germany to move to Brazil and work on designing a new combat plane and a revolutionary helicopter. The government agreed to pay their salaries, finance the projects, and to create within CTA a new research institute (IPD). The Germans left about four years later when the whole venture was declared unworkable and a failure. The Germans and their Brazilian counterparts could not work together effectively for a variety of reasons, including language problems and salary differentials between the two that were regarded as unfair by the Brazilian engineers. The experience cost the government dearly, and the benefits, although significant, were regarded as being out of proportion to the costs. The movement to develop Brazilian designs for aircraft thereby suffered a major setback, and the government was content, for more than a decade thereafter, to leave the growth of the aircraft industry to private-sector initiatives.

Of all the private firms seriously producing aircraft, three stand out. The first, CAP, lasted from 1942 to 1948 and produced several hundred units of a single-piston-engine plane that was supplied mainly to aero clubs throughout Brazil. The second, Neiva, was founded in 1953 but introduced its first aircraft, also a single-piston-engine trainer, for the Air Force. The third, Aerotec, was founded in 1962 and has produced more than a hundred units of its version of a single-engine trainer. Thus, none of these firms produced twin-engine aircraft on a commercial scale or outgrew their very strong dependence on the Air Force for a market.

Not until 1965 was a major new project initiated again by the Research and Development Institute (IPD), this time led by Captain Ozires Silva, a 1962 graduate of ITA and an officer of the Brazilian Air Force who headed the aircraft design group. The proposal involved developing a Brazilian design for a small twin-engine turboprop transport plane that could replace an aging fleet of Beech-18s for the Brazilian Air Force. The proposal was reportedly approved by the aeronautics minister in 1965 on the condition it would be "costless," i.e., it would not require any budgetary allocation, because he was unwilling to earmark funds for aircraft design projects after what had happened earlier with the German projects. The IPD design team working on this project was headed by a French aeronautical designer, Max Holste, who had decided to move to Brazil.

Holste had earlier designed in France the MH-250, a small twin-piston-engine transport that was eventually developed into the Nord 260 with turboprops and a pressurized fuselage. The possibility of producing the MH-250 in Brazil was also considered by the CTA, but it seemed too small and to have insufficient range for Brazilian operations. An 8–10-seater, nonpressurized, twin-engine, turboprop transport plane, the IPD-6540, seemed the optimal project for the IPD group to embark upon.

Silva persuaded the "materials commander" of the Air Force to pay Holste's salary and to provide some of the materials needed for building the prototype. The CTA, headed since May 1965 by a very supportive officer, Major Brigadier Paulo Victor Da Silva, bore some of the other costs and made its research facilities and labs freely available to the design team. Because of the complicated way this "costless" project was financed, no one knows what it actually cost to implement.

Despite several complications, the design work on IPD-6504 proceeded on schedule, and production of a prototype began in 1966. The first prototype was successfully flown in October 1968. It became clear at once that the aircraft, with some significant but manageable modifications, would make a functional, reliable, and efficient aircraft. The government's attention then shifted to the question of how this unexpected success of the aircraft design group should be exploited to launch a Brazilian aircraft industry of some sophistication. Meanwhile, doubting Brazil's ability to mass-produce an aircraft as large as the IPD-6504 in the foreseeable future, Holste moved to Uruguay, leaving the design in the hands of two Brazilian engineers who were a part of the original team. One of them, Fontegalante Pessotti, later became Embraer's first technical director and still held that job in 1978.

THE BIRTH OF EMBRAER

The Brazilian government strongly desired that series production of IPD-6504 be carried out in the private sector. The government was willing to provide the design free of charge and to place an initial order for about 80 planes. But sustained efforts by Silva, the air minister, and others yielded no private party (including Neiva and Aerotec) willing to invest in what was regarded as a risky proposition. In the context of Brazil's economic boom in the late 1960s, private firms could earn much higher rates of return on alternative projects entailing very low risks. Moreover, private firms were reluctant to start a venture so heavily dependent on the government for its success. Multinationals, too, showed little interest in starting aircraft manufacture within Brazil, least of all of an unproven indigenous design; they were more interested in exporting to the Brazilian market.

In sheer frustration and for want of an alternative, the Brazilian government decided in 1969 to create its own enterprise, the Empresa Brasileira de Aeronáutica, to produce IPD-6504 planes in series. The government's wish to involve the private sector in this activity led to the creation of Embraer as a "mixed enterprise," or a joint venture between the government and private shareholders, although the government retained full control over the enterprise and attracted private capital to the venture through an unusual scheme.

INSTITUTIONAL MODEL USED FOR EMBRAER

Presidential Decree No. 770 of August 1969 creating Embraer stipulated that the company's stock be divided into two categories—voting shares (or "ordinary shares") and nonvoting shares ("preference shares")—and that the Brazilian government always control at least 51% of the company's voting shares. There was no minimum level of holding stipulated for nonvoting shares, which private investors would be encouraged to buy. The government's voting shares would be managed by the Aeronautics Ministry, which in 1969 also supervised the Air Force and the CTA and regulated the domestic airline and aircraft industries.

Although Embraer was a state-controlled enterprise, it was managed like private companies by a board of directors. The president of Brazil, with the advice of the ministers for planning, finance and commerce, and industry, appointed the president of Embraer and three other directors. Two directors were elected at the general body meeting of shareholders to represent the company's private shareholders. The "director-superintendent," or managing director, was the only full-time member on the board. The corporation's daily affairs were managed by an executive committee composed of the managing director and functional directors for industrial relations, production, technology, finance, and marketing. The company's bylaws required that executive directors be "residents of Brazil and of proven technical and administrative experience," and that the director-superintendent "be someone of recognized competence in aeronautics and general management."

In keeping with the general philosophy surrounding the creation of Embraer, the Presidential Decree of 1969 stipulated that, as it grew, Embraer must observe rational, economic criteria, including the need to operate at the minimum scale for efficient production of all products. It was also required, wherever possible, to draw upon the production capability of existing or potential private firms. The presidential decree also gave Embraer some special privileges. The Ministry of Aeronautics and all other federal agencies would give priority to the use of Embraer's prod- ucts and services. Embraer was exempted from paying taxes and duties on imported raw materials, parts, components, and equipment not available locally. The government designed a unique arrangement for attracting private capital to the Embraer venture, employing what has come to be known as the "fiscal incentive scheme."

This scheme permitted Brazilian corporations to invest up to 1% of the income tax they owed the federal government each year in Embraer shares and to offset income-tax payments to the government to the same extent. The scheme was voluntary, but few companies preferred to pay taxes to the federal government rather than buy Embraer shares on which there was at least a small chance of earning a return. Originally, Embraer was to enjoy this privileged means of financing until 1975, but it was extended to 1980. The same privilege was extended to a few other enter- prises in priority areas. The fiscal incentive scheme yielded Embraer substantial amounts of low-cost capital, amounting to $26.5 million dur- ing 1978 (see *Exhibit 1*). As a result, the Brazilian government's share in total equity (voting and nonvoting stock) fell steadily from the initial level of 82% to as low as 11% in 1978, but its share of voting stock increased from 51% in 1969 to 54.5% in 1978. Among the largest nongovernment shareholders of Embraer were other state-owned companies, but the vast majority of shares are owned by more than 175,000 shareholders, com- posed mostly of small and medium-size Brazilian companies. Individuals could not buy Embraer shares, and the share was not quoted in the stock market, but an informal market reportedly existed for the shares. The only shareholder who regularly attended general body meetings was the nominee of the aeronautics minister, who exercised the vote on behalf of the government's controlling interest.

Silva became Embraer's first director-superintendent in 1969, and two of the functional directors who joined him were members of the IPD team that had worked on the Bandeirante project. Brazilian law required that all Air Force officers retire from the Air Force before joining Embraer. About 150 engineers and technicians who had worked on the prototype construction formed the nucleus of the Embraer organization, which grew by 1970 to 595 employees and by 1978 to well over 4,000 employees. Some production personnel were gained from other metalworking indus- tries, but most were trained by Embraer. A virgin tract of land close to CTA's offices in São Jose dos Campos (55 miles from the industrial city of São Paulo), was earmarked for Embraer's offices and factory buildings so that the company could continue to use the specialized labs, test facilities, and airport owned by CTA.

THE INITIAL PRODUCT LINE

Embraer began with three product lines in 1970. The first was composed of derivatives of the IPD-6504, which became known as the Bandeirante after the daring seventeenth-century explorers who undertook long expeditions into Brazil's interiors. The Bandeirantes manufactured in series for the Brazilian Air Force and designated as EMB-110 had more powerful engines than the first prototype flown in 1968, and they seated 12 passengers as against only 8 earlier. The first EMB-110 was handed over to the Air Force on February 9, 1973, at a ceremony presided over by the Brazilian president, Emilio Medici. In December 1972 Embraer received certification from the CTA for a 15-seat civil version of the Bandeirante (EMB-110C). In subsequent years Embraer developed nine other versions of the Bandeirante, including an 18-seater for foreign commuter airlines, a private passenger-cargo transport for export, and military models for aerial photography, paratroopers, and maritime patrol.

The second product line that Embraer took on in its first year was an agricultural spraying aircraft. This, too, was an indigenously designed aircraft, whose development work was started in IPD in1969 (IPD-6909) but was transferred to Embraer soon after it was created. The plane was designed to be effective in the climatic and farming conditions prevalent in Brazil. The first prototype was flown in July 1970; the first deliveries of this aircraft, called the Ipanema (EMB-200), were made in 1972. In this case, too, Embraer improved the original design from time to time, introducing new models in 1974 and 1976. The main market for Ipanemas consisted of private farmers and firms that rented out agricultural spraying aircraft to small farmers. Each plane sold in 1978 for $60,000–$80,000, depending on the options included.

The third product that Embraer began in its early years was a jet trainer and ground attack aircraft called the Xavante, named after a Brazilian Indian tribe. In 1968 the Brazilian Air Force required a jet trainer to replace an aging fleet of T-33 aircraft and selected the Italian firm Aermacchi's MB-326 as the best available replacement. But with the creation of Embraer, the government decided to allow the state-owned enterprise to assemble and test the Aermacchi jets, and it persuaded Aermacchi to enter into a licensing agreement with Embraer in 1970. The Air Force ordered 112 jets from Embraer in May 1970. Embraer technicians and engineers received initial training in Italy, and Aermacchi sent 20 technical representatives to São Jose dos Campos to begin initial production.

Although the production of Xavantes contributed to Embraer's early financial results, the most important benefit to Embraer was the opportunity to learn from the Italians the nitty-gritty of series production of aircraft. According to Mr. Pessotti, Embraer's technical director:

It was a very interesting cooperation, because it brought a lot of technology and expertise that we did not have at that time in Brazil—for example, in areas such as tracing technology, assembly of planes, organization for the procurement of materials, quality control, technical documentation, organization of assembly lines, etc.

We did not manufacture any parts for the Xavantes here since for that small a number of planes it would not have been economical. But we did redesign some parts of the Bandeirante with the cooperation of Aermacchi engineers. For instance, at that time we didn't know how to design integral tanks. So we sat with Aermacchi and learned how to do it for the Bandeirante. This was an important change with respect to the original prototype.

A NEW MARKET OPPORTUNITY

Even as Embraer began to execute the Air Force orders for the Bandeirante, an opportunity to market the plane to commercial airlines in Brazil cropped up much sooner than Embraer's officers could ever have expected. In April 1973, four months after the civilian version of the 15-seat Bandeirante (EMB-110C) had been certified, Transbrasil, one of the four privately owned commercial airlines operating in Brazil, placed an order with Embraer for three Bandeirantes. The planes were delivered in a record period of just sixty days be diverting planes manufactured for the Air Force, which agreed to a deferral of its own deliveries. A few modifications that took barely a month to incorporate were made to the Air Force version before supplying the Bandeirantes to Transbrasil. A few months later VASP, another commercial airline, controlled by the state government of São Paulo, ordered ten Bandeirantes. And as still more orders came in, the Air Force agreed to an arrangement in which every other plane originally intended for the Air Force could be diverted to the civilian market. "It was not that the Air Force did not need the Bandeirantes in a hurry," one Embraer official explained, "but rather they saw that a whole new market was opening up that Embraer should be given a chance to capitalize upon."

The sudden surge in demand from commercial airlines was to a large extent the result of a decision made by the Aeronautics Ministry in 1973 to introduce a three-tier airline network in Brazil. The first tier would comprise two international airlines; the second would comprise Transbrasil, VASP, and two other airlines, which would link the different regions of Brazil; and the third would be composed of five commuter lines, one in each region, which would link small towns and cities to regional centers. The second and third tiers were relatively weak in the early 1970s, since private airlines had not found it worthwhile to operate their fleet, composed largely of jets, on short, low-density routes. The Bandeirante offered itself as an attractive aircraft for use in these two tiers.

The government introduced a scheme to subsidize regional operators, whose operations would otherwise have been unremunerative, and raised funds for the subsidy program by imposing a 3% levy on all long-distance routes. Part of the funds was initially used to provide subsidized loans to the airlines to buy the Bandeirantes. Furthermore, any regulatory hurdles to the use of the Bandeirante in the second and third tiers were eliminated. Embraer's officers had a hand in the Aeronautics Ministry's shaping of these new policies and regulations, but the speed with which orders came in 1973 and 1974 surprised them, too. By 1977 the four national airlines and the five regional airlines operated more than 45 Bandeirantes. Not only was the Bandeirante attractively priced and financed, but, according to one industry analyst, its design was optimized for tropical conditions and could therefore operate in Brazil with as much as 15% more fuel efficiency than comparable U.S. aircraft.

PERSONAL AND BUSINESS AIRCRAFT

In 1974 the oil crisis and the resultant Brazilian foreign-exchange crisis found Embraer getting pushed by the government into manufacturing light single- and twin-piston-engine aircraft to replace imports of similar aircraft from the United States and other countries. Demand for such aircraft skyrocketed because of Brazil's economic boom in the early 1970s, resulting in the import of 540 planes costing nearly $600 million in 1974. Cessna accounted for almost 60% of all these planes, followed by Piper with 20% and Beech with 15%. Brazil was Cessna's biggest export market, accounting for 17% of that company's total exports in 1974.

The government directed Embraer to seek an agreement with one of the foreign firms to manufacture the planes locally. Embraer invited the three leading U.S. firms to come up with proposals for an "industrial cooperation" agreement with Embraer that would, among other things, (1) allow Embraer to manufacture a progressively greater share of the planes' components and parts within Brazil; (2) involve no royalty payments; (3) allow Embraer to modify the foreign partner designs, whenever necessary, to make the aircraft more suitable for local conditions; and (4) envisage the joint development, manufacturing, and marketing of aircraft by the two partners at some time.

Cessna and Piper entered into serious discussions with Embraer, but Cessna apparently proved unwilling to yield to almost all of Embraer's main demands, insisting that even the paint used should not be purchased locally. Although Embraer is believed to have initially preferred Cessna because of its dominant position in the Brazilian market, Piper was eventually selected as the partner. Piper's annual report for 1975 proudly announced the news of the agreement with Embraer and the access it provided to the Brazilian market; Cessna's report was totally silent on the sudden loss of its largest export market. One Embraer official commented:

> It was a good agreement for us. Frankly, some of us were surprised that Piper accepted all our demands and more. But it was also a good agreement for Piper. Their business in Brazil increased tremendously.

Piper's compensation over the ten-year agreement was mainly a percentage return on the components it shipped to Embraer. As Embraer progressively substituted locally produced components for these imports, Piper's returns would decrease, although it was to be paid a certain minimum flat fee even if Piper models were produced 100% by Embraer. At the end of a three-phase import substitution plan, Embraer expected over two-thirds of the Piper product to be of Brazilian origin. So far, Embraer had chosen to manufacture five single-engine and two twin-engine Piper models (with seating capacities of 3–8 passengers), each selling in the local market under a Brazilian brand name. After the Embraer-Piper agreement, the Brazilian government jacked up the import duty on similar aircraft from 7% to 50%. Cessna's exports to Brazil fell to a mere five planes in 1976, while Piper sold 352 kits for local assembly by Embraer in that same year.

Embraer's engineers did not regard the Piper line of products to be as sophisticated as the planes they had designed or were planning to design. One young aeronautical engineer commented: "We don't think of the Piper products as part of Embraer. We had to make them and so we are doing it!" By 1978 Embraer had manufactured and sold 1,039 Piper aircraft in Brazil.

MANUFACTURING OPERATIONS

Embraer's manufacturing operations were largely confined to the airframe and total aircraft assembly operations. It had so far not sought to integrate backward into aircraft engines, landing gear, avionics, or similar equipment on the grounds that it would be uneconomical to do so. Since Embraer did not pay import duties on these items, it could import them from abroad at a lower cost. Currently, imported components and equipment accounted for 38% of the total cost of production in the case of Bandeirante, 41% of the Xavante, 27% of the Ipanema, and 47–71% of the various models of the Piper aircraft.[1] For similar reasons, Embraer relied on local subcontractors to the utmost extent possible, rather than manufacture everything in-house. Among Embraer's 50 subcontractors was Neiva, which did most of the work on two Piper models.

All of Embraer's manufacturing operations were concentrated at São Jose dos Campos. Its facilities were regularly updated to include the latest numerically controlled machine tools. Embraer's engineers prided themselves on their quality control systems, something Silva attributed to the fact that quality consciousness was built into the organization's culture from the very beginning. Embraer's production of all its product lines from 1970 to 1978 is set out in *Exhibit 2.*

RESEARCH AND DEVELOPMENT

Embraer had consistently emphasized research and development, spending $13.3 million on it in 1978, or roughly 13% of sales. It had also recovered significant amounts of its development costs from the Air Force.

A distinguishing feature of Embraer's R&D strategy was the consistent emphasis on turboprop technology. One engineer said:

We have no illusions or desire to be a leader in jet aircraft. That game is not for us. We want to be the best in the world in turboprops, something that is within our reach and capabilities.

In the mid-1970s Embraer developed a derivative of the Bandeirante that could serve as a business executive turboprop plane with a seating capacity of 6 or 7 persons. The development of this aircraft, which at current prices would have cost $80 million, represented Embraer's first attempt at building a pressurized aircraft. The aircraft was named the Xingu (pronounced "shingoo"), after a famous, very large river in the Amazon basin. Embraer claimed that with this achievement it joined a select group of four countries that had developed and produced a twin turboprop executive transport. The Xingu was the first plane Embraer developed on its own that was not intended mainly for sale to the Air Force. By 1978 Embraer had manufactured 8 Xingus, each selling for almost $1 million.

In 1978 Embraer also launched work on a new military trainer for the Brazilian Air Force to replace its obsolete trainers. The cost of developing

[1]Mainly because of this strategy, Brazil's imports of aviation equipment exceeded $100 million in 1977. U.S. firms had the largest share in this, supplying more than $50 million worth of aircraft parts and avionics equipment to Brazilian companies.

this single-engine, two-seat turboprop trainer was expected to be picked up by the Air Force. The Air Force was expected to place an order for more than 100 of the T-27 trainers. While the T-27 project built on Embraer's previous design experience, according to one executive, its wing design was an adaptation of the wing design of one of the Piper models.

The most ambitious of Embraer's new products was still on the drawing board in 1978. It was a twin-engine, pressurized 30-seater for commercial airline applications, called the Brasilia, and designated as EMB-120. It would employ a new generation of turboprop engines being developed by Pratt & Whitney with a 1,500-horsepower rating. Development costs were estimated to be over $160 million; an estimated total of 165 planes (each costing about $4 million) would have to be sold to break even. The Air Force and the local commercial airlines were expected to buy some Brasilias. Embraer hoped to persuade the Air Force to pick up at least part of the development costs. But the main target market for this new passenger plane was the export market, especially the United States, where it was hoped that at least ten planes could be sold annually. A study by Embraer had shown that there was likely to be a big gap in the availability of fuel-efficient transport planes in the 30-seater range and that the Brasilia would be an ideal plane to meet that demand. The first prototype was expected to make its maiden flight by the end of 1982; deliveries were expected to begin in 1984. The plane was being designed so that it could comfortably meet certification standards in foreign markets, including the United States.

In the field of military aircraft, there was some talk of Embraer's launching a joint project with two Italian firms, Aeritalia and Aermacchi, to develop a new generation of tactical fighter, the AM-X. Whereas Embraer had been a licensee of Aermacchi in 1970 when the Xavantes were being produced, it was expected to be a full-fledged partner in the development of the AM-X. The cost of developing the AM-X was estimated at a staggering $600 million, which would be divided between the Italian companies and Embraer in the ratio of 2:1. Embraer's share of the costs would be recovered from the Air Force. Each AM-X plane was expected to cost $10 million.

FINANCE

The company's balance sheet and income statement for 1978 are set out in *Exhibit 3.* As of 1978, Embraer's total assets stood at Cr.$5.29 billion[2]

[2]The Brazilian currency is the cruzeiro, which was worth about 5 cents in December 1978 (i.e., US$1 = Cr.$20 approximately).

(US$264 million), and its sales had increased to Cr.$2.08 billion (US$104 million) from only Cr.$0.22 billion (US$37 million) in 1973. The company had earned a small net profit since 1973 and had paid a token dividend to its shareholders since 1974. The dividend rate amounted to about 6% of the par value of the shares but only about 1% of the shareholders' invest-ment, after adjusting for inflation as per standard inflation accounting practices in Brazil. Embraer, like private companies, was required by law to pay out a minimum of 25% of its net profits (after deducting accumu-lated losses) as dividends. In some years Embraer had paid dividends slightly greater than the required amount. One officer explained:

> We believe it is important to pay at least a small dividend so that the companies that have bought Embraer shares know we are still around and operating profitably. That also makes them more willing to go through the headache of continuing to buy Embraer shares every year under the fiscal incentive program.

The annual amount received by Embraer under the "fiscal incentive scheme" increased steadily, reflecting the rate of inflation and the conse-quent increase in the amount of income tax companies were paying the government. Embraer officials were relieved in 1975 when the scheme was extended for five more years, thereby providing Embraer with funds to invest in developing the various versions of the Bandeirante, the Xingu, and the Brasilia. Embraer did not have long-term debt of any significance in 1978 and did not have to obtain funds from the govern-ment on an annual basis.

ORGANIZATION

Embraer had all along enjoyed considerable freedom in determining its personnel policies. Most employees, especially at lower and middle levels, were paid salaries comparable to those paid by other private and multina-tional firms in the São Jose dos Campos region, such as General Motors and Volkswagen. As in the rest of Brazil, Embraer had generally been free of union problems. Embraer was allowed in principle to lay off workers, if necessary, and actually did so in 1977, when local demand for Ipanemas and Piper models slumped after a government-imposed credit squeeze. At senior management levels, Embraer's compensation package was re-ported to be significantly lower than that offered by large private firms and multinationals, being governed by the principle that no employee of a government-owned company should draw a salary greater than that of the president of Brazil.

Embraer's work force was young, dedicated, and motivated. The typical employee was twenty-eight years old, married, and had one or two children. Several of the aeronautical engineers working in Embraer were graduates of ITA.[3] In Embraer's offices there was an air of efficiency, and people at different levels and in different departments intermingled and communicated freely. One American engineer, visiting Embraer to conduct business on behalf of a U.S. company, commented:

> I was talking to some Italian firms in this industry a few weeks ago, and I can say without hesitation that I found Embraer's engineers better prepared for discussions and much more eager to learn. Embraer's engineers don't believe they know everything, and so they are more willing to listen and more concerned about catching up and staying abreast. I think this is a first-rate outfit.

The team of executive directors of Embraer had not changed since the company's creation, although three of the directors once interchanged their functional responsibilities. In the same period, the aeronautics minister had changed twice, and the director of CTA four times. Asked why Embraer's top management team had survived intact for so many years, although their formal contracts ran for only three years at a time, one of the directors quipped: "There is a saying in Brazil that if the football team is winning, why change the composition!" Another officer explained:

> Silva and his directors work as a team. He always keeps a low profile, insisting that it is the team effort and not his personal effort that counts. If he goes, the whole team may go, and the government cannot afford to let that happen. Nobody knows Embraer's business as well as they do, and the company is in a critical position in its growth now.

By all accounts, Silva was the father figure at Embraer, revered and respected. Under his leadership, Embraer was reported to have operated with a good deal of autonomy. Silva explained that the government played its legitimate role as a controlling shareholder, but no more. The government approved the company's objectives, strategies, investment plans, issues of stock, compensation policies, and the disposal of fixed assets, but it gave the company considerable freedom on matters such as personnel selection, pricing, marketing strategy, sourcing decisions, make-versus-buy decisions, technology selection, etc. In 1978 Silva was also appointed the president of Embraer, i.e., the chairman of the board, although according to most people he was the *de facto* chairman even in the earlier years, when the board of directors was formally headed by a part-time president. Silva commented on his job:

---

[3]About a hundred aeronautical engineers graduate out of ITA each year and work for the Air Force, Embraer, and private aeronautical firms in Brazil.

I know the story of every brick in this company. A lot of my life has been dedicated to it. I think of Embraer as my own company. For me this is much more than a job.

I never sought to be a very powerful man. If I did, I should have stayed in the military. And I have never desired to be a very wealthy man, for if I did I should not have joined the military. My personal life is very modest. As long as my salary is enough for me and my family, I am satisfied. I enjoy the sensation of creation that I get from Embraer. I keep receiving offers from the private sector for jobs, but they are only jobs! None of them could be like this one.

DOMESTIC MARKETING

In the domestic market, which accounted for two-thirds of Embraer's sales in 1978, the Brazilian Air Force was the single largest customer (50% of domestic sales). All Xavantes and two-thirds of all Bandeirantes sold by Embraer in the home market had gone to the Air Force. Embraer's ties with the Air Force had been positive, partly because both organizations were under the same minister, and partly because the Air Force thought of Embraer as something that grew out of the Air Force organization. These ties were no doubt further strengthened by Silva's personal relationship with former Air Force colleagues, some of whom were generals now.

Embraer's sales to the domestic private and corporate sectors were protected from international competition by tariff and nontariff barriers. The import tariff ranged from 50% for Piper-type general aviation aircraft to 0% for aircraft not manufactured in Brazil. In recent years, as Brazil's balance-of-payments problems worsened, the government considerably tightened the issuance of import licenses and required all importers to make a one-year, interest-free deposit covering the full price of manufactured goods to be purchased from abroad. (See *Exhibit 4* for details on Brazil's balance of payments and external debt.) These measures made imports of planes comparable to the Bandeirante, Xingu, Ipanema, or the Piper models almost impossible. But Embraer officials pointed out that this had not resulted in higher prices for local customers: The domestic prices of all these planes, with the sole exception of the Piper models (which had high import contents), were reportedly not very different from what Embraer charged for them in export markets.

A network of ten franchised dealers and eight additional authorized overhauling facilities provided after-sales service to Embraer's customers, especially for the large number who owned Piper models. Embraer regarded this as an important part of its effort to build a base of loyal and satisfied customers.

At a broader level, Embraer worked hard to maintain a favorable public image. Journalists were treated like kings, according to one official. People were encouraged to visit Embraer's factory, and almost 200 did so every week. Apart from weekly press releases, Embraer participated extensively in the first Latin American international aerospace show held at São Jose dos Campos and São Paulo to coincide with the birth centennial of Santos Dumont. After 1975 Embraer started to participate in international fairs and exhibitions, as the company's products began to find their way into foreign markets.

INTERNATIONAL MARKETING

As Embraer gained experience with manufacturing, selling, and servicing its products in the large Brazilian market, it gained the confidence to seek markets for those products overseas. The prime candidate for exports was the Bandeirante, which was performing very well in Brazil and had become quite competitive after the oil crisis of 1978 made fuel-guzzling jets much more expensive to operate than the noisy but fuel-efficient turboprops. Moreover, the Bandeirante was probably the most recently designed aircraft among the turboprops available in the world in the 15-20-seat range. One of Embraer's international competitors, Beech Aircraft, offered the 7- to 10-seat Beech 99 at a price of almost $1 million and had plans for developing a larger turboprop with 17 or 25 seats. But turboprops were not the core of Beech's operations, and its financing terms very stringent: All payments had to be made in U.S. dollars, and deliveries to non-U.S. buyers were made only after full payment was received. Cessna began developing its first 8- to 13-seat turboprop, the Conquest, only in the mid-1970s and apparently faced several technical problems in doing so. Piper did not manufacture turboprops that could seat more than 8 passengers. Sweringen produced the metroliner, a turboprop that was pressurized and much larger than the Bandeirante and therefore also much more expensive. And Sweringen reportedly often demanded a down payment of 40–60% of the price of the aircraft. Outside the United States, the Bandeirante's main competitor was de Havilland's less expensive Twin Otter, but this 19-seat aircraft had fixed landing gear, was slower, and had a much shorter range than the Bandeirante.

The Bandeirante had demonstrated in the domestic market that it was dependable, fuel-efficient, and simple to maintain—all very important characteristics for commuter operators. An Embraer, like other Brazilian exporters of projects and large manufactured systems, could provide very attractive financing: a down payment of only 15%, and the balance payable over seven years at interest rates of 7.5% to 8.5%. Furthermore, Embraer could offer very short delivery periods, often just 5–6 months, since planes were manufactured in anticipation of orders.

Embraer did face several problems in trying to sell its products overseas. Principal among these were its lack of experience in selling abroad, lack of a reputation or brand identification among potential customers, problems in obtaining certification as per the regulatory standards applicable in each country, problems in translating manuals and technical documentation into foreign languages, problems in finding good agents and in providing reliable after-sales service to customers, and so on. But Embraer invested considerable effort in dealing with each of these problems. A particularly striking feature of the organization was its deep awareness of international trends, strategies of competitors, and regulatory conditions in foreign markets. Virtually every national and international industry journal was available at Embraer's library and was eagerly devoured by its managers. Besides, many of Embraer's engineers had visited, studied, or worked abroad. Silva himself had spent a year at Caltech (in the United States) in 1966 earning a master's degree in aeronautics; others had studied or worked in Europe before joining Embraer. And Embraer's engineers learned a great deal about some foreign markets through their regular interaction with foreign suppliers of equipment, who also supplied some of Embraer's competitors. Nevertheless, the process of breaking into the markets of the industrialized countries was slow.

Embraer's initial export efforts were focused on the Latin American region. The first export order came from Uruguay for five Bandeirantes and ten Ipanemas in August 1975, followed by one from Chile for three Bandeirantes six months later. The first order from outside Latin America came from Togo for three Xavantes in November 1976.

In early 1976 Embraer saw the first serious opportunity to sell its planes in the United States when the Federal Express Company approached it with a request for 25 units ($800,000 each) of a modified version of the Bandeirante that would be stretched in length and have a door in front as well as a much larger door in the back for loading and unloading cargo. Embraer invested in the development of such a design, only to find that Federal Express was no longer interested in the aircraft. But this stretched design led to a passenger-cum-cargo plane, EMB-110K1, of which 20 were eventually sold to the Brazilian Air Force. The same stretched version was also developed into the EMB-110P1, a plane that could quickly be changed from an all-passenger aircraft to a passenger-cum-cargo aircraft and vice versa. Another derivative, the EMB-110P2, used the same airframe as the EMB-110K1 but did not have the large rear cargo door and was meant for commercial operations with up to 21 passengers. It was the stretched versions of the Bandeirante that proved later to be Embraer's best sellers abroad.

In April 1977 Embraer participated in the Paris Air Show at Le Bourget Airport for the first time, displaying the stretched Bandeirante (EMB-110P2) and the newly developed Xingu (EMB-121). Shortly before the air show, Embraer signed its first contract with a European customer when Air Littoral of France, a commuter airline, agreed to buy one EMB-110P2 Bandeirante. The sale terms were apparently favorable to Air Littoral, including the appointment of the French airline as Embraer's agent for most of Europe and the Middle East. A French airworthiness certificate for the Bandeirante came only in December 1977, and the Bandeirante began operating in France for the first time in 1978. Since the Bandeirante used a number of components supplied by European companies, it had a sufficiently high European content to escape import duties in the EEC. This landmark order was followed by more from Air Littoral as well as from operators in Australia and in some African countries. By 1978 Embraer could claim that its Bandeirante was flying in about a dozen foreign countries, but the United States was still not one of them.

With the deregulation of the U.S. airline industry in 1978, several large airlines had canceled their low-density routes, and new commuter airlines were taking up those routes. Embraer thought the Bandeirante ideal for the growing number of commuter operators, but entry into the U.S. market was being hindered by special regulatory and political barriers.

Embraer had applied as early as 1973 for U.S. certification for the Bandeirante, but the Federal Aviation Administration (FAA) had turned down the application for two reasons: (1) Brazil and the United States did not have a bilateral agreement on aircraft certification; and (2) the FAA could provide its services only to American taxpayers and not directly to Embraer, i.e., Embraer had first to find an American company interested in buying the Bandeirante and then get that buyer to apply to the FAA for certification. Meeting the first condition involved setting in motion a political process between Brazil and the United States that culminated in 1976 in a U.S.–Brazil bilateral agreement on certification. But meeting the second condition posed a classic Catch-22 problem: no customer, no certification; and no certification, no customer!

Embraer was confident that the Bandeirante could satisfy FAA requirements since Brazilian certification standards were modeled after American ones, and a good proportion of the Bandeirante's 28,000 parts came from established suppliers in Europe and the United States. But the prospects for exploiting the U.S. market were adversely affected by the political lobbying of Cessna and some other American companies, which apparently saw the Bandeirante as a threat to their home market business. Cessna, in particular, was believed to be eager to get even with Embraer and the Brazilians for having been shut out of the Brazilian market. Apparently its strategy was to create delays in the Bandeirante's certification and to urge the American government to impose an import duty on Brazilian aircraft unless the Brazilians eliminated the 40% import duty and the nontariff barriers that kept American general aviation aircraft out of Brazil.

Embraer was determined to get around these constraints. The temporary slackening of demand in the home market due to a credit squeeze made it even more critical to do so soon. Silva wondered if he should visit the United States to argue Embraer's case with concerned individuals and agencies in that country. As he and some others mustered arguments that could be used on such a trip, they also began to plan how Embraer should get organized to serve the U.S. market. Several questions needed to be answered: How should Embraer find its first customer in the United States who would also be willing to start the certification process with the FAA? How would other U.S. and non-U.S. competitors respond to Embraer's entry into the U.S. market? Should Embraer sell through a local agent who would also provide after-sales service, or should it set up a subsidiary in the United States? (Setting up a subsidiary would require a decree from the president of Brazil.) Should Embraer offer training to its customers' pilots in Brazil, as it normally did, or set up a simulator within the United States?

Silva knew only too well that getting the Bandeirante flying successfully in the United States was only the first step to invading that country with the much more expensive 30-seat Brasilia aircraft. And breaking even on the Brasilia project would depend critically on whether Embraer could capture a share of the expected demand for that kind of aircraft in the United States in the eighties.

EMPRESA BRASILEIRA DE AERONÁUTICA S.A.

Exhibit 1
Key Financial Data: 1973–78

	Unit	1973	1974	1975	1976	1977	1978
Sales	US$ mil.	37	54	80	112	104	104
Exports	US$ mil.	—	—	5.0	20.7	12.1	38.0
Total assets	US$ mil.	113	136	185	242	258	264
Net profit after taxes	US$ mil.	4	7	8	5	—	3
Dividends	US$ mil.	—	1	1	2	1	1
Expenditure on R&D	US$ mil.	NA	NA	6	7	7	13
Receipts under "Fiscal Incentive Scheme"	US$ mil.	10	16	21	21	29	26
No. of shareholders	('000)	96	118	118	126	160	177
Govt.'s share of total equity (voting and nonvoting)	%	21.7%	16.3%	16.0%	14.0%	12.7%	10.8%

Notes: Original Brazilian Cruzeiro (Cr$) amounts converted to U.S. dollars at following exchange rates and rounded off to neare. . million:

	Cruzeiros					
	1973	1974	1975	1976	1977	1978
US$1.00 =	6.1	6.8	8.1	10.7	14.1	20.0

NA = not available.

SOURCE: Compiled from company records.

619

EMPRESA BRASILEIRA DE AERONÁUTICA S.A.

Exhibit 2

Production of Aircraft by Embraer, 1968–78

Model	Production (Units)											
	1968	1969	1970	1971	1972	1973	1974	1975	1976	1977	1978	Total
Bandeirantes												
110:military liaison	1[a]	1[a]	1[a]	—	2	5	14	20	19	—	—	60
110C:commercial tpt.	—	—	—	—	—	8	12	11	6	—	—	37
110E/J:executive	—	—	—	—	—	—	—	12	5	—	—	17
110S1:geophysical survey	—	—	—	—	—	—	—	—	1	—	—	1
110B1:convertible pass-cum-photography	—	—	—	—	—	—	—	—	1	—	1	2
110B:aerial photogrammetric	—	—	—	—	—	—	—	—	—	6	—	6
110K1:cargo/paratrooper	—	—	—	—	—	—	—	—	—	10	10	20
110P2:pass, feederliner	—	—	—	—	—	—	—	—	—	2	13	15
111:maritime patrol	—	—	—	—	—	—	—	—	—	7	7	14
110P1:mixed pass.-cargo-tpt.	—	—	—	—	—	—	—	—	—	—	6	6
110P:pass feederliner	—	—	—	—	—	—	—	1	14	5	—	20
Total	—	—	—	—	2	13	26	44	46	30	37	198
Xingu:EMG-121	—	—	—	—	—	—	—	—	1[a]	3	5	8

Ipanemas

200:Original design	1[a]	—	13	33	3	—	—	—	—	49
200A:Improved version of 200	—	—	—	—	24	—	—	—	—	24
201:More power and payload	—	—	—	—	27	78	98	—	—	203
201A:Improved version of 201	—	—	—	—	—	—	3	94	15	112
Total	—	—	13	33	54	78	101	94	15	388
Xavante:EMB-326GB	—	7	23	19	23	24	15	21	17	149
Piper Models										
710:"Carioca"	—	—	—	—	—	50	90	88	29	257
711:"Corisco"	—	—	—	—	—	29	82	103	30	244
712:"Tupi"	—	—	—	—	—	—	—	—	12	12
720:"Minuano"	—	—	—	—	—	21	27	29	7	84
721:"Sertanejo"	—	—	—	—	—	—	52	68	11	131
810:"Seneca"	—	—	—	—	—	27	58	90	50	225
820:"Navajo"	—	—	—	—	—	4	43	30	9	86
Total	—	—	—	—	—	131	352	408	148	1,039
Total Embraer	—	7	38	65	103	277	514	556	222	1,782

[a] These are prototypes and are not included in totals.

EMPRESA BRASILEIRA DE AERONÁUTICA S.A.

Exhibit 3

Financial Results: 1978

(Figures in US$ millions)

A. *Balance Sheet as of December 31, 1978*

Cash and marketable securities	$ 33	Loans	$26
Accounts receivable	59	Supplier's credit	19
Inventories	105	Advances	11
Others	1	Others	12
Total current assets	$198	Total current liabilities	$ 68
Long-term receivables	17	Long-term loans	7
Net investments	2	Supplier's credit (long term)	39
Plant and equipment	29	Total long-term loans	46
Deferred expenses	18	Advances for capital increase	33
Total long-term assets	66	Capital (voting and nonvoting)	42
		Capital reserves	
		(i) Share premium	9
		(ii) Price level restatement of:	
		Capital	13
		Plant and equip.	15
		Working capital	30
		(iii) Retained earnings	1
		(iv) Other reserves	7
Total assets	$264	Total shareholder's funds	117
		Total liabilities and capital	$264

B. Income Statement for Year Ended December 31, 1978

Sales		$104
Less: Cost of sales		(72)
Gross profit		32
Plus: Other net operating income		13
Gross operating profit		45
Operating expenses:		
Administrative	$8	
Commercial	11	
Financial	7	
Depreciation	1	(27)
Operating profit		18
Price level adjustments		(15)
Income before tax		3
Income tax provision		negligible
Net income		3
Dividends declared		1
Profit per share — 0.4¢ per share		
Dividends per share — 0.1¢ per share		

Note: All figures rounded off to nearest million.

SOURCE: Embraer Annual Report, 1978, Exhibits I and II.

EMPRESA BRASILEIRA DE AERONÁUTICA S.A.

Exhibit 4

Brazil: Balance of Payments and External Debt

(In millions of U.S. dollars)

Description	1970	1971	1972	1973	1974	1975	1976	1977
Exports	2,739	2,904	3,991	6,199	7,951	8,670	10,128	12,139
Imports	2,507	3,245	4,235	6,192	12,641	12,210	12,346	11,991
Balance of trade f.o.b.	+ 232	− 341	− 244	+ 7	− 4,690	− 3,540	− 2,218	+ 140
Net services	− 794	− 966	− 1,245	− 1,695	− 2,433	− 3,162	− 3,763	− 4,019
Balance of payments on current account	− 562	− 1,307	− 1,489	− 1,688	− 7,123	− 6,702	− 5,981	− 3,879
Balance of payments on capital account	1,015	1,846	3,492	3,512	6,254	6,189	6,651	4,863
Overall balance of payments[a]	545	530	2,439	2,179	− 936	− 513	+ 670	+ 984
Gross external debt	5,295	6,622	9,521	12,571	17,166	21,171	25,985	32,037

[a]Includes miscellaneous items.

SOURCE: Banco Central do Brasil (Central Bank of Brazil).

The Cut Flower Industry in Colombia

In late 1979 Señor Simón Parra, co-owner and general manager of Flores El Dorado, sat in his office in downtown Bogotá looking at the latest statistics on cut flower exports from Colombia. Estimates for total exports in 1977 were around US$37 million. He couldn't help recalling the great struggle his firm and others in the industry had had in the last decade. Starting from scratch in 1967, the industry had experienced high growth by penetrating the European and American markets. It was estimated that some varieties of Colombian flowers had as much as 35% of the total U.S. market in 1977.

Despite this success Parra was worried about his firm's and the industry's future. The Colombian penetration of the U.S. market had angered U.S. producers, who asked the U.S. International Trade Commission to impose quotas on imported flowers. A further problem affecting the Colombian grower's competitiveness was rising costs stemming from Colombia's 30% inflation rate in 1977. As chairman of the board of directors of ASOCOFLORES, the Colombian Association of Cut Flower Exporters, Parra was to lead discussion of the industry's future strategy in the next meeting. An important point on the agenda was formulation of a set of recommendations the association would present to the newly appointed general manager of PROEXPO, the Colombian agency for financing and promoting of exports. The recommendations would concern government support, which the flower producers felt necessary for the industry's further development.

SOCIOECONOMIC PROFILE OF COLOMBIA

With an estimated population of 24 million by mid-1976, Colombia had the third largest population in South America. The annual population growth rate averaged 2.8% during 1966–76. About 45% of the population was under fifteen. By 1976, 68% of the population would live in urban areas.

This case was prepared by Felipe Encinales, under the supervision of Professor James E. Austin, as the basis for class discussion rather than to illustrate either effective or ineffective handling of an administrative situation. Abridged with permission.

Unemployment in 1973 was estimated at about 14% and was heavily concentrated in the urban sector. Urban underemployment was around 15%. All the main cities, especially Bogotá, were encircled by poverty rings reflecting rapid migration from the countryside. GNP per capita in current US$ increased from $350 in 1960 to $550 in 1975. But the top 20% of the population was thought to receive as much as 60% of the national income, while the lowest 20% received only 5%. Estimates of land ownership showed that the top 10% of owners had 80% of the land; the lowest 10% had only 0.2%.

In 1971–75 GDP grew in real terms at an annual average of 6.4%, while inflation averaged 24%. Agriculture contributed most to GNP at 26% in 1977, but its relative importance was declining. The high growth rate of the Colombian economy started back in 1968 as a result of several factors, one being the government's promotion of exports. The different governments in power since then had continued to give exports a high priority within their development plans.

TRADE POLICIES AND PERFORMANCE

Before 1967 Colombian exports consisted almost entirely of coffee and oil. In 1952, 95% of total exports came from those two products. In 1966 the percentage of nontraditional exports (all products other than coffee and oil) reached 19%; by 1976 their share climbed to 42%, while coffee fell to 54% and oil to 4%. Four main policy actions stood out in the government's effort to strengthen its trade sector: the formation of PRO-EXPO, foreign-exchange controls, import restrictions, and export tax credits.

PROEXPO

In 1967 PROEXPO was set up to "increase the foreign trade of the country and strengthen the balance of payments (see *Exhibit 1*) through the promotion and diversification of exports." PROEXPO was created as a subsidiary of the Central Bank so it could profit from the bank's financial flexibility and its well-established organizational structure. The function of PROEXPO was threefold. First, it financed working capital needs of exporting companies and, to a lesser degree, investments in fixed assets. In the case of the cut flower industry, credits from PROEXPO had evolved as shown in the accompanying table.

PROEXPO Credits to the Floriculture Industry

Year	Col$000	Exchange Rate	US$000
1973	44,766	23.8	1,880
1974	72,586	27.1	2,678
1975	156,450	31.2	5,014
1976	165,577	35.0	4,734
1977	94,925[a]	36.6	2,594[a]

[a]First six months.

PROEXPO had recently agreed to finance two important projects for the flower growers. The first involved financing a large refrigerated facility in Miami so that imported cut flowers could be kept at the adequate temperatures while clearing customs and sanitary inspections before being shipped to their final destination. The second involved financing Avianca Airlines for the installation of refrigerated compartments on some of its planes for the transportation of flowers.

Traditionally, interest rates charged by PROEXPO had been well below the market rates. In 1977 PROEXPO's lending interest rate was 13%, while commercial bank rates were around 32%. To make funds more available to borrowers throughout the country, several lines of credit were established with the various development finance corporations and commercial banks. PROEXPO's loan portfolio expanded rapidly to US$173 million by 1976.

PROEXPO's second major function was external promotion. Commercial offices were opened in several cities in Europe, North and South America, and Japan. Through them PROEXPO studied export possibilities for different products, gave information to potential importers, and established contacts between Colombian export firms and local buyers.

A third role for PROEXPO concerned internal promotion. Several regional PROEXPO offices were established in Colombia's major cities to decentralize the activities of the institution and make PROEXPO's services more available to exporters of different regions. These services included technical assistance, selection of regional participants to international fairs, information about foreign markets, and organization of commercial missions to different countries. The efforts of these regional offices helped create an exporting mentality among Colombian industrialists and increased their understanding of the different problems and opportunities of participating in international markets.

PROEXPO was financed through a special tax imposed on CIF imports and through debt from the Central Bank. Initially, this tax was only 1.5% on the value of imports, then it was raised to 3.5%, and again to 5%. This mechanism provided constantly growing capitalization to PROEXPO that enabled it to afford subsidized interest rates to exporters without depending on appropriations from the national budget (see *Exhibit 2*).

Foreign-Exchange Policy

In an attempt to have greater control over the balance of payments the government had instituted foreign-exchange controls. All foreign-exchange transactions had to be done through the Central Bank at a rate specified by the bank. A rigid exchange-rate policy had been overvaluing the peso constantly. A new policy of minidevaluations was established by which the peso would devalue continuously against the dollar, averaging between 7% and 9% per annum. This policy brought the exchange rate from Col$15.76 to US$1 in 1967 to Col$38.20 per dollar in 1978.

Import Restrictions

To protect local infant industries and to have further control over the balance of payments, Colombia had a very strict import regime. Goods were classified in three major import categories: free, those requiring license (80% of present imports), and prohibited products (including nonessential luxury goods). Various import duties ranged from 0% in a few products to 200% of total cost for products like cars. Of 1976 imports 50% were intermediate goods (fuels, industrial and agricultural imports), 39% capital goods (mostly industrial and transportation equipment), and 11% consumer goods. The number of products in each category changed in accordance with government policies and the balance of payments situation.

   One major drawback of these restrictions up until 1959 was that many industries found their export potential limited because of restrictions on the import of raw materials and fixed assets that were required to manufacture their products. Consequently, "Plan Vallejo" was instituted in 1959 whereby special import duty concessions were given to those products that were to be reexported or that were basic for the production of export goods. By 1976 imports under the plan were US$89 million and exports US$337 million.

Export Tax Credits (CAT)

At time of export, a CAT bond (Certificado de Abono Tributario) was given the exporter, who could use it to pay taxes or sell it in the financial market. Initially, the face value of these CATs was established at 15% of the exported value. Over the years several classifications had been defined. In 1977 most agricultural products received 7% CATs, most manufacturing products received 5% CATs, and some other products not needing this support received 0.1% CATs. Cut flowers were included in this last category in 1974, after the U.S. Treasury determined that due to the CATs flowers from Colombia would be subject to an additional countervailing import duty of 10.2%. The cost of all CATs to the national government (in the form of forgone taxes) peaked in 1974 at US$84 million and declined to US$28 million in 1976.

THE FLOWER INDUSTRY IN COLOMBIA

Origin

The origins of Colombia's cut flower industry can be traced to 1962 when Señor Edgar Wells, an old-time floriculture hobbyist, decided to come to the United States to learn about the latest techniques used in producing flowers at an industrial level. Upon his return to his country, he joined a company that had been recently founded to produce flowers for the local market. But Wells had in mind what he considered a much more profitable business: exporting to the United States. After a long struggle to implement the different techniques he had seen in America, Wells was able to persuade one of the U.S. wholesalers to buy a trial shipment. The first shipment was sent on October 18, 1965.

During the same year, a series of studies about the meteorological conditions for the cultivation of carnations was made at the University of Chicago. The U.S. Department of Agriculture disseminated the results in 1966 among several countries, including Colombia. It became evident that the Savana de Bogotá (the plateau surrounding Bogotá) presented ideal conditions for the cultivation of carnations. This conclusion led a number of wealthy Colombian and American entrepreneurs to start a few floriculture farms around Bogotá. In 1969 there were six of these companies with more than two hectares[1] specializing in producing carnations for export exclusively to the United States. Ministry of Agriculture data in the accompanying table reveal the quick expansion of flower production during the following years.

By 1969 the number of firms in the industry had grown to 50, and by 1974 to 63. The six largest firms accounted for 60% of total exports. The Colombian Ministry of Agriculture indicated that the largest 15 firms

---

[1]One hectare = 2.471 acres.

Area Planted in Flowers for the Export Market
(Hectares)

Year	Savana de Bogotá	Rio Negro[a]	Cauca Valley[a]	Total
1968	8	—	—	8
1969	16	—	—	16
1970	30	—	—	30
1971	48	—	—	48
1972	99	6	—	105
1973	144	20	—	164
1974	210	15	5	230

[a]Rio Negro and the Cauca Valley are regions with equally acceptable meteorological conditions, located in the vicinity of Medellín and Cali, respectively.

accounted for 80% of total production. In 1976 there were about 550 hectares cultivated with flowers for the export market.

All the firms in the industry were privately owned. The largest companies were run by professional managers and had wide access to the financial markets. Most of the firms had debt-to-equity ratios of about 3 to 1.

Industry Association

Under the auspices of PROEXPO, the Colombian Association of Cut Flower Exporters (ASOCOFLORES) was founded in 1970 to represent the industry in the public and private sectors, both locally and internationally. In 1977 its members accounted for 95% of the country's total flower exports.

ASOCOFLORES played a key role in securing support for the flower producers from different government institutions. The Association, based on information provided by its individual members, prepared different studies of the industry's impact on regional employment, foreign-exchange generation, land use, etc., that were presented to the different government agencies that dealt with the industry.

In recent years ASOCOFLORES had started buying, both locally and internationally, some of the basic inputs its members used, such as fertilizers and packaging. This volume buying reduced input costs for the members. ASOCOFLORES represented the local producers in international disputes, directed and contracted for market research studies in the United States and Europe, and bargained with airline carriers for transportation prices for the cut flowers.

In 1973 the Association promoted the creation of a cooperative of small producers. Through this cooperative, 24 growers with less than 1 hectare each shared technical, administrative, and financial assistance provided by different government institutions and hired experts. In 1974 cooperative members accounted for about 6.5% of the total production of the country. As a group they were members of ASOCOFLORES and consequently enjoyed all its services.

Production and Transport

All production was made under prefabricated structures of wood and plastic to protect plants from extreme temperatures and insects. Since there are no marked seasons in Colombia (because of its geographical location), there was no need for the more solid and formal facilities used in the United States and Europe.

Seeds were planted on specially prepared land maintained at a certain temperature and irrigated periodically. After 15–20 days, what was called the "mother" plant was ready to be transplanted. Initially, Colombian producers imported the "mother" plant already grown; later these were produced in Colombia with excellent results.

"Mother" plants were transplanted to "growing beds," rectangular structures, 1.5 feet deep, that were constructed 3 feet above the ground. The soil in these beds was sterilized with steam and fertilized. Halfway down in these beds, a metallic net was laid in the soil. This net was electrically heated to provide the precise temperature needed. The amounts and timing of fertilization and irrigation were also carefully controlled, for they determined the quality of the flowers and their freshness capabilities once cut.

When the plants reached a certain stage of development, they were again transplanted, this time directly to the ground where the actual production of flowers took place. Requirements of irrigation, fumigation, and fertilization were again carefully controlled in this last stage of production. The productive life of a plant was estimated at around three years.[2] A carnation plant yielded about 18 flowers per year.

The timing of cutting was also extremely important, for it determined flower quality and the plant's productivity. How soon and how low a flower was cut determined the quality of that flower and the time necessary before the next flower was ready to be cut. Each flower variety demanded different production conditions and care. The Colombian producers had to acquire this know how by bringing in experts mainly from the United States. Only in later years had leading producers actually started serious research and development programs. Despite these tech-

---

[2]The actual life of the plant was usually longer, but only during its first two or three years was the quality of its flowers good enough to be exported.

nological efforts, productivity is only 60% of that achieved by U.S. producers. The estimated annual production per hectare for the main types of flowers was as follows:

Carnations	1.6 million flowers
Pompons	432,000 flowers
Standard chrysanthemums	225,000 flowers

Once cut, flowers are extremely perishable. Their life varies with the type of flower, but it seldom is more than three days in a nonrefrigerated environment. If kept refrigerated, their life can be extended to eight or nine days.

Flowers were shipped in boxes by planes adapted with refrigerated compartments. One major problem of Colombian exporters was the very limited number of airlines (mainly Braniff and partly government-owned Avianca) serving routes to Miami[3] and Europe. Each grower contacted the airlines individually, although transportation rates were usually negotiated by ASOCOFLORES and were basically the same for all producers. The bulk of the business for these airlines was passengers; cargo was only a marginal and secondary concern. Despite this problem, Colombian producers were able to place flowers in Miami as quickly as their California competitors.

It was estimated that the flower industry employed 25,000 direct workers in 1977. Workers were mainly women (80%), and no particular skills were required. The average pay for the unskilled workers was about US$2.90 per day. Production costs were broken down as follows:

Labor	59.4%
Packing material	10.6
Chemical products	9.2
Construction maintenance	4.9
Consumption materials	3.2
Energy and fuel	1.0
Cuttings	11.7
	100.0%

It was estimated that total production costs for the average major producer were US$4,000–US$4,500 per hectare per month. In the case of carnations, this gave an average production cost of about 3.2¢ per stem.

---

[3]Exports to the United States were shipped almost entirely through Miami, which had the largest distribution center in the country.

After marketing, overhead, finance, transportation, and import duties,[4] total costs added up to about 6.8¢ per stem. Total investment per hectare in 1977 was about US$75,000.

Crops other than flowers were often subject to greater government regulation, sometimes forcing growers to sell in local markets at prices below the international price for that commodity. In 1975 a farm cultivating corn had average yield of 1.3 metric tons per hectare, which could be sold locally at about US$120 per metric ton. Costs were estimated at $80 per ton.

Year	Exports	Percentage Increase over Previous Year	Percentage Participation in Nontraditional Exports
1968	782	—	0.4%
1969	909	16%	0.4
1970	1,221	34	0.5
1971	2,308	89	0.8
1972	4,974	116	1.2
1973	9,691	95	2.1
1974	14,310	48	2.1
1975	18,036	26	2.3
1976	26,884	49	3.5
1977	37,000	38	NA

Colombia's 1968–77 cut flower exports (in US$000) are shown in the accompanying table. Although these exports came from many flower varieties, a few of them accounted for a very large share. Unit exports in 1977 were distributed as follows:

Carnations	74%
Pompons	20
Standard chrysanthemums	2
Roses	0.3
Others	3.7
	100.0%

("Others" comprised statice, miniature carnations, daisies, etc.) Only 10% of total production was sold in the local market and consisted mainly of export rejects. In 1977 the exported 90% were shipped to the destinations shown in the accompanying table.

[4]Import duties were 17% ad-valorem in the winter and 24% in the summer.

	Carnations	*Pompons*	*Standard Chrysanthemums*	*Roses*	*Others*
U.S.	64%	92%	96%	86%	79%
Europe	33[a]	2	1	1	14
Other	3	6	3	13	7
	100%	100%	100%	100%	100%

[a]Germany 12%; England 6.3%; Sweden 4.2%; Norway 2.1%; Switzerland 2.1%; Others 6.3%.

Although recently diversification was recurring, most local producers have concentrated their production in one or a few varieties. Different types of flowers demanded different production requirements that had to be met with substantial care if the desired quality was to be achieved. In a market so sensitive to quality, adding an additional variety to a farm could be a major undertaking. Agronomically, it was feasible to grow other types of flowers.

THE U.S. MARKET

As shown in *Exhibit 3,* U.S. consumption of cut flowers increased slowly during the 1970s. Average annual growth in current dollars was only 5.4%. Meanwhile, total imports averaged a growth rate of 52.1% per annum. The relative importance of improts varied significantly within different varieties. The accompanying table shows the performance of imports of the individual major varieties in terms of their share of the total U.S. market.

Year	*Carnations*	*Pompons*	*Standard Chrysanthemums*	*Roses*
1967	0.3%	0.6%	0.5%	NA
1968	0.5	1.5	0.9	NA
1969	0.8	2.0	1.2	NA
1970	2.4	4.1	2.4	0.1
1971	5.1	5.7	6.4	0.2
1972	8.3	10.5	9.1	0.4
1973	16.9	15.5	12.7	0.8
1974	22.0	21.0	13.4	0.8
1975	21.1	24.4	9.7	0.9
1976	25.9	32.9	7.0	1.3

The three leading suppliers of cut flowers to the United States in 1976 were Colombia, Mexico, and Guatemala, which together accounted for over 95% of total imports. Twenty-one other countries shared the rest.

Colombia alone accounted for 91% of U.S. imports of carnations, pompons, standard chrysanthemums, daisies, roses, and statice imported in
1976, up from 64% in 1972. Colombia's share of imports during 1976
varied from a low of 31% for statice to a high of 96% for carnations.
Exhibit 4 indicates the evolution of import shares of leading producer
countries.

Per capita consumption of flowers measured in units had increased less
than 4% since 1970. The following list compares the U.S. annual consumption per capita with that of other European countries in 1975:

	US$
United Kingdom	4.65
Italy	8.75
France	9.75
United States	15.46
Sweden	19.25
Netherlands	23.15
West Germany	28.15
Switzerland	32.20

Among U.S. producers, there was a shift from many small local growers
in the Northeast and Midwest to a few large, efficient growers in California, Florida, and Colorado, where there were more favorable meteorological conditions. *Exhibit 5* shows the trend of the number of growers of each
variety. In 1977 about three-fourths of total U.S. production came from
one-fourth of the growers. A high proportion of the output was produced
by the top 10% of growers of any particular variety. For example, in 1975
the top 8% of chrysanthemum growers accounted for about one-third of
the total production.

The accompanying table shows the concentration of production among
U.S. carnation growers in 1975. *Exhibit 6* shows the unit participation of
U.S. growers and imports as suppliers for the U.S. market for three of the
major varieties.

Sales in 1975	*Number of Growers*	*Percentage of U.S. Production (units)*
Less than US$100,000	615	30%
US$100,000–US$500,000	240	50
More than US$500,000	36	20
Total	891	100%

Most U.S. growers concentrated their production on one particular
type of flower. *Exhibit 7* shows a joint profit and loss statement of 13

growers of carnations as compiled by the International Trade Commission.

Sales of cut flowers in the United States were highly seasonal, peaking
on Mother's Day, Memorial Day, Valentine's Day, Easter, and the Christmas holidays. Colombian exports, as measured in kilos, indicated this
seasonality. The following table gives a monthly percentage breakdown
for sales of 1977:

January	5.6%	July	5.1%
February	6.9	August	6.7
March	11.2	September	12.5
April	3.3	October	12.0
May	8.2	November	9.3
June	6.0	December	13.2

Prices received by importers and U.S. growers moved in the same
direction; the former were usually higher than the latter. According to a
study made by the U.S. International Trade Commission, the difference
was accounted for by the "generally superior quality . . . owing to superior
climatic conditions prevailing in Colombia, which is the main supplier."[5]
Exhibit 8 shows wholesale prices.

COMMERCIALIZATION

Colombian growers had distributed their flowers by establishing fixed-
price contracts with U.S. and European importers or by selling directly to
wholesalers on consignment. Under the latter arrangement, the wholesaler charged a fixed percentage of the price paid by the retailer.

The larger, more aggressive producers had established marketing organizations in the United States and Europe, thus selling their products
directly to wholesalers or retailers.

Once the flowers arrived at the U.S. port of entry (usually Miami), they
were distributed throughout the country in refrigerated trucks. The distribution network allowed the flowers to reach retailers only a couple of
days after having been cut.

Cut flower retailers in the United States considered quality, durability,
and price as the three most important product characteristics. Traditionally, U.S. retailers were predominantly flower shops, whose target client
was the "special occasion" buyer. More recently there was a trend toward
distribution through mass merchandisers. The accompanying table shows
this trend.

[5]"Fresh Cut Flowers," U.S. International Trade Commission, August 1977.

Percent of Total Sales in U.S.

	1970	*1977*	*Average Annual Growth*
Retail florist	63%	56%	7.6%
Nonflorist retailer	37	44	11.2
Total	100%	100%	9.1%

Some flower types, especially carnations, were able to penetrate the European market successfully. But high transportation costs[6] and high import duties placed Colombian flowers in a difficult competitive situation. Furthermore, some European countries gave special concessions to previous colonies and other countries.

RECENT EVENTS

Some recent developments in the local and international scenes had Parra concerned about their impact on the flower industry.

One of the most important events was the creation by the monetary authorities of the foreign-exchange certificate. The government, in an attempt to control the impact of increasing foreign reserves on local prices, had instituted a new foreign-exchange mechanism. Its main effect was to force exporters and others wanting to convert dollars into pesos to wait for three months before being able to receive pesos after the presentation of the corresponding foreign exchange to the Central Bank. If certificate holders wanted pesos immediately, they were forced to take a sizable discount. With the same objective of controlling the money supply, the peso's devaluation against the dollar had slowed to less than 10% per annum, causing an overvaluation of the peso.

On the other hand, inflation threatened to be particulary hard on the flower producers because of expected increases in the cost of labor (between 40% and 50% during the next year). Land values had also increased dramatically, particularly near Bogotá. Furthermore, the industry had been strongly affected by the drastic government credit squeeze on financial markets.

On the international side, the Growers Division of the Society of American Florists and Ornamental Horticulturists had filed a petition with the U.S. International Trade Commission, asking for the establishment of quotas for the imports of cut flowers into the United States. Just recently,

---

[6]Because of the relative scarcity of direct flights to Europe, part of the flowers going to that market were transshiped through Miami.

after a detailed investigation, the commission concluded that imports were not a cause of "major injury" to the local flower industry. But it was felt that this investigation had been a warning signal for the Colombian growers. Furthermore, the minister of agriculture had sent a letter to ASOCOFLORES urging it to ask its members to restrain from further expansion of production facilities of carnations and pompons and to plan the future supply in accordance with the absorption capacity of the U.S. market. The Colombian growers, however, felt that the imbalance of supply and demand in the American market was due mainly to a lack of proper marketing and distribution. A report on this issue by a prestigious American consulting company identified several weaknesses in the marketing of flowers, especially at the retail end. It was felt that an effort from retailers to market their products more aggressively could interest the nonoccasional buyer, thus expanding total demand for flowers and also smoothing the very sharp seasonal cycles to which the industry was subject. The increasing interest of mass merchandisers and, in particular, some large food retail chains was expected to contribute significantly to the future growth of the industry.

Parra reflected on the implications of these concerns for the recommendations he would present to his fellow flower growers regarding the industry's strategy generally and in particular the petition to PROEXPO.

THE CUT FLOWER INDUSTRY IN COLOMBIA

Exhibit 1
Balance of Payments
(US$ millions)

	1970	1971	1972	1973	1974	1975	1976
Exports	788	752	979	1263	1494	1694	2258
Imports	802	900	848	982	1510	1480	1814
Trade balance	-14	-148	131	281	-16	214	444
Service receipts	212	222	228	285	364	406	523
Service payments	347	-142	-162	-180	-139	-196	-158
Other current	-153	-142	-162	-180	-139	-196	-158
Current account	-302	-453	-191	-56	-351	-176	187
Private capital	100	106	72	25	28	32	45
Direct investment	39	40	17	23	36	43	45
Loan (net)	61	66	55	2	-8	-11	—
Utilization	128	145	139	60	50	76	—
Amortization	67	79	84	58	58	87	—
Public capital	161	130	255	285	158	249	195
Utilization	236	222	351	417	364	383	376
Amortization	75	92	96	132	206	134	181
SRD allocation	21	17	18	—	—	—	—
Errors and omissions	14	118	10	-41	-224	-13	-157
Net reserve changes	-6	-82	+164	+213	-389	+118	+584

SOURCE: DANE.

639

Exhibit 2
PROEXPO Balance Sheet
(*$000 Col. pesos*)

	1967	1970	1974	1975	1976
Assets					
Deposits in Central Bank	1,135	14,940	16,386	541,340	172,297
Other deposits		35	378	439	67
Loans & discounts	61,954	269,880	2,567,486	4,369,491	6,562,223
Investments	5,304	79,486	35,428	12,783	112,680
Fixed assets	—	—	907	104,112	106,101
Other assets	3,604	17,978	141,112	71,617	82,367
Other receivables	—	91,960	498,148	—	—
Total assets	71,997	474,279	3,259,845	5,099,782	7,035,735
Liabilities					
Debt to Central Bank	39,547	175,529	2,152,659	3,108,919	2,878,211
Accounts Payable	118	236	44,666	43,607	18,958
Other Liabilities	1,117	10,952	23,587	109,663	159,956
Equity	31,215	287,562	1,038,933	1,837,593	3,978,610
Total liabilities	71,997	474,279	3,259,845	5,099,782	7,035,735

THE CUT FLOWER INDUSTRY IN COLOMBIA

Exhibit 3

U.S. Cut Flower Production, Imports and Exports

Year	Production (1,000 dollars)	Imports (1,000 dollars)	Exports (1,000 dollars)	Apparent Consumption (1,000 dollars)	Ratio of Imports to Production (percent)	Ratio of Imports to Consumption (percent)
1967	195,208	902	1,978	194,132	0.5	0.5
1968	221,321	1,886	1,755	221,452	.9	.9
1969	233,831	2,948	1,908	234,871	1.3	1.3
1970	229,944	5,782	2,228	233,498	2.5	2.5
1971	233,901	8,901	3,554	239,248	3.8	3.7
1972	251,754	14,908	4,258	262,204	5.9	5.7
1973	256,094	22,706	4,412	274,388	8.9	8.3
1974	258,596	31,330	5,246	284,680	12.1	11.0
1975	266,189	30,862	8,680	288,371	11.6	10.7
1976	282,863	41,711	13,982	310,592	14.7	13.4

SOURCE: International Trade Commission.

THE CUT FLOWER INDUSTRY IN COLOMBIA

Exhibit 4

Fresh Cut Flowers: U.S. Imports of Carnations, Pompon Chrysanthemums, Standard Chrysanthemums by Specified Sources, 1972–76, 19-Week Period Ending May 8, 1976

(In thousands of stems)

Source	1972	1973	1974	1975	1976	1972 Market Share of Imports	1976 Market Share of Imports
Carnations							
Colombia	47,828	119,287	163,638	157,097	196,069	85%	96%
Mexico	2,491	3,748	5,907	6,001	6,644	4	3
Guatemala	*	*	1,714	366	774		4
Ecuador	3,867	4,594	7,755	4,023	66	7	—
All other	1,967	4,591	955	781	898	4	4
Total	56,153	132,220	179,969	168,268	204,451	100%	100%

Pompon Chrysanthemums

Colombia	13,181	24,759	52,053	70,158	104,978	52%	91%
Guatemala	8,035	12,931	8,965	3,262	8,287	32	7
Ecuador	1,197	1,762	1,791	1,801	781	5	1
Costa Rica	2,612	2,509	1,356	321	634	10	1
All other	216	228	183	251	82	1	—
Total	25,241	42,189	64,348	75,793	114,762	100%	100%

Standard Chrysanthemums

Colombia	4,945	9,705	13,767	12,233	9,614	31%	77%
Guatemala	6,716	9,137	7,456	3,375	2,387	42	19
Mexico	*	*	514	332	333	—	3
Netherlands	294	455	*	*	148	2	1
Ecuador	2,672	2,823	3,595	1,064	77	17	—
All other	1,239	1,232	560	380	0	8	—
Total	15,866	23,352	25,892	17,384	12,559	100%	100%

*Data not available.

SOURCE: U.S. International Trade Commission.

THE CUT FLOWER INDUSTRY IN COLOMBIA

Exhibit 5

Number of U.S. Growers

Year	Carnations		Chrysanthemums		Gladioli	Roses	
	Standard	*Miniature*	*Standard*	*Pompon*		*Hybrid Tea*	*Miniature*
1966	2,175		2,972	2,976	581	376	
1970	1,717	443	2,236	2,342	366	367	284
1974	958	301	1,402	1,380	176	300	231
1975	891	302	1,346	1,366	163	309	236
1976	808	318	1,238	1,203	144	278	221

SOURCE: International Trade Commission.

THE CUT FLOWER INDUSTRY IN COLOMBIA

Exhibit 6

Carnations, Roses, and Pompon Chrysanthemums: U.S. Production, Imports, Exports,
and Apparent Consumption, 1967–76

(Carnation, and pompon chrysanthemums in millions of stems; roses in millions of blooms)

Year	Production	Imports	Exports	Apparent Consumption	Ratio (percent) of Imports to Production	Ratio (percent) of Imports to Consumption
Carnations						
1967	524.6	1.6	1.4	524.8	0.3	0.3
1968	599.9	3.0	1.3	601.6	.5	.5
1969	647.8	5.1	1.4	651.3	.8	.8
1970	656.3	16.4	1.5	671.2	2.5	2.4
1971	623.5	33.2	2.5	654.2	5.3	5.1
1972	623.0	56.2	3.0	676.2	9.0	8.3
1973	657.4	132.2	7.0	782.6	20.1	16.9
1974	646.3	180.0	11.0	815.2	27.9	22.0
1975	624.3	162.5	15.0	771.8	26.0	21.1
1976	603.6	204.5	20.0	788.1	33.9	25.9
Roses						
1967	388.4					
1968	437.3					
1969	457.1					
1970	469.4	0.7	1.5	468.6	0.1	0.1

(continued on next page)

645

Exhibit 6

Carnations, Roses, and Pompon Chrysanthemums: U.S. Production, Imports, Exports, and Apparent Consumption, 1967–76 *(Continued)*

Year	Production	Imports	Exports	Apparent Consumption	Ratio (percent) of Imports to Production	Ratio (percent) of Imports to Consumption
1971	458.6	1.0	1.5	458.1	.2	.2
1972	461.6	1.7	1.5	461.8	.4	.4
1973	446.8	3.4	2.0	448.2	.8	.8
1974	473.6	3.6	4.0	473.2	.8	.8
1975	463.4	4.2	8.0	459.6	.9	.9
1976	466.6	6.2	10.0	462.8	1.3	1.3
Pompon chrysanthemums						
1967	180.6	1.2	3.6	178.2	0.7	0.6
1968	199.8	3.0	4.2	198.6	1.5	1.5
1969	215.4	4.2	4.8	214.8	1.9	2.0
1970	212.4	9.0	4.2	217.2	4.2	4.1
1971	225.6	13.2	6.0	232.8	5.9	5.7
1972	220.8	25.2	5.4	240.6	11.4	10.5
1973	237.0	42.2	6.6	272.6	17.8	15.5
1974	247.2	64.3	6.0	305.5	26.0	21.0
1975	240.6	75.8	6.0	310.4	31.5	24.4
1976	240.0	114.8	6.0	348.8	47.8	32.9

Exhibit 7

Profit-and-Loss Experience of 13 U.S. Growers on Their Fresh
Cut Carnation Growing Operations, Accounting Years 1972–76

(Money figures in thousands of dollars)

Item	1972	1973	1974	1975	1976
Sales:					
Fresh cut carnations	1,312	1,255	1,255	1,273	1,469
Fresh cut chrysanthemums	1	3	5	4	8
Sales of other flowers and plants	28	30	47	62	117
Total sales	1,341	1,258	1,307	1,339	1,594
Other income	27	38	14	20	13
Total sales and other income	1,368	1,296	1,321	1,359	1,607
Total growing and operating expenses	1,035	1,050	1,060	1,082	1,228
Net profit before income taxes and officers' salaries	333	246	261	277	379
Ratio of net profit (before income taxes and officers' salaries) to total sales (percent)	24.8	19.6	20.0	20.7	23.8
Ratio of fresh cut carnation sales to total sales (percent)	97.8	97.4	96.0	95.1	92.2
Range of individual growers' total sales:					
Low	29	23	22	32	25
High	222	192	242	217	306
Median	87	106	99	101	104
Range of individual growers' total profit or (loss):					
Low	(24)	(7)	(22)	(17)	(7)
High	78	47	142	110	189
Median	18	20	7	9	16
Number of growers reporting losses	2	2	4	2	2

SOURCE: Compiled from data submitted in response to questionnaires of the U.S. International Trade Commission by U.S. growers of flowers.

Exhibit 8
Average Wholesale Prices Received by U.S. Growers
(Cents per bloom)

| Year | Carnations | Chrysanthemums | | Roses |
		Standard	Pompon	
1967	7.9	18.3	13.8	11.7
1968	7.7	20.2	14.0	12.0
1969	7.6	19.6	13.8	12.6
1970	7.5	18.3	13.7	12.3
1971	7.6	19.0	14.2	12.7
1972	8.6	21.2	14.8	13.8
1973	7.8	21.6	15.2	14.8
1974	7.8	20.5	13.7	15.3
1975	8.2	21.9	14.7	16.4
1976	9.4	20.9	16.0	17.6

SOURCE: International Trade Commission.

Daidong Mould & Injection Co.

One hot summer day in July 1985, Jung-Myung Kang, president and chief executive officer of the Daidong Mould & Injection Company (a Korean manufacturer of high-quality plastic components for electronic products), returned to Korea from Japan. As an export-oriented company, Daidong had achieved 300% growth of exports during the past three years, reaching US$15.3 million in 1984. As a result of its impressive export growth, the government had given the company a "Successful Exporter Award."

During his three-week visit to Japan, Mr. Kang had confirmed export orders to a number of major Japanese electronic manufacturers, including Sanyo and Sony, but he did not get as many orders as he had expected, and he learned that the Japanese had recently become interested in finding other, more cost-competitive suppliers from Korea and other Asian countries. On the way back to Korea, he also realized that the company's export sales for the first half of 1985 had reached only 65% (US$5.1 million) of the previous year's level for the same period.

As Mr. Kang entered his office, he called for a board meeting in thirty minutes. He lit a cigarette and thought about the agenda to be discussed at the meeting.

THE COMPANY

Daidong Mould & Injection Co. was a supplier of plastic cabinets and internal components for various electronic products, such as radios, cassette players, TVs, stereos, and telephone sets. With a sales volume of $17.2 million in 1984, Daidong was not a large-scale company in Korea, but it was well known in the industry for its high quality and pioneering history. Since its establishment in 1972, the company had introduced the best-quality products and the most advanced technologies in Korea and had almost monopolized the high end of the domestic and export markets. In the early 1970s, when the other Korean producers had been small

This case was prepared by Research Assistant Seok Ki Kim, under the supervision of Professor James E. Austin, as the basis for class discussion rather than to illustrate either effective or ineffective handling of an administrive situation. Abridged with permission.

and technologically backward and the industry had been in an embryonic stage, Daidong had been the only exporter with first-class world technology and efficient plant management, both brought from Japan. (The company had two Japanese staff members serving as plant manager and operations manager.)

Almost 90% of Daidong's sales in 1984 were exported to a few big buyers (*Exhibit 1*). As to the current situation of the company, Kang said:

> We have worked for a small number of Japanese buyers for a long time, and we know each other very well. They know how to take care of their own suppliers. Though we are independent in ownership and management, our relationship is so close as to make us and our Japanese customers act like a single vertically integrated firm. In bad times, they acted as a buffer for my company; we have been less severely affected by fluctuations in the world market than our competitors because our clients, like many other large Japanese firms, have maintained a philosophy of "coprogress through coexistence." Unlike other buyers, their orders have been regular and profitable.
>
> This year [1985] our sales became sluggish; sales of the first six months fell short of last year's performance for the same period, and future orders from the Japanese seem uncertain. I feel the Japanese are concerned with our rising costs and Korea's recent economic-political development. Moreover, we are no longer the only leader in the industry. Though we are slightly ahead of our competitors in technology and quality, they are growing fast and becoming more cost competitive. They work as hard as (maybe even harder than) we did years ago and are willing to take small, unattractive orders from many domestic buyers. With increased competition, high turnover of workers is another problem; our people are the best trained and naturally become a target for scouting by competitors. One of my staff reported that the turnover ratio of our factory workers was 100% for the last twelve months.

COMPANY HISTORY

The history of the Daidong Mould & Injection Co. dates back to 1960, when Mr. Koh-Won Kang, father of Mr. Jung-Myung Kang, set up the Mode Plastic Co. in Japan. In 1920, when Korea was under Japanese occupation, Koh-Won Kang's family had moved to Japan.

When the family moved to Japan, Koh-Won Kang was only eight years old. His father had decided to go to Japan, hoping for a better life and better education for his children. But the reality was different. Koreans were considered second-class citizens and excluded from many opportunities and activities. The life of the Kang family was at a subsistence level, and young Mr. Kang could not go to high school. They were disappointed but too poor to go back to Korea. When he was thirteen, he got a job at a small grocery store as an errand boy. One day a few years later, he delivered some food to a nearby factory that was manufacturing things totally new to him. It was a very small (though very big to him) factory with 15 workers producing plastics. In the following year he moved to that factory as a cleaning boy. He worked very hard, from dawn to late at night, and frequently slept at the plant. People began to like him; later he became an assistant to the lowest-level craftsman. He worked even harder and was gradually promoted. He always thought, "Honesty, trust, and sincerity are my guiding philosophy." Thirty years later the company became one of the leading manufacturers in the industry, and he became a co-head of the plant, which had been merged with Sony.

In 1960 he resigned from the company and set up the Mode Plastic Co. with his savings and severance pay. He recalled:

> As a Korean in Japan, I realized my limitations. Also, as head of my family, I felt responsibility for my growing sons. I did not want to be a father working for a Japanese company. I wanted my son to inherit the company and hoped that all my family could go proudly back to my country.

Though the business was not big, the family could live on it, and the company maintained its reputation as a high-quality producer in the industry. As Jung-Myung grew up, Koh-Won Kang began to teach him all he knew about the product, production, and customers. As soon as Jung-Myung graduated from college, his father appointed him a director of operations. Soon the son proposed to move the business to Korea, where labor was substantially cheaper. He thought the combination of his technology, customer relationships, and cheaper labor would give him a substantial advantage over the Japanese competitors. He conducted all the studies and formulated a plan. Mr. Koh-Won Kang remembered: "That was exactly what I had dreamed of for a long time, but I said nothing because I thought it was time for me to retire and I wanted him to make decisions of his own."

In 1972 the Kangs finally established Daidong Plastic & Injection Co. in Korea with a minimum production scale and $250,000 of initial capital investment, which was financed by a sale of 50% ownership of the Mode Plastic Co. in Japan. The company began its first operation in October 1972 as a typical cottage industry, with two plastic injection machines (see the following section for the production process) and 30 people. In anticipation of market growth, the company expanded its facilities by 300% through a capital investment of $500,000 in early 1973. Mr. Kang sold the rest of his share of Mode Plastic and arranged a loan ($200,000 equivalent in Korean currency) from a local Korean bank to finance the expansion. But struck by a recession after the oil crisis in 1973–74, the company had a serious financial crisis. President Jung-Myung Kang recalled:

> It seemed obvious to me that I, with my limited scale, could not compete effectively against many Japanese counterparts. Moreover, our old Japanese clients worried about their geographical and psychological distance from my newly created Korean operation. Their primary concern was quality assurance and delivery schedule. To produce exactly what we had produced in Japan at much lower cost, capacity expansion was indispensable. With a global recession, the Japanese did not give me the minimum order necessary for our survival because I, as a foreign subcontractor, could get only secondary attention from them. I also thought about domestic [Korean] buyers, but my high-quality, high-priced products were beyond their interest, and I could not compete in the lower-price product range. I concluded that the key was to reestablish a trust- and loyalty-based relationship with my good old Japanese buyers. But even before I tried, I encountered a financial crisis. I was not familiar with business management in the modern sense. I knew only about plastics, and it was my life, as it was for my father. I was new to Korea and had no personal contacts. Fortunately, my father-in-law (at that time my fiancée's father), who was running a sizable construction company in Korea, saved me.

As Mr. Kang recovered from the first crisis, he tried everything he could to develop trust- and loyalty-based relationships with major Japanese buyers. He explained:

> It was a long and painful process. Sometimes I had to decline some very attractive orders from other buyers to meet the delivery schedule for the small, unattractive orders from the Japanese buyers. We all worked very hard; the plant operated twenty-four hours a day, seven days a week; sitting up all night was not unusual for many of us. I personally handled everything between my company and them. I never sent anybody else to the Japanese buyers, and I was the only president who came to pick up the orders and specifications and to discuss technical matters with their operational-level people at the factory. I visited them once or twice every month and did not forget to visit their families with gifts on major Japanese holidays and their birthdays. Finally, they began to trust me and help me by giving me continuous orders and providing technical assistance by sending several key technicians to my company.

In 1977 the company set up a mould manufacturing division as a step to vertical integration and changed its name to the Daidong Mould & Injection Co. It invested $200,000 to produce moulds, which had previously been provided by the Japanese with each order. (Moulds are the solid frames in which liquid plastic is injected to shape hard structures.) As soon as the new factory was completed, the company got into another financial crisis. In 1978, with a recession caused by the second oil shock, one of Sony's subsidiaries went bankrupt; as a result Daidong could not collect a $300,000 receivable. Fortunately, a month later Sony provided financial assistance (a large personal interest-free loan) and gave compensating orders despite the global recession. As the market turned upward from 1982, the company grew rapidly (see financial statements in *Exhibits 2* and *3*). It expanded again by setting up the precision mould division to produce moulds for highly sophisticated plastic components for computer and telecommunications products. As the technological leader, the company virtually monopolized the high-end market (both export and domestic) in Korea. The company was in a position to choose the best orders and best clients.

PRODUCTION AND TECHNOLOGY

Production at Daidong was driven by specific orders. In the received orders, buyers gave the product quantities and specifications. The moulds were internally produced by the Mould Division or the Precision Division. Moulds were made of iron or very fine sand and required highly specialized expertise. Making each mould required three steps: design, crude modeling, and fine finish. Design was a manual process performed by eight designers, who were graduates from vocational schools or professional junior colleges and had three to five years of field experience. In this industry in Korea, computer-aided design was not done. The design team's manager said, "Human hands cost much less." An experimental mould was made according to the design. To approximate the specifications, about three or four crude moulds were made. Once an acceptable mould was made, it was installed in an injection machine to produce an experimental product. Fine finish was a process to correct errors in the crude mould to meet the specifications exactly.

While the moulds were being made, such materials as chemicals and inks were ordered. At the same time, silk screens were prepared to print letters and pictures (such as company logos) of various colors on the surface of the plastic products. The Production Technology Department determined the proportion of chemical materials (e.g., polystyrene, ABS, acrylic, AS, polycarbonate, polypropylene, thinner, and paint) to make the liquid to be injected into the mould in the injection machine.

After the moulds were installed in the injection machines and the liquid plastic was injected into the moulds, it took from a few seconds (for small components such as buttons or keys) to two minutes (for a large TV or stereo cabinet) to produce each solid plastic frame. Once a solid frame was made, grinding and polishing followed, using sandpaper and fine knives to smooth the surface. The next step was painting with a spraying machine, silk screen, or both. Finally, after passing inspection, the frames were packed and shipped.

The total process took in general 30–45 days, depending on the size of each order; everything except injection was performed by hand. The company began with two injection machines in 1972; by July 1985 that number had increased to 42.

All the technology of the whole production process was simple and standardized except for mould production and silk screening. Industry experts believed that Japan possessed the most advanced technologies for precision-mould production and silk screening for electronic products. In general, order size and yield ratio were the two critical elements determining profitability, because there was a substantial learning effect specific to each order. President Kang modified the technology in the Korean operation to increase yield ratios by establishing recycling loops for rejected outputs. In Japan plastic frames that did not pass inspection were either wasted or melted for reinjection. At Daidong they were returned to the middle of the process according to the specific defect(s) of each frame, which had been individually inspected and handled at several stages of the process. While painting was done by spraying machines in Japan, Daidong used labor, because Kang thought it was more economical.

MARKETING AND ORGANIZATION

Daidong never had a marketing organization. Every marketing activity was exclusively and personally performed by the president. One executive commented:

> In Korea we are the best and the largest. We select customers. We do not need any marketing activities because they are costly. Our president knows everything: He knows the product, technology, and, most important, he knows how to handle big buyers and how to get good orders. He is our Big Boss. We simply do what he orders us to do.

As for marketing, Mr. Kang said:

> I am more a technician than a businessman. For me my plant is like my palm. Even when I am in my room, I know exactly what is going on in every corner of my company. I feel less comfortable, however,

with accounting, finance, or advertising. All our customers are good, old people whom my father and I have known for decades. I believe they will not abandon us so long as we keep our trust and loyalty to them. Since I was brought up in Japan, my Korean language is not perfect, and this is a critical handicap in doing business in Korea. I ask Mr. Jong-Bae Lee, executive vice president, to handle all external relations [with banks, the government, etc.] in Korea.

As of June 13, 1985, there were 213 white-collar employees and 852 blue-collar workers at the production line at Daidong. Of the latter group, about 80% were women in their late teens to mid-thirties. (For an organization chart, see *Exhibit 4*.)

THE INDUSTRY

As of July 1985 there were about 300 firms in the plastic component manufacturing industry in Korea. Since this industry was loosely defined and most firms were small (only ten had more than 100 employees) and financially weak, no statistics were officially available. One industry expert speculated that the size of the plastic components industry was 15% (for TVs) to 20% (for most audio products) of the consumer electronics industry. The export growth of the electronics industry had dropped from an annual rate of about 30% in 1984 to about 7% in 1985, mainly because of the recession in the United States, which accounted for 53% of Korea's electronics exports.[1] Antidumping duties in the United States and Canada on Korean TVs led some buyers to switch to cheaper Taiwan models. But exports of VCRs and car stereos were rising in 1985. The Korean domestic market for electronics was experiencing a 10% growth rate.

In 1985 Daidong was the largest and highest-quality producer in the plastics components industry. Kang believed that Daidong's premium quality was based largely on its moulds. Though there were two other Korean mould manufacturers, their quality was not comparable to Daidong's, and Daidong did not sell its mould products to other companies. Large manufacturers of electronic products maintained different degrees of vertical integration depending on product lines: For some lines, they produced all the intermediate goods in-house (including moulds and injected plastic components); for others they specialized in producing only key components and subcontracted the production of moulds and plastic parts to such firms as Daidong. For large Japanese

[1]"Has the Bubble Burst?" *Korea Business World*, September 1985, p. 30.

manufacturers (Sony, Sanyo, etc.), subcontracting was more common, because the mould and plastic-injection industry was relatively well defined and highly specialized. In Korea, large firms did not subcontract moulds and plastic-parts production for their core items. Samsung, for example, subcontracted only audio products, which were not their core items.

In the industry segment for high-quality injection and production of plastic components, ten firms competed, including Daidong. In general the prices of Daidong's products were at least 10% higher than those of the next leading Korean supplier. In 1984 Daidong supplied 100% of Sony's Korean sourcing, 60% of Sanyo's, and 30% of the Samsung audio division's. Though exact figures were not available, Mr. Kang estimated that his company's portion in his major clients' global sourcing of plastic components was around 10% for Sony, 15% for Sanyo, and over 20% for other Japanese customers. The biggest advantage of Daidong over Japanese suppliers was its low price: Daidong's price was less than half that of its Japanese competitors. But Japanese quality was superior to Daidong's. Mr. Kang commented:

> When I first set up my operations in Korea thirteen years ago, our technology and product quality were at least as good as the Japanese, but now I must admit that I did not catch up with Japanese R&D. Updating technology is costly: I have to hire more expensive people and buy expensive new plant equipment. I did not think it was necessary because I could still prosper with a cost advantage.

GOVERNMENT POLICIES AND MEASURES
TO PROMOTE EXPORTS

Since the early 1960s, export-led economic growth had been a backbone strategy of the country, and the Korean government had used various policies and measures to promote exports. As a resource-poor and labor-abundant country, Korea had to provide about half a milion new jobs each year for its increasing labor force, to pay the bills for importing energy and raw materials, and to service the world's fourth largest foreign debt. This meant that the economy had to grow at least 7.5% per year through export promotion (see *Exhibit 5*).

To boost exports, the Korean government maintained the following policies and measures as of June 1985:

- Flexible adjustment of the foreign-exchange rate (For historical exchange rates, see *Exhibit 6*.)
- Practical and timely adjustment of export financing (An exporter

having L/C could get a loan from any bank for a certain proportion of the face value of the L/C. For example, an exporter could borrow up to 710 wons for $1 as of May 1985.)

- Extended financing for export
- To facilitate supply of raw materials for export (For materials supplied domestically, the international price was applied; for foreign-supplied materials, tax and tariff exemption was granted.)
- Extensive financial support for investment in export industries (In 1985, 600 billion wons were allocated.)
- Simplification of custom-clearance procedures for export samples
- Control of freight fare charged by domestically owned shipping liners.
- Close cooperation between government and exporters: (1) monthly meetings chaired by the minister of commerce and industry to discuss detailed issues with exporters; (2) expansion of the General Trading Companies' (GTCs) role in export marketing; and (3) appointment of 20 high-level government officials to monitor continuously export situations by product group
- Expansion of export market: (1) market expansion by GTCs; (2) collective effort by firms in the same industry; (3) increased information service by export-related government agencies (e.g., Korea Trade Promotion Corporation, Korea Traders Association, etc.); and (4) support of exporters' direct participation in distribution channels in export markets
- Increased effort of government to establish/promote relations with foreign governments at high levels
- Selection and support of "Promising Small and Medium-Size Companies" (PSMSCs)
- Establishment of a division in the Ministry of Commerce and Industry to administer the selection and support of PSMSCs
- Simplification of import/export procedures

Among the Korean government's measures to promote export listed above, Daidong had used only "export financing." The company's designation as a "successful exporter" qualified it for preferential access to the scarce export financing.

SOME RECENT DEVELOPMENTS IN THE KOREAN ECONOMY

Over the period 1962–82, Korean economic growth was marked by one of the highest growth rates of GNP (average 10% per year) and exports (average 35% per year). Korea's economic development was a process of export led industrialization. During the period 1960–80, Korea's growth of manufacturing value-added was 17.2% per year, the highest in the world.

At the heart of such rapid growth was the relationship between business and government, characterized by close cooperation and strong government interventions across a wide range of economic activities. To sustain a high GNP growth rate, the government promoted exports by keeping wages low and allocating resources selectively to a few large private firms. As a result, labor activities were largely controlled, and big business groups known as *chaebols* were created. In 1984 the aggregate sales of the five largest *chaebols,* which were listed within the top 100 in the *Fortune 500* outside the United States, accounted for 54% of the GNP. The average annual growth rate of the big five was 30% for the past two decades, as against 10% for the national average. Only five countries—Japan, Germany, the United Kingdom, France, and Canada—had more firms than Korea in the top 100 list. But the domination of large firms and an increasing deterioration in income distribution had brought criticism. Workers began to demand their fair share of the benefits of economic growth, and the general public started to criticize the relation between government and *chaebols.* As a result, wages began to increase dramatically (see *Exhibit 6*), and the government recently changed policies in favor of small and medium-size companies.

In the past, unlike other successful exporting countries in Asia, the Korean government had often considered being small a problem. Though employing half of Korea's industrial work force, smaller companies had been neglected and discriminated against by the government. Aware of public criticism of the large *chaebols* and Korea's staggering export growth rate, and stimulated by Asian rivals' export success (led largely by small firms), the Korean government changed its strategy to favor smaller companies. A special agency for small and medium-size companies (SMSCs) was created to promote technology transfer and cooperation among them. The government ordered bankers who had preferred to deal with well-established *chaebols* to make 40–50% of their total loans to SMSCs. The government was concentrating its efforts to select 5,000 "Promising SMSCs" by 1987 for intensive support and guidance, in the hope of fostering successes and thus an entrepreneurial tradition. SMSCs would also be granted a collective monopoly in some areas. The government also simplified export procedures for SMSCs, which, unlike large firms, could not afford the staff to cope with complicated paperwork. As of June 1985 the government had selected 2,282 Promising SMSCs and had designated 110 product groups as off limits to big business. Daidong's product was not one of those protected items. (The overall plan of the Korean government for the SMSC sector is summarized in *Exhibit 5.*)

In his spacious and nicely air-conditioned room, Mr. Kang extinguished the cigarette and looked out of the window. He recalled a scene he had witnessed about twenty minutes earlier, when he had entered the Kuro Industrial Complex (in the southern part of Seoul) where Daidong was located. He had seen one of his neighboring companies surrounded by a riot squad and had heard some blue-collar workers shouting with white bands around their heads and pickets in hand. The executive vice president of the company, who had come to the airport to greet his boss, had explained in the car:

> There have been some strikes asking for wage increases and political freedom. Several weeks ago there was a large-scale strike and demonstration at a garment plant, and shortly thereafter another demonstration took place at a neighboring plant announcing that they were only trying to support their neighbor workers. Now everything is under control and no significant damage or casualty was reported.

Kang also recalled a remark that his brother-in-law, an elite member of Korean society, had once made:

> If you do not grow further, you may find it impossible to exist. Government does not care about individual small and medium-size companies, because the impact of each small company is almost negligible. Without support and attention of the government, you may find it difficult to compete against large integrated companies belonging to giant business groups. If you ever get into trouble, they will take you over at an unreasonably low cost as a step to vertical integration. In Korea, small companies are at a disadvantage in attracting good people, because good people go to big companies. A lot of people I met at small companies are short-sighted.

Mr. Kang felt that his brother-in-law was correct, especially regarding the people, because he saw hardly any of his staff making innovative comments in meetings. When the door was opened and his staff came in for a meeting, he felt a unique feeling of responsibility for his business and his people.

Exhibit 1
Sales, Export, and Profit of Daidong (1980–85)
(In US$)

Year	Sales	Export	Profit (Before Tax)
1980	$ 6,855,000	$ 6,163,000	$332,000
1981	6,617,000	5,396,000	(493,000)
1982	7,325,000	5,810,000	252,000
1983	12,089,000	10,864,000	329,000
1984	17,274,000	15,288,000	658,000
1985 (Jan.–June)	7,587,000	5,074,000	NA

Sales by Buyers in 1984

Buyer Name	Amount (US$)	%
Export:		
Sanyo	$ 6,219,000	36.0%
Sony	3,800,000	22.0
Orion	3,110,000	18.0
Tandy	2,159,000	12.5
	$15,288,000	88.5%
Domestic:		
Samsung	1,727,000	10.0
Gold Star	86,000	0.5
Others	173,000	1.0
	$ 1,986,000	11.5%
Total	$17,274,000	100.0%

SOURCE: Company reports.

Exhibit 2
Income Statement
(In US$)

	1984	1983	1982
Net sales	$17,274,000	$12,089,000	$7,325,000
Cost of goods sold	14,468,000	10,912,000	6,407,000
Cost of purchased materials	7,629,000	5,477,000	NA
Cost of labor	2,555,000	1,634,000	NA
Other (transportation, utility,			
subcontractor fee, packing, etc.)	4,284,000	3,801,000	NA
Gross profit	2,806,000	1,177,000	918,000
SG&A	2,539,000	1,085,000	851,000
Operating profit	267,000	92,000	67,000
Other income	828,000	593,000	415,000
Fees charged for mould			
production[a]	552,000	403,000	310,000
Others	276,000	190,000	105,000
Other expense	366,000	354,000	230,000
Interest expense	294,000	244,000	181,000
Others	72,000	110,000	49,000
Other deduction	71,000	2,000	0
Profit before tax	658,000	329,000	252,000
Income tax	184,000	43,000	0
Profit after tax	474,000	286,000	252,000

[a]Daidong charged separately for production of moulds.

SOURCE: Company reports.

Exhibit 3

Balance Sheet

(In US$ as of December 31)

	1984	1983	1982
Assets			
Current assets	$2,419,000	$3,032,000	$2,475,000
Cash and equivalents	670,000	897,000	339,000
Receivables	747,000	774,000	646,000
Inventories	656,000	1,194,000	1,272,000
Other current assets	346,000	167,000	218,000
Properties, plant and equipment			
less accumulated depreciation	3,495,000	1,394,000	1,026,000
Deferred charges	15,000	90,000	101,000
Investment and other assets	993,000	177,000	90,000
Total assets	$6,922,000	$4,693,000	$3,692,000
Liabilities and Stockholders' Equity			
Current liabilities	$4,684,000	$3,370,000	$2,755,000
Accounts and notes payable	1,075,000	881,000	1,146,000
Short-term debt	2,669,000	1,651,000	1,255,000
Advances received	334,000	267,000	18,000
Accrued expenses	289,000	272,000	197,000
Other current liabilities	317,000	299,000	139,000
Long-term debt	311,000	362,000	416,000
Accrued severance benefits	497,000	236,000	62,000
Total liabilities	5,492,000	3,968,000	3,233,000
Stockholders' equity	1,430,000	725,000	459,000
Total Liabilities and Stockholders' Equity	$6,922,000	$4,693,000	$3,692,000

SOURCE: Company report.

DAIDONG MOULD & INJECTION CO.

Exhibit 4 Organization Chart

(as of June 13, 1985)

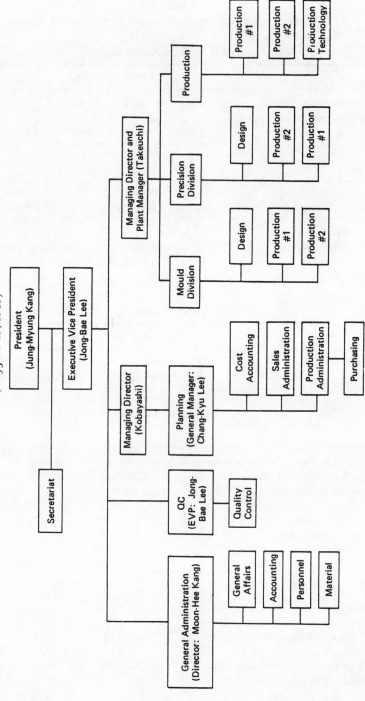

[a]Indicates Japanese national.

Exhibit 5
Export and Small and Medium-size Companies in Korea

Role of Export in Korean Economy

	1981	1982	1983	1984
Contribution to GNP, growth (%)	48.4	23.2	38.9	50.7
Direct contribution to total employment (%)	15.1	15.0	15.5	15.7

Small and Medium-size Companies in Korea

Legal Definition[a]	Number of Employees	Asset Size
Manufacturing/mining/ transportation	less than 300	less than W500 million
Construction	less than 50	less than W500 million
Service	less than 20	less than W50 million

Growth (1960–79)

	Sales	Value-Added
SMSCs	218 times	226 times
Large companies	928 times	820 times

Resource Allocation (1960–79)

	SMSCs	Large Companies
Total resource allocated	30.0%	70%
Capital/person (K/L)	57.9	100
Depreciation/person	31.3	100
Profit b.t./person	54.9	100
Value-added/person	61.9	100

Government Plan

	1981	1991	Change
Contribution to GNP growth (%)	17.9	32.0	+14.1
Portion of value-added (%)	35.4	44.8	+9.4
Resource allocation (%)	30.0	43.7	+13.7
Contribution to total employment (%)	47.7	54.3	+6.6
R&D participation (%)	9.7	40.0	+30.3
R&D expenditure/sales (%)	0.1	2.0	+1.9

[a]For administrative purposes for governmental support, the above definition was extended for firms that employed more than 700 persons in labor-intensive industries; had fixed assets valued less than W2 billion; or had outgrown the above two numbers within the previous three years.

SOURCE: Ministry of Commerce and Industry, Korea, 1985.

DAIDONG MOULD & INJECTION CO.

Exhibit 6

Wage, Export, Import, Prices, and Exchange Rate in Korea

	1980	1981	1982	1983	1984	1985 (June)
Monthly industrial wage (1980=100; in Korean currency)	100.0	120.7	139.7	155.1	171.8	NA
Export/import	17.5/	21.3/	21.9/	24.5/	29.3/	13.3/
(in US$ billions)	22.3	26.1	24.3	26.2	30.6	14.3
Consumer prices (1980=100; in Korean currency)	100.0	121.3	130.1	134.5	137.9	140.7
Wholesale prices (1980=100; in Korean currency)	100.0	120.4	126.0	126.3	127.5	128.0
Export prices/import prices (weighted average in US$; 1980=100)	100.0/	103.0/	99.2/	96.4/	98.4/	95.9/
	100.0	104.0	98.7	94.4	94.3	91.0
Exchange rate, Korean won per US$1 (as of the end of the period)	660	701	749	796	827	875
Prime bank lending rates	20.0	17.0	10.0	10.0	11.5	11.5

SOURCE: National Bureau of Statistics, Economic Planning Board, Korea.

Comparative Change in Unit Labor Costs
(1975=100; in national currencies)

	1972	1973	1974	1975	1976	1977	1978	1979
Korea	65.4	71.1	85.5	100.0	126.7	147.0	173.2	196.9
United States	74.6	76.6	84.9	100.0	100.7	107.3	115.7	123.2
Japan	59.8	62.0	80.4	100.0	99.4	104.0	102.0	99.1
Taiwan	65.2	70.5	100.9	100.0	95.3	94.8	90.1	94.3
Singapore	NA	71.4	90.7	100.0	99.7	120.4	NA	NA

[a] Average for January–September.

Countertrade and Merban Corporation[1]

In December 1981 Indonesia issued a new set of regulations that required all foreign companies selling more than US$775,000 worth of merchandise to the Indonesian government to export an equivalent amount of Indonesian goods. Suddenly, if a company wanted to sell the Indonesian government $2 million worth of computers, it might have to pay a huge penalty or not receive payment until it arranged for the export of $2 million worth of Indonesian rubber, coffee, plywood, or assorted other Indonesian products. Although this sort of regulation was not very new—many countries had required these so-called countertrade obligations for specific contracts—it was relatively rare for nations to require counterpurchases for a large percentage of imports and exports. While such practices were common among communist countries in the late 1970s, many people were shocked and disturbed that a noncommunist nation would enter the countertrade arena in such a big way.

For Merban Corporation and its president, Charles Baudoin, the Indonesian announcement raised a number of important questions. Should the Indonesians succeed in compelling firms to engage in countertrade, there could be substantial profits for trading companies like Merban. Many firms exporting to Indonesia would need help to meet their countertrade obligations. Furthermore, if Indonesia's countertrade policy appeared to succeed, there was a good possibility that countertrade could spread throughout other Third World countries.

Yet Baudoin and his associates at Merban were not convinced that countertrade was about to become a global phenomenon, or that Indonesia could force foreign firms to engage in countertrade. Merban had developed a profitable countertrade operation in Eastern Europe and considered itself a leader in the countertrade field. Therefore, if countertrade practices were to spread, Merban wanted to be at the forefront. But Baudoin was unsure whether the Indonesian announcement represented a fad or a real step toward more international barter. Indonesia's regulations were vague and perhaps unworkable, and Indonesia was

[1]Merban is a privately owned company and its financial statements are confidential, thus all financial data included on Merban have been disguised.

Assistant Professor David B. Yoffie prepared this case with the assistance of Research Associate Jane Kenney Austin as a basis for class discussion rather than to illustrate either effective or ineffective handling of an administrative situation. Abridged with permission.

known in international business circles to be problematic because of corruption among some government officials. Finally, Indonesia was under heavy fire from both its trade competitors and its trade partners. No one, except trading firms and the Indonesian government, seemed to want the countertrade regulations to work.

COUNTERTRADE IN THE 1980S

In 1982 observers suggested that global countertrade activities ranged from a low of 10% of world trade to a high of 30%. If these assessments were accurate, it would mean that anywhere from $200 billion to $600 billion in international commerce per year was tied to some form of barter.[2]

Part of this countertrade was handled through government-to-government diplomacy. When Italy exchanged naval frigates worth $1.5 billion for Iraqi oil of similar value, for example, the two governments negotiated the deal. A more common pattern was for foreign governments to sign countertrade contracts with private corporations. In many government-to-company deals, the company used its own in-house expertise to market countertrade goods. McDonnell Douglas, for instance, sold $2.4 billion in aircraft to the Canadian government and took it upon itself to sell $2.9 billion of Canadian goods and services. Levi Strauss sold Hungary a plant to make blue jeans and agreed to buy back 500,000 pairs of jeans per year, which it would market in Europe and Africa. Northrop Corporation offered to market millions of dollars of Turkish goods, if Turkey would buy Northrop planes. And in one of the biggest countertrade deals in history, Occidental Petroleum arranged to ship phosphate fertilizer to the Russians in return for Occidental marketing Soviet ammonia. The twenty-year, $20-billion contract called for Soviet imports of fertilizer, plants, and technology purchased from Occidental to balance with Soviet exports of ammonia and other products.[3]

Firms such as General Motors and McDonnell Douglas handled countertrade demands with their global organizations. But many smaller or less experienced companies needed help. Sometimes the smaller firms have bought trading expertise from multinational corporations that have their own trading subsidiaries, such as Sears Roebuck or General Electric. More often, firms requiring countertrade have turned to specialized trading companies or international banks for assistance. Five or six large American trading firms—such as Philbro/Salomon Brothers and Associ-

---

[2]International Trade Commission, *Analysis of Recent Trends in U.S. Countertrade,* March 1982; *New York Times,* July 26, 1981; Pompiliu Verzariu, *Countertrade Practices in East Europe, the Soviet Union and China,* U.S. Department of Commerce, April 1980.

[3]*Business Week,* July 12, 1982.

ated Metals & Minerals (Merban's parent corporation)—had strong positions in this market. Since governments often demanded that unusual
goods be taken in countertrade deals (such as one barter deal in which
Yugoslavia insisted that McDonnell Douglas buy canned hams), success in
countertrade required a company to have extensive international networks able to locate buyers and sellers for a variety of products on short
notice. American trading companies, although few in number, were well
suited for this business. Their existing organizations stretched around the
globe, and their personnel were expert in finding markets for diverse
goods. The corporate culture of trading companies also emphasized fast
action, which has been critical for countertrade.

Merban's competition included large U.S. banks, such as Citibank and
the European American Bank, that were trying to enter the countertrade
business in the early 1980s. The banks hoped to use their trade finance
experience and the resources of their global lending networks to identify
potential customers for countertrade products. Unlike trading companies, however, American banks were historically restricted by U.S. law
from buying and selling goods. As a result, U.S. banks were able to act only
as brokers in countertrade deals, which limited their competitiveness.[4]
Outside the United States, the major firms competing for Merban's countertrade business included Metallgesellschaft, a German trading company, and specialized banks in Vienna and Zürich known for expertise in
East–West European countertrade. These European banks were more
flexible than their American counterparts, but their range of operations
tended to be geographically limited. Finally, Japanese trading companies
handled most of the countertrade obligations for Japanese firms and
occasionally competed with American and European traders for non-
Japanese business. The close relationship between Japanese exporters
and Japan's general trading companies sometimes gave Japanese firms an
advantage in bidding for countertrade contracts.

Despite all these players, the demand for countertrade skills out-
stripped the available supply in the early 1980s. Countertrade expertise
was scarce because few players had anticipated the sudden explosion in
barter. Companies and governments were caught off guard partly because
countertrade statistics were very sketchy. In most cases, countertrade
contracts were negotiated without direct reference to the countertrade *deal*.
When Control Data signed one contract to sell computer peripherals to
Eastern Europe and then another to purchase ball bearings, the countertrade obligation was not mentioned in either agreement. When Brazil
required bidders on a $130-million space satellite to import Brazilian
products, there was no formal method to record the transaction as a
countertrade deal.

---

[4]Under the Export Trading Company Act of 1982, U.S. banks could create trading subsidiaries. This could enhance the role of banks in future countertrade deals.

MERBAN CORPORATION AND COUNTERTRADE
IN EASTERN EUROPE

Merban's Baudoin viewed countertrade as a central part of international business. In a letter in the *Wall Street Journal,* one of Baudoin's associates pointed out important advantages to countertrade:

> Most countertrade transactions are self-financing. During the boom years of Euro-currency lending, countries borrowed (and bankers lent) with little regard for the source of repayment. Countertrade requirements focus attention on transactions where their economic justification can be clearly identified. As the international credit markets contract further, an increasing number of countries, like Mexico for example, will have to make some use of these nonconventional payment methods in order to stay in business. If this results in closer analysis of the economics of each transaction, then buyers, sellers, and bankers will benefit.[5]

Baudoin added, "Theoreticians may wrinkle their noses, but governments and businessmen have to deal with reality." Baudoin's views on countertrade reflected his forty years of experience in countertrade. As president of the Dutch American Mercantile Corporation from the 1940s to the 1960s, he was involved in hundreds of switch and barter deals. Calling himself a switch banker, Baudoin never purchased merchandise. His firm would finance trade with Eastern Europe and act as an intermediary, matching buyers and sellers, whenever countries or companies ran into problems with bilateral clearing accounts. In the late 1960s Baudoin joined forces with Associated Metals & Minerals, a privately owned trading company with about $4 billion in annual revenues and a $250-million net worth. The new company, Merban (short for merchant bank), was infused with new capital but remained relatively autonomous.

Merban's main businesses changed in the 1970s. As the number of clearing accounts diminished in the early 1970s, Merban became more active in lending, syndication, and foreign-exchange trading. Acting like an international investment bank, Merban would make loans in $15–$20-million lots, financing them through its bank lines and gradually selling them within the syndicated loan market. Throughout the 1970s Merban's loan portfolio ranged from $100 million to $150 million, while it syndicated about $750 million in loans every year. At the beginning of the 1970s, almost 80% of Merban's loans were to Latin American countries. This declined to 60% by 1979 and to about 50% in 1982.

The countertrade part of Merban's business started to take on greater significance around 1978. As margins for its loans were being squeezed

[5]*Wall Street Journal,* November 11, 1982.

and fees for its syndications declined, Merban concluded that syndication was a declining business for firms of its size and that cross-border lending would not be as profitable in the near future. At that point Baudoin decided that countertrade was likely to become more important in the 1980s.

Merban was well positioned to expand its countertrade operations since few companies had its expertise in both traditional trade finance and nonconventional payment methods, such as barter, switch, and clearing deals. Merban also had a strong foothold in East–West countertrade. In 1979 it entered into a joint venture with the nationalized French bank, Crédit Lyonnais. The bank wanted countertrade expertise; in return it gave Merban access to French firms needing countertrade services. Through the joint venture with Crédit Lyonnais, Merban was able to expand its East European countertrade operations. But its resources were limited: Baudoin described Merban as an executive-intensive operation. Professional staff was required for most deals, and Merban had only 17 professionals in New York, Hong Kong, London, Paris, São Paulo, and Mexico City. Although the staff was aided by agents acting as Merban's representatives in dozens of other countries, it had to choose its deals carefully to avoid spreading its personnel too thin.

Merban's decision to concentrate on East European countertrade was well-timed. In 1980–81 Merban was already developing a network of contacts throughout the East European bloc when the doubling of oil prices and the Soviet invasion of Afghanistan led Western banks to reduce their East European lending. Suddenly Poland, Romania, and several other nations discovered that they lacked sufficient funds to cover their import costs or pay the interest on their debts. As a result, most of these communist countries started to require countertrade for some or all of their imports. Romania, in particular, took a hard line. With almost $10 billion in debts, Romania established a 100% countertrade requirement in January 1981. The government told foreign companies that henceforth all Romanian imports had to be accompanied by counterpurchases.

Initially some doubted whether East European governments could successfully require such broad countertrade obligations, but companies quickly learned that countertrade expertise was essential. When General Electric sold Romania nuclear plant turbines for $142 million in 1981, it had to agree to buy or market abroad a full $142 million worth of Romanian goods. Even though Romania badly needed alternative energy sources, and even though GE had superior technology and could provide below-market financing from the U.S. Export-Import Bank, informed sources believed that the countertrade offer was essential for closing the deal.[6] With sales of power plant turbines dragging in the West and energy consumption down around the world, many companies from the United

[6]*Wall Street Journal,* April 9, 1982.

States, France, the United Kingdom, and Switzerland were competing for the same contract. This allowed the Romanians to play one company off against another until they could negotiate a satisfactory deal.

The core of Merban's East European operations developed in Romania and East Germany, where Merban's close government contacts gave it a head start in handling growing countertrade demands. As one of the early countertraders in those two nations, Merban established a strong reputation and a network for obtaining advance information about which companies were doing countertrade business, which goods were being traded, and which deals had government backing.[7] Baudoin felt that Merban's relatively high ratio of success was due largely to its ability to get referrals directly from Romania and East Germany. He described a typical deal in which Merban made money.

> Late in 1981 our contacts in Romania gave us and our joint venture with Crédit Lyonnais a list of firms that had outstanding counterpurchase obligations. The Romanian government asked if we could help these companies because they were in danger of paying a penalty unless they could complete their countertrade deals by the end of the year. One such firm was Brunswick Corporation, which had sold $900,000 worth of valves and filters to Romania's petrochemical industry. Brunswick had agreed to buy an equal amount of Romanian goods and pay a 10% penalty on any portion of the counterpurchase commitment that was not fulfilled. To secure the penalty, Brunswick had to open a letter of credit with a Belgian bank that would guarantee payment if the countertrade was not completed.
>
> When I discovered Brunswick's problem, I called the company in Skokie, Illinois, to offer our services. I arranged to assume Brunswick's countertrade obligation for a fee of 9%—or $81,000. Even though the going rate was around 6%, we were able to extract a higher fee because it was close to their deadline. Furthermore, I assume this was not a problem for Brunswick. Brunswick probably factored the 10% penalty into their selling price, in case they couldn't find Romanian goods.
>
> The next step was for Brunswick to tell the Romanians that Merban accepted its obligation. Since Merban had good relations with the Romanian FTOs [foreign trade organizations], Romanian approval of the switch proved to be no problem. Now, it was Merban's job to find export rights that the Romanians would count toward fulfilling Merban's obligation. This, too, was relatively easy. The Romanians

---

[7]This kind of inside information can make a difference between a profitable and an unprofitable company. Although many deals may be under consideration in a country at any given time, only 3–4% are usually completed. Baudoin noted that whenever demand for an import was high, a country would allocate foreign exchange despite its countertrade requirements.

had created a system that allowed exporters from Romania to earn credits that would offset Brunswick's sale. The only catch was that Brunswick was supposed to satisfy its countertrade obligation by buying from the same FTO it had sold to in 1981.

We had two ways to accomplish the deal. First, I knew of an American oilfield equipment dealer that bought Romanian goods from the same FTO as Brunswick, and negotiated for the right to use these purchases for countertrade obligations. I could then arrange to purchase these rights for about 4%. This was relatively cheap, but since the rights were about to expire, the company was willing to sell. The second possibility was to work through a client of Merban's that annually purchases about $4 million in furniture from Romania and sells it to Kmart, Zayre, Pier I, and other discount stores. As one of the furniture company's bankers, we asked the company to negotiate a deal with the Romanians whereby its purchases could be used to offset countertrade requirements. The Romanians had no objection to the request, but they would allow only 50% of the furniture purchases to offset general countertrade requirements. The other 50% had to go toward countertrade obligations with the FTO that specifically handled furniture.

Since we were financing the furniture company's purchases of Romanian goods, the Romanian government tended to look very favorably upon Merban's activities. This turned out to be helpful when we wanted to use the furniture credits to offset Brunswick's obligations. We told the Romanians that we would provide additional credit to the furniture importer, which would help it buy more Romanian goods, if the Romanians would allow all the furniture export credits to be used for general countertrade obligations. When Romania agreed, we were able to satisfy Brunswick's requirement. Merban paid 3.5% to the U.S. importer for the credits, 4.5% to our joint venture with Crédit Lyonnais for arranging the linkage, and kept 1% for its profits.

In 1982 Merban and its joint venture with Crédit Lyonnais each expected to earn close to $1.5 million gross profit from its operations in Eastern Euope. (Baudoin estimated that the net profits were 8–10% less than gross profits.) This compared with $650,000 in 1981, $250,000 in 1980, and negligible profits from countertrade in 1979.

INDONESIAN COUNTERTRADE

According to Baudoin, no one was surprised when East European countries required countertrade. Since countries like Romania planned the

number and type of goods that they export, countertrade helped to reduce the uncertainty of the international market. Furthermore, authority
for trade in communist governments tended to be centralized. As a result,
most communist nations were usually able to organize quickly for countertrade and negotiate effectively with multinational corporations.

Although countertrade fitted the East European context reasonably
well, 100% countertrade requirements like those enforced by Romania
were not easily implemented elsewhere in the world. No capitalist economy had engaged in wide-reaching barter for anything other than military sales in more than thirty years. Thus, when Indonesia announced a
sweeping countertrade policy in late December 1981, the world was
caught by surprise. The Indonesians said they would require foreign
companies awarded government contracts to export Indonesian goods
equivalent to the amount of the contract. Since Indonesian government
contracts were expected to range from $3.5 to $6.0 billion annually, this
policy could have a significant impact on trade in Southeast Asia.

Merban, as well as dozens of companies and governments around the
world, pondered the meaning of the Indonesian announcement. The
immediate concern for Merban was to determine whether Indonesia was
pursuing a well-thought-out program to promote exports or a series of *ad
hoc* measures that could never be implemented. Although Indonesia could
possibly be the biggest profit opportunity for countertrade business in
years, Baudoin would not start operations in Indonesia unless Merban
could realize a return in a relatively short time. Baudoin felt that some
firms, such as Japanese trading companies and large American banks, had
the resources to send people to any country where countertrade might
develop. Merban, by contrast, had to be selective about where to open
operations. Baudoin felt he did not have professionals to spare if a new
venture would not be self-sustaining in the short run.

Yet equally important to Baudoin was Merban's longer-run status in the
countertrade business. He was not sure if countertrade was going through
another cycle, as it had in the 1960s and 1970s, or if countertrade was
becoming a truly global phenomenon. But if the Indonesian announcement was signaling a boom in countertrade—if Indonesia was successful
and others followed the Indonesian example—Merban's reputation
would be greatly enhanced by establishing a strong position in Indonesia.

Background to the Indonesian Announcement

Indonesia is an archipelago of more than 13,000 islands sprawled across
3,000 miles along the equator. With 155 million people in 1981 and a
wealth of natural resources, Indonesia held an enviable position among
developing countries. It was an oil-exporting member of OPEC and had

just completed a decade of extremely rapid growth. After a real increase in GNP of 9.6% in 1980 (*Exhibit 1*), Indonesia could boast a comfortable reserve equivalent to US$10 billion and a healthy balance-of-payments surplus. Although some of its reserves were borrowed, the country had a high international credit rating. Indonesia also enjoyed a favorable investment climate, taking in one-third of the annual investment flowing into developing Asian nations.

Despite these successes, many of Indonesia's development goals were yet to be achieved. Its average per capita income was US$350, but almost 40% of the population subsisted on less than US$90 per year. About 3 million people were going to enter the work force annually in the next decade, which made a high rate of growth a social and economic necessity. Finally, a few special interests controlled large segments of the Indonesian economy. The military government of President Suharto maintained tight control over the nominally democratic state. And pervasive corruption seemed to be a drag on development.

President Suharto recognized many of these problems and wanted desperately to maintain Indonesia's rapid economic growth. Part of his strategy was to diversify exports by shipping more labor-intensive manufactured goods and cutting down on imports. In the meantime, however, Indonesia was importing expensive, capital-intensive projects to build infrastructure and domestic industry while exporting traditionally unprocessed commodities. But heavy reliance on exports of primary commodities can be risky. Indonesia was among the world's leading exporters of petroleum, liquified natural gas, wood, rubber, coffee, tin, and other commodities (*Exhibit 2, 3*). As demonstrated in *Exhibit 4*, it was also in direct competition with other members of the Association of Southeast Asian Nations (ASEAN).[8] Prices for some of Indonesia's exports were influenced by international commodities agreements, and the rest were subject to wide price fluctuations in world commodity markets. This meant that Indonesia and its fellow ASEAN countries were constrained in setting export prices. If any ASEAN nation tried to increase its commodity prices, others would take its market share; any effort to cut prices could lead to a price war or a violation of an international commodity agreement.

By the end of 1981 soft commodity markets were beginning to threaten the foundation of Indonesia's ambitious development program. Declining global demand and lower world prices for Indonesia's nonoil exports caused the greatest concern. Nonoil exports in the fourth quarter of 1981

---

[8]ASEAN was formed in 1967 as a loosely knit organization facilitating political, social, and economic cooperation among its member states: Indonesia, Thailand, the Philippines, Malaysia, and Singapore. ASEAN has made headway in diplomatic cooperation, but despite preferential trading arrangements only about 15% of ASEAN's total trade is among ASEAN countries.

were only 65% of their 1979 level. Growth in domestic consumption of oil and signs of weakness in the international oil market further aggravated the Indonesian situation. Although many observers felt that Indonesia had ample foreign exchange to pay for needed imports, the Suharto government felt compelled to take several strong measures.

One of Suharto's first responses was to limit government spending. On January 5, 1982, he announced that government expenditure would nominally increase only 12.3% in the coming year, as against a 32% nominal increase the preceding year. The budget included cutbacks in food and fuel subsidies and a salary freeze for all civil servants.

At the same time the government announced its countertrade policy. By way of explanation, the government said it had two choices: cut imports drastically or maintin imports and expand exports. It claimed that choosing the latter was in the interest of world trade. The countertrade policy would allow foreign nationals to sustain high levels of exports to Indonesia without disrupting the Indonesian economy. The most important elements of the new policy were a 100% counterpurchase requirement for government tenders over US$775,000; a 50% penalty for noncompliance; counterpurchased goods had to be shipped to new markets rather than existing ones (i.e., sending Indonesian goods to traditional customers at historic levels would not be sufficient); and petroleum and natural gas exports would not count toward countertrade.

International Reactions

Some reactions to the Indonesian announcement were sharply negative. One observer decried the Indonesian policy as creating "artificial barriers to the free flow of trade,"[9] noting that countertrade "is close to barter trade, which is a concept which we thought died about 150 or 200 years ago." But most countries withheld judgment because they were unsure whether the regulations would work. For example, Australia sent a delegation to Jakarta to discuss Indonesia's purchase of US$100 million in Australian wheat. The delegation pointed out that Indonesia already had a trade surplus with Australia and that Indonesia needed the wheat. Japan, Indonesia's largest trading partner (see *Exhibit 5*), also opposed the counterpurchase policy but did not take a strong position. Since Japanese trading companies have extensive international networks, many believed that Japan would easily adapt to the regulations. But MITI (Ministry of International Trade and Industry) believed countertrade would discourage world trade and fostered a tacit agreement among the largest groups not to submit bids complying with the Indonesian policy. MITI did not

---

[9]Quoted from an article in the *International Herald Tribune* in Merban's files.

"raise a big fuss in the early stages," because it hoped Indonesia's insistence on rigorous implementation would make the policy unworkable.[10]

MERBAN'S DECISION

Merban found out about the Indonesian countertrade requirement early on, and in March 1982 a Merban executive met with the Indonesian trade counselor in Washington. Baudoin's associates also talked with other firms doing business in Indonesia and other trading firms. Information from those companies suggested that if Indonesia's countertrade worked, the fees (and profits) would be high. And as soon as one company in a large tender agreed to the counterpurchases, everyone would scramble to join in the game. Yet through the first four months of 1982, there were no solid counterpurchase contracts. No one seemed to understand how the policy's terms could be implemented.

If Merban wanted to establish a profitable position in Indonesia, it had to create a network similar to the one it had in Eastern Europe. This meant that one of its higher-level executives from New York or Paris had to spend several weeks in Indonesia finding exporters whose products qualified for countertrade, locating potential markets for those products, and arranging to assume countertrade obligations of firms selling to the Indonesian government. Baudoin's dilemma was that he could not afford to send one of his countertrade executives on a wild goose chase to Jakarta. Since many countries had some countertrade requirements, Merban had to be selective in its choice of target countries. In addition, all qualified personnel were busy on existing business, including a very complex switch deal between the East European bloc and South America that promised Merban almost half a million dollars in profit. Thus the costs of sending someone to Indonesia were not only direct expenses but also the loss of assured business in Eastern Europe and elsewhere. An Indonesian trip would be worthwhile, but only if there was some degree of certainty that Indonesia's policy would succeed.

Baudoin was confident that if countertrade were successfully implemented, Merban would be very competitive even though it would be starting from scratch in Indonesia. The company's only contacts with the country were a substantial short-term loan in the mid-1970s to Pertamina, Indonesia's national oil company, and Baudoin's short trip there in 1969 at the suggestion of the East German and Hungarian governments. Indonesia had accumulated substantial debt with Eastern Europe in the 1960s, and the socialist countries thought Baudoin could advise the Indonesians

[10]*Far Eastern Economic Review,* December 25, 1982.

on how to use countertrade to settle that debt. But a week in Jakarta produced no business for Merban. In retrospect, Baudoin suspected that his refusal to make "appropriate payments" to the appropriate person might have been responsible.

To discover if Indonesia was more serious this time, Baudoin sent one of Merban's vice presidents, Stephen DeGot, to Jakarta. Since DeGot was already in the Far East on lending business, Baudoin hoped this would be an inexpensive way to determine the status of Indonesia's countertrade. In his subsequent report, excerpted in the *Appendix,* DeGot noted that countertrade rules were more complicated than Merban originally thought. DeGot also discovered that the countertrade policy was creating serious problems: Many foreign contractors were unwilling to commit themselves to countertrade, which was delaying the import of critical products.

As more information came to Baudoin's attention in late April and early May, the picture became more clouded. The deepening world recession in 1982 was creating a huge buyer's market: Everyone was anxious to sell products. Indonesia was negotiating big tender bids for fertilizers and power plants, two industries facing intense competition and weak sales. Yet everyone Baudoin talked to in these industries was convinced that there were ways to "get out" of countertrade obligations. Some exporters seemed sure they could escape the 50% penalty. Even the *Far Eastern Economic Review* noted, "There is a feeling that those Western companies which enjoy a strong market position can usually get away with the least inconvenience."[11]

In the meantime, Indonesia published the list of commodities that could be exported to satisfy countertrade requirements (see *Exhibit 6*). The list raised the stakes for Merban, because success in Indonesia seemed to heighten the possibility that countertrade could spread throughout Southeast Asia. One publication Baudoin received in April stated:

> Any effort to press exports on today's soft markets could lead to major price distortions and dislocation of existing trade. Certainly Indonesia's partners in ASEAN, Malaysia and Thailand, would not take lightly a sudden decline in the price or volume of their tin and rubber exports. . . . As a senior purchasing agent . . . in Indonesia put it, "The real worry is that other countries in the region might enact similar policies in response. Then what are we supposed to do, throw the Indonesians over in favor of the Thais or Malays?"[12]

---

[11]*Ibid.*

[12]*East Asian Executive Report,* March 1982, p. 9.

The senior purchasing agent's dilemma could be the trading firm's delight. If Merban wanted to lead in the countertrade field, it had to make the right decision about how to position itself in Indonesia. Yet in early May 1982, the opportunity costs seemed high and the future of Indonesian countertrade remained uncertain.

APPENDIX
EXCERPTS FROM MERBAN MEMO ON INDONESIAN COUNTERTRADE

To: Merban, New York City
From: S. DeGot, Vice President
Date: April 24, 1982
Subject: Indonesian Countertrade

It is not a regulation or a law. There was merely a ministerial declaration for certain government organizations for projects not financed by ADB, World Bank, etc. The Indonesians have published guidelines . . . and explained it to whoever cares to listen. . . . If the government feels a project is especially important or a high priority, it can drop the countertrade requirement. . . .

The countertrade idea is a strictly commercial initiative on their part to penetrate new markets for Indonesian goods. They perceive real direct and indirect trade barriers for Indonesian products, and they hope that counter trade will open these markets. They perceive that countertrade will enlist the aid of powerful partners who traditionally have had only a one-way interest in Indonesia.

Regarding the rules . . . requiring counterpurchases to go to new markets, they have set these up because they recognize that otherwise:

1. The Japanese will perform 100% of the business and dump the products in their regular distribution channels.

2. They wish to limit commodity market disturbance, but recognize that they will disturb some channels.

3. They want to use countertrade to prevent exports from going to Hong Kong, Singapore, Malaysia, and Taiwan, and then being reexported to existing markets.

Regarding the 50% penalty, they pick the number to show they "mean business." The comment was that they felt it would be "impossible" for a supplier to increase a price *by 100%* (to cover a 50% penalty). Therefore, they would have to have a "serious" attempt to comply with the export requirement, rather than simply mark up and walk away. He [an Indonesian official] agreed that nonperformance by a supplier would have other negative impacts beyond the penalty. They recognize there will be a "markup" for countertrade. They admit this markup will result in greater costs, but the cost impact will be felt over the economic life of the asset.

The alternative is export subsidies, which are bad for a number of reasons:

1. Trading partner complaints (other governments)
2. Direct budget expense
3. Possibility of abuse between private exporter and government officials
4. Favoritism

Regarding price increase of the export product, this they feel is a market function, but abuses can be brought back to the attention of the Department of Trade. (Obviously there will be market cost to get a shipper to specify "countertrade" in the contract of purchase. The buyer of a nontraditional/noncompetitive commodity will need a price break. The exporter of a traditional commodity may also need a premium to specify the export as qualifying for countertrade.)

The question of base export versus incremental exports was strictly case by case. For example, they have certain bilateral arrangements in the East Bloc. The exports under these deals won't count for countertrade.

We discussed the role of the countertrade firm. I said we cooperated with the authorities in the countries that operated countertrade. Basically, I pointed out many companies were not organized to face unknown risks in dealing outside their business line. If we backed them directly or indirectly, we basically would lower the costs to Indonesia of countertrade. We discussed countertrade inefficiencies, including the fact that profit must be a factor in the costs, i.e., all benefit does not flow to the export side. He [an Indonesian official] recognized that to really develop a market required a real financial incentive to get it done.

Equipment suppliers are still expected to come with "finance packages." Ten years is the norm. Doing a countertrade does not release this aspect. This, of course, puts "teeth" into the Penalty Factor since they could repudiate a debt (except that international finance institutions [banks] will fight). Nonperformance of countertrade will not be allowed as a debt excuse.

He said the countertrade was not a "bilateral" effort, i.e., they want to penetrate markets but have no interest in balanced trade country by country. (As an oil exporter this makes sense. Bilateral balancing would be counterproductive.) He also stated that this was not an effort to "get money." He said they had enough money and enough borrowing power. What they want is "markets for goods," and this is a method of pushing it. (This also is a key factor.)

He said that a few people have put in weak letters of intent, best effort, etc. But if they are finally awarded, the tender agreement will bind them absolutely in spite of preliminary weak letters.

COUNTERTRADE AND MERBAN CORPORATION

Exhibit 1

Indonesian Domestic Indicators, 1976–81

	1976	1977	1978	1979	1980	1981
National accounts (billions of rupiahs)						
Exports	3,430	4,466	4,935	9,940	13,898	14,183
Government consumption	1,591	2,077	2,659	3,733	4,688	5,788
Gross capital formation	3,205	3,826	4,671	6,704	9,485	11,064
Private consumption	10,464	12,458	13,851	17,261	25,364	32,543
Less: imports	(3,222)	(3,817)	(3,370)	(5,614)	(7,990)	(9,901)
Gross domestic product	15,467	19,011	22,746	32,025	45,446	53,677
Less: net factor payments abroad	(432)	(679)	(892)	(1,536)	(2,103)	(2,097)
Gross national expenditure = GNP	15,035	18,332	21,854	30,490	43,343	51,580
National income, market prices	14,028	17,097	20,371	28,400	40,381	48,046
Gross domestic product, 1980 prices	33,187	36,094	38,925	41,359	45,446	48,897
Consumer prices (1975 = 100)	119.80	133.10	143.90	175.40	207.90	233.40
Exchange rate (rupiah per $, end of period)	415.00	415.00	625.00	627.00	626.75	644.00
Population (millions, mid-year est.)	138.24	140.71	143.15	145.58	148.03	150.52

SOURCE: *International Financial Statistics Yearbook*, 1983, IMF, p. 279.

681

COUNTERTRADE AND MERBAN CORPORATION

Exhibit 2

Composition of Indonesian Exports, 1975–81

(Quantity in thousand metric tons, value in US$ millions)

Exports (f.o.b.)		1975	1976	1977	1978	1979	1980	1981
Maize	Q	50.7	3.5	10.5	21.1	6.8	14.9	—
	V	6.4	0.4	1.2	2.4	0.8	2.1	—
Coffee, not roasted	Q	128.4	136.3	160.4	215.9	220.2	238.7	210.6
	V	99.8	237.5	599.3	491.3	614.3	656.0	345.9
Tea	Q	46.0	47.5	51.3	56.3	53.6	74.2	71.3
	V	51.5	56.6	118.5	94.8	83.4	112.7	100.8
Pepper	Q	15.2	30.8	33.2	37.8	25.2	29.7	34.0
	V	22.9	47.0	66.2	69.2	46.8	50.1	47.2
Copra cake	Q	296.1	392.8	335.7	334.7	317.0	394.3	321.8
	V	24.7	33.4	37.4	34.1	41.3	47.4	35.8